1 MONTH OF
FREE
READING

at

www.ForgottenBooks.com

By purchasing this book you are eligible for one month membership to ForgottenBooks.com, giving you unlimited access to our entire collection of over 700,000 titles via our web site and mobile apps.

To claim your free month visit:
www.forgottenbooks.com/free664239

ISBN 978-0-483-61983-8
PIBN 10664239

REPORT

ON THE

MANUSCRIPTS

OF HIS GRACE

THE DUKE OF PORTLAND, K.G.,

PRESERVED AT

WELBECK ABBEY.

Vol. VII.

𝔓𝔯𝔢𝔰𝔢𝔫𝔱𝔢𝔡 𝔱𝔬 𝔟𝔬𝔱𝔥 𝔋𝔬𝔲𝔰𝔢𝔰 𝔬𝔣 𝔓𝔞𝔯𝔩𝔦𝔞𝔪𝔢𝔫𝔱 𝔟𝔶 ℭ𝔬𝔪𝔪𝔞𝔫𝔡 𝔬𝔣 𝔥𝔦𝔰 𝔐𝔞𝔧𝔢𝔰𝔱𝔶.

LONDON :

PRINTED FOR HIS MAJESTY'S STATIONERY OFFICE

BY MACKIE & CO. LD.

And to be purchased, either directly or through any Bookseller, from
EYRE AND SPOTTISWOODE, EAST HARDING STREET, FLEET STREET, E.C., AND
32, ABINGDON STREET, WESTMINSTER, S.W.; or
OLIVER AND BOYD, EDINBURGH; or
EDWARD PONSONBY, 116, GRAFTON STREET, DUBLIN.

1901.

[Cd. 783.] *Price 2s. 3d.*

CONTENTS.

INTRODUCTION.

THE letters calendared in this volume were written by Dr. William Stratford, canon of Christ Church, Oxford, to Edward Harley, afterwards Lord Harley and 2nd Earl of Oxford. Dr. Stratford, who, previous to his appointment as canon, in 1703, had been chaplain to Robert Harley, was son of Dr. Nicholas Stratford (successively Warden of Manchester College and Bishop of Chester) and godson of Thomas Harley, minister to the Court of Hanover.

The letters begin in the summer of 1710, and the first great political event noticed is the fall of the Whigs, and Robert Harley's advent to power; news so welcome at Oxford, that Stratford feared excess of joy might make vacancies amongst the headships (p. 9). The only drawback, to the minds of the ardent Tories at Christ Church, was that Lord Chancellor Cowper was appointed Lord Lieutenant of the county of Hertford, which made them fear that the Queen meant to allow him to retain the Chancellorship, especially if Sir Simon Harcourt should refuse it. Dr. Stratford shrewdly suspected, however, that Harcourt's coyness was only meant to raise the terms (pp. 11, 13); and perhaps it was so, for shortly afterwards he took the Great Seal.

At this time Christ Church was enjoying a peaceful calm under the gentle rule of Dr. Aldrich. The eight canons were Dr. South, now an old man; Dr. John Hammond; Dr. Thomas Burton, Sub-dean; Dr. John Potter, Regius Professor of Divinity; old Dr. Woodruffe, who died in 1711 and was succeeded by Dr. George Smalridge; Dr. Roger Altham; Dr. Francis Gastrell; and Stratford himself. With most of his "brothers," as he calls them, Dr. Stratford was on very friendly terms; but his intimates appear to have been Gastrell and Smalridge.

In December, 1710, Dean Aldrich died, and the appointment of his successor was long delayed. "We are headless indeed," Dr. Stratford observed, "but not for that reason miserable, only as we have lost our old head, not for want of a new one . . . The College is as full as it was and as regular, without a Dean, and Peckwater goes on without money, and in both cases we subsist well enough yet upon the stock of our old credit" (p. 24). Reports were circulated of riots in the House, but they proved to be quite unfounded. In June, 1711, a rumour reached Oxford that Dr. Atterbury, Dean of Carlisle, was to be transferred to Christ Church. It was not believed at the time, but in August positive news of the appointment arrived. Stratford received it calmly. "Our new Governor," he wrote, "will find his subjects in a better disposition to obedience than I believe he expects . . . I hope we shall have discretion enough, as well as honesty, to preserve peace amongst ourselves." But he thought the appointment a great mistake. "None," said he, "but one blinded with passion, would have desired to have come where he knows so many stories of former failures are yet fresh, and where no one can have the authority that is requisite to this place whose youth was not without blemish in it." But he was mad, and would hear nothing from any friend he had" (pp. 49, 50). From this it will be seen that the Doctor's prejudice against Atterbury was very strong. In fact his prejudices on all subjects were very strong. He was a good lover and a good hater. He appears to have had an extravagant faith in Harley (even allowing for the fact that the letters are written to Harley's son), and very little faith in any other minister at all. His views are interesting, not because they are unbiassed, but because they seem to represent the opinion of the honest Hanoverian-tory party at Oxford, whose hatred of "the enemy," i.e. the Whigs, was counterbalanced by loyalty to the Anglican Church, and dread of a Roman Catholic successor to the Crown. With the intrigues with the Pretender, Stratford and his friends had nothing whatever to do, and he apparently had not the slightest suspicion that his patron had anything to do with them either.

Atterbury accepted the deanery, and re-adjusted his minor offices, resigning the chaplaincy of the Rolls, but keeping that of Bridewell, in order, it was said, that he might have lodgings in town during Convocation. Christ Church was anxious and not hopeful. "Do what he will," wrote Stratford, "he will fall short of his predecessor, and in other things as well as his speeches. He may be without some of that poor man's infirmities, but he will never have all his virtues, either intellectual or moral" (p.59).

On September 24, a message was received that on the next day, at such an hour, the new "Governor" designed to be at the foot of Shotover, where it was hoped his students would meet him ; and every one who had or could hire a horse was advised to oblige him. On September 27 he was installed, with a "very noble" entertainment, and the new reign began (pp. 61, 62).

Before long the College was in an uproar. "Whilst we hope for peace abroad," Stratford declared, "we expect nothing but war at home " (p. 64). The Dean claimed the sole disposal of the College "curacies," overhauled the muniments, took possession of the books, disputed the rights of the Canons, and tried, not very successfully, to ingratiate himself with the students, by treating them with tea in an afternoon. The "brethren" were united entirely among themselves, his attempts to divide them having only cemented them more closely, and an open rupture appeared to be unavoidable. At the end of the year 1711, Stratford laid down his office of Treasurer, and a new Sub-dean had also to be appointed. After some demur, Dr. Potter accepted the latter office and Dr. Gastrell the former, the Chapter resolving to bear anything save the surrender of their rights, in order to avoid a breach. About this time however, they complained that the Dean was adding illegal proceedings to arbitrary ones, for at the admission of the new students, having forgotten to bring a Bible, he swore them on a statute book instead. "Had any other done so, he would have made the kingdom roar with it " (p. 84).

There are no letters of the year 1712 of earlier date than August, when Stratford and his friend Gastrell were travelling in the west of England. At this time, Charles Aldrich, nephew of the late Dean, brought an accusation against Stratford of having embezzled books, papers and money from his uncle's study. Stratford, believing that the whole thing was got up by Atterbury with the hope of provoking him to "a great passion," resolved to defeat this design by taking everything quietly and submitting to a strict inquisition (pp. 85, 86). A Chapter was

called to consider the matter, and some of the Canons began
to take notes of the proceedings, upon which the Dean declared
that if they were going to write down what was said he should
leave the Chapter, rose from his seat, cried "Good-bye to you,"
and so departed. A deputation was sent to beg him to return,
but he received it very rudely, would not ask the Canons into
his study, and called after them "I despise you," as they left
the house (p. 96). Dr. Smalridge thought his rage was real,
but Stratford, on the other hand, suspected that he wished to
break up the Chapter in order to prevent Aldrich from having to
submit to examination.

Atterbury was apparently uneasy at the presence in Oxford of
Dr. Smalridge (p. 97), who had succeeded him as Dean of Carlisle
and had brought strange accounts of his doings there (p. 94).
Dr. Stratford thus describes the situation at this time:—"We are
in a state of as great confusion as it is possible to imagine any
body corporate. He will not allow us to propose anything in
Chapter but what he likes. He will not allow the Registrar to
enter anything in our register but what he bids him do. If we
put any question to him, he will give us no direct answer; he
will exercise what power he pleases without saying that he claims
it. . . We have no remedy against this but to throw ourselves
at the Queen's feet." And this remedy, Stratford goes on to
show, was attended with great difficulty, for Atterbury would
probably forestall them by appealing to his friend, Lord Keeper
Harcourt, and thus the Canons' complaint would seem to lie not
only against their Dean, but against the Lord Keeper, who would
do his utmost to have his own sentence justified. There was
apparently considerable doubt at this time, both at Christ Church
and other Colleges, as to who was their lawful "visitor," which
increased their perplexities (pp. 121, 126, 131).

One thing was not at all doubtful. The Dean was very angry
with Dr. Stratford, and accused him of writing letters against
him to the Lord Treasurer, and of blasting him all over England.
If Stratford said a tenth part to the Lord Treasurer of what he had
said to his son, the accusation can hardly be alleged to have been
without foundation. But that Stratford was not alone in his views
is shown by a letter from Dr. Smalridge, written about this time,
in which he praises the temper and patience shown by Dr.
Stratford, under the "ill, inhumane and unchristian treatment"

of the Dean. "I don't look upon myself to be a very fiery man," he continues, "but I could not promise that I could be so easy under so grievous provocations. My temper has been pretty much tried, but not in such a manner as my poor brother's. Mr. Dean is very much nettled at our disproof of his false accounts of brother Stratford about the meadow money ; he has protested with all the solemnity in the world that he never gave a copy of the paper laid before us to any person whatsoever. But it so happens that none of our body give any credit to his most solemn asseverations" (p. 103). The allusion here is to another accusation brought by the Dean against Stratford, as Treasurer, of falsifying his accounts, in support of which, as the brethren had positive proof, the Dean had sent certain papers to the Lord Keeper, in order that they might be laid before Lord Treasurer Harley. On November 4, Stratford made a formal protest against the charges concerning Dr. Aldrich's study. He reminded the Dean that in former times, he had given him (Atterbury) a key to his house in Westminster, where for two years he went in and out at pleasure. During that time, he continued, "several things were missing in it. When I removed to Oxford, there were some books wanting in my study. Should I desire you, at this distance of time, as I do not, to declare upon oath what you did in my house, whilst you had a key to it for so long a time, and used that key so often; and what books, papers or other things you removed, would you think such dealing like that of a gentleman, a friend, a Christian, a clergyman ?" (p. 107). By this time the Dean had found out that it was useless to continue this particular struggle. Young Aldrich had himself given Stratford receipts which completely exonerated him, and the Dean's own friends urged him to abandon the matter. At the next meeting of the Chapter, the Canons pressed him with uncomfortable questions, and at last he could stand it no longer, "bounced out of his chair, and ran out of the Chapter House" (p. 109).

About this time a diversion occurred, by the adjudging of the prizes for the new *Certamen Poeticum*, a project of Atterbury's, for which he had diverted funds hitherto used for the college buildings (p. 91). There was a great ferment among the young candidates, who declared that there was false play ; that certain persons had private notice of the theme before it was given out and that others had had their verses written for them. When the three victors were announced, and the first two proved to be Thomas Bromley, son of the Speaker of the House of Commons, and William Le Hunt, a kinsman of the Lord Keeper, the suspicions of a "juggle" were much strengthened, and shortly afterwards Dr. Stratford even learned that Noel Broxholme was the real author of the verses for which Bromley (in order, as it was believed, to make his father the Speaker easy "after the disobligation laid upon him" in the summer), had received the prize (pp. 110-113).

At the end of this year, 1712, a new source of dissension arose from the Dean's determination to turn out the Chapter clerk, an old and valued servant of the House. The Canons retaliated by refusing to sign a "great glut of fines" which were about to come in, and of which the Dean's own share would be some 400*l*. (pp. 123, 124). At the next meeting of Chapter, the Dean proposed a reference of the dispute to two persons, one to be chosen by each side, and, according to Dr. Stratford, was non-plussed when the Canons at once agreed to it (p. 130). He tried to modify his suggestion, proposing to submit the matter to the Lord Keeper as Visitor, but the Canons, ignoring this, answered that they embraced his offer, were ready to name their arbitrator and were quite willing that all their differences should be referred in the same way (p. 131). Upon consideration, however, the Canons decided that, if they declined to submit the disputes to their Visitor, it would look as if they mistrusted their cause, and that it might be well to accept the Lord Keeper "as Visitor under the Queen." They prayed the Lord Treasurer for his direction in this matter (p. 133), and he evidently advised compliance, for, a few days later, Stratford told Lord Harley that they had acted in obedience to the Earl's wishes, but believed that it would do no good, as the Dean and the Lord Keeper had evidently made up their minds to bring it to a public hearing. The only thing which might draw him to a speedy decision would be want of money. There was now 1,000*l*. lying in the Treasurer's hands, and as much more expected shortly. The Dean had hoped that lack of funds would have brought the Chapter to submission; but their resolution was taken. They would neither comply nor appeal. The Dean was as much afraid of going to the Queen as the Canons were of going to the Keeper, and it was shrewdly suspected that the "Visitor" was by no means anxious to exercise his function ; in fact, he had declared that he would rather quit the Seal than do so (p. 136). The audit came to a full stop. The Dean demanded his money, fell into a violent passion, hopped up to Dr. Gastrell, pushed him with great violence several times and bid him get out of his house for a pitiful fellow. "This whole storm proceeded from three words. Dr. Gastrell had said in answer to very provoking language 'Mr. Dean, do not use me so; you know that *I know you*'" (p. 137). When he calmed down, an attempt was made to arrange something, but things were still at a deadlock when the news arrived that Atterbury was made Bishop of Rochester and Dean of Westminster. Christ Church was astonished and angry. "Nothing," Dr. Stratford remarked to Lord Harley, "that has been done since your father's ministry, has struck such a damp upon the hearts of all that have honour or honesty, as this promotion. All of any weight here . . . wondered that such a one should be permitted to act as he did here, but they lift up their hands to see him preferred for it" (p. 140).

The deanery of Westminster had first been offered to Dr. South but declined by him. Stratford went to visit him soon afterwards, and wrote "My brother South begins now to fail in his understanding. I am afraid his head will go before his legs. It was a providence of God that he retained his faculties enough to know that it was proper for him to refuse the deanery. He is complete eighty in next September" (p. 161). Dr. South's letter to Lord Oxford is printed in the 3rd Volume of the Harley Papers (p. 295), but it by no means gives the impression of being written by one who was failing in his wits. "Alas," he wrote, "that answer which Alexander the Great once gave a soldier petitioning him for an office in his army, may no less properly become her Majesty to my poor self (though not petitioning for, but prevented by her princely favour) : 'Friend,' said he, 'I own that I can give thee this place, but I cannot make thee fit for it.'"

Atterbury's appointment brought about complications at Oxford. He was on the point of being installed as Dean of Westminster, but he had not resigned his office as Dean of Christ Church, and had sent down a proxy to Dr. Smalridge to act on his behalf. There were grave doubts as to the legality of the proxy, and whether, when once admitted to his new dignity, he could continue to exercise the functions of his former one. Everything was at a standstill; no degrees were granted, the doctors could not "proceed" (p. 142). At the end of June, Atterbury came to Oxford for a parting visit, and Stratford believed he had discovered the reason of his "scandalous practice of holding two deaneries together" in his anxiety to secure his share of "the grass" which was only now being cut (p. 147). He met the Chapter, and to his claims of money the Canons replied that he should have "every style of payment" which had been made to his predecessors; that they themselves had no interest in the matter, for they would "only have the same share, whoever had the Dean's." The Canons stood firm, but Atterbury's "easy successor" gave way, and urged them to agree to what was demanded. The easy successor was Dr. Smalridge, who succeeded Atterbury here as he had done at Carlisle; and is said to have observed that Atterbury went first and set everything on fire, and he followed afterwards with a bucket of water. In the end, the Canons agreed to fall in with Dr. Smalridge's suggestion on condition that the retiring Dean should give up all the books, own Mr. Brooks as Chapter clerk, renounce all further claims, and sign for the money with his own hand (p. 149). Thus ended the stormy period of Atterbury's connexion with Christ Church. The picture is a curious one, but Dr. Stratford, as before said, was a man of strong prejudices. He did not do justice to Atterbury's abilities, gave him credit for no principles at all, and attributed to meaner motives the actions which more probably arose from an overbearing disposition and love of power.

Peace now descended upon Christ Church. "I have nothing to tell you," wrote Stratford, "but that you are not likely to be troubled with such long letters for the future as you have for two years past. We shall have some quiet ourselves and allow a little to our friends; we breathe another sort of air than we did" (p. 150).

On July 18, 1713, the new Dean was installed, but without the usual ceremony, partly because he was out of health, and partly, Stratford declared, because it was usual for the successor to make mention in his speech of his predecessor, and in this case the successor "could not with safety to his own conscience speak any good of one of whom he not only believes but knows so much ill" (p. 155).

The seat of war was changed, but the war itself was not at an end. Only a fortnight after Atterbury's final departure from Oxford, the news arrived that he had begun a new campaign at Westminster, where the vestry of St. Margaret's were already up in arms against the new Dean. He objected to their choice of Lord Guernsey as a vestryman, and "desired them to have a care of bringing Lords into the vestry, and to put them in mind that when they chose Lord Halifax, they had soon after the Palatines brought in upon them" (p. 157). He tried to dictate their choice of a vestry clerk, but by a majority of fourteen to four they elected their own man, and left the Dean to seek his remedy (p. 165). He "fell foul" of old Mr. Only, the "curate" of St. Margaret's, who had supported the said vestry clerk, and "used him worse than he ever did any one" at Oxford. Stratford believed that the war would last as long as that between France and the Confederates, and did not hesitate to suggest that the Bishop's aim was "that the peace of Westminster may be an argument for removing him to Lambeth" when there should be a vacancy there.

For several years after this there are only casual notices of Atterbury—"Ruffe" or "Ruffian," as Stratford usually calls him after his elevation to the see of Rochester—but in 1722, Stratford informed Lord Harley that war had begun again at Westminster, about the Receiver's place, and also that "Ruffe" was "making pretences to the good Duchess of Buckingham," and was caressing Pope, with a view to making him useful in the matter. The Duchess had dined at Bromley Palace, taking with her the young Duke, the late Duke's natural daughter, Pope and Chamberlain, and to say the least of it, "this was an odd condescension to one who had not then been a widower a full month," if she designed no further (pp. 325, 326). Following close upon this came the discovery of Atterbury's intrigues with the Pretender, made through the incident of the dog "Harlequin" sent to him from Rome, which revealed to Government "the cant name by which Ruffe goes in the letters," a name well known as that of a Jacobite plotter, but not hitherto identified with the Bishop of Rochester (pp. 326, 328, 330).

Atterbury's committal to the Tower followed, and now, when his old enemy was in trouble, Stratford began to relent towards him. In giving an account of a quarrel between the Bishop and

Col. Williamson, he shows plainly that he thinks the former in the right, and he repeatedly speaks scornfully of the manner in which Lord Harcourt had abandoned his old friend. The sentence of banishment seemed to him worse than imprisonment, to one of "Ruffe's" age, and with his ignorance of foreign tongues (pp. 332-337, 344, 355, 356, 362). Soon after Atterbury went to France there was a gossiping rumour that he had fallen out with his son-in-law, Morice — "the poor man," Stratford observed, "must have somebody to quarrel with." The last notices of him are at the Court of the Pretender, where he was reported to have quarrelled with all his intimates, and to have "roused amongst those poor desperate wretches as great a bustle as ever he did elsewhere." In fact Stratford believed that he had set them all by the ears, and that the Government had never done a wiser thing than in sending him thither (pp. 385, 386, 390). In this connexion may be mentioned some curious details given of the rupture between the Pretender and his wife, "Madam Sobieski."

The news from Oxford in Dr. Stratford's later letters is not so interesting as in those written during Atterbury's rule at Christ Church. Amongst other matters, he mentions the settling of prebends upon the Colleges (pp. 170, 171); the struggle over the Margaret Professorship (p. 211); the quarrel with the soldiers quartered in the town (pp. 216-218); the setting up of the "Constitution Club" (p. 222); the parliamentary election of 1717 (p. 231); Hearne's difficulties (pp. 234-236) and his assiduity "in publishing those useful pieces of monkish antiquities by which he is to immortalize his own name and reform us all" (p. 249); the election of a new Rector of Lincoln (pp. 256-259); the deaths of Dean Smalridge and Dr. Hudson and the appointment of Dr. Boulter in Smalridge's place, and of Mr. Bowles as librarian (pp. 260, 262, 265); and the election at All Souls (p. 263). On Candlemas Day, 1720, he chronicled the serious fire in Christ Church Hall, caused by the burning of the evergreen decorations there on Candlemas Eve, "to put out Christmas." The cost of repairs amounted to 600l., but this included replacing the "rotten lantern" by two chimneys, arching the hall, and repaving it (p. 268-270). "Our governor" Townsend, making a survey of it on this occasion, declared that "there was never in England a better building for fineness and curiosity, as well as for strength and the goodness of the materials." This is no doubt Townsend, the architect, whom Hearne mentions as surveying the ground for the new printing house (*Collections*, ed. Doble, III. 347). There are many notices of the deaths and appointments of Professors and "Heads," including a detailed account of the struggle between Cockman and Dennison for the Mastership of University College (pp. 340-343, 346, 349-351).

In 1723, Dr. Boulter was made Archbishop of Armagh, and Dr. Bradshaw succeeded him as Dean of Christ Church. His first act was to promote an address to the King on the royal donation of a History Professorship to the University. Over this address there was much discussion and diversity of opinion. The Dean wished to insert the clause, "the only support of the Church of England, of all the Protestant interest abroad and of all the Protestant Universities." Dr. Stratford had his doubts whether either the Dean or any of the Ministry could even give the names of a tenth part of the "Protestant Universities," so little had England to do with them. In the end, the clause was rejected, the address was taken up by some of the "grandees," and was kindly received and graciously acknowledged. But the poor Vice-Chancellor—who had never been at Court before or ever seen a King or a Secretary of State—"to the no little surprise of the company, made no answer to the compliments" (pp. 327-390).

In his later years, Dr. Stratford spent much of his time at a "cottage" on the Berkshire Downs, probably built by himself, in the parish of Little Shefford, of which he was rector. Nothing is more curious in the clerical life of that day than the universal system of pluralities which prevailed. One Canon of Christ Church was Bishop of Chester, another was Bishop of Hereford. Yet Gastrell and Smalridge were not ambitious politicians, but quiet students and earnest Christian men. Stratford himself, when asked one autumn when he had last seen his parsonage, vaguely replied "this summer." He had the excuse apparently that there was no rectory house, as he added that he "designed to build"; but there is no hint of how the services of the Church were carried on there during his life in Oxford; no mention of any intercourse with the curate who presumably supplied his place.

That some sort of line was drawn between what was right and what was wrong appears evident, for Atterbury was blamed for keeping the chaplaincy of Bridewell when he took the Deanery of Christ Church, though he seems to have held it without comment—and that of the Rolls also—when he was Dean of Carlisle; and Stratford distinctly declared that the rectory of Presteign ought not to be held by any one who could not reside there. But the rules by which they were guided are not very apparent to a modern eye.

The letters of these later years contain comparatively little Oxford news. Stratford did not like Dean Bradshaw, and gave gloomy accounts of the state of Christ Church under his. rule (pp. 441, 447). But though much away from his old haunts, he kept to the last his love for the "lads" of the House. In 1726, he wrote to his friend (now Earl of Oxford) that he wanted to beg his charity. "I have not been troublesome to you or my lady on that head," he says; "I have always forborne you while the poor late Bishop of Chester [Dr. Gastrell] and others were picking your pocket for good purposes. But I now want a few guineas, beyond what I can afford myself, to help some poor lads with necessaries, bare necessaries, to go on with their studies." It is evident from a letter written a few days later, that Lord Oxford responded to this appeal promptly and generously (pp. 432, 433). In November, 1726, the Earl offered his old friend the valuable living of Presteign in Radnorshire, but, though much gratified, Dr. Stratford did not accept it. Had he been fifteen years younger, he wrote, he would most thankfully have done so; but at his age, he ought not to think of beginning a new course of life, and whoever took the living ought to spend most of his time there. He could not feel it right to put a curate into such a place that he might have the overplus to put into his purse and to spend at a distance, doing nothing for it (pp. 443, 444). After this his health gradually declined, and on May 8, 1729, his servant wrote to Lord Oxford that the evening before his beloved master had peacefully passed away.

This volume does not give us much fresh information concerning the Harley family, but there are two or three letters of Dr. Stratford's (of earlier date than those calendared here) which throw an interesting light on Edward Harley's college life, and show that as regards the love of books, the boy was father of the man. Young Harley went up to Oxford in 1707. Stratford, already a canon, could not be his tutor (that office being shared by Mr. Terry and Mr. Keill), but he evidently had charge of him, as in July 1708 he wrote to Robert Harley, "it will be the endeavour of my life to lay hold on all opportunities to express to the utmost of my poor power the sense which I have of my obligations to you; but the favour which you are pleased to allow me of Mr. Harley's company is a very great addition to them." In December following, he sent up the half-year's account, which, with part of the letter commenting on it, may perhaps be worth giving here.

	£	s.	d.
Mr. Harley's Account.			
Commons.—Michs. Qr. - - - - -	1	10	4
Xmas. Qr. - - - - -	1	6	0
Buttery.—Michs. Qr. - - - - -	1	10	0
Xmas. Qr. - - - - -	1	9	10
Tutors, ½ year - - - - - -	20	0	0
Servitor - - - - - - -	1	0	0
For washing for himself and man - - -	1	5	0
Barber - - - - - - - -	1	10	0
For a set of microscopes - - - -	3	5	0
Recd· of Dr. Stratford - - - - -	26	1	4
To his man for board wages - - - -	2	19	2
Bookseller's bill - - - - - -	25	15	9
Bookbinder's bill - - - - - -	16	3	4
Tailor's bill for morning clothes ° - - -	8	19	10
	£112	**15**	**7**

1708, Dec. 19. Christ Church.—"I have enclosed Mr. Harley's account for this last half year. I am afraid you will be surprised, as I was, at the bookseller's and bookbinder's bills. It was unknown to me till within this week that he owed anything to either of them. When I inquired why he had not called in for their bill sooner, he told me he hoped to have discharged those bills without troubling you with them. But he could not tell me how he proposed to do it. ˙I told him I thought myself obliged to acquaint you with any debts he contracted here, that all the comfort I could give him was, that if you must pay bills I believed you had rather pay these sort of bills than others. I wish you would be pleased to order him to send up the bills to

---

° Perhaps mourning clothes for the Prince of Denmark.

you, two-thirds of the bookseller's bill are for very trash, and I am afraid at least half of the bookbinder's is for gilding and Turkey leather. He is very uneasy at the apprehension of your displeasure on this account, and any notice that you are pleased to take of it will, I believe, be a sufficient restraint to him for the future. I bless God, in all other respects he is as you would desire he should be. If you will be pleased to order Mr. Bateman to pay the money to Mr. King in Charter House Square, I will discharge everything here. Mr. Harley would have me put in full pay for his tutors, but I am obliged to acquaint you that five pounds for this last quarter to Mr. Keill ought to be deducted. Mr. Keill was here at the beginning of the quarter, when Mr. Harley was at Brampton. But since Mr. Harley's return, Mr. Keill has been attending at London, and has not read to him this quarter."

In the Calendar of the Harley papers proper is the note sent up by the culprit at the same time. "I am extremely ashamed," he wrote to his father, "of the two articles that have so great a share in it; I mean what's paid to the bookseller and bookbinder. I have nothing to say in excuse for my fault but only that as it is the first of this sort that ever I was guilty of, so I assure you it shall be the last."

It is curious to note, in this connexion, that concerning another item of expense, which would seem much less legitimate, he makes no apology whatever, but merely informs his father, "I gave Mr. Broxholme two guineas for the Ode that is printed in the Oxford verses with my name under them." This is not the only occasion on which Mr. Broxholme is mentioned as writing other people's verses for them. (See p. 113 of the present volume.) He ends by saying that if he may have the set of razors promised him, the expense of a barber will be needless in the future.

Edward Harley does not seem to have kept his terms very regularly, for in a letter of August, 1710, Stratford wrote to him, "I now begin to despair of seeing you within your usual time of half a year. . . . Your tutor, not expecting you some months yet, takes this opportunity of your absence to go himself upon a ramble" (p. 9); and in a rather earlier letter, not calendared here, the doctor asked him if, at least once while he was at college, he could not return "in less than half a year's time."

In August, 1710, Robert Harley was made Chancellor of the Exchequer and practically Prime Minister, and from that time his son paid only flying visits to Oxford.

There are allusions in the letters to Guiscard's attempt upon Lord Oxford; to Lady Betty's marriage to Lord Carmarthen and to her early death (pp. 97, 114, 173); to the unhappy married life of the Earl's other daughter, Lady Dupplin, afterwards Countess of Kinnoul; and very warm letters of congratulation when the rather prolonged negotiations which preceded Lord Harley's marriage reached a satisfactory conclusion, and the heiress of the Duke of Newcastle, Lady Henrietta Cavendish Holles, became his wife (p. 166). In February, 1715, the little daughter, Margaret, was born, who was destined one day to unite the House of Cavendish to that of Bentinck. It was remarkable, Dr. Stratford thought, that she should arrive on the very day when her mother came of age. Many allusions in the letters show how greatly Lord Harley desired a son; but when at last (after the father had succeeded to the Earldom of Oxford) little " Lord Harley " made his appearance, he only lived a few days (pp. 402, 403) and Lady Margaret remained her parents' only heir.

The letters of the early summer of 1714 are full of anxiety concerning the Lord Treasurer's position, all the more so because Stratford believed that he was "too stout" to take means to insure his own safety (p. 189). On July 29, the news of his fall had reached Oxford, but other than personal regrets were speedily much lessened by the fast following news of the downfall of his enemies' hopes in consequence of the Queen's death.

"The disposition of the staff," Dr. Stratford wrote, "was indeed lucky; if [the Queen] had recovered, all the new measures would for the most part have been broken by it; but I could wish, however, that it had been in your father's hands at this juncture, and so I believe they do who wrested it from him." Stratford was not without hopes apparently that Lord Oxford would return to power, especially as Thomas Harley had been a *persona grata* at the Court of Hanover. " Do you hear how your own family are like to be with the new powers?" he asked on August 8, and two days later he observed : " The Regents drive fast; it is to be hoped he who is represented by them will like a gentler race when he is in the saddle. He has it in his power to establish not only himself but his family, if he would take the way which I believe your father would suggest to him. If they who are his justices should be his counsellors, his reign will be uneasy" (p. 198).

Lord Oxford was in much financial embarrassment after his fall from power, and his son also, in spite of his wife's wealth, appears to have been in difficulties. There was talk of the two households sharing an establishment, but although Lord and Lady Harley were very willing to have the Earl with them they by no means wished to have the Earl's second wife, who evidently was not popular with her husband's family. Dr. Stratford declared that Lord Oxford's private debts were above double anything he had, without computing the encumbrances on the estate, for which interest must be paid; and he strongly urged Lord Harley to put a stop to all unnecessary expenses and not to think "any frugality, be it never so little, useless," in order to bring his expenditure within the compass of his income (p. 208).

The birth of Lord Harley's daughter at this juncture was considered a great blessing, giving the prospect of the permanent settlement of the great fortunes of the Cavendishes in the Harley family (p. 212, 213).

There are no letters in relation to Lord Oxford's committal to the Tower, and only a casual mention of his release (p. 220). After this, there is nothing beyond slight allusions to his health and movements, until his death in May, 1724, when Dr. Stratford offered his condolences, dwelling upon " the integrity with which he served his country in the midst of temptations as well as perils, his universal capacity for it, and the unblemished honour with which he is gone out of the world" (p. 379).

There are many references to other members or connexions of the Harley family; especially to "Mr. Auditor" and his son Edward (afterwards his cousin's successor as Earl of Oxford), and to the Foley family. Lord Foley is usually spoken of as Abel; his wife as Abelina or the Termagant, his son as Abelin. Thomas Foley, of Stoke Edith, is the " little captain" or the "little captain of Stoke."

Sir Simon, afterwards Lord Harcourt, Lord Keeper and Lord Chancellor, is very frequently mentioned, at first with respect, but afterwards with a bitterness only second to that shown towards Atterbury. His son "Sim" or "Simkin" appears chiefly in connexion with his attempts to get into Parliament. He died abroad, to his father's great sorrow, whilst still young (p. 278).

Dr. Stratford appears to have been very intimate with Mrs. St. John, afterwards Lady Bolingbroke, and keenly resented her husband's neglect of her. "I was last week to pay a visit," he informed Harley in the summer of 1711, "to a poor disconsolate lady in Berkshire. I met nothing there but sorrow and disorder. That unfortunate gentleman is more irregular, if possible, in his private than [public] capacities. A sad instance to all young gentlemen of quality, how the greatest parts and expectations may be made useless and be disappointed by the folly of vice— the only way in which that unhappy gentleman will ever be of any use in the world " (p. 39). In the midst of his plottings, in the summer of 1714, to turn Oxford out, Lord Bolingbroke wrote to his wife praying pardon for all his ill-usage, promising amendment, and expressing his intention of coming to her shortly at Bucklebury. Stratford professed himself at a loss to understand his reasons, but believed it was either that he thought he should lose the day and have occasion to retire, or that he had been advised by his new ally [? Atterbury] to treat his wife better for their common credit (p. 193). Lady Bolingbroke clung to him in spite of his ill-treatment of her, and after the Queen's death was in great distress. " She burst into as great concern for one who has deserved so little of her," Stratford told Lord Harley, " as Lady Harriot could have done for you . . . and would part with all she has in the world to save him " (p. 203).

She died during her husband's exile, and when he returned to England, it was with a second wife, a French lady, whom he had married abroad.

There are several allusions scattered through the letters to sayings of Dr. Radcliffe's, the noted physician, as that "a man might as well draw a face as prescribe for one that he did not see" (p. 334); that Bath was good for the colic, but good for nothing else (p. 385); and that he knew not what to do for babies, and so was for giving them as little as possible and leaving nature to do its own work (p. 403). On Radcliffe's death, in 1714, Stratford supplied Lord Harley with some details of his will, observing " 120,000*l*. in charity is what can scarce be paralleled in any age from a private man, and all gotten by himself by the fairest practice that ever any of the profession used " (p. 206).

Swift and his writings are occasionally mentioned, and Dr. Stratford confessed to a great liking for " Gulliver," although he did not dare to own so much to his friend " grave Thomas " (*i.e.* Lord Foley) who was full of wrath against the book (p. 445).

When Pope's " Dunciad " appeared, Stratford at once guessed who was the author, being confirmed in his suspicions by a newspaper report that there had been " some insult lately made on him " (P. 464).

There is a rather interesting criticism of Burnet's History of his own time, on p. 367, and several letters about the wordy war which raged round the "Epistles of Phalaris," in which Dr. Stratford, like most other of the learned men of the day, believed Bentley to be in the wrong (p. 487). Notices of books and the writers of books occur so frequently throughout the letters that the reader can only be referred to the Index.

On p. 417, mention is made of Dean Berkeley's design to build a college in Bermuda. Another matter which is repeatedly alluded to is the struggle in relation to the wardenship of the Collegiate Church in Manchester (pp. 272, 390, 391), for the better understanding of which it may be well to remind the reader that in 1718 the Rev. William Peploe, a zealous Whig, was appointed Warden, and not having the necessary doctor's degree, obtained one from Archbishop Wake instead of going to his University for it. Gastrell, then Bishop of Chester, his diocesan, demurred to the Lambeth degree, but, by a decision of the Court of King's Bench, its sufficiency was declared, and the Bishop, silenced though not convinced, proceeded to the institution. On Gastrell's death, Peploe was made Bishop of Chester, with permission to hold the wardenship *in commendam*. This raised a fresh difficulty, for the Bishop of Chester was, *ex-officio*, visitor of the College, and Peploe could not visit himself. But Ministers came to the rescue of their ardent partisan, and passed a bill vesting the office of visitor in the Crown whenever the bishopric and wardenship were held by the same person. To this bill, the High Church party objected strongly, holding " that the authority which takes upon it to alter a statute relating to a

Visitor may do it in any other point," and that "if this power of altering charters and statutes by Act of Parliament for sinister ends be allowed to Ministers, no one knows when any foundation is secure, be it never so firmly established by law" (pp. 475-477).

There are a few notices of the new Palace of Blenheim and its mistress. The stoppage of the works there is mentioned (pp. 19, 20), and the consecration of the chapel (p. 467). The position of this show place, so near to Oxford, was not without its disadvantages. "I am almost foundered," Stratford wrote, "with showing sights to people that take us in their way to Bath or Blenheim. That Blenheim is a curse upon this poor place; I would at any time make one in a rising . . . to raze it to the ground" (p. 55). Of the imperious temper of the great Duchess, one or two instances are given. She forbade her grandson, young Lord Sunderland, to accept a post in the Royal household, and even obliged him to decline the Garter, telling him that "if he would despise their baubles, she would give him somewhat better." And when "Mr. Coke of Norfolk" (afterwards Earl of Leicester) took his bride to Blenheim, it was said that the Duchess "sent them word they should not see it" (p. 243).

Sir Robert Walpole's financial schemes are often alluded to, and there is frequent mention of the South Sea Company, in which, by Lord Oxford's advice, Dr. Stratford.bought some stock (pp. 112, 124), although he appears to have sold it again before the bubble burst. On pp. 275, 284, are allusions to the danger which Law, of the Mississippi scheme, ran in France, and to his pluck in meeting it. When he afterwards came to England, he brought introductions to Dr. Stratford at Oxford, and spent an evening with him. He talked very readily of his affairs, and seemed to regard it as a great reflection upon himself that anyone should imagine the South Sea Scheme to have been formed on the plan of his Mississippi one, evidently deeming the projectors of the former to be great bunglers (p. 335).

A gossipping letter from Bath, written in 1718, reminds us of an old custom in connexion with the drama. "My Lady Harley's play last night," Dr. Stratford wrote to her husband, "was crowded more than any that has been acted this year, but . . . Lady Katherine Edwin would not go to the play, nor let Lord Manchester's or her own daughter go, and was so well-bred as to own her reason to be because it was bespoke by Lady Harley. But the ladies stand by us bravely, and have vowed revenge upon Dame Edwin, if she dares to bespeak a play this season " (p. 237).

Two or three anecdotes show the anxiety felt by the upholders of the House of Hanover, in the early days of its rule, in regard to the spirit of the English people. In 1718, the Bishop of Salisbury, Dr. Talbot, had a great quarrel with his Dean and Chapter for letting the anthem " By the Waters of Babylon " be sung on the 1st of August, the anniversary of the Queen's death. " The thing," Dr. Stratford told Harley, " was perfectly casual, a new boy who was to be tried having desired it might be in that anthem." If it was really an offence, he suggested, his Lordship had better get an Act of Parliament to have it left out of the ordinary course of the Psalms (p. 240). Two or three years later, great offence was given to the Court at the production of Handel's new opera, " Floridante," in which a rightful heir is imprisoned and afterwards triumphs over his oppressor, at which "last circumstance, there happened to be very great and unseasonable clapping, in the presence of great ones " (p. 311). While on the subject of music, we may draw attention to the account of the " Act " of July, 1718, when Croft, the well-known church musician, received his degree of Mus. Doc., offering as his " exercise " settings of two odes by the Oxford Professor of Poetry on the peace of Utrecht. " Croft's music," wrote Stratford, "was as fine as ever I heard, and will be worth your hearing in town "; and again ; " the music, which was very extraordinary, made our guests tolerably easy . . . The English music was preferred, and very deservedly, to the Italian, though the last was very fine, I believe, in its kind " (pp. 153, 154).

Many of the passages quoted in this introduction have shown Dr. Stratford as a good hater. Perhaps we may fitly conclude the notice of his letters by showing that he could be a good lover too.

The most charming passages in the letters are those in which he writes of his friend Dr. " Robin " Morgan. Stratford greatly desired to get him to Christ Church. " There is one you know well," he wrote on Dr. Woodroff's death, " beyond Snowdon Hill, who is of too great value to be buried in that obscurity, but who yet is of so peculiar a temper that we can never hope to see him here, unless he is forced to it by such a call which . . . he would look upon to be God's Providence " (p. 44). In 1711, the vicarage of Ross was offered to Dr. Morgan, but Stratford much questioned whether he would leave his Welsh retirement. "The difference of the profit will have no manner of influence on him. That which he has is scarce subsistence, but if it pays his journey to attend Convocation, he looks no further . . . He acts not by any of those motives by which we other poor mortals are influenced." And again, "If his own motives do not tell him it is proper for him, you can no more persuade him to take such a considerable preferment than you could our Dean [Atterbury] to bate one shilling in a fine. If one could but have an art of transfusing souls, I would not have my dear friend's pure gold alloyed with any of our Governor's copper, but the least tincture of Robin's would burnish strangely the other's coarse ore. But it is a peculiar mercy in God not to leave Himself without witness in the world, but to raise up such pure bright souls to show others what human nature even in its present state is capable of " (pp. 71, 78).

The selection of Dr. Stratford's letters for publication was made by Mr. Richard Ward and the Secretary to the Commission. To Mrs. S. C. Lomas the Commissioners must express their acknowledgments for the Introduction and Index to the Volume.

THE MANUSCRIPTS

OF

HIS GRACE THE DUKE OF PORTLAND.

Vol. VII.

HARLEY LETTERS AND PAPERS.—VOL. V.

Letters of Dr. William Stratford of Christ Church, Oxford, to Edward, afterwards Lord, Harley.

1710, June 24 [Oxford °].—Your letters are like a man's first paper when [he] sits down to make a sermon; a great many hints very proper to be enlarged upon. But I make the proper allowances for one who has so many visits to receive and return, in so short a time as he designs to stay in town.

Where did you meet my friend Henry Hoar? I supposed he was the person you dined with, and not the eldest brother. When you see him again my most hearty respects to him.

The insolence of these fellows is without example, but as our actions have often consequences that are little expected from them, I believe this may too; not only in the general indignation which is of great use and must weaken their interest, but this very insolence of theirs, if duly managed, as no doubt it will be, may prevent that only inconvenience that was feared upon a change, and by which, as their last resort, they thought to awe the Queen, I mean any failure in the public credit.

We are as ready as you can wish us to be for a new Parliament. Nay more than you wish us, for we think your proceedings too slow, and are afraid you are terrified by the Bank. But should the power of the Bank come down to Kensington, we must call up Dr. Sach[everell] and his posse to encounter them.

1710, July 7.—I bless God I am safe at home, I have taken so sound a rest after my journey that I have yet seen nobody. I am sorry you and I should differ in any thing, but I speak only

---

* All succeeding letters are dated from Oxford, unless otherwise stated.

upon my own experience. I find rest more sound and refreshing at this season here, than it was in London. I suppose I shall see you, when the Parliament is dissolved, in your way to some borough in Herefordshire.

My most humble duty and thanks to your father for the great kindness he was pleased to honour me with when I visited him. Be pleased to let him know that if any letter comes to me from abroad, it will be immediately delivered to him. When your father has read it, pray do you enclose it to me. I know not but it may oblige me, much against my mind, to see your wicked town again. You shall hear by the next post about Lord Strathallan.

1710, July 8.—I had some discourse with Lord Strathallan yesterday, he readily agreed to that I proposed, said he had re-solved before to have turned him off, and that he had been told from other hands that his credit had suffered for this fellow's faults. You may be certain I was much pleased with this, and looked on his Lordship's ready compliance as a good argument of his own innocence. It was agreed to discharge the fellow this morning. I enquired this evening and found it was not done, his Lordship pleaded that, upon second thoughts, he was afraid it would be thought unhandsome to turn off one so nearly related to him at so short warning, that Lord Drummond would take it very ill, and much to this purpose, and he desired to keep him till Michaelmas. This unexpected change has raised some suspicions in me. I shall not trouble you with all that passed between us, I insisted that the fellow should be gone immediately and told his Lordship that I had hitherto stopped the complaints from coming to the Dean, that if his Lordship would not, the Dean, when the complaints were laid before him, must dismiss him. And that I thought it most fit for his Lordship's, and his cousin Gann's credit too, to have him discharged as soon and as privately as might be. We agreed at last that he should be discharged on Monday morning. You shall hear by Tuesday's post if his Lordship keeps his word with me. I have not intimated to his Lordship yet, that I suspect there is any truth in the reports that have been upon his Lordship, through this fellow. I thought it not proper to take notice of them, till the fellow is gone. He is more willing to part with him, whilst he thinks he is not suspected himself. As soon as Gann [or Gunn] is gone, I shall examine his Lordship as to himself and let you know what I find.

It is hot discourse here that the Duke of Marlborough has left the army in discontent and is coming over, with all speed possible. You need not be told who spread it or believe it.

1710, July 10.—Gann has taken a place in the coach to-morrow, though to my knowledge his countrymen, of as great quality as he pretends to be, have used no other conveyance than their own legs, for longer journeys. I am glad we are rid of him. This afternoon I had some discourse with my Lord about himself. He protests his innocence; I hope he does it truly.

Though to deal plainly with you, I cannot say that I am altogether cured of my suspicions. His Lordship is to [be] with me again this evening at eight o'clock.

Yours last night revived us. No one I think can doubt now of seeing these changes they wish for—were the conjurer once out, I think it would be for our advantage if the dissolution were deferred for some time.

Dr. Morgan left me this morning, with express charge to desire you to accept his respects. He was much pleased with your letter and thinks you a very notable statesman for your years. It is a dangerous trade, but if it is your fate to follow it, I hope you will make more advantage of it to yourself than your father has done.

Postscript. One of Corpus Christi tells me that a lawyer in town—whom he named not—says that the Queen has granted to Mr. Harley the Remembrancer's Office for three lives. I wish you could confirm this news to me and give me a good account of the value of it, it would be more welcome news than any I have yet heard.

1710, July 13.—The letter at last is come round to me from Exeter. Van Brug (Vanbrugh?) passed through this place on Tuesday and dined with George Clark. He said it was now agreed on all hands that there would be no new Parliament, that all differences were made up, and that Lord Halifax had been very instrumental in reconciling the contending parties. You see what opinion they have of us, when they think this will pass upon us from poor Van.

1710, July 16.—Mr. Palmer is here, but never surely was man sent upon such an errand with so little instructions from his friends what to do. The Bishop of London and Dr. Gastrell could not but know that the Chancellor's letter would be necessary for anything he had to desire here. Nay in my letter to Dr. Gastrell I mentioned it, that he might not fail to bring it with him, and to have it as much in his favour as possible. There will be a week's delay unavoidable in sending for the letter, and it is at the end of the term, when many will be uneasy to have the term continued. Indeed it may be done out of term, but not so well. The letter which your father received from the Bishop of London for the Vice-Chancellor never came to his hands, if he does not lie. The President of Corpus is out of town, thus we are under all the disadvantages possible. I have pawned my credit to the Vice-Chancellor—how far it will go with him I know not—that your father received a letter from my Lord of London for him, and sent it to him. I desire you would enquire what became of that letter. We have drawn and sent a letter this post to be signed by the Chancellor. I have presumed to let Portlock know that your father is much concerned for Mr. Palmer and to desire the utmost despatch. I shall take upon me to use the President of Corpus's name to his Society, and shall do Mr. Palmer all the service I can in all other colleges.

Though I heartily fret at the management of his business, and I desire you would chide my brother Gastrell severely, for instructing one so ill whom he would serve; I hope we may get it done, but it will be with more trouble, and charge too, to him than he would have had, had he taken proper measures.

The Remembrancer's place is no secret here, your friend Colonel Trelawny had it in a letter last night, as he was at supper at the Dean's, that it was given to your father and to you after him. The Colonel immediately published the news.

My Lord Carteret says you are not a man of honour, you promised to meet him here before he left us. He takes leave of us on Tuesday or Wednesday.

Postscript. Dr. Smith, Principal of Hart Hall, is dead. The Hall is in the gift of the Duke of N[ewcastle?].

1710, July 17.—The letter that should have come last night has miscarried again, and I suppose by the same mistake, of putting it into the Exon instead of the Oxon bag. I desire Mr. Thomas would superscribe it Oxford and not Oxon to prevent such mistake. I am the more concerned at this mistake, because I hear from my friend in the city that he had received a letter for me which he had sent to yours.

1710, July 19.—To put you out of pain, the letter which should have come on Sunday came to me last night, the post mark on it was on the 17th; at the same time, I received yours with the enclosed, which were written on Monday. I immediately dispatched the Bishop of London's letter to the Vice-Chancellor. We shall have greater opposition than I expected in Mr. Palmer's business. The Vice-Chancellor pretends to be sorry for it, but I wish he does not secretly foment. It is very unlucky for me that the two persons of most weight here, and on whom I could most depend, are absent; the Principal of Jesus and the President of Corpus Christi. Those who oppose the degree have a more plausible pretence than I thought they could have had. It seems when Mr. Palmer wrote against Wesley he reflected upon the universities, and upon Dr. Hudson by name, and said his dedications were such as a school boy should be ashamed of. I had sent for Dr. Hudson, and represented Mr. Palmer's case to him, and desired him to do what service he could. He was very unwilling and very uneasy; this surprised me so much, that I expostulated with him somewhat warmly upon it. After much talk at parting he told me, for my sake he would do what service he could, but that when the business was over he would convince me I should not have asked him. I was still in the dark, and telling a common friend with some wonder what had passed between the Doctor and me, he smiled and told me the reason, of which I was ignorant, having never read either book. I perceive this will be the greatest objection, but I hope to get over it. I shall apply to every college in turn, by myself or by my friends. I have had friends from different colleges with me about it all this morning. It happens unluckily, that at the time I should be going about, I shall be obliged to attend for the most part at

home, on Sir Simon [Harcourt] and his brethren. But I hope I
have secured Magdalen on the account of our late merits on
Dr. Sa[cheverell]'s account. I reckon too upon Jesus, Corpus
Christi, most of New College and Lincoln and St. John's. And
should any peevish men persevere to oppose it, I hope we shall
have some friends too in other colleges. I hope we shall receive
the Chancellor's letter to-night, we have no further occasion for
the Chancellor's interest.

Postscript. Since I wrote, I understand Sach[everell] comes to
town to-day, and under pretence of going to meet the Sheriff, who
comes to wait on the judges. Town and country are going to
meet him, and he will be brought in by a vast multitude. I am
sorry for the bustle that is like to be, but it will make well for
us. By Sir Simon and our own merits we shall secure this great
Doctor and do Mr. Palmer's business.

1710, July 21.—Mr. Palmer's letter came last night and was
proposed this morning to the Heads of Houses. We did not
apprehend any difficulty there, for which reason many did not
attend. But it was opposed violently by two extremes, the
Master of Balliol and the Warden of Merton, the Bishop of
Oxford's chaplain. I am told, among other things, these
gentlemen were pleased to say that he was Mr. Harley's convert,
and that his converts were not to be trusted, and to instance in
Roger Griffith. The Vice-Chancellor was very fair and would
not come to a question, but adjourned the meeting till
three o'clock this afternoon, when the Dean will be there and
has sent to his friends to meet him there; and the Principal of
Jesus who is to come to town, and on whom I have waited, will
be there too and hearty for us and no doubt we shall carry it
amongst the Heads this afternoon, and in the Convocation too, I
hope to-morrow morning. A report has been spread here that
your father has had a meeting with the great Duchess at my
Lord Halifax's and composed all differences. These are very
slender shifts indeed.

1710, July 22.—Mr. Palmer is now a Master. Upon the Dean
and the Principal of Jesus appearing, all opposition was dropped
amongst the Heads, but the struggle was great in Convocation.
I was afraid of our neighbours at Corpus. They are refractory
fellows. The President very fortunately for us came home on
Thursday; I waited on him to know if he had received a letter
from my Lord of London to recommend Mr. Palmer, he said he
had heard nothing at all from my Lord of London about him. I
was a little surprised at this strange neglect. I had desired
Dr. Gastrell to let Mr. Palmer know that the Bishop's letter to the
President would be of more moment to him than any other
recommendation. Upon examining Mr. Palmer, I found the
Doctor had told him, but he had not yet any letter. But the
President was very kind, and was pleased to say that the concern
Mr. Harley had for him ought to command all the respect this

place could show to Mr. Palmer. The Principal of Jesus said the same. The President came to-day to the Convocation and kept his House in order. The Principal came not to Convocation, but sent to every fellow in his House a particular request from himself to desire them to be there. When I waited on the Master of University, he said the kindness which he understood Mr. Harley had for this gentleman was an obligation to him, without any other reason, to serve him. His conversation with Greg has done him great service upon this occasion. When we met this morning, the cry was, we should lose it. We had brought all our own strength, which happened by reason of the Act term to be more than ordinary. Dr. Sacheverell came himself, but brought not the party with him he had promised us he would. I did not see above four Magdalen men that I knew. Just before we entered the Convocation House, Dr. Sacheverell came to me and said he had discovered a combination against us, and the letter would be thrown out, unless Mr. Palmer would come into the Convocation, and make a recantation of all he had written or done against the Church; that if he could prevail with him to do that, he, Dr. Sacheverell, would engage the letter should pass. I said I thought it was very odd, when we proposed to show respect to a gentleman, to require him to do penance first; that I should make no such ridiculous proposal to him, that I, who was his friend, had rather he should be without that he asked for, than have it upon such terms. The House was very full. The Heads and Doctors, who were above twenty, were unanimous for him. There was opposition, but to no purpose, amongst the Masters. Pray do not pity me, I hope I shall never think it a trouble to do my duty.

I brought an ugly cold with me from London which hung on me till Mr. Palmer came. A little exercise this hot weather has been instead of a bagnio and I hope cured it. Mr. Palmer knew this place so little, as to have designed whilst he was here to have gone over to Waterstock to pay a visit to Sir Harry Ashurst, but I have desired him to forbear it, if he has any concern either for his own or his friends' credit in this place. He will be in London on Monday night.

When may I hope to see you here? By Mr. Auditor [Harley]'s going into the country, I conclude the writings are finished and sealed. I suppose the State now detains you. You must allow us to be uneasy here, till the Parliament is dissolved. The judges insulted all who came near them, and said they could assure them there would be no new Parliament. This morning they were very positive in it, upon letters they pretended to have received last night from London. I need not tell you how much they are credited, when I tell you who they are, Blencow and Dormer. One of them, Dormer I believe, said he wondered how any one could imagine any such thing, that no new Parliament could be called without it was first proposed in Council, and that he would not give three years' purchase for any one's life that should venture to propose it.

1710, July 22.—Since I wrote I have some reason to think our new ally Dr. Sacheverell played booty with us; he voted himself for us, but I am afraid every one of his House who were there, except Tom Collins, my old acquaintance, were against us. The Doctor's cavalcade into this place was a trick upon the Sheriff and his company; they little expected the Doctor's company; he came along with Sir John Walters, who had appointed the Sheriff to meet him near Woodstock. The Doctor had secretly appointed some of his own House to meet him at the same time and place. The companies met much to the surprise of the Sheriff. Sir John desired the Sheriff to join companies and to wait on the Doctor to his college. For fear of quarrelling with Sir John, he complied.

1710, July 25.—This place now affords nothing to entertain you we are here in a perfect calm, expecting to hear somewhat from you, that will put us into a new ferment.

Lord Carteret left us on Wednesday last; I may tell you, but let it go no farther, that I think his Lordship has not left us very handsomely. You know the respect and kindness with which he has been used here. He told me at parting he would order a plate to be sent. I desired his Lordship would be pleased to let us have that sum, and no more, which he designed for the plate, to the building. I told him we did not desire it to increase the expense to his Lordship, that the very sum be designed for his plate would be as creditable to his Lordship as a plate, and much more acceptable to us. I could not prevail; he said it did not suit with his quality if he gave money, to give so little, and urged Lord Hatton's example, who has given a plate. I gave him many other examples of those who had given that which they had designed for a plate in money, and withal said, I must have leave to tell him, that I thought we had reason to expect more kindness from his Lordship and my Lord Hatton than others, since they had brothers who would enjoy the benefit of the foundation. He was nettled I perceived at that, and said he knew not how he was more obliged because his brother was to be there. I said I hoped his Lordship would think he had more reason than another to keep our buildings in repair, when so near a relation was to have the advantage [of] it.

So we parted, and I am afraid I have lost some of his favour for presuming to be so free with him; I wish he may not be so very full of himself as to think all the kindness we endeavoured to show him here as strictly due to him for the honour he did us in living in our society. Lord Strathallan is heartily glad that cousin Gann is gone. Drummond has still some power over him, and, as I perceive, upon the point of Jacobitism, and writes to him, I believe frequently, to enquire whether he keeps his principles. He was afraid of displeasing Drummond by dismissing Gann, and thought too lest Drummond should suspect him for that to have lost his principles as he calls them; but he says Drummond is easy at it, for which reason his Lordship is now glad that he is rid of the fellow. He owns he was a saucy and clumsy servant, and I believe he thought him too a spy upon him, who gave Drummond an account of all he did.

Postscript. Blencow showed scandalous partiality to Dormer at his trial. All in court cried shame and perceived from the first moment that it was concerted to acquit him.

1710, July 27.—I must tell you one story of our ally Dr. Sacheverell, but it is not proper yet that it should be known. He told Mr. Palmer that he had reconciled the *Proto-Bibliothecarian* to him, that word was (*sic*) more stately than *Dr. Hudson.* I was sure that must be a lie, because I knew there was no correspondence betwixt them, but an aversion on Dr. Hudson's side. I asked him when I saw him; he said he was never but once in his company, but that as to his speaking to him about Mr. Palmer, it was impossible to be other than a lie, for he had not seen his face since his return till they met in Convocation.

1710, July 29.—We are much obliged to you for accepting so kindly any endeavours here to express our respects to you, but we have been upon another foot with you than with any one we ever had to do with. We have been paid beforehand for any service that is in our power, and the utmost we ever can do must fall short infinitely of that we are obliged to, supposing we were brokers bred at the exchange, and not scholars at a university. We have reason to bless God, if such excellent dispositions have received no prejudice by conversing with a Society that has so long been under so ill a name. The justification you will be of us to the world would be an ample reward, could we deserve any from you, and had no other.

I have been so used to meet with little thanks from those I have desired to serve, that I am not in the least now shocked at it, nor should any wise man, if he can recollect himself a little, ever repine at. It is of mighty use to us in the frail state we are, and inures us by habit to that which the gospel requires so positively of us, to do good upon no other motive than the apparent goodness of the action. Till a man can act upon that view, however good his actions may be, he has no great reason to applaud himself for them, or to hope they are acceptable to God, not to mention the disquiet he must be often in, from the struggle within him of different motives to action. But in the weak state we are, I am afraid disappointments are necessary, as well as reason, to work in us such a temper.

That Lord [Carteret] and I parted with great civilities to each other. Whatever I may think of him, I shall live with him as I have always done. Indeed he had a mind to have had some of my books, and said he hoped I who was his friend would let him have them cheap, and he would have bought them at the rate of a dividend in a bankrupt's estate, at half a crown in the pound. But I did not think myself obliged to carry my compliments so far. It is lucky for him he comes into the world, with an alliance into Lord W[eymouth]'s family, and at a season when honest men are coming in play again. These accidents may contribute to preserve his credit, I say not his conscience, for if I mistake not much, he would have been for advancing his fortune upon any terms, and with any that had been in power. I think I told you my thoughts of this long ago. I find he expects the court should soon take notice of him, and he expects too, more upon his own intrinsic merit than the merit of his alliance to Lord W.

You will easily think that I have made what enquiries I could, how men voted in Mr. Palmer's business. I heard one thing very remarkable I think. Every Whig and low churchman in the university was against him. This may afford matter for reflection.

Postscript. My Dutch friend [Drummond?] sent me word he had dined with Mr. H[arley] and said in his Dutch English, *to more one knows him, to more one is in the love with him.*

1710, August 1.—I am afraid Dolben's last will must be good, I am sorry though it should, he has used his family so unkindly in it. You were mistaken though I believe in one point, I think you told me that he had left the Vice-Chancellor's wife 50*l.* in it. It is an 100*l.* that he has left her. He was more a cavalier than to leave such a lady so little as 50*l.*, as he was more a merchant I suppose than to part with money without a consideration for it.

Who is it that at this time dares open your father's letters? I thought Frankland had been his servant, the other indeed is Lord Treasurer's nephew, but he too is now near allied to Sir Simon. But methinks either of them might discern the weather well enough, not to offer at any such thing.

I am sorry to hear your father has occasion for cupping. Was it to remove or to prevent a cold?

1710, August 4.—Your weeks that you propose to be absent when you leave us, will in time be prophetical ones. I now begin to despair of seeing you within your usual time of half a year. Be pleased to deliver the enclosed with my duty. Your tutor not expecting you some months yet takes this opportunity of your absence to go himself upon a ramble.

1710, August 10.—You have relieved me with a strong cordial indeed, our spirits were just failing. The Principal of Jesus was with me on Monday evening, but nothing I could say or could give him could cure his despondency. He gave all for gone, and your father's being turned out of commission, which I laughed at, was a sure sign to him that the party were confident of no dissolution. The news you have sent is too good, I am now only afraid of the excess of transport. Such sudden transitions from the extremity of one passion to another are as dangerous to the mind as any quick changes from heat to cold would be to our bodies. For myself, I have been rallying my philosophy this morning, and hope to bear this great event without suffering any considerable alteration in my own compositium. But I much fear how it may work amongst some of my friends of the grave Heads. I wish some who may now think themselves in a fair prospect of being Bishops yet, do not find too much joy make vacancies amongst the Headships.

I shall not quarrel with you for staying, since you do it to so good purpose. I suppose the compliment will in a few days be returned to the Lord Chancellor. When you have cashiered him, I think you may see us again. You may leave what remains to be done to others, I shall want to hear from you how this late great man and his friends bear his disgrace.

I have written this morning to my correspondent to press for a positive answer by next post, whether we may expect him or not. They have had such accounts sent to those parts, that they could never believe that would be done which, I bless God, is done. I believe that has been the occasion of his delay. I am apt to think this news will both determine him and hasten.

I ought I own to be satisfied with that I had last night, but I know not how, it only makes me more eager. I hope you will not fail me every post, I shall long to know to whom I am to make my compliments.

1710, August 13.—The joy we were in for so great an event as your last gave us notice of would not let us reflect on it at first as we ought to have done, I have now recovered myself enough out of my transport to be able to consider it a little, I find it grows upon me. I could hardly hope to see such a point gained, but I was still more afraid how my master would keep his ground than how he would get it. I was able in my little sphere to foresee mighty difficulties he must have to struggle with, but it seems to me that they are all provided against, and begin already to vanish. The inconvenience we feared at home, the point of credit, is over I reckon, and I fancy my Lord Rivers is instructed to prevent any we were afraid of abroad. Every one upon the news of his going made that reflection, that he was to offer the army to the Elector, and to command under him. It is all wonderful and he who could bring about these great things, I trust in God, can support them too.

I hope you do not think I am so impudent as to expect now to hear from your father, it was too much honour for me that he was pleased to honour me with his letters when he had not this business on his hands. I shall think myself honoured much more than I have reason to expect, if he will be pleased to throw away so much time as to read this I have enclosed.

I am much obliged to my dear Lord Dupplin for his very kind letter. That which took up the greatest part of it and pleased me most was the great gratitude he expressed to his father Harley, and his great sense of the tender kindness he has found from him, and of his own happiness in being allied to him.

I heard from Mr. Drummond by the last mail. Harry and his lady too are your admirers and heartily your servants. Pray don't you supplant me there, I have been served two or three such tricks by my bosom friends. He tells me that all their wise men heartily repent that ever they meddled in our affairs. I am sure he does good service at this time in Amsterdam. I should visit a poor disconsolate lady at Bucklebury [Mrs. St. John], but I have made my excuse, because I would be ready to come at an hour's warning, when I hear my correspondent is expected. Come when I will, I suppose I may find lodgings empty at Mrs. Beresford's.

Mr. St. John writes to me, that Mr. Harley and Dr. Freind had told him that I was expected every day in town. By Mr. Harley I suppose he means you, but how came Dr. Freind to know that I designed to be in town. Had he it from you? I suppose he does not know on what occasion I am to come.

All here begin to despair of seeing you again, especially since the late turn; they say you are of age, and now entered upon the government of the nation, and not likely to relish any longer the poor entertainments this place affords. I would fain flatter my-self that we are not yet to lose you. At least for your own sake I could wish we might have you for one quarter of a year more, but since I perceive you are too much engaged in the state to think of us suddenly, I can wait for my 'snush' no longer. Pray send me such a little paper as my godfather [Thomas Harley] is used to send you, by the post.

I had almost forgot to tell you that I saw in a letter last night that came from Lord Dartmouth's office, that the Lord Chancellor was made Lord Lieutenant of Hertfordshire. It astonished all the company, but all agreed it must be a mistake. Surely as affairs are now, it is impossible. Let me know what is in it. I could not but observe a little alteration in the style of the same letter. The post before it said the Lord Treasurer was turned out, this last post upon mention of him, it said, having resigned his staff.

1710, August 14.—You will perceive by mine yesterday how much all here were surprised at the news of the Lord Chancellor's being Lieutenant of Hertfordshire. Did any of the remainder of the old Ministry, upon the strength of the Queen's old promise, put this in the Gazette, without acquainting her and having her leave for it, or did she give way to it without acquainting her new Ministry with it. Satisfy me if you can which way this was, many fancy from this that the seals will continue in the same hands; but that surely is impossible if the change that we expect is to be. It is much easier to take away the seals than the staff. Whatever the present gentleman's personal qualifications are, he is not surely one of that interest that he can do much hurt to any one if he is dismissed, or service if retained. The difficulty in this case I take to be in supplying the vacancy, if Sir Simon, as he declares he will, should be obstinate. But betwixt ourselves, perhaps that may be to raise the terms.

Postscript. Remember my 'snush' on Tuesday, master.

My peaches and nectarines begin to be ripe and are the finest in the country. Won't this tempt you?

1710, August 17.—I thank you for the 'snush' which is very good, and for your letter I should have thanked you, if it had been somewhat longer, and had answered all my queries.

Has Harry Guy been to make his visit at your house, though I think I need not enquire that, if he is not bedrid. I expect that you should make that use of this juncture as to get us another 100l. out of him. When you see him next, let him know that we are going to build up the west side, and that you are commissioned to desire his kindness to us. If he excuse himself, be importunate, and sour too if there be occasion, he will not refuse you if you insist upon it.

I suppose one thing that may detain you is the great pleasure you have in the daily application that is made to you for places. I have discovered myself within this week to be of much more moment in the world than I could have thought I had been. I have been honoured with several epistles to desire my recommendations, but whatever opinion the gentlemen have of my interest, I find they have a good one of my modesty. But there is one thing, which is a sort of charity, which I wish you would do if there be any room for it, it would be very kindly taken here. You know Seb. Smythe, that was master here. I suppose you know the story of his marriage, and how hardly his father has dealt with him—particulars are too long for this letter, but you may have them, if you know them not, from Dr. Smalridge who was his tutor. His father has taken the wife's portion and will not settle one farthing more than an 100l. per annum on him. He must have when his father dies 1,000l. per annum, which his father cannot [put] him off. His father, who uses him so hardly now, will I believe leave him his whole estate at last, and then he will have 2,000l. per annum in this county. But his circumstances are very hard indeed at present. His utmost ambition is any clerk's place, of 50l. per annum value. If there should be any vacancy to which you should think fit to recommend him, you would oblige one who now wants it, and may live to be in a condition to thank you. If there be no vacancy in your offices, let me know and I will try what I can do for him with Mr. St. John. He writes a very good hand and is very sober and diligent. You may know more of him from Dr. Smalridge. Though he was a master of arts here, I cannot boast much of his learning, but he has enough for the place he pretends to.

I am told one Dr. Strahan will be recommended to your father, as one proper to be employed abroad. I have known him before he went abroad, a young man at Balliol, and since his return. He is a good-natured, sensible, and I believe a very honest man, that would give satisfaction to those who employ him. He has been abroad several years. He was secretary to Sir Philip Meadows at Vienna whilst he resided there, but his relation to Sir Philip should be no prejudice to him, for he always was and is heartily with us. I expect to see Sir Simon here to-day, if the haste he is in to take possession of the seal does not hinder him from calling.

Lord Rivers' illness is somewhat ominous, as though all designed for a place of that importance should have some lets.

Mr. St. John's heart will be at ease, he will be in the post he has long wished for. I pray God he consider himself under his new character, a Secretary of State must not take all those liberties one of War might think perhaps proper to his station.

1710, August 19.—You have Sir Simon now in town : he did me the honour to lie here on Thursday night. He still says he will not have the seal, but I perceive it is only to raise his terms, that which he will insist on I believe will be somewhat considerable for life for the young gentleman.

The Bishop of Winton is hastening into Cornwall, he told the Dean at the election that when he had heard he was going into Cornwall, he might be sure there would be a new Parliament. I am afraid he will scarce do himself more credit by his future than he has by past recommendations, but it is to be hoped his influence will not be so great as it has been. The Colonel [Trelawny] owns that Liskeard designs to revolt from him, but he hopes however they may have a struggle for it. The Colonel is gone this morning to go with his father into the west.

Postscript. We are told Lord Marlborough has written a very submissive letter, owning all her Majesty has done to be for the best, and offering his own service at what terms she pleases. But I suppose no messenger can be returned from him, since the staff was broken.

1710,. August 21.—You are too kind in saying you would endeavour to make Mr. Smith easy, that expression may seem to import somewhat more than is aimed at. The lowest clerks places in your offices as well as in the Secretaries' are I suppose worth 50*l.* per annum. That is the utmost that he pretends to, or that I would desire you to intercede for. I would not undertake for more than that he writes a good hand, and would be diligent and faithful. If he should be able to recommend himself to somewhat better, it will be well, but I believe he aims only at getting somewhat, that with that he has may enable him to live without contracting debts, till the Jew his father, who though he is tough yet is old, shall be pleased to leave him in better circumstances. I have some credit with the old fellow and could get any thing from him but money. He has many tenants, and though he had always been with us, yet at the last election he declared he would be neuter, and said it would not be safe, for such a one as he was, to oppose the Duke of Marlborough. I was sent to him, and it cost me from one o'clock till six to persuade him that he would suffer nothing by voting with us. Since this turn he takes me for a conjurer ; and says he will vote as I would have him so long as he lives.

, Not only I, but much better judges, like the "Examiner" extremely. I now know the author of it, but what he writes I perceive has been supervised.

Is that old sinner [Guy?] so weak that he cannot crawl out? If I come to town I will make him a visit, and beg you to go with me. I may hope to prevail of you to assist me. The son of a Premier minister will weigh more with him still, than one of our profession.

We have digested the staff, and our appetite is very sharp. You must furnish out some more entertainment, if you would not have us clamorous.

Postscript. The debt to the workmen at Blenheim that is known is above 60,000*l.* They owe to Strong the mason for his share 10,500*l.* It will go hard with many in this town and the country who have contracted with them. Their creditors begin to call on them, and they can get no money at Blenheim. One poor fellow, who has 600*l.* owing to him for lime and brick, came on Saturday to Tom Rowney [M.P. for Oxford] to ask for a little money he owed him. Tom paid him immediately. It was about 5*l.* The fellow thanked him with tears, and said that money for the present would save him from jail.

1710, August 24.—I thank you for yours, but pray never refer me to others. They do not think themselves bound to be punctual in their correspondence with us poor fellows, that live at such a distance from the chief wheels that move the politic machines. It is a favour if those gentlemen will let us have a line from them when they have nothing else to employ their time in. I had no letter last night from my brother Gastrell, or any other of my correspondents but you and Mr. St. John. Some of them might have been so civil as to have given me some account of their address and their reception. Not that I think it of so much moment to be duly informed of the ecclesiastical part of the politics, but I would not have been at a loss for an answer to those who enquired what I heard of it.

I had letters from the camp by the express, they seem to doubt whether they shall be in a condition to attempt another siege. There is a great sickness among the troops.

Mr. Harcourt is treating to-day at Wallingford, where Hucks and Nevil spend freely to oppose him. I want to have you in. I will be content to let you go to town on that occasion, but on no other. And that too on condition that you shall see us for some time in the recess, though you may be too great to wear a gown then, but I have known Senators wear pudding sleeve gowns.

1710, August 27.—We have worse news of Lord Scudamore than I perceive you have. Our last account said he was given over and could not live. This is very melancholy composition of the differences in your country. You see what comes of riding foolish horses. I hope you will take warning, and mount only such sober beasts as I do.

The address is certainly very well penned, but I cannot see any reason there was to carry it to Lord Anglesey, for his approbation either of the thing or the style. No doubt it galls the godly, since it cuts off in a great measure one of those means by which they might hope to recover ground again. This will prevent the effect of any insinuations that we are at the bottom in the interest of the Pretender. If they cannot make that believed, I know no other way they can have any advantage, unless by our own foolish jealousies and divisions.

I long to have a little discourse with you. I wish you would come to me, or that my Dutch correspondent would bring me to you. Let me know if you can how the change here has worked with the great bully abroad.

1710, August 28.—I could not omit this opportunity of writing one line to you. I had by this mail a letter from your very humble servant Mr. Drummond. He tells me all are satisfied in that country, except at the Hague, where malice and wrong emissaries abound. All modest men are vexed at their impertinent meddling, to which, they allege in their own excuse, that they were not only encouraged, but half forced. They care not for that which is past, but they want to have the Duke continue in command. I suppose they have found their own account better with him than they can hope to do with any other, and they hate the name of a Sovereign Prince to command. I have not troubled your father with this, because I suppose he may have it more fully from Mr. Drummond himself, or from better hands. He tells me there are already at Hanover before my Lord Rivers, emissaries from the Montagu family of Northampton; that is his expression. One thing he mentions which I wonder is not taken notice of in any of the public papers, that Cadogan is turned out of all, to the joy of the whole army.

Postscript. This day I have set the workmen to begin to pull down another side of Peckwater.

1710, August 29. Bucklebury.—I had not time in my last to reflect upon the news we have from Spain. If the victory proves as great as the first report of it is, it must bring with it at once all we can wish for. There is an end of all difficulties we feared, either at home or for our allies, about the command in Flanders; there will be no occasion for any General. We have nothing now to ask of the French but that they have already offered, and they will give more now I suppose if we insist on it, rather than not have peace; but this victory will not only give us peace I hope abroad, but at home too. The change of affairs upon it must give such authority at home to the Queen and her ministers, that they will be able not only to subdue enemies, but to control too unreasonable friends. It is to be hoped they will, without any further delay, take the measures they think proper, without thinking themselves obliged to enquire whether every one they have to deal with is in a humour to be pleased with them.

I owed a visit to the lady of this place. I did not see any time I could have but these two days. I came over hither last night, and have appointed the coach to meet me again at the end of the Downs to-morrow morning. I shall be at home by noon. I believe I may find Mr. King at my house at my return, if that may be any encouragement to you to come to me, but your taste I suppose is quite altered. The last " Tatler " or politics have spoiled your relish of microscopical observations. I want your assistance though in my own affairs. Upon the pulling down of this side of Peckwater, I shall take the advantage of the old materials, to build anew my own outhouses. I shall have a kitchen, a brewhouse, a woodhouse, I shall have lodgings over for servants, and a large room to dry clothes, or lay lumber in, I shall [have] two new bog houses, and a little greenhouse and a little bagnio. I have a plan which will be very pretty I think as well as very convenient, but I should be glad to have your approbation of it, before I execute it.

The lady of this place commands me to give her respects to you and your father, and she hopes her husband [H. St. John] did her the justice lately to make her compliments.

1710, August 31.—The fame of credit so effectually established, when all at home and abroad expected to hear we were bankrupt, will be more formidable to France than our arms, and dispose them more to peace than even this blow in Spain, if it hold true. It seems, there is more money to be had than is wanted. Mr. Decker wrote to me, that he would engage for 40,000*l.* but there was no occasion for him.

I wonder "Dyer" took no notice of the bills posted up in Spittle Fields. That is the true spirit of the party. When the changes that are expected are made, and the Parliament dissolved, there will be an end of the noise of the Pretender.

Mr. King and I spent the evening yesterday with Tom Rowney and I am desired to tell you that you are so slow in your changes that we have not yet new healths enough to last for three bottles of wine amongst five, but we hope you design to proceed *à la* Cohorn, not to fire at all till all your batteries are ready to play together, and then to fire without any intermission till the enemy surrender.

Postscript. In the printed catalogue, which I had from the bookseller I deal with, of new books which they lately have got, one is "*Histoire secrète de la Reine Zarah et des Zaraziens.*"

1710, September 2.—I had several of the letters to the "Examiner," as many as cost me fourteen pence for postage. I suppose they were sent by direction of the author. I soon guessed him. I had heard most of them in discourse. Lord Haversham's speech is much approved, but the "Queries" please wonderfully; I and several had parcels of them by the post. I had two besides that I received from you, and I have this day sent them into different parts of the country.

1710, September 5.—You are very kind in consulting our health so much as you do, you keep us to a very slender diet, you give us, when we are ready to expire, just enough to support life, and take care we shall have time to digest that we have had before you send us more news. We are now alarmed with a coalition, we are told those who threatened to throw up are willing to keep their places and to join with those already in, and the visits your father is said to have paid of late to Lord Halifax have given no little disquiet to us. I am sure of visits every morning after a post-night. Her Majesty ought to make me some allowance for the tea and coffee which is spent in curing her well-affected subjects in these parts of their fears and jealousies.

1710, September 6.—I was told last night with some assurance, by one who has pretty good intelligence, that the Duke of Argyll is in great discontent. It is said a commission was ordered to make Duke Hamilton Governor of Edinburgh Castle, that upon this news the Duke of Argyll had written a very angry letter—it is not said to whom—threatening the utmost revenge, if that place was so disposed of. That at the same time he had sent a copy of his letter to several friends, desiring them to publish it in all coffee houses, that amongst others a copy was sent to Dr. Garth, who had gone round all the coffee houses to read it. There are many circumstances that would make me think it a lie, but it was told me with so much assurance, that I desire you would let me know, if you can by to-morrow's post, whether there be any ground for this report.

1710, September 7.—I can return you nothing but account of our horse races, for the account you are so kind to give me of the State. The Duke of Beaufort's horse won the plate the gentlemen subscribed for. The Tories look upon this as a good omen. Sir John Walter and Sir Robert Jenkinson sat with me last night, they tell me they expect no opposition in the county, and that they hear Rialton, as well as Reade, has declared he will not stand. Fail not to bring or send those almanacs I sent up to your father. I can now complete the whole set, with very fresh and fair ones. I have duplicates, of imperial paper and of the first impression, of almost all of them. The gentlemen seem secure of carrying it in Gloucestershire for Berkeley, but all on the Oxford side of that county are very indifferent for Howe and many will be single votes for Berkeley. John the father, at our last election, forced a poor honest parson, who had some dependence on him, by open menaces to come against Sir Robert Jenkinson. This was the only vote he could any ways influence in Oxfordshire. The son however applied to Sir Robert for his interest in Gloucestershire, where his estate is much more considerable than in this county. Sir Robert refused him.

1710, September 9.—I saw a letter this morning from a gentleman of good interest in Cornwall, he says they are so well disposed there, that he believes Boscawen might be thrown out, if any one would oppose him. They expect Mr. Granville with new commissions for the county, and are impatient for his coming, they want somebody to head them there.

I forgot to tell you, that Sacheverell had been making interest to be chosen by this diocese Proctor for the Convocation, but he has found little encouragement from either the laity or clergy from whom he most expected it. He is thought much too forward. It is taken ill by the clergy, that one who has no preferment in the diocese should set up to be their Proctor. They look on it as a reflection on themselves as though no one amongst them were fit to represent them. It is so ill relished, that I believe he must drop it, for which I am not sorry upon some other accounts.

18

Postscript. We are at a loss to account for the delay of that which must be done at last. No one but thinks they have gone too far to stop; and we fear we lose ground by deferring that which is designed, and by not having taken advantage of the fear of the people. The enemy too has had time to retrieve their interest in some places, but this may be of an excellent use to you, who are now entering on the world. Learn from the difficulties your father meets with, what you are to expect; do not think, as many have too fondly, that because your designs are honourable and disinterested, therefore the execution will be easy. I grant you this is a thought that but offers itself to all honest minds, that have yet had no experience, but I think all the records we have of time show the contrary, and let any one try, and he will be soon convinced by his own experience. They who act upon other motives, have not only the more profitable but more easy part. If ever you hope to do any good in any station, high or low, you must be content, not only to forego your own interest, but prepare yourself to deal with the perverseness of friends as well as the roguery of knaves and the malice of enemies. The case seems somewhat hard on an honest man's side, and would be so, if he did not hope to have the better of it in another place. But this very constitution of human affairs would be a good argument for such a place, if we had not better.

1710, September 27.—You judged very truly of the reason of my not writing. I have not stirred out this week, that I might be at home when you came, but I perceive you are a courtier; you must take your chance now whether you find me at home or not. I will not be disappointed any more by trusting to you; it is some satisfaction for having so often disappointed me, that you promise to spend the winter with me. We did indeed suspect you would have been put up at Lympster (Leominster).

I must give you a pleasant account of the event of a great cabal last week at Althorp, though perhaps you may have heard it from better hands, I had mine last night from Dr. Keill. The Grand Duchess, Lords Godolphin and Rialton were there to direct, but not appear openly. All of the party were summoned in from all parts of the county. Upon a great council, it was resolved that the old members could not be thrown out but by breaking the Tory interest. Mr. Bretton of Norton was desired to appear. He is a young gentleman, half mad, who has got a great interest in the common people by an extravagant expense amongst them, always in the Tory interest, but has thought himself disobliged by Sir Just[inian] Isham, who voted for Sir Child against him for a verderer's place. His estate is not above 1,000*l.* per annum. Bretton objected that he could not bear the expense, they engaged to supply him with a 1,000*l.* towards it, upon this he declared he would stand, went that night to Northampton and set the bells to ring. Messengers were dispatched at the same time with great joy from Althorp, to give notice of it in every town in the county. Bretton went home, and his brother, as it is said, prevailed with him to desist. Whoever did it, he sent word the next morning to Althorp that he would not stand. Upon this the cabal there are become the jest of the county.

I have a little parcel of very good wine ready for me on the other side of the water, it is a present too, not from Mr. Drummond, but from my old dear friend Mr. Watkins. Can you protect it for me, if it comes over, it would help us to pass the winter with a little more comfort and to remember our friends in town. But do not give yourself any trouble, if it is not to be done with ease. I will write to Mr. Decker, to have it seized and to buy it out again for me, but one would save that money, if it may be done easily.

We are surprised at that which "Dyer" says that Mr. Smith is to be Teller of the Exchequer. Is he so formidable that it is requisite to buy his silence with so considerable a place? Surely he has merited nothing from this Ministry. We are somewhat angry in this county that Lord Rialton will not give us an opportunity of showing our interest.

1710, October 1.—You will perceive by the postmark from what part the enclosed came, it is from some one I suppose who thought you knew your own mind, and that they might take your word when you assured them you would be here by such a day.

Dr. Smalridge has given me an account of the impudence of the party in printing a list of names that was of dissenters to one amendment, to another that concerned the Hanover succession and which had passed without any opposition. Were care taken to make the detection as well known as the lie, they would fall into the pit they had digged for others.

By your letter the Lord Hyde and Lord Anglesey seem to be sharers in the Vice-Treasurer's place, indeed I have heard it is of value enough to satisfy two, if they can be reasonable.

We are much at a loss here, when Tom Rowney and I meet to settle the nation, to account for Jack Smith's having any place. We remember how he insulted Sir Simon, and what returns he made to your father.

1710, October 4.—I beg my most humble duty to my good Lord Dupplin, though I am glad he is in England, yet I know not how he can be spared at this time in Scotland. Are the hearts of his countrymen so turned that there is no occasion for one of his interest and authority to countenance the elections there? For you I give over all expectation of seeing you, I suppose I must hope in a short time as little for your correspondence as for your company, if I may judge by the gradual abatement in the length of your letters, which have grown each at least six lines shorter than the precedent for this last fortnight. We had this day notice that all who were at work at Blenheim, of all sorts, even to the weeders in the garden, were discharged yesterday by Vanbrugh sent down on purpose by the Duchess.

The uproar in the town upon this is very great, and I believe endeavours will be used to make some advantage of their resentment, and to set up somebody unexpectedly at the election which comes on upon Saturday.

The elections for the University and town were over this morning in a few minutes. I am afraid Mr. Harcourt will be hard set to-morrow at Wallingford.

I thank you very kindly for your enquiry, but since it must be seized, I need not trouble your friend. I will write to Mr. Decker to take care of it.

I am sorry I shall miss your letter on Friday. I have put off the journey I designed upon this bad weather. I now look upon myself as laid up till next April. I suppose Sir Richard Leving is put up in opposition to Lord Dupplin; he must set up upon the dint of money. He has no acquaintance surely or interest in that country. But we say here, that you who are at the helm are afraid of having too good a Parliament and take measures to cool the affection of the country. You put us in good humour last week, but we are somewhat puzzled at the commission of the Admiralty and at the disposal of some other places. We are told Walpole would have resigned his place of the Treasurer of the Navy, but that his resignation would not be accepted. I know not who has the merit of these things among the Whigs, but care is taken that your father should have the blame of them among the Tories.

Postscript. In one month more, Blenheim would have been covered so as to be secure against any injury from the weather. Their orders were positive to break off, and if it continue in the condition it is left, the frost and wet will ruin all that has been done this summer.

1710, October 9.—You made some omission in yours last night, which though small, would be of great use to me to understand the sentence. The words are—*My father says that this week and that day I shall go,* you designed to have interposed somewhat I believe betwixt *week* and *and,* which through haste you forgot. I suspect this the more, because Lord Dupplin tells me that your father designs for Herefordshire, and that he is to attend him, and that I shall have the honour of seeing them in their journey. This I suppose you designed to have told me; if you know the day your father designs to be at Oxford, I beg you would let mek now by to-morrow's post. I wish you would prevail with your father to do me the honour to take his lodging with me, and not to lodge, as he has been used to do, at an inn. If my Lord Dupplin takes part of a bed with you, you know I can accommodate both your father and his Lordship. I believe they may be easier here, than they can be in an inn. If your father will not consult his own convenience, I could wish he would be pleased to do me such an honour.

Why should you enquire whether I will go to the election at Berkshire ? I believe you do not doubt of my zeal to the main cause, but I am not so ill [a] courtier as to be wanting in my personal respects to a Secretary of State. Other ministers of State may not be of so singular a temper as your father is, as not to observe whether the respect and duty of their servants is not increased in proportion to the augmentation of their own honour.

By yours I should guess that Mr. Drummond has sent a bill in which I am concerned to your father. I am heartily troubled at it, and protest to you it was without my knowledge. I hope I have a little more manners than to have been so impudent, and I shall let Mr. Drummond know as much. But for your comfort, that is not the wine I expect from Mr. Watkins, I hope that will be better than Mr. Drummond's will be.

1710, October 12. Christ Church.—I thank you for yours, but I am so far from expecting you within this week or fortnight, that I have no hopes now of seeing you at all. I do not believe your father's business will permit him to take a long journey into Herefordshire, and as for yourself, I think you may have a much better pretence for being in the town in the winter, than you have had hitherto. There will be more company then and more business. Pray let me know your mind whenever you are able to know it yourself, and when you come to a resolution of not coming, pray send the key of your study to me.

We lost the opportunity of throwing out Sir Thomas Wheate at Woodstock, because we were not provided with' one to set up there. The town sent round the neighbourhood and could not prevail with any one to appear, nor could our gentlemen in three days' time find any among themselves that would accept it. And Lord Abingdon was unluckily called away to Westbury, whence he had news that Cornish was come thither with 3,000l. to turn that election.

Postscript. Since I wrote what is before, I hear that the petition of the Warden of All Souls, about which I presumed to trouble your father, has been delivered to the Queen and brought before the Cabinet Council. The gentleman who put it into the Lord Dartmouth's hand was written to not to deliver it before he had farther notice. I had desired it might be stopped till I had received your father's direction, but Mr. Hill had delivered it to my Lord Dartmouth before he received the letter, and my Lord Dartmouth had delivered it to the Queen before Mr. Hill could be with him again to stop it. I hear it is now referred to the Attorney. We hope his answer will be in our favour.

1710, October 15.—The visitation at All Souls was opened on Thursday, no more was done than to adjourn till three o'clock the next day, and to order every one who had any complaints to make them in betwixt three and five o'clock on Friday in writing. I believe the Commissioner did no more then than to receive the writings that were brought to him, and it is thought he will do nothing but carry up the papers to the Archbishop. As far as can be guessed by the Commissioner, it is supposed the Archbishop will not enter into any other complaints, but those about

the monitions to take orders, and that he will only give them a
new injunction to determine how many shall be allowed to study
physic. That will indeed lay the disputes in the college, but any
such allowance will be contrary to the intention and end of the
founder. There is some obscure intimation in one statute of
some who studied physic, but in the days in which those statutes
were made the practice of physic and study of divinity were
usual. There were many Bishops of Ely; and then in the University, I believe, there was no distinction in the degrees.

Your tutor is returned, and tells me you talked of being here
at the end of this week. I perceive you have had the pleasure
of imposing on him, he really was so credulous as to think you
were in earnest.

1710, October 16.—Do you stay in town to drink my tokay,
those very numerical bottles which you had were I believe the
same which were promised to be given to me upon the change of
the Ministry, and which you have now intercepted. I believe
you were conscious of this, and to cover yourself the better you
prevailed on Lord Dupplin to go a share in your robbery. You
depend upon it that I shall acquiesce in my loss rather than call
his Lordship to account for it but I may retaliate upon you if I
can. If ever I see you here again, I shall way lay the next
plum cake or pigeon pie that your mother or Mrs. Betty sends
you.

Do you know or did you ever hear of one Anderton or Anderson,
a Presbyterian minister? Do you know where his meeting house
is in town? He came hither lately to marry Burroughs the iron-
monger's daughter, she had been married before by her mother
to Woodcock, the Presbyterian minister who died here not long
ago. The mother was resolved she should not marry again but
to another of the same tribe, for reasons no doubt that are of
great weight with the sex, and perhaps from her own experience.
This man was sent for to marry her at the first sight. The
sisterhood in town, who had been desired to provide a yoke-fellow
for the young widow, had pitched upon him as the most proper;
but the reason why I enquire if you ever heard of him is, because
he affected whilst he was in town, to talk as though he was very
familiar with your father. He was always mentioning somewhat
that he said had passed betwixt him and Robin Harley, that was
the most respectful term he ever was pleased to use.

I was surprised to see the Solicitor General chosen for Bishops
Castle. I suppose he was chosen there by your father's
recommendation, at least by his permission, but I thought Lord
Dupplin had been designed for that place. Pray where does he
come in? I have not the bill of lading yet from Mr. Watkins, but
I have written to him to send it, and to make it too, to Mr.
Decker. I thank you heartily, but I shall not presume to give
you more trouble, I am ashamed of that which has happened
already, through Mr. Drummond's presumption I assure you and
not mine.

Postscript. The Tories here are not a little pleased with the success of the elections, and the more because there was no previous change of the lieutenancies and commissions of the peace. That circumstance makes us think our obligation much less to you at Court for the Parliament we hope to have.

1711, March 30.—It was dark last night before we could reach Tedsworth; the ways are much worse than when we came up before Christmas. We were out again this morning at four, in hopes to have got home before prayers, but we were obliged to stay at Wheatley to mend some tackle that was broken; there I got on my pad and came home. But they were got to church before I could get hither. I leave you to judge how tired I am who have been up for two mornings at four, no very usual hour with me.

I hope to hear to-night that the matter which came from the contusion is quite discharged. I could not have left the town, had not Dr. Radcliffe assured me that he could not now have any apprehension of danger. I hope your father has nothing now to do, but to improve the uses that are to be made of such a villainous attempt to the good of his sovereign and his country. And I trust that what we have seen is an earnest to us, that if the malice of his enemies is not extinguished by these visible interpositions of Providence, any future attempts of it will be directed by that Providence which watches over him, as all past have been, to his honour and the public advantage.

My fellow traveller Tom Rowney tells me that Dr. Sacheverell last week presented my Lord Keeper with a large bason and ewer double gilt. I wonder his Lordship would accept of it, for he cannot now plead the merit of having served gratis in that cause. There is a very pompous inscription upon it, but the Doctor has so interwoven his own praises with my Lord Keeper's, that his Lordship is afraid he cannot make any public use of the plate. It is said to be given *ob meam causam* upon such an occasion so defended.

Postscript. The title of the book is, as I told you, *Reinesii Apologia pro variis Lectionibus.* Rostock, 1653. I bought it single for Mr. Bernard, I suppose he bound it up with those with which it is now, because they too, as I remember, were written by Reinesius. If you are an adventurer for it, pray let me know what your success is.

1711, April 1.—I thank you for yours, it was the best cordial I have had since my tiresome journey. I rejoice for your father's sake, I rejoice for the public's sake, that he is likely to be abroad again so soon. I rejoice for my own sake, since I have his word, that when he goes abroad I shall immediately have you here again. You cannot think how lonely this place seems to me without you. The concern I have had for you has bred in me sentiments of another sort than I feel for any friend. I can almost as little brook your absence as your father, but I must begin to wean myself from you. Should I get you again this

time, I must not hope to keep you long, or to recover you whenever I part with you again; either a ramble, or a closer confinement than any you have yet had, will in a little time deprive
me of you.

The enclosed perhaps will surprise you, as it did me very
much I assure you. I found it when I left you, lodged for me at
the Speaker's. It would tempt me to think myself much more
considerable than I ever yet durst do. The words *ought to have
done* have relation to somewhat which he has pleased to throw
out, when we dined with Mr. St. John, and for which I had
presumed to expostulate with him. I did not expect such a
submission from so high a spirit. You see what is desired of
you, but take notice that I do not move you to do it. God
forbid that I should desire you to misrepresent so far a body
that has the honour to have you one of its members. We are
headless indeed, but not for that reason miserable, only as we
have lost our old head, not for want of a new one. I know not
one instance, since the vacancy, in which the authority of a
chief Governor has been wanted. The College is as full as it
was and as regular, without a Dean, and Peckwater goes on without money, and in both cases we subsist well enough yet upon
the stock of our old credit. But pray return my letter to me, it
may be of use to me perhaps, some time hence, to be able to
produce it.

Dr. Bayly's son is with Mr. Terry, as you desired. Dr. Potter
has left the College, without a design of returning till
Michaelmas, he has not read one lecture since last Trinity Term.
He never preached his own cause but once; Clemens Alexan-
drinus, in which he was to raise his credit, is laid aside. Alles-
tree and Jane, after having served twenty years, were used to
plead their age, once in a term, for missing a lecture. He is the
only professor who ever made a sinecure of their chair, and that
too upon his first entering on it; but the saints always had and
will have their peculiar privileges.

The Sub-dean [Dr. Burton] designs to be at the election, but I
hope you will not see him there.

1711, April 2.—I received the enclosed on Sunday, there is
nothing very material in it, but that the Dutch themselves begin
to be sensible that the French think not the change that has
been there to their advantage. This possibly may dispose the
French to make new offers of peace, but I wonder my correspondent should think the French as little pleased with the late
Ministry. I believe they had more hopes from the late Treasurer
(St. Germain certainly had) than from any one employed here
since the Revolution, and my correspondent might have thought
so too, if not from his own observation, yet from that which he
had often heard from me.

I have had time to look about me. I was alarmed, before I
came down, with reports that there were frequent riots in the
House, that the gates stood open all night, and that most of the
gentlemen had left it. I could not believe all I heard, but I was

afraid there might have been some occasion given to those who might think it their interest to improve such things. But upon a strict enquiry, I find [nothing] has happened since the late Dean's death, that could deserve any other notice than the ordinary ones of an imposition or cross. Many of the gentlemen who had fled from the small pox are returned. The number of commoners is near doubled in my absence, above forty undergraduates commoners resident and in commons in the hall. But though the reports are the reverse in every point of the truth, the reason of giving them out is pretty plain.

My most humble respects to my Lord Dupplin. I shall send by the barge on Thursday the books he has written [for?]. I will not send Maundrell's voyage because I will not cheat him, for there is a new edition ready to be published with some additions.

I shall send in another box the Irenæus, and the letters of King James, King Charles, and the Duke of Buckingham and his Duchess, with most of the originals of those published in the "Cabala." I beg your father would be pleased to let them have room amongst his noble collections.

Can you send me no news of the Archbishop? Can His Holiness get on yet his slipper on his toe? You are very brief, but very full as to the main point, and that makes me willing to excuse you for allowing me so little of your leisure.

This comes by John. I would have advised him not to venture to town whilst warrants and messengers are so rife, but he relies upon you to vouch for him, if he should be snapped and carried before Mr. St. John.

1711, April 7.—Brother Potter has brought himself into a snare from which I know not how he can well disengage himself. The parsonage of Newelme was given by King James the First to the University, in trust for the use of the Regius Professor. They were aware that a professor who had institution might, if he should ever leave the chair, retain the living, and defeat the end of the donation. In the grant therefore it is said that an Act of Parliament should be obtained the following session, to enable the professor, whilst he was such, to hold it without any institution to it, but no such Act was ever had. What other professors did I know not, but Dr. Jane wisely took institution upon a presentation from the university, and the university took his word that he would resign the living when he quitted the chair. Potter took no institution and has lately quarrelled about tithes with one Tipping, the chief man in his parish, and as notorious a Whig as is in the county. Tipping pleads great merit in helping him to the chair, pretends that the Archbishop employed him to get the Duke of Marlborough's favour to Dr. Potter. He says he had a promise from the Doctor that he should rent the whole tithe. He has written to the Archbishop to complain of our brother Potter's ingratitude, and has upbraided him with it to his face. But all this not weighing against that serious thing called money, Tipping has fallen upon another method that will give our brother much trouble. He insists that no tithes are due to him, for that he never was rector of Newelme, that he never had institution, and that the sequestration which was laid on upon Dr. Jane's death was never taken off. The lawyers I believe have advised brother Potter that the plea is good, and that he can have no remedy but by an Act of Parliament. He desired the university would be at the charge of procuring an Act. They thought that unreasonable, he now offers to bear half of the charge. That is to be considered, but the living is certainly lapsed if advantage should be taken, whether to the Queen or Keeper I know not.

I thank you for my letters. I shall preserve one of them, the letter was written for the sake of the postscript. It surprised me almost as much as the same person's earnest and repeated application to me, that I would pass by what Delaune had said of me to Dr. Smalridge. I could not help thinking him the most improper man in England to make such a request to me. His concern lest Delaune should suffer by it, looked as though he had not been ignorant of that he did, but Delaune has returned the compliment to him, for he has said here since his return with great seriousness and assurance, that if the Archbishop goes off, my friend the Prolocutor [Atterbury] is the most likely to succeed him, I hope, for the Prolocutor's sake, that Delaune has better ground for making him Archbishop, than he had for making me Dean, though perhaps both may come, though with a different intent, from the same place. It is pretty well known, where Delaune's chief application at present is. I heard the same thing mentioned there, but I was so dull as to think no more was meant by it than a high compliment. This would be a compensation that would be accepted of for our poor Deanery. I found Dr. Blechingden in town and had the honour of a visit from him. He brought the President's service and desire too, if I could be at leisure, to wait on me that evening. I returned my thanks for the honour designed me, but said I owed the President three visits, if not more, and that I hoped he would not trouble himself to come to me, till I had paid my debts to him.

John Davies is fallen down with his boat to Iffley this evening; on Monday he goes on, and I hope he will be with you on Thursday or Friday. He has two large chests with all the books my Lord Dupplin desired, and a little box with the Irenæus and all the papers that I had of any value, and some too that I am afraid are not of much, for your father. Many of the letters are in the "Cabala"; there are some, which are of most moment, that are not. You will find a letter from the Duke of Buckingham to King James I. about a letter which he was to write to Pope Urban VIII. You will find by King James's letter how he desired it might be altered before he could sign it. You will among the papers find the letter as it was first proposed and as it was altered and signed by him, though the original signed by him being here, it should look as though it had not been sent. You will find a letter from the Duke of Buckingham to the Queen of Bohemia, which I have put with some of hers to him, which makes it very probable that there was ground for the report that he broke off the match in Spain, upon an offer from her of marrying his daughter to her son. There are some copies of letters from our King Charles the First to his Queen, dated from Newcastle, which are not among his letters which are printed, but they confirm that odd story in my Lord Clarendon of Sir William Davenant being sent from the Queen to persuade the King to give up the Church. I suppose the King's constancy in that point was the reason why the Archbishop got copies of those letters, and preserved them. Some of the Duke of Buckingham's letters to King James agree with the account that is in my Lord Clarendon, of the state of favour Buckingham was in, after the breaking off the match with Spain. I cannot guess who wrote the account of Prince Henry, but it must be one who was very near him, and is the most particular account of his illness some time before and at the time of his death, that is anywhere to be met with. Beecher's account of Henry the Fourth's amour with the Princess of Condé, and of the mighty preparations he made upon it, for a war with Spain, is a very entertaining and valuable piece. There is no such account in any history that has been written of that court and time, but I could never hear that one of so good sense, as he appears to have been, was ever more at home than a clerk of the Council. Sir Th. Morgan's account of the battle of Dunkirk is very different from the French ones and not much for Lockhart's credit, but I believe it is printed somewhere.

How does Lord Strathallan do? Some care should be taken of his servant here. My Lord, when he went up, said he would send for him in two or three days. My Lord never wrote to him. There are half a year's wages due to the poor fellow, and he has nothing to subsist on. They should pay him, whether they will entertain him still or discharge him. He would make an excellent servant to one who wanted a good one and would use him well.

I had almost forgot to tell whence I had my news of the new Archbishop. The President of Corpus told me on Tuesday that he had it from one newly come from London, who seemed positive in it, and thought he had reason to know, but he named not the author. This afternoon the Warden of All Souls told me, and was surprised that it seemed news to me. He immediately quoted the President for it, as a thing that he reported every where with great assurance, and he seemed to have as little doubt of the President's authority as he reported the President to have of his news.

Postscript. There are some letters in the parcel from Sir Horace Vere, one of your ancestors I think—I do not remember any of them in the "Cabala," but in a hand as little legible as mine is. There is one from Prince Charles to the Duke of Buckingham, that is much to Sir Horace's honour.

1711, April 9.—I am sensible how I tired you last post, I will now be more reasonable. I hope to hear that your father is in the House again before the end of this week. Won't you see Robin Morgan and Charles King, before you leave the town? Robin Morgan is your neighbour, he lodges at a gunsmith's, at the Cross Guns at the bottom of St. Martin's Lane, at the same side with the church, and about five or six doors below it.

I should be glad to hear what fortune you have had in Bernard's auction. You may remember I showed you a book, in which there was a very odd translation of a copy of verses of Beza. They were the verses which gave occasion to Mr. St. John, though without any ground, to say that Beza had written lewd verses, which I had. That book I suppose is in Bernard's auction—he had it, and I never saw any one, but his and my own. The title of it is—".The Disputation concerning the controversit Headdis of Religion, haldin in the Realm of Scotland, the Yier of God, one thousand fyve hundreth fourscore Yeiris, betwix &c. Imprented at Parise the first day of October, 1581. 8vo."

I exhausted all that this place affords last post, but we are told you will be able to furnish us soon with some news that will be acceptable to all, such as is not only highly proper, but indeed as our affairs are, absolutely necessary, a thing long since due to the person chiefly concerned, but probably deferred by Providence to a juncture in which it will come with the best grace, for his honour and the public service too.

1711, April 12.—I hope the box is with you before this can reach you. I have no apprehension of any miscarriage, there is not a more trusty or careful fellow than he is who has the charge of it, he would swim with it in his hands as Cæsar did with his Commentaries, if there was occasion, and sink before he would part with it. It is your own fault if you had not any books you had a mind to, I gave you the refusal of them all. I forget what the books were that I mentioned at Abel's ; I think they were two or three of the Elzevirs which you said you had ; you consented that I should send up Epictetus, and the fragments of the poets. However I empower you to take any you have a mind to, but if you should be complaisant, I believe I can procure you another Epictetus in large paper. All the other books, which you wrote in your note, are reserved for you.

I left the town with sad expectations of hearing things I should not care to hear of my old friend the Secretary [St. John]. I had the honour of free conversation with him for the first month I was in town ; for the last two months I was there, though he was very civil when I waited on him, yet he was much on the reserve, and seemed as though he was willing to avoid with me. I did not understand it at first, but upon hearing some things, I looked on it as a kindness and true compliment to me. God forbid that I should desire to be thought one that is in his favour, when he holds such a conduct, that no one, of my gown, can be supposed to be intimate with him, without hazarding his own credit, and such a conduct, too, as must at length make it impossible for the best friends he has to support him. I have no hopes now of ever seeing it otherwise. This post was the last remedy; since that cannot restrain him from extravagances at least, it would be foolish to think any thing can ever alter him.

I pity the poor lady [Mrs. St. John] from my soul, she is a flagrant instance, amongst many others, who are made the most miserable creatures in the world, by having had so great a share in it. Whilst I had opportunity, I did her the utmost service that an honest servant and sincere friend could, but the person with whom I worked is now beyond my reach, and got out of the activity of my poor sphere. I can do nothing but pray for her; that I shall do, and I am afraid there is too sad occasion for it.

The passage you mention of Guiscard's letter is remarkable, it can have but one sense. I hear I have been much obliged for some kind things that have been said of me, since I left the town. A young statesman, that undertakes to manage in the House of Commons, is I am afraid one of my friends, and a young Lord from whom I thought I had reason to expect other things is another I believe, but these things will be me (sic). I ought not to complain, when the poor late Dean, that had merited so much more than I could, is not exempted though he is in his grave. Tom Rowney sends me word that the young statesman is in great wrath that our poor Deanery is not yet disposed of. I suppose he thinks it an indignity to himself, since he has been pleased to declare himself for one of the competitors.

Postscript. I think I remember now some of the books I mentioned at Abel's, and they are not sent. I have a variety to part with. I have got the few "Transactions" I wanted, and have now a duplicate of the History of the Royal Society, and of a complete set of the "Transactions." I sent my Lord Keeper lately two small presents which concern his family. One was a short Journal of the famous Siege of the Busse in 1629. In the last attack in which the town surrendered, and which was the only one in which there was hot service, Sir Simon Harcourt (his grandfather as I take it) commanded, and came off with great honour. The other is an account of Guiana, dedicated to Prince Charles in 1613, by Robert Harcourt, esquire, of Staunton Harcourt, who had a patent for it from King James, and attempted a settlement there.

There are among the letters some from the Duchess of Buckingham to her husband, which I would humbly beg leave to recommend to my Lady Dupplin's imitation, when she has occasion to write to my Lord.

Bring down Barnard's Catalogue with you, with the prices marked. Forget not my godfather's snuff.

1711, April 16.—I know there is a great intimacy between old Craggs and the S[ecretary St. John]. The S. thinks he has always been able to get secrets out of old Craggs, though I am afraid the contrary is true. For his sake he would do anything for the son, who is a very idle silly vain young fellow as you would be satisfied by some stories I could tell you. But I should be sorry to hear Stanyan was sent to Berlin, he would be more improper there at this juncture too, when the Queen is recommending episcopacy and the liturgy to that King, than at any other. He is one who, when he was in England, endeavoured to recommend himself by professing to be a downright atheist. You tell me in yours, *that the Archbishop is much since these last two days,* but you leave me at a loss to know whether you mean better or worse. Your friend Sir Henry Ashurst is dead. I know no one that will be so much lamented, except the good man at Lambeth, if he should go. Sir Henry sent for Ludwell; when Ludwell had written his prescription, he desired to be carried home again, but Sir Henry would not let him have the coach to go home, till he had heard Sir Henry sing a psalm, and a good man that was there pray extempore by Sir Henry's bed for an hour. The next time Ludwell was sent for he would not go.

1711, April 21.—I should be glad to have notice of your health, though I cannot of your coming. I hope you do not stay to see the Sub-Dean at the election, that will be no new sight. The late Dean, in the last vacancy, made the election as Sub-Dean, and after all the noise that has been about keeping this place vacant, it has not been void yet so long as it was the last time. Massey left the College in the night on St. Andrew's eve. The late Dean went up to town as soon as the new roll of officers had been fixed up on Christmas day; he returned not to the College till.the night before he came to be installed on the 17th of the next June. During all that time, the College was not only without a Dean, but a Sub-Dean too.

I heartily wish the session of Parliament were over for the sake of the Convocation. I am satisfied the bishops will not at present fall in with the Lower House to do any thing that is proper for them, but I hear the country clergy go off very fast. I wish the number do not grow so small, that the other side be the majority. Should that happen, the other party may not only hinder any good, but lay hold of that opportunity to do some mischief. This place affords no news, we expect that from you, especially upon this news of the Emperor's death. It is very unseasonable at the opening of the campaign, I should be glad to know your thoughts of it. I wish the retarding of a peace may be the least evil consequence of it.

Postscript. I told Lord Dupplin that I am afraid Mills' Testament in the large paper is not to be had. One was bought lately of a private gentleman, but six guineas were given for it. I have taken care to secure for each of you a copy of the "New Year's Gift" in large paper; I think only one hundred and fifty were printed, and they will be sold only in private, not publicly by any bookseller.

1711, June 9.—I hope you are safe at home, though it is nine o'clock and I have yet no notice, nor must I expect any I am afraid to-night. I have missed you much every evening since you left me, the want of you is more uneasy to me, because I thought myself so sure of you till the opening of a new session, and I begin to suspect now that I shall see you no more, at least not much otherwise than as a traveller, for two or three days. But you employ my thoughts more now than when you were here, and I shall trouble you with some of them when I hear how you are disposed of, whether you return to town, as I am much afraid, after your election, or stop here for sometime, as I would fain wish.

I was fast asleep for some hours after you were gone, indeed you were in bed some hours before me, for my guests were dusty and thirsty and stayed not to hear, but to cool themselves with liquor. Did not you think Mr. Chetwynd talked with the air of one who expected to be dismissed? Mr. King took him off from me at the proper season, when he was very willing to have entered into politics.

I have other guests now in town, my Lord Digby and Sir Charles Holt, you have lost a visit by being absent when my Lord Digby is here. I ventured to open your news letter and Mr. Thomas's, I return you Mr. Haye's; another letter which came yesterday by the courier was sent in your box by the coach this morning, the waggon was so loaded that it could not take the box that has the livery, it shall go by the next.

I have read the preamble designed for the Lord Keeper's patent; I think I may say of it *Est quod amputes?* I thought your father's not full enough. Here is in this somewhat that may be spared, I should think, I cannot say how right my notion is, that no virtues should be taken notice of in the preamble to such an instrument, but those which regard the public and by which he has merited of it.

I am told the archbishop is not so well as he would be thought, that he is not able to go abroad yet.

Postscript. Since I wrote yours is come in. I thank you heartily for it. I find I guessed right of my guest Mr. Chetwynd, I suppose he took his journey now on purpose to be absent when he was to be cashiered. I think I told you before you left me that Delaune's Headship, as well as his other preferments, was now under sequestration; but a worse thing breaks out, he had gotten 2,000*l.* of Holloway who was Coggs' partner, which is now reckoned by Coggs' creditors amongst the desperate debts, as well it may.

1711, June 11.—I thank you for the favour of yours, but I should have been more obliged to your Lordship if you had executed your intention of writing me a longer letter. Deny yourself for half a dozen minutes to those who came to make their court to you, and bestow them upon an old friend; they will be employed at least as profitably this way as in the other. I beg your pardon for presuming to rebuke you now, but I have a little good news to make my excuse; I have stole for you, that which you wanted so much, an Epictetus in the large paper, it is extremely well bound too. I looked in your study this afternoon for those pieces which you have of Xenophon, but could not meet with them, I think it is the Agesilaus which you want.

You tell me not how you are like to be disposed of; whether you go to the country or no? or whether,—which I am most concerned to know—I may hope you will stay there some time as you return from your election.

I had last night a great honour, I received from my Lord Keeper's chaplain, by his Lordship's order I suppose, the preamble that is designed for his patent, as I had before his Lordship's speech in the Exchequer to the Lord Treasurer. If this fit of kindness hold, I shall be put I am afraid to exercise my self denial, by the offer of the next prebend in his Lordship's gift.

Mr. Laughton and Mr. Stuart spent the evening with me, and I believe you think we remembered you.

Pray what opinion have you in town of the sailing of the Brest squadron so much superior to ours, on the same day, as "Dyer" says, that ours set sail? We are alarmed here, and in great pain for our ships and our forces too. Pray afford me a few more lines, being known to have the honour of your correspondence I am supposed to be furnished with the earliest and surest intelligence. I have a levee every morning to enquire what news I have from my Lord Harley; if I say I have none, they wont believe me, but think it ill nature in me, or at the best great reserve.

1711, June 14.—I see already what I am to expect, not only to lose you, but to be forgotten by you. I depended not only upon a letter, but a long one too last night, when you had excused yourself the post before for writing one so short. But I hear where you were, but you left your burgundy and champagne soon enough for the post, and did not drink so much of it as to disable you for writing. I hope you told Decker that you are to return to me, or there will be a drawback upon the burgundy when it comes. I suppose your Lordship is now above the dispensation of a poor pint of wine and water and dry bread and cheese for your evening repast. *Alia vita alios mores postulat*, but I must tell you a few of my own thoughts, before I take my leave of you, when you let me know how you are to be disposed of, whether you now fix in town, or go first to the country.

I have services and congratulations to your Lordship from your humble servant John Drummond and his and my lady. He tells me he is preparing a cargo for your father, and I am afraid will presume without my knowledge to thrust amongst it a little parcel for me; if he should, I must make interest to you to take care of it.

1711, June 16.—I must now tell you somewhat that nearly concerns you. I hear your father before he had a Staff was ready to sink, and had mortgaged his whole estate to the Duke of

Newcastle. But to make you some amends for this sad news, that he designs now to pay off the mortgage by marrying you to his daughter. I heartily wish the story may not be all of a piece, but this has been given out here. I cannot say it was by the same person who made remarks on the patent, but he who gave me the account of that told me this too, though he would not name from whom he had this, but it certainly came from some of that gang, if not from the same person.

I shall not be surprised at any thing I hear of Lord [Carteret?] you know what I have prophesied of him for this last two years. There can be no security of any thing trusted to that other gentleman. Anyone that will think him up to his pitch may have anything out of him. When he is in that condition he is less retentive in his head than in his tail.

Here is a visitation at University college, one of the fellows has appealed against the Master for turning him out before his year of grace was expired. All the Doctors of Divinity in the University are the visitors, I am now to sit in judgment upon the Master, and I will attend him.

1711, June 19.—I have sent your Lordship the proposals for printing the second volume of Spanheim *De usu Numismatum.* Your Lordship I think has not the first, you will perceive by the proposals, that you may have both and in what paper you please. I believe your Lordship and Lord Dupplin too will think fit to have the book; if you should desire it in the small paper, pray come in with me to make a set, and then we may have the advantage of a seventh amongst us.

Tom Rowney came to me the other day to tell me we had a Dean, but not as he said to give me joy of it. He had a letter dated on Thursday from my Lord Keeper's family, to tell him the Prolocutor [Atterbury] had that day been declared Dean of Christ Church. I know not the meaning of such news; if the policy was in expectation of hearing of great joy upon it, they were much disappointed. I could not but smile. He was angry I would not believe his intelligence, but I could not but think, that in a point in which I have some concern, I should have had as good intelligence from your Lordship as he could have had from the other place.

The great living of St. Mary's in Reading is void, it is worth above 300*l.* per annum, in the Keeper's gift. It was pressed upon Blechingden; he declined it, having too much the spirit of a gentleman to deal in any thing but dignities. Afterward he offered to keep it till the President was translated to a bishopric in Ireland, that he might resign it then to Archer, on condition that he should make over his interest in the College to him for it. This was the first plan, but I hear there is some alteration in it now, and that Blechingden absolutely declines it, but I know not to whom it will be disposed.

1711, June 20.—I must ask you how you do, though I have nothing else to trouble you with. I hear my Lord Keeper is to

c

be at Cockrop as this day. He stays only till Monday. I know not whether it will be proper to wait on him when he makes so short a stay. At least I think in good manners I ought to wait till I hear whether he is willing to admit of a visit. I had a very welcome letter last night from my brother Gastrell, he tells me I may expect to see your Lordship here in your way to Brampton. Pray contrive your journey so if you can, that you may spend an evening here. If you come in here, without baiting by the way, at three or four, we may have some hours together, and you may be in bed and up again as early as you please. Dr. Grabe is very desirous to know whether he may meet with you in town a week hence, he designs if you are in town when he returns to wait on you and my Lord Dupplin with the Alexandrian manuscripts.

1711, June 25.—Your Lordship judged very right when you thought I should not be insensible of the honour that was designed me, but your Lordship might have continued your correspondence till I had begun to break it off. I am just returned home, and find neither any letter from your Lordship nor the news letter. I was in hopes to have had notice last night, to expect your Lordship and my Lord Dupplin here tomorrow. On Friday night Mr. Rowney and I were desired by a special messenger to come over to Cockrop next day; we thought to have returned in the evening, but his Lordship laid a very kind embargo on us, and obliged us to send home for linen. On Sunday in the evening we offered to take our leave again, but were not permitted to go till this morning. His Lordship was very easy and allowed us more freedom than we would take, though I know not whether we did not take more than we should have done. We were very cheerful, I pleaded for Mr. Rowney's case and he mine. I told his Lordship I hoped he would now remember Tom's long and faithful service to him. Mr. Rowney put his Lordship in mind that he had promised me before him, that when his servant Blechingden was provided for, I was to have the refusal of what was in the gift of the Seal. His Lordship was very merry with us both upon our several pretensions, but methoughts he was a little deaf too as well as somewhat blind. No one was with us but Sir John Stonehouse and Mr. Harcourt. His Lordship has promised me to bring the Great Seal to Christ Church, if I could prevail with my Lord Treasurer to meet him there with the staff. I owned to him that would be a very impudent request indeed, but that however I would try by you what I could do to obtain an honour that had never been bestowed upon a poor Canon, since the institution of such societies as ours are. The young gentleman was, as he always is, much upon the reserve before his father, and would not oblige us with any of his politics. He was very sweet to me. Father and son, I find, have both a design to deprive me of you, and concur in opinion that it is by no means proper for your Lordship to return to me any more. They think your Lordship has been brought up too long in the shade, that

you are unacquainted with the world, and ought to be brought
into it as soon as possible. I made the best excuses I could for
your Lordship's bashfulness, it had been reckoned a virtue in the
days of our ancestors, though I could not but own but it was
not very common at present in those of your Lordship's age
and quality. I know not indeed whether your Lordship is master
of so much address as Mr. Harcourt has gained from his travels,
but you have one quality fit for a man of business in a greater
degree than he has ; I had some secrets from him, that I could
not get from you. He told me some dismal stories of my old
friend Mr. St. John. I was amused that he should tell them,
and to me especially, but I soon perceived that there is a personal
pique in the case. There is a coldness between that unhappy
[man] and his father that has happened of late, and though I
know not the cause, I am convinced that the Lord Keeper is as
much dissatisfied with him as your father has reason to be. This
was new to me, for I thought there had been an intelligence there
that could not have been broken. His Lordship was pleased
with a smile to enquire if we had a Dean yet. I cannot be
wanting on this occasion to my own pretensions, his Lordship
having when I was in town engaged to me that I should be so
within a year, I think it is not worth while to make any other
for the little remainder that is yet unexpired. If I mistake not
much, he is not so hot upon that scent as he was. I have given
you some account of our conversation, and would give you more
if the post would allow me longer time.

1711, June 26.—The post cut me short yesterday, or I should
have given you some further account of my conversation at
Cockrop. His Lordship did me the honour to talk with me
about the great living now void at Reading, he seemed to have
some thoughts of offering it to my brother Gastrell, but I question
whether he has a constitution to endure the labour that will be
necessary in so large a parish. He mentioned the Master of
Balliol as one who had been recommended to him, and that
could be by no one but the Prolocutor. He then talked of Dr.
Tonke and Mr. Hinton. I find he is not yet determined. He
was pleased to impart to me a project he said he had been
thinking of, to annex four prebends of those in the gift of the
Seal to four of our poorest headships. That would be very
gracious indeed, and welcome to those who were to have them,
but I suppose it is not yet ripe, and may be thought of for some
time longer before it is resolved on, but the very rumour of such
a thing may be of use to recommend Mr. H[arcour]t to this
place, especially to all those colleges who could have hopes of being
cf the number to whom such a benefaction was to be annexed.

I gave you an account of what the young gentleman said of
Mr. St. John. The more I reflect on it, the more I am surprised
at it. I believe he was in earnest and spoke his father's sentiments. If it was thrown out—though I do not think it was—
with a design to lead me into a discourse of him, he was disappointed, for as he broke into the discourse without any inquiry

from me to bring it on, so I heard it without replying to it.

Have you been wanting to return any civilities that have been paid to you, because both father as well as the son complained, though not in any unkind manner, that you knew nothing of the world? I ask the rather because of a very ridiculous odd story which is got into the College, but I cannot find from whom it came, that when the Lord Keeper complimented you upon your honour, you asked when you should return the compliment to him, and that he replied to you, the Lord of Oxford knows. This was told me last night by John Urry, but I cannot hear or imagine whence so silly a story had its rise.

1711, June 28.—Since your journey into the country is delayed so long, I regret my having parted with you. Why could not you have passed these three weeks with me, and have been called on here by your fellow travellers? Is the town more entertaining than any other place at this season? If your uncle's business still detains him, why should not you come hither in the mean time, and let your uncle call on you when he is at liberty to go? I know your uncle must be much distracted with the variety of business he has, and may possibly not think of our little affair amongst so many of more importance, but I beg you would put him in mind of giving some orders about it before he leaves the town. We have an impudent fellow to deal with, we have a debenture for our money, it appeared by the accounts we had made up with Auditor Jett before Easter that he had money enough in his hands to answer our debenture, and yet we cannot get it. Surely there may be some way of dealing with such a knave.

I have a very proper present for your Lordship. I know your love of antiquities makes you a little superstitious. I have an elder stick, that was cut in the minute that the sun entered Taurus. Such a planetary cutting of it gives it a virtue to stop bleeding to which you know you are subject. If you desire to know more of the time and manner of cutting it, of its virtues, and of the manner of applying it, you must consult Aubrey's *Miscellanies*. You may meet with it without doubt amongst your father's collection of mad books.

The Speaker was pleased to give me notice last night that he was going to the country. Must not we direct to any Privy Councillor 'Right Honourable,' pray tell me in your next?

1711, June 29.—I have just now the sad news that poor Dr. Hutton died at Aynho on Wednesday night of an apoplexy; he was well at nine o'clock, read prayers to his family and went to bed, and was dead before eleven. I regret his loss most heartily on many accounts. I have lost a worthy friend, the church has lost one who by his life and learning was truly an ornament to it; there is not any one, that I know, that had a more sincere respect, esteem and love too, for your father. These sudden deaths have been more frequent of late than they ever were known. I pray God preserve us from them, or prepare us for them, but I beg of you by all the interest I can pretend to in you not to dally with yourself, as you are used to do when you are out of order, and refuse to lose a little blood. I am as often as I think of you, which is not seldom, in pain, lest your obstinacy in this point should at some time or other bring some fatal stroke upon you.

1711, June 30.—I hope you have ·received the things you wrote for ; I am afraid by your sending for them that I shall not see you in your way to Radnor, which will be no little disappointment to me. You cannot save above five miles by any way that you can pass by me.

I know not that Philips you mention, I never saw but I have heard much of him. Mr. Harcourt is in the utmost rage against him. I chanced once when I was at Bucklebury, to give Mr. Harcourt a gentle hint of what he had done abroad ; he flew into a passion, and said I believed all the lies that rogue Philips had told of him. Mr. Drummond recommended Mr. Harcourt to Mr. Forrester, a very ingenious and I think an honest man, who had then the care of Sir Richard Grosvenor. Mr. Forrester being to leave Mr. Harcourt in some place in Italy recommended him to this Philips. Forrester told me that Philips had been very serviceable and kind to Mr. Harcourt, and been very ill used by him. Mr. Harcourt afterwards had great quarrels with Forrester. Forrester had designed at his return to practise the law, and was afraid misrepresentations might be made to Sir Simon of what had passed, which might be of prejudice to him in his profession. I advised him to wait on Sir Simon and to give him a true account of every thing. He did so, and Sir Simon then pretended to thank him. It is news to me that Sir Simon should have bought Philips's silence ; I think he had better have let him'say what he could, if he had been disposed to tell tales. The money given will be an argument for the truth of any thing he tells, if he should not be so honest as to hold his tongue. The chief thing about which they first quarrelled, was upon Mr. Harcourt's drinking a health in all companies to a young person abroad, and saying that he knew enough who were for him and able to bring him in, and that he was sure his father was in that interest. When this was told Sir Simon he said his son might have called him a Mohammetan as well as a Jacobite. This is all I know of it, and let it not go abroad. Mr. Stawell sends me word that Mr. ———— is dangerously ill ; I hope, by your silence, that Mr. Stawell was misinformed. Give me notice of your motions. If I must not expect you here, I intend in the assize week, to avoid that hurry, to make a visit for two or three days to the poor widow at Bucklebury.

1711, July 2.—It is somewhat hard that you will not call on me when you pass so near. Would your calling here have retarded your journey, you might have had some pretence to excuse yourself, but had you contrived your journey so as to have lain here, you would not have lost one moment. I know not how my Lord Dupplin can disengage himself from the promise he so often has made me, that he [would] never go to Herefordshire without calling at Oxford. I suppose all the blame must be laid upon Mr. Auditor. You pretend to be under his direction, but I have observed that the youngest in the company are for the most part the governors.

If this should not find you in town, I suppose it will follow you. I hope you will let me hear from you when you are in the country, and let me know how to direct to you.

I had last night a very great honour, I received a warrant for a buck from my Lord Bishop of Winchester; within, a letter, a most kind one, all of his own inditing. I was amused at it, and can account for it no otherwise than that it is at the desire of the good Colonel. It is very kind of him, if it was, to remember his old acquaintance at this distance, but his Lordship had forgotten to sign the warrant. I have returned it to-day to be signed, but when I have it again, I am afraid I shall have no benefit of his Lordship's intention, for they have refused for this last year to serve any of his warrants in Whichwood Forest. His Lordship was pleased to tell me that he had employed George Clark to agree with Gibbons for a statute for Cardinal Wolsey, and that Gibbons had sent to have the measure of the niche. I suppose his Lordship means that over the great gate towards the street. We will get the statue, and we will then find a place for it, but I am afraid we dare not put any statue in that place but Henry the Eighth when we can get one.

1711, July 7.—The Bishop of Winchester has agreed with Gibbons for one hundred guineas for Wolsey's statue in marble; it is to be placed in the niche that is in the passage to the hall stairs. I have by this post sent up the dimensions of the niche.

Had not your Lordship of me *Aristæneti Epistolæ?* I think your Lordship had, but yet I cannot find it among your books, there were two of them in Bernard's auction, each sold for 2*l.* a piece. A prodigious price for so small a book. Those in Bernard's auction are said to be printed at Paris 1596, but I believe it is a mistake, mine is a very fair one of Plantin's edition 1566, and I never heard of any other edition. Upon looking over the catalogue, I find I have most of the books which sold at such extravagant prices; I believe I should part with mine if I could have so good a price for them.

I hope the answer to this will come to me franked ' Harley,' and give me notice that within a week I may expect to see you here. I can allow you one week to converse with your dogs and to hunt, and I think that allowance is fair enough, but I am afraid now you are a Senator you will pretend to be *tui juris*, and not allow me to prescribe your time to you.

Postscript. I have written to secure Dr. Hutton's manuscripts if they are to be parted with.

1711, July 18.—I thank you for the honour of yours, I allow it to be a very reasonable letter for one so much engaged as your Lordship must be at this time. If your Lordship has not that book, I have one of them I will desire you to accept of when I see you. The print is beautiful, it is nothing but love letters, not always so decent as they should be, had they been in a tongue more understood than Greek is. The matter of the book and the variety of it, is that I suppose which raises the price of it, I am sure it cannot be the intrinsic worth of it.

Archer and Tilly preached the Act sermons. Tilly preached in the afternoon, his whole sermon was a panegyric upon Sacheverell and railing at those who had not preferred him. He did not forget himself, but did Dr. Sacheverell the honour to associate himself with him in the merit of saving the nation. *We have stood in the gap and others run away with the prefer- ments.* He plainly pointed out Lancaster and abused him. Lancaster was at church and Sacheverell too, which gave occasion to suspect that this was preached by concert with Sacheverell. But the author was resolved that more than the few persons present should enjoy the benefit of it, and designed to print it, but with much ado Dr. Sacheverell was made to understand, that it might not be for his interest that it should appear, and by Dr. Sacheverell's entreaties, though he could not by any other motive, the author is prevailed with not to print at least at this time.

Mrs. Hutton is left sole executrix to her husband, she is willing to part with his collections to your father, but I perceive she will expect a good price for them.

It must be a round sum indeed that can ever prevail with me to consent that you should mix with such blood. I think no consideration of fortune can make amends either to yourself, for the uneasiness you would have with one of such manners as those of her education often have, or to your family, by corrupting it by mixing with such a strain.

I beg the lady's pardon, she may be a little angel for aught I know. No rule to which there is not an exception, but I suppose there is no danger. The father, though rich, will hardly bid high enough. I cannot think you would sell yourself, now you have the whole female part of the nation out of which you may pick and choose as you please, under 100,000*l.*

My brother Gastrell is come with bag and baggage. Charles King is with me, but we want you to make our society complete. I believe you may find him here when you return.

I have compliments to you from Mr. Drummond and his lady, they design to be in England in the beginning of August.

I was last week to pay a visit, as I told you, to a poor discon- solate lady [Mrs. St. John] in Berkshire. I met nothing there but sorrow and disorder. That unfortunate gentleman is more irregu- lar, if possible, in his private than [public] capacities. A sad instance to all young gentlemen of quality, how the greatest parts and expectations may be made useless and be disappointed by the folly of vice—the only way in which that unhappy gentleman will ever be of any use in the world.

1711, July 27.—I was struck indeed with the death of the great man [the Duke of Newcastle]; it seems to have crossed a project that I well hoped had been pointed out by Providence to establish your family at once, and to leave your father entirely at liberty to pursue his own designs for the public. I know not whether your father can have as good an interest in the Lady as he had in the Lord. If he could it would be worth while still to pursue it. Though the young lady is now less by some thousands per annum than she was before supposed to have, she is still the greatest fortune in the nation. What a prodigious fortune is fallen to the Pelhams! I am afraid it will be employed to worse uses now than it was before.

I may give you joy, I hope, of some little comfort under this great disappointment. I hear from all hands that you will soon have occasion to be chosen again. We have made you Teller of the Exchequer, I heartily wish it may be so, I think it is a very proper post for you. It is time for your father to think a little of his domestic concerns, it will not only be prudence, but strictly his duty to raise his estate so far that it may with credit support his honour.

We are afraid we shall suffer a loss here, that we shall sensibly feel. My Lord Carteret upon the accession he expects from the Bath estate, is going to live with his mother and to set up a family. He has by Dr. Freind endeavoured to inveigle Mr. Herbert from us, to live with him. Dr. Freind has not done well in it, the poor young man was engaged before I had the least notice of it. The proposals are 40l. per annum, kind usage, and the reversion of a parsonage worth 300l. per annum, on which there is a sickly incumbent, and which is in that part of the Bath estate which my Lord expects will fall to his share. I think the proposals are by no means an equivalent for the certainty he must quit and the fair expectations he has. if he stays here, and the poor youth little knows what it is to give up his liberty and depend entirely upon any one, though he were more generous and of a fairer temper than I am afraid that Lord will be. I have done what I could to make him sensible that the conditions are not worth his accepting, and the way of living will by no means be so agreeable as he seems to hope it will; but he seems much inclined to it, and I am afraid will accept of it, though some others will endeavour to dissuade him.

1711, July 30.—I have had a letter from the Speaker, which I want you to explain to me, he complains mightily to me of the practices of some—whom he names not—on whose friendship the Speaker thought your father might have depended. I reserve the letter for you, I cannot guess whom he means. I have desired him to enlighten me a little. I know your father has reason to be dissatisfied with a young friend, but he is not the person meant ; he may not behave as he ought to do to him, but he cannot be considerable enough, by his practices, to obstruct or disturb your father.

I expect Mr. Drummond will be in London within a week, he leaves his wife in England and returns himself by September to Amsterdam. He insists with me to see him before he returns, I shall go for three or four days and no more. I can be punctual to my resolutions in such a point, but I shall not stir till I see your Lordship here; and if he be come to England before your Lordship returns, if you will give me leave, I believe I shall wait on you to town, for I begin to suspect, nay I more than suspect, that you will only pass through and not make any stay with us.

Dr. Blechingden told me this evening that my Lord Keeper with his family came to Cockrop last night; his Lordship desires to be *incognito* for the first week. I send my compliments by Thomas to-morrow. I hear some good news, Mr. Harcourt told Dr. Blechingden that my Lord Dupplin is Teller, I beg you would pay my most hearty compliments to my Lord upon it. I daresay you are as well pleased as if yourself had been named to it.

I perceive you have parted with your servant, he is come to Oxford ; he says you were very kind to him, and promised to recommend him, if any of your friends wanted such a servant.

Has not the Teller several clerks in his office, I mean under clerks worth about 50*l.* per annum or so ? Had you been Teller I had a design on you for one I had formerly recommended to your charity. If there are such places and should be any vacancies, you must assist me in behalf of that poor man ; but perhaps my Lord's countrymen will expect he should employ none but of his own nation.

I believe you are weary of company you are so little fit for, but these uneasinesses will induce your Lordship to make reflections on human life, that there is no state of it that is wholly free from some alloy, that may admonish us not to be over fond of it. You who have the chief stations in the world have encumbrances which attend your greatness, that inferior mortals are strangers to. When I see you again I shall accost you with Evander's compliment to Æneas :

> *Aude Hospes contemnere opes et Ti quoque dignum*
> *Finge Deo.*

Mr. Cowley says this was a greater compliment than ever was made in the Louvre or Escurial. Can your Lordship relish it, now you have had a taste of the word ?

1711, August 10.—The enclosed is the best account I can get of Dr. Hutton's manuscripts, I desire your farther directions about them. If your father desires a sight of them, I will borrow them and send them to you. I waited yesterday on my Lord Keeper and was graciously received. I am sorry I must condole with you for a disappointment you have had. Lord Keeper said that if the Duke of Newcastle had lived your Lordship would have had his daughter and his estate. I know no one on whom both of them could have been so well bestowed, if he had any design of bestowing either of them well, but I hope Providence has in reserve for your Lordship some thing to make up this loss, if it was one to you. His Lordship was very easy, but nothing of news of our Deanery, except that he wished a bishopric would (*sic*), but not one of the ordinary ones, for that would not do he said. I told your Lordship of a letter I had received; in a late order made about Dr. Hannes' estate, the money left to us was ordered to be paid to the *Treasurer* of Christ Church. I understood that they had inserted in the minutes *Dean and Chapter* and that one of the executors designed to take advantage of those words to delay the payment of the money. I applied to his Lordship to desire he would command his own order to be observed. He answered me by Mr. Harcourt, to whom he dictated, that he had sent, if it was not too late, to have the mistake rectified; but that if it was too late, and we found the objection should stick with the executors, my Lord Treasurer when I represented to him the inconvenience we suffered would instantly remove it. I believe those words in the order had been altered on purpose to have a plea to press for the supplying of this place.

Decker writes me word that he has found my wine and will take care of it. I will give your Lordship no trouble about it.

Postscript. Here was a story about a riot in which Lord Gore was concerned and a man killed. The story was carried to London and to Windsor. Upon enquiry I find there was very little ground for it. A saucy fellow was beaten indeed, but not hurt, and no more beaten, by what I hear, than he well deserved.

This should have waited on your Lordship on Saturday, but my servant was too late for Friday's post. I have nothing to add but that my brother Gastrell has discoursed me, as my Lord Treasurer was pleased to order, what plate it might be fit for your Lordship to give when you leave us, but I immediately told him, what he says was his own opinion, that there can be no occasion to consider of that, there can be no expectations of that kind from your Lordship. It is not very agreeable to me to talk of any thing that implies you are about to leave us.

I must tell you that I am in full favour with my Lord Keeper, for he has promised to dine with me before he returns to his winter quarters, and to bring his whole family along with him. I know not how I shall do to support the envy here of such an honour; all our Heads will conclude me to be next upon his Lordship's roll.

Dr. Pelling is with me, and will stay here I hope some time. I expect Mr. Jennings and Mr. Nelson next week; these are some little reliefs to me under the disappointment I have had from your Lordship.

We hear Sartre cannot last long, I hope Dr. Freind will succeed him, and that use will be made of it to engage him to keep the school, which betwixt ourselves I am afraid he has no design of keeping but till his house at Witney is fit for him.

1711, August 13.—There has been lately a very handsome offer made to Dr. Smalridge, and one that would have been very convenient for him, should [it] be his and our fortune for him to be settled here. Mr. Cartwright offered him the parsonage of Aynho; it is worth 250*l.*, a pleasant place and a good house, but there was one condition which would not allow Dr. Smalridge to accept it. Mr. Cartwright expected that whoever accepted should reside constantly in winter as well as in summer. I cannot blame Mr. Cartwright for insisting on so reasonable a thing, in a living of such value, which he bestows with great honour. But Dr. Smalridge must then have quitted a more profitable post, though not a more easy one, for it, and that his family would not allow of. It has since been offered to another worthy man, Mr. Edgely, Convocation man for Surrey, who lives [with] Mr. Hewer at Clapham, the gentleman who was executor to Mr. Pepys and had all his manuscripts and curiosities. But the expectation Mr. Edgely has from Mr. Hewer, whose niece he married, would not allow him to accept of it on Mr. Cartwright's terms.

I am afraid I have caught my Lord Keeper in a trap, I believe I shall find in a few days that the order which he made in Court was certainly altered by concert betwixt his Lordship and the Prolocutor, that his Lordship might have a pretence to insist for the supplying of this place, because we could not without a Dean receive the money due to us. He seemed surprised that I had notice how the first order was, and of the alteration that had since been made in it; he promised that his first order should be observed, if the order was not signed before his letter could reach London. Now the order is not yet signed. His Lordship when I was with him would not enter on the discourse, but turned it off when I mentioned it to him, and I have notice last night from town, that the order will go at last with the words *Dean and Chapter*, notwithstanding his Lordship's late promise to me that it should not. If it does pass so, I shall be convinced that I was right in my suspicion; but should it be so, this will be playing at very small game. For to tell you the truth, I applied to him only to find out whether this was not concerted between him and the Prolocutor, and not for any occasion that we have for the money, for I have more now in my hands than will answer all due by our agreements with the workmen till next midsummer.

1711, August 14.—Your travels must be very short if you go abroad at this season, I conclude you must be at home again against the meeting of the Parliament. There is one thing indeed you may see now, which you will not have an opportunity of seeing probably at any other time, the Coronation of the Emperor, and perhaps you will have no other leisure but this in your life for such an excursion, for I hope affairs of greater importance to you and your family, before the next year, will not allow you any such thoughts.

We have a strong report here that Woodroffe is dead. Christ Church is your own, under your protection, it belongs to you to answer for all that come in to any vacancies here, and if we endeavour to do our duties and can be of any service to our country, I hope God will remember it in blessings to you and your family. If you are not under any other engagements or inclinations, you may perhaps have an opportunity of doing an action as generous in itself, and of as great use to this place, as ever was done. There is one you know well, beyond Snowden Hill, who is of too great value to be buried in that obscurity, and who ought to be transplanted into a more southern climate, but who yet is of so peculiar a temper that we can never hope to see him here, unless he is forced to it by such a call which, for being without his knowledge, he would look upon to be God's providence. I find my acquaintance Dr. Blechingden is very eager upon the scent, he was to enquire news of Woodroffe of me. I was abroad. He left a note to desire intelligence, if I had any. Woodroffe's living in London is in the gift of the Seals. It is one of the smallest in compass and greatest in revenue of any within the walls. By houses lately fallen in, which are not yet leased out, it may be made as it is said worth 400*l. per annum.* Blechingden has no design on this for himself, that is too mechanical a part of our profession for so fine a gentleman to deal with, but he certainly aims to get some very good prebend, Windsor I believe if he can, in exchange for it, and to make such a composition for this as he would have done for Reading.

Oakely preached at St. Mary's last Sunday. He prayed for your father. "*Spartam quam nactus est hanc ornet.*" He must be confined to his Orientals.

The Bishop of Bristol [Robinson] is in town. I paid my compliments to him and desired the honour of seeing him here; he said he must return to Hasely to-night, or he would have seen (*sic*). He dines upon invitation at Queen's; those Northern men have good noses.

1711, August 15. Christ Church.—I had last night a long letter from the Speaker, who has sent for his son into the country. He tells me he hears the Bishop of Worcester is grown a child, and weak in body as well as in mind. But that is not the thing I chiefly designed to give your Lordship notice of; I find he is much concerned both about his chaplain and his brother Mr. Stawell, and says it is a month since he wrote to my Lord Treasurer about his brother, but had never yet had the honour to hear from his Lordship. I thought it might not be improper to let you know this, I have written to him what I could judge proper to-day by his son.

Postscript. I perceive the place which the Speaker had hoped for for Mr. Stawell was that he should be one of those sent to Spain.

1711, August 15.—It proves as I expected, the decree for Dr. Hannes' estate was not drawn up till last Saturday, and was not signed I believe till Monday. The words *Dean and Chapter*

were continued, though his Lordship had promised me his first
order should be observed, and though I had put his Lordship in
mind of his promise when I waited on him on Thursday last.
But I have another very material circumstance of this noble
intrigue. The secretary, being asked why he had not observed
his Lordship's orders in the minutes he took, said he had
observed it, but that when he brought the minutes to his Lord,
he ordered him to strike out *Treasurer* and insert *Dean and
Chapter*, and said if there was not a Dean in a little time, the
college might then move the Court, and he would order the
money to be paid to the Treasurer. This I find to have been his
own express order which, in answer to me when I applied to him,
he said was the clerk's mistake. What paltry doings are here,
to compass a Dean who may promote his own poor ends in this
place, the greatest of which is to make son Sim burgess for the
university, which no Dean he can send, nor all the preferments
in his gift, either can or shall compass. Sim's giving out those
notorious lies at Windsor was for no other end but to furnish an
argument for the necessity of a Dean, because of the extravagances
that happened here. The thing that was done was not here but in
a gentleman commoner's chamber of University College. Lord
Gower was in the company but had the least hand in it, the person
chiefly concerned was Skeiler of All Souls, who had certainly most
of poor Lord Strathallan's money. The fellow who was beaten
was one of those who had broke the windows of the room where
the gentleman were sitting, he was so little hurt that he and
all concerned in beating him appeared before Charlett as soon
as it was done, and the fellow went straight to a coffee
house and told how he had [been?] beaten. Lord Abingdon
came next day to Dr. Hammond, and sent for
Lord Gower, to assure him the fellow was dead and
to offer to be his bail. Lord Gower told him he believed the
fellow was then in the street very well, and upon going out they
found him there.

I will endeavour to make Mrs. Hutton set a price on the
manuscripts. You may certainly have them, if you are willing
to pay for them. But if I could know so as not to take notice to
her what the utmost is my Lord Treasurer is willing to give, I
should be able better to bring her to terms.

1711, August 18.—This day the gentleman whom I employed
to Mrs. Hutton came over to me ; he said the indexes to all the
volumes, upon an exacter search, are all near finished. There
are thirty-two volumes now in the widow's possession, and three
lent out, which she has called for in. In these books is the
whole labour of that very industrious man for the last forty years
of his life. I cannot tell how material all his observations and
extracts may be, nor is it easy to judge of that. Good use may
be made of things which seem trivial to those whose thoughts
are employed on other subjects, but his exactness and fidelity
may be depended on to the utmost, but I am afraid the widow
expects too much for them. This gentleman says Kennett is very

earnest to have them. I suppose he is employed by some other person to buy them, by the price he offers. He has already bid above 100*l.* for them. The gentleman tells me he is afraid the widow will expect 200*l.* Let me know what my Lord Treasurer is willing to give, and I will endeavour to get them at the rate you desire. She will not part with them upon any terms, till I send her word that I have no more to say to them.

I cannot say that I am sorry to hear that your going abroad is likely to be deferred for three months, I wish it may be so for two months longer. I shall deliver up all my business here to my brother Gastrell at Christmas. Should not you go abroad till after that season, I believe I should see you safe on the other side of the water, but if you stay longer in England, why should you not spend your time here till the session of Parliament comes on? What diversion or employment can you have in town in this vacation? But I must tell you, that if you come here only to take leave of us, it will be expected, I find, that you should accept of your Master's degree at parting. It will cost you indeed twelve or fifteen guineas, but it has been usual for those of your Lordship's quality, who have lived with credit here, to receive that compliment at parting. But I find by the President of Corpus that it is expected from you, since the Vice-Chancellor had sent to compliment you with the offer of it, immediately upon your father's honour, and when it was thought you would have made some further stay with us I have other reasons too why I wish you should accept it.

I thank your Lordship for your account of that which passed at Windsor on Sunday last. My brother Burton, who returned last night from his waiting, though then at Windsor, had heard nothing of it. So incurious or so great philosophers can some be, on the scene of the greatest business. But how came those three persons you mention to go to make their complaints to the Queen? I suppose that Duke had taken no notice of them, since they were called into the Queen's service.

I fancy there is some ground for that the Speaker said, of the Bishop of Worcester's being very weak. My reason is, because the Bishop of Oxford is in great haste to speak with my Lord Keeper, and has sent that he may have immediate notice when he returns to Cockrop, that he may come to him, I suppose to concert measures for succeeding the old man.

1711, August 23.—I hope to hear you have kissed her Majesty's hand for somewhat more than the bare honour of kissing it. I wish you were with me or I with you for two or three days. To us at this distance the affairs at Court seem somewhat perplexed and embroiled, which we cannot account for, for want of a little light to clear the dark part of them. I pray God direct your father in the choice of those who are to be brought into the service. His high station, though it has augmented the number of those who attend his levée, has not I am afraid increased the number of his friends or lessened that of his enemies; but our circumstances are very unhappy. Though

God gives your father discernment to choose those who are most proper, yet we have none out of whom he can choose. His own merit must support not only himself, but those who are brought in by him. I believe it is plain of many, that he can so little expect any help from their character or abilities, that nothing but his own could bear them up. Not to say, that there may be want of faith in some, as well as of sense in others. It is unlucky too that at this juncture, they are not I am afraid at liberty to take the measures that would make this little part of the nation very easy. But we of this House are prepared for any event. I foresee indeed in one case what sort of interest will be chiefly cultivated here, and to whose use all that can be raised will be chiefly applied.

There is a lady now in London that had the honour to be gallanted by you, when she was here. Pray do not you take the opportunity of my absence to supplant me, but be so honest, since you have the whole female world before you to choose out of as you please, to leave to me my old mistress.

We are to have great doings here next week. The Lord Keeper comes to show himself in his greatness and to receive the compliments of this place. His Lady, son, daughter in law and the daughter's mother come too, and his Lordship designs to spend three or four days in this place. I know not yet where he designs to fix his quarters, whether with me, Tom Rowney, or at the President's lodgings of St. John's which are now empty, he being at Winchester. I shall certainly have them one day at dinner, but I cannot well lodge them. I can make but two beds, and one of those is now taken up by Dr. Pelling. I suppose now will be thrown out the design that has been much talked of of late, to annex four of the prebends in the gift of the Seal to four of our poorest Headships, and which I believe he designs as much as he does his own estate to build alms houses. You shall hear what passes.

Postscript. I believe I shall be able to get the [Hutton] manuscripts for 150*l.*, if you are willing to give so much for them. You need not fear, care will be taken that they will neither be sold nor embezzled.

1711, August 25.—I see in the Prints notice of a paper called the *Hermit*, a weekly paper from one retired from the world, I know not the contents of it, but I fancy the title not very improper for the letters I trouble you with. I am here almost in as great a solitude as any of the old anchorites were in the Egyptian deserts. The little conversation I have with the world I owe chiefly to you. Whenever my thoughts go into the world, it is when the remembrance of you calls them into it, and then they rest chiefly on you, as that part of the world for which I am most concerned. Can you in the gay scene in which you are ever think of your old hermitage? Can you, after the relish you have had of another life, be content to spend a week or two here? I should then be at ease, and think you may be trusted safely in the world, if I find that you can retire from it at any time without

regret. I am afraid you will think this more like a sermon than
a letter, truly I was making one this morning, and I know not
what influence that may have on my thoughts this evening.
But I have much to say to you upon this great change in your
life, on the first years of which all the comfort and honour of the
remainder of it depends, but I reserve it till we meet, and I give
you notice that you must bear with me. For be your station
never so elevated, I shall always think I have a greater right to
be concerned for you than any one but your own father. But
to return to my cell, as humble as it is, two great men were
pleased to take their breakfast in it this morning, Mr. Harcourt
and Dr. Blechingden. We had a little mundane conversation,
Mr. Harcourt was more communicative than you are (which is
somewhat hard) of what passes at Windsor, and has told me who
is to be Privy Seal, and our own Governor. But not one word
of that which I chiefly expected, when I was to see the
family here, which was odd, for Tom Rowney tells me they
will certainly be here on Tuesday, males and females, and
take up their quarters with me. I hope his Lordship does not
design to surprise me ; if he does, he must fare accordingly, and
take up with that you were forced to submit to, when you were
under the ascetic discipline, bread and cheese, and half a pint
of wine to a pint of water. But how to behave to the content
of the ladies I know not. I was but very indifferent at it in the
gayer part of my life. My comfort is, that I believe a poor
hermit may look on them, without suffering any thing from the
sight in his spiritual estate.

Mr. Stawell has given me notice of his obligations to my Lord
Treasurer. He will be here this week to take his leave of me,
but whether as he goes to or returns from the Speaker I know
not. Pray think if you have any commissions for him in any
parts he is to go to.

I have this day received somewhat that may invite you, I had
a parcel of books which I bought in the last auction in Holland.
Some very good indeed, some very proper for the taste of a man
of quality, that have nothing but the scarceness of the edition
to give a value to them, and I am not yet old enough to leave off
buying such baubles. But my burgundy is come along with
them. Pray enter among your debts two dozen due to me,
which I have lost by your not being here.

1711, August 28.—I find you are now grown a regular courtier, I
doubt not but you have got the air of the place, and shine in it with
a grace that becomes the only son of the greatest minister that
ever was at the head of our affairs. I hope I shall hear no more
complaints that you are unacquainted with the world, but shall
be told that you [have] worn off the ungraceful habits you had
contracted here, by the advantage of a more polite conversation.
I doubt not but you receive the addresses which are usual to the
son of the first minister. That which I want to know is how
your Lordship is affected with them. I own to you, I either know
the world or at least value it so little, that I should not be at all

displeased to hear you are so unpolished, and of so ill a taste, as
not at all to be exalted with the court that is paid to you, or to
think one jot the better of yourself for it.

I have enclosed the answer which I have just received about
Dr. Hutton's manuscripts, you will see the widow still insists
upon her first price, or would have any abatement of it looked on as
an obligation. Be pleased to show it to my Lord Treasurer and
to let me know his pleasure. You may be assured there will be
no other bargain struck up, till I send her word I have no more
to say to them.

Though I had not "Dyer" last post from your Lordship, yet I
borrowed it, to see if there was any thing in it about our
vacancies. I was not deceived in my expectation. My friend
the Prolocutor had found the way to convey a paragraph once
more to John Dyer. If you are at a loss to understand this.
Master Cunningham can explain it to you. Tom Rowney came
for his breakfast to me this morning. He told me Mr. Harcourt
and Dr. Blechingden were with him on Sunday in the afternoon
when "Dyer's letter " came in. Upon reading the last clause Mr.
Harcourt fell into a great rapture, that the point was gained at last.
Dr. Blechingden said he must now be Bishop of Oxford and then
we have done. Tom made a little demur, and asked if he thought
the Dean of Carlisle would have both the Deanery and Bishopric.
Blechingden replied, it is his sole aim, he has set his heart upon
having both, and then he will be quiet. Tom asked if he thought
Oxford would be removed to Worcester. He said it must be for
the Bishop of Oxford's sake, and to make way for the other.
These projects are idle in themselves, and for purposes in which
they will certainly be disappointed if I know any thing of this
place and how the interest of it lies ; one year will convince both
my Governor himself, and those who have been so zealous to
have him here, that he will never make that figure, or have that
interest in it, it is proposed he should.

1711, August 29.—I beg my most humble duty and thanks to
my Lord Treasurer, for the notice he has been pleased to give
me by your Lordship of our new Governor [Atterbury]. The conferring of the Deanery of Carlisle, as well as this vacant canonry,
on Dr. Smalridge, is a very peculiar mark of kindness and respect to
him. But I dare answer for him that he would have been content with the Canonry only. Our new Governor will find his
subjects in a better disposition to obedience than I believe he
expects. We could indeed have been better pleased we must say
with old Canon Gardiner, a Herefordshire man of whom you
have heard me tell many stories. That we are content, but we
could have been better content. I hope we shall have discretion
enough, as well as honesty, to preserve peace amongst ourselves,
if it be possible, though we shall never enter into
some projects that are already on foot. But now this
struggle is over, I tell you my serious opinion, that I
believe our Dean himself, if he can be convinced of any
thing, or at least will own that he is so, will be satisfied in a short

time that they were his truest friends who wished him in some other part of the world. I can have no reserve to your Lordship, because I know I am safe in you. I will now tell you that which would [not] have looked so fair to have told you, before this business was over. If he had not been bewitched with two things, the pride of carrying his point and the project of joining the diocese to the college, he himself would have desired to have had his lot in any other ground rather than in this. None but one blinded with passion would have desired to have come, where he knows so many stories of former failures are still fresh, and where no one can have the authority that is requisite to this place whose youth was not without blemish in it. But he was mad and would hear nothing from any friend he had. I have just now an account from one in whom he thought himself safe, to whom he came straight, when he had been with your father last week. He was in the utmost exultation, that he had carried his point, and that he had pinned down Dr. Smalridge to that he believed he cared not for; that his own and Dr. Smalridge's patents were then drawing, and Dr. Smalridge knew nothing of it; that it would be offered to him, without leaving him liberty of choice, and let him at his peril refuse it—by the bye I know not why he should think there was any hazard that Dr. Smalridge would be such a coxcomb; that he had staked his all upon the point, and that he was resolved to come hither to show he could not be bustled, though he were to stay here only half a year. I pity the poor man, he is in a proper disposition to manage so many and so different tempers as he will have to deal with, who has so little power over his own. Since it is over, as wise men I hope we shall look only upon the advantages that we shall have by it. Now I shall get my money for Peckwater, without being obliged to my honourable sincere friend my Lord Keeper for it, but I promise him I will never forget that very ingenious trick he played me. Now I hope to have a little business stirring in my own office, and to have the college seal employed again. It has grown rusty, I have ordered it to be new oiled. I cannot indeed tell your Lordship that our bell ropes have been worn since I had your letter, but that was the Sub-Dean's business to order and not mine. But I will acquit my good brother of any malice in the case, I was I own malicious enough, though I observed that he forgot it, not to put him in mind of it.

Mr. Stawell came to me last night from the Speaker. I find the Speaker is in very good humour again. I will transcribe the last paragraph of his letter *verbatim*. "I shall be very glad to have Lord Treasurer think rightly of me, I look upon it that we are embarked in the same bottom, engaged in the same interests, and I am therefore very sincerely and unfeignedly his humble servant and shall do my utmost—as far as I have any power to do it—to support his ministry, and I do hope that such reasonable care will be taken to satisfy and make our friends easy, that I may be able to serve him."

1711, August 30. Christchurch.—Your Lordship's goodness in excusing the freedom I took with you is alone sufficient, though I had no other reasons, to convince me that it was unnecessary. After my letter was gone I myself began to reflect on it, and was sensible that nothing but the truth of my concern could be an excuse for my impertinence. But we monks as well as the ladies are subject sometimes to vapours, and in many the cause of them is the same, and your converse in the world, that secures you from these irregular fits, gives you too freedom enough of spirit to make allowances for them in us that have them.

Your Lordship will perceive by my last, that I thought your Lordship had gone to Windsor on Saturday with my Lord Treasurer. That which you did me the favour to write to me last Saturday came not to me till yesterday, which is odd, since that which your Lordship wrote on Monday came safe on Tuesday. Your Lordship will perceive by the letter I enclosed what the widow Hutton still insists on. She may be beaten down I believe to 150l. I have told her my opinion that I think that more than she could have expected. The offer she has of other chapmen encourages her I suppose to insist on her first price. I must expect your Lordship's directions in it.

I beg your Lordship would be pleased to pay my most humble duty and thanks to my Lord Treasurer for the honour he was pleased to do me in your Lordship's letter. That which his Lordship was pleased to mention was indeed surprising, and cannot but be understood by all the clergy, as it is designed. The only doubt is, whether it be not too great instance of respect and kindness to us. The laity ever since the Reformation, in days better disposed to us than these are, have been very uneasy when any of our gown, how great soever their abilities were, have been admitted to any share of secular honours. The gentleman for whom this is designed will be able, if any can, by the character of his ability as well as integrity, to support the envy of such a kindness to our order.

Last night my brother Gastrell and I drank my Lord Treasurer's and your Lordship's health with Tom Rowney in some wine he had from his brother Walters. I had notice there that we are not to expect our great guest yet, his coming is deferred till our new Dean is with us. And as Tom gathered from Mr. Harcourt, his Lordship designs to do the new Dean the honour to grace his installation with his Lordship's presence. That will be a particular honour indeed and needs no comment. [At] the installation of a Dean of Christ Church, if the present Dean enters upon his office with the same pomp his predecessors did, every head of a college or hall, and most of any character in the University, are present. The whole entertainment is at the Dean's expense. The charge of the last Dean on that day was considerably above 100l. I believe. I shall save my bacon by it; I may say so properly, for his Lordship was to have had a ham with me.

I am afraid the town is mistaken in the report of Dr. Freind and Mrs. Bovey, though there may be seeming grounds for it. It is no secret that he is not at liberty to enter into such engagements. Should the widow list him for her service, there is one, who is a virgin much against her will, would send an apparitor to take him out of her custody.

1711, September 1.—I forgot in my last to answer some of your Lordship's questions. The Prolocutor designs to quit the Rolls, but not Bridewell. He keeps Bridewell that he may have lodgings in town during the Convocation. It is the first time I believe that ever a Dean of Christ Church kept the honour of Bridewell since our foundation with this Deanery. But those lodgings lie very convenient and near to Harry VII's chapel where he is to attend. I know not who are competitors for the Rolls; Dr. Fowke is one of them. I believe Dr. Smalridge will have no thoughts of quitting New Chapel [Westminster] yet. Nor will he have any occasion; he will be here in the summer. There will be no occasion for greater residence unless he had an office, but that will not strictly come to his turn in some years. He certainly quits St. Dunstan's, and I believe the Master of the Temple will succeed him in it.

I begged your Lordship when you were in the country, to mention to my Lord Treasurer, when you saw a proper time, Rymer's *Fœdera*, which his Lordship was pleased to give me leave to promise to Mr. Lewis.

Brother Gastrell and I had last night letters from our new Governor, though through his very unusual modesty he will not yet take the title on him. He tells Gastrell there are uncertain rumours of a Dean, but none yet named. He desires him to let him know what it is proper for a new Dean to do, and promises him that he will communicate it to the new Dean whoever he is, and that he doubts not but he will have his thanks. He tells me that he has seen the "Post Boy," in which there is some mention of a new Dean, and many people coming to visit him, who is confined by the gout, and talking the same way. He does not know whether there may be some thing in it. In my answer I have told him that there must be some great mystery, that that should be kept as a secret from him, who is at Chelsea, on Thursday, which was sent to me from a good hand on the Monday before, and that the uncertainty he is in as to his own fate agrees worse still with a piece of intelligence I had on Friday se'nnight, that the day before he himself should have said, that he knew both the patents were then drawing. It is a little hard that he should begin his government with so gross a banter upon his old friends.

The news of the Privy Seal by the last post was very surprising to all, you may be certain it is very acceptable here. I believe the laity will murmur. I expect the run in the pamphlets will be that the clergy are grasping at power again. That will not signify much ; but the several pretenders will be uneasy to see themselves disappointed by one they never suspected. But the Archbishop in all probability will drop before the end of the

next winter, and then the Queen may be at liberty to dispose
again of the Privy Seal where she thinks fit.

1711, September 2.—I hope there is no such combination as
your Lordship has heard of, and I believe there is not yet. Our
Dean is upon a better foot with the Principal of Jesus than with
any other Head in town, but he is old and concerns himself little,
though whenever he does he is of weight. The President of
Corpus, who has the greatest authority amongst the Heads, is too
wary a man to enter into an open opposition of any one, unless
the occasion should be very extraordinary. What he does of
that kind will be by private influence. He has the utmost distrust of our Governor, and will never enter into any common
measures with him, and be always jealous of any thing that comes
from him. Most of the other Heads are at present in the same
disposition to him the President is. I know not one with whom
he can think he has any true interest; whom he may gain, I
cannot tell. That which is likely to be of most use to him for
that purpose is the interest he is supposed to have, and which
he takes all the methods he can to persuade others that he has,
in the ministry, and the plain signification that has been given
that whoever in this place expects favour from the Seals must
apply through him. These probably may procure some applications to him, but I believe he sees so well upon what foot he is
here that he will be very cautious, and not concern himself in
any business out of his own house till he has got a surer footing.
I do not yet foresee any open difference that is likely to be, but
between him and Lancaster. It is no secret how they are affected
to each other, and that they will oppose each other to the
utmost, and there are some who are under Lancaster's direction.

I take this plan to be a pretty true one of this place. Our
Governor has great skill, and I wish he may be able to change it.
There is no one with whom he is as yet in any confidence but
Delaune. He invited his brethren to sit with him on Sunday
night; when they came there, they found it was to meet Delaune
and Sacheverell, which was no great compliment to them.

I have had an answer from Mrs. Hutton, she is willing at last
to take 150l., and a very fair sum it is for them; when I wait on
my Lord Treasurer, I shall take his directions about it.

I assure your Lordship I was surprised to hear of the Bishop
of R[ochester]'s courage, though he was so well supported. It
is a sure indication that his Lordship thinks it is set in for fair
weather.

1711, September 4.—I presumed in my last to put you in mind
of Rymer's *Fœdera* for Mr. Lewis, and my letter was scarce gone
when I received a letter from Mr. Lewis to put me in mind of it.
I have enclosed the letter to your Lordship. You will see he
wants to pay his duty to my Lord Treasurer, if he were encouraged
to do. You will see too what they think in Holland of the Scotch
medal. This is the first day of our horse-race, the town is very
full but we are never so quiet in the College as at such a season.

1711, September 8.—I wonder Lord Keeper should continue to give out things so very foolish, because known to be so far from truth. For our parts we are resolved to make the best we can of that we have, but I assure your Lordship, in all the visits I have made, since the vacancies here were disposed of, at Christ Church or Jesus, the Vice Chancellor's &c., the first health to me was joy of my new brother and neighbour Dr. Smalridge, but no mention of the other, nor any more notice taken than if no such vacancy had been filled. I leave your Lordship to judge by this fact of what the Keeper told you; but it was like that he told Ned Jennings last Sunday at Windsor. He had a great deal of discourse with him about Dr. Smalridge, that he was not his enemy though he had opposed him, and that it was in a great measure owing to him that Carlisle was given to Dr. Smalridge.

Our Governor told you true, in saying that every one was leaving the place as fast as he could, but he would not be willing the true reason of it should be known. I wish he may be able to compass that he designs. We have taken care to provide lodgings for all he can bring. We have built from the ground and covered one side during the vacancy. If his influence be as great as he thinks it, surely we shall build another side, now we have such a Dean at the head of us, in as little a time as we reared one without a Dean. A year's experience may show him perhaps what he can do. I wish he do not find that to such a post as this is credit is altogether as necessary as ability. But why was he so officious with your Lordship about Mr. Terry? Mr. Thwaites is ill indeed, and I am afraid in a consumption, but I do not apprehend he will go off suddenly. Possibly he may linger out as long as our Governor will be willing to stay with us, but I believe there was no occasion to put your Lordship in mind of Mr. Terry, nor had our Governor any reason to think that I should forget it when it was proper.

The Scotch nobleman who is coming hither is my Lord Glenorchy's son; his mother was Lord Jersey's sister. His father and mother are in town with him. I was an utter stranger to his Lordship, but he sent yesterday to give me notice he would visit me. He told me he had seen my Lord Treasurer, and that his Lordship had been pleased to tell him that he supposed he would see me here. He said one thing, which you will easily believe pleased me not a little, that your Lordship's character had determined him to have his son bred here. He has taken a house over against the Theatre, and designs to live here whilst his son is with us. His son's tutor is to live in the same chamber with him, and he designs to capitulate with him that he shall take no other pupils whilst he has his son. I know not who recommended Mr. Broxholme to him, but he may be proper for such terms, because he has yet no other pupils. I waited on his Lordship to see some chambers; he has pitched I think on those which were Colonel Trelawny's. They were designed for Dr. South, when that side in which his now are was pulled down, but though that side would have been down this autumn, had the late Dean lived, yet I fancy we shall not now be in so much haste, and Dr. South does not like those chambers. He would have had Mr. Periam's chambers if he could have had the whole floor, but poor Lord Strathallan's chambers had been taken before by Sir Charles Holt for his son, who is to [be] brought in student. The Speaker must get him in, he wrote to me, and bid me deal freely with him, whether I had a mind to be asked or no, but I had fixed already, and I have referred him to our new Dean's, let one of them pay for his honour.

Had the Lord Chamberlain [Kent] made any stay in our neighbourhood, I should have gone with Tom Rowney to have paid my duty to him. He lay one night in Oxford, but no one knew he was here. The next morning about eight, he with the Duchess drove in their coach round both our quadrangles. My servant came in to me to tell me, I put on my gown and went out to have offered them any respects I could pay them, but they were gone before I could get out.

If your Lordship goes abroad, I am afraid we must give over all hopes of seeing you here before the session.

I suppose I must let the affair about Dr. Hutton's manuscripts rest as it is. The widow possibly will be glad of that which has been offered, when she finds she cannot meet with a better chapman.

I am very sorry for Mr. St. John's sake, that his behaviour to your father is so much known. Should this end, as it must at last if it continues, in dismissing him from his post, he is undone. I know so much of his present condition, though I am far from being at the bottom of it. But this is the consequence of that which was instilled into him last winter, by some who took that way to make their court to him, that he was of capacity enough to stand upon his own legs.

1711, September 11.—We have yet no news of our Governor, I believe he will not be able to take possession of us so soon as he designed. The late Dean was above eleven weeks from the date of his patent before he could be ready for his installation. Our present Governor will [lose] sixty odd pounds by not being installed before next Friday, but we are a poor House and it will go towards the paying of our debts, where it will be better bestowed than in any private pocket. Our Governor has written to the Keeper to let him know he is afraid he cannot be here soon enough to pay his duty to his Lordship before he leaves the country. The whole family leave the country on Friday next. This letter has altered his Lordship's design. I am afraid we shall have the whole family here this week, and I am told by Blechingden still that the head-quarters will be with me.

I will never pass the months of July and August here again. I am almost foundered with showing sights to people, that take us in their way to Bath or Blenheim. That Blenheim is a curse upon this poor place, I would at any time make one in a rising of the University, town and county, to raze it to the ground.

I hope your Lordship has prepared your mind for any change of fortune. The Whigs give it out with great joy here, that there will be a new scene, or rather the old again, before Christmas. I believe too it is concerted to hearten their friends with the same news in other places too. A gentleman was with me yesterday who was lately at Worcester and dined there with the Bishop of Oxford, the Bishop read a passage out of a letter, to this purpose some things have happened here which it is not safe to commit to paper, which give us reason to hope that things will take a very different turn next winter. This was as near as I can judge, by the account the gentleman gave me, about the time the Duke of Somerset would have come to Council. You see what use has been made of that affair.

I am quite out of snuff, and I hope you will give me leave to beg a little recruit of your Lordship; you may send it to me by my brother Smalridge.

1711, September 13.—We are once more baulked, the Lord Keeper sent his gentleman over on Friday last to tell Tom Rowney he would be with him in the beginning of the week. Blechingden brought me the same notice, but not by order. I declared I would not lay in a college crust till I had notice in form. Tom sent to his friends and tenants to send in capons, pheasants, partridge and all other provisions. We expected our guest, but heard nothing of him. This morning the mystery came out, it was thought our Governor's gout would not have let him be here before his Lordship left the country, but they met last Sunday at Windsor, and then concerted their measures, as we suppose, for meeting here next week, for Blechingden says his Lordship was resolved if possible to see the Dean in his new government. I suppose, as we at first thought, he will honour his installation. But this week his Lordship went on a visit to Sergeant Banister, without ever giving his friend Tom notice that he had altered his purpose. The Senator is in a pet, I have a double advantage over him, I have saved my own provisions and shall have a share in his.

1711, September 15.—As much as I desire to see you, I am not sorry that I shall not do it till the installation of our Governor is over. He will be much disappointed if he expects, as I hear he does, that the House should meet him on the road. Their proper attendance on him is in several stations, in several bodies, according to their different degrees, when we wait on him to the Hall after his installation. He will have all the respects paid to him, which were paid to any of his predecessors, but no other, though I believe he may desire more. But he will find it is not the way to make himself greater than they were, to endeavour, as he has done for this last year, to lessen them in all companies, and to raise his own credit upon the ruin of theirs. I hear now he will not be with us till Tuesday se'nnight. I gave him some account of the late Dean's speeches; I believe upon that, he has taken more time for composing his own. But do what he will, he will fall short of his predecessor, and in other things as well as in his speeches. He may be without some of that poor man's infirmities, but he will never have all his virtues, either intellectual or moral.

The Lord Keeper can wait no longer it seems for our Governor's coming, he has sent me word this evening that he and his family will be with me on Monday. After such an honour, I hope you think I shall not envy either of the new Deans.

I have heard great complaints this summer of both the Blunts. If that I heard was true, your father's interest and that of the South Sea Company have suffered from nothing but the prejudice that is in the city against those two men.

I have not heard from Mrs. Hutton since I sent the last letter I received to your Lordship; she expects to hear from me again. I will let her know next week that I can give her no hopes of any more than I have already offered.

Our Governor gives one reason for not coming down next week because Sunday se'nnight is Ordination Sunday, and that he might avoid any difference in the beginning with the Bishop of Oxford, who might claim as his right to ordain without leave in our church. But that point has been settled ever since the visitation of the college in 1628, when Bishop Laud and others did what they could to support the students in their complaints against the Dean and Chapter. The Bishop of Oxford at that time was by a civil message, by one of the canons deputed from Duppa—then Dean—and the Chapter, told that he could not be admitted without leave first asked. He answered he would not be beholden to them, and ordained in another place ; and none of his successors have ever since ordained here, without first asking leave. But by what I hear we shall have no ordination, because it is supposed that the new Dean will be here at that time, and the Bishop of Oxford has as little mind to meet him as he can have to meet the Bishop.

1711, September 18.— I beg you would pay my most humble duty and thanks to the lady whose fair hand was pleased to do me the honour to direct the last letter I received from your Lordship, and I am very glad to find that the ladies of members, as well as members themselves, have the privilege of franking.

I had notice from other hands as well as your Lordship that Buys was to come. I am glad of it, as it must be interpreted by all as a public mark of the respect of the States to my Lord Treasurer, and their confidence in him. It is a very good omen too for peace, which would at once remove all difficulties, and I am afraid nothing else will. Decker gave me an account of the doings at Pontacks, he says the hearts of all the citizens that were fit for anything but to go to the devil were charmed, but his head seemed to be at least as full of the entertainment as of the speech.

I have a very odd story to tell you. Not many weeks since a man and two women went about the country begging with a pretended pass, the Mayor of Stamford suspected that the pass was counterfeited, and designed to seize them, but they escaped them. He gave notice of them to one Mr. Kirkham, a Justice of Peace, of a very good character in the neighbouring parts of Northamptonshire, near to whose house he heard these people were. Mr. Kirkham seized them and took away their pass. I cannot tell whether he punished them otherwise too, but the next morning one of the women came to desire to speak with Mr. Kirkham, she had put off her beggar's weeds and was dressed in a very handsome riding habit, with cap and feathers. He was surprised to see her in that dress and says he thought her then one of the most beautiful women he had ever seen. She addressed herself to him with great manners, assured him those he had seized were persons of no ordinary condition, desired he would restore their pass and give them no more disturbance. When she could not prevail, she fell into a great rage, bid him at his peril trouble them any more, for he should hear of it again in a little time. Within a month, Mr. Kirkham was fetched up by a warrant for high treason from Mr. St. John ; he was surprised, but suspected whence it came. When he was brought before the Secretary he desired to see the depositions against him, and to be confronted with the witnesses, but neither was granted. After a great deal of charge and trouble he was discharged. He was not satisfied, but insisted upon the expense and trouble he had been at for that which he had done in the execution of his office ; he demanded reparation, and to know who had accused him. He could have no other answer, but that he might if he pleased go about his business. The story needs no comment. I cannot vouch all the particulars to you, but your Lordship has them as they were brought to me out of Northamptonshire last week by my brother Gastrell, where the story makes a great noise, as well it may. I need not desire your Lordship not to publish it, at least as from me.

I think I am very good that have found time to write so long a letter in the midst of the great guests that are now in my house.

Postscript. Mr. Harcourt says the Peace is made. I am glad of so good an authority for it. You would not tell me this, though no doubt you are in the secret too.

1711, September 20.—I promised your Lordship some account of what passed at the great honour I received on Monday. His Lordship designed to have lain only with me and to have dined with Lord Abingdon on Monday, to have supped with me at night and to have dined the next day with Tom Rowney. But my Lady Abingdon being ill of the gout, his Lordship had excused him for not being able to receive them. Tom Rowney and his whole family went out of town on purpose to be even with them for having disappointed him the week before. By these means the whole honour was devolved on me, but his chaplain prevailed to have the honour of his company yesterday at St. John's. The ladies were much at a loss, being disappointed of the conversation which they had expected of their own sex, and this was no small addition of care to me, the ladies being that part of my guests I knew least how to deal with. His Lordship was pleased to tell, which I knew very well, that he had delayed his coming in hopes of having been here when the Dean came, but since that could not be, he would not leave the country without seeing me. The next morning the Vice Chancellor, the Warden of All Souls, President of St. John's, and the Canons in town paid their compliments to him. His Lordship went with me to see Dr. Smalridge's lodgings, observed that the garden was run to ruin, but hoped the Doctor would not lay out sixpence in a place in which he was not likely to stay. He was pleased to wonder too why I had laid out so much, since he supposed I designed to leave my lodgings if I could. I told his Lordship that I should think Providence dealt very bountifully with me, if it allowed me to lay my bones where it had now placed me. He asked me when I had seen my parsonage, I told him this summer, and that I designed to build there. He said if I would build, he thought I should build upon a better parsonage, and such a one might be had—a gracious intimation to me to apply to him. I told his Lordship this little one best suited all the aims I had in the world, as well as my abilities. Not one word of our Dean, but a very odd expression I thought of his friend, before Lord Abingdon and Sir John Walters after dinner. We were observing that one of my brother Gastrell's and the Dean's election was at this time Dean of Christ Church in Dublin and Bishop of Kildare. His Lordship said it was well it was an Irish bishopric, for he could answer for the Dean that he would let none of them have an English one before him.

When we were at St. John's the President dined there, his Lordship began the Dean's health and told brother Gastrell and me that we must not expect to keep him long. Upon that I told his Lordship that I wondered my friend the Dean would be at the expense and trouble he must, for that which he could keep so few weeks. How few, said his Lordship. Why, he can hold it but three months. Who says so, said his Lordship. One, my Lord, who I hope has honour as well as power to make his word good, even your Lordship ; you were pleased to promise me last January that I should be dean before the year was out. I observed that his Lordship's friend the President, though by nature not much inclined to blushing, was somewhat out of countenance upon this as well as his Lordship was.

We parted after dinner with mutual compliments. I was pleased to observe Mr. Harcourt very fond of his lady, she is indeed, by all I have seen, a very good young lady. My friend Dubber, his Lordship's old servant, told me she was the only Christian in the family, and that he knew not what would become of them if they were not all saved by her prayers. Mr. Harcourt said he would not exchange her for the Duke of Newcastle's daughter and all her estate, if he could have them. The latter part of the expression was modest, the former a noble compliment to a good lady ; I will not enquire whether there was any other meaning. His Lordship has procured venison out of all the neighbouring parks for the Dean, and to make his compliment entire, has paid the fees in all places, or left money with me to do it. There is the strictest alliance that is possible between them, which is somewhat surprising to me, who a few years ago knew the opinion which each had of the other, and was employed by our Dean, when the present Keeper first came in power, to bring on an acquaintance between them. It would be worth while, if one could get at it, to know the true ground of this mutual change.

I most heartily thank your Lordship for my snuff, I like it very well. John Urry was robbed as he came down, but my snuff escaped.

1711, September 23.—I shall I believe have no opportunity of hearing more circumstances of that story, all I had were from my brother Gastrell, who had been in some parts of Northamptonshire, not far from the place where Kirkham lives. There can be no doubt of the truth of the main part of it. I wish there be not too great a proof of it by some public complaint.

I troubled you with a very impertinent letter last post, but I was willing to play the fool to divert you. I thought indeed some part of the conversation odd enough betwixt such old friends. His Lordship will now make his chaplain easy; the prebendary of Gloucester, whose prebend his Lordship had disposed of last spring, is now dead. There is a living in this county in the gift of the Seals, near 300*l.* per annum, void by the same man's death; I hear his Lordship's chaplain is in some doubt whether he shall accept that too, because if he does he must quit his fellowship and his college living. I promise you I won't make use of the hint that was given me.

There was much talk when I was in town in the winter that Mr. St. John was to go to Holland. Can the office be carried on in his absence? or would he quit it for the other post? Absence might be of service to him, if he would make the proper use of it, but he must be more discreet at least than he is here, if he would be acceptable there.

1711, September 24.—I had last night a letter from John Drummond, to give me an account with the utmost joy and gratitude of the very kind reception he had met with from my Lord Treasurer. I leave your Lordship to judge how much this pleased me, you know how dear all his concerns are to me, I value him as an old true friend, and as one who has as hearty and sincere an honour for your father as ever any one had that was so happy as to be known to him, one who I know would hazard all he has for the sake of that interest which is under your father's protection, and who is as able too to serve it as any one of his condition ever was. I am to thank your Lordship for your kindness to him, he tells me he had been so happy as to see you once, and acknowledges your favour with the gratitude an honest man should. He tells me he returns soon, and desires to see me before he goes over again. I design to be in town as soon as I have paid my duty to my Governor. God willing I shall be there sometime next week, and at home again the following week. He tells me too that he hopes you will go over with him, that alone would bring me up, for I cannot let you go abroad without seeing you once again before you go, and giving you my prayers, though I cannot my benediction.

Dr. Blechingden reckoned it seems too fast upon a new parsonage, the prebendary of Gloucester now dead is not the prebendary who has the good living in this county which is in the gift of the Seals.

Our students have been employed this afternoon in hiring hacks. Last night came letters from Dr. Freind, the physician, and others to give notice that the Dean designed to be to-morrow precisely at such an hour at the foot of Shotover, and that it was hoped the students would meet him there. The late Dean forbade any one to meet him, but since we are given to understand that our Governor thinks such a compliment from the young men may be of use to him, we have advised every one, that can hire a horse, to oblige him.

Postscript. The Speaker, upon my writing to him, has returned his son to assist at the solemnity. Though he tells me he parted with him with great regret, he is extremely pleased with him, and the satisfaction he has in him I believe makes the loss of the other pretty easy. He will indeed much better support his family than the other would have done. He is in very good humour upon all other accounts and much pleased with the hopes of a peace. He tells me he hears the Duke of Beaufort has been the most angry man of all the laity at the promotion of the Lord Privy Seal [Bishop Robinson]. That is pleasant enough. Had he any pretensions to such a post?

1711, September 27.—I suppose your Lordship will see an account of our cavalcade in Abel Roper. The Dean could have no other end in being at so much pains to procure it. Excepting the students of the House, Williams the upholsterer was the person of the greatest quality in the whole cavalcade. But I have some pleasant stories of it to divert you, which I reserve till I wait on you.

I write this in the morning before our ceremony is begun, for I shall have no time in the afternoon. I must stay till the next post to give your Lordship the account of any thing which passes then, but I can now tell you, the ceremony will be deficient in one main branch of it. The Dean has no speech, as his predecessors had, to the whole company, which was always the large speech, and indeed the only one of the moment. He designs only to answer the three persons that speak to him, in very short speeches, and that it may not be observed, he has invited his company at one o'clock, that the speeches may be over long before they come. I told him it was unusual, that the whole company invited had attended his predecessors from the Dean's lodgings to the hall, that I was afraid they would take it ill to be invited only to his meat. All the Canons seconded me. The only answer he had was, that he had promised a dinner for them,

but no speech, and that it was too late now to remonstrate that
to him.

Brother Smalridge came last night and will be installed to-day
too. Brother Gasse [Gastrell], Smalridge and I drank the Lord
Treasurer's and your Lordship's healths together, as we are all
in duty bound.

1711, September 30.—I promised your Lordship some account
of our solemnity, if there was any thing in it that could entertain
you. The Sub-Dean installed the Dean, and then the Dean
installed Dr. Smalridge. The Dean was disappointed in his
design of not having his speeches heard. The company would
have his Latin as well as his meat, and most of them though invited at one were got to his lodgings before we came from church.
The Dean read his speeches, he used a pretty artifice to cover his
want of one speech. He answered not the rhetoric reader, as
was usual, at the fire place, but went straight up to the top of
the hall, whither the masters followed him, and there spoke to
the masters, where his predecessors used to make their last
speech to the whole company. He disappointed me in one thing,
he spoke very handsomely of the late Dean. The entertainment
was very noble and managed without any confusion; the most
remarkable thing in the whole solemnity was the Psalm which
happened to be the first of the day. It was the 120th. I and my
two brethren were struck together with it, and could not but
observe it to each other. The fines which begin to come in put
us all in good humour. We are all very easy together and I
hope we shall continue so. Our Dean says he has now got all
he desires in this world, that he will never ask for any thing
more, that he will employ for the future all the interest he has
in the Lord Treasurer for others. He told J. Keill he would
not be quiet till somewhat was done for him, but John does not
think there is any occasion for the Dean's application in his
behalf when your Lordship has been so kind as to declare you
would be his friend, nor will he let the Dean into any share of
the merit of that which he must owe wholly to your goodness.

I shall come up to town, God willing, with my brother Smalridge on Thursday. The coach (flies?) still, and it will be late
before we can get thither, I cannot hope to wait on you that
night, but I shall beg leave to drink a dish of coffee with
your Lordship on Friday morning. Should you not be stirring
when I call, I hope you will allow me, as I have done here, to
come to your bedside and wake you.

1711, October 21.—I most heartily thank you for the favour of
both your letters, they are always dear to me, but these have
relieved me from the concern in which I left the town on your
father's account. A concern which I have not only as his
servant, who owe all I have to him, but on account of my own
little share too in the public stock. There is but one life in
England on which the quiet or confusion of these kingdoms
more depends. Since your father is abroad again, I doubt not
but we shall soon hear the stocks rise again. He certainly has a

great majority of the nation with him for peace, and he is thought to have those arguments for it which no one who would oppose, either abroad or at home, can answer. If our allies dislike it, let them make good their own quotas ; if our senators are against it, let them provide for the war ; it is supposed the impracticability of either will oblige both to agree to it.

I have made your Lordship's compliments to the President of Corpus, he drank your health with me last night, and will take it for a great honour to see you when you are here. I am very glad it will be so soon. It must be this week if you are here before our Governor is out of waiting ; he has promised to be here on Tuesday se'nnight. I reserve an account of ourselves till I see your Lordship. Our Governor took the advantage of my brother Gasse, George's and my absence to bully our poor brethren who were left here. If he goes on, we shall all soon be better known in the Court of Chancery, or at the Council Board. Our tenants will summon us into one place, and we ourselves shall be obliged to appeal to the other. I have written to him with all deference possible about some things, in which his own credit alone will be concerned. Were I his enemy, as much as he thinks me, I would give him as much rope as he desires.

Yesterday we chose a new beadle in the room of Rogers. We carried it by a great majority for Rawlins, our singing man. You must bear with these small occurrences in the midst of the important affairs you are engaged in.

1711, October 23.—I hope my Lord Treasurer is abroad again, and that he will be prevailed on to have a little more care, than he has hitherto had, of a life in which every one in the nation has a greater concern than he himself has.

I wish you could send me some hopes of the peace going on, we at this distance judge of it only by the rise or fall of stocks, and I am not able to answer their fears who guess at a peace always by the last clause in the " Post Boy."

I cannot say that our number is yet much increased since we have ceased to be a headless society. We have had two gentlemen entered, who came upon Mr. Terry's account, being Kentish men. One is a son of Sir Francis Lee, sent by the Bishop of Rochester, the other is one Desboverie, whose relations are in the Turkey trade, and his uncle a director of the South Sea Company. I hear yet of no more, and more are leaving us than are yet come. Poor Heysham must be taken away, he is now with his father, but we have discovered an intrigue with a girl for marriage. His friends have notice of it, so I suppose we shall not see him again, but this to yourself.

1711, October 25.—I hope my Lord Treasurer was able to go to Hampton Court on Tuesday, and that your Lordship was with him. For want of better news to entertain you, I must give you some account of our own affairs. It is due to you too, since you are pleased to have so kind a concern for us. Whilst we hope for peace abroad, we expect nothing but war at home. Our Governor claims to dispose of all the college curacies by his sole authority, though given to the Canons as well as the Dean by the Charter, and disposed of always under the Common Seal, nor has he the least colour but his own will and pleasure for such a pretence. It looks as though he were resolved upon a breach, thinking to carry any point by the Lord Keeper, before whom I suppose he believes it must be brought. But in that he may be mistaken ; he had agreed to let Mr. Gore's fine remain as it had been set in the late Dean's time, by whose death he has the advantage of it. The fine is 240*l.* His agreement to it was entered in the minute book, upon which I sent to the Receiver to call upon Mr. Gore's agent for the money. Three days after I was gone, he moved the Chapter to have the former order revoked, and a new one made that the consideration of Mr. Gore's lease should be respited till his return, or his further direction. Every one in Chapter begged of him to let the first agreement stand, but he was positive, and they to be easy complied. No notice was given to me of this new order, nor did he mention it when I was with him in town. In pursuance of the first agreement, the money is paid in town, and received as a fine. He now insists to raise the fine 160*l.* above the sum agreed to. Mr. Gore may certainly call us into Chancery and force us to make good our agreement. I have written to him with all due deference to represent the case to him. I suppose I shall have no answer till I see him here on Monday or Tuesday. Not one of the Chapter is with him, even Hammond leaves him and thinks it too shameful. Mr. Gore, when he was first our tenant, gave us very frankly 100*l.* to Peckwater. We are likely to have benefactors when we make such returns. His friend Hammond supposes this to be out of some private pique to the Bishop of London, to whom Gore is related by marriage. But all this to yourself. I had only a mind to let your Lordship know the temper we have to deal with. I believe he will soon convince all our friends that those who know him had reason to wish him elsewhere. We shall, if it be possible, prevail with him to desist in both cases. If we cannot we hope to manage it so that any public complaint shall come from the tenant against him, or from him against us, and that we shall not be aggressors.

1711, October 27.—Yours last night brought me doleful news indeed, but the loss the public will have in Dr. Grabe extinguishes almost the sense of my private loss. I lose indeed a very intimate and very instructive friend, but I know no one man of our profession, whose life is of more concern to the Church at this juncture. Nor can one determine whether we lose more, by the want of his piety or his learning, of his prayers or his writings. No man in Europe can finish the Septuagint as he has begun it, and I am afraid we shall entirely lose those observations which he had made, but never I believe digested into any order, towards the reconciling the Hebrew and Greek texts. His loss looks somewhat ominous as to the Arian heresy, which is so openly revived. Had he lived he had effectually quashed it, by exposing the forgery of those constitutions on which it is chiefly grounded by Whiston. He had communicated to me a discovery which he had made of those very books from which those constitutions had been forged, and which he had designed to have printed *verbatim* on one part of the page, with the text of the constitutions, and marks to show every particular interpolation in it, on the other. He stayed only for the copy of a manuscript in the Vatican to publish this work. I know no one who can do it, when he is gone. He was as remarkable for his gratitude as for any other virtue he had. My Lord, your father will lose in him a sincere, earnest, daily suppliant to Almighty God for the prosperity of him and all who belong to him, but I hope those who were his patrons, though they lose him, will not lose the merit of their kindness to so good a man.

The loss of this friend naturally increases my apprehension for your father; not only Church, but State would feel a convulsion upon such a loss, should it be at this juncture. We should unavoidably fall into the utmost confusion, but you must excuse those, who are sensible how much depends on it, for fearing danger where there may be none, and for pressing your Lordship, whose interest in his life gives you a right to intercede with him, to beg he would have a little more care of it. If the pain he has ends in a regular gout, I hope it will rather be a remedy than a disease.

Postscript.—Thanks for your good news, not of the Bishop of London's illness, but of your father's amendment. I had rather bear my share of his temper than be eased of it at such a price. Though he may be perverse, perhaps, he hopes that may be an argument for his preferment.

1711, November 1.—The comfort your Lordship gives me as to my chief concern alleviates in some measure that I have for my poor friend Grabe. That indeed is a much less concern, but no little one. I hope the re-establishment of my Lord's health will allow you to make good your intention of seeing us. I hope it will not be before the end of next week, then our Governor must be again in town. We will be as cheerful as those who love you can be upon a visit that is to be parting too. ·If we may be allowed *recepto furere*, we may too *abluto merere*.

All are pleased that her Majesty has vindicated her own honour so much in resenting, as she has done, the insolence of the Imperial minister. The party for peace grows every day, if that can be called a party to which there is no opposition. I hear not of any one in the country that does not pray for it.

I beg my duty to my godfather, and be pleased to let him know that we yesterday chose Dale, whom he recommended to me, one of Bishop Fell's exhibitioners : it will entitle him to 10*l*. per annum for ten years, if he resides here so long. The lad appeared extremely well, and has made very good use of the little time he has spent here.

Our Governor I believe will not complain when he comes up again that I do not visit him ; I spent yesterday with him from one o'clock till nine at night ; we were very easy. I made his lady as true compliments as I could, and told her the door of communication should on my side be always unbarred. If he should be jealous of me, I believe he will be the first man ever was so, but that may be, for the least thing works with him of any man I ever knew, and I had spite enough to try what I could do with him.

I am afraid we shall not adjust other points, but we will prevent any difference by keeping them if we can in suspense. At least I will defer the decision to the audit, when I hope to have some more of my brethren here as auxiliaries. I told him the Bishop of London was ill, he pricked up his ears at it, and said it was news to him, but I have damped him again to-day with the news that he is better. Your Lordship I suppose may have heard that we have lost two students in the expedition to Canada. Captain Twisden that was lost in the storm, and Hicks that went chaplain, who died in the return of a fever. The great living, by which poor Herbert was tempted to leave us, is fallen, and the co-heirs have presented Herbert, but the Bishop of Exeter has given institution upon George Granville's presentation. Herbert must now try his title. Does your Lordship think Lord Carteret will bear his expense ? I am afraid he will have little reason to think he has gained by leaving us when he sums up his expense, if he should get the better.

1711, November 3.—The recovery of poor Grabe, when we had given him for gone, would make it much more welcome. I am full of hopes upon the account your Lordship gives me, and am willing to believe that God will preserve him to finish those things which no one but he can do. I hope my Lord Treasurer will not venture out too soon. I like not that paragraph in your Lordship's letter about the Parliament. If it is prorogued, we shall have our Governor longer with us. It will be a sore disappointment to us, if he does not leave us at the end of this week. We are heartily weary of him, though his crest is fallen a little, and we shall oblige him to relinquish both his points, about Gore's lease and the curacies. The only thing that sticks at present with him, is how to retreat with honour. We treat with him, as great princes are used, by an ambassador. We have no discourse ourselves with him about the points in which we differ, we transact them with him by the most acceptable person of our body to him, his confident Hammond. He offers to agree with us about Mr. Gore's lease, if Mr. Gore waits on him when he returns to town and begs the favour of him. Since he thinks such a deference of moment to him, if we have the substance we shall for peace sake let him please his own dear self with the form. As to the curacies we insist stiffly, we know our own right to be upon the very same ground his is, and we shall oblige him to give up that pretence, without any salvo to his honour. I hear he has somebody in your family with whom he corresponds, from whom he has had constant accounts of my Lord Treasurer's health. It can be only Wanley I believe—keep this to yourself— but find out if you can, without telling Wanley that you hear of it, whether he writes to him.

The Whigs have outdone themselves in their behaviour upon [Count] Gallas's disgrace. This is telling the Queen very roundly what they would do with her, if they could; but it is well they are so open, it will have its use with the people as well as with the Queen.

There is a great struggle at All Souls', only one vacancy. George Clarke is come down himself to support the interest of one he recommends; but it is. thought the Warden and he will lose it.

Postscript. Our Governor has been looking into our muni- ments—as he calls them, you and I should call them writings. He is amazed to find the Dean has no greater a power than he appears to have in those he has yet seen. He suspects we are all in a combination to conceal from him those that make most for him.

Dr. Clarke has carried his election by one voice. The man's name is Wilbraham. The opposite party have protested against the election because the Warden took the scrutiny which they say, though I believe without ground, ought to have been taken by the two deans.

1711, November 5.—Our hopes it seems for poor Grabe were very short-lived, we cannot at present be sensible as we ought how much we have lost by him. We can know it only as occasions happen that will require him. He is happy; one so much above this world as he was could not but be ready for the other. The difference there was betwixt the souls of that poor man and our Governor's, who is glad the poor man is gone! Upon a private pique, in which our Governor was the person who did the injury, and a shameful one it was. When Grabe could not agree with Bennet about his Septuagint, Bennet to force him to his terms threatened to print another edition at the same time, and got leave to use our Governor's name, as though he would be the editor, though he no more designed it, nor was any more fit for it, than I. Grabe, for fear the sale of his own edition should be spoiled, offered Bennet to let him have half the profit if the person he employed would do half the work. Our Governor proposed not to work separately but jointly with Grabe. The poor man saw this was to throw all the trouble on him, when the other was to have the credit of his labour. He refused it, but offered to take one part to himself and to leave the other to our Governor, and to let our Governor have his choice of the books he would publish. The sham then appeared, but our Governor never forgave him, but from that moment did all he could to lessen the credit of his learning, he durst not attack his piety, and the other was too hard for him.

Our Governor and I met last night in my little parlour *tête-à-tête* at his own desire; he sat from seven till nine; he returned after prayers and sat till twelve. He began with Gore's fine, and grew very warm; I was prepared and rebuked him very seriously for his passion, and took the liberty to tell him how little I thought it became him, whether it were affected or real. To be short, I got the better of him, and he agrees to let it go as we would have it, if I will write to Gore to wait on him when he came to town and desire his consent. I told him I did not see the great use of that; he insisted that it was not for his dignity as Dean to have such a lease go without a personal application to him. I said if that was all, we would not break with him for form, he should please himself in that. We then went on the general business of the College, I gave him in every point the fullest information I could, and made my reflections with decency to him, but freedom enough as to my own opinion. I told him by all that I knew of the College, its security from its first foundation to this time against intestine sedition, and assaults from without, had been the unanimity of the Dean and Chapter. He took occasion in his discourse to drop graciously that when he was most angry with me, he took me for an honest man. At twelve, the Judas threw his arm about my neck and kissed me, and desired we might have no more squabbles, for he hated them. I asked him if he could say that with a good conscience, he smiled at that. As to the thing itself, I told him he might be certain it would be his fault, not ours, if we had any. He has been looking into our muniments and finds he has not so uncontrollable a power as he took himself to have. He does not think he can run us down so easily as he once thought he should, he will quit his other point in a day or two, and it was lucky for us that he pitched on those at first which he could so little defend. He is likely to engage in the quarrels abroad sooner than I thought he would have done. He owns he designs upon the first opportunity he can meet with to attack Lancaster. They are as well met as any two I know. I did not discourage him. The more he is embroiled abroad, the less leisure will he have to be troublesome at home, and more occasion too to be easy with us. Your Lordship yourself heard how hard he was on the memory of the poor late Dean. Indeed his infirmities were our Governor's constant topic, but what cannot wise men do. He finds that is not popular here, he has changed his language, and now is full of projects how to do honour to him. He designs to put his picture over the chimney in the study, and talks of putting up his statue in the middle of the area of Peckwater, with the model of Peckwater in his hand. But that I believe upon second thoughts he will judge improper. Mr. St. John offered the late Dean to give 100*l.* for the Duke of Marlborough's statue to be put in that place. The Dean told him he could place no statue there, but one of the Royal family.

Mr. St. John was angry, but he had an excuse for giving us nothing.

Your Lordship was pleased to make an excuse to me for writing so long a letter to me, if it wanted an excuse; I have revenged myself on you in writing one four times as long upon much more impertinent matters. If it be a true instance of friendship, as I think it is, to write any occurrences without restraint to one you trust, I have showed by mine to your Lordship that I am not insensible of it.

If Herbert be not too bashful he certainly may have the lady. The Bishop of St. David's began upon less encouragement, and was not a cleaner fellow. Rob Freind might have her without doubt, if he was not hampered already, and had a mind to her. I have had it from those who were present that she has encouraged him in plain language to say what he would to her. I wish Herbert may fall into hands that may give him proper instructions. I will try what I can do with him, when I come up after Christmas.

1711, November 7.—I had an account from my brother Smalridge of poor Grabe. May God give his grace to all those who have lost the advantage of his conversation, to profit by the memory of his example. The most truly pious soul that ever I knew, always excepting Robin Morgan, is now gone into bliss, I heard very near his last breath was employed in that he was so truly sensible of, in paying his duty and thanks to my Lord Treasurer. I doubt not but your Lordship and your posterity will find the effects of my Lord Treasurer's great goodness to that saint.

Diram qui contudit hydram, must be my motto I think. If you do not check me, I am much disposed to be vain, but I think your Lordship ought to have the greatest share of the honour. If I do any thing it is by the advantage of the instructions I had from you in town. You said I could not dissemble; if you don't believe I can, I dare say my Governor does. This day has mortified him more than his noble cavalcade exalted him, his greatness was so gracious as to give up to-day both his points in a full Chapter. A train was laid, which he could not avoid, to bring in the business of the curacies. When we mentioned it he said he was yet in the dark, and desired further time till his next return from London, that he might search the Treasury. But I would not let it go, I told him it would be soon dispatched, and called for the leiger books. I offered him that of Bishop Fell's time; he is used to appeal to him, as one who he thought stretched the authority of the Dean to the utmost. He declined that, and would know only what his predecessor had done; he thought that a time of negligence, in which we had no instances against him. We acquiesced in that and immediately produced him several collations under the Common Seal, within these last six years. With much ado he owned he was satisfied, and an order was made that all who had not collations under the Common Seal should be obliged to take them. Never man started such a pretence, without the least colour for it. Then he brought on Tring and offered again his very scandalous expedient. Every one was against it and requested him to let it go as it had been agreed ; he said at last he would have no hand in it. His proxy might do what he would in his absence, provided Mr. Gore waited on him when he came to town, and desired his favour. As he and I came home together he took me by the hand, and desired me to learn from him to *yield*. I told him that when he and I were students together, I was always for submitting to lawful authority ; but that he knew he had been an old mutineer. I believe his courage is cooled a little, and that he will not advance any more new pretensions so hastily as he did these.

But what excuse shall I make to your Lordship for the trouble I have given you of all our impertinent squabbles ? It may be of one use to you indeed, to convince you that nature can be subdued by nothing but grace ; neither sense, nor education, profession, nor even sense of interest can restrain it. It would be a pretty diversion to the world to see us embroiled as much as Trinity College, and about many points too of as little moment. To our shame be it spoken; we have not been more remarkable for our obstinacy in our quarrels than for the trifles about which we squabble, but I hope we shall disappoint our Bentley.

I hear not a word of any reformation designed but that of our revenues, there we are in hearty earnest, though I cannot well call it a reformation. When men reform they retrench, we may do that in our expenses, but not in our gains. We design to extend them to the last farthing, and that will be the point in which we shall have perpetual squabbles, but I believe the canonical part of our Chapter will always be in that on the favourable side.

1711, November 11.—Reports here in town, and some letters which I have had from London, tell me I must wish you joy ; I wish I may. Should it prove true, the joy I should have would dispose me to forgive you for concealing from me that in which you know I should take so great a part. But I do not like one circumstance of the report, it says you were married on Thursday last in Henry VII's Chapel by the Bishop of Rochester. Neither the place nor the hand seems likely. Of late persons of your quality have dispatched that affair without the ceremony of going into a church. I stand not much upon the manner, if you can but give me assurance of the thing, that it is done or will be done. I will then let you know my reflections on it. But I am not so impudent as to desire to know any thing that you may have your reasons to conceal, but it is talked of here with that confidence I could not avoid mentioning it to you. If your Lordship sees us within a fortnight you will find our Governor here. This prorogation, however necessary for the public, is unlucky for us. He is now delighted so much with his new government that he will not leave us till the Convocation sits. Your Lordship remembers the letter he left for me with the Speaker, in which he desired me to represent by your Lordship the *miserable* condition of our headless Society. I then told him, that were it proper for me to meddle in it, I could not say we were a *miserable* society. That I promised him when he came, notwithstanding all disadvantages, he would find it in a better condition than any society in Europe of the same number. He has now changed his note, and is full of the good condition in which he finds every thing but his stubborn Chapter. But though I did not think we were miserable, yet I still think there are many parts of our discipline which ought to be revised, but I perceive by his discourse that is not at all in his thoughts. He says plainly he must be on his guard not to disoblige his subjects. That is, in other language, that he has other use to make of them, than to oblige them to be such as they ought to be.

I have enclosed a ballad upon the cavalcade that was sung in our streets. I know not whether even such as this might not give some little satisfaction, if the Canon had not had unluckily a share in it. I believe you have as bad poetry as this in your collection.

Our Governor has news that a vacant prebend of Bristol is given to Peter Foulks. He has good luck if it is so. Tom Rowney tells me it is given to Harcourt of Jesus, a good young man.

I hope your Lordship will find R. Morgan here when you come.

1711, November 12.—I was much pleased with so long a letter from your Lordship till I came to the close [of] it. This relapse of my Lord Treasurer was unexpected, I hope there is no danger; but the continuance of this pain is as unreasonable for the public as it must be troublesome to him. My Lady Dupplin's safe delivery was very welcome, I have made my compliments to my Lord. It will cure my Lord Kinnoull of the gout if he should be in a fit, to hear of another boy. Had the news we had here two days ago held true, I should have hoped to have seen my Lord Treasurer a grandfather by your Lordship, but by your silence I guess there was no ground for the report. I beg my most humble duty to my Lord Treasurer. Be pleased to assure him that Mr. Buys and the gentleman that comes with him shall have all the respect that I and this place can show them. I am sorry you can think me so insensible of the honour of this recommendation, that you should make any excuses for it.

The greatest inducement Robin Morgan would have to come into Herefordshire would be your Lordship's neighbourhood, I am sure. He has a very sincere respect and esteem for you, but I much question whether he will quit his Welsh retirement. The difference of the profit will have no manner of influence on him. That which he has is scarce subsistence, but if it pays his journey to attend Convocation, he looks no further. Ross as I take it is a large market town, and the business there may not be so agreeable to one who gives himself so much to speculation. I expect him here in a few days, but I am afraid he will have come to a resolution before I shall see him. Not that any thing I could say would move him, if he has his own reasons against it. He acts not by any of those motives by which we other poor mortals are influenced. What a disparity betwixt the soul of that man and our Governor's? But our Governor will make us all Robin Morgans; we shall all be philosophers. If any thing can bring a man to perfect patience, it is continual squabbling about things of no moment in themselves, and where there is not the least ground for dispute, but only the pride and perverseness of him with whom you have to deal. As the town fills there will still be more in it for peace, I believe no one that comes out of the country but is for it.

Postscript. John Urry begs leave to give his duty to your Lordship and desires to know whether he did not lend to you a letter from Herne (*sic*) to Bagford about Chaucer.

1711, November 13.—The report I mentioned to you in my letter on Sunday grows stronger. All the letters on Sunday night mentioned it as a thing certainly done. They had altered the day indeed, the last letters say it was done on Wednesday. Tom Rowney had a letter which said the young lady was sick of the measles; I hope that is false. I see no one who does not enquire of me, what I know of it; my answer is, that I neither hear of the thing nor of any ground for such a report, that I had the honour to hear from you, that there was no hint of any such thing in my letters, that if such a thing had been I believe you would have been better employed than in writing to me. If after all you should have compassed it, I heartily as I told you forgive you for not letting me into the secret. It is an exploit worthy of you at your first entrance on the world, and a good pledge of what may be expected from you.

We are at present pretty quiet here, the curacy of Caversham is vacant, but we hear no more of any pretences to the sole nomination of it. We now talk of setting our young men at work; a good thing if proper hands are employed on subjects that may be of use. Broxholme is to put out a new edition of Virgil, I know not though how he will mend those we have. Fairfax to put out the Iliads, to answer the late Dean's edition of the Odyssey. But John Urry, because he is an antiquary, must put out a new edition of Chaucer; John scratches his head, and says he is at [our?] mercy and must not disobey, but he hopes our Governor he says will be a bishop before he can gather the materials for his work. These are all the projects that are yet in our view at home; our thoughts indeed seem to lie most abroad, and to aim at framing a party without doors, in which we shall certainly be disappointed, more than we have been in any thing at home. By Sacheverell we hope to make Magdalen and Christ Church go together. Delaune is reckoned as dependent on us, and we court Shippen, because so corrupt a man will certainly fall in, if we can make him hope to find his own account in it. But these noble allies put me in mind of Hoppy and Toppy, and yet I see not any one besides with whom we are likely to be upon any other terms than of bare civility. I believe we ourselves see and are not a little mortified at it, that all others instead of courting us, as we expected, seem to be in the utmost distrust of us. Lancaster has certainly been beforehand with us and will be too hard for us, especially whilst we stand upon our own counsel and our own bottom, without any aid from the credit or advice of our old friends.

I hope my Lord Treasurer's last fit was the last effort of his distemper; pray put me out of pain, by telling me he is so.

1711, November 15.—You needed not to excuse the shortness of your letter, it had in it all that I desired to hear. Since my Lord Treasurer is likely to be well again, I can rest in hope that every thing else will go as we wish it should.

Mr. Buys and his kinsman dined and supped with me yesterday, they were recommended to our Governor by Mr. St. John. We dine with him to-day. I had provided Mr. Terry to wait on them round the university; our Governor thought I should have the sole credit of that mighty business, and therefore he would have one he said to represent him too; they are his own words. He deputed Mr. Alsop, so they have two attendants. Lord Privy Seal had recommended them too to a very honest man of Oriel. I have a very pleasant scene to tell you when I see you upon this occasion. Our Governor was angry that the Secretary had recommended them to him, and yet angry too that your Lordship had recommended them to me and not to him. He grudged them a little meat, and was yet afraid too lest I should outdo him in my entertainment; and all this to my face, in as plain words as I write to you. Poor man, his soul is under the torment of very different passions. I left it to him to take which day he pleased to entertain them, he said he would have Thursday, but if they should stay only one day, it would be proper for him, not for me, to entertain them; and therefore desired I would provide for them on Wednesday, and if he found they stayed no longer, he would take the dinner I had provided. I humbly begged his pardon for that, I said if I bespoke victuals for any one, they should eat it in my own house or not at all. After some squabble upon so decent a point, he agreed to take his chance whether they stayed Thursday or no. There was another difficulty too, for he was under an appointment to dine with Sacheverell at St. John's; that was put off. I pity Delaune. If he could not sell his victuals to the college kitchen, it may go hard with him to make new provision. Well, if we can but give content to our guests, it is no matter for our own squabbles about doing of it.

Our Governor is now sitting to a Dutchman who is here for his picture, it will soon appear in the world in mezzotints. He is very uneasy, and has observed it openly, that we have had no custom at our shop since he was our chief, not one of any degree entered since he came except two, which were coming before solely on Mr. Terry's account. He thought his name would have drawn the youth from all parts of the nation. Since his name won't do, he is going to try what his picture (*sic*).

As I am writing I have received a very angry message from my Governor, which I suppose will produce another quarrel. A tenant came to pay his rent, and complained that another of our tenants who joined to him, pretended to some part of that which was granted to him by our lease. Not going to dinner I sent him with Mr. Brooks to the audit house, that he might dine there, and have the leiger books looked into to see to whom the ground in dispute belonged. I did not think the Dean would have come in. He happened to come in, and found them talking about it, he was in a great passion. He goes out and calls Brooks and sends him just now to me, with a formal message, that I take upon me to hold chapters without him—though I have not been out of my study to-day—and he is "displeased" at me. My dear Lord, what shall I do? As soon as I have ended this letter I am going to submit myself to him, and to assure him that this was nothing but what is constant practice and could not be designed to encroach upon his authority. Guess what a comfortable life I lead, somewhat or other of this nature is started every day.

1711, November 17.—I hope the Parliament will be in good humour when they meet. I wish your Lordship could contrive that the Convocation may not be adjourned at Christmas. We would be glad to eat our mince pies in quiet; no victuals we have had for this last month have done us any good. You will find me, if you do me the honour to see me again, as spare in body as I am grown humble in mind. I told you in my last of the message which I received from my Governor as I was writing to you, it was the first reproof I believe that was ever sent by a servant to a Canon, and much more an officer who has served seven years, I hope without any great blemish. His predecessors were so gracious as to own us for their brethren, and if they had occasion to reprove a brother, which I believe no one of them ever did, would have done it by themselves and not by a servant. When I waited on him humbly to know the reason of it, he denied it, he said he only said in general that he took it ill. When I pressed him with the words of his message which were delivered by his express order, he put on a passion, said he would not talk with me, and went off with a toss of his head. But I will digest it. My good friend my Lord Keeper shall not have any hold to complain of me. Our Governor is now in a great rage with his friend Dr. Hammond; the occasion was that a gentleman who came from a tenant to desire an abatement of a fine, and had been personally known to Dr. Hammond for many years, came to him to talk with him about it. Dr. Hammond told him it would be to no purpose to desire any alteration, and advised him not to trouble himself about it. Dr. Hammond told the story innocently at dinner, there were no expressions of wrath at that time, but when I waited on him, there were many dark words about Canons presuming to treat of the College business with persons who had not first waited on him. I cleared myself, as I easily could, but upon enquiry of another I

found, to my no little joy, that brother Hammond was the person
who had given this great offence, without knowing that he had
done so.

Our Governor is now going to enter the lists with the Vice
Chancellor, about the nomination of a beadle of beggars. I
believe he is entirely in the wrong, but by what he said this
afternoon he seems resolved on it. I had imprudently said
somewhat to dissuade him, but upon recollection I stopped short,
and I hope what I said has had no effect. But take no notice of
this, till the noble quarrel breaks out.

We have not yet done with him about our curacies, though he
has given up the pretence of a sole nomination, yet now he would
have them have no instrument under the Common Seal, nor
their nomination so much as registered. This is to leave room
to start his pretence whenever he sees a fair opportunity, and to
cover as well as he can the disappointment he has had. We
must have new conferences upon this point; you see, my good
Lord, how difficulties multiply upon us. He leaves us on Friday;
if I can hold out till that day, I hope I may recruit enough in his
absence to go through another month at his return.

Postscript. Since I wrote I have discovered one thing which
our Governor thinks a great secret, and little dreams how I can
come by it. The project about annexing some of the prebends in
the gift of the Seal to some of our Headships is now set on foot
again, whether sincerely I cannot yet determine. The Lord
Keeper is to ask the Queen's leave, and our Dean is to have the
choosing of the Colleges. The end of this is too plain to need to
be mentioned. It must draw applications to him, to be sure too
before the places are determined, and is to make his Lordship
absolute here, where our Governor is to be his Viceroy. The
ultimate end I can yet see is to make Sim [Harcourt] our member.

Pray let my Lord Treasurer know it and then keep it to yourself.
There may be reasons I think to doubt whether the Queen should
permit it.

1711, November 20.—I will be very willing to buy my peace of
my Governor, with letting him have the whole credit of any thing
in which I had a share, if that will do. The Dutch coming in so
fairly into the Queen's measures has given the dead blow to the
last ministry. I hope all will be as easy as we can wish at home,
since they go so well abroad. This last attempt of the W[hig?]
T[raitors?] is a sign they look upon their case as desperate. Surely
many must be concerned in it, and it may be easy to come at the
bottom of it. I hope it won't be stifled as Guiscard's was. A
full discovery of it might be of use at the meeting of the
Parliament, and help to unite them and to put them in a good
humour. All are in joy upon the hopes of a speedy peace.

I hope, now my Lord Treasurer is able to go abroad again, that
John Drummond's business will be soon settled. I believe it
would be a great ease to him to be at a certainty of that he is to
expect, and be of a great use to him in the measures he must
take as to his own private affairs.

Our Governor says he leaves us, as he says, on Friday; say and hold (*sic*). It would be a cordial indeed to my spirits, if I should see your Lordship next week. Our Governor begins to treat his students with tea in an afternoon, but I would tell him that won't do, if ever he attempts, of which we have yet no appearance, to revive discipline. I have given them wine, but that would not do, if I gave any good advice along with it. I must on this occasion tell your Lordship a story of Bishop Fell. He had suppressed the breakfast, which used to be somewhat riotous, of the bachelors on Egg Saturday before Lent. He came out at his back door, to put himself at the head of his House to go as usual to the Schools. He found nobody there, he sent to call the House together, nobody would stir out of their chamber. At last, upon his enquiring with some earnestness the reason of it, one answered him, *Si placet domine nolunt convenire sine vino.*

I beg you would let my Lord Treasurer know that the money due from the House to Dr. Woodroffe will amount as it comes in course of payment to about 280*l.* We hear there is a debt due from him to the Queen. We had rather the Queen should have this money than his creditors. He who had the sequestration upon his canonry had a sequestration for 839*l.*, of which he has received above 700*l.* The original debt was but 200*l.*, all the rest interest upon interest. There is indeed somewhat due from the Doctor to the House, and I hope we shall be allowed to pay ourselves first, but when that is done, the Queen may get more of the debt here than I believe will be found in any other place. I thought it my duty to give this notice that, if his Lordship thinks fit, the College at least may be enjoined not to pay elsewhere, till further order.

Mr. Urry gives his most humble duty to my Lord Treasurer and your Lordship, and with great thankfulness accepts of my Lord's offer. He will concert that with your Lordship when we see you here. We this day have once more come to a sort of truce with our Governor. It looks as if we should have a little fair weather again, at least I hope it will hold up till Friday. He goes up then with Sacheverell, the rendezvous is to-day at Delaune's.

1711, November 22.—Your Lordship will have a little ease for some time at least. You will neither have so long nor so impertinent letters from me, as you have had. We shall correspond as we used to do about ourselves or our friends. No more for some days of our ridiculous squabbles. We all hope here the peace cannot be defeated, we presume to drink my Lord Treasurer's health by the name of the Peacemaker. We are not surprised at anything we hear of the W[hig?] T[raitors?], these are the last efforts of the rage of disappointed villains. They know when the peace is made that they are at mercy, but surely so desperate a project, in which so many were concerned, may be searched to the bottom. We are more afraid here of your lenity than their villainy.

Pray let me know if you think there will be any occasion for a full House on the first day. Tom Rowney designs to be in town on Thursday, but if there were any occasion he would be there by Tuesday noon.

Poor old Moore that was Proctor for this diocese in Convocation is dead. Our Governor is making interest to set up Rob Freind, who is rector of Witney. I believe it might be easily carried if the Archbishop would let a writ go out to fill the vacancy ; but he never yet would upon any such occasion.

1711, November 25.—I have now for three days tasted the comfort of my old life here, but the joy of it almost oppresses me. I am like one who passes from one extreme to another, or rather I have passed so from a perpetual contention to a profound quiet. But the present calm makes me think how I shall bear a much greater joy about six weeks hence, when I shall have delivered up my staff, and have nothing to do but to study how to spend my time to my own satisfaction. I promise my Governor who thinks now he has too much of me, that he shall find it no easy matter then to get a sight of me, except at prayers.

I begin now to despair of seeing your Lordship till I wait on you in town. When you are entered into the House, you will scarce leave it, unless you go to the congress. If you design that, you would do well to be going before Christmas day, if you stay till after the holidays you shall take me along with you. Lord Dupplin is tied at home, by a better reason than his employment. But whilst you are a free man, I see not how your Lordship can divert yourself better than by being at so famous a negotiation. You will see there at once an epitome of Europe, and be within a due call if any affair of more consequence should require your presence at home.

We want to know a little more of your pageantry plot. We are as suspicious as you can [be] with us, of the designs of it, but we think you know more than you will impart to us and, like other wise men, we cannot see the reason why you conceal it. We want to know who promoted and contributed to the subscription. Your Lordship I hope is entering upon the world in a happy time, when we shall have peace established not only abroad, upon the extinction of so bloody a war, but at home too upon the crushing of a more bloody faction. The last attempt they will endeavour to make will it is likely be in the Parliament this session. But it looks as though they had not great hopes of doing much within doors, when they form such desperate projects without. I suppose you will soon see our Governor, pray let me hear what account he gives you of his brethren or his College. We are as yet very thin. We have one gentleman come who had always been designed for us, his name is Hill, his father is a Shropshire gentleman, I think he was one of the late Dean's parishioners at Wem. Mr. Terry is his tutor.

1711, November 27.—I will be a faithful steward for her Majesty, but I hope his Lordship will allow us to pay ourselves first. That which is due for bread and beer, &c., though it come out of Dr. Woodroffe's share dividend, is not so properly his money as the College money.

We have this day done a very honest thing that will put our Governor, when he comes to know it, into a great fit of passion. He had charged his proxy Dr. Hammond, if any of the greatest leases we have should be offered in his absence to be renewed, not to proceed in them. It was a very extraordinary strain to pretend to tie up our hands from carrying on the College business in his absence. The very next post after he had left us, were sent offers from one that is the very best estate we have, and from another very good one. His friend Dr. Hammond has left him in the lurch, he called a chapter and we immediately set the old fines. He will never be persuaded but that I was in intelligence with the tenants to send their proposals just upon his leaving us; and Hammond is dipped, he will never forgive him, though he could do no otherwise than he did. Had he pretended to stop up we should all have been about his ears. I wish the Archbishop would keep the Convocation sitting till Christmas, we should then hear no more of our Governor probably till May, and might have a little breathing time.

Some company who were with me last night said the Queen had been already applied to about annexing those prebends I mentioned to our poorest headships, that my Lord Treasurer had moved it to her Majesty and that she had consented. If your Lordship knows whether any such thing has been done, pray let me hear in your next. If such are to be annexed, the librarian's place would be a more proper object of her Majesty's bounty than any headship, both on account of the great deservings of the man and the scandalous salary of his place.

1711, November 29.—I have this day heard of R. Morgan, though not from him ; he is now at Hereford, and may have if he will both Ross and the canonry, but cannot yet determine with himself whether he shall take them. I told your Lordship where it would stick. If his own motives do not tell him it is proper for him, you can no more persuade him to take such a considerable preferment than you could our Dean to bate one shilling in a fine. If one could but have an art of transfusing souls, I would not have my dear friend's pure gold alloyed with any of our Governor's copper, but the least tincture of Robin's would burnish strangely the other's coarse ore. But it is a peculiar mercy in God not to leave Himself without witness in the world, but to raise up such pure bright souls to show others what human nature even in its present state is capable of.

May I give you joy yet of being a member ? or are you not to be introduced till the Parliament sits. If you are easy in the House of Commons, as I hear from very good hands you are likely to be, surely you may lay the spirit of faction in the Lords. There is a little wand in your family that has never failed to charm on such occasions. I am glad my friend the Speaker answers all your desires, as I hear he does.

1711, December 1.—To show you how little I am concerned in any thing that passes out of my own doors, I assure you I knew nothing of Weston's degree till some days after it had passed. Your Lordship knows I always admired my godfather. In imitation of him I am turned hermit. I may indeed creep out of my cell after Christmas, to see how the world goes ; but only to do as he does, to laugh at it for its madness, not to have any concern in it.

But I have [a] piece of news brought to me, which if true will afford you and the world a little sport. I am told there is an open quarrel betwixt Sacheverell and his friend Tilly. Upon Dr. Smalridge's resignation, Tilly is one of the competitors for St. Dunstan's. He desired his dear brother Sacheverell's interest, but the great man told him he was already engaged for another. The little angry man resented this to so great a degree that he bid him defiance, and threatens to publish him to the world. Tilly is obliging the world with a volume of his own compositions ; he designs to print one sermon, which he lent as he says to Sacheverell, and which Sacheverell preached at St. Mary's as his own. Perhaps the famous Paul's sermon may prove to be Tilly's at last ; but I hope our Governor will endeavour to compose any difference betwixt two such worthy friends.

Our Governor sent word last night to Dr. Hammond, that Mr. Gore had been with him, but that some new matter offered itself, which he was not apprised, and which he would lay before us when he returned. He had solemnly promised us in chapter that when he had seen Mr. Gore he would send his consent to his proxy. He vouchsafes not to tell his new objection, nor can he have any, but this is some new device to bring that matter about again if he could. I believe it will be determined at last in Chancery.

Tom Rowney desires your Lordship would let him know if the House will sit on Friday and if you think there will be any occasion for an honest man to be there on the first day.

1711, December 4.—Lord Dupplin was so kind as to let me know how his own family did and all too in York Buildings. I perceive by his Lordship that some spurs have lately been sent to Scotland and that his countrymen are posting up to town. I suppose galloways may be had within a fortnight at reasonable rates.

The book of the management of the allies and the late ministry &c.* takes as much as you could wish it. It will put the country gentlemen in the temper you desire, they are very ready to battle it at home for a peace abroad. I am sorry I cannot be in town at the beginning of the fray, but you cannot do much before Christmas, and I will not be out of town many days after it.

Your acquaintance Sir Copleston [Bampfylde] drank your Lordship's health with me on Sunday night, he is come so far in his way to the Parliament and goes forward again to-morrow.

---

* Swift's "The Conduct of the Allies" was issued at the end of November this year. See "Journal to Stella" about this date.

Your Lordship enters into the world at a great juncture, the negotiations at home as well as abroad will be so important, that they who are so nearly concerned for you as I am know not well where to wish you. You have indeed a more immediate concern to be informed in that which relates to your own nation, and whilst you are here private concerns, that may be of some importance to you, may be attended as well as the public; [so] that I know not whether I should not recant the wish I had that you would go abroad. I only stick to my condition, that if you do go, I will go with you.

1711, December 6.—It was well our Governor was only a spectator, not a *convira*. The sight of John Drummond would have spoiled his stomach. That same thing, conscience, will be impertinent sometimes, and come in upon those that think they have got rid of it.

I had heard from other hands that you hint about Lord N[ottingham ?], it would be a strange part in one of his years, and at a time, too, when not one of those upon whose interest he has valued himself, will go along with him. It shows that passion can make fools of old men as well as young ones. If he is to be wrought upon, and it be thought worth while to do it, I believe the Speaker is the person that would have the greatest influence with him. There has been a great correspondence betwixt them.

Postscript. Since I wrote I have seen in the "Courant" Bothmar's memorial, I suppose it must come from himself or some of the Junto to whom he communicated it to the press. It looks as if done in concert with them; it has a very odd aspect at this juncture. May one ask you what you think of it in town? I fancy they will repent of it before the session ends.

1711, December 9.—You now know *Quantum nova gloria in armis et prudenter decus primo in certamine possit.*

I give you joy of the entire rout you have given the enemy in the left wing. You have lost a little ground in the right I hear, but I hope it will soon be recovered. Such a Treasurer at the head of such a body of gentlemen will secure himself and every one too. We hear how Lord Dismal [Nottingham] has behaved. Every one is sorry that he should throw away his reputation at such an age, but the advertisement in the "Post Boy" gives great diversion.

I wish I could write to you as cheerfully about our domestic affairs, but my heart is as heavy as the weather about them. You will hear from my brother Gasse [Gastrell] a full account of our Governor's pretences, which he has at last openly owned to Dr. Smalridge; an open rupture I am afraid will be unavoidable. All that we can do will be to manage so that he shall be obliged, if he will insist on his extravagant pretences, to make the complaint. We claim nothing but what we are able to show to have been the constant practice from the oldest registers we have within eleven years of our foundation. He says openly, if there is a breach, it must be determined by the Keeper [Harcourt] and he doubts not of having justice from him. Whether he says this only to intimidate us, or whether he really has assurance from the Keeper of being supported by him I cannot yet judge. Some things look indeed as though he acted in concert with the Keeper, but he will be the first Dean who would ever own any other as our Visitor but the Queen. We shall certainly appeal to her and desire her to take immediate cognizance, by appointing a committee of Council to examine as has been usual, or any other commissioners she shall think fit. Perhaps the Keeper may insist upon it that he is Visitor ; if he does, and carries his point, we know our fate, though we should appeal from him, as our predecessors have done, if the Queen will receive it. I must tell you one very odd thing of myself, I had asked the Keeper when he was here with me, what I must do with Dr. Woodroffe's money upon his death, I being to leave my office at Christmas, and yet the order of court being to me personal, and not to the Treasurer for the time being. He then would give me no answer. When I dined with him in town, as I sat next to him, he took me by the hand, and said " Cardinal, you were enquiring what you should do about Woodroffe's money, move me this term, it will cost you only two guineas, and I will give you an order to pay it to your successor." I reported this to the Dean and Chapter, our solicitor was ordered to have such a motion made, it was made by Mr. Jeffryes, and the Lord Keeper refused it, though he had put me upon it, and the thing itself was no favour but common justice. When our Dean was told of it, he said it was odd, but he indeed had not spoken to my Lord Keeper about it. This was to give me to understand that it was refused because I had not applied through him for it, but the extent which I expect from the Queen will make me easy. Adieu to the peace of my place, which was never yet broken from the first foundation of it to this unhappy hour.

1711, December 10.—I doubt not but the tide will soon be turned in the upper House. . Not a mortal that does not exclaim against the dismal Lord; but it was barbarous in him to clip his poor son, whose future credit must depend in a good measure upon his behaviour at his first setting out. But I hope allowances will be made for the necessity the poor Lord is under.

I long for the next post to know what the good news will be that you give me hopes of, whether public or domestic, I hope rather the latter. We expect our Governor on Wednesday, and are saying our prayers to prepare ourselves for a state of squabble and contention. We are united entirely amongst ourselves; his attempts to divide us, and dealing with one and then with another, have only cemented us more closely. Dr. Hammond, his proxy, has made use of his full powers to seal Mr. Gore's lease, to prevent any more trouble on that head. It will make him flounce, but as he tells us that we may seek our remedy, let him seek his.

1711, December 13.—Our Governor is under the highest degree of resentment for our having signed Mr. Gore's lease, but he yet smothers it, and we know it only by his looks and his behaviour to us. But I suppose we shall have it all this evening, for he has summoned the Chapter then to attend him, and he can have no other business that I know of.

1711, December 16.—I have been out of order for two or three days, and am now in a little physic. But I would ask your Lordship how you do, and enquire whether I may depend upon seeing you on the 21st.

Our difficulties grow upon us, we have now some that arise amongst ourselves. Potter refuses to be Sub-dean, and insists that old Altham should bear office before him. Altham had been Treasurer for three years when he was Canon by King William's patent; since he came in by her present Majesty's patent he has had no office. Potter insists that being upon a new patent he ought not to plead the service done upon a former patent, in excuse of himself. This is very hard, and though perhaps true by the strict letter of the law is not so in equity; nor do I believe the Queen if appealed to by the different parties would give it against Altham.

I had no "Dyer" on Friday.

1711, December 18.—The news of the Occasional Bill is an extraordinary piece of policy indeed, I did not believe the first rumour of such a design. If they persist in it, they are infatuated. Do they think any one else will oppose it when it comes from them? Will there be any occasion to tell the Dissenters to whom they owe it? Now they have brought it in, I do not see how they can recover the false step they have made, if they should see it. If it comes to your House, that Bill will make the October [Club?] easy for this session, nor will there be any fear least they should think themselves obliged for it to those who brought it in. I told your Lordship in my last of the difficulty we are like to have in choosing officers amongst ourselves. We know not yet how we shall get over it. We shall I believe choose Potter, he will I fancy refuse to serve or take his place as Sub-dean, though he is chosen. What course we shall take in so new a case, if it should happen, I yet see not. We must contrive to put him upon the complaint. We could manage these points much better if we could act in concert and confidence with our Governor. But the true reason why Potter declines the office is because he will not if he can help it serve under our Governor. He was desirous of the place under the late Dean, but no mortal will have to do with him than can help it. I pity poor Gasse, but I say nothing to him till he is fast. I think I have reason to know both, and am persuaded they can never agree for one hour together. Gasse will not bear to be snubbed as I have been; he looks on himself, as he well may, as his equal in all points but dignity, and as to obligations he is under great ones to Gasse, and Gasse under none to him.

I am somewhat better than I was, but no place agrees with me in this muggy weather but the town. I am hastening to it as fast [as] I can. I am afraid I shall not see you till I wait on you there. The Warden of All Souls is going to be married to one of Sir Sebastian Smith's daughters, a strapping lass, of a proper size for him.

1711, December 20.—I wish I could say I were well, but I have not yet got clear of my illness; and the vexation I have from the difficulties we have I am afraid helps it a little. Potter is obstinate and cannot yet be prevailed with to take the Sub-dean's office. An appeal I am afraid will be unavoidable on that account. Our Dean to-day in the audit has made his demand of all quarterly payments from the date of his patent. Never since the House was founded was any one paid but from the day of installation, and the advantage of all the time of vacancies went to the House. He offers to refer it to two lawyers, but we think we cannot alter the disposal of the revenue of the house but by particular order from the Queen. If he will petition the Queen and get us such an order we shall not oppose it. What he will do this afternoon we know not, we offer him to enter his claim in our books, that the passing of the accounts may be no prejudice to the rights he thinks he has, but I am afraid that will not do. I wish he does not break off the audit, and refuse to go on unless we comply with him. We have hitherto by management been too hard, and avoided all the occasions that he daily invents to provoke us to an open quarrel. On Tuesday night he sat with me and Gasse till two in the morning. You may guess what calm discourse we had, but his greatest quarrel with me at last was that he could not put me into a passion.

1711, December 23.—I thank God the audit is over, we prevailed with our Governor at last to let the account be signed, upon our signing a memorandum at the bottom [of] it, that the signing of it should be no prejudice to his claim. I suppose he will do by this as he has done by other things when he has blustered for a while, and finds it won't do; he will drop it. Our next difficulty comes on to-morrow about the choice of a Sub-dean. We are resolved to choose Potter, and try whether he will refuse to serve. We can justify ourselves in doing it to all the world. Our Governor seems wholly unconcerned at it, he must have some end of his own in his view that makes him so easy. I know of none that he can, unless he hopes he may have occasion of applying to my Lord Keeper on this point, and of having him owned as Visitor, which he may use afterwards in his own claims, but that [he] shan't do.

Our Governor yesterday admitted the new students, and forgot to bring a Bible with him to give them their oath on upon their admission, but when he found his mistake, he would not send cross the chapel for a Bible, but actually swore them upon a common university statute book. When the Sub-dean told him of it afterwards in Chapter, he said it was all one, they had kissed the oath. He certainly is the first of our gown, or any other, that made a statute book in case of an oath equivalent to a Bible. The poor lads' admissions are certainly illegal, and can give them no right to anything they should claim by it, but let our Governor look to that. Had any other done so, he would have made the kingdom roar with it.

1711, December 24.—I bless God the audit and all our other difficulties are for the present quite over, we have chosen our officers, we have prevailed with Dr. Potter to be Sub-dean, we have had some contest with our Governor about jurisdiction, some points we have gained, others we have deferred to further consideration, and we have now a year to look before us. We were all resolved to bear any language to avoid coming to a breach, if that could be done without giving up rights, and we have been contented with entering our claims, and then to suspend them to a farther opportunity. I hope we shall have a little time to breath till the end of the session at least.

I beg my most humble duty and thanks to my Lord Treasurer for his great favour to Mr. Terry. If your Lordship is so kind as to give him notice of it only by sending his patent, be pleased to take care that the grant be to Thomas Terry, bachelor of divinity. Surely you will be able to control the Lords in a little time.

1712, August 27.° Hereford.—[At Gloucester] Brother Gasse and I spent the evening at the deanery with Mr. Dean [Chetwoode] and our schoolfellow Prebend [ary] Baines. The Dean had very good wine, and we had both entertainment and diversion very good from him. We dined yesterday at Ross, think the situation one of the most beautiful I ever saw, we came hither easily in the evening.

I forgot in my last to let your Lordship know that when the Lord Keeper said those things of our Dean amongst other company the Vice-Chancellor was there. The Vice-Chancellor was received with a great deal of stiff civility, and I believe those things were thrown out before him, to let him know how he must behave to the Dean if he expected favour at Cockrop.

We brought Bob [Freind] to confession at Burford, he owned the Dean had set his heart upon London, and that he was persuaded that he would refuse Worcester if it were offered to him.

1712, September 1. Bath.—I got safe to Bath on Saturday night, but most heartily tired, and with a great cold which I got upon the road. The night I came here I met with a packet from Oxford, which informed me, as I expected, that the Dean was not idle in my brother's and my absence. One attempt was directly against me, but the most extraordinary and most malicious one that I believe was ever made—a humble

---

° There are no letters written in the earlier part of 1712 in the collection.

representation of Charles Aldrich to him the Dean, a paper, a long one, drawn up every one word by the Dean, and which he had got Charles Aldrich to sign. It is levelled against Dr. Hammond and Dr. Burton in some points, but there are plain and many insinuations against me, as though I had not only embezzled his uncle's books and papers, but had stolen several hundred pounds of his money, and concludes with a request that Dr. Hammond and Dr. Burton would give under their hands what papers were taken out of his uncle's study, when they went in with me upon his uncle's death, and whether they saw any considerable sum of gold there; and that the Dean and Chapter would influence me to do him justice, and that I would declare upon oath what I did in his uncle's study, between the time of his uncle's death, when the key was sent to me by this gentleman himself, and his uncle's interment. This is our Dean's last blow I suppose, and he has used this poor wretch, after he had prevailed on him to deliver up his uncle's letters to him, to insinuate such villainies against Dr. Hammond and me, to whose kindness this poor fellow owes all that ever he had from his uncle, and I may say that the aversion which his uncle for many years had to him was removed by us only. As soon as I have leisure I will transcribe this paper for you, it speaks its author, and will need no comment upon it. I do not believe there ever was in the world a more infernal spirit, but he shall have my oath, though my Governor would discover little by that if I were guilty, if I had as little regard to an oath as I can prove he has. I have yet met with nothing here to entertain your Lordship. Here is much company, but not many of quality.

A letter that came hither this morning from the Secretary's office says Lord Bolingbroke is very ill, pray let me hear if there be any ground for it.

1712, September 3. Bath.—I have sent your Lordship the copy I promised you of the charge exhibited against me in my absence. I beg your Lordship would be pleased to show it to my Lord Treasurer. I am certain, as I could show by undoubted proofs, that it was every word drawn up by the Dean himself, and I am as certain too that he would deny it, if charged with it. His Lordship may in some measure judge by this of the temper of the man we have to deal with. It has been very grievous to be forced to employ our time wholly in ridiculous contests with him, and in fencing against him, but this shows a malice blacker than I could have suspected to have been in him. He begins with me, but others I doubt not would have their turn too, could he succeed in this. I am sorry there is any one of the profession capable of such actions. I believe, in the temper he is, he would not stick at any subornation that he thought he could promote safely to himself, to compass the lives of either me, brother Gasse, or George Smalridge. Let my Lord Keeper, who trusts him so much, have a care of himself. Should his Lordship ever disoblige his man, he perhaps too may

find what it is for one in so public a post to have trusted him.
I had once thoughts of sending a copy of this with a letter to my
Lord Keeper, but I know not but it may be better to defer it till
I have held up my hand and my trial is over. I shall disappoint
Mr. Dean. He depends upon it that he shall provoke me, and
put me into a great passion by this. I shall be patient beyond
his expectation and submit to as strict an inquisition as he can
desire, and when I return, in full Chapter, the prosecutor present,
I will have it examined line by line, and offer him my oath upon
every article. I bless God, Dr. Hammond and Dr. Burton were
with me when I first entered into the Dean's study, and are
witnesses of all that was done and themselves assisted in
sealing up the drawers. Though that was a caution, it was
great odds I had not taken, considering the entire confidence
in which I had lived with the late Dean for so many years, and
the kindness I had showed to his nephew. And this poor wretch
has been prevailed upon to sign this paper at near two years
distance from the facts, and without ever asking me before about
any one thing mentioned in the paper. But I will do him justice
in the utmost manner he can desire, and when the impudent
falsities of this paper are laid open, I shall leave the Dean to
enjoy the honour of the malice of it.
Copy of memorial from Charles Aldrich enclosed.

1712, September 5. Bath.—Your Lordship may be certain I
shall not fail to keep up my correspondence with you whilst my
neck is in danger. By your Lordship's taking no notice of that
I said in my first letter, I believe you thought I was in jest, but
the paper I sent you in my last has convinced you, I believe,
that I was in too good earnest. Upon the advice and importunity
of friends, I have sent a copy to my Lord Keeper, with a letter
humbly to express my own resentment and upon the score of old
friendship to beg his Lordship would advise me what method I
ought to take for my own justification. I have sent the letter by
trusty T. Rowney, I shall at least discover by this how his Lordship approves of this way of managing differences in his friend
the Dean. I am advised to bring an action in the Vice-
Chancellor's court. This will not only bring me upon my oath,
but him too, to discover who abetted him in his design and
assisted; and perhaps too I may be able to make the Dean himself a party to my bill, and oblige him to take oath whether he
was not concerned in it. I do not believe though I shall discover
any thing by that, but since I am likely to come upon my oath, I
must desire your Lordship to return to me those poor things you
had from me, of Clemens' Epistle, the Satires of Horace, and the
copies of the Geometry, the perfect and imperfect one, and the
Epictetus. I must have it in my power to produce every scrap
I had out of the study. I shall send you another Epictetus
which I had designed in the place of this, though not quite so
well bound, and this itself was a supernumerary one in the upper
study. Be pleased to pack them up in one bundle directed to me
at Christ Church, they will stay till I return. You see how I am

put to it to make good my honesty, when this villain, who is encouraged to sign this paper against me, is obliged to me for not demanding a good sum of him for books which I had bought for his uncle for some years before he died, as I bought all his books abroad, and which through forgetfulness his uncle never paid me, and I never demanded of the executor. I design, when I hear what Lord Keeper says, to write a letter to Mr. Dean himself, to remind him of his private obligations to me, to recapitulate all his life in short as far as I know it, and to ask him how he dares to receive such a paper against me, when he knows how much I have him in my power.

Here is a very senseless story that came down in a letter by the post to-day hither; that my godfather had invited a fool that is at the Court of Hanover—suppose there is more than one there—and given him money to ridicule the Duke of Marlborough, that the fool carried the money to old Sophy, who sent for my god-father, and reprimanded him.

Lord Bolingbroke has presented the fine ring to his lady; that will go a great way with a lady, but will not make full amends.

I am an utter stranger to Davies [of Hart Hall]. The design to support the namesake at Jesus is the greater for his Lordship's silence. Mede, Taylor the solicitor, clerk of Bridewell, our Dean's creature, and Dr. Henchman have been sent for to Oxford. They have been there for above a week, and may be there still perhaps, and have been several times over with our Dean and Harcourt at Cockrop.

The Vice-Chamberlain's Lady is here, and he is expected on Monday; Lady Mansel is expected to-night. It is said Lord and Lady Wharton will be here next week. Old [Master of the] Rolls [Trevor] is here, and does me the honour to converse with a poor Welsh relation; he asked me how old Altham [did], I told him he was very infirm; he laughed and said then your Dean will make a breach upon you if he can, and bring in a canon of his own, "Doctor, as well as I wish to your Dean, I do not desire that he should make the canons of Christ Church." I wonder why the old "veterator" said this, unless it were to pump me. I had not said one word to him of the College, nor did I make him any reply to this.

1712, September 7. Bath.—Were I with your Lordship to make my observations on the paper I sent to you, I could show, I think to a demonstration, that it is every word indited by the Dean himself. What is there that he is not capable of, who could do so mean as well as a malicious thing? How might this man serve any one who should indeed trust him with any thing of moment, that might be made use of against themselves? I told your Lordship in my last what I had done, and what I am further advised to do. I shall have time whilst I am here to turn it [in] my thoughts, but I could wish to know, if your Lordship could think it proper to enquire, what my Lord Treasurer thinks would be proper for me on this occasion.

Lord Huntingdon has been designed above three years for our House; some stop was put to it for some time by his guardian, who is Archdeacon of Leicester, upon our present Dean's being preferred to us. His guardian, though no extraordinary man, yet had personal acquaintance with George Smalridge and Jonathan Kimberley, and had designed Jonathan's son for the young Lord's tutor. Alsop has a sister who lives with Lady Betty Hastings, she has been made use of to desire Lady Betty Hastings to recommend Mr. Alsop to the Archdeacon for her brother's tutor. The Archdeacon stuck at it, but the Dean who is at the bottom I hear is resolved on it, if the Lord comes. His enemies could not wish him to do any thing more to his disadvantage than to put one of that quality into Alsop's hands, who, as your Lordship knows, is so infamous for his neglect of Lord Salisbury and all others that ever were entrusted to him ; and if I am not mistaken Mr. Dean could not do a thing that will more alienate those very students whom he sets up to court so much. It will be too a great encouragement to draw more men of quality to his House. Surely this man thinks himself above observing common measures with any part of mankind.

1712, September 10. Bath.—I hear from Oxford that care has been taken to make the noise of that scandalous paper so public that it will be absolutely necessary for me, for my own vindication, to have all parties upon oath in the Vice-Chancellor's court.

Lord Keeper has been at Oxford and dined and lay at the Deanery. Mede and Taylor and Judge Upton of Ireland were there to attend him; brother Gastrell waited on him in the morning. His Lordship talked to him of accommodating our differences, and said he would try what he could do, when we were all together in town next winter. Brother Gastrell told him somewhat had happened, which was personal betwixt the Dean and me, which he was afraid would not be determined but by a public decision. His Lordship protested he knew not of it, and was very inquisitive to hear it. Brother Gastrell told him that I designed to acquaint his Lordship with it, and he would not prevent me. In the afternoon Tom Rowney carried his Lordship in his own coach alone to Sandford; as they went Tom told him of it, his Lordship said he had heard it. I can scarce believe he had been alone with the Dean betwixt Dr. Gastrell's and Tom's speaking to him. His Lordship said further, he did not believe I would be guilty of any dishonest action, but I might be overseen in some matters, and not have acted so prudently as he could wish. But I hope to be able to justify my prudence as well as my honesty, though I perceive I must not expect much assistance from his Lordship to do it. However I am not sorry that I have written to him, I never expected other than I find, but I have left him without excuse. He cannot complain now that I did not apply to him. Where these things will end I know not, but I fancy they will recoil at last upon the person that contrives and foments them.

Lord Pembroke has been at Oxford and received the appeals of both parties; ordered the government to be carried on by the other officers, till he had decided their differences; told them he would decide them when he returned to London with all the impartiality he could and should have regard to merit. He received J. W[ynne] with great kindness, he told him he had received several letters about their affairs. They must all come from the other side, for John had written none nor any for him that he knew of. I hope that affair will go as it ought and that all their wicked contrivances will be baffled. Since Harcourt has appealed to the .Visitor, I do not believe it can be brought now to common law. That was what they would have done if they could. The Dean had not waited on Lord Pembroke, when my letters came from Oxford, though his Lordship has been a constant friend to us. He gave us 100l. to Peckwater. Lord Herbert gave 50l., and Mr. Herbert 30l.; such benefactions deserve the respect of a visit at least.

When Tom Rowney asked the Dean himself how such a paper came to be given in against me in my absence, the Dean said that might seem hard indeed to those who did not know that Aldrich had come to town on purpose to offer it, and that no one knew of my going or when I would return, but that there were orders to send a copy of the charge to me.

1712, September 13. Bath.—I look on your advice as an instance of that sincere friendship I have had so much experience of from your Lordship, and I am resolved to follow it. It perfectly agrees with my own judgment; if I had written, it would have been in compliance with the opinion of others, who thought it might frighten. But that itself may look as though I desired to have this paper stifled, and thought to oblige him to it by threatening him with reprisals. It was out of submission to others, and not to my own judgment, that I wrote to my Lord Keeper himself. He may take that handle from it, if he suspect the Dean may be brought in at last, as to advise me to measures which may screen him; and he may pretend to resent it, if I should refuse to take his advice when I have asked it. But I should not have much regard to that, if he should advise me to any thing I think improper for me. I long to know what my Lord Treasurer says to it, and I hope your Lordship's next will bring me an account of it. I have enclosed a letter which I received last post from my brother Smalridge, it is so remarkable that I desire your Lordship should see it, and wish too you would show it to my Lord Treasurer, and then return it to me. Your Lordship will perceive by it that our Governor was the same at Carlisle that he is now with us, and by some gentlemen come from Exeter, whom I have met with here, I find they have the same opinion of him in the west as they have in the north.

On Tuesday the Archdeacon and minister of this place, Mr. Kimberly, and I dined with the Master of the Rolls; he entertained us for two hours after dinner with stories of his chaplain, our Governor, which were very diverting to us, though not much to the honour of his chaplain.

1712, September 15. Bath.—I beg your Lordship would be pleased to give my most humble thanks to my Lord Treasurer for the favour of his concern for me. I think it is a duty which I owe to his Lordship, as well as to myself, to have this matter laid open; that his Lordship may not be reproached for having received into his service such a rogue as I am represented to be. I hope I shall not have occasion to give any trouble on this score to any of my friends. I have nothing at present to beg of his Lordship, but that his Lordship would be pleased as far as he shall think proper to express his sense of these proceedings to my Lord Keeper. The Lord Keeper may say what he pleases to excuse his friend the Dean, but his Lordship I am confident *believes* as much as I do that every word was indited by the Dean. I wish his Lordship does not *know* it. I think it no great instance of kindness in his Lordship to say that he does not think me *dishonest*. I think he had experience of that for some years, when every groat of rent or what he got in the circuits was always left with me. And when he was used to draw on me, when I had no money of his in my hands, for whatever he had occasion for in the country, I am confident I lost money by it in some bills, which I had forgot to put down, and never drew on him again for.

[*The subject of Dr. Stratford's grievances against Dean Atterbury is continued at very great length for the rest of this letter.*]

1712, September 17. Bath.—I can come to no resolution till I know whether an action will lie in the Vice-Chancellor's court against Aldrich. It is worded with all the art possible to avoid being reached by the law, but I have sent to enquire of those who are best able to inform me. I shall then better judge what I am to do.

Though Lord Keeper thinks the Dean had no hand in it, the Dean will not say so much for himself. When brother Gastrell charged him with it in Chapter, he did not confess it, but he did not disown it; he only said, brother Gastrell had nothing to do to examine him. But some days ago the Dean was in brother Gastrell's counting house; upon mention of my name brother Gastrell said to Him, "have not you done yet with brother Stratford?" He grinned and went grumbling out of the room and said, "I have not done half I could do." Gastrell replied, "We are sure you will do what you can, we expect the worst." I think this was fairly owning the libel to be his own.

I have at last heard of his project for his *Certamen Poeticum*. Never surely was so wild a design as that he has for a fund for his prizes and to save his own pocket; but brother Gastrell will give your Lordship a full account of it; I will not prevent him.

1712, September 20. Bath.—I beg my service and my thanks to my friends in Scotland Yard for their kind concern for me. It would be of use to me if Mr. B. could remember from whom he heard of it, I might perhaps by that be able to guess at some of those who are employed by our Dean to disperse scandal for him—uncommon care has been taken to send this into all parts. J. Urry was over here this week from Longleat; care had been taken to send John a copy of it. He owned not this to me, though he told me he had heard of it, but to Mr. Trevor. But I could not learn from Mr. Trevor from whom John had the copy.

The fund for the reward of achievements in poetry could be no one's project but his own, and is a signal proof of his own generosity, and of his honesty to the College, to design to divert to so ridiculous a use the chief fund we have had for fifty years past for our building, and the only fund we have any prospect of now, for paying that which is still due for the third side of Peckwater, and for finishing the inside of it. When my brother Gastrell waits on your Lordship at Windsor you will have from him a full account of our miserable condition.

1712, September 22. Bath.—The Dean has no just authority to invite a chamber fellow upon poor Palmer; it is the right of the Dean and Chapter to determine which chambers shall be single and which double, though when chambers are so distinguished, it is the Dean's right by custom to appoint who shall have them. Dr. Hammond and I went together to view Palmer's chamber. Upon our report it was agreed that it could not with any convenience be made a double chamber. Then at my request, Dr. Hammond, who was at that time the late Dean's proxy, a little before his death, gave it to Palmer. The Dean has no right to alter this without the concurrence of the chapter, though he may dispose of it to another single person, should it become vacant. When Palmer first apprehended a chamber fellow put into him, he applied to me. I was a very improper solicitor to the Dean; however I took an opportunity at a Chapter, when the Dean was by chance calm, to let him know upon what previous care the chamber had been disposed of to Palmer, and desired him to view it. He told me he would and seemed satisfied. If he now puts in another to him, it can be only to give an instance of his power, and in spite to me, because I had procured the chamber for Palmer. But how can we help ourselves in this or other cases without a public complaint of him? But I well hoped the concern my Lord Treasurer had showed for Palmer would have secured the poor lad from so notorious an injury.

Your Lordship took the most proper way in applying to Terry. And perhaps when our tyrant knows that your Lordship concerns yourself in it, he will forbear. He still has a respect for power and those who can do him further service; and that in this case and others too, if applied, would be a restraint to him. But till you who are in power signify to him that if he does not mend his manners he must expect nothing more from you, he will persist in everything, for he is above conscience or shame.

I am now resolved on the measures I shall take, upon advice on which I can rely. I shall bring one action against Charles Aldrich in the Vice-Chancellor's court for defamation. I shall bring another, as having an interest as canon in the late Dean's

- - will, to oblige him to show that he has executed the late Dean's will. This last will bring in Mr. Dean himself. Charles Aldrich must forswear himself, or own what papers belonging to the late Dean he has given up to this present Dean.

1712, September 24. Bath.—I shall find greater difficulty I am afraid than I apprehended at first in coming at my point, and be obliged to change my measures in some part. Your Lordship knows well that we have not one in Oxford of common sense in the civil law but old Bourchier, and his son is now assessor in the Vice-Chancellor's court, and is [of] no capacity himself, but does all by the father's direction. I sent brother Gastrell over to old Bourchier to get his advice how to proceed against Charles Aldrich, I have sent your Lordship a copy of his opinion. By that and by what passed betwixt him and brother Gastrell, I entirely agree with my brother Gastrell that the adversary had been with him before, and had his opinion and direction too. He was for excusing Charles Aldrich in every point, even in that of delivering up his uncle's letters.

Opinion of Thomas Bourchier enclosed.

1712, September 27. Bath.—We have a report here that the Duke of Beaufort is much out of order, not from any acute distemper, that I hear, but from a general ill state of health. He would be much missed in these parts, he has been of great use in the elections.

1712, September 29. Bath.—The prebend of Canterbury is certainly worth 200*l. per annum* or somewhat better, but not near so good as Windsor. I do not expect your Lordship should have any success, nor, had I been consulted, should I have advised the gentleman to apply to your Lordship upon this occasion. It is too forward, even if he had not lately received an instance of my Lord Treasurer's favour. Such forwardness must be to his prejudice with such a one as my Lord Treasurer; but I am certain that this is the effect of the new friendship he is entered into with our Dean, he has put him upon it, though I hear T. begins to be staggered a little at some of the Dean's proceedings, and to wish himself disengaged.

I shall long to hear what passes betwixt Lord Treasurer and Lord Keeper. By Lord Keeper's early application to Lord Treasurer before he had received any letter from me, one would be tempted to suspect that he had not been altogether a stranger to it. God alone knows what the consequences of such proceedings will be. Very ill to be sure, be the matters managed with never so much temper and prudence on our side, but the man grows every day more frantic, as you will hear from my brother Gasse.

1712, October 4. Bath.—I have been on a visit at Wells to the Bishop, or I had not missed your Lordship last post. I should makes excuses to your Lordship for the trouble I have given you, and not expect to receive them from you, though if my Lord Treasurer's indisposition should continue, I must beg that I may hear every post from your Lordship or Mr. Thomas.

I had sent to the Speaker a copy of the paper. This morning I received an answer, of which I have enclosed a copy to your Lordship. I beg you would show it to my Lord Treasurer, and to no one else. You will perceive by it how extensive as well as restless the malice of the gentleman is, though I bless God, in all points he has yet started, impotent. This scandal is wholly founded upon the meadow money, which in his paper he supposes to have been divided among the Canons. If it had been so, seven others had been equally guilty with me. But what is our condition who must be quiet under all these efforts of frenzy rather than malice? He ventures on that he does, because he presumes our hands are tied up from exposing him. Nor can we make any effectual or proper return to him in any place but the Privy Council.

May I enquire who wrote to your Lordship about the prebend of Canterbury, did Mr. T—— write himself, or the Dean in his behalf? If the latter wrote, he did it to lay an obligation on T—— though he never expected or desired any success in it. If it were so, I hope your Lordship will let T—— know that you expect he should apply to your Lordship, when he has occasion, by himself and not by another hand.

Enclosure—[William Bromley, Speaker, to Dr. Stratford.]

1712, September 29.—I thank you for the curiosity you sent me, it is a very extraordinary one, but of such a nature that it can do you no harm, for it is impossible it should gain credit with any, even of those that are not your friends, but must reflect most on the author and abettor—if any one can be so abandoned—of the scandal; but their malice does not stop here. I will transcribe a paragraph out of a letter I received last post from Sir Charles Holt. "Here is a surprising report got among the clergy of my neighbourhood, that our friend Dr. Stratford has been detected of making false accounts to the College, during his office of Treasurer, and has endeavoured by vile practices to defraud the College of great sums. I cannot believe there is any truth in this, but I am very uneasy till I am enabled to justify him from this scandal. The story is publicly talked of, and variously reported."

I have taken care to enable Sir Charles to justify you, and withal told him what I believe to have been the foundation of the report.

1712, October 6. Bath.—Here is a report given out here by the Whigs that there is a great breach betwixt my Lord Treasurer and Lord Bolingbroke. I hear Lord Bolingbroke is at Ashden Park with Sir W. Wyndham to hunt for some days. It is not a proper season for diversion, if he has acted a part that must be fatal to him, but I hope it is only given out by those who wish it.

I have just received the favour of your Lordship's. I am sorry it brings me no better news. I pray God preserve a health of such moment to us all. There is but one in Europe upon which more depends. Pray do not trouble my Lord whilst he is out of order with our impertinent squabbles.

I go to-morrow to Longleat with the Master of the Rolls. We return on Wednesday.

1712, October 8. Bath.—I went yesterday with the Master to Longleat, we returned to-day. I was ordered by the Viscount [Weymouth] to make his compliments to my Lord Treasurer and to your Lordship. Your Lordship is highly in the Viscount's favour. He spoke nothing but what your character will justify, but greater .things than I expected from him of you. I suppose your Lordship is obliged to your humble servant John Urry, who is there, for the Viscount's good opinion.

I have now done my rambles. The Bishop of Bath and Wells will be here on Friday or Saturday. As soon as I have seen him I shall look homewards, and hope to be there again on Tuesday. I cannot be blamed if I am not in haste to go to execution. I have been learning my neck verse. I had much talk with the . Master as we were alone on the road in his chariot. He is positive that I should not bring my action, but treat the matter with contempt; and give the Dean and Aldrich notice before witnesses that if Aldrich has any demands on me I am ready to answer them when they are made in a proper place. And then I shall have all the advantage of a defence, which will be much greater than if I am the actor.

1712, October 11. Bath.—I have not much malice in my heart, but I own I have a little in one point. I should not be sorry to see Lord Keeper, who has buoyed up this gentleman, and by his extravagant countenance of him fomented all our differences, himself embarrassed at last with him, and forced either to withdraw himself from his new friend, and then he will certainly hear of him, or be engaged by him in somewhat he will have reason to repent of. I have a strong persuasion on me that I shall live to see this, and I believe no advantage his Lordship can have from his alliance with the Dean will be an equivalent to him for the servants he will lose by espousing him.

My brother Smalridge and I have adjusted our journeys so as to meet on the same day at Oxford. He brings up with him memoirs of his predecessor's tyrannical reign at Carlisle; of his insolent behaviour to his brethren of the Chapter; of his exactions upon the tenants, and his extraordinary attempts for sole power; which may help to convince the world that our complaints are not without ground, since such practices are not new in him.

I was disappointed this morning in not hearing either from your Lordship or Mr. Thomas, but I hope that is a proof that Lord Treasurer is perfectly well.

The waters this last week have begun to reach that part for which I chiefly wanted them, the right side of my head, which was struck with a cold last winter of which I never was quite clear. I find it sensibly better. I am pressed much to stay and not to leave that, till they have had all the effect I wish for from them, but I must go home, both for my own affair and the College business.

1712, October 16. Oxford.—I got home very well, I bless God, the last night and met here the favour of your Lordship's. My Lord Treasurer's approbation of the Master's advice has determined me, I shall do nothing at present, but take some of my brethren along with me to the Dean, and desire a Chapter may be called to consider what to do about the paper given in by Mr. Aldrich. If he calls a Chapter, I shall then desire Aldrich may be summoned to appear on a day appointed to answer such questions as the Chapter shall ask him. If he appears, after we have put such questions to him as we shall think proper, I shall tell him I am ready to answer all his demands on me when he brings them in a proper place. If the Dean either refuses to call a Chapter, or to summon Aldrich, or to answer the questions we ask, it will still increase the presumption of his being the contriver of the paper. The Dean of Carlisle, who met me here yesterday, had this morning a great deal of free discourse with our Governor. He would not own that he had anything to do in the paper. He said he did not countenance it, nor would he discountenance it. I believe we shall oblige him to quit the neutrality he affects, and either to declare against it or openly to abet it.

I believe my godfather [Thomas Harley] is very easy in quitting both the title and habit of his Excellency. I beg my duty to him, and my congratulations for his safe return. Did your Lordship receive the letter in which I had enclosed a copy of one I had from the Speaker? Your Lordship does not take any notice whether my Lord Treasurer had any further discourse with my Lord Keeper.

We all conclude my Lord Strafford would come upon no other errand than a general peace. God send it, then every place at home, except poor Christ Church, will be quiet. Perhaps too our Governor may be more temperate when the waters are less troubled about him.

1712, October 19. Christ Church.—I have received the box. I am sorry your Lordship had been at the trouble of binding those sheets, I hope to be [able] to make you amends for your loss, though I know not whether ever even these will be demanded of me. I believe I shall not part with them, but by due course of law.

I have one satisfaction since I came home, if it were allowable to take pleasure in it, to find that the gentleman who has attempted to make a rogue of me has effectually proved himself one by it. Not one man that I can hear, those who correspond with him as well as those who do not, who does look upon him not only to have countenanced the paper, but to have written every word of it. Indeed upon comparing notes with brother

Smalridge there appears so many particular expressions which are peculiar to him, and besides the turn both of thought and style, and some facts which Aldrich could have from no one but him, that it is demonstration to any one's private judgment, though it would not amount to a legal proof in court, that the paper was written by him.

His only support is the confidence he has in Lord Keeper, and I am afraid that is too well grounded. Since my Lord Treasurer spoke to Lord Keeper I hear from a sure hand that Lord Keeper in private discourse with one about our differences said the Dean would be too hard for us; at least he could mean nothing by this, but that the cause must come before him, and that he would give it right or wrong for the Dean.

We are told Lord Strafford has brought a new plan for peace. May we be allowed to ask what it is?

I can tell your Lordship some news that will be welcome to you. On Thursday last Decker came to an agreement with John Drummond's creditors, by which he is to pay them 30*l*. *per cent*. in two months' time and 20*l*. *per cent*. in six months' time more; and to pay besides to Guybons 2,500*l*. out of Mrs. Drummond's money now in Decker's hands. By this agreement, that honest unfortunate man will be at liberty again in eight months at farthest.

1712, October 22.   Christ Church.—A Chapter was called to-day to consider about Aldrich's paper. The Dean came; Aldrich was without, and Dr. Smalridge proposed, in order to our peaceable proceeding, a question, whether every member of that board had not a right to propose such questions to Mr. Aldrich as he should think fit. Mr. Dean said "To that question I will give no answer, but I will acquaint you with something that looks towards an answer." The Canons took pen and paper into their hands, upon which the Dean said, "Nay, if you write down what is said here, I will go out of the Chapter." He rose out of his seat and cried "Good bye to you" and went out. Dr. Hammond, Dr. Burton, Dr. Smalridge and I followed him to his lodgings, in order to desire him to return to Chapter. He came out of his study, he would not let us speak; he bid us not to offer to come into his study, he did not desire to see us in any room of his house. He would neither hear any thing we had to say, nor give us any answer to any thing we asked. I must leave it to Dr. Smalridge to give you an account of the rage with which he treated us. Though no words can describe it, nor can any thing but a sight of it give any one a true idea of it, no footmen could be treated with the contumely we were. As we went out he cried, "I despise you." Dr. Smalridge thinks all his rage was real, I think it was in good part affected, and that he took the first opportunity he could to break up the Chapter, and to prevent Aldrich from being examined there. I am at present at a stand, but when I see further what I am to do, I will let your Lordship know.

1712, October 23.—Nothing more has happened since Tuesday. This day was appointed for examining into the ground of the Dean's own claim about money, but we have heard nothing of him. He will I believe keep his word with us. He told us at our parting from him, that he would never meet us again in Chapter till the previous points were settled. We fancy he has written to the Lord Keeper to know how far he may depend upon being supported by him. It is so, I believe, or else he acts this part to avoid having any Chapters whilst Dr. Smalridge is here. He is very uneasy at his presence. We are in a state of as great confusion as it is possible to imagine any body corporate. He will not allow us to propose any thing in Chapter but what he likes. He will not allow the Registrar to enter any thing in our register, but what he bids him do. If we put any question to him, he will give us no direct answer, he will exercise what power he pleases, without saying that he claims it. If we desire to know whether he claims such powers as he exercises, he will not he says tell us whether he claims or disclaims it. We have no remedy against this, but to throw ourselves at the Queen's feet. That we cannot do till my Lord Treasurer is pleased to give us leave; and yet we lie under a great disadvantage in this case. Should he complain first to the Keeper, we can have no remedy but to appeal from the Keeper to the Queen. In which case, besides the double trouble, we complain not only against our tyrant, but the Keeper himself, who would use all the interest he has in that case to have his own sentence justified. Our circumstances are to be pitied.

The Dean in all companies now lets them know what reasons he has for resentments against me; that I have written letters against him to the Lord Treasurer, that I have blasted him all over England, &c. He begins to be sensible that he is generally thought to be a rogue, and would, to excuse his own character, pretend that it is owing to my aspersions of him. But I look on all this talk to be, in other language, a plain confession that he wrote the paper himself, and would find reasons if he could to excuse himself for doing it.

My Lord Dupplin is pleased to give me a hint, of which I have had nothing from your Lordship, that I may shortly expect to hear of a marriage in the family. He leaves me entirely in the dark, whether it be of Lady Betty or your Lordship. There is no one will rejoice more heartily at either, or pray more earnestly than I do, that you may both be disposed of as I wish, but I will not press to know more of this than your Lordship is at liberty or disposed to communicate.

1712, October 26.—Indeed I heartily rejoice with your Lordship for the good news you have sent to me. I had I must own some intimation of it from another hand. I am pleased with it not so much on the account of the circumstances of quality and fortune, which are all very proper, as on the disposition of the young gentleman on which good Lady Betty's happiness must depend. It is, by all that I have heard, such as will make her very easy, and the gentleman who promotes this will, by the influence he must have on the young gentleman, be very proper to do all those good offices, which may be a means to fix an unalterable affection betwixt them upon their first coming together. My old friend Phil [Bisse], will by this provide effectually for himself as well as for his nephew Carmarthen. He has a long head. He had open breach with our villain this summer, and they parted in terms of utter defiance to each other. It was my good fortune at that time to do my friend Phil some service with your father, in undeceiving him in some which our villain had conveyed to him by Lord Keeper, for no other end but to prejudice him against the Bishop of St. David's. Nothing can be a greater stab to our villain's heart than the news of the access which Phil must have to your father by this match. This treaty gives your Lordship without doubt an opportunity of seeing the Bishop of St. David's often. Pray inform him of everything that has passed here, if he knows it not already. Gastrell will do it when he comes up to town, but I should be glad his Lordship knew it as soon as may be.

Our villain's behaviour in Chapter was such as no one would have been guilty of whose judgment was not entirely overruled by his passion. I hope your Lordship diverted my Lord Treasurer with it. The gentleman himself begins to be sensible that the report of it may be to his prejudice. We had a Chapter again yesterday; amongst other things, he owned he was in a passion then, but said we had deserved from him every thing that was fit for him to say. He endeavoured to restrain himself, and to keep his temper with every body, but when he spoke to me he had no command of himself, and rage and spite flushed in his face. I told him I knew of no indignity that had been offered to him in the former Chapter; he turned upon me, in a rage, "You! you would think it no indignity if you s—t upon my head." Dr. Smalridge asked him if he thought such language proper to be used in Chapter. He replied, "You may write it down if you please, though I must own there is one word not very proper to be written." I then told him, any thing that was not proper to be written by us was not proper to have been spoken by him.

As we were reading leases, Charles Aldrich sent in to let the Dean know that he was there. The Dean said, "He had no orders from me to attend, ask him what he would have." He sent in word he desired to be admitted to the Chapter when we were at leisure. The Dean asked us if we would admit him, the Canons told him they would not admit him then, because it would be proper to have a public notary present when he was admitted, and our Chapter clerk was not present; and because they desired some matters in relation to the method of our proceedings might be adjusted before we admitted him, and that the Chapter clerk might be present when we debated on those matters. I then desired him to call another Chapter as soon as might be when the Chapter clerk was present. I could have no other answer, but that it would depend on accidents when he should have another

Chapter. I happened in discourse to say "*we* are of opinion," he turned upon me and cried, "*we!* what have you the whole Chapter in your belly, learn to be more modest." I told him I had, besides my own vote, the votes of Dr. Hammond and Dr. Gastrell as their proxy, and might without breach of modesty use that expression. But my poor belly it seems was an eyesore to him. He had ordered Charles to offer himself to this Chapter, because he knew we would not admit him in the Chapter clerk's absence, and then he might have a pretence to say that Aldrich offered himself and the Canons would not hear him. If your Lordship is tired with this stuff, you must blame yourself for laying your commands on me to acquaint you with what passed.

I must beg leave to pay my duty and compliments to my Lord Treasurer upon his receiving the Garter, by your Lordship, unless your Lordship thinks it more proper for me to write to his Lordship. I would not be wanting in any point of my duty, nor would I be impertinent. I consult your Lordship in this case, not as my Lord Treasurer's son, but as my own friend. Dr. Smalridge when he comes up will inform your Lordship that I have observed your commands, and kept my temper, as Dr. Smalridge says, beyond what he expected. Though the gentleman has pointed all his rage at me in Chapter, ever since I returned, he has been able yet to provoke me to nothing but a smile.

I have but one thing now to pray for, and then I shall be at ease in relation to your family, to hear that your Lordship is disposed of as I could wish, but I will ask no question, but wait for information as you are pleased to give it to me.

Postscript. Our Governor will not let his wife visit Mrs. Smalridge because she is in my house. She herself told Mrs. Smalridge that she could not wait on her because she was in the house of one with whom she was not acquainted; that if she went to her own house, whilst she stayed, she would wait on her. This must be by order, for the poor woman knows that brother Gastrell and I have had more than an ordinary acquaintance with her, and have been her counsellors and comforters.

Perhaps I may see your Lordship before the marriage. I hear Aldrich now gives out that he will go up this week to file a bill against me in Chancery, that he has *assurance* of success, that he pretends not to make good what he has insinuated against me, but that if he can but prove that I took a pin out of his uncle's study he shall carry his point, which is to expose me as he thinks and to put me to charge. The Dean's proceeding looks as though some such thing were intended. He ordered him to attend the Chapter when he knew he could not be admitted, that he might have a pretence to say that, since he could have no remedy from the Chapter, he would seek it elsewhere. I am told, too, he designs to drop all those impudent lies that insinuate felony, and only simply to desire that I may declare upon oath what I took out of the study. I am apt to think he will bring an action somewhere, which is that which I desire, but I am sure he cannot bring it in Chancery without being liable to imprisonment and fine, and expulsion. But I shall not tell him this, and I believe the Vice-Chancellor is entirely disposed to do all he can in my favour. I had rather the cause were in Chancery than in any other place.

1712, October 28. Christ Church.—Your Lordship will have less trouble from me this post than you have had in some former. Nothing new has happened here since my last. We hear nothing from Mr. Dean about a Chapter. Aldrich went out of town on Saturday. Whether he be gone to town to file a bill against me I know not. I wish it may be so, though most are of opinion that his director will not let it go so far. A little time will show us what we are to expect, but I hear Mr. Dean himself is sensible that he has done some prejudice to his own cause by his late behaviour to us when we waited on him. He owns he was in the wrong, and has gone farther; so far as to say that he could be willing to live well again with Dr. Smalridge and Dr. Stratford.

This was said to us by one who heard him say it, but said he had no orders from him to say it to us, but we have had experience enough of him not to trust too easily to him, or to deal [with] him without good security.

I have had a letter from John Drummond, who begins to be somewhat easier upon the prospect of accommodating his affairs. They lose by Dick Hoare 3,000l., for which they are forced to come into a composition of 12s. in the pound, to be paid in two or three years.

1712, October 30. Christ Church.—God Almighty begins to reward your father's virtue with those blessings which are most real, though not the most glittering, domestic ones. The next blessing to the having of such children as he has is to be able to dispose of them so much to his own satisfaction and their happiness. I doubt not but as good a Providence waits on your Lordship as on your sisters. I am pleased to hear the affair will be in a little time ended one way or other. The best thing for your Lordship, next to the accomplishment of it, would be the breaking of it.

My own affair has somewhat in it of the nature of Greg's, si parva licet componere magnis. I am now easy, for I think I see the very utmost they can make of it. And I thank God there will be nothing that can in the least reflect on my credit, and very little on my discretion. The utmost they can make of it is to instance in one or two things, which a man of caution would not have done if he had known he had had very rogues to deal with, but which any one would have done in my circumstances, that had to do with those who had been much obliged to him and whom he at that time thought honest. But, however, yesterday we prevailed with the Dean to appoint Tuesday next for considering this business; I shall then be able to give your Lordship some further account. We have reason to think here that he is writing; his pen is that which he trusts to most, next to my Lord Keeper.

But I fancy he will find his account as little in that as in any other of his measures; we shall give him an answer which he little expects. We shall not employ ourselves so idly, or in a work so improper for our profession as to revile again, and to divert the world with our abusing one another. We shall only, in some solemn short paper to be signed by us, observe that this place from its foundation to his coming was at peace, that no place where he ever was before could be in peace, that we leave the world to judge of his character and ours. That we should think it improper for us as clergymen to follow the example he sets us, but that we hope we are able to justify our conduct in every point to the Queen when she is pleased to call upon us to do it.

I must conceal nothing from your Lordship, but you must keep that I tell you secret as yet. Bob [Freind] has renewed his *amour* with his old mistress, and entirely reconciled himself with her. It will be a match in a few months, that will bring him into a close correspondence again with his old friends and entirely take him off from the Dean. Then that gentleman will not have so much as one of his friends left that will converse with him.

This day was appointed to examine in Chapter the meadow money. When I produced my receipts from the workmen for that particular money the Dean was astonished, he desired to have them home with him to compare with the books, he said he was not good at these things. Dr. Smalridge asked him if he would not agree with them to declare that the money had not been divided amongst the Canons, nor put in my own pocket. He said if it appeared clear to him he would agree to declare it as soon as any of us, provided we would declare first that it was irregular not to have entered this in the public books. That was in effect that we would declare that though I was innocent yet he had reason for his suspicions. We told him reasons why it was not only improper but absurd to enter this in the public books. None would be allowed good by him. Dr. Smalridge said if he would nòt come in to declare his opinion, he must desire to know of his brethren what theirs was. He turned upon him, " You collect votes here, why don't you take this chair, you want to be in it, it is not come to that yet." After much noise, when he was desired to hear answers to what he said but would not, he declared he never suspected me of putting one farthing of this in my own pocket or any other money whatever, that he knew me to be a generous man. He took occasion to repeat this thrice, for what purpose I know not, but he said that I had contrived to conceal this matter from him, out of spite to him, to prevent his coming at it. Potter told him that there had been near a year's vacancy betwixt Dr. Jane's death and his instalment; that he had received nothing that was due during that vacancy. This was a stabbing blow to all his pretences, he parted without doing anything. At parting I put the receipts into his hands, and told him he might compare them with the books if he pleased against our next meeting.

This morning Dr. Altham had a letter from Charles Aldrich, to let him know that he had written one to the Dean, to be communicated to the Canons, to this effect: that he had waited some months for an answer to his representation from the reverend persons concerned in it, that since my return he had offered himself twice to the Chapter but could not be admitted; that since he could not be heard by us, he concluded he was permitted to endeavour to be heard elsewhere, &c. The Dean has stifled the letter he received and never mentioned it to us. There seems to be some change in the gentleman's measures, though he is ready to burst still with spite and passion. We shall see on Tuesday what he drives at.

1712, October 31.—I had not time in my letter yesterday to acquaint your Lordship with one matter of importance. When your Lordship was so kind as to give me notice at Bath that Lord Keeper had put the Dean's papers about his own claims, and about the Canons stifling Bishop Fell's Exhibitions, into my Lord Treasurer's hands, I remember not whether your Lordship said that the Dean had sent those papers to my Lord Treasurer by my Lord Keeper, or only that my Lord Keeper had put them into my Lord Treasurer's hands. I should be glad to know that. But be it as it will, I have kept myself within proper reserves. But yesterday when I insisted upon a resolution of the Chapter to vindicate me, Dr. Smalridge told him that, upon this paper, he had met with a report in Warwickshire that the Dean had openly in Chapter detected me of cheating the College of great sums. I told the Dean I had received the same account from Warwickshire, and further, that I had reason to be confident that this paper had been put into my Lord Treasurer's hands. I could not say it was sent by the Dean to my Lord Treasurer, or by whom it was delivered, but that my Lord had seen it. He said then, it must have been sent to my Lord Treasurer by Dr. Gastrell, and he laid his hand upon his breast and called God solemnly to witness that he had never given a copy of it to any person whatsoever. This was a rapper. It was necessary your Lordship should know it, that you may judge of the man we have to deal with by it. But I would be glad to know how far your Lordship would give me leave to take notice that I know how that paper came into my Lord Treasurer's hands. Your Lordship may be sure I shall not own any thing but what you allow me, but if it were so that my Lord Keeper did not deliver these papers as a secret to my Lord Treasurer, but owned that he had them from the Dean, or was desired by the Dean to deliver them to my Lord Treasurer, if I could be permitted to tell this to the Dean and to fix it on him, I should spoil his new trade, and make him incapable for ever of 'ing a suborner. But I shall not speak the least tittle in this ma.' . without your Lordship's express allowance.

Dr. G. Smalridge to Lord [Harley].[9]

[1712, October 31.]—My brother Stratford gives me leave to endorse his letter with my most humble respects to your Lordship, and I gladly take this opportunity of doing my brother the justice to assure your Lordship that I never yet in my life saw any man bear so ill, inhumane, and unchristian treatment with so much temper and patience. I don't look upon myself to be a very fiery man; but I could not promise that I could be so easy under so grievous provocations.· My temper has been pretty much tried, but not in such a manner as my poor brother's. Mr. Dean is very much nettled at our disproof of his false accounts of brother Stratford about the meadow money, he has protested with all the solemnity in the world that he never gave a copy of the paper laid before us to any person whatsoever. But it so happens that none of our body give any credit to his most solemn asseverations.

Dr. William Stratford to Lord Harley.

1712, November 2.—Your Lordship was pleased to let me know at Bath that my Lord Treasurer was pleased to say that if he could do me any service in my affair, I should without scruple let him know it. His Lordship may do me if he pleases a very great service, by a thing to which no one concerned can take any just exceptions. I would only beg his Lordship would give that paper which was put into his hands, about the meadow money, to your Lordship, with orders to transmit it to me, and to let me know that his Lordship required to know what I could say to it. No one can take it ill that his Lordship should give a servant an opportunity of answering for himself, before his Lordship believes the accusation against him. But this would give me an opportunity of confounding of our tyrant, not only by returning to your Lordship an account of that affair attested by all my brethren, but by confronting the gentleman in open Chapter with the paper given out by himself, after he had solemnly called God to witness, before the whole Chapter, that he had never given out a copy of it to any one person whatsoever. Since our great men will not directly interpose to restrain this satanical fellow, they may I hope allow us such honest means as these are to humble him a little.

I told your Lordship that he pretended he was slow at accounts, and could not in chapter examine the receipts which I gave in to prove the disbursement of the meadow money, but desired to have my bills and the book of accounts home with him. This was what had never been desired by or granted to any Dean or Canon since the foundation, to examine public accounts in any other place than in Chapter. However I frankly put books and papers into his hands, and let him carry them home with him. What end does your Lordship think he had in his ·, when he pretended not to be able to settle

---

the account in Chapter, but desired to have the bills home
with him? And what use do you think he has made of my
ingenuity in giving the bills into his hands? He copied them, and
sent privately for the workman, and ordered out of his book (*sic*)
and bring him the account of the work of the meadow. It is a
year's distance since the first bill was brought in and paid.
Should there be any difference in the bills the workman is
ordered to bring in now and in those he gave in a year ago, he
may have a pretence to say the account is not yet clear to him,
but that there was a collusion betwixt me and the workman.

We yesterday, as usual, invited him to dine with us at Bishop
Fell's commemoration speech, though he had forbidden four of
us his house the week before.´ We expected, according to
custom, to have been invited after dinner to the Deanery, but he
could not bring himself to that. He should not have accepted
of our invitation, or have returned it. He preached this morning a sermon about conscience, a very good one, every word of it
applicable to himself. He surely is under the highest degree
that ever yet was, either of ignorance of himself or hardness of
heart.

Postscript. I forgot to . . . to your Lordship that . . . the
Dean did not invite any of the Canons to his house after dinner,
yet he invited Dr. Newton and the students, who dined with us.
We were not much mortified with it.

1712, November 4. Christ Church.—Charles Aldrich was this
day before [us?], he desired to have an answer to his representation.
Dr. Hammond and Burton desired to know whether he had ever
made such a demand on them before. He said he would give no
answer to any questions till he had an answer to his
representation. We desired to take in writing what he desired
and what he answered. The Dean ordered him to withdraw and
would not let either his demands or answers be taken down
whilst he was present. Then in his absence squabbled about his
answers and would not let any words be written down but what
he approved. If he liked not Aldrich's answers, he would dictate
entire answers to him and say, you would say so and so; he
would often alter part of his answers for him. When his
answers had been written down and owned by Aldrich,
the Dean upon second thoughts would insist to have them
altered, lest they . should be misunderstood. When Dr.
Smalridge told the Dean that the Chapter desired Mr.
Aldrich's answers, and not his, the Dean's, he said the poor man
was in a consternation, and he thought himself obliged as a
judge to put him right. It is the first time that a judge declared
himself for the plaintiff, and would not let the plaintiff's depositions be taken in the plaintiff's (*sic*) presence. I then desired leave
to give my answer to Aldrich's demand, that I was ready to
deliver all I had out of his uncle's study when he would come to
my house for them, and that I was ready to answer any demands
upon oath when he desired it, before those who had authority to
give it. I desired him to appoint a time when he would come

to receive what I had. The Dean bid him withdraw, and consider what to answer. I thought there had been no great need of study for an answer to such a desire. The Dean would not let him give any other answer but that he would come to me after dinner, but would not say that he would then appoint a time when to receive the late Dean's books and papers. I desired to ask some questions. The Dean told him it was his advice that he should answer no questions which I asked him out of a written paper, till the question was given to him in writing, and time allowed him to consider of it. This was the substance of what passed with Aldrich. I desired then the Dean would agree with my brethren to consider of the paper itself and to give their sense of it. He said he could not give his sense but in proportion to the evidence for the facts, and that he could not enter into an examination of the evidence lest it might forestall the evidence and blow upon it, which Mr. Aldrich might have occasion to use in court. I took occasion to put the Dean at parting in mind of his having had a key to my house for two years, and asked him how he would like it if I should at this distance of time desire him to declare upon oath what he did in my house every time he was [there]. I will send your Lordship when I have time a copy of what I said. He impudently said he had forgotten, if I had not told him, that ever he had a key to my house, and that he had never used it five times. He was there at least five times a week. The perjury is now owned. As the Dean was coming with Dr. Smalridge from divinity disputations, he called to him, and desired him in the dark, with great hesitation and reluctance, to tell Dr. Stratford that he was sorry he had affirmed that he had never given out a copy of that paper, for upon recollection he owned he had given out a copy of it to a certain person. He found I had discovered him, and was afraid I should fix it on him, and thought the best way to lessen the guilt would be to own it, before I fixed on him. But I hope my Lord Treasurer will still be so kind as to send the paper to me and to require me to give an answer to it. I have enclosed a copy of a paper signed by the Canons, which I desire you to communicate to my Lord Treasurer.

1712, November 6. Christ Church.—I beg my most humble duty and thanks to my Lord Treasurer, and a thousand thanks to your Lordship for your kind concern in my behalf. If I receive that paper from my Lord Treasurer, with orders to give him what answer I can to it, it will give effectual means to put him to as much shame as he is capable of having. I have sent your Lordship my answer beforehand. I had sent you last post in haste an incorrect copy. I have now enclosed a more correct one. I have sent your Lordship too a copy of that which I spoke to the Dean at parting in Chapter. I had almost added *man servant* and *maid servant*, but having reproved him for want of gravity in Chapter, lest I should offend myself, I left them out. But let no one have a copy of this, I care not who has copies of the other paper.

On Tuesday in the afternoon Aldrich came to me with a proctor of the court, and demanded of me what things I had that had belonged to his late uncle. I gave them to him, and took his receipt; his proctor soon went off. Dr. Smalridge and Brooks were with me. Aldrich was going off, when I told him that he had now only things which I had taken out betwixt the time of his uncle's death and interment, but that I had other things of which he had made no demand. He might remember he had put the key into my hands a second time. He owned he had ; that I had then taken out some books for my own reading, that I had exchanged some of the many duplicates his uncle [had] with those to whom his uncle had owed money for other books, and that I desired he would receive one, and give me his hand that he approved what I had done in the other, it being for his service. He did both; I then asked if he had any further demands. He said he would consider. Yesterday he was with Dr. Hammond and Dr. Burton, and they under their hands gave him a full answer to what he had demanded of them, and he under his hand acknowledged it. In the evening we sent to him not to go out of town till he heard more from us. He came to me this morning. Dr. Smalridge was with me. He told me he insisted on my oath, I told him he should have it when he pleased, but I expected he should call me before those who could tender it as soon as he could. He told me I should hear from him in a day or two. I suppose he will put me in the court to-morrow. When he was first with me, he was in such confusion, that if Dr. Smalridge had not out of too much candour hindered Brooks and me from squeezing him a little, we had brought him I believe to confess all. Dr. Hammond, by upbraiding him with his uncle's and his own kindness to him, put the poor fellow into great agonies. But the Dean had him to himself all the last evening and has steeled him, though he could hardly speak one plain word this morning; but I now see the end of this affair. Within a month we shall have gone through the forms of the court, and then, as Dr. Hammond told him, he must expect to hear from us. I pity the poor fellow, he is likely to be undone by it, but when we come upon him for the execution of his uncle's will I fancy the Dean himself will be forced to appear upon the public stage. I hope my Lord Keeper will come down and vouch in court for his honesty.

I told Mr. Aldrich we expected he should stay in town to be ready to appear if he were called before the Chapter. He said he would answer no questions till his own demands were fully answered, and he would stay in town if the Dean bid him. We shall do nothing with him till all is over in court lest, the Dean should say we do it to deter him from seeking justice.

Enclosure.

Endorsed by Lord Harley:—" A copy of what Dr. Strat[ford] said to the Dean in Chapter " [on November 4].

From the manner in which this paper was introduced to the Chapter, and from the countenance which you have now given to Mr. Aldrich, besides many other reasons, I have cause to think you had a share in the contrivance of it.

About March 1703 I was possessed as tenant of the Reverend Mr. Evans' house in the Little Cloisters, Westminster ; soon after I was in possession of it, you desired that I would allow you a key to my house, by which you might come in at all times at your pleasure. I need not recite the reasons which you then alleged to me why a key to my house would be in many respects convenient to you, your condition was not then so plentiful as through the good providence of God it is at present. I had that affection for you, and confidence in you, that I gave you that proof of an entire friendship, which few persons give to any one, and I gave to no one but to yourself, the allowing you a key to my house.

By the advantage of that key, you had access to my house, to my study, and to all that I was at that time master of ; you came in as *often* and as *privately* as you pleased ; not only when I was there, but when I was absent in the country ; you came often *alone*, and at other times brought others with you ; you stayed there not for *three hours* only, but for days and nights together ; you were possessed of this key, not only for *eight* days, but for near two years. During the time that you were posssessed of a key to my house, several things were missing in it. When I removed to Oxford there were some books wanting in my study. Should I desire you at this distance of time, as I do not, to declare upon oath what you did in my house, whilst you had a key to it for so long a time, and used that key so often ; and what books, papers, or other things you removed, would you think such dealing like that of a gentleman, a friend, a Christian, a clergyman, I had almost said of a brother of the same Chapter ?

Mr. Dean, it is insinuated in this paper that I robbed the late Dean. I hope I can declare with a good conscience that I not only never broke the eighth commandment in relation to the late Dean, but that I never broke the tenth ; that I never coveted any thing that was his.

1712, November 8.—My affair has had a much shorter issue than I expected ; Mr. Dean on a sudden changed his measures. I had intelligence from a sure hand, which I must not trust to letter, that on Thursday evening the Dean sent Aldrich with his proctor to a person on whose advice the Dean has been directed by Lord Keeper in all extremities to rely. But this was the first time that he ever vouchsafed to ask advice. This must be a secret, because I had the whole in the utmost confidence from one to whom that person imparted all that passed. The person and I have had occasion to correspond about business. Aldrich was to lay all before him, and to be determined by him whether to proceed or not. The person would take no fee, that he might be more at liberty to give his opinion. He told him it was a shameful business; he was so kind to me as to say he thought they had pitched upon the most improper man in the university to fix such scandals on. He advised them as a friend to stop, and to get clear of it as soon as they could. When the report was made to the Dean, it was resolved to stop, and this is the first time that ever he followed advice, as well as asked it. But the true reason was not to [be] owned, and a pretence was to be found out why Aldrich did not proceed. The Dean had been very angry with Mr. Aldrich for signing receipts for me; he was sensible Aldrich had cut the throat of his cause by it, and the Dean did not know how to draw up minutes for the libel, lest Aldrich's own receipts should contradict them. Aldrich came on Thursday night with a witness to Brooks and sent him to me, Dr. Hammond, and Dr. Burton to require copies of all that he had put his hand to. I bid Brooks tell him I expected he should come himself, if he had any thing to say to me. The Dean next morning sent Brooks to me, to know if I desired to have a Chapter. I sent him word I should be glad of a Chapter at any time. Soon after Aldrich came with his proctor to demand a copy of the receipts he had given me, for he could not proceed without them. I told him I did not know that I was obliged to give him a copy of receipts which he had voluntarily given to me before witnesses. His proctor said that he came only to let me know that Mr. Aldrich had been consulting those with whom he advised in this affair, and that they were of opinion he should stay and consider a little before he proceeded further. Dr. Smalridge told the proctor it was very well known with whom Mr. Aldrich consulted on this occasion.

As the Dean and Dr. Smalridge came together from prayers, the Dean said things were come to a great height, and he would be glad to talk with him about them. Dr. Smalridge went to him; in his conversation he pretended a concern for me, though he did not expect I would believe him, that every step I took was wrong (?), that I would find it so at last, especially my denial of a copy of that which Aldrich had subscribed. After a great many turnings and different ways of application to Dr. Smalridge, all ended in insinuating that if I was for the peace of the College, if I would take a voluntary oath, all might be ended. Dr. Smalridge told him he believed I would not think of that, for that he was certain I desired to have this matter examined to the bottom. Dr. Smalridge then expostulated with him for his usage of me; he said there is no treatment so bad which I had not deserved from him. Dr. Smalridge told him, were I so bad, yet there might be treatment which, though I deserved, he as a Christian should not give. He said it might be so, but then I had deserved from him all the treatment that a Christian might lawfully give to a heathen. No divinity that I know of but his own would allow a Christian to use a heathen ill. But this was not very consistent with the tenderness he had pretended for me at the beginning of the conference.

The Chapter met at one, I told Mr. Aldrich that I before the Chapter told him that which I had said in my own house, that since he insisted on my oath, I expected he should call me as soon as he could before those who had authority to give it to me. All the Canons present told him they expected the same. I then asked him since I had answered his demands as far as I could, and that it was not my fault that I did not answer them further, I desired to know whether he was yet ready to answer the questions I should propose to him. He said he would answer no questions till I had given him copies of his receipts. Mr. Dean, when I insisted that Aldrich should be obliged to call me into court, said that might be inconvenient, but that if I would give a voluntary oath it might be ended. I told the Dean I would give no oath but in court. The Dean said I had a mind to get rid of it. Dr. Smalridge asked him with what face he could say so, when I pressed to be called into court. The Canons proposing some questions to Aldrich, the Dean interposed to tell him what he should answer, upon which Dr. Hammond said, since the Dean makes himself so much a party, I think we should take Mr. Aldrich's answers by themselves, and the Dean's by themselves. The Dean upon this bounced out his chair and ran out of the Chapter house. Several of the Canons called to Aldrich to stay, but he followed him. It was intimated to Aldrich that the Canons would suspend their proceedings till they saw whether he entered his libel against me, that it might not be said that any thing was done to deter him from seeking justice; but that if he did not soon do it, they would proceed to censure his paper and to punish him, though the Dean should not concur—and so they will. The tide is now turned, and I have only to consider if I can come at this fellow, and oblige him by any means to own who made him a tool.

At that Chapter I desired Mr. Dean to own that before my brethren, which he by Dr. Smalridge had owned to me in private, that he had called God to witness to that which was not true. He said he did not swear it, he owned he affirmed it. Dr. Smalridge told him he called God to witness. If he did, he said he was not concerned, for he had forgot himself, and he owned it as soon as he remembered it. I asked him if any poor wretch should for hire forswear himself in a court of justice and be indicted for it, whether he thought such a one would save his ears by saying he had forgot himself. He told me I was very rhetorical. Somewhat passed between him and Dr. Altham, and he used the old man very scurrilously.

In the morning at his own house, he owned to Dr. Smalridge that he had received from Aldrich many letters which had been written to the late Dean, but they were only such as related to the College. Dr. Smalridge pressed the late Dean's will on him; he said the Dean's will extended only to papers in his own handwriting. Dr. Smalridge told him that after the words *in my own handwriting* followed, *and all other papers whatsoever that he shall find me possessed of at the time of my decease, excepting papers relating to accounts.* He would not own that he knew of those words. I have now time to breathe a little, which is more than your Lordship will do after reading all this stuff.

1712, November 11. Christ Church.—I had a letter yesterday from Robin Morgan, to let me know that he was hastening to Hereford, because he heard the Bishop was much indisposed. By the same post came a letter from Dr. Smalbroke, now at Hereford, to his wife here, in which he tells her the Bishop was dying.

My own affair is now at a stand, and I believe it will rest where it is till the audit. We shall allow the Dean's poor wretched tool full time to call me into court, that he may not say that we do any thing to deter him from seeking justice. When we meet again in a full Chapter, at the audit, we shall reassume it, and think in the mean time what measures to take about bringing the Dean and Aldrich into Court about the late Dean's letters.

Your Lordship has heard that my Lord Keeper has set aside the appointment of the Heads, by which Sir Thomas Cooke's benefaction was appointed to Magdalen Hall. It is now thought that it will be settled on Gloucester Hall. I know not in whom the nomination of the Head will be placed, probably in the Chancellor. Dr. Hudson would be glad of it I believe, I know my Lord Treasurer has been pleased to design some kindness for him, and for that reason I thought fit to give your Lordship this notice. He would be a proper person for the place, it would be some provision for him, and it would be done without any expense to the Queen of her preferments.

1712, November 13.—Another prebend of Canterbury is void, and your tutor Mr. Terry desires I would beg your Lordship's intercession in his behalf. I expect your Lordship should tell me you will do what you can, but you are afraid it will not do ; but it might not be amiss if you should insinuate that, if a canonry here should be vacant, or the Hebrew professor's place, you believe you could have more hopes of success than for this place.

The judges are now upon examining the exercises of those who are candidates for the prizes of the *Certamen Poeticum*, but there is a great ferment amongst the young candidates ; they say there is foul play. They have discovered that some had private notice of the theme, a long time before it was given out in public ; that others have had verses made for them, and they suspect that it was resolved to whom the prizes should be given before the theme was published, and say already they will never more make verses upon this occasion. It would be pleasant enough if the lowest part of the College should be the first that takes up arms to rescue themselves from oppression. ·

Since my Lord Keeper was pleased to receive an accusation against me, I hope he will be so just as to be at the trouble of reading what can be alleged for my vindication. I could wish my

Lord Treasurer would be pleased to put the paper signed by the Canons into my Lord Keeper's hands. If his Lordship does not think it proper, I hope your Lordship will take an opportunity of showing it to my Lord Keeper. One in his station should not take it well that any one should use his favour, only to impose upon him and to use him as an instrument to convey gross lies.

Postscript. I heartily rejoice with your Lordship for the disappointment of the hellish design of which I had an account from Mr. Thomas. It is the most extravagant piece of wickedness that I ever heard of, and so diabolical that I can scarce think any one, but our Dean, could have thought of it. I hope you will not, as usual, neglect it, but do what you can to discover from what hand so kind a present came.

1712, November 16.—I hope your Lordship has been very well pleased with the entertainment you have had at Windsor, and I suppose you will still be better pleased with that you will have in town this week. I hear the marriage is then to be solemnized. I am pleased to hear my friends are in joy, though we are in a comfortless state, which every day grows worse and worse, and without the least prospect of any end, but by a visitation. I look upon my own affair as over. I think the fiend has done all he can to me, though he is as restless as he is malicious, and I must expect always that he will do me some mischief if he possibly can. But I have still a share in the common interest, and that is in such confusion that I see not how we can subsist two months without an appeal. We shall have a general meeting at the audit of all that belong to the Chapter except brother South. I believe then we must come to a resolution of joining in a petition to the Queen, and desiring her Majesty to appoint commissioners to examine and compose our differences. All we do without this is but patchwork. As fast as we stop the mischief in one place, it breaks out in another. For my own part I had rather throw up my canonry, than hold it in the wretched state we are; and I would lose not only that, but all my own little private fortune, sooner than submit to the insolence of one who persists in that he does upon no other ground but some assurance, which he thinks he has, that we shall never be permitted to prefer a complaint against him.

Dr. Smalridge yesterday desired of him to see the chief register of the College which he has in his hands—he positively refused him. Dr. Smalridge renewed his request to-day; he had thought better of it, and said if he came to his house he should see it, but he would not let it go out of his hands. At the same time he claims a right of taking what papers he pleases out of the treasury, and this very book ought to be kept in the treasury, but he has got it into his possession and will not restore it.

The victors in the *Certamen Poeticum* were declared this morning; it proved, as was expected, that Bromley was first, Le Hunt a commoner, Lord Keeper's kinsman, second, and the third was Prescot. I truly believe there was a juggle, as was all along suspected, and that measures were altered as to the last man and

Prescot was brought in, who is known to have been made student by me, and to be one to whom I am kind, to cover better the juggle in the two former. Terry owns to me that he is [of] opinion Bromley's verses were made for him, but not one word of this I pray. I must not own any thing I discover of this kind. This was contrived to make the Speaker easy again after the disobligation laid on him this summer.

1712, November 17. Christ Church.—You must allow me to be in the condition of a lady, who has not heard in some post from her lover ; she may be uneasy at his silence, not from any suspicion of his unkindness, but from the concern she has for him and her ignorance how it is with him.

I anticipate to-morrow's post, that I may desire your Lordship to send to the Oxford waggon which will be in town on Wednesday for a little box directed to your Lordship. I did not forget to enquire of the Vice-Chancellor about the Xenophon, he has one single volume in large paper, but not that which your Lordship wants, but the Cyropaedia. Since I cannot complete your Lordship's books, I must make good my own promise of sending your Lordship my own ; it is the fairest in England, it was picked out by the late Dean of all the bundles to be given to his friend and father (sic) my old cousin Sheldon. Two volumes the Dean bound before he gave them to my cousin, the rest he gave in sheets, but I bound them like the others and lettered them. Your Lordship must do me the honour to accept of them; I am in your debt too for the poor trifles I lately called out of your hands again. I cut them out of their binding before I gave them back to the villain, though he might perhaps have a title in law to the paper, he had none to the binding.

I have private intelligence that Lord Keeper designs to be at Cockrop for a week betwixt the end of the term and the Seals. Nothing can induce him to such a journey at this season, but a desire of conferring a little with our tyrant. I will certainly go to him, if I can swim through the waters betwixt this place and Cockrop; and unless he orders his doors to be shut upon me I will let him know somewhat he may be willing enough not to hear. I bless God, I am not afraid of showing my face to him either out of court or in court.

I had a letter this morning from Robin Morgan, he is returned to Hereford, he tells me the Bishop continues to rise and to go to bed at his usual hours, and that he comes down every day to his parlour, but that he certainly wears away apace, and that a revolution in that place cannot in all appearance be far off.

I am glad to perceive that South Sea rises, I had that faith in my Lord Treasurer as to venture all the little ready money that I have in it, I hope it will be at par before the Parliament meets. I expect some strange turn, for the worse I am afraid in my own soul, now I am got into the funds, which I never was before in my life. I may with more likelihood now be accused of stealing than I could two years ago.

One Houghton, an attorney, a known rogue, shot himself through the head here on Friday. When I heard of it, it shocked me, for I could not suppress the thought that I might live to hear some such thing of our Dean. This fellow had stolen a woman, a week before, whose father was able to give her 4,000*l.* It is said he had forged a licence by which they were married; he quarrelled that morning with his new bride, and went from her straight into his closet and shot himself. The under cook at Queen's had hanged himself but two days before.

The account of Duke Hamilton and Lord Mohun is very dismal. I suppose now the Parliament will begin to think again of a law against duels.

Postscript. Broxholme made Bromley's verses; this to yourself.

1712, November 20. Christ Church.—I suppose this good weather tempts your Lordship to stay at Windsor. My brother Smalridge leaves me to-morrow, he will wait on your Lordship as soon as he comes to town. Your Lordship will have from him many particulars of what has passed here, which could not be conveyed to you by letter.

We are told here that my Lord Keeper presses hard for the Bishopric of Raphoe for the President of St. John's. It would indeed be very convenient for the President's circumstances, there being 8,000*l.* which will come in to the next successor immediately, besides the yearly income which is 1,200*l. per annum.* But it seems somewhat odd in my Lord Keeper to expect to have such a bishopric for one he recommends, whilst his Lordship will do nothing to extinguish quarrels in a place where my Lord Treasurer desires to have peace; which quarrels must cease if they were not supported by my Lord Keeper.

We hear the Duchess of Newcastle has carried her cause in the Commons, against the validity of the will. I should be glad to hear this news confirmed by your Lordship.

1712, November 22.—I have read Thursday's "Examiner" with a great deal of pleasure, but I understood not all the persons that are referred to in it, nor who it was that Macartney offered to kill. I should be glad if your Lordship would send me one with a cipher in the margin. I think one thing very necessary, that my Lord Treasurer's friends should have a little care for him, since he has so little for himself. Every one is not of his Lordship's temper to live unconcerned in the midst of daggers, pistols and subornations. Though the world has no concern in my life, yet I have so much concern I own for myself as not to be altogether easy in the neighbourhood of one who would take me off by any of those means if he could hope to do it with indemnity to himself. But we cannot live in the state we are; our great friends will not show any dislike of what this man does. A dissolution is preferable to our present condition. I think we are now come to a resolution to throw ourselves at the Queen's feet. None are not ready for it but brother Gastrell and ·

Smalridge, and if they see the rest resolute I believe they will not let the petition go up without their names. Perhaps we may not be heard, but when we have lodged our complaint we have done all we can. We must then wait for the interposition of that God whose name our perjured Dean has blasphemed, by appealing to it in the denial of that which he was forced afterwards to own to be true.

When will your Lordship send J. Keill to us ? I hear he stays in expectation of the decipherer's place. Is he likely to succeed ?

1712, November 27. Christ Church.—I hear from all hands of the rage of the party about Macartney's villainy. It is said public collections are made for his support. This looks as though there was a combination of assassins. I cannot be without my fears on my Lord Treasurer's account. I hope his children and his friends will prevail on him to go better attended, to ease their fears, though he has himself none.

When I have notice of Lady Betty's wedding day, I will take care to celebrate it that evening here. I think I had a promise from her Ladyship that I should have the honour of doing that good office to her, but my old friend the Bishop of St. David's [Bisse] supplants me. I shall live to see him in Durham or London. Pray tell him he can make me no amends for the injury he does me, in taking this honour from me, but by giving me at least the best preferment he has in his gift when he comes into a better bishopric.

It would be very hard indeed if my Lord Treasurer should not be allowed to recommend to his own diocese the person that will be most acceptable to him.

I have sent your Lordship an odd account of a dream, but it is not more remarkable than it is true.

Enclosure.

Some few days before the news of Dr. Aldrich's death came into Ireland, the present Bishop of Londonderry dreamt that he saw Bishop Fell, who though dead was in great agonies of mind for his College ; he foresaw that Dr. Aldrich would soon die, and then he did not know what would become of that society. The Bishop of Derry told him he had no reason to be so much concerned for them, that Dr. Smalridge would in all probability be made Dean, and that he was so excellent a man in all respects, and so well qualified to be a governor, that it was impossible but the College must flourish under him. To this Bishop Fell replied, if it was so I should have no uneasiness ; but I know it will be otherwise, Dr. Smalridge will not be the man, Aldrich is to be succeeded by one who will do a great deal of mischief and bring all things into confusion amongst them. The Bishop of Derry told this dream to several of his family the next morning, at least three days before it could be known in Ireland that Dr. Aldrich was dead.

The Bishop of Derry is now in London.

1712, November 28.—Poor Wyat died this morning. St. Mary
Hall is now in the gift of the Chancellor. There has not been
one scholar in it for many years, but there will be the advantage
of lodgings to any one who has it. Dr. Hudson would be glad
of it for the present for the sake of the lodgings, and if any one
can fill it again with scholars he will. Application will be made
for him to the Duke of Ormond, and it will be hard if his Grace
should refuse it to one of his great merit. Would my Lord
Treasurer be pleased to let the Duke know that he has an esteem
and concern for Dr. Hudson, I doubt not but the doctor would
succeed in so reasonable and so small a desire.

I hear of no one yet that appears for Orator, but Dr. Newton.

Fenton and the elder Fowke carried the prizes yesterday in
the *Certamen Oratoricum.*

1712, November 29.—Blechingden is actually Principal of
Gloucester Hall, he had notice of it last night. This is to secure
him to be Head when that hall is made a college. He will never
resign his principality, but in favour of himself to be sure. I
own this to be very dexterous in Lord Keeper.

Simon Harcourt yesterday took possession of Newnham, it was
the estate of Mrs. Robinson, that married Lord Wemys. It is a
very pleasant situation, and a fine estate. Lord Keeper pays for
[it] 17,000*l.*, and Tom Rowney, who managed this bargain for him,
tells me it is the cheapest pennyworth that ever was bought in
Oxfordshire. His Lordship has laid out within two years 4,000*l.*
at Cockrop. He has bought Sir Edmund Warcop's estate that
joins to Cockrop for 10,000*l.* and now this purchase for 17,000*l.*
It is plain there is money to be got by the Seals, and formerly
money was got in the Treasury, but I do not hear that your
father is about any purchase.

Digby Coates of All Souls is competitor for the Orator's place
with Dr. Newton.

Mr. Dean begins to revive a claim he had once after two
months given up openly in Chapter, the sole disposal of all
College curacies. I suppose he will next claim the whole revenue,
he has altogether as much pretence for it. He has actually put in
one to officiate at Cowley by his own authority, but the pay goes
through our hands. We shall stop that at quarter day. Great
is the expectation of the College of what will pass at Christmas.
I foresee disorder enough. I believe at Christmas eve we shall
be in greater confusion than Trinity in Cambridge is.

It is thought Lord Keeper will be at Radley on Monday to see
his new purchase. I shall endeavour to see him before he
returns.

1712, December 2. Christ Church.—I hear from my brother
Smalridge that he has been allowed to have an hour or two of
your time. We are all sensible, as we ought to be, of your Lord-
ship's concern for us, and I for the particular share I have in it.
But our evils require a speedier remedy than that which your
Lordship thinks we should wait for, nor are we so wicked as to

wish ourselves eased of that which is evil to us by that which must be greater to the public. God forbid that a son of perjuries should under this ministry be preferred to the mitre! Promotion surely is very improper for one to whom a pillory would be an unjustifiable mercy. Lord Keeper is much mistaken if he thinks we will spare his friend, that we may be rid of him. Be the event what it will, he shall be laid open to the world.

The denying the use of our seal to us, by which we lose the presentations to our curacies and livings; the refusing to let what all the Chapter besides himself agrees to be entered in our register or published in the hall; the leaving the College half a year without a proxy, are such things as no society but we would have borne with so long. But then if we come to other parts of his behaviour, his perjuries, his common swearing upon trifling occasions, his dreadful imprecations on himself and others, his lies, his insolence, his extortion from tenants, &c.; such a catalogue will appear that without doubt indeed he will be pinned down here; but I hope there is as little doubt that he will be humbled here. In Queen Elizabeth's time, Sampson, Dean of Christ Church, was deprived by the High Commission court for that which was but a peccadillo to any one of those hundreds we can prove upon this man. We can hope for nothing from Lord Keeper's interposition. He seems resolved to make good what he said at Cockrop in the summer, that he would stand by him in all things against all the world. I am fully persuaded that he consults Lord Keeper in all things, and acts by his direction. He would not dare to do that which he does, but that he is assured of support, or that we shall not be allowed to complain.

I have now had as good advice as the nation affords about the points in dispute betwixt us. We insist on nothing but what is undoubtedly our right by law. All advise us to have recourse to the Queen as the most certain and most honourable remedy for men of our profession. Can any one think it reasonable that we should defer it any longer? Surely those who say they are our friends will allow us to seek for a remedy where we can have it, since they think it not proper for themselves to give the least rebuke to this man. What has he deserved more than others, or what reason is there to fear him more than others, that all must be obliged to acquiesce under what he does? We are desirous to put all upon the issue of a public complaint. If the commissioners appointed to visit us decide against us, we need not have a greater punishment than we shall have from insults on us. But there are many reasons why no wise man would advise us to defer our complaint one day; we are now unanimous; we have several who were Canons in King Charles's time, and whose age will give weight to their testimony, as well as be an aggravation of his insolence. We are sure the Queen, whose life God preserve, whilst she lives will, from the opinion she had of this man before, be disposed to hearken to us. It is for our interest to lodge our complaint with the Queen, before the Lord Keeper possesses himself of the cause he will right or wrong give against us. We can indeed then appeal to the Queen, but

then we are under the prejudice of appealing against a Lord
Keeper's sentence, who will use all the interest he has to support
his own sentence, and many may be less willing to do right to us
then, lest in doing it they should disoblige him and condemn
what he has done. Let us come immediately to the Privy
Council and not by appeal from the Keeper, and I venture my
canonry upon the issue of the cause.

Dr. Gastrell, Dr. Smalridge, and I shall never I hope show
ourselves unmindful of the obligations we have to my Lord
Treasurer and the duty we owe to him; but consider, my
- Lord, there are five other Canons, who received their canonries
from other interests. They do not look on themselves to be
under those obligations we may to forbear a complaint, nor will
their complaint be of less weight if we three should not sign it.
If we are not parties to their complaint, they will summon us in
as witnesses, and then we must confirm the truth of all they
allege. Nor will it be of any service to our great friends to have
this complaint deferred; for if they remove this man, and do not
subdue him, they will certainly in a few weeks have as great
complaints of him from any other place where they put him,
and where they who suffer may not bear so long as we have done.
It is force and power, not reason or kindness, that must work on
him. I gave your Lordship notice that he was reviving his claim
to the sole disposal of curacies, he now encourages Alsop not to
ask us for his year of grace, but tells him he shall have it without
the consent of the Canons. If it is not asked before Christmas,
· we are resolved to strike his name out of the Treasurer's books
and to stop his allowances upon every article. He designs to
claim at Christmas the sole nomination of officers, which we shall
never allow, but shall break up I believe without naming officers
or making a new roll. And then we are in a state of as great
confusion as any enemy we have could wish us. We are almost
so already. After all his boast of the unanimity of the students,
never was society in a more wretched state; not two persons in
the House that converse with one another with any confidence.
They are jealous of each other, and of his little spies; not one
man in the House that would be of use if he stays in it, that is
not resolved to leave it the very first opportunity he can meet
with. But this day will show what this man's interest is in his
own House, as well as in the university. There is an universal
opposition to Newton because he is recommended by our man.
Newton's best friends have advised him to desist, but the Dean
will not let him. On Sunday Newton gave out all over the
university the enclosed paper. No copy was sent to Christ
Church. The design was to insinuate to the university that,
if they would choose him, he would revive the claim of the
Orator to a canonry. It was certainly indited by our
man, who never designed it in his heart, but hoped
to get votes by it. It was to have been a secret to us till
the election was over. A copy of it was brought to me, and I
communicated it; it has worked as I expected. Half the
students are resolved to vote with the Canons against the Dean and

Newton, and the Proctor of our House puts himself bravely at the head of the revolters. The Dean last night came into the common room; desired their votes for Newton; and begged, whatever the event was, they would be unanimous. He was disordered in his looks, and faltered much in his speech, but he could not stir a man. This day ends the so much boasted of dependence of the students upon him. Of those who stay with him there are not six but do it only out of fear. This day too confirms an interest in the university against our man, which he will never be able to surmount, and crushes all the little designs for Mr. Harcourt. Clarke has declared he will not quit the county, and the gentlemen will not desert Mr. Clarke. Now the thoughts are on the University again for Harcourt, and this day will convince my Lord Keeper, if any thing can, how far our great Governor is able to serve him here. Harcourt has been in town since Sunday; he spent Sunday evening at the Deanery; he dined there yesterday : he passed by my lodgings both times without calling. I am not much mortified. I have known the time when father as well as son would have been glad to come here; when they could be admitted into no other house. I shall have opportunity to return his civilities when he tenders his sweet person to be our representative.

What goes before was written before dinner. The Dean has thrown up the game; Dr. Newton desists, and has been with Dr. Hammond, Dr. Altham and me, to assure us he had no ill intention in his paper. Mr. Dean has done himself some service by preventing that which never happened before since our foundation, a division of the College upon a public election; but that will not cure the division of his students at home, which will not only last, but, *si rite auguror*, increase, every day—every one now knows his character.

Your Lordship asked Dr. Smalridge what could be done. I know no way so probable as if he were told that if he did not immediately alter his conduct, we should have leave to complain to the Queen. We shall never submit to Lord Keeper's determination; if we are summoned before him as a judge, though we shall not refuse to appear, we will at the same time petition the Queen. I know not whether my brethren might not agree to refer themselves to my Lord Chief Justice Trevor, or the Attorney, or both of them. Lord Chief Justice Trevor was of our House, and has a kindness for us, and is not more acquainted with one party than the other.

Postscript. The Dean yesterday at dinner before Harcourt and Delaune, by way of upbraiding other heads, said aloud, every vote in my House goes along with me to-morrow; he keeps close to-day.

1712, December 4.—I am afraid I have tired you with the account of our impertinent squabbles, but you shall have ease. I shall only tell you that Mr. Harcourt is still here; how much longer he will stay I know not. Here are little cabals held every day, but amongst such I believe as will not be able to serve him as he desires. He has gone by my door every day, but never yet called here, no doubt it is by order. You will think so, when I tell you what I desire you would mention to no one but my Lord Treasurer. I have now reason to think Lord Keeper himself saw the paper signed by Aldrich before it was delivered into the Chapter. I would not have this take air; it may prevent my coming at a full proof of it. Should it prove so, I leave your Lordship to judge whether we can expect anything fair or honest from his mediation. The meaness of the action in one of his station is almost incredible, but what can be the motive to one, whom I have endeavoured to oblige by all the ways in my poor power, to take such sordid means to ruin me, if he could? If this prove true, I believe your Lordship will think I have reason to be on my guard, and to judge that it is determined betwixt him and his friend to compass my ruin by one way or other. Your Lordship may be sure I shall not mention it, till I find more of it, and if I should be certain it is, I shall think a little how far it may be proper for me to take notice of it.

I am afraid Dr. Freind is going to play a worse part than he ever has done hitherto. He renewed his love to his mistress, begged pardon for what was past, gave her the utmost assurances that man could give that he would make good all that he ever promised to her. Our neighbour has had notice of it and has been doing all he can to persuade him to break off again, I am afraid with success; but all this to yourself. I am sorry for Dr. Freind's sake; if he does it, he will no more have ease in this world than happiness in the other.

Postscript. Pray enquire, if you think it proper, whether my Lord Treasurer did not write a letter lately to Lord Keeper about our affairs. Last night in company where our Dean and Mr. Harcourt were, one who was there told me the Dean received a letter; upon opening there were two letters, one as the gentleman thought in Lord Treasurer's hand, the other from Lord Keeper. The Dean immediately gave both to Harcourt to read.

1712, December 7.—I am afraid I am under your displeasure. I think I have not heard of your Lordship in ten days past. In my last I told your Lordship I had some reason to suspect that Lord Keeper had seen Aldrich's paper before it was given in to the Chapter. I have now proof of it, not sufficient indeed to be allowed in a court, but to convince your Lordship when I wait on you. And yet when my brother Gastrell first told him of it at Christ Church, he denied having heard of it, as strongly as the Dean did his having given out a copy of the other paper. This is very hard upon me, and a warning to me to be on my guard, and yet young Harcourt sups with me to-night. He called on me last night; I asked him if he [had] not gone by my door every day this week, he owned it, but that he still designed to call on me before he left the town. I told him I believed I was obliged to the weather for seeing him. After a short visit, he appointed to come with T. Rowney and to sup with me this evening. I hope you will allow me to have learnt somewhat since I belonged to the court, when I can be upon a point of compliments with the son after I have been used so by the father. If I go on to improve in this way I may in time be qualified for better preferment. Brother Gastrell has given me an account of what passed betwixt him and Lord Keeper. He has only convinced me of that which I always thought, we [are] not to expect anything that is fair from his Lordship. We can never think it safe for ourselves or successors to submit our cause to him either as arbitrator or judge, though I had [rather] appear before him as judge than refer it to him as arbitrator. We may appeal from his sentence as judge, though if he summon us, though we shall not decline his jurisdiction, we shall at the same time appeal to a higher power. But since Lord Keeper thinks it beneath him to admit any others to be with him on any other terms than as advisers, methinks he should not desire to be concerned at all. Nor do I see why he should act at all but as judge. It is beneath him to act as a referee, and we will refer it at any time, if Lord Keeper is left out. Let us have Lord Trevor, the Dean have Judge Powell, and if it be thought necessary to have a third man, let them two pitch on him, and we will stand to that award.

If you think it proper, I wish you would let me know whether Lord Dupplin wrote any letter to our Dean on Monday or Tuesday last about St. Mary Hall—it is a very odd question that I ask, but if your Lordship thinks fit to give me an answer to it, I will let you know why I ask it. I hear from brother Gastrell, but not before, that Lord Dupplin is removed into Poland Street; that will be very convenient for me when I am in town. But I beg your Lordship would enquire whether my Lord Dupplin received a letter from me directed to him in Queen's Square, in answer to that which I had the honour to receive from his Lordship.

1712, December 8.—I can give your Lordship no other account than I have already of your father's letter. All I know was from one who was in company with Mr. Harcourt and the Dean on Wednesday last at Pembroke; he was one who knew your father's hand. The Dean's letters were brought to him, there was one from Lord Keeper and another, which this gentleman thought to be from your father, which when the Dean had read, he put them both into Mr. Harcourt's hand.

Your Lordship seems not to have heard of the disposal of St. Mary Hall, till you had it from the Speaker. Did not your Lordship receive a letter from me on Saturday se'nnight, which I wrote the day Wyat died, to beg my Lord Treasurer's favour with the Duke of Ormond in behalf of Dr. Hudson? Your Lordship takes no notice of your having received any such letter from me, and yet the Dean on Thursday last in the morning could tell Dr. Hudson that my Lord Treasurer had sent to the Duke of Ormond to beg St. Mary Hall for him, and that the Duke had readily granted it. If this were so it is unaccountable to me

that your Lordship should not have heard of it sooner than from
the Speaker. The Dean told John Hudson further that he had
had notice of it from my Lord Dupplin, the Treasurer's son. I
am sure John Hudson could not dream of this or feign it, for he
asked me simply if there was not one Dupplin that was the
Treasurer's son, and this was the reason of that I desired to know
in the letter of yesterday's post. And I beg your Lordship would
let me know, if you can, whether Lord Dupplin wrote to the
Dean, or whether his Lordship was sent to the Duke of Ormond
about it or if his Lordship was no way concerned in it; but [if]
the place however was granted to Dr. Hudson at my Lord
Treasurer's desire, how came the Dean to have so early notice of
it, before any one else here knew of it? If all this should be
without ground, I can guess whence his intelligence came, and
for what purposes other circumstances were invented.

I am afraid it would be to no purpose to trouble your Lordship
with any further accounts of our squabbles. Our condition
admits of no remedy but that from which we are debarred; but
though that may be delayed, yet it will be recurred to at last, if
this man lives here a year longer. For my own part I have
given over all thoughts of our affairs, I foresee a terrible confusion, but the greater it is the sooner we may be delivered from
it. Our condition may speak for us, though we speak not for
ourselves. I see the whole design, and where the support of it
is expected. It is all in concert with Lord Keeper; but by that
I told you in my last, your Lordship will easily think we shall
never acquiesce under him as our Visitor. Should he, if we
appeal to the Queen, insist, as he said he would, to be appointed
by her to visit, we certainly would except against him and
petition for commissioners less partial, and we have practice on
our side; since upon all complaints, whether from the Dean and
Chapter or from the students, the Crown always indeed
appointed the Lord Keeper as one, but never as sole commissioner to decide our differences, indeed usually it was a committee
of Council did it. But the scene now begins to open, and the
reason of this strict alliance with our Dean to be seen by all the
world. It is the very same we suspected from the beginning. All
the bustle to make this man Dean, all the unjust support of him
in all his villainies since he has been Dean, was only by his
interest to influence things here as Lord Keeper should think
most proper for his own turn, and to make young Simkin our
representative. Now it appears that the young gentleman came
not down to take possession of Newnham, but the university.
For this reason he has been with the Dean from day to day
round with some of his poor creatures. I suppose I owe the
honour of his supping with me last night to the same purpose.
We hear from several quarters that it is dropped in discourse
that [Sir Wm.] Whitlock is old, that he will not desire to stand
again, that if he should it would not be proper to choose
one past service, and where can we choose better than
Mr. Harcourt? To-morrow he is to be presented in
Convocation to his master's degree. This is to be a sort of public

recommendation of him to the whole university, but all will not do. If I am not very much mistaken, the tide is strong against him. Could it be turned for him, as I believe it cannot, I have in reserve that which will quash this noble project at once. I foresee no common resentments from Lord Keeper upon such an occasion; then I suppose he will come in upon us with a high hand as Visitor to crush the poor Canons. The noise will be great, but I know not how it can be avoided, nor what it will end in; in other sort of quarrels perhaps than ours are, and between persons of more importance to the quiet of the world. But this was not unforetold before this man had the broad seal to be the destroyer of this Society. It is hard that we of this place must be the most unfortunate part of the clergy under this ministry. But let things go as they will I purpose to drink the Marchioness [of Carmarthen]'s health on Thursday night, and to wish that two sisters who are so equal in their goodness may be so too in their happiness, which depends on their husbands.

1712, December 9.—We were in expectation of Mr. Harcourt's inauguration to-day, but it is deferred, for what reason I know not. He stays here some time longer, as Mrs. Rowney tells me. Frequent cabals are held.

What I told your Lordship of Bob [Freind]'s relapse was true, but brother Gasse endeavoured to fix him once more before he came away. Time must show us whether he has done it.

We had a Chapter to-day; we were calm, though we differed. The Dean proposed to have one instrument sealed, we insisted to have another sealed first that had been first entered in the leiger book. We offered him to seal that he desired, if he would agree to let that we proposed be sealed afterwards. He told us roundly it should never be sealed whilst he was Dean, so we parted.

1712, December 11.—I would not interrupt your Lordship long in this time, as I suppose, of joy to the family, only if the marriage is over, I would beg your Lordship to make my compliments to my Lord Treasurer and all his family, and to present my most humble duty to my Lady Marchioness of Carmarthen, and to assure her that no servant that belongs to the family prays more heartily for her Ladyship's and her Lord's happiness. When I have notice from your Lordship of the marriage, I shall beg leave to present my duty to the Marquis of Carmarthen by the Bishop of St. David's.

I wish your Lordship could have leisure to write me one line only about that I mentioned concerning St. Mary Hall.

1712, December 12.—I am very sensible of your Lordship's great kindness in favouring me with so many letters when you are engaged in business of so great concern and satisfaction to yourself and to your family. I did suppose that which was said about the letter to be an impudent lie, and told for no other end

but to possess John Hudson and others that should hear of it by
him with an opinion that it had been done by my Lord Treasurer
at his desire. When I wait on your Lordship I can divert you
with a great many stories very ridiculous, coined and given out
for the same end, but I shall now trouble your Lordship with
somewhat of more moment. Measures are concerted betwixt the
Dean and his great friend to bring our affairs to an issue, but it
will not be such I believe as they design.

Tom Rowney has acted the part of a friend to me in our late
quarrels, in such a manner as I must never forget whilst I live.
I have had intelligence from him which has been of great
use to me, which I could have had from no one else. Tom was
yesterday at Sir John Stonehouse's; after dinner Harcourt said
he believed by that time a thing was done at Christ Church
which would bring their differences there to a decision. That
the Dean had resolved to turn out Mr. Brooks, the Chapter clerk,
as on that day, and he believed it was done by the time he spake
of it. That the Dean supposed the Canons would then appeal;
that if they did, but refused to concur in business with him,
then he himself would appeal. Mr. Harcourt added that the
Canons had a notion that my Lord Treasurer would be joined
with my Lord, his father, to determine their differences, but the
Canons would find themselves mistaken, for his father was resolved
to have the sole determination of them. Tom made a pretence
to come away when he had heard this, and rode up straight to
my door to tell this to me. I desire no one may know this but
yourself and my Lord Treasurer. The Dean has attempted
nothing yet, and I am apt to think he has laid aside
this project or at least deferred it. He finds upon enquiry the
pretence he designed to have taken for turning Brooks out to
fail him. It was an instrument entered in our leiger book,
which he thought had been entered by Brooks, but which we had
taken care to have entered by his clerk, when Brooks himself
was at London. Should he pretend to turn him out before
Christmas, we should have no officers elected then, nor any
removes from the several tables; but there is a thing which still
weighs more with the Dean than all other reasons. A great glut of
fines is to come in within six weeks; the Dean's share will amount
to about 400l.; should he pretend to dismiss our Chapter clerk,
all these would be at a stand, we would not seal nothing (sic).
I am apt to think if he ventures to do it, it will not be till a day or
two before he comes up to town, but I will not however answer
for what he may do; he goes not by any rules that other men
do. A packet was sent over to Mr. Harcourt this morning,
whether to give notice of a change of counsels, or to
desire Lord Keeper's approbation of those already taken, I know
not. Harcourt will be in town again on Saturday. They are
mistaken in all their points; the Canons never expected the
Lord Treasurer should be joined with Lord Keeper, nor did they
ever think it proper that Lord Treasurer should have any trouble
about their impertinent quarrels; but the Canons are resolved, if
they can help it, that Lord Keeper shall not have the sole decision

of them. We shall not appeal, let the Dean do what he will, but lie still, and put a stop to all business. South Sea stock rises, I hope I can hold out half a year without my canonry. If the Dean appeals, we know what we have to do, but we shall have time enough to consider, and we shall do nothing but with Lord Treasurer's leave and approbation. We are in hourly expectation of this noble stroke or some other of the like nature. I do believe he will do somewhat very extravagant betwixt this and Christmas.

Tom Rowney, brother Gastrell, John Urry, Tom Terry are to meet at my house on Monday night to drink the bride's good health. I will be so impudent as to say we shall do it in as good wine as any you will have at the bridal supper.

1712, December 13.—The blow is struck; it was struck whilst I was writing my last letter to your Lordship. The Dean sent for poor Mr. Brooks a little after three o'clock on Friday, and told him he dismissed him from his place. That you may see what passed I have sent your Lordship a copy of what Brooks could recollect when he came home. The Dean came to-day to the Canons as they were at dinner without giving them any notice. I was not at dinner. Brooks was with them. He told them he had turned out their Chapter clerk, and had put another in for various reasons. They desired to know his reasons; he gave none that I could hear. Dr. Hammond and all there told him they could not allow him to put out or put in a Chapter clerk without their consent. He told them he would hold no more Chapters but in the presence of the Chapter clerk whom he had nominated. They told him they would hold none but with their old Chapter clerk. Then, says he, it will be to no purpose to call any more, and so he went off. We must meet again on Thursday, though not capitularly, yet as trustees to dispose of an exhibition; we shall then offer the Dean, for the sake of carrying on the business necessary for the support of the College, to proceed without any Chapter clerk, either his or our own, and to attest our acts ourselves as our predecessors did before they had a Chapter clerk. If he refuses this, as I believe he will, we are as it were dissolved. We shall have no officers at Christmas, nor will there be any one that I know who will have sufficient authority to receive or pay the money necessary for the support of the House.

I cannot tell how to account for this proceeding, if it is done without the knowledge and allowance of Lord Keeper it is down right madness, and I should think Lord Keeper would not allow this. Lord Keeper had a particular kindness for this man, has in his time received many guineas from him, promised him just before he was Keeper, in my house, to do somewhat for him, has his son now in his service; and always employed this man in all his own business here in the country. The Dean had last winter written to Lord Keeper to tell him he could do no good in the Chapter whilst this Chapter clerk was in, and to desire his consent for turning him out. Lord Keeper then said, "Hold! not so fast neither, John Brooks must not out." I can scarce think this is done with Lord Keeper's knowledge and allowance, but the Dean for this fortnight has had constant correspondence with Lord Keeper, either directly or by Mr. Harcourt. Mr. Harcourt was acquainted with it some days before it was done. If it was done without Lord Keeper's privity it could be done with no other view but to make any accommodation by way of reference impracticable. I suppose Lord Keeper had given him notice that he would be pressed to that to prevent it, therefore he was resolved to put things into such a condition as should be capable of no determination but by a public decision, in which he supposes Lord Keeper will be the sole judge.

We are now, my Lord, much at a loss how to proceed, it is some comfort to us that it will appear to all the world that the extremity we are in is not owing to us in the least, but how to get out of it we do not well see, without such measures as have not yet been thought advisable. If we do not appeal, we believe he will. That which we apprehend is, that he will bring on us an injunction from my Lord Keeper to command us to act with the new Chapter clerk, named by the Dean, and to acquiesce in all other points till he can hear and decide our quarrels ; that would be a short way to enslave us. He may never proceed to hear, and in the mean time subject us to the Dean's tyranny; we can indeed appeal from such an injunction, but it would be easier to prevent it than to appeal from it. Since our differences must now be decided by public authority, they can no longer be a secret, they will be as much known to the Queen, if we are summoned before my Lord Keeper, as if we petition her. But it concerns the Queen's prerogative, as well as our own interest, that we should apply first to her. We would desire leave for no more than to set forth in a short petition, that whereas there are many differences which put a stop to the business of the College, we humbly beg her Majesty would order things to continue as they were before the present Dean came, till she shall think fit to order commissioners to hear and decide our disputes. We hope this may not be thought unreasonable ; this is the shortest way of making us quiet. Might we have leave to petition for such an order, we should not be concerned for any further proceedings. We should rest contented under it, unless the Dean himself should force a visitation. I cannot see any other way we have of subsisting as a Society, without an immediate visitation. But we shall do nothing without my Lord Treasurer's leave. Our brother Smalridge is desired by us to wait on my Lord, as soon as my Lord's leisure will allow him access, to lay our state before him, and to desire his Lordship's advice and direction. We would desire only to have leave to have a petition ready, that in case the Dean appeals to the Lord Keeper, we may be able to lodge it with the Queen before we can receive a summons from the Lord Keeper. This acting is very surprising, I thought my Lord Keeper, at my Lord Treasurer's desire, would at least have restrained the Dean from any new outrage, if he had done no more.

I have sent your Lordship a copy of the most solemn decision that ever was upon any complaint from this place. It appears by it that the Lord Keeper was not then thought our Visitor, but only one of the committee of Council that heard it.

In Queen Elizabeth's time, the committee used to be the Archbishop of Canterbury, the Lord Keeper, and the Chancellor of the University. Afterwards in 1632, two Canons quarrelled about their lodgings and appealed to the Lord Coventry; he sent an injunction. Your Lordship will see the petition of the Dean and Chapter upon it, and the King's answer, by which though the King allows them to have recourse to the Lord Keeper and requires them to obey his orders, yet at the same time he allows them, whenever they desire it, to have immediate recourse to himself, or they may appeal from the Keeper to him. In fact ever since that time, upon all occasions, which have been many, we have always applied directly to the King, and had his orders by the Secretary. There is too in a book which the Dean has got into his hands one letter from King Charles I. in 1643, in which he declares himself our sole Visitor.

I have laid our miserable state before your Lordship; I believe it cannot be longer concealed. We could wish, but my Lord Treasurer knows best, that her Majesty heard of it from my Lord Treasurer, before she heard of it from any one else. Mr. Harcourt retired to Radley whilst this noble feat was to be done here, but your Lordship will perceive by my former that he had been let into it. Yesterday the Dean sent his servant to bring him to town again. He came in the evening. The Dean and Delaune went with him to the Vice-Chancellor, to desire he might be presented to-day to his Master's degree. The Vice-Chancellor invited them to dine with him to-day; called a Convocation this afternoon, and Mr. Harcourt was presented by the new Orator. As the Dean was coming from the Canons to-day, he met me in the quadrangle, and came up to me; Terry was with me; he told me *Lord* Harcourt was to be presented in the afternoon to his degree, and he hoped I would be there; I told him I should certainly attend his Lordship. It is not yet publicly owned, but every one understands that he is to be put up to be our representative. The opposition will be great, and I believe very effectual; then the Dean will have the honour to have put the University into as great a flame as he has done his own College. The University has been in perfect peace for twelve years past, and this, for aught I can see, is the sole end for which our Dean is espoused, and such combustions are to be raised. These are rare politics! Blechingden's being made Principal of Gloucester Hall has quite spoiled the credit of the Lord Keeper's decree. His Lordship disowns his having had any hand in making Blechingden Principal, but nobody will believe. That alone has fixed no small party against his son. I am sorry I must trouble your Lordship with such stuff as this, at a time of so much joy to your family. But the prosperity of every branch of you, as it will be my prayer, so it will be a comfort to me, in any condition we are in, be it what it will. I told you in my last who are to meet in my parlour on Monday night to drink the bride and bridegroom's health.

Postscript. Poor Brooks's case is very hard. He has I think nine children; he was put in by Bishop Fell and the unanimous consent of the Canons. After thirty years' service and more he is to be turned to the wide world for a new livelihood. I believe he is as honest and as able a servant as ever belonged to a Society. I am sure our business cannot go on without him, but our Christian Dean is *hard* upon no one but when it is for his own *ease.* Is the "Divel" himself more? This poor man has been in hourly attendance upon the Dean ever since he came, he has been forced to neglect all other business to wait on him. He has often, I believe, between six in the morning and nine at night, been sent for twelve times in a day. He has made collections and extracts for the Dean out of all books he could have any occasion for, he has done his own private business for him, he never had a farthing from him, he has been used with the utmost insolence, he has been sent on errands I would not send my footman, and now the Dean would kick him off, just as he did his wench, when he has had his use of him and wants no more of him, to introduce one who would attest right or wrong whatever he bids him.

When St. Katherine's Hospital was visited, Lord Somers was appointed one of the commissioners. Before the commission was opened, I think, he entered a protestation to save his own right of being Visitor as Chancellor, but afterwards sate with the commissioners and acted as one of them.

Jeffryes the chaplain, who was put in by the Dean at Cowley, came to the Treasurer to require his quarterly payment. The Treasurer asked him by whose order he officiated there, he told him by the Dean's. The Treasurer paid nothing. This is the next step to the sole disposal of our revenue.

Enclosure 1.

Dean Atterbury's interview with Mr. Brooks, the Chapel Clerk.
Between three and four, 12 December, 1712.

Dean. I am sorry to tell you what I am about to tell you, you know I gave a hint of it long since, that is, you and I must part; you shall no longer be Chapter clerk here. I am now resolved to turn you out, and have within this hour put another into your place. I know you to be very fit and capable of being our Chapter clerk, and that it will be many years before another can come to your knowledge of the place, but I cannot be easy till you are out.

Brooks. This is a very hard thing, Mr. Dean. Pray, give me leave to ask you, for what cause you would turn me out.

Dean. I am never hard to anyone but for my own ease.

Brooks. I declare to you I know of no cause, unless it be that

I have refused to do my duty to the Canons, in obedience to ou.

Dean. Yes, Mr. Brooks, you know you wrote against me, you have omitted to enter several leases in the leiger book, you have kept counterparts of leases by you, and not brought them into the treasury, gone out of town without my leave six days together, and many other just causes I have against you.

Brooks. Mr. Dean, what I wrote was by the Canons' orders, and was I think no more than an account of what things were necessary to have been done in Chapter, and I thought, if that was a crime, it had long since been forgiven. As to your other particulars, they are such very small faults, as would not I think forfeit a man's place, in the judgment of any unprejudiced person.

Dean. I am never hard to any one, unless it be for my own ease.

Brooks. I must say it is hard that I who have had the honour to serve this Chapter for above thirty years, and can say it without boasting, faithfully and with credit, and have applied and spent all the best of my time in it, should at last without any cause be turned out with disgrace, and be now to seek a new way for a livelihood.

Dean. You may if you will avoid the disgrace. There be two ways of your going out, one is that you may leave the place and say that there being great differences between the Dean and Chapter you was weary of serving them any longer, and the other is, you know you must go out. Consider of it till to-morrow morning.

Brooks. No, no, Mr. Dean, this usage is no surprise to me. I have well considered this matter before this time. As I came into this place with the unanimous consent of the Dean and Chapter, so I hope to continue in it till they are pleased to put me out, and I hope never to leave it as a fool or a knave. But, Mr. Dean, I never thought you would have offered this, till you had paid me what you owe me.

Dean. I owe you! I owe you nothing.

Brooks. Yes, Mr. Dean, you know you do, you owe me for your instalment, four guineas. You know it to be the second item in the account of all my fees which you was pleased to exact of me. You owe me for many other things. A bill of which I shall make bold to present you with, and for many attendances. More particular services have I done for you and some slavery than I have ever done for all the deans together in the space of thirty years, and never yet saw sixpence of your money. Your humble servant, Mr. Dean.

Dean. Good night to you, consider on it.

Enclosure 2.

Copy of proceedings at the Court at Whitehall, the 30th of January, 1629[–30], on the complaints of the students against the Dean and Canons of Christ Church.

Enclosure 3.

Copy of the Dean and Chapter's petition to Charles I.; and of
his Majesty's declaration, at the Court at Whitehall, 2 November,
1632, that the Dean and Chapter and the Students of Christ
Church shall acknowledge the Lord Chancellor or Lord Keeper
as their Visitor under his Majesty, the King nevertheless
reserving to himself all power and authority, whensoever he shall
please to take immediate knowledge of any business concerning
them.

1712, December 16.—My friend Mr. Rowney's intelligence was
very exact; the feat was to have been done on the day Mr. Harcourt said it was done, but Hammond had the Chapter book in
his hands, and was gone a roguing. The feat was deferred till
next day, that the Chapter book might be got out of Dr. Hammond's
hands before it was done. Upon different pretences the Dean
had got all our leiger books and all our Chapter books into his
hands, and the most material of our writings before he attempted
this. But we know pretty well what he has, and we hope the
royal power may oblige him to give them up again.

Lord Keeper we hear will be in our neighbourhood in Christmas
week; preparations are made for him at Cockrop. We are afraid
it is concerted that he should give us a visit and do somewhat to
our disadvantage. This makes us more anxious to know what
we may have leave to do, and what measures my Lord Treasurer
thinks most proper for us. Our tyrant pretends lameness and
keeps within; I suppose he is digesting his materials to be laid
before his Visitor, not ours. He had the gout though last
Christmas to excuse himself from preaching upon Christmas day.

I beg your Lordship would give my duty to my Lady Dupplin;
I have been forced to stay longer than I thought I should have
done for some brawn, till I could meet with such as I would
presume to offer to her. I shall on Friday or Tuesday next beg
her to accept of a collar.

1712, December 18. Christ Church.—The enclosed is what
could be recollected and written down by the Canons, the moment
the Dean left the Chapter. He did not expect we would so
readily and unanimously have agreed to a reference. When we
had taken him at his word, he used all the evasions he could
think of on the spot to retract what he had offered. I believe
he has been pressed by Lord Keeper to make a tender of a
reference in hopes we should decline it, but it is secretly agreed
betwixt them that points of greatest moment shall be left solely
to his Lordship. Now surely it is not proper for his Lordship
to be concerned at all unless he came as Visitor. We only beg
my Lord Treasurer would be pleased to think how the Dean may
be obliged to stand by his own offer. We shall choose Lord
Trevor, let the Dean choose any one he pleases, we are ready to
refer everything to an arbitration. I hope your Lordship will get

our brother Smalridge access to my Lord Treasurer as soon as you can.

Postscript. We have met the Dean again since dinner to dispose of an exhibition; not one word more to us of reference, but only a declaration that he would hold no more Chapters till our disputes were adjusted. I have added what passed to the morning account; we fancy by his silence as to a reference that he now designs to appeal to the Lord Keeper. If he does and we are summoned, we hope we may have leave to remove the cause to the Queen by a petition setting forth our summons and desiring to know whether her Majesty will not be pleased, as her predecessors did, to take us into her immediate protection, or refer us to the Lord Keeper. He seems to endeavour to manage so that Lord Keeper shall think himself obliged to insist on it, as his right, to have the sole cognisance of our disputes.

Enclosure.

Dean Atterbury's proposals.

The Dean proposed to us to refer all matters in dispute betwixt us to two persons, he to choose one, and we another. The Canons immediately cried they agreed to it. Then he said he would refer this of the Chapter clerk first. Dr. Gastrell desired all might be referred at the same time. The Dean insisted to refer the dispute about the Chapter clerk first. Dr. Stratford proposed that should be referred first, if the Dean would agree to let the Canons choose what point on dispute should be next decided. The Dean would give no other answer to that, but that other things would come on in course. Then the Dean said he would refer some things in dispute to some persons and some to others. The Canons insisted to have all proposed to the same persons. Dr. Gastrell proposed that the Canons should have but one referee on their side for all points, but that the Dean might change his as often as he pleased. The Dean said he would refer the Chapter clerk and his claims about money to any two referees, but that other things he should refer only to my Lord Keeper as Visitor. The Canons were of opinion that the same referees might decide all points, the Lord Keeper, if he acted as Visitor, not being properly a referee. Dr. Stratford put the Dean often in mind of his first proposal to refer all matters in dispute to two persons. The Dean would not at first own that he made that proposal, but at last said if he had made such a proposal he now rectified it. The Dean said he would send his proposal to us in writing. Mr. Barber being called in about his lease, the Dean was in a heat upon some discourse that passed and when Mr. Barber went out, the Dean followed him. As the Dean went out he cried out, you are not in a referring humour, I will talk no further with you. The Canons told him they were very ready to agree to a reference, that they thought he was in a heat and not they. The Dean called for Mr. Perrot, and the treasurer upon that calling out Mr. Perrot, the Dean told the treasurer he was a rude beast.

Three o'clock in the afternoon, Dr. Hammond requested the Dean that we might have some of the books and papers belonging to the College again. The Dean answered we are no Chapter now, and said "I will tell you further I will have no more Chapters till these matters in dispute are adjusted, I am willing to go on with business that may be done without a Chapter, as the audit, but I will hold no more Chapters."

1712, December 19.—We received to-day the enclosed paper from the Dean ; it is plain he would come off from his first offer of submitting to an arbitration, by explaining it so that he thinks we will not accept of it. I must observe too one alteration, as to the arbitration of those points he still agrees to refer. He does not now offer fairly to refer them to two arbitrators, one to be chosen by him and another by us, but *to arbitrators to be agreed on*, by which he seems to leave himself at liberty to recede if he does not like the arbitrator named by us. But we shall do what we can to disappoint. The answer we design at present to make is, to embrace his offer of referring those points he mentions; to desire they may be referred as soon as possible, and to tell him we are ready to name our arbitrator ; to tell him we are ready to accept his first offer too, of referring all other differences to the same arbitrators, with all respect due to the authority and interposition of our Visitor ; to offer in the mean time, for peace and the business of the House, to proceed without any Chapter clerk, as our predecessors often did, and we can show many instances particularly of the election of officers at Christmas, no Chapter clerk present, but the election attested only by the Dean and Canons who made it ; to offer, if he insists upon the presence of a notary, to act with any indifferent one, to be called in by common agreement. I think no more can be expected from us by any who are most concerned for our peace. When we mention our *Visitor* we shall do it in general without naming either Queen or Lord Keeper to avoid any offence, but we think we cannot accept that which he has proposed of desiring Lord Keeper to take cognisance of our differences. Though we will not decline my Lord Keeper's jurisdiction, we think we dare not submit to it without asking the Queen's leave, without injuring the prerogative. He pretends not to be Visitor, but under her Majesty, and it might be want of duty to her for him to appeal to him in points of such moment without her knowledge and allowance. We wish we could be so happy as to know my Lord Treasurer's opinion by Sunday night; we shall not give in an answer to the Dean's paper till Monday. We would do nothing without my Lord Treasurer's approbation, and should be glad to know if he thinks any thing more proper for us than that we design.

1712, December 20.—I sent your Lordship on Friday a copy of the paper which we had just then received from the Dean, with our first and hasty thoughts upon it. Upon further consideration we are satisfied we must not decline the Dean's offer of referring

all our disputes to the Visitor. It would give the Dean a great
advantage, and look as though we distrusted our cause; we have
only a doubt to which Visitor we are to appeal. If my Lord
Keeper visits us, I believe the quarrel will be as public, and can
no more be concealed from the Queen, than if we are visited by
a commission from the Queen; nor do I believe Lord Keeper
himself will visit us without acquainting the Queen. But it
would be more to our advantage to desire the Dean to join with
us in a petition to the Queen, and, if he refuses, to petition by ourselves. This would be more dutiful in us to the Queen, and
according to the constant practice of our predecessors;
and commissioners from the Queen would have power
not only to settle present disputes, but to prevent
future, by giving standing rules to us, which Lord Keeper
cannot do, who can only judge of past usages and declare
which he thinks so. But we throw ourselves at my Lord
Treasurer's feet, and beg to know his pleasure what would he
have us do. If he would have us close entirely with the Dean's
proposal, and desire my Lord Keeper as Visitor under the Queen
to take cognisance of our disputes, Dr. Gastrell and I will
endeavour to bring our brethren into it, though at present they
are very averse to it. We shall put off our answer to him for two
days by telling him that though we have no objection to that
he proposes, yet we cannot give a full answer to it till we know
the mind of our absent brethren, who are as much concerned in
it as we are, and propose to him in the meantime the expedients
I mentioned in my last for carrying on the business of the College.
But I beg I may have a letter from your Lordship on Wednesday
night, at farthest; or if your Lordship receive this soon enough on
Monday, I wish I could hear on Tuesday what my Lord Treasurer's
will is, to which we shall entirely submit. If I should hear nothing
from your Lordship, you will give us leave to presume that it is
indifferent to my Lord Treasurer what method we take. We
foresee a great deal of trouble and confusion, but I hope it is
evident by whom we are brought into this extremity. He receded
from other methods of accommodation which he himself proposed,
the moment we accepted them. Should we decline this he now
proposes, he would load us with the envy of it, as though we
were averse to peace or distrusted our cause. It now appears
that all the steps which he has taken since he returned from
London were in order to this at this very time. I believe he
has had notice from Lord Keeper himself, or by my Lord
Treasurer's letter, which I believe was sent to him, how unwilling
my Lord Treasurer was that our disputes should come to the
Queen. He depends upon it that we shall never be allowed to
come to the Queen, and he thinks we would never agree with him
to appear before my Lord Keeper; but he will be mistaken. We
shall trust to the goodness of our cause against any favour he
presumes on, and do in this what will be most agreeable to my
Lord Treasurer.

1712, December 21.—I know not how to beg your pardon for all the trouble we give you, or to thank you for all your concern for us. By the letter I wrote yesterday, your Lordship will perceive we had some thoughts of altering the measures we had at first resolved on in relation to the Dean's proposal. We were apprehensive, and are still, that he would take great advantage of our declining to close with his offer of going with him to our Visitor. He will load us as though we were averse to any accommodation and doubted of our cause. We are very sensible of the noise and scandal that will be upon a public visitation, whether it be before the Lord Keeper or the Queen. An arbitration would be more quiet and less expensive, and if that shall be thought more proper, we can bring our brethren to offer that to him once again. We have kept ourselves at ˙ liberty to do that which we shall be directed to. This day we gave in the enclosed, by which we shall gain time till Wednesday to know what my Lord Treasurer would please to have us do. We shall entirely follow any directions we receive, either from Dr. Smalridge or your Lordship. No one can imagine any in his wits desires˙ the trouble or noise of a public visitation, if [it] may be avoided, but so far as my brother Gasse and I can judge, our Governor is resolved on it. If we will not appeal ourselves, or join with him in a petition, he will appeal I believe by himself to my Lord Keeper, nor can any thing stop him or make him come to an arbitration, unless my Lord Keeper could be prevailed on to let him know that he would not receive the appeal, if he brought it, but refer it to the Queen. And if my Lord Keeper should do so, he would immediately fly in his face. No one knows this gentleman thoroughly, but we who have been so long acquainted with him and have had so much to do with him. He will certainly endeavour to prejudice the Lord Keeper against us for not immediately closing with his proposal, but seeming as he will represent it to decline Lord Keeper's jurisdiction. But we hope my Lord Treasurer will do us the justice to let my Lord Keeper know that we were willing very readily to have joined with the Dean, and that the reason of our giving another answer was only to gain time to see if any expedient could be found to prevent coming to the extremity of a visitation. We beg your Lordship would give our duty to my Lord Treasurer and assure him that we are ready either to petition the Queen, the Keeper, or to agree to an arbitration of all differences whatever, or to take any other method his Lordship shall think most proper for us. No one can think but that this life we lead is very uncomfortable to those who have all their life lived in perfect quiet and friendship. But if this man has not secret assurance of support from my Lord Keeper, he must act still upon a worse principle. He must [be] desperate. He may think he has behaved so that he may have lost all hopes of quitting this place upon the terms he would desire to do it. He is now very warm. He has no concern for what the world says of him. He thinks he cannot be dispossessed of that he has, and resolves therefore to disturb and vex to the utmost of his power all he has to do with. God of His mercy deliver this place from him by the means He shall see most proper! No one that was not desperate would venture to stand the things that would be produced against him at a visitation. If Lord Keeper has not privately allowed him to do that he has done, surely he will show his dislike, and let the Dean know how much he is concerned at such violent proceedings.

1712, December 25.—The enclosed will show your Lordship what effect our last paper had with the Dean, and the answer we have made to his proposal. I believe our answer is in the main agreeable to that which my Lord Treasurer thought proper. Last night at five we went to his chamber to choose officers and make our removes. He pretends to keep in with the gout, though we all know he walks as lustily as ever he did. We desired our Chapter book to proceed by, he said he had put that and a great many other books into the hands of the new Chapter clerk, and had taken a bond of a 1,000l. of him for restoring them, and therefore it could not be brought in unless it were by his Chapter clerk. We insisted upon the necessity as well as right of our Chapter book, that surely no dean ever pretended to deny his Chapter the use of their own book. He said he would justify what he had done, that we should not have the book unless we would let it be brought in by his Chapter clerk, or gave our solemn promise to restore it to him, if it was brought. He offered to proceed by the Buttery book after much squabble, we protested against it as irregular, but however for the peace of the College said we would submit to it. We did our business with some intervenient squabbles. We desired to know of him whether Mr. Alsop had not desired him to propose to us a year of grace. After the most intolerable shuffling that ever was known, when he saw we were going to order the Treasurer to stop his allowance he owned Mr. Alsop had desired him to propose it, and he proposed it accordingly. We offered to attest the roll of the election; he would not allow that. We desired to know how it should be attested. He said he would be plain; he designed his own Chapter clerk should transcribe it and sign it *vera copia per me Carolum Perrot Decani et Capituli Ecclesiæ Christi Registrarium.* We told him that was not according to the agreement which we understood had been betwixt us, that we should look on it as a breach of faith. He said he would consider of it; if we find at noon that he does so, we have a roll ready attested by our own Chapter clerk, which we will put up.

Your Lordship sees our case, and I hope my Lord Treasurer will be satisfied that we have done more than any other men in our case would have done to prevent a public hearing; and I must beg leave to say that we have done it purely in obedience to my Lord Treasurer; but after all it will be to no purpose, for I am convinced that it is not only designed by the Dean, but concerted betwixt him and the Lord Keeper, that this should be brought to a public hearing before my Lord Keeper. Young Simon owned, when he first (blabbed?) this, that it was done only to force us to the neccessity of an appeal. Since we do not, I believe the Dean will appeal alone, for he certainly has taken those measures, upon notice he has had from my Lord Keeper, that will not suffer us to come at the Queen, and that therefore if there is an appeal it must be to Lord Keeper only. But surely, my Lord, we are in the hardest case that ever poor men were, who, as my brother South says of himself in another case, have our hands tied behind us with a strong cord whilst a knave buffets us. But if it must come before Lord Keeper we had rather it should come before him as a judge than as a referee. He himself has declared he will not accept of it as a referee, and we are glad of it, we shall have more restraint on him when the hearing is public. The cause shall be as well pleaded and attended as ever cause was, and such a heap of scandal shall be produced, that if his Lordship will justify his Privy Councillor's doings he shall run the hazard of his own credit by it. But should the Dean appeal, as I believe he will, to my Lord Keeper, we are not then without remedy if we may use it. We cannot refuse to appear before the Lord Keeper, but we may at the same time lodge a petition for redress of our own grievances with the Queen, and should we in that case be still forbid attempting to come at the Queen it will be in effect to require us *praebere jugulum*. And whatever Dr. Gastrell, Dr. Smalridge, and I may do, I believe the other five will not think themselves bound to submit to our measures. What can we expect from Lord Keeper, who could use me so hardly as to receive a paper so entirely false against me, and without giving me the least notice of it, to communicate it to ——? What can such a poor fellow as I expect, when his Lordship to support this man should betray to him the letters which he has had from —— himself? Can it be advisable to submit to him as a referee? If he acts as a judge, what he does must be in the face of the whole world, and at the worst there will be an appeal to a higher power. Our case is very deplorable, we can see no end of it in the way we are at present; we must not use the proper method, nor is any other way of relief proposed to us. But should Lord Keeper have sole cognisance of this affair as Visitor, that will by no means end this quarrel. Lord Keeper as Visitor cannot give away the private right of the poor man to be our Chapter clerk. We have as good advice as can be had that the man has a right which Dean and Canons together cannot take from him, that at the last it must be tried in Westminster Hall, and if lost there, in the House of Lords. Nor can Lord Keeper, though he should declare as Visitor that the Dean has power to put out this man, ever oblige us to act with another. We are not under any obligation to have a Chapter clerk, he is not an officer appointed by our Chapter. Lord Keeper as Visitor may *jus dicere*, but he cannot *jus dare*. He may interpret the present clauses in our charter, but he cannot add any new ones to it. The Queen only can give us a new charter. But what is this man we have, that he must use all the world with that insolence he does, and yet no one in power will shew the least discountenance to him?

I wish your Lordship a merry Christmas, it is the most melancholy one I ever knew. I thought to have been in town at the beginning of the next week, but I believe now it will be the end before I shall be there.

Postscript. The Dean put up the roll as he said he would, signed by his Chapter clerk. When we went up into the hall, we stopped and made our servants nail up another roll, subscribed *Ita testor ex fide digna venerabilium virorum J. Hammond, &c., canonicorum nunc praesentium J. Brooks Registrarius.* The Dean durst not stand the odium of not choosing officers, but he now declares he will act in no other matter without his own Chapter clerk. As though he could act without a Chapter in business of greatest moment to the College, the choosing the officers and making the removes, [yet] might not, with much more reason to do it, in affairs of much less concern to us. He was such a cripple last night that he hopped upon one leg, and was led by his servant from the fireside to the bottom of his bed. To-day he walked down to dinner, and has company to dine with him and to sit with him in the evening.

His whole aim has been to force us to appeal first. He said to us last night, "If you are grieved, why do not you bring things to a trial."

1712, December 27.—I have written to you of late in pretty much haste and confusion ; I am afraid what I wrote has had some resemblance to the state of my mind. We have had no answer from our tyrant to our last paper, but I think we have brought it to that pass, that matters must be accommodated in the way my Lord Treasurer desires they should, if his Lordship can prevail in one point with my Lord Keeper. The want of his money will certainly put the Dean upon taking some method for a speedy decision. There is now lying in the Treasurer's hands above 1,000l. to be divided, and we expect as much more in a little time. The Dean thought such a sum would either oblige the old Canons, or those who wanted money, to submit to his Chapter clerk, that they might get their money, or force them to appeal. Upon this prospect he ventured on that stroke, and all his measures of late seem to have been to force us to appeal. He finds nothing will do. We shall neither comply nor appeal. Now we begin to hear loud complaints of his own want of money, he has no way to get it but by an arbitration or an appeal. If my Lord Keeper could be persuaded not to receive an appeal if it is tendered to him, but to tell him he would have nothing to do in it, and refer him to the Queen, the Dean must come in to an arbitration. The Dean will be as much afraid of going to the Queen as we are of going to Lord Keeper. If my Lord Treasurer could prevail with my Lord Keeper in this point, our matters must certainly be determined in the way my Lord Treasurer thinks most proper, and there is this ground for expecting this from my Lord Keeper, that his Lordship declared to my brother Gastrell, the Dean of Carlisle, and me, that he would sooner quit the seals than come to visit us. And he told my brother Gasse the day before he last left the town that he should look on it as the great misfortune of his life to come amongst us upon a visitation.

We go on very slowly in our audit, the Dean told brother Gasse to-day roundly that he would give him as much trouble as he could. He starts impertinent objections upon the most common things, he has been convinced hitherto that he has been in the wrong in every thing, and that his malice has only betrayed him to expose his ignorance. It would be tedious to trouble your Lordship with particulars of such trifles. Our broils have obliged me to defer my own journey for a few days, but I shall be there God willing by Saturday next.

1712, December 29.—We are now at a stop in our audit; the Dean had tried several methods to oblige us to break off, we were resolved to bear every thing, and that the step should not come from us. When we had this morning gone through the first quarter of the disbursements, he declared he would not proceed further till his claims were stated and the money actually paid to him. We desired that might be no stop, we told him we were ready to refer it when he pleased. He said he would be paid all before he proceeded. He fell on a sudden into a violent passion; he hopped up to Dr. Gastrell from whom he had not had the least provocation; he pushed him with great violence several times, and cried "Get out of my house, you pitiful fellow." We all expected he would have struck him, it was plain he had much ado to forbear it. I never yet saw any man so much under the power of rage, his face looked black and every joint about him trembled. I was in the bow window at the further end of the room. Dr. Burton and Dr. Potter, who were nearest, ran in between the Dean and Dr. Gastrell, and Dr. Potter begged the Dean to sit down again. As he was sitting down, he held up his cane and shook it at Dr. Gastrell, and cried, "Dare to give me any indecent language in my own house." This whole storm proceeded from three words. Dr. Gastrell had said in answer to very provoking language, "Mr. Dean, do not use me so, you know that *I know you*." When he was sat down again he fell into bitter language, and at last turned from Dr. Gastrell to me. I had not said one word, nor did I return one word, I only made him a low bow. At last I came up to him, and only said "Mr. Dean, the two persons you now treat so have done you services, and considerable ones in their time, and they desire to know if you pretend ever to have done them any." He replied, "If you have done me services, you have made amends for it this last year." When he was a little calmer, I offered to proceed with him to examine all the precedents he alleged for his claim. He called for book after book, the two first alleged by him appeared to be directly against him, and he acknowledged before us all that they were so. He would then go no further; upon one point he said there was no instance since the year '60; that he had examined all, and if I could produce an instance he would give up the point. This he said openly before all; I called

for a book and showed him an instance, and pressed him to be as
good as his word. He said he meant there was no instance
among those he had in his paper. All would not do, he would
not proceed. The Treasurer tendered him a note of all allowed to
be due to him, and offered either to pay the money here, if he
would sign the disbursement book, or to order the money to be paid
in town if he would barely sign a receipt for it for so much money
and for such particular sums without saying *in full.* He said he
would be paid all he claimed or the audit should stop ;
his claim should be determined by the proper judge before
he would proceed; that if the audit was stopped that would hasten
the determination. After dinner Dr. Hammond, Dr. Burton,
Dr. Gastrell, Dr. Altham, and I waited on him. Dr. Potter dined
abroad. We made him the same offers we had done in the
morning, and desired him to proceed. He said he would do
nothing till the money was paid him. We could get no other
answer. He thinks he shall force us by this to appeal, but he is
mistaken. We have gone through all the accounts but three-
quarters of the disbursement book. We are resolved to meet
to-morrow morning and to go through with it, and attest every
page with our own hands, that it may appear to be a just account
if the higher powers think fit to examine it. We will then state
the balance and settle the arrears, that the Treasurer may be
able to go on with the public business. We doubt not but the
necessity of the house will justify us in doing this ; if
he thinks it irregular let him complain.

It appears every day that he would, if possibly he could, have
provoked us to be the appellants. He expostulated with us
to-day about the paper we put up in the hall. We told him we
were obliged to it, because he had broken his word with us. He
replied, "If I did that which did not become me, why did not you
complain of me?" We told him we thought the method we had
taken to be easier and more proper. If he cannot force us, as he
shall not, to complain of him, I believe he will himself appeal.

I am sorry your Lordship happens to be now at Wimbledon. In
my last by Sunday's post, I told your Lordship that if my Lord
Keeper can be prevailed on not to accept the appeal, if one is
tendered to him by the Dean, the Dean must submit to an
arbitration, and all our disputes must be decided in the way my
Lord Treasurer thinks most proper. My Lord Keeper may waive
his right in this case without renouncing it. He has said he
would quit the seals rather than visit us. He said lately to
Dr. Gastrell that he should think it the great misfortune of his
life if he should be sent to visit us. These I think are good
reasons, besides some others much stronger, why his Lordship
may fairly decline receiving an appeal if tendered to him.

1713, June 9.—I heartily thank you for your good news ; you
will have no more trouble this session.

Upon the report here of what Lord Chancellor had said to
Blechingden when he asked him whether he had been to ask

blessing of the new bishop, White, the Censor, and some others threw up their caps in the quadrangle and huzza'd to a new dean. Some of the present Dean's friends got together upon it; much bickering there was, but no blows. At present the College is divided into two parties, the Dean that is wished for has the most valuable party on all other accounts as well as on the majority, but woe to the poor wretches that declared themselves too soon, if the old Dean returns again.

The Vice-Chancellor is disposed to deal with Aldrich with all the tenderness that can be without leaving a precedent against their own jurisdiction. Any submission I believe will be accepted, but I have some reason to suspect he is ordered not so much as to appear before the Vice-Chancellor if summoned, but he is to run the hazard of expulsion, and that his expulsion is to be made a pretence for giving him some preferment. I have slept so soundly since I have been at home that my eyes are yet scarce open. I will be longer by the next post.

1713, June 11.—I hope your late success in the Lords' house is a pledge to you of success in everything else, and that all other difficulties, as well as those of the session, will at last be surmounted.

I find upon my return that the Lord Chancellor's interest runs as low in the county as it does in the university. The design to have set up Sim for the county was pushed farther than ever I thought it had been. We were informed of it by Mr. Cole, of Euston, who is our tenant; he says Lord Abingdon was so alarmed that he spent money to oppose it; his Lordship was certainly then in earnest. There was a meeting of the gentlemen at which Cole was to take measures to oppose it. Clarke would have desisted, but continues at the desire of the gentlemen that there may not be any opportunity for setting up Sim. That which surprised me most was that Sir Robert Jenkinson was more eager than any other against. I thought he had been upon very good terms with the family, but he came to Cole and told him he would never join his hand with that fellow, meaning Sim, and asked Cole if he would stand by him if there should be occasion, which Cole very readily engaged to do. They say it will go very hard too at Wallingford; I believe they must have recourse at last to Cornwall. But I am afraid they will require the father to pay for his own election there, which he has not yet done, before they choose the son.

We shall have two Doctors of our House this act, honest Periam goes out as well as his brother Terry, but neither of them can proceed unless our Dean comes down, and we hear nothing of him. We cannot hold a Chapter to give them their degrees in the House. We shall have more proceeders in divinity than we expected. One who is chaplain to the Bishop of St. David's, of Trinity, takes his degree of doctor, and obliges, by doing so, five who are his seniors to take their degrees too. We have not yet any proceeder in law or physic.

Our Dean has now but one Head here who entertains any correspondence with him; it is [Robert] Shippen of Brasenose, one fit for his purpose, but who certainly proposes to serve himself by the Dean. I suppose his aims are at somewhat from the Court by the Dean's recommendation. The Dean to engage him lately introduced his brother, who is one of the Inquisitors, to the Lord Chancellor's acquaintance.

1713, June 12.—I hear from London, though not from your Lordship, that warrants are passing for making our villain Bishop of Rochester and Dean of Westminster. You may think I give him a hard word, but I am persuaded he is the greatest either in or out of a gown in the three kingdoms, except the person that supports him. The world is no stranger to both their characters, but some late affairs have given us occasion to collect memoirs of both their lives, and they shall, God willing, be better known to the world than they yet are, as much as it is thought they may be now known. One of them passed the first years of business in the neighbourhood of this place; what has passed lately has given occasion to revive many things which were then done for which even necessity cannot be an excuse. You must allow me to say that nothing that has been done since your father's ministry has struck such a damp upon the hearts of all that have honour or honesty, as this promotion. All of any weight here, it is true that I tell you, wondered that such a one should be permitted so long to act as he did here, but they lift up their hands to see him preferred for it. I perceive this was determined before I left the town, but your father was pleased to keep it a secret from me when I took my leave of him. I desire your Lordship would be so kind as to let me know for what part of my behaviour, since I had the honour to belong to your father, I have deserved this. We shall be at quiet however, though we might have been so, had your father pleased, at a much less expense. We shall now have leisure to study the art of being troublesome, in order to be preferred.

Postscript. I beg your Lordship would, with my duty, mention Mrs. Hutton to your father. She is clamorous and very troublesome to me for her money.

1713, June 13. Christ Church.—Your Lordship will perceive by my last that I had been informed how the vacancies will be filled. The Speaker informed me, and was surprised as much as I was, after what he had heard, at the disposition. But your Lordship does not tell me what occasioned the change of those measures which I thought had been resolved on when I left the town. I beg your pardon, if I impertinently press for that I am not to know. It is lucky for the fellow that he has got off; that proud soul would have been humbled had he stayed here longer; he is talked of no otherwise in this place than as a common rogue. Now he is going, they, who have been tampered with every day own some new roguery he would have drawn them into. If your father had occasion to forge plots to support his ministry, this gentleman would have served the government much better as a solicitor to succeed honest Aaron Smith than as a bishop. I wish my Lord Treasurer do not find those most concerned at this promotion who had the truest respect for him. Where will you find Bishops to consecrate him? I am sure not one on the whole bench would do it, if they did not incur a *premunire* in case they should refuse when commanded. It is a brave fellow that can carry his point, when it is certainly true that there is not one person that he leaves, or that he goes to, that does not hate him; but I pity this poor Church. Had this man been kept out of power, and we had lived to see a new archbishop, there was a certain prospect of peace amongst ourselves and of our uniting to do business proper for our calling. All hopes of that are over, now he who certainly will obstruct it is put into a capacity of doing it.

I am not surprised at that I hear of Francis Annesley. I told your Lordship my thoughts when I parted with you. It belongs to others to enquire into the reason of his conduct. Lord Chancellor can certainly influence him, if he would.

The Speaker tells me he has talked with Lord A. and hopes he has made him easy. I hope you will still go through with the Commerce bill. It would be a slur on the Peace to drop it, and I am afraid it would give the adversary some advantage in the elections.

Since our fellow has got his point I hope his instruments will be soon dispatched, or else we shall have what we never had yet, a public act, without a Dean of Christ Church. I am certain this gentleman with all his assurance will not appear there; he had better too not come down here again for money, unless he acts with our Chapter clerk, and renounces his impudent claims; we will seal no leases, nor pay any money. And if he comes, he shall have a peal in the Chapter House as well as the steeple, at parting, such as he never had yet, and shall be better attended out of town when he leaves us than he was into town when he came to us.

1718, June 14. Christ Church.—I have sent away the letter I had written to your Lordship, but I have just received notice that Dr. Bridges solicits very earnestly for the canonry, and that his friends say openly he designs to hold it *in commendam*. This looks like our Dean's project, who has many views on it. That which I had the honour to hear from my Lord Treasurer when I took leave of him gives me hopes that Dr. Bridges cannot succeed, but I beg leave to furnish your Lordship with an argument against any importunity. This College cannot subsist if the canonries are to be made sinecures, and are not supplied with those who are able and willing too to take their turns in bearing the offices; and the discharge of the offices here requires somewhat more than bare attendance, which alone may · be sufficient in other cathedrals. We have struggled many years with great inconveniences, by reason those who ought to have borne the offices were disabled from doing it by it (*sic.*) No one will answer the duty more to the satisfaction of all concerned than the person my Lord Treasurer was pleased of himself to mention; he is young too and may serve the College for many years, without any inconvenience to himself. And our new Dean will not be able to go through the business without a proper Sub-dean to assist him and to relieve him too upon occasion. I beg your Lordship would represent this with my humble duty to my Lord Treasurer; but your Lordship or my Lord Treasurer will hear more of this from the Dean of Carlisle [Smalridge] himself.

1713, June 15. Christ Church.—Last night the Dean of Carlisle received from the Dean of Christ Church a general proxy; it was said to be sealed such a day and delivered in the presence of; but there was neither seal nor witness to it. The Dean of Carlisle returns it to him to-day. He served Dr. Altham the same trick at Christmas 1711, in hopes to have ensnared him to act by a proxy that was not valid. To-morrow we hear he is to be installed Dean of Westminster, and whether after that installation he can act and sign a proxy as Dean of Christ Church we are not lawyers enough to know. I am sure if he can, it is scandalous that he should, and that he should seal a great many leases which lie ready for him at Westminster on Wednesday as Dean, whilst in the mean time all his appointments here, which are payable weekly with us, go on to him; but his unreasonable profit will be the least damage. Should he send a proper proxy, several of my brethren doubt whether it will be good if signed after he is installed at Westminster. I am afraid we shall not get a sufficient number to act by it; in the mean time all our business is at a stand; no degrees granted; and our Doctors who should appear this act cannot proceed, or if they should be able to go out, they will lose their seniority. I hope my Lord Treasurer will have so much compassion on us as not to oblige us to wait for a vacancy till this man's *desecration* is over, but will require him to make a resignation of this deanery upon his instalment into the other, and will be pleased to order the new Dean's patent to be despatched with all possible haste. We have suffered enough already, it will be hard if upon so solemn an act we should be in confusion, and without power to relieve ourselves. Were our new Dean now in possession we shall never be able so soon to remedy our late evils as to appear with the advantage we used to do on these occasions.

1713, June 18.—What I wrote to your Lordship was grounded on what I had heard from my Lord Treasurer and from your Lordship too when I parted with you. If your Lordship has changed your opinion since I had no means to know it. Had I known it I should not have vented my thoughts so frankly to you. I shall not presume to use the same freedom again. Had we not been under restraint from your father's command, we could have made ourselves easy by that which would have stopped this man's promotion; a plain representation to the

Queen of his behaviour since he has been here. He is turbulent indeed, but he, like other cowards, never is so but when he foresees he can be so with impunity, and is sure of support from some and permission from others. But I shall say no more of him; but the manner in which he is promoted is still harder upon us than any thing that has yet happened. It belongs to others to consider of the consequence of the precedent of allowing the same man to enjoy together two of the best deaneries in England; but the end, that is said to be aimed at in removing him, will be so far from being attained that our condition will be worse than it was before he was preferred, and the trouble to those above greater, and that every thing is likely to be brought on by his promotion which was designed to have been prevented by it. I believe your Lordship will soon see that it was not without reason that we hoped he would have been obliged to resign this deanery, and to have renounced his extravagant claims before he was installed at Westminster. He has now possession of both deaneries, and I have good ground to believe that he will defer his confirmation and keep both his deaneries unless we will allow his claims, which we never shall do. He will now insist upon his terms, and how anyone can oblige him to quit I know not. You may think this very extravagant. It would be so in any other but in him; but should he be in haste to be in the Lords House, yet he will either commence a suit against us in Chancery on account of his claims, or appeal to the Lord Chancellor as Visitor. In the first case we have lawsuits entailed upon us, in the last we are unanimously resolved, upon any summons from the Chancellor, without any more delay to throw ourselves at the Queen's feet.

My Lord Chancellor is not our Visitor, but were he Visitor, yet as Visitor he has no power, only to gratify the insolence of one man, for no more than 25l., to alter the disposition of the revenue of the College, which has obtained from our very foundation, and to allot to him that which has always been applied to the public use of the society. The Queen only can do this, who is Founder as well as Visitor, and before her I foresee it will come at last. We shall come too late, but however we shall have an opportunity of telling our tale, and of laying before her Majesty all the insolence, the claim and exercise of arbitrary power, the frauds, the imprecations, the curses, the oaths, and the perjuries of this man. I beg your Lordship's pardon for troubling you with our wretched affairs, but you shall hear no more of them; they must now take their fate whatever it be.

I am sorry for the account I had last night of the quarrels that are likely to be in both Houses about the Commerce bill. This party has been forming ever since Christmas, I then or soon after gave your father notice of it. More than one of those, for whom he has shown so much complaisance, have been at the bottom of it, and [if] some who pretend to be greater friends to your father dealt as honourably by him as the Speaker has done, your father had not had this trouble. But these matters are out of my sphere.

1713, June 21.—Tom Rowney gave me an account of what passed on Thursday. I was in hopes your Lordship would have written on Friday, though it was too late to write on Thursday night. There is no account yet of it in this place, but what I had from Tom on Thursday night. It was very unexpected, I did not apprehend it could have gone so in that quarter. I thought no intriguing could have brought about a majority there. Surely there was either some treachery or at least neglect or carelessness in some of your own friends. I am heartily concerned for the difficulties your father has to struggle with, and the returns that are made to him, as well as for the public. It is to no purpose to enquire into the causes of what is passed, or to guess at the consequences. They are obvious enough. One should prevent them as far as one could. If you have a mind not quite to break with these men, but are willing if it could be done, to piece again with them, the Speaker is the only man who has credit enough with both sides to be able to attempt a reconciliation. If the breach is not to be made up, it will be uneasy to him, I know, to act differently from a great many of his old friends, much more in opposition to them; but yet he thinks their opposition in this point so unreasonable and groundless that he might I believe be brought to it, and you ought at this time to secure him; for whilst you have him, you are sure of a standing body of the church and gentry with you. But you will forgive me for talking of these things as I do in the dark, when I am ignorant of the situation of affairs with you. It is well, however, that this has happened at the close of the last session. Had such a division been in the beginning of a Parliament, all in it had been listed probably for the whole Parliament. It is to be hoped now that this new party may not have time enough to take a deep root, and that in a new Parliament there may not only be many new members, but that many old ones may come up to it with new dispositions. I wish, however, that such emergencies may be an admonition to your father to make some provision at least for himself and for you.

1713, June 23.—We were not uneasy without reason. We know what my Lord Chancellor since his friend's instalment at Westminster has threatened to do to us, by his own power, if we should refuse to comply with any of his friend's demands at parting; but we hoped his Lordship had been convinced by late experience that we are not to be bullied.

Your Lordship says you believe, if the Dean had not had Westminster, he would have insisted to have held Christ Church *in commendam* and have been supported in it by the Lord Chancellor. If he would not have taken Rochester without Christ Church what hurt would it have been if he had continued at Christ Church without Rochester? We were willing to bear him, and we were sure his credit was such here that he never could have lived again in this place. But my Lord Chancellor would have supported him in it! Does my Lord Chancellor's place entitle him to recommend to the Queen on these occasions?

Is he first minister? Is he to give the law to, or to take it from, your father? Or is he so very useful and necessary, that he may on that account insist on what he pleases? But I shall say no more; your father alone is concerned in this. We heard he was introduced by the Bishop of Norwich to the Archbishop and received very graciously. As we were mentioning this at table, brother Potter smiled and said he knew the Dean had kept a constant correspondence with the Bishop of Norwich both by visits and letters. Brother Gastrell seemed surprised and said he was sure the Dean could not hope to bring over the Bishop of Norwich to his opinions. Potter replied, smiling, "No, that is certain, but it is as I tell you."

I am very glad to find by your last that you are so easy in town after Thursday's debate. I hope you, who are the best judges, do not fear those consequences from the issue of it which we did here. Some of Sir Th. Hanmer's topics might have been urged betwixt man and man in private, but were surely very improper for the House. I am very glad honest Tom Rowney was with your Lordship.

We had to-day the Dean's parting legacy, and such as was suitable to all the blessings we have had from him since he has been here. Mr. Periam takes his doctor's degree this Act, does all exercises, bears all the extraordinary charges of it, and only begs of the Convocation to be dispensed with for a few terms. The Dean's creatures had entered into a combination to deny this gentleman's letter in Convocation. They had sworn secrecy to each other, and obliged all that they had got into the design both at home and in other colleges to the same. They hoped to have carried it by surprise, few, when no opposition is feared, attending Convocations. I need not tell your Lordship Mr. Periam's character to convince you of the malice of this design. A day or two ago, a false brother, to make court I suppose to the successor, betrayed them, and gave us notice of the design. We had scarce time to send round to our friends to appear. The enemy, though detected, yet persisted, and demanded a scrutiny this morning in Convocation, but we carried our point and the Proctor pronounced, *placet longe majori parti hujus convocationis.* This Christian attempt, which is to prepare him I suppose for the imposition of the bishop's hands, was not only with a design to have put an indignity upon this honest man, but to have fomented a party that should have been under his direction here when he is gone; but it is quashed.

On Friday last the Lord Chancellor's order for dissolving his injunction was read in court, and Aldrich summoned to appear *ad videndum ulteriorem processum.* Aldrich has since sent to the Vice-Chancellor to offer to make any submission he pleases. The Vice-Chancellor said he knew not but he might be prevailed with to change his mind before the next court day, and therefore appointed him to come to him on Thursday next in the evening. The next court day is on Friday. The Vice-Chancellor was so kind upon this as to send to me, to know if I had any demands on Mr. Aldrich. I thanked him, but said I should not think it worth my while to give him any trouble about my private concern, if he was satisfied as to the interest of the university. My Lord Chancellor may see that the university that (*sic*) dare proceed, though his Lordship since his sentence was pleased to tell the Speaker that Aldrich should be torn in pieces before he should submit, and that the university should not touch a hair of his head.

We have yet no news of our Governor, and yet letters by last post said the consecration was to be next Sunday. If that be so, I suppose we shall hear no more of him, unless he comes to-night.

What wretched stuff are the Cambridge verses!

Postscript. Mr. Periam's grace, I hear, when the Convocation was over, was denied in the congregation. But that is but impotent malice; any one regent can deny a grace thrice, but then he must [show] a reason to be approved by congregation, or the grace passes.

1713, June 25.—I heartily bless God and rejoice with your Lordship that your late division is likely to have no worse consequences. The Speaker was so kind as to write me a long letter to put me out of pain. It is hard that these gentlemen's understandings cannot be opened till the whole nation smarts for their mistake.

The Vice-Chancellor had a letter last night from G[eorge] Clarke by the Duke of Ormond's order to desire that the proceedings against Aldrich might not be *rigorous*. No such were ever intended unless he had been obstinate, but the High Chancellor upon notice of Aldrich's citation immediately begged our Chancellor to interpose in the poor wretch's behalf. No punishment of that fellow could give me that satisfaction as I have to see so great a man so much concerned to prevent his punishment. This would be thought a plain confession that he had been at the bottom of that business, if we wanted Aldrich's own confession, but we have it now in some measure, and I believe we shall have more of it. The person employed by him to the Vice-Chancellor said that Mr. Aldrich alleged in his own excuse that he was unwilling to have come into Chancery, but that the *Lord Chancellor* pulled him in, and would have the cause in his own court; but I believe he wishes now it had never been there. But this is not the only thing he has been fond of that perhaps in time he may be weary of. He may possibly in a little time more wish he had never had to do with the promoter of the cause, as well as the cause itself.

I hear the war is begun already at Westminster about the clerk of St. Margaret's. This is somewhat sooner I confess than even I could have expected it.

Postscript. We are told that just after the Dean's instalment at Westminster there was a terrible storm; the moment he got out of his coach here yesterday, the clouds gathered, and there was immediately as great a storm as I ever knew of, thunder, lightning and rain for an hour together.

> When shall we "nine" meet again
> In thunder, lightning and in rain.

The more thoroughly the nation is convinced of their damage by the loss of the Commerce bill, the more your father's interest will be established.

Last night came another about Aldrich in the Duke of Ormond's own hand, to desire their proceedings might not be severe, and that before they executed any sentence they would acquaint him with the method they had taken, and that he hoped they would show their *civility to my Lord Chancellor*, by avoiding any severity to Mr. Aldrich. How comes *lenity* to *Aldrich* to be an instance of *civility* to the *Chancellor*; was ever so great a man in such an agony about so sorry a wretch? This is palpable.

The Dean this morning told Dr. Smalridge that he desired to make void a chaplain's and a chorister's place, and to fill them before he left us. This is very unreasonable that he should be allowed to turn out and put in here, when he has now several vacancies which he is to dispose of at Westminster. Two such deaneries at one time is very great indulgence to him, and no little hardship on us.

1718, June 28. Christ Church.—I shall give your Lordship a short account of what has passed at parting. The Lord elect came hither on Wednesday; his first care was to convince us why he had desired to be indulged in that scandalous practice of holding two deaneries together. In equity he had right to no more than the profits of half a year of the meadow, but by the letter of the law he might claim all his share of the grass, as soon as it is severed from the ground, which is at least four-fifths of the yearly profit. He was afraid lest all the grass should not be cut down before his consecration; he spent an afternoon in the meadow, and observed they had begun to cut very late. He was told the orders were not to begin either sooner or later one day than the grass was fit to be cut. He said perhaps such orders might have been given by the Sub-dean, but he believed not by the other Canons. He was told the orders were given by all the Canons in the place. He observed very few hands were employed. He was told, more were employed now than ever had been in any former year. He bargained with the mowers to give them two shillings to drink, if they would promise him not to leave that work for any other till all the grass was cut down, so solicitous is he to make the utmost use of the indulgence allowed him to defraud his successor. When it began to rain last night, he observed it was very fortunate the rain should fall at that time, because the mowers could not have gone on with their work on Sunday, if it had been fair. On Friday he met us in Chapter, and desired to know what we designed to do in relation to two things; his claims of money, and the fines which had been paid in, but not divided because the leases had not been sealed. He desired our answer the next day. We met again in Chapter on Saturday, the Sub-dean gave our answer; that we were willing the Treasurer should pay him upon every style of payment whatever had been paid to any one of his predecessors; that we were willing he should pay this immediately, upon the Dean's giving such a receipt as the Dean himself had declared under his hand he had once proposed to give. He said the answer was general and he desired a particular answer whether we would pay his claims or not. I told him he ought [not] to be displeased who from his coming hither had never vouchsafed to give us any other answers. He said that might have been formerly, but now he was ready to give a particular direct answer to any thing we desired. We adhered to our answer and would give no other; he asked if we would refer our claims; that he was ready to give such a receipt as we desired if we would subscribe to it that we agreed to refer the money in dispute. We told him we should give no other answer than we had already. He said he looked on the share of the fines as his due, and should not easily part with them. We said the Canons had no interest in that; we should only have the same share, whoever had the Dean's share; that it was not our business to decide betwixt him and his successor. He said he did not expect any sealed in his successor's time, nor did he pretend to set any new fines, but that the leases for those already paid might be sealed before he left us. That he should not be confirmed at soonest before next Saturday, and he could defer it. We asked him if his predecessor at Carlisle had ever received any profits at Carlisle after he had been installed at Wells, though he did not quit Carlisle till some time after his instalment at Wells. He said the resignation of Carlisle was dated from his instalment at Wells. He told us he insisted upon sealing the leases; we said when any leases were brought regularly before us we should do what was proper, but that we insisted to have all our books and papers delivered up to us before we would seal any lease. He said he could not stay to seal the leases, but that the man he had named Chapter clerk should deliver up all the books, and give us no further trouble; that he would leave a general proxy; that we might if we pleased employ our own Chapter clerk again if we would seal the leases before his confirmation, and he desired to meet us again at five o'clock. We told him we could not meet then; he desired to have our answer by the Sub-dean, and left us. We were resolved to stick to our point, but his easy successor thinking it would be a reflection on himself, as though he had prevailed with us to do it, because he alone had interest in it, desired we would seal the leases, if all other points were given up to us. After much entreaty, we made the Sub-dean our plenipotentiary to agree to what he would, but upon the following conditions, that all powers and books should be immediately given up to us, by himself and his pretended Chapter clerk; that any extracts taken out by either of them should be given up, upon such a solemn assurance as both would be ready to confirm by their oath; that he should be told that we should employ

Mr. Brooks the Chapter clerk to draw up these leases only; and that he should act as such and be owned as such without any pretence of restoring him by the person who had his proxy; that the Dean should solemnly renounce every claim he had made of any farthing beyond what we had offered to pay him; and that for the money which we paid he should sign every sum in the public disbursement book with his own hand. If he agreed to these things, at the request of the Sub-dean, we might perhaps seal the leases, if they could conveniently be sealed before his confirmation, but that we gave him notice he must expect no share of the copyhold fines which were paid, because we could not now conveniently hold our courts. If he did not like these terms he might defer his confirmation, and say his points could be decided by a visitation. The Sub-dean went to him betwixt three and four and told him he believed he could prevail with his brethren to seal the leases upon the terms I have mentioned. He immediately agreed to all, but signing the books with his own hand; he said that would be mean, and desired he might do it by proxy. He desired too he might meet us again. Our plenipotentiary reported what was offered to us, we insisted that he should sign with his own hand the public book for every particular sum. We said it was our duty, when called, to meet him in Chapter, but that he had not deserved so well of us that we should meet him only to hear his compliments. When our plenipotentiary returned to the place of treaty, he found other company there. At nine at night his Lordship elect told our plenipotentiary he would come to his lodgings. He came and desired again to be excused from signing the books; he was told that was insisted on as the chief preliminary. He said if he could [not] be excused he was ready to do it, but that it was late and he had left company at his own house, and desired therefore that he might do it to-day. Our plenipotentiary told him it would not be proper for him to do such work upon a Sunday, who was to be consecrated a bishop the next Sunday. Upon that the books were called for, his Lordship elect made a solemn disclaim before witness of all the claims he had ever advanced, and then signed our books and cried several times as he was signing, "You have gained your point." He was asked if it had been worth his while to make the disturbance he had done about that which, if it could have been gained, would not have amounted, according to the way of the payment we should have insisted on, to above 8l., according to his own reckoning not to above 25l. He said the point was of more importance than the money. He promised, when he had done signing, to deliver every thing else this evening, and upon oath if we desired it—but upon experience we know that to be as weak a security as his word—and to refer himself entirely to our honour, which is more than we should do to his after his confirmation. Thus has this man for the sake of his money given up every point for which he had raised such a flame in the world, and which he has so often called God to witness he would never quit, unless he was compelled to it by Westminster Hall or our Visitor. This would afford many reflections; I shall make but one, that we have shown your father how he might have brought him to terms, if he had been pleased to do it, though I doubt not but he knew it well enough, if other reasons had not intervened. Can you have patience to read the detail of this important negotiation? Our Governor leaves us to-morrow at four in the morning to prevent being saluted with a peal at parting.

We hope our new Dean [Smalridge]'s patent will have such dispatch that he may be in possession if it be possible before the Act, both for the sake of business and of authority too at such a time. It would be very inconvenient if he should be obliged to come up to wait on the Queen.

Endorsed by Lord Harley : " An account of what Dr. Atterbury did when he left the College."

1713, June 30. Christ Church.—I have nothing to tell you, but that you are not likely to be troubled with such long letters for the future as you have for two years past. We shall have some quiet ourselves and allow a little to our friends; we breathe another sort of air than we did. Our climate is in the state the poets would suppose any part of the world upon Alecto's return to her native region, after she had been permitted to be abroad for some time.

We have a report that the poor Bishop of London lies past all hopes of recovery. I will lay your Lordship a bottle of burgundy that our fellow puts in for a translation before his consecration.

My diocesan the Bishop of Chester is here, he will be with me I suppose to-morrow. He will let me I suppose into the secret of the Trade bill. I shall know from him all your faults; I think he shows himself to be disinterested, since he can leave the town when there is likely to be such a vacancy in the hierarchy. It is more than the Lord elect of Rochester would have done.

I hope your Lordship left all well at Leather Lake.

Our Act begins on Friday se'nnight. I hope the patent for the new Dean will be here so soon that he may be installed before the Act is opened. We must, I am afraid, defer the solemnity that usually attends the installation to another time, but this only to yourself or your father. The present state of our business, and the season of the Act, will oblige us to install him the day after we receive the patent, and not to wait for ceremony.

Postscript. We have had one discovery already of our departed Governor. He was actually so mad as to have had a design to claim the sole propriety of the copyholds of the College. He had not only commanded Brooks to draw a patent for a game keeper in our manor of Binsey in the name of the Dean alone. And one reason why he pretended to turn Brooks out was because he told him he knew not how to draw such a patent. But at Christmas last he sent the bailiff of the College with an instrument under his own hand, and signed with the sign manual, he called it the seal of his office—a little seal that never was used to any thing but testimonials for orders—to give notice to all who belong to the homage within twenty miles of Oxford, in any of our manors, that they were to own no authority but his. When the bailiff returned he took the instrument from him and enjoined him strict silence; the bailiff owned this to us to-day. All this pretence was grounded only on this, that the steward brings the copies to be signed by the Dean, and this custom was only of thirty years' standing, and never practised by any steward but Brooks, who did it for the security of the College, that he never granted any copies but what the Dean and Chapter knew of.

1713, July 5. Christ Church.—Our late Governor could have no reason to think we designed him ill language but his own consciousness that he deserved it. Had he been paid as he demanded from the date of his patent all his claims—according to the custom from our foundation, which is to pay in proportion to the number of weeks any one is in possession—would have amounted only to 7*l.* 8*s.* 0*d.*; but he afterwards said he could, if he pleased, advance his claims, and demand all profits from the day of his predecessor's death. Upon that foot his claims would have amounted to about 830*l.*, not 500*l.*; but that would not have affected us only, but every other Cathedral in England of Henry VIII.'s foundation, who are under the same methods of payment that we are. He ought to be more thankful for 174*l.* which we have given him at going off, in fines, of which he would not have had one farthing if his successor, who only was to have the advantage, had not been the intercessor for him, and yet though his successor had got this money for him, and had bought his goods of him to a considerable value, he left orders with the housekeeper to demand to be paid for a little movable reading desk and a step in his study, neither of them worth sixpence, which he had forgot to insert into the catalogue of the goods agreed for. He had ordered her too to take off all the locks on the doors unless his successor would pay [for] them, though all, within two as I take it, belong to the House and have been paid for by the College; and he went himself to my Lord Abingdon, as he is Justice in Eyre, to insist that of the two bucks which her Majesty is usually pleased to give to the Dean of Christ Church he might have one, because he had continued Dean for one moiety of the year, though certainly he who is Dean at the season when her Majesty's favour is bestowed has the fairest title to it. It is a pity but his preferment were suited to his soul.

Lord Chancellor has not yet digested all the wrath he had conceived against the university. We are told from hands we can depend on, that lately in court, upon some mention by Whitlock of laying men by the heels, his Lordship in a fury cried, "Sir William, I know not whom you mean, but if you mean your client the Vice-Chancellor, there is no man in England whom I would sooner lay by the heels." His Lordship best understands the prudence of such language from such a bench. It will not, I am afraid, retrieve the lost game here.

J. Keill says your Lordship and my Lord Dupplin design to honour us with your company at the Act. Upon this notice, I

have put off a little journey I had designed at that time, and will
certainly be here. I hope you will give me notice when I may
expect you. To the credit of the university the proctors cannot
meet with any one that will be a *terræ filius*. The greatest part
of our guests will be disappointed of the chief part of the entertainment they had hoped for. Our late Dean, who had nominated
the poets of our House last Christmas, has taken care to have due
compliments in the verses to my Lord Chancellor and to himself
too.

I am sorry to hear of my Lord Treasurer's illness, I wish him
soon rid of his troublesome distemper. Brother Gastrell had a
fit last week, voided a little stone, and was immediately well and
continues so.

1718, July 7.—I have enclosed to you the Bishop of Rochester's
evening meditation betwixt his confirmation and his consecration.
He had received during the year and three quarters he was Dean
here 1,500*l.*; by the largest computation he never spent in this
place 200*l.* He must have carried off clear 1,300*l.* The bill for
painting which was sent with the enclosed amounted to 3*l.* 5*s.* 8*d.*
All the wainscot he so much boasts to have put up never came
to 5*l.* No Dean or Canon ever yet had sixpence allowed them by
the College on account of painting. The person whom, as presuming
him to be his successor, he would have this bill paid by, this very
day paid a bill of 14*l.* for painting in his Canon's house, yet this
poor Bishop could have leisure from his prayers on Saturday
night to write his letter to desire he might be eased of so
unreasonable a charge. Pray return it to me safely, for I design
to lay it up in the archives of the College, with proper notes upon
it for the information of posterity. Had there been a *terræ filius*,
it should certainly have been published in the Theatre. The locks
which he mentions are stolen by him directly; we can prove
them to have belonged to the College.

We have had very seasonable rain this last week, above a quarter
of the meadow, in the part where the best grass was, is yet uncut.
We shall not allow my Lord of Rochester one blade of it. I hope
we shall have a law suit about it.

Postscript. If this fellow were Archbishop of Toledo, no one
would have his preferment to have his soul with it. He ought to
belong to no one but the Duke of Marlborough.

1718, July 9.—The Dean of Carlisle and all of us are obliged
to return your Lordship our hearty thanks for your kind concern
for him. It is no worse with him than it was when I first gave
you notice of his misfortune. I hope he is in no danger at all,
and I believe he will not have much trouble with it if he can once
get an instrument that is fit and easy too. I cannot imagine
what end there can be in giving out such a report. Now there is
a vacancy, he is well enough to be installed, if we had a patent
for him. There is one ready in the office to make all the
dispatch that may be as soon as the warrant comes.

I thank your Lordship for the favour of your venison, we shall remember you over it, but not more for it. I will send a piece to your true friend and servant, Mrs. Rowney. Your health, and another's in conjunction with you, will be drunk there upon that occasion.

We had an account from eye witnesses how very liberal our new bishop was at his landing at Paul's of the privileges of his new office. He pulled the officers of the trainband to him, when they were in a hurry and never thought of him, and would make them have his blessing. This is strictly true, and there may be reason for it, for if he gives his blessing only to those who desire it, I am afraid he will have little occasion to exercise that part of his office.

He bade a man before he came down last, who was to pay in a very considerable fine, but had lapsed the time set him, to hasten the payment of it; this was concealed from us. On Tuesday night last came letters from the man to the late Dean and to the Treasurer, to give notice to them that he was ready to pay the money. I own I have malice enough to be pleased with this, and the more because I am sure he will be persuaded that the man came three days too late by concert with us.

1713, July 10.—I am to thank your Lordship for a noble buck which I received this morning, the man said they could not kill another, and so he brought none for Dr. Terry, but he has settled with Dr. Terry when he would have another brought, but it was lucky for Dr. Terry that his buck was not brought now, for the weather has been so bad that the venison has suffered a little in the carriage. It can be owing only to the weather, for the bucks which I had in former years came as sweet as if they had been fresh killed, and I shall spend this immediately. And it has not suffered so much but that I can use most of it, only Mrs. Rowney will be disappointed of drinking Lord Harley's health over his own venison. Tom was with me this morning, and desires me to put you in mind of your father's promise to subscribe five guineas to their Oxford race.

Postscript. I am told Lord Chancellor has quitted Wallingford, and is going to try what he can do at Abingdon for his son.

1713, July 12. Christ Church.—All hitherto in our Act has gone extremely well and without the least disorder. Croft's music was as fine as ever I heard, and will be worth your hearing in town. You will perceive through all the exercise of all sorts all the endeavours that could be to pay respect to your father, and it certainly proceeded from the disposition of the persons themselves who were concerned in them, and was not suggested to them by others. In two copies of verses there was mention of the Lord Chancellor, you will easily guess by whose order.

Lord Leominster and Captain Herbert are in town, they did me the honour of a visit yesterday in the morning. I was obliged to attend in the afternoon the exercise of the inceptor doctors, and could desire his Lordship's company, but they have promised to do me the honour to spend this evening with me.

We have found upon enquiry that those folding doors, on which the Bishop of Rochester would claim so much merit, were actually put up at the charge of the College, and charged and allowed in our bills. The little stools for which he insisted to be paid by Dr. Smalridge, and which are now carried to London, had never been paid for by him, nor were the[y] valued by the carpenter when he appraised the shelves in the study for Dr. Aldrich's executor, as he did lately for the Bishop of Rochester.

He thought himself so sure of his point, to hold the canonry *in commendam*, that he had said to several that, upon his return, having found the *commendam* drawn without the canonry, he had *expostulated* with your father about it, and had *obliged* him to agree to have a new warrant drawn. He has lately too complained how unfortunate he was that the Bishop of Rochester should drop before the Bishop of London.

1718, July 14.—I did not give your Lordship notice of the misfortune of your kindness, with a design to beg more of you.

Our Act is over and without the least disorder ; nothing more to be done, but seeing plays and eating and drinking for a few days more. The music, which was very extraordinary, made our guests tolerably easy without a music speech, or *terræ filius*. Since they have been once dropped, I suppose they will never be revived. The English music was preferred and very deservedly to the Italian, though the last was very fine I believe in its kind. I attended all the exercise, and there was not one single exercise in which the respect that was due was not paid to my Lord Treasurer, in those which will not be printed as well as those which will. The poorest exercise was the Vice-Chancellor's speech at last—pray though take no notice of this—it was honest enough, but it was the meanest I ever heard, but the Theatre at that time was thin, and not many left to hear it that were likely to report it to our prejudice. He should not have trusted to himself.

My Lord Berkeley brought his son hither yesterday, and we have notice of so many noblemen and gentlemen that design to come to us shortly that we are under great difficulties how to provide rooms for them. We are going to finish as fast as we can the third side of Peckwater, though we do it upon credit.

I thank your Lordship for the favour of the accounts you have been pleased to give me, some good must come out of the confusion you mention, though it may be likely to be attended with difficulties ; but were the main point over, I fancy others would be adjusted.

I shall strictly observe your order as to the letter, but how comes that man to be in such strange subjection to the other ? Is he at his expense to make amends for the other's extravagance ? There is somewhat at the bottom more than any one guesses, when the other too can so easily do it out of places which are in his own disposal. No bishop in England has so many and so good temporal places in his gift as the Dean of Westminster.

Better late than never, though the compliment from Lord A. is somewhat unseasonable, when all the mischief has been done that could be.

1713, July 16.—If I go any where this summer to stay for any time, it will be to Bath, but I am not yet resolved on that. Does your Lordship design for Brampton? I hope you will be prevented, by somewhat more agreeable and more important to you.

I suppose the Parliament is up, and that we shall now soon hear how the vacancies in church and state will be filled. Why did the Lords reject the Tobacco bill?

1713, July 18.—We this day installed our new Dean; neither his illness nor the confusion of our affairs would allow us to do it with all the ceremony that has been usual on such occasions. There was another reason too of as great weight as any that obliged us to waive it, which regards his predecessor. It has been usual for the successor always to make mention in his speech of his predecessor; it was not thought proper to speak truth of him; and his successor could not with safety to his own conscience speak any good of one of whom he not only believes but knows so much ill.

A canonry is now vacant, and there is an opportunity for your Lordship to show your generous kindness and favour to your tutor. Your Lordship will be pleased to give notice, if any warrant is ordered for him, that care may be taken to have the offices attended. After so long an abstinence, we are pretty hungry for renewals; dispatch may be of use to him as to his profits. We shall hardly pay him the compliment of refusing any leases that offer themselves in the vacancy.

The Queen has parted very kindly with her Parliament, and has given them a very gentle admonition only of their ill treatment of her in the Commerce bill.

Postscript. Since I wrote I have notice of a very sad accident. Bayly, whom your Lordship recommended to me, had been missing ever since Monday night; his tutor, Dr. Terry, had made enquiry after him, but could hear nothing of him. He was the less surprised because the young man would be missing sometimes for two or three days. Upon enquiry, it appeared that he was last seen on Monday night about nine at night, going in his night gown to the house of office in Peckwater; they had the curiosity to look there, and found the poor young man smothered there. His poor tutor is in the utmost affliction. This accident could not happen through any disorder in drink, he was never given to it, nor could he have had enough that night; the whole hall was cleared immediately on Monday night as soon as supper was ended. The under graduates had allowed at their table only one bottle of wine betwixt four; and by the time the poor lad was last seen, this happened as soon as supper was over. But I have often wondered that no accident of this nature ever happened in that place before. The seats are large, and without any backs to them, that if any one leans back on a sudden, he must tumble in; when I have mentioned it, I have been told they had been so without mischief ever since the College was founded. His tutor is in such concern that he was not able to give your Lordship an account of it, but desired me to take that sad part on me.

Upon further enquiry we find this poor lad was alive some hours probably after he fell in. Bagshaw, a bachelor student, Dr. Gastrell's kinsman, went into the house of office about eleven o'clock, and heard such a groaning that he was frightened and ran away, but never mentioned it to any one till the body was found. Wainwright went about twelve to fetch a pitcher of water from the pump that is near, and heard a sad groaning, but thought it had been somebody sick in Bear Lane.

There was a great bruise on one side of his head; it is probable he fell asleep on the seat and slipped in double. There had been a great crowd and bustle, in the undergraduates' gallery especially, that afternoon in the Theatre. We were often afraid they would have tumbled over by dozens. He might be spent and tired and nod as soon as he came on the seat, but he was very unfortunate. I now hear that Jenkinson went into the house of office about twelve, heard groaning and held down his candle to see if he could discover any thing, saw nothing and concluded it was some dog thrown in.

1713, July 21. Christ Church.—I sent your Lordship the first accounts I had of the sad accident that happened here. Upon a further enquiry I am afraid the poor lad had got more drink than was fit for him, for I hear he had gone out of the College when supper was over. No one gave notice to his tutor that he was missing till Thursday morning, and he was the less surprised, because the lad had once run to London for three weeks. Dr. Terry had a year ago given his father notice that he [would] not mind his business, and had advised his father to remove him, but the mother, who was very fond of him, had employed one to write to the Doctor to desire that he would let her son stay in the College, and not make any further complaints to the father. The Doctor however wrote again to the father, but believes his letters were intercepted by the mother.

I am much troubled to hear of my Lord Treasurer's illness. I pray God, Radcliffe may be mistaken. I hope it is only gravel, that will often give as violent pain as a stone.

I have sent your Lordship's letter to the Dean, and I expect that he will come to me, but I can tell you of my own knowledge, from what I have heard from all the gentlemen of those parts, that Gibbons has the best character of any clergyman in those parts, and Todd the worst. They are the reverse of each other's characters in every part; one will be the most acceptable, the other the most ungracious, that can be pitched on. I am a stranger to both. Todd was the Bishop of Rochester's tool when he was at Carlisle, and not only privy to all his rogueries there, but the instrument by which he managed them. The Lord Chancellor is I am certain a stranger to Todd, and can have no concern for him but at the desire of the Bishop of Rochester.

But it is strange that Lord Chancellor, who has the disposal of fifteen hundred ecclesiastical preferments, cannot be content with so fair a share, but must think that he ought to recommend too to other vacancies. But this is an instance, amongst many others that appear every day, of the entire ascendancy the new bishop has over the Chancellor. By what he commands him I know not, whether by flattery and by some secret. I believe rather the latter, or else his power would not be so absolute as it is. But they who have to do with Lord Chancellor ought, for their own conduct, to know that there is nothing, be it of what nature it will, that is trusted to Lord Chancellor which the Bishop of Rochester is not master of.

We hear the war is proclaimed at Westminster, and I can tell your Lordship somewhat, which you may not have heard. Both Lord Chancellor and Bishop of W————r used their utmost endeavours to persuade the new Bishop [Atterbury] to comply with the desires of the parish, but could not prevail. The vestry sent to desire Lord Guernsey to be a vestryman. The new Dean immediately sent to them to desire them to have a care of bringing lords into the vestry, and to put them in mind that when they chose Lord Halifax they had soon after the Palatines brought in upon them. This has provoked Guernsey, as well it may. This quarrel will be very fruitful and produce others I doubt not, which will never be ended whilst he is there. But I believe it may be designed that the peace of Westminster may be an argument for removing him to Lambeth when there is a vacancy there. He might have been humbled, had we been allowed to lay a true account of him before the Queen. We should have put it out of his power to give any further trouble to the world, but the opportunity was slipped, and I wish they who have been concerned not only to cover him, but to prefer him, be not the first who feel him.

The Faculty place was disposed of on Saturday to Harry Watkins. I should have been proud to obey your Lordship's commands, but Mr. Broxholme had put it out of our power to serve him. I always looked on him as a fair tempered man, that had much of a gentleman in him, but he was drawn into that paltry malicious combination to have denied Dr. Periam his degree. But I hear since that he is ashamed of it.

I had a letter this post that the Bishop of Bristol was declared Bishop of London, but I suppose it is not so, because your Lordship is silent.

The Dean is with me, he is full of company and begs your Lordship would excuse him for not writing to-day; he will write to your Lordship to-morrow, and observe your orders. He is not at the liberty he could wish he were to declare his opinion about a successor at Carlisle, because he has often declared he would [not] pretend to concern himself about it. But he entirely agrees with me that Gibbons on all accounts whatever is the most proper for the service of the Queen and the church, too, in those parts. He tells me a great deal more than I knew of Todd. I can only assure you my Lord Chancellor never recommended an "erranter" knave than Todd, *excepto semper* the Bishop of Rochester. He is hated and despised too both by laity and clergy. Should he be made dean, that church would once more be in a flame again. He would certainly as far as he could imitate the Bishop of Rochester and act there by his direction.

I am heartily glad the Speaker has acquitted himself to the last so much to your satisfaction. I wish some others who pretend to greater friendship with your father, and who I am sure are under greater obligations to him, would deal as honourably with him.

Every one is pleased with the Speech, and think it was very right to part so kindly with the Parliament and to touch so tenderly what had passed about the Commerce. If there be any thing amiss in it, I think it is rather too short in enumerating what things this Parliament has done.

Postscript. Young Sim[on Harcourt] is put up at Abingdon, and Knap is promised to be made a Welsh Judge for his interest in the town. They were beaten out at Wallingford, and I believe they would lose it too at Abingdon, should there be any opposition.

1713, July 22. Christ Church.—I had little time yesterday to answer the favour of your Lordship's, nor was I very well, but that which I wrote was as to the substance of it true. I have since had more discourse with our Dean; he had reason to know both those gentlemen when he was at Carlisle from his own experience of them, as well as from the different characters they had of them from all he conversed with there. Gibbons is the most beloved man, and as the Dean believes very justly, in the whole country by clergy and laity; the other the most hated, but it cannot be determined by whom most, his own profession or others. I had many particulars to confirm this, but they will be said only to me. The Dean had promised not to concern himself about his successor. When he was pressed by Todd to recommend him, he would go no further than to promise not to meddle in it. He could not, he says, with safety to his own conscience have recommended Todd. Should Todd succeed, you may expect to hear that church is in the same condition it was four years ago, nay greater, for both the bishop and clergy will be more provoked at Todd's preferment than they were at Atterbury's. The last was unknown to them, till they had had experience of him, but it amazes me that they who cannot be ignorant of the state of that country, should yet press for Todd.

Postscript. It is amazing to me that Lord Chancellor and Bishop of Rochester should offer to press for Todd when they cannot but know that your father is more disposed to favour Gibbons. Ought not they to be satisfied with having carried their own points ? Do they press the Queen in this case by and through your father? Or do they go directly to the Queen for Todd without him and in opposition to him? I wish you would tell me that. If the latter, by whom can they apply? I have good reason to think no application from themselves would be acceptable, where their persons are otherwise. If they press by your father, he may [be] certain the more he yields to such importunities, the more he will be troubled with them. This looks as though those gentlemen were in a confederacy to overbear your father whenever they thought fit.

Your Lordship said the loss of the Excommunication bill was a mortification to the Bishop of Rochester. Not in the least; he never had any concern whether it passed or no. He did put [it], as your Lordship observes, into Lord Guernsey's hands. I gave your father notice of that, but he did that for other purposes than for the bill itself—he was then in a ticklish state. He was casting about for new friends, and how to form new parties. He had a design to apply to Lord N[ottingham]. He had made two or three offers there to no purpose. He knew the aversion both the brothers° had to him. He was to recommend himself by giving them an opportunity of doing somewhat that what was to be popular amongst the clergy. This was the reason of putting that bill into Lord Guernsey's hands. Since that he has got clear of his difficulties and gained his points. He was as unconcerned now for the bill as for Lord Guernsey himself. He is now going to be at open defiance with him, and, as I told you in my last, opposes his being chosen into the vestry at St. Margaret's; and I will tell you further, that you will find he will pretend to make his quarrel with Lord Guernsey a piece of merit with your father.

1718, July 28. Christ Church.—There is come out a little pamphlet called "The Proceedings of the Lower House of Convocation, upon her Majesty's most gracious messages and letters, &c." being the substance of a report drawn up by a committee of the Lower House, brought into it and received by it—July 1, 1718. There is a fallacy in saying it was received by it; it was not indeed refused; nor could it be either received or refused; for there were not enough to make a House, or to pass any judgment on it. The design is to reflect on the Upper House, and to be a ground for reviving all those Convocation controversies. There are many tokens in it by which the author may be known, though I think there is one which alone would be sufficient, that there is but one man whose interest it is now to continue those disputes. But I wonder he will let his friend be out of the Convocation, when he has aim still at supporting a party there. Not that he would be of any other use than as a tool to carry orders and to give him an account of what passes, but since he has resigned his interest in Gloucestershire, out he must be, unless he can get a deanery before the session.

I have received a sermon from the Bishop of Bath and Wells [Hooper]. The critics may perhaps nibble a little in some

---

° The Earl of Nottingham and Lord Guernsey, made Earl of Aylesford in 1714.

passages at the language as somewhat stiff, but all honest men will approve the sense of it. There are a great many notions in it that seem, methinks, to agree with what I have heard on several occasions in York Buildings. There is much more life and fancy than one would expect from one of his years.

1713, July 25. Bucklebury.—I am an utter stranger to Gibbons, and could have no aim in what I wrote but the Queen's or your father's service. If it may be of any use to either of them I shall be glad. I had come from Oxford before the letters came in yesterday, but I left a servant to bring them after me. I could not give the Dean notice to send up his resignation on Sunday, but I propose to be at Dr. South's [at Caversham] on Tuesday and at home again on Wednesday. The resignation shall come up on Thursday; there will be no loss in it, for it will bear date from the time of his installation at Christ Church.

The Speaker tells me he fears, in the disposal of the Bishopric of London, that respect will not be paid to his friend the Bishop of Bath and Wells which he the Speaker could wish and thinks due. I believe, if it had been designed to give the Bishopric to him, it might have been as safely offered to him, as the Deanery of Westminster was to Dr. South. But I find the Speaker more concerned at the neglect, as he apprehends, of the Bishop, because the Speaker had been used to bring him out of the country when no other means could do it. But I have good ground that my Lord Chancellor and his sworn, or rather forsworn, ally, value themselves more upon stopping that Bishop's removal than upon gaining all their other points. The Speaker tells me no other news, but of your new lord,° and that the Auditor's place is disposed of. But you need not apprehend that the Speaker will be troublesome, for he has sent for his horses, and goes next week for Warwickshire.

Your Lordship asks me what I think of your new lord. They who made him know best what to say for it. It was justly alleged in the late creation that all of them were of ancient families; no one I have met with is much acquainted with the new lord's pedigree, nor are his merits in the House from whence he is removed sufficiently known. I am afraid the creation of your new lord will be of as little use to the public service as [that] of your new bishop.

I am sorry I cannot be of your Lordship's opinion on one point, I believe not only Knap, but any other, will be not only a Welsh judge, but bishop too, if my Lord Chancellor pleases.

I do not desire your Lordship should withdraw any of your favour from Broxholme. That which I mentioned would not have permitted us to show the kindness he desired at this juncture, but it would not hinder us upon another opportunity, where he could fairly pretend to it. But there are so many his seniors who think they have as fair a claim as he has, that if there had been more vacancies we could not have chosen him, without doing that which others would have thought, though not strictly unjust, yet unkind to them.

---

* Robert Benson, M.P. for York, made Lord Bingley.

I beg I may meet a letter on Wednesday to give me notice if you receive this, because it goes by a by-post to Reading.

I wonder your father or any that wish well to him can expect he should be without some distemper, when under such a fatigue as he has undergone. He never allows himself any time, either to take waters, exercise, or so much as a little fresh air.

Accedunt anni et tractari mollius aetas imbecilla volet.

1713, July 28. Bucklebury.—I most humbly thank your Lordship for the favour of yours to this place, and for your goodness in giving Dr. Terry notice that his warrant was signed. One would have been appointed to take care of it, could he have thought it proper for him to presume so far upon the Queen's favour to him as to appoint one to take care of the warrant, before he had notice that it was signed. I am sorry there are still such remains of my Lord Treasurer's distemper as to require so severe discipline as your Lordship mentions. No difficulties in the public affairs can be equal to those he has overcome, the public cannot for the future require so much of his time as it has done for some years past. I hope he will be prevailed with to allow some part to take care of himself.

I go this day to Dr. South's. You will have received, I hope, before this reaches you, the respects of the Lady [Bolingbroke] of this place, in the manner which will most recommend them to you.

1713, August 2. Christ Church.—I am heartily glad poor J[ohn] D[rummond] has given so much satisfaction. I always took his capacity to be equal to his integrity, and when I presumed to recommend him to your father, I thought I recommended to him as able as well as faithful servant as he ever had employed. I believe the event has justified my opinion. It will be an action worthy of your father to enable this poor man to look the world once again in the face. The poor man has not only his service but his sufferings, too, to plead for him. Agatha I believe will be in town again before your Lordship returns from Windsor, she designed not to stay at Bucklebury above three or four days.

I am amazed at Lord B[olingbroke]'s demands, but I believe there is ground for the report, and perhaps he may succeed. He will not be the only example where impudence has been of more use than merit, but the love I have for your father makes me wish he would think a little, whether it can be for his service to let the world see that he can be overborne. Methinks one who has stood so firm as he has done against public noise from any quarter, should be able to be above private importunity.

There is no instance of respect which the university can pay to your father, but what they are I believe in a disposition to pay, but I have not yet heard of that particular instance which your Lordship mentions.

My brother South begins now to fail in his understanding. I am afraid his head will go before his legs. It was a providence of God that he retained his faculties enough to know that it was proper for him to refuse the deanery. He is complete eighty in next September; should decays come on fast now, he has no reason to complain, nor his friends to be surprised.

I suppose your Lordship will see Lady Carmarthen and Lady Dupplin too at Windsor, I beg my humble duty to them. My prayers always wait on them, that they may long enjoy the reward they have of their own goodness, in such good Lords.

Your Lordship durst not or at least were not allowed to see me last summer; the objection is now removed, you may venture into Christ Church without fear of being obliged to declare for one side or other. I hope you will remember that there are some promises which you have never yet made good.

1713, August 6. Christ Church.—Your Lordship's Canon was installed this morning. I hope your Lordship will be pleased to take this place so far into your protection as not to allow any one but yourself to recommend to any vacancies that shall happen here. Your Lordship's favour to your particular servants will be the greatest security that can be had for the public welfare of the College. On Saturday we shall confer on Dr. Terry another dignity which is in our gift, but which he is made capable of by that he has received from your Lordship. We shall make him sub-dean, but I do not pretend that we do it so much out of respect to your Lordship or to him, as for our own ease.

I suppose you are returned from the solemnity at Windsor, and I hope to-morrow to hear from you again.

1713, August 8. Christ Church.—There were published here last week Chronological tables by Marshall who was lately student of our House, the Bishop of Worcester's nephew. The tables are really old Worcester's, though he lets his nephew put his name to them. Every gentleman should have a general scheme of chronology in his head, and perhaps these tables contain as much as is necessary for a gentleman to know of it. They certainly are more exact than any yet published. I shall beg leave to present your Lordship with a set.

The incumbent of Fladbury is dead. It is the best preferment in the Bishop of Worcester's gift, worth 500 l. per annum. Will Floyd has it, and Offley the son-in-law will have the living W. Floyd leaves. I suppose Will now will not want a prebend of Worcester.

I have now direct proof that Lord Chancellor saw the bill which was filed against me, and gave his directions upon it before it was shown to Lutwych, the counsel that signed it; and I have probable, but not direct, proof that Perrot was named Chapter clerk by the late fellow, upon Lord Chancellor's recommendation, and that Perrot paid his Lordship money for his recommendation. That was the reason why the late fellow put the Chancellor in mind of his repeated promises to do something for Perrot.

1713, August 10. Christ Church.—Why do you loiter in town? Get you gone into Cambridgeshire. I will throw an old shoe after you. You should be ashamed to show your face any

more in town till you can show another along with it that is
better than your own, though that be an honest one.

I was out of my house when the letters came yesterday, or I
had answered yours then. I was surprised with the account you
sent me of the disposition of the preferments. Methinks an
ancient baron with a noble estate should not *desire* a bishopric,
but not *accept* a deanery ; he should leave those things to those of
the profession who want them more. We hear the Bishop of
Westminster will not be well pleased, nor do I know whether the
Dean here will be in a condition to take the kindness designed for
him. But how comes it that my poor brother Gasse is forgot still
in the disposition of preferments? He had the honour to be my
Lord Treasurer's servant before either the Bishop of Hereford,
Rochester, or the designed Bishop of Bristol were known to his
Lordship, and to introduce all of them to my Lord Treasurer.
And yet they have all changed bishoprics or deaneries twice or
thrice since he was first Canon here, and I believe he would do
as much credit to his patron and as much service to the public
as any of them.

Our late sultan made seats in the windows of two of his bed-
chambers ; there were only single windows in the room. The
two seats had as usual two cushions in them, the deal board was
to be painted, but he frugally considered with himself that there
could be no occasion to paint that part of the seat which was
covered by the cushion. Accordingly this was not painted. He is
computed to have saved at the utmost five farthings by it. This
was not discovered till the workmen came in for the alterations
that are now to be made. This is so great and so new an instance
of frugality, that the whole town is invited to see it, and the
workmen have pence apiece for showing it.

1713, August 13. Christ Church.—Here are accounts to several
hands in town of the rupture betwixt the mother [Duchess of
Newcastle] and daughter, and of the daughter's choosing your
uncle for her guardian.

I have now no more concern in this world. I have lived to see your
father clear of all those difficulties which proved greater than he
himself could foresee when he entered on his administration.
The nearest wish I had, your settlement in the world, is now
upon the point of being accomplished. Providence has made
that provision for you, which your father never would nor could
have done. My own College, after the highest ferment that ever
any society was in, is at perfect peace. Now these things are
over, which were the only things that ever engaged my thoughts
with any concern, I can go to Ross, and spend the remainder of
my days with my friend there. There was indeed another thing
for which I had some grudging ; it was to have seen a great rogue
humbled, and not preferred. I desired this not out of a spirit of
revenge, but charity to the fellow's soul. If he escapes here, he
must have it elsewhere, and I do not wish that to him, either as
he is a rogue or my enemy. But since for *Ragione di Stato* or

some other motive that is ordered otherwise, let us bless God for our own peace, and leave to Him other men's punishment.

If this finds your Lordship still in town, you will give me leave to desire notice when you leave it, and when the affair is finished. I will not put you to much trouble, I know how busy you must be at such a juncture, one line would be more than I should expect, two words, *l'affaire est faite*, will serve my turn.

I have obeyed your orders to our Dean. If her Majesty still continues disposed to promote him to Bristol, I believe you will hear of no more excuses from him, though he had contrived to convey by some other hand besides your father's notice of his own inabilities to support that dignity. I could not learn by what hand, but the chief objections I believe are removed. There are friends who have undertaken to supply him with what he will want on such an occasion, without bringing him under any obligations that may be hazardous to his family. But had I had notice that this thing had been designed before I heard that it was done, I might perhaps have suggested somewhat to your Lordship, which would not be proper now.

I guess by somewhat from Tom Rowney, that the Lord Chancellor has given Tom notice that somewhat is designed for him. It cannot be placed upon an honester man, but I wish any thing of that kind may be managed so that others may not have the merit of what your father does.

I had last night a long and kind letter from the late Speaker; he owns the new honour that is designed for him, but great part was to rejoice with me very sincerely and heartily at your Lordship's establishment, which he looks upon now as certain.

1713, August 16. Christ Church.—I expected no other end of Lord B[olingbroke]'s management, I wonder it has lasted so long. He is a sad warning to gentlemen of how little use the greatest parts are to one void of all sense of honour and religion. How soon will this great blaze be extinguished! His private affairs are in the utmost confusion; he will be desperate when he is cashiered. What the end of all will be I cannot guess. I from my soul pity this poor lady; she has not yet I am afraid seen her worst days.

I have obeyed your orders, and I hope the Dean will have the sense he ought of your father's extraordinary kindness to him; but my last I believe satisfied you that he will not be obstinate. The good man is aware of the difficulties of the post, but Mademoiselle will not I fancy hazard the loss of a new title, though it be only a title of courtesy; but I cannot yet find out the other hand by which he sent to make his excuse to the Queen. Pray learn it if you can, and let me know it.

I was sorry to hear from your Lordship last post, I hoped you had been in another place; but I am more troubled that you give me hopes of seeing you soon, as much as I wish it. But if you are at liberty to attend your election, pray let me know in your next when you think of going. You may be certain I shall not allow of your going either by Abingdon or Woodstock, but I still hope your journey will be prevented.

The war I hear is now declared at Westminster. On Thursday last the vestry of St. Margaret's by a majority of fourteen to four chose their own clerk, and have left the Bishop to seek his remedy. The labouring oar is on his side. I doubt not but this war will last as long as that betwixt France and the Confederates.

But the great man is now going to engage a mightier enemy, no less than her Majesty herself. On Thursday last he called, as we hear, a Chapter, and supposing there would be a vacancy at Newchapel, had an act of Chapter made and entered, that the Chapter would assert their right of nominating to the chapel. Were there a vacancy, it would be in the Queen's gift, but I see not how there can be a voidance, where there was no institution. He may perhaps say it is void because it was never full, and that Dr. Smalridge never had a legal title to it. That I believe may bear a dispute, and if the Dean and Chapter of Westminster name one, he may try the title, but I believe if he should get the better, he would not be much the richer for it, the profits depending on the rent of pews or free gift. I am apt to think that will be the method, and that the Bishop will persist, since he has once engaged, though the Queen should signify her pleasure to the contrary; but it should be considered that the Queen is not only Visitor but Founder there, and as such may dispose, I believe, of that chapel as she pleases if it belong to the Dean and Chapter. But perhaps my Lord Chancellor may come in once again to help his friend at a dead lift, and claim to be Visitor, not under but in opposition to her Majesty. This is pretty well for the first two months. I doubt not before Christmas to hear of more. It will come to the Chapter itself at last. There have already been warm words betwixt him and Brodrick.

Harry Watkins and his brother candidate Brough called on me yesterday in their way to Brackley. I examined what bank bills they had. They have to do with as experienced a corporation as Weobly itself.

1713, August 18. Christ Church.—I hope this will not find you in town, but it may follow you, though I cannot think you will have much leisure to read letters if you are where I wish you. I shall be shorter than usual for that reason.

I am obliged to desire your Lordship's [favour] to Mr. Ince, a student of our House. He has studied the law for some years, and desires to go Attorney to Barbados. He is a very ingenious young man, and a very honest one; he is young, but I believe as old as they have usually been who have been sent to that place. The Attorney and Solicitor General will both certify that he is qualified for it. His old father is one who has been very useful to this College for many years. We are concerned for the son for the father's sake as well as his own.

[To the EARL OF OXFORD.]

1718, September 5. Bath.—The relation I have had the honour to have to my Lord Harley will excuse me I hope for presuming to trouble your Lordship with my joy upon his marriage.

I hope I take the part I ought to do in my Lord Harley's establishment in being possessed of a lady whose fortune, though so great, is allowed to be that which is least valuable in her. But I must beg leave to say, from the knowledge I have so much reason to have of my Lord Harley, that the world, as well as Lady Harriot, will be convinced that all the advantages which my Lord Harley may have from this marriage, are too little for him.

The tenderness which I know your Lordship has for such a son assures me that your Lordship will be pleased, if God thinks fit to bestow His temporal rewards on your Lordship, for your own hazards and cares in the public service, in His blessings on my Lord Harley.

[To LORD HARLEY.]

1713, September 5. Bath.—I can now say my *dimittis*, since I have lived to see your Lordship possessed of that which you have so long wished for, and more, to my knowledge, out of affection to the lady than for any other advantage you could hope for from so great an establishment. You must give me leave to say that my joy would not be so complete as it is were I not certain, from the long experience I have had the honour to have of you, that you will make all the returns that are in the power of the best of men to so excellent a lady, who has deserved so greatly of you.

Compliments though due from all who have the honour to be your servants, yet ought to be short I think, to one who is employed so much more agreeably as you are at present. I would only beg leave to tender through your Lordship my most humble duty to my Lady Harriot. The relation I have had the honour to have to your Lordship, is the ground of my presuming to offer my duty to her Ladyship, and the pledge too of having it received by her.

1718, September 19. Bath.—When I was used to wish the excellent Lady you now possess might fall to your lot, you know it was for the sake of her character as well as her fortune. Your Lordship writes like one that had got possession of that he had long wished for, but bystanders, who may be thought more impartial judges, own that nothing can be said of her by a fond husband which would not bear the scrutiny of a sour philosopher. May you still continue, as I doubt not but you will, to find every thing in your new condition to exceed not only your hopes but your imagination too.

Your Lordship is pleased to allow me the honour to suggest my poor thoughts to you. Your Lordship will always command every thing in my power. That which I am to guard against is lest the concern I have for one whose welfare is so dear to me should make me so forward as to be impertinent. But your

Lordship must allow me to observe that one who in your circumstances can be so good as to ask the advice of a poor friend will have little occasion for it. To show it will be so, I shall only instance in the first and the chief thing that I should presume to suggest, which is certainly needless to you. What has your Lordship to do, upon the entrance upon so much happiness, but to take all the methods that prudence and affection can suggest to make your happiness as lasting as it is great, and to lay at this time the foundation of a friendship betwixt your excellent lady and yourself which may make you both, in this adulterous generation, more remarkable for your mutual affection than for any other circumstance in which God has placed you. This is certainly your interest, but your Lordship is above that motive, and I hope I never preached it to you. Even gratitude, though a noble principle of action, though due from your Lordship to such a lady, is too mean a motive for you to act upon in this case. I am for nothing but pure affection, an affection so entire as not to need the sense of gratitude to enforce it.

Mr. Auditor has done me the honour to communicate to me somewhat that he was obliged to suggest to your Lordship, the friendship that is to be betwixt your lady and yourself for your whole life entirely depends upon the first management of it. And it is of so great moment to your Lordship to rivet that so fast that it shall not be in the power of any accident to weaken it, that I cannot but agree with Mr. Auditor, that what he suggested is not only advisable but strictly necessary. Your Lordship's own prudence will furnish you with the methods by which you may do it with most ease to yourself.

Your father, with all his experience, could not have suggested to you a wiser reflection than that which you have made, that your future quiet and honour depend upon the conduct you observe at your first appearing in so new and so great a scene. A steadiness in the first opening of it, will make you master of yourself and your time for the remainder of your days. Should your Lordship give way to any thing now, which you may afterwards find inconvenient, it will be very difficult, if possible, to get clear of it then, though it may now with ease be prevented. I suppose your Lordship will use your utmost skill, in ordering your time so as to save as much of it as you can to yourself. If you reflect how much of your time must unavoidably be given up, by one of your quality, to the common forms of life, you will perceive that all that you can save will be less than is necessary for your business. Your estate will require your first care, I mean of worldly cares, and I am afraid it will leave little of any time you save for any other use. If you have any leisure hours on your hands, fear not but there will be studies in which you may employ them, and such studies, and to such you ought to confine yourself, as will enable you to answer the great ends of the high station in which God has placed you. At the distance I am I can suggest nothing to your Lordship but what is general. I should think it the blessing of my life, if I could promote a happiness which I so cordially pray for; but I shall carefully preserve the letter I have had the honour to receive, that I may produce your Lordship's own command as my excuse if I should happen at any time to be impertinent.

I beg my most humble duty and thanks to my Lady Harriot for the honour she has been pleased to do me in owning me for her servant. I am prouder of it than a late bishop was of his rocket on the thanksgiving day. I can say nothing greater. I shall endeavour to show my sense of it, in that which I know will be most acceptable to her Ladyship, my zeal for your Lordship's service.

Your Lordship must expect all your dependents will now be putting in their claims. To show I have learnt a little of the world I shall be as early as I can in mine. Your Lordship may remember when we used to drink Lady Harriot's health at Christ Church, I had a promise of your picture, if it should be your fortune to get the prize. I do not desire but insist to have the promise made good to me, and it must be by Sir Godfrey, and as well as he can do it, and as soon too. Unless it may be convenient to defer it till a star may be drawn on the coat; but it will not be delayed long I suppose on that account.

The waters agree extremely [well] with the Auditor. I prescribe to him. If I can but prevail with him to stay long enough, I doubt not but I shall send him up to town as plump as I am.

I must beg leave to observe that your Lordship has improved your hand since your marriage. I wonder not at it, since you have so fair a one to imitate. If I could meet with one that could teach me to mend my hand, I am sure I should have one good reason to alter my condition.

1713, October 27. Christ Church.—Since I was so happy as to know your Lordship, I never was so long without hearing from you, as since the last I had the honour to receive at Bath. I know how agreeably your Lordship has been engaged, nor am I so unreasonable as to hope to enjoy as constant a correspondence for the future as I have had for some time past. But your Lordship must allow me to enquire sometimes how you do, especially since you are doubled and have got another self. And though I am prepared to expect an abatement in your correspondence, pray let it be gradual, that it may be easier to me. I hope it may not be unseasonable to enquire how my Lady Harley does. Your Lordship will believe by my enquiry that I do not hope to hear that she is without complaint, but none I hope but such as will produce their own recompense. I beg leave by your Lordship to presume to offer my most humble duty to her Ladyship.

I hear the Lord Chancellor has ordered the dragoons he had quartered on you to be discharged.

Now Newcastle House is free, I believe the weather will soon oblige your Lordship and my Lady to think of the town.

I could not prevail with the Auditor to stay at Bath, nor did he return, as he promised me he would, before I left it. I left your aunt Abigail with a cold, but I hope it was going off. Your aunt Harley had found much greater advantage than she could have hoped for. If she stays long enough, I doubt not but her health will be entirely restored.

I have now Hoffman's Lexicon in sheets, and a complete set of the Transactions of the Royal Society, and the History of it, to part with at easier rates than can be had elsewhere. I think I once got Hoffman for your father; but if your Lordship or my Lord Dupplin desire either of them, you may have the pre-emption.

I have in store some accounts that will divert you when we meet. I shall only tell you now that young Simon is very much displeased with the present management and is resolved to model the ministry anew. He never gave himself such airs as he does at present. I am afraid he is not aware that many judge of his father's sentiments by what he says.

1713, October 31.—I beg my most humble duty and thanks to my Lady, for her great goodness in permitting me to pay my duty to her at Wimple. I must reckon this honour the greatest of those many advantages I have had by my relation to your Lordship. My desire has been with you ever since the happy hour you were joined. I could not but long to see those together I have so often wished so, and I had waited on you this season if the Auditor had returned to Bath as soon as he promised he would when he left it, but new "purchases," the business of you great men, made him break his word. I am afraid it is now too late to think of such a journey, there are some rotten vales between this place and Wimpole, and I, as well as my predecessor Falstaff, have a great alacrity in sinking. Should I attempt the journey, I should be stuck in the middle of it. Could I get at you, I should not be concerned if I could not get home again, but God willing next spring I will wait on you, as soon as you are there.

Your Lordship enquires whether I have been to wait on a distressed Lady [Bolingbroke]. Not since I wrote to your Lordship from that place. I had designed to have called as I returned home, but I had a friendly notice given me not to do it. The country was full, and upon some words that fell, when I was mentioned, it was feared I should be *affronted* if I called. This to yourself, I perceive the displeasure is as great to me as ever the favour was. I shall know what was said as soon as the coast is clear, but I hope I can stand anything, since I have stood a bill in Chancery.

There has been a rendezvous indeed, and a famous one too, if all be true that is reputed here. A young gentleman, for whose lady your Lordship has a hearty concern, I am afraid, is thoroughly initiated.

There are differences I believe among the great ones, and with others than him your Lordship mentioned. I hear some are displeased at the late promotion, and with reason. It is the greatest blow to them, and security to somebody else, of any thing that has yet been done. I gave you a hint of this in my last, which I do not perceive your Lordship had received before the date of yours.

Here are great discontents here, and much talk of an appeal to the House of Lords against a late order of Chancery about Sir Th. Cook's charity. Somebody is so apprehensive of this, that all means are tried to bring off particular votes, and to prevent a majority of the trustees from concurring in it. Promises of preferment fly as thick as hail. Public notice has been sent that there are orders for settling a prebend of Gloucester on Pembroke, and one of Norwich on Oriel and a vacant prebend of Bristol is to be bestowed on the Master of Balliol. We shall see in a little time whether this be given out only to serve a present turn ; but there is no expense will be spared to prevent the storm that is feared. Your Lordship shall know what effect all this has.

We have now another public trial of interest with the Bishop of Rochester ; he recommends Mr. Hinton for chaplain to the new Speaker ; our Dean recommends Dr. Pelling. The commissioners of the public accounts join with the bishop in recommending Mr. Hinton. The Duke of Ormond and Mr. Secretary Bromley use their interest for Dr. Pelling. We are apt to think we have the better end of the staff, and that we shall show the bishop we can beat him any where, and that we can get the better of him though he gets the better of the ministry.

I think I have tired you, and have convinced your Lordship that I think you in earnest when you allow me to use you so freely. I thank your Lordship for all the kindness in your last; I never doubted of your Lordship's indulgence to me, but I hope I am not so vile a wretch as to presume upon the goodness of a noble friend. The more willing your Lordship is to allow me freedom, the more cautious ought I to be how I use it.

1713, November 7. Christ Church.—I really am ashamed to write to you ; you beat me out of all the little play I have. I know not how to acknowledge kindness so much beyond what I can have any reason to hope for from your Lordship. But I should be as great a rogue as the Bishop of Rochester if ever I could make any other use of it than to promote, as far as is in my poor power, the honour and good of him from whom I receive it.

I heartily give your Lordship joy of my Lord Danby. God will reward your father in the way that affects most a great and good man, in blessings on his family. They have hitherto been the most remarkable in every branch of any this age affords, and I hope we shall see the completion of them within eight months more in my Lord Ogle. I hope there is some work coming for me. I hope I am not to be cut out every where. If I had no title to marry you, I have a better to christen the fruit of your marriage than the Dean of Wells can pretend to.

A little French air added to the accomplishments gained in former travels has made the young gentleman your Lordship mentioned as complete a coxcomb as any Great Britain can show.

I have some choice stories for your entertainment when I next wait on you. I have some new ones of the father, but they are of another nature, and such as will raise other sort of passions than those which produce laughter.

I gave your Lordship an account of favours that were to be bestowed here. I wonder how one your Lordship and I know gave way to it, but of that when we meet; but the end that was aimed at is not likely to be gained. More are disobliged than gained by it; some I believe will now declare who before were doubtful.

Mr. Bromley is your servant, the young gentleman here I mean ; he tells me he wrote to pay his respects to your Lordship upon your marriage, but is afraid you never received your letter. I forgot to let your Lordship know the raptures your old friend Mrs. Rowney is [in]. I believe she could not be more pleased if young Tom had been married to her satisfaction. She is resolved to come and see you in Newcastle House.

1713, November 16. Christ Church.—I am heartily glad my Lady and your Lordship stay so long in the country, it will certainly be for the health of both, but it may conduce to that which is of more moment to both of you. So much conversation as you must have together, where you are upon your marriage, must give you a thorough knowledge of each other and endear you to each other, and be the foundation of that inviolable affection which must be the mutual comfort of your lives. For believe me my Lord who have a few more years of my head than your Lordship has, that you must expect no satisfaction in this world, besides what arises from a good conscience, but what is domestic and to be had at your own home. It is well if all the rest, as great as your part is like to be in the world, be only an amusement to you. You must not be surprised if you should often find trouble from it.

The prebend of Gloucester on Pembroke is settled as far as it can yet be, by the Queen's warrant for doing of it. That which is to be annexed to Oriel will not be done till the Bishop of London comes over, who is to have the honour of it, having been bred in that College. The Master of Balliol has the vacant prebend of Bristol but that is not to be annexed to his College, and it is said Charlett will have the vacant prebend of Worcester, but I do not hear that is to be annexed. But all would not do. Since it was perceived that votes were valued, every one was for getting something, a promise at least. There were persons here who had a full commission to give them, and they have now brought off so many that they have a majority by one, and it was done so openly that some who had given their word desired to be released from it and named the preferment of which they had a promise, if they voted as they were desired in this case. The storm is stopped I believe that was apprehended, but they have been obliged to pay dear for it.

I have now a full account of the displeasure against me that I mentioned, but it is such as I cannot convey to you by letter.

I will order one to wait on you when you come to town and acquaint you with it. My crime is that I am supposed, and very truly I own, to be more in the interest of a relation of your Lordship's than in that gentleman's. For this I am called ungrateful; I can scarce think him weak enough truly to think me so in his own breast, but it will appear evident to your Lordship from the whole story that this has been infused into him by my sure friend at Westminster.

Nature, or rather the devil, is broke loose at last there, he has begun now with one of his own Chapter. He perceives that he is entirely in the wrong in the dispute about the parish clerk, and that he should certainly be baffled in it. He has got some of the prebendaries to join with him and has fallen foul upon Only, who as curate of St. Margaret's had given his approbation to Turner. Only was prebendary there many years before the Bishop was of the school. He is a quite harmless old man betwixt seventy and eighty. The Bishop has used him worse than he ever did any one here. I cannot say more, but it has affected the old man so that it is thought his head is disturbed and that his days will be shortened by it. Your Lordship will have the whole story from brother Gasse when you come to town. I believe the uproar is very great in the neighbourhood.

1713, November 19. Christ Church.—You shall be obeyed, though your last, as it increases my obligations, ought also to my acknowledgments, but I will receive your friendship in the way you are pleased to prescribe to me, though I hope you will allow me to be as civil to you as I am to others. One of the heaviest accusations against me has been want of breeding, it is somewhat hard to alter one's manner after forty, but I am trying if I can be a little more complaisant than I have been. I would not have those I love best be troubled with the worst part of me.

Dr. Pelling has written nothing against Whiston, but there is now a prosecution against Whiston—not at the instance or charge of Dr. Pelling—but in all prosecutions some name must be used, real or feigned, in which the prosecution runs. The late Bishop of London desired Dr. Pelling to let his name be used, though it was carried on by the order and at the charge of the Bishop; that is the reason of this letter to Dr. Pelling.

There is earnest solicitation made for an Irish bishopric for Delaune, your Lordship will guess by whom. He meets with great difficulties, and it is questioned whether he can overcome, but I wonder a friend of ours should give way to it. Should it be done the noise will be great upon it, our friend will have the scandal of what another does. He who permits it will suffer more by it than he who promotes it.

Your Lordship without doubt has had an account of the new spirit which has risen up in Ireland, by which the Tories, beyond all expectation, are three to two in that Parliament. This unexpected turn will occasion I believe a certain person to alter his measures as well as his humour.

[To the EARL OF OXFORD.]

1713, November 24. Christ Church.—I cannot presume to think myself able to offer any consolation to your Lordship under your just grief. As I am one who have had the honour to be your servant, and to be known to the excellent lady who is gone, I beg leave to take the part which all who belong to your Lordship ought to do in so great an affliction to your family, and which is the chief amongst those very few of a private nature of which your Lordship could be sensible.

The sense of my Lady Carmarthen's having been an eminent example to her sex, in every relation she bore, though it makes the loss easy to your Lordship on her account, yet it must embitter it to yourself.

Your Lordship had lived to see a prospect of peace to your country after struggling for it through difficulties which, though not too great for your courage, were beyond I believe even your own expectation. Your Lordship had lived to see every branch of your family, by the especial providence of God, and not by the means of your own wealth or power, in so flourishing a condition as to be the envy of your friends, as well if not more than of your enemies. Such a calamity as the death of my Lady Carmarthen, in such a state of your affairs, ought to teach us all how uncertain those things are which we most value, and how entire our dependence is on God for every thing that is dear to us.

[To LORD HARLEY.]

1713, November 24. Christ Church.—I never wrote to your Lordship with so heavy a heart or so unwilling a hand. The loss of my Lady Carmarthen must be a damp to your Lordship in the midst of your own felicity, though such a blessing as you have in a lady is the greatest support you could have under the loss of such a sister. She was an example to her sex, in every relation she bore. . She had as many of those virtues which are the ornaments of her sex as ever any of her years had obtained to, nor could any one I believe name the fault that was a diminution to them. Such a loss when the family had so fair a prospect of prosperity, after all difficulties, public and private, seemed to have been surmounted, should make us all sensible how much we are every moment in the power of God, and depend on Him for that which is dearest to us. I will be so vain myself as to pretend to have had the loss of a most sincere friend in the poor lady that is gone. I had lately received some letters from her which I shall preserve to my dying hour, as testimonies of her opinion of me, and of the confidence with which she was pleased to honour me. I shall not allow place to any other thoughts in a letter on so sad an occasion. Possibly this calamity may hasten your Lordship to town sooner than you had designed, if it does I beg I may know. I have somewhat which should be known elsewhere, but I shall not give notice of it by any hand but your own, nor shall I convey it to you by the ordinary way.

1718, November 26. Christ Church.—On the 22nd of this
month I made a visit for one day at Bucklebury. I there learnt
that the gentleman was much out of humour whilst he was there,
and amongst other signs of it, broke out into these expressions
against your father, "I and *Lady Masham* have bore him upon
our shoulders, and have made him what he is, and he now leaves
us where *we* were." I know my old friend will rant sometimes,
but the person he joined with himself made me take notice of
the expression. I must leave it to others to make reflections on
it. Your Lordship will perceive this is to be communicated to no
one but your father, because of the person from whom I had my
intelligence. When you have read this, I hope you will burn it.

I heard one odd thing more, he and Lord Lansdowne have been
very cold to each other for two years past; they were so when I
left the town. Their common friends were once afraid there
would have been an open rupture. They are lately reconciled,
and old friendship renewed, or a new league struck up. I know
Lord Lansdowne, when I left the town, pretended to be full of
discontent.

1718, November 29.—This is only to enquire how your Lordship and my Lady do, since the sad news from town. I presume
not yet to trouble you with any occurrences here. I know
thoughts must be too much engaged, to be able [to] attend to
such things. I allow your sorrow to be not only just but great
for the loss of one who was tied to you as closely by friendship
as by blood. But there are succours to be had both from reason
and religion, which are proper to be called for after the first gust
of grief [has sp]ent it self. [Your] Lordship has the most
effectual consolation in your own lady, whose relation to you as
it is nearer to you than any other can be, so it yields a friendship
dearer than any other can.

I should be glad to hear if those which I have lately directed
to Royston have come to your hands. I hinted to your Lordship
that I had somewhat to communicate to you, what I should not
send by the ordinary conveyance; I have had an opportunity of
sending by Dr. Keill to London.

1718, December 5. Christ Church.—I bless God that you and
your Lady have borne your late affliction without any disorder to
your own health. I have now nothing more to wish, than that
we may all make that use of poor Lady Carmarthen's death, to
endeavour to be as well prepared for it as she was. Nothing
could so effectually convince your Lordship how little that we
most eagerly pursue here is to be depended on, nor can any
lesson be so proper at the time you are entering upon the
possession of so great a share of it.

I was in hopes your Lordship would have been in town by this
time. Remembering that your Lordship thought Juggins had a
good hand at brawn, I had presumed to prepare a collar, which I
designed, by your Lordship, humbly to beg my Lady Harley to
accept of. I had one ready too for poor Lady Carmarthen, but

that shall go to no one now but to myself, but I must beg to know what I must do with that I had designed for my Lady Harley. It will be spoiled if it stays in town till you come up. That which [might] not have been unacceptable in town will be of no use I am afraid in the country, where you must have much better. But if your Lordship, for the sake of your own fancy, would be pleased to have it [sent] to you into the country, let me know as soon as you·can to whom I must direct it for you in town.

Londonderry is now vacant, which is the most valuable bishopric in Ireland next to the primacy. The Chancellor presses earnestly for Delaune for one [of] the vacancies. He has yet importuned without any effect; no one knows what perseverance may do, but the Delegates of Accounts have written to the Duke of Ormond and to Mr. B[romle]y, to desire, if a grant is made to Delaune and not before, that they would represent to the Queen the debt due to the university, and beg the grant may be stopped till security is given to the university for it. The Chancellor storms at this, and thinks it designed as an affront to himself; it [may] perhaps help to let the Queen see what regard ought to be had to his recommendations.

They have at last *bought* off as many, and that too not very secretly, as to make a majority to agree for Gloucester Hall. Whether some of the others will not appeal still I know not; they may if they will.

A citation went out of the Vice-Chancellor's court on Friday was se'nnight against Aldrich. Since that he has sent notice to the Dean that he is married. I believe the university will proceed without taking any notice of that, but we are at a loss to know here what the woman is to whom he is married. She is a Scotch woman, about two years older than he, who had married to her first husband one who had married to his first wife Aldrich's mother's aunt. This man was said to have left her a great deal of money. Aldrich's mother persuaded her to come and live with her at Henley; there she lived for a year, and she and the mother often comforted themselves plentifully at a famous inn which is there. This summer she went away for two months with Aldrich; the day she returned she bid Aldrich's mother and sister begone out of the house. The mother asked if she were married to her son; the woman would not then own that, but 'bawd' and 'whore' flew about betwixt them plentifully. The sister within a few days went away, poor creature, with a big belly, the father of it is not yet owned. Soon after Aldrich and the woman went away again to town. The Dean sent to him, to know if he was married; if not, he must summon him for giving scandal by living with that woman. Upon this he has owned his marriage; some say the woman is worth thousands, others that she is not worth a groat.

Lord Treasurer sent lately to me to enquire of the character of one Lewis that is here. I sent what I could learn, and I heard nothing to his prejudice. If Lord Treasurer would have him a student, now is the time for your Lordship to recommend him to Dr. Terry. We shall make a new roll at Christmas. I give your

Lordship this early notice, that you may, if you think fit, write to Dr. Terry, before he has engaged himself by nominating another. Were I at liberty, I should be glad to serve him, but my place in the next roll was mortgaged last act to Dr. Hammond to bring in Sir Ch. Holt's son, Mr. Secretary Bromley's nephew and godson. But that is made a pretence by a great man for breaking off with me, and giving me very hard words.

1713, December 14.—Had the Chancellor consulted his own interest, he would never have run the hazard of letting the Queen be informed what sort of men are in his favour, but we have had more instances than one, within this last year, that his passion can overrule him against his interest. He was in the utmost rage when he had notice of what the delegates desired, he redoubled his own applications upon it for D[elaune], but all to no purpose. The application is not to be made to the Queen unless a grant had been obtained. They who stop it, and by doing so prevent the Queen from being informed more fully of D[elaune]'s character, do as great a service to the Chancellor as they did who persuaded him not to deny us our privilege.

I believe the Duke of Ormond thinks himself very ill used upon Aldrich's account. I believe a promise was made to the Duke that Aldrich should make a public submission, if his Grace would interpose to excuse him from any further punishment. Upon this promise the Duke interposed. The university upon the Duke's desire were willing to remit all other demands, he took advantage of their indulgence to delay his coming till he thought fit to own his marriage, when he supposed he was out of their reach, but I believe the court will still proceed either to expulsion or excommunication.

1713-14, January 5. Windsor.—I am got to Windsor, but I have not relish enough of the honour of my attendance to think it can make me amends for the trouble of my journey. My godfather was here on Sunday, I had a little usual conversation with him, you know he is always open and communicative, that is his foible. But I was pleased with one thing, the account of your Lordship's impatience to return to Wimpole, that was right, and I doubt but the impatience for your absence was, [as] it ought to be, mutual.

I have seen all the great men, I think that is honour enough ; I may even return home, and live upon it till the next year. The young gentleman, my old friend, is very fair and smooth in appearance, I desire no more. The great man [Harcourt] and I met at supper at your father's lodgings, I was in the room first, he came in to me—never was man more surprised than he was when he found me there. We were alone near a quarter of an hour, till Secretary Bromley came in and relieved him. I leave your Lordship to guess how much he was at a loss for conversation.

The Queen continues lame in both her hands, she now begins to complain of her knee, it is hoped the gout will fall into her feet.

I have no more than to wish you and my Lady many years, and may you love each other in the last as well as you do now. I shall return on the 16th to Oxford. I must own I had a desire to have seen you and my Lady together, but I ought to be satisfied that I hear you are happy in each other. Now I have seen that I have wished for as to you over, I have no other concern in this world, nor anything to hinder me from passing what time I have to come in it with Robin Morgan in preparing for the next.

1713-14, January 22. Christ Church.—I left Windsor on the 16th ; I reached Bucklebury that night, and returned home last night. Your Lordship may perceive by the Gazette, that I shall be obliged to be in London by the middle of March. If your Lordship is not before that time settled in Newcastle House, I will make no stay in town, but wait on your Lordship as soon as my turn is over. If your Lordship continues at Wimpole, I will concert my journey with you, against I come up to town. I beg my most humble duty to my Lady, and my thanks for her goodness in allowing me to pay my duty to her; you won't believe me, but there is somewhat of truth in it, that I have as great a desire to see my Lady, now your Lordship is married to her, as your Lordship had before you were married.

I long to give your Lordship an account of my conversation at Windsor, but I must reserve it till we meet. Lord Chancellor and I were alone in your father's room for a quarter of an hour, he came in upon me there, and was not a little surprised to find me there. Never was man more at a loss for conversation; he would not come to church the day I preached. All very fair in appearance between the young lord and me.

You have heard I suppose of the poor wretch who poisoned herself, for love, as it was given out, of Colonel Killigrew; his friends to excuse him reported that she forced herself into his bedchamber, and would have come into his bed, and because he would not let her, she took ratsbane. I believe your Lordship never heard before of a Joseph amongst the soldiers; the truth was this. He had solicited her long; that he could not for fear of losing his place marry her in the common form, but she should be his wife before God ; that the intervention of a priest was no ways necessary, but only a trick of the priests to get money; that she should be his wife as much as Sarah was Abraham's; that he would never know any other woman, and would allow her 50*l.* per annum besides presents which he would make to her. Upon this she complied with him on a Monday. She found when it was too late that he slighted [her], and attempted to speak with him on Tuesday, but he avoided her. On Wednesday she met him alone at the chocolate house, and desired him to provide for her as he had promised; he bid her begone ; she told him he had ruined her; he answered "God damn me, because I have ruined you, must I ruin myself?" She went away and immediately tried to get some ratsbane. On Thursday she got some of an apothecary's boy, and mingled it with some sugar and put it into

M

warm ale, and drank it up as ale and sugar before several people.
She had lain for several days in great torture when I left Windsor,
there was a bare possibility, but little probability of her life.

1713-14, January 27.   Christ Church.—I know not how
to express my duty and thanks to my Lady for the honour she
does me. I am very glad to hear I shall find you in town
when I come up. I shall certainly beg leave to wait on you
at Wimpole as soon as you return thither in the summer. Your
Lordship will have a neighbour this winter at Newcastle House
that you will like. I believe Tom Rowney will have the corner
house in which he lived two years ago.

I have received all the letters your Lordship did me the
honour to write to me, and I hope your Lordship received the
last I wrote to your Lordship from Windsor. I think I told
your Lordship in that how kindly I was received by Lord
Bol[ingbroke], though he could not help dropping some expressions by which I understood how far I was to rely upon
appearances.   I have since had a further account from
London, that all that civility was perfect hypocrisy, but that
is as much as I desire. If he breaks not out into open quarrels,
I will never press him for old friendship. Your Lordship will
have an account from my brother Gastrell, before I shall see
you, of the reason of that minister's wrath against me.

I am sorry to hear of Lord Treasurer's cold, I think he was
too complaisant to go out yesterday, before his cold was quite
gone, to the christening in Lincolns Inn Fields. I suppose your
Lordship has had an account of it. The Bishop of R[ochester],
who was to do the office, would by that have an opportunity
of speaking with your father, which he complained he could
not get, and said he would never attempt any more. I cannot
but reflect on the proceedings of great men one to another.
To see your father pressed to such a compliment by those
who but three months ago were in concert to have ruined
him—but let that pass.

1713-14, February 5.   Christ Church.—I know not whether
this will come soon enough to Wimpole to wish your Lordship
and my Lady a good journey to town. I suppose the approaching session obliges your Lordship to think of leaving the country.
You must have some days I suppose to prepare for your going to
the Upper House. There I expect to hear of you as soon as the
Parliament is opened, and I wish there may not be an occasion for
more strength there. If there be any ground for the reports we
have here, the opposition there will be as obstinate as ever.

Our governor is gone to London, I suppose he will have the
addition of a higher title before we see him again. There is
now more matter for those of our gown who are intriguing for
better preferments. The poor Archbishop of York is dead. The
two chief competitors for that see, I believe will be Hereford and
Chester. I may tell your Lordship, whom I can trust, that our
friend the Bishop of Hereford never at first desired a bishopric

so much as he now does a better. He gave so many proofs when he was at Hereford of his designing to leave them the first moment he could, that he had lost himself in that diocese before he was well in possession of it. Chester [Dawes] will certainly vote against you if he has not York, and I am afraid will not be firm to you if he has it. He will then hope for no more from you, and think himself at liberty to do as he pleases, and the best you can hope for from him will be to be whimsical. It is a very unaccountable part that he has taken on him ever since the change of the ministry, to reflect publicly in all companies on your father, and for that too for which no other person ever pretended to tax him, for want of sense. But I hope my brother Gastrell will not be forgot amongst the vacancies that are likely to be by deaths and removes.

I suppose your Lordship has heard that young Mr. Bromley is gone with my godfather to Hanover. I am glad of it for the young gentleman's sake, and it is very proper too on the public account.

1713-14, February 10. Christ Church.—I hope you have had charity enough to have made a visit in Duke Street. I am afraid cordials may be wanting there; the disappointment will try all the remains of philosophy. I do remember when there was a great stock of philosophy there, at a time when I could not boast of much of it. But what cannot ladies do! I am afraid it was all given in dowry to the noble lady. I could give a little comfort, but I have ill-nature enough not to do it. I could tell him that I believe he is reserved for London upon the next vacancy; but what poor creatures are we to have our peace depend upon these things. Your Lordship may allow me to talk a little at this rate now you are provided for to the utmost of your wishes.

If the new promotion° is for the Queen's and your father's service, it is well. It is lucky for him, he could not have lived any longer where he was. You may not easily believe this, but I think my intelligence in those parts is sure. He was sunk to a degree, scarce credible, for his votes in the last session. Not one gentleman, I repeat it without exceptions, not *one*, would converse with him, of those amongst whom he had been very popular. He has had prodigious luck there, in the short time he has been there he has received more in fines than my poor father did in eighteen years. Two good estates fell in entirely. Bishop Hall had charged on one of them, besides the usual rent, 48*l. per annum* for the augmentation of the salaries of the petty canons, which are wretchedly mean. They petitioned this bishop for the continuance of it, but though he had such fortune as never man had in that place he would not hearken, but gave the whole estate to his son. I suppose your father did not promote him on account of the particular friendship and respect he had for your father. If your father did he was much mistaken, as, with submission, the greatest men may be, but if it is an

---

° Of Sir William Dawes, Bishop of Chester, to be Archbishop of York.

expedient to make some unreasonable men easier at this time, there may be one reason given for it. His successor will smart for his good fortune. I have a sort of a hint from S[ecretary] B[romley]that my brother G[astrell] may be the man; if he should, it will be well for the diocese, to which I wish well, though I never got anything by it, but G [astrell] will be undone unless he has a good *commendam.*

1713-14, February 12. Christ Church.—I should be glad to know where you are, and whether you received the last I wrote to you. I would not willingly it should fall into other hands. I wrote my mind in it, before I was aware, a little more freely than a cautious man would, by such a conveyance. The competition is as I expected, both equally desire it, but one is too stiff to ask for it, he expects it should be offered to him; the other is a little more supple, *non modo petit, sed pulsat.* I believe we may foretell that *petenti dabitur.* I hope he will be satisfied then, though I will not answer for him. There will be one step still higher.

I remember your Lordship was saying once, that one edition of Speed was better than the other, pray which is the best? Can your Lordship tell me, where you are, in what year and by whom that was printed? I ask because one is offered to me to be sold. I would not buy the worst edition.

1713-14, February 13.—It is plain which way the W[hig]s hope to play their game. Their aim is to offer themselves to join with the T[orie]s who either really are against the Commerce bill, or make that a pretence to pursue other discontents. You must humour your new Lordship a little, you must leave him at liberty to differ from you some times; he will look on that as a point of honour, and do it without much hurt to you. One thing I fancy you will find in him, that he will make it a point of honour not to be against any thing he has ever openly declared himself. You must let him take his own way if he will be content with his own private dissent from you, and not cabal against you.

Grabe's "Spicilegium," that is reprinted, is only on small paper; there are none of them on large. The faults in the former edition are corrected and several additions are made in this.

Postscript. I shall bring up with me to town a note of some books of the late Bishop of Hereford? If you have a mind to pick any out I can procure them for you.

Pray be pleased to think of going to Sir Godfrey's for my picture, I have a design too on my Lady.

1713-14, February 16. Christ Church.—I cannot blame you for thinking of Wimpole again, there is nothing by what I hear in town that can make it agreeable to any honest man. They have put me in the Lent list, were not that on my hands I should have no other motive to come to town, nor business when I am there, but to pay my duty to my Lady and your Lordship. When I have done that I will retreat again as fast as I can to my cell.

I can easily believe there is confusion enough, and it will be as great in church as in state, but I hope there was no good ground for the report you had met with of Sir T. H[anmer]'s refusing the chair. Not that he is such a one as I could wish there, but I know not where at present you would have a better. My kinsman would be as mercenary as you would desire him, he would do any thing you would have him, but if he were in that chair he would be paid for what he did. But if he were in the chair, he would be of no weight or authority in the House. But I may spare my reflections. All will be over before this can reach your Lordship. I hear John Ward has thrown up his Welsh judge's place, I know he thinks he has been unkindly used, and I convinced him that it was owing to my Lord Chancellor. But his throwing up now is no proof of any fresh discontent, for he told me when I met him in [the] summer at Bath that he was then resolved to quit it, but it may be of use to you perhaps to know that if Sir Th[omas] H[anmer] be in the chair he will be more under the influence of J[ohn] W[ar]d than of any one man whatever, even more than of Mr. B[romle]y.

I had wrong information about the person that is likely to succeed at York. It is said now it will not go to him that asks for it. I suppose he is reserved for another place, but I expect now to be informed by your Lordship how those things will go.

Tom Rowney and his wife go up to town to-morrow, but he could not have the house in your neighbourhood; he is in Covent Garden.

I hear there is a design in which many Tories have combined to move to bring over H[anove]r. If this be so, it is either by distressing your father to force him to their own terms, or what is worse, upon a supposition that the Queen cannot last long to make their court to H[anove]r. If there be such a design my Diocesan of C[heste]r is in it, and I believe you will find some considerable ones in your House come in on this pretence, because they once voted for it, they think it would be dishonourable to be now against it. They will not move. for it, but if others move it they cannot be against it. No one in his wits can expect anything from it but immediate confusion.

1713-14, February 28.—Your great neighbour in the Fields [Harcourt] interposed with great warmth, to oppose Dr. Pelling and to recommend Mr. Hinton to the Speaker. And out of mere despite for J. P[elling's] success he did a very extravagant thing in giving the schoolmaster's place at Ewelme to one Newcome, when the Queen had signed a warrant to give it to Mr. Ivy of our House. It is certainly not in the Chancellor's gift, and he has taken upon him to dispose of that which he has no more right to than your Lordship has. But if it had been in his own disposal, he might have had the manners to have given way to the Queen's warrant. But he has lost more by this disposal of it, than ever he will get by obliging the Principal of Brasenose or the Bishop of Rochester. The man to whom it is given is very infamous, his story is too long for a letter, and all here are astonished at his getting of it. The place instead of a school will be a bawdy house—perhaps his Lordship may call in as he goes to Cockrop.

The talk was here for my brother Gastrell for Chester. I wish the bishopric were as fit for him as he is for the bishopric. I know of no bishopric in either province that will give more trouble to one who makes a conscience of doing his duty, nor any one that requires more a good man, a man of sense and a discreet man. But his predecessor has so stripped it, that brother Gastrell will be undone if he should not have something *in commendam* with it.

1713-14, February 25. Christ Church.—I am [in] no little pain for my dear godfather, there are no letters yet of his safe arrival [at Hanover], and I am told there are reports in town as though he had been cast away in the stormy night. Pray let me hear from you, or order some other to write to me as soon as you have any account of him.

It is as I guessed it would be, the poor man wants a cordial. I had a letter last night, he could not help owning how very uneasy he was. This is not very episcopal. I am afraid he wants grace upon more accounts than one, had he a little more one way he would not be so much concerned for missing of it another way, but this *entre nous*.

In looking over my pamphlets there were three or four I had forgot, which I know not but you might desire :—Guthry's "Memoirs," worth your having, if you have it not; Burnet's "Account of John, Earl of Rochester"; "The Emperor and Empire betrayed, how and by whom," a famous little pamphlet towards the latter end of Charles II. ; Wolsey's "Life"; "Narrative of the Proceedings against James, Bishop of St. Asaph." If you would have any of them I will bring them up with me.

' 1713-14, March 1. Christ Church.—I heartily thank you for putting me out of pain about my godfather. I do long to see you, but were it not for that I should come up with great reluctance; there is nothing there that I want, and I leave everything here unwillingly. I see not how I can be in the least of any service, but I will obey, and I hope I shall be able to be in town in the beginning of the next week. But you must engage to protect me against your great neighbour. Tom Rowney sends me word—this betwixt you and me—that the wrath is as great against me ; I know not the reason, nor do I much care. If things here are not exactly as he would have, I must have the honour of being the cause of it. He says I talk against him, but he will not instance in what. I hope I shall keep myself out of the reach of *scandalum magnatum*. But I have not conversed with above five persons in the university for this last half year, and have purposely avoided any discourse of things in which he had any concern. But I can easily guess at his intelligence. His Bishop keeps his hold on him, by furnishing him with stories, but he is now in the utmost rage at J. Pelling's success and my brother Gastrell's promotion. He is come to that pass as to declare that he looks on all at Christ Church as his enemies. I believe his Bishop has possessed him to that degree that he looks on any opposition as designed ultimately against himself, and that when any who are not friends to the Bishop are preferred it is in order to strengthen an interest against himself. The choice of the Almoner may perhaps throw him into as great a fit as he had last year, upon the university's proceeding against Ald[rich].

1713-14, March 4. Christ Church.—The Speaker I heard invited those gentlemen because they had spoke for him. I am told it is usual to invite all those that speak to recommend him, but I suppose he will be allowed to take his own way in things of no great moment; he will more easily be persuaded to go right in matters of weight.

I will come up if I can on Monday, but I am afraid it will be Wednesday before I set out. I shall be wanted here till then for the College business, and I believe I shall scarce be able sooner to pick up my own poor rents to enable me to take my journey, but that shall be the latest.

Postscript. I do not believe that you would most labour to prevent will come on in the beginning of the session. I like not the beginning in the Lords' House. Have you not strength enough to protect your friends? This censure will be construed by many as a public approbation of the other. Perhaps it may be a forerunner of it. What if the printer [of the "Spirit of the Whigs"] should squeak, what will become of ———— [Swift?] Pray give me some account of this. Was it really through want of number that so little opposition was made to W[harton]?

1713-14, March 6. Christ Church.—Things seem by the Lords' Address to go better in that House than we might have hoped from the first day's work. I hope Barber is a sturdy fellow; I believe no law can touch him. I pity poor D[octor] S[wift] if Barber should squeak. The pamphlet is very well written, you are obliged in honour to protect the Dean.

Freeman of the "King's Head" is made a justice of peace, no doubt by the interest of a bishop, at Alsop's desire. The reason Alsop had to procure this honour to Freeman can be no secret to your Lordship, the great man has no reserve of complaisance for his ecclesiastical friend.

[To ABIGAIL HARLEY?]

1714, May 1.—Madam, though I durst not presume to enquire directly of yourself how you and Mrs. Harley and my little mistress did, yet I failed not to enquire of Dr. Bettenson. But since you have done me the honour to mention me in yours to my Lady Dupplin, I think I have a title to trouble you directly.

I hope Mrs. Harley will not be in too great haste to leave the Bath, after so great a struggle as she has gone through, I believe the waters will now take place, and restore her to a condition of health she has not known for many years. Pray do not interpret what I wrote as though I was capable of a thought to the disadvantage of my little mistress. What I said I think imported rather that she needed no improvement, than that she would have none. Be pleased to assure her with my most humble respects, that Lady Harriot has . . . . ° her, but longs very much to see her. I never had the honour to wait on Lady Harriot, but I began her health to her (*sic*). It is with the greatest satisfaction that I can assure you that I believe there are not in the world a happier couple, and upon truer grounds, than in Newcastle House. Both exceed my expectations, though not my wishes. I hope too in a little time we shall see them easy in a fortune which they may call their own. If it be not as great as one of her birth might have expected, yet it will be as great as one of her sense and goodness will desire. But though the composition should be upon harder terms than it was once thought it might have been, yet what has passed within these last two months makes it highly necessary.

Lady Dupplin commands me to write you some news, and yet she will not furnish me with the most proper materials, which as a lady who receives and returns visits, she is best able . . . . . . Those of the public affairs for . . . . . two months, are such as would astonish you, but not much entertain you, especially that part of them which has been the most pursued, though it appears least. My poor master has narrowly escaped stabs, of another nature indeed than that which he had from Guiscard, but which were aimed at him with as much malice, and had they taken place might have been near as mortal. No malice so virulent, as well as base, as that which is heightened with ingratitude. I hope he is not only past the danger of it, but may, if his own temper would give him leave, by turning it on the authors, prevent any revival of it. I hope one, who perhaps may [have] had some share in it, begins to see the issue of it would have been her own ruin. There is an accommodation in appearance with others, but after such attempts I believe there can never again be any true confidence.

The ladies I am afraid will have a great disappointment. It is said they have been preparing to set themselves out to the greatest advantage upon the Duke of Cambridge's . . . . . . every one hoping to be the happy lady that will engage him. Some begin to be of opinion that all their pains will be to no purpose, not for want of charms in them, but for his not coming. I cannot on this occasion forbear thinking of the widow you were pleased to mention. I hope she has qualities in her more

---

° A few words at the foot of each page of this letter are lost from decay.

valuable than her beauty, though that is beyond what a poor parson ought to hope for. Had she been here, as you suppose, there would have been somewhat in town to have make my stay very agreeable to me. I have met with enough to make it otherwise, but the pretty widow is not many miles distant from you. I have a great inclination not to trust to Dr. Bettenson's report, but to wait on you at Bath, and see with my own eyes how you do. But you are so given to suspect me, though I thought I had not been liable to much suspicion on that account, that I am afraid you would not take the compliment to yourself, but be apt to think that I came to Bath only for an opportunity of going a little further.

[To LORD HARLEY.]

1714, June 1. Christ Church.—I thank God I am safe at home, and my relish of my own cottage at present is very strong. How long it will continue I know not, but the change of the scene is so agreeable to me, that instead of envying your Lordship for your greatness, I heartily pity you upon all accounts but one, for your having Lady Harriot; for having herself, and not those appendixes of her dirty manors and woods, which many may think the chief part of your good fortune. But from my soul I think the possession of herself a blessing for which even as great a philosopher as my fellow traveller may envy your Lordship.

I am scarce recovered of my journey, you must be content this post with a short letter. I hear the Dean of St. Patrick's [Swift] is in town. I suppose he will call on me.

1714, June 3. Christ Church.—I was in hopes of a line last night from your Lordship. Your Lordship will excuse a little curiosity when we are in so great a crisis, but I take your silence for a good sign, at least it is a proof that no mischief has happened.

I saw not the Secretary before I left the town, but I received the enclosed [missing] from him at eleven at night. I had told him, that I thought things would be brought to an issue in a few days. You will see what his apprehensions were upon it. I leave it to you to show this elsewhere as you shall think fit, but return it to me again.

Lord Anglesey last Friday at dinner at the Speaker's, before the Lord Almoner [Smalridge], said that your father had spoken to him to desire him to speak to all his friends to be for giving the arrears to the Hanover troops, and told him that it was the Queen's desire they should be given. Lord Anglesey said he spoke to Lord Boling[broke] upon it, that Lord Boling[broke] told him it was not the Queen's desire. Lord Anglesey asked him which he must believe, your father or him. Lord Bol[ingbroke] said if he would go along with him to the Queen he should hear it from herself, that it was not her desire.

The Dean of St. Patrick's came hither on Monday, in the other coach, but we met not on the road. He was in the College on Tuesday, and met Dr. Altham, who told him I was in town, but he called not on me. He is gone to one Mr. Gery's, who has a parsonage near Wantage, one who lived formerly in Sir William Temple's family, and was afterwards a fellow of Corpus Christi, and went off about four years ago to this parsonage, which is in the presentation of the College. By what I hear the Dean will be at full liberty to converse with himself, and to sort his papers without any interruption from his landlord, and will be obliged for his entertainment to his own reflections.

Postscript. It is resolved to attempt in the Lords to extend the Seminary Bill to Ireland also. They will first pass the Bill and then offer the amendment. The Primate solicits Lord Anglesey to do this. Lord Anglesey had been twice with the Bishop of Rochester about it; he was received at the first time coldly, but at the second time his Lordship promised to be assisting in it.

1714, June 5. Christ Church.—I had this day a full account from the Bishop of Chester of yesterday's debate and division. The Lords our friends, who were for admitting the petition, are such known friends of your father, that you must expect the Bishop of Rochester and Lord Bolingbroke will say they voted so by his order. One may perceive already how it will go; if the bill is not dropped, it will be garbled, and any amendments that can be desired will be admitted.

Honest John [Drummond]'s coming over was very providential, he has done greater service at home than abroad. It will be hard if he should not reap some little advantage from those services, from which they for whose sake they are done reap so great. It is high time there should be a mar mission [?], but can you guess in what manner it will be, will there be a submission or a dismission. There can be no reconciliation I am afraid, that will be safe.

The Dean of St. Patrick's left not Oxford till Thursday morning, one saw him then going out of town with a portmanteau behind his man, big enough to contain his library as well as his equipage. I heard not of him whilst he was here, nor can I learn either where he lodged, or with whom he conversed.

My Lord Treasurer told me on Sunday that he would order the money for Dr. Hutton's books to be paid; if it be paid to Hutton at Somerset House it will be sufficient, but his Lordship was pleased to say that all the manuscripts were not there. I thought Dr. Freind had got in all that had been lent out. If his Lordship suspects any to be wanting, if he can guess what they are, I will order immediate enquiry to be made for them.

I heartily wish to hear that Lord P[elham] and your Lordship were agreed in other points as well as in this which was last in dispute. My dear Lord, let no happy turn tempt you to defer the conclusion of that matter, as far as it is in your power, but rather make use of the sunshine to hasten it. That is of too great moment to be left any longer to chance. When I hear that is over I can lay down my head on my pillow, without fear of waking before daybreak.

1714, June 8. Christ Church.—I found upon my return that there had been too much ground of complaint against Lewis. He had for six weeks past absented himself from the chapel, the hall, and from his tutor's lectures, and had often lain out of the College. These were all just grounds of suspecting somewhat worse than appeared. I could not meet with him in four days after my return ; at last I had him seized in bed in a morning and brought to me. I said what I thought proper, and at last told him if he lost the provision designed for him by your Lordship's intercession, and did not make his peace with the Sub-dean, he must expect nothing more from your Lordship or your father, and might look upon himself as undone. I then ordered his tutor to carry him to the Sub-dean. I have since spoken with the Sub-dean as by your Lordship's order. I told him your Lordship would not press him to do any thing he thought improper, that he was to be the judge, who was fit to be nominated by himself, but that I did not know that your Lordship had any thoughts of recommending any other, if Lewis should be unfit. That I believed your Lordship could still wish Lewis might have his favour, if he should by his future behaviour endeavour to recommend himself to it. The Sub-dean said what I allowed, that after so much negligence, it would be necessary to have a proof, as well as a promise, of his future behaviour ; that he could only recommend Lewis to the acceptance of the Chapter, that he should be ready to do what your Lordship desired, if Lewis should behave himself so as to be fit for his kindness. In short what has been done may be passed over, I suppose, if he be regular for the future. And I believe the Sub-dean will not have any nomination this year, so that we shall have time enough to have proof of Lewis's manners. I am afraid the lad has very ill habits. I wish your Lordship would take [care] to have him told, severely, that he must expect nothing either from your family, or his own friends, unless he take care by exemplary diligence to make amends for what is passed. I will not fail to watch him and to send for him sometimes.

Here are reports with us that Lord B[olingbroke] designs to surrender his seals. They are pleased to compliment me so far as to enquire if I know any thing of it, but I very safely answer that I am a stranger to his Lordship's intentions.

1714, June 10. Christ Church.—I am very glad to hear your Lordship mention hand and seal. I hope your Lordship remembered to tell Lord Treasurer what I took to be the true meaning of an odd expression dropped by a certain person to him. He was certainly vexed that your father had taken out of his hands the opportunity he would have had of making his own terms by having the management of such an affair.

I was in hopes you would have been up in a week. Surely
the business might have been dispatched sooner; this delay I am
afraid gives advantage to those at home, who endeavour to do
mischief in that we are chiefly concerned with abroad. Our letters
tell us the French commissaries and ours are agreed, and that
the bill of commerce will be brought in. Is this true? It may
be worth while to protract the session for that bill, though it
comes in unseasonably if there should be any opposition to it.

I do not expect any issue of other affairs until the session is
over, but methinks assurance might in the mean time be given
of what shall be then done.

1714, June 12. Christ Church.—I hear the Queen expressed
great concern to Lord Al[moner] about the success of the Schism
bill; this was on Thursday last, and she was afraid lest it had
been spoiled by the alterations that [had] been made in it the
day before. This looks not well. This concern must come from
some impressions made from a wrong quarter, and I just now
hear that affairs are in as great confusion as when I left the town.
I cannot say I have this from a hand that I can entirely depend
on, but it is from a friend and one too who has good acquaintance.
If there be any ground for this I hope your Lordship will let
me know it in your next.

I forgot to tell you that the man who governs the Speaker and
infuses all his ill humours into him is Mr. Hill.

Sign and seal the first moment you can, no one can guess
where a wind that shifts from one point to another so often will
at last settle.

Postscript. I hear Sir Charles Hedges is dead. I hope some
of his many places will fall to the share of my [friend], Dr. Henchman. He would be a credit to the greatest of them; there is no
one of his profession who upon the test of merit can be a competitor with him. I have just now received the honour of
your Lordship's and at the same time one from J. D[rummond].
I perceive by the last letter, in what a dismal way we
are. Your Lordship in yours seem to dart a little ray
of hope. Pray let me hear, though only on one bare
line, how things go and who gains ground, be it good or bad.
I suppose the lady [Masham] has the chief hand in this. What
is it that she pretends for this new turn in herself?

1714, June 14. Christ Church.—I have not at present much
to say to you, but I am in no little pain till I hear from you. I
hear by Tom Rowney to-night that which explains to me the
expression in your Lordship's letter of going back to ways and
means. Pray who were the occasion of that? I hear too that it
is resolved to lay aside the old commissioners of accounts in the
new bill. Who is it that opposes them? They are not, as I take
it, unanimous amongst themselves, but in different measures, and
for following different heads. The quarrels at court certainly
begin to spread elsewhere, and will diffuse them every day
further, unless a stop be put at the fountain of them.

Which way will the Duke of Shr[ewsbury] go, I hear which way he voted yesterday, but with whom will he side in another place? As soon as you are at any certainty, p^{ra}y let me hear, be it good or bad.

1714, June 17. Christ Church.—If the new scheme prevail, I hear the Bishop of Rochester is to be Lord Privy Seal. I truly believe there is some ground for this, and that we should see, if not this, somewhat in relation to him altogether as extravagant.

I am glad of the new accession of strength, but I am afraid there will be a difficulty in keeping up a good correspondence there and with Anglesey at the same time. The latter is not of that moment as the other, but if he can be kept, he is a hearty enemy to the new minister.

My letters tell me alterations are talked of, and I find all good men wish, if they are to be, that they might be before the Parliament is up. The alarm begins to be taken. You may tell your father from me, that by the accounts which I have, I perceive that if the alterations talked of go on, some declarations which were lately made with great solemnity will immediately sink in their credit.

I wish J. D[rummond] may be in the right, but it is good to expect the worst. I am preparing myself to be a malcontent. I have been used to it, and never found but that I was as easy when the wind was in my teeth as when it was in my back. John has been a faithful servant to you in this, as well as all other cases. If you do go off, methinks it should be a matter of remorse to you that you have not provided better for him whilst it was in your power to do it. I must tell you the vogue is against you, as far as I can learn it. It is thought you cannot keep your ground, though no one thinks others can hold it longer than the next session, nor even to the end of this, at near as it is, if the alteration be before it is up.

My duty to my Lady and my most humble thanks for the great honour she does me in vouchsafing to allow me a place in her memory. I wish these domestic broils do not bring a trouble on her she does not suspect. If the war goes on, and I should be driven from Christ Church, I shall certainly retire for protection to Wimpole.

Stanley may be of use. if there should be occasion to fix Lord Shrewsbury. He heartily hates the new minister, and has good reason to do so.

1714, June 20. Christ Church.—My accounts every post still give me less hopes, I find the expectation of a change grows every day, and it is impossible to express men's apprehensions of it. All I find run into the same suspicion. It is not hard to guess at the consequence of so general a suspicion. But the Lord Treasurer is too stout to do what is necessary to prevent this, in his own account; yet he for the sake of the public and others too should set all hands at work to stop it. They know they have it in their power to expose the chief drivers. As late

as it is in the session, I should think some at least of their
practices should be brought into the House of Commons, at least
so far as to show them what they are to expect next winter.
This possibly might check those who are running so warmly
with them. But all who are of any weight, who have honour or
fortune, and are engaged in the public service, should agree
amongst themselves to withdraw from it, if the alteration happens,
and should let that agreement be known. It may be too late
to treat for a remedy till the next session, it is probable we
shall be in confusion before. If this go on, I am afraid it is
upon the prospect of somewhat that must be attempted before
the next session.

What party was it in the House that were for continuing
the old Commissioners, and who were warm for new ones?

Pray who was it that, when the supply was closed, stood up
and said he hoped none of it would be applied to the Hanover
troops? I hear a friend of ours thought himself reflected
upon in that and could not forbear answering.

1714, June 22. Christ Church.—Has your Lordship heard of
the Bishop of Rochester's congratulating Mr. Nelson upon the
likelihood of your father's removal? Mr. Nelson gave him an
answer the Bishop did not expect, but such as he deserved. I
take this to be a proof [of] the Bishop's politics, as well as of his
honesty and gratitude. There can be but one point upon which
that Right Reverend could suppose such a removal could be agreeable to Mr. Nelson. I hope your Lordship will take care that the
right Reverend's goodwill be known where it was intended.

I trust the Colonel's hope is upon some good ground, and not
merely the result of his courage.

That which has been started in your House will be of mighty
use, if it can be made good. I need not tell your Lordship that
others than appear in it are supposed to be at the bottom of it.
I hope they are sure of their point. The transferring of stock
looks very like a confession of guilt. I have not heard of the
Dean of St. Patrick's [Swift] since he went hence, he does not I
believe like these shifting winds, and will scarce appear till the
wind comes to be settled in one point or other.

1714, June 26. Christ Church.—I like not the present face
of affairs, I know not where it will end, but it seems not to forebode anything that is good. I long to hear that your own affair
is finished. I should be sorry if the storm should break upon us
before that is over. If that were done we might hope to meet
it without being overwhelmed by it. I thank you for the hopes
you give me of seeing you here soon; it cannot be I suppose till
the session is over, and as warm as you are at present yet I
fancy the session will be like the days we have now, the hottest
at the close.

J. Davies will be in town as soon as ever there is water enough
in the river to carry up the barge; at present there is not, the
channel may be passed without wetting your shoes in many
places betwixt this and Abingdon. I will order him to call on

your Lordship when he goes, and give your Lordship notice when he will be there.

I was in some danger, but came off without hurt. The adventure was so odd, I cannot help smiling when I reflect on it, it will be more proper to be told than to be written, but pray from whom did your Lordship hear anything of it?

Postscript. I have good reason to believe the Bishop of London has of his own accord, at this juncture, done the part of an honest man to somebody, and of a friend to your father. I know not the success.

June 27.—I perceive by the letters just come in that the talk of the town runs on the Captain's side. I hope care is taken to have the Colonel's friends kept steady against such an accident. I hear Lord Treasurer is to be president of the Council, this agrees not with what I heard, that he had left them. I take him to be wiser. It is said Lord Anglesey is to go to Ireland. I know not how such a post may tempt him, but he and B[olingbroke] are mortal enemies and can never hold. All agree the lady [Masham], your quondam friend and cousin, is irreconcilable.

1714, June 29.—I have no news to send, but I expect some from you, and such as must be of greater consequence, be it good or bad, to us all, than any event that has happened in my days. We may learn by what we [have] seen since Christmas last, how foolish all our presumptions of quiet and security are. When we think we are past all difficulties, and that every thing is easy, somewhat we never expect breaks out that gives us more trouble than all we foresaw. But I think the present posture of affairs ought to be a lesson to your Lordship, who are just entering upon the world, though not to avoid any share that is proper for you in the pub-·lic affairs, yet never to depend on it, and always to keep your own private affairs upon such a foot, that you may at a moment's warning quit any public post not only. with honour, but without any inconvenience too to yourself.

1714, July 1. Christ Church.—I shall [write] more freely to your Lordship than I do now, to-morrow by old Mr. Jenks, who then sets out for London. I hope I have pleased the old man, I have had his boy entered, and have prevailed with Benson to take care of him. I shall desire Mr. Jenks, if he meets not with your Lordship at home, to leave the letter for you, and not to fail to do it on Saturday.

Postscript. I told Mr. Benson that Mr. Jenks was one for whom your Lordship was concerned. Mr. Benson upon this promised to recommend the lad to be servitor to and to live with my Lord Lemster, who will be here in a few weeks and is to be under Mr. Benson's care.

Mr. Jenks gave me some diversion ; he saw the Lords' address on my table. He was mightily pleased, I perceived, and seemed to look on it as somewhat providential that the Queen was desired to renew her alliance with the Emperor. He thinks the Emperor, I perceive, a sure friend and support to the Protestant succession; but the Queen's answer did not give him entire content. It did not seem to him direct enough that she would do what the Lords desired; he owned it was, as it were, tantamount.

1714, July 1. Christ Church.—I can by this conveyance desire you to explain a line in your last. Your Lordship says, " Certainly, Anglesey will be theirs if he has Ireland, the Duke of Ormond, I believe, will leave." Do the words "If he has Ireland" refer only to Anglesey, so as to mean that Anglesey would be theirs, in the condition only of having Ireland? Or do those words belong to that which follows, so as to mean that the Duke of Ormond would leave them, if Anglesey had Ireland? But whether those intermediate words belong to those which precede them or those which follow them, it is plain that your Lordship supposes the Duke of Ormond at present to be with them, which amazes. I did not think my friend your father had any one surer to him, or more averse to the new ministry. Nor can I imagine what can have brought him off, unless the Duke of Shrewsbury being with your father. Perhaps he may think if your father continue here, the Duke of Shrewsbury will continue in Ireland, but if your father quit, the Duke of Shrewsbury will not go again to Ireland, and then there may be room for them (?) to hope for him. I would [not] willingly think him capable of such mean thoughts, but I know not otherwise how to account for his being with them. Pray explain this a little to me. I never had that opinion of Anglesey's honour that I had of the Duke of Ormond's, but Anglesey has so often called the others villains and said he knew them to be so, and sworn solemnly that he would never serve one hour with them, that if he does after all this join with them, he must be as great a villain as any of them, and has only played the part he has done to wait for an opportunity in troubled waters of selling himself to those who would buy him with this place. But I would be glad to know how long he has been with them. F. Annesley must have been the man who has negotiated this matter, if it be done. Pray let me know who you think do stick with you, who will to the last do so ; and who have, or who you think will leave you. How does my friend the Secretary hold? I ask because I am told he has seemed to favour A. M[asham?] and to enter into measures for bringing him off. I believe the Secretary will do nothing dishonourable. If the Duke of Ormond and Anglesey should upon a change fall in with the new ministers, I am not certain how far the Secretary might be prevailed with to continue too. Though if he has any due sense of his own safety, he will throw up, and if I can be of moment with him, he shall not want to be pressed to do it. If you think I can be of any service on such an occasion, I will come up whenever you summon me.

Pray tell me upon what foot my Lady Abigail puts herself at present; what does she give out as the reason of the open war which she declares at present? Has she no friend to tell her that if your father should give way at present, his own private and the public interest must bring his affairs where they were again. If her Ladyship should be routed, she is gone without resource.

I must now tell you one thing which must not go to any one, except your father and my godfather. I heard this morning from a certain lady, her spouse [Bolingbroke] tells her that he shall certainly be with her as soon as the session is up and stay a month. He writes this so often and with such protestation, that I perceive she has no doubt of it; what is more, he has begged her pardon for all his ill usage and promised amendment for the future. That would be somewhat more surprising than any thing that has passed since Christmas: but now to account for this. I know no meaning of it, unless he thinks he shall lose the day, and have occasion to retire. If he stays in and is chief, he can have no leisure, any more than he would have thoughts of retiring to her. There may possibly be another reason for the good words he gives her; he may have been advised by his new ally to treat his wife better, for the sake of their common credit, and to answer objections in the world, and that somebody may with a better grace confide in him. If that be the case, then this sweet letter is a sign that he thinks he shall get the day, but that will not account for his coming down.

Answer this by Mr. Jenks, if he returns, as I believe he will, by Oxford.

1714, July 8. Christ Church.—I beg my most humble thanks to my godfather for his kind remembrance of me by Tom Rowney. I find Tom is full of my Lady Harley's goodness to the female part of his family. I have not yet seen them. Tom either knows not, or will not own he knows, the story of the duck pond and Brudenel. But Tom tells me that this very night, the new junto are to hold their cabal at Bromley. Perhaps what passed on Friday may either put it off or make the meeting more necessary. I wish we had a more perfect account of it. I hope to have it by to-morrow's post. By the account we have the Lords came unanimously into the address, upon a short debate, but we cannot yet guess by what we hear where the address points, nor who drew or advised the signing of the three articles, nor whether any of the ministers owned or desired their having any concern in them. To-morrow's post I hope will give us a little light.

I hope your Lordship has received the letter I sent by old Mr. Jenks. I believe you were surprised at the last part of it, and know as little as I what to make of it. It is certainly all villainous hypocrisy, but for what end is the question. I must tell you one thing to prevent any mistake in judging. The letter I received should have been with me a week before, so that I conclude the letters written to the person who wrote to me were at least a fortnight ago, if not earlier. New hopes since perhaps may have induced him to change his style. I hope your Lordship will bring poor Lady Carmarthen's picture down with you.

1714, July 6. Christ Church.—I have just now the answer to the Lords' address; it looks as though it were resolved, if possible, to cover those who have been concerned. I am afraid it is plain by this answer who has the ascendant at present, and if they can be covered it is easy to guess what may be expected when the session is over. I wish no desperate measures may be thought of in the interval of Parliament to prevent what may be expected when it meets again.

On Thursday last Lord B[olingbroke] had no less than three personal conferences with the Bishop of Rochester, besides notes that had passed betwixt them. If the new project cannot be prevented, they who are chiefly concerned in it are now so blasted that they must stick at nothing to support themselves.

No rain yet with us, nor can we tell when our river will be navigable again.

1714, July 7. Christ Church.—I think I understand your letter, and foresee what we must expect, and that we must expect it quickly. I am sorry there should be any occasion for any one to interest themselves with the Secretary in this point. I know not what I can do, but I will do what I can, and if you continue to think it proper for me, send by Thursday's and Saturday's posts; I will come up on Monday. That will be soon enough for any use I can be of in that place; but take no notice to any strangers of my coming, I shall not stay above two days, if your Lordship's affairs should not allow you to leave the town as soon as you at present design.

Postscript. Are your own affairs in that condition that the other party cannot fly off?

1714, July 8.—I had little time to write in yesterday, but upon further thoughts I have nothing more to add. If by Saturday's post you think it proper for me to come up, I will sup with you, God willing, at Newcastle House on Monday. I am sorry you have any doubts of that person, because if he stays I am afraid some others will, from whom I did not expect it. We must do what we can, and leave the rest to Providence.

I just now receive your Lordship's of yesterday, I will not fail to be in town, God willing, on Monday. I would be there on Saturday, but that I expect both our bishops then, and, besides business of the House, I would inform myself from them in what humour they leave people in town. I hope one day will "break no squares." I shall come up in the stage coach, Acton road, but it will be too great a trouble for your Lordship to meet me there. I perceive we are coming to extremity. Let me hear from you by Saturday, and how things are.

' *Postscript.* If you would have me come sooner, send a servant to me as soon as you receive this, and I will be in town on Sunday.

1714, July 11. Christ Church.—If you give yourself the trouble of meeting me, this will not I believe be with you before I see you. If you stay at Newcastle House till I wait on you, this is to desire that you would be able if you can to inform me when I wait on you, when and where I may pay my duty to your father. He lies at Kensington and I cannot be certain of him at the usual times in York Buildings, and my stay must be so short that I would wait on him as soon as I can, and would not if I could help it call to no purpose. I should be glad to see my godfather as soon as I could.

The close of the Queen's Speech is to me a proof of the resolutions that are taken. If I meet you not, I hope to be at Newcastle House soon after eight.

1714, July 23.—I hope this will find my Lady and your Lordship well in Newcastle House. I must beg your Lordship to present my thanks to my Lady for the honour she has done me. Her Ladyship forgot her cap, but it shall be sent by Eldridge's coach to-morrow, which lies at the "Checquer" in Holborn. I am afraid her Ladyship wanted it on the road. I shall be desirous to know the issue of the present struggles, but I suppose things were yesterday as we left them, because I hear not of any change by this post.

1714, July 24. Christ Church.—I thank your Lordship for the good news of your safe journey, and bless God for it. My most humble duty and thanks to her Ladyship, she has left impressions of herself here that will be as lasting as the College. I thought your Lordship has a tolerable interest in this place, but I must tell you plainly—I have great authority for the expression—that her Ladyship has, if it be possible, I think the better of the two. I never knew any one who had the honour to know her that was not from that moment sincerely her servant.

It is good news that you can tell me none, I reckon every day's delay to be to our advantage. I suppose the Attorney [Harcourt] was not sent for upon the errand young Simkin seemed to hope as well as said he was. I rather believe it was upon the project the Duke owned to me, that if somebody would not do them the kindness to throw up, they would threaten to do unless he were turned out. I fancy the Attorney was sent for to a further consultation about that matter. I hope your Lordship remembers what passed betwixt me and the Duke and betwixt Baron P[rice] and the Attorney.

I forgot to give your Lordship the Greek Testament you had left here printed by Wechely (sic), and Daniel's Poems in quarto, stitched but without covers. I shall give them to Sedgely to be sent up with your other books, but if you would have Daniel bound by him, let me know.

I send your Lordship the enclosed to show you that you have prevented our impudence, and that if you had not given we were ready to beg. It was made by Wigan of the last election. The theme was given him by the Dean as an imposition for missing

prayers, but the Dean did not think of the application the lad
would make of it, nor had the lad I suppose heard of your
Lordship's bounty. He is a very bright lad.

Postscript. I have your Lordship's. We must all prepare to act
the part that becomes us on this occasion. I hope your Lordship
will now see a greater necessity of that I presumed to suggest to
you, with relation to the management of your own affairs. I
hope Lord T[reasure]r will not think of any other place than
Wimpole to retire to. I wish some who have given reason to
think they would run your fate do not act another part when the
blow is struck. The reverend person who was with you here
will certainly behave decently to your father, but he will adhere
to Mrs. Margery [Lady Masham?].

1714, July 27. Christ Church.—We live in expectation of hearing
of the change, and in preparing ourselves for the consequences
of it; the last will employ the most serious thoughts we have.
One thing occurs to me which I will presume to suggest to
your Lordship. I would only premise, that it arises purely from
my own thoughts, and is not hinted to me by the man himself,
or any other on his account. There can be no doubt I believe
but that poor Mr. Thomas will run his master's fate, and be
dismissed by those who succeed your father. Perhaps it may be
burdensome to your father to entertain him, though he will not
care to dismiss him. If your father should be willing to part
with him, why should not your Lordship take that opportunity
of securing to yourself the unvaluable treasure of such a servant,
No one can express the advantage of such a servant to one in
your Lordship's circumstances, who are entering upon so great a
fortune, in which for the first years at least you will have so full
employment. And I take Mr. Thomas, for his ability, his
honesty, and his temper, to be the very best servant that ever I
knew or heard of to any great man.

I hope your Lordship will let me know as soon as Lord Pelham
and you have signed. I have then nothing more to pray for, but
that you may take the most proper and speedy methods you can
to secure and perfect that agreement, and to clear off all encumbrances whatever from the estate that falls to your lot.

The post is come in, and I have no letters from the town. I
conclude the blow is not yet struck, though their own confusion
is I suppose the only occasion of the delay. It is what never yet
was known, that they who have power to vacate should not have
credit enough to be able to fill places.

1714, July 29.—The affair is now over ; we must now guard as
well as we can against the consequences of it. I may now say
that they who most rejoice in it will, I believe, have the heaviest
share in the consequences of it. But there is somewhat in the
manner of this transaction which seems still obscure to me. I
thought your father had been resolved to have had the staff
wrung from him, but it does not appear to me whether he was
turned out or resigned. It is given out, and by young Simkin,

that he goes out upon a composition. If there be any thing of this, I hope you will let it be known to one who is determined to put in all his own little stake upon your bottom. One thing has come to my knowledge by a sure way, though one you cannot guess, that a certain ———— has dealt not only cunningly, but somewhat more with your father. I expected dissimulation, but I did not think my good master could have been snared by one of whom he has had so much experience. You may hint this if you please, but I cannot explain myself till I see you or him, or have the opportunity of another conveyance.

Postscript. When does your Lordship and Lord P[elham] sign?

Our misfortunes come together. I am afraid Lord Weymouth has not made provision for our hall. The surveyor has been here and settled all and was to have made his report the day Lord Weymouth fell ill.

1714, August 1. Christ Church.—I heartily congratulate your Lordship upon the conclusion of your own private affair at such an extraordinary juncture. My heart is at ease as to your Lordship, and now our thoughts must have another turn as to the public. It is to no purpose now to tell you that young Sim came over and met Sprat and some other such at Delaune's, to rejoice at your father's dismission. I had an account of all that passed, they are now as dejected as they were rampant. Your poor father was to have been loaded, as the ruffian said, as far as such wretches could have done it, with every thing that could have made him odious. The disposition of the staff was indeed lucky; if [the Queen] had recovered, all the new measures would for the most part have been broken by it, but I could wish, however, that it had been in your father's hands at this juncture, and so I believe they do who wrested it from him. You do not think I gave much credit to Simkin, but he was not the only one who gave out such reports. God be blessed that your father quitted it with as great honour as he had kept it.

Late accidents have somewhat in them very remarkable as to the time in which they have happened. We ought to begin our reflections from the death of the Princess Sophia. I hope all tends to public tranquillity. Upon this next half year our future peace in great measure depends. I suppose your journey to Wimpole will be delayed, if not laid aside, but if you attend the Parliament I could wish my Lady had lodgings in the air somewhere near the town.

Mrs. Margery may be safely left to the punishment of her own reflections.

I had received notice to expect our friends in Scotland Yard to-morrow, perhaps upon this accident they may defer their journey.

1714, August 2. Christ Church.—We have no certain news yet of the poor lady's death, but we suppose it. Any particulars of what passed in her illness would be a favour. Is there any_

will ?   Were there any gifts or grants to Mrs. Margery or others?
What becomes of Mrs. Margery ?   How look the Chancellor and
Lord B[olingbroke]?   Here is a strong report, and I have seen
it in some letters, that high words passed betwixt your father and
Lord Chancellor the night he resigned his staff.   I have seen it
in letters.   Was there any ground for it?   If there was, what
were the words ?   The gentlemen here who were rampant four
days ago begin to turn upon their heel very quickly.   Delaune
ordered King George to be prayed for yesterday morning in St.
John's Chapel, when it was objected that it was not certain the
Queen was dead.   "Dead," says he, "she is as dead as Julius
Cæsar."   At the ordinance on Wednesday night the President of
Trinity toasted the Earl of Oxford.   Delaune said then, "He is
out, what do you toast him for?   What have we to do with him?"

When Sim was here, amongst other stories he said the Duke
of Argyll came up to Ruffian [Atterbury] in the House of Lords
and asked him if he might give him joy of being Privy Seal.
That Ruffian answered, "My Lord do not insult me, I know who
it is that has given that out, but I may live to have it in my
power to be even with him."

Is the black box opened?   Who are our Regents?   I hope you
forget not what passed betwixt the Chancellor and B [aron] Price.
Not the story of Nevil.

Postscript.   The late apprehensions we were under make this
affliction much easier than it would otherwise have been.
They had already begun with Lord Almoner [Smalridge].
Mr. B[romley] had written to let him know that he was represented as one who endeavoured to make the administration·
difficult by insinuating to all people that the protestant succession
was in danger, and desired that he would enable him to justify
him.   What scenes of wickedness would have been opened!

1714, August 3.   Christ Church.—The remainder of the prints
are coming.   You will desire Mr. Thomas to take care of the
enclosed.   Pray let one of your servants write out a copy of the
list of those prints you received from Vaillant, and send it to me
by the next post.   What think you of the list of Regents?   Is it
such as my godfather expected?   Can you yet guess, or do you
hear, how your own family are like to be with the new powers?
You will thank nobody for safety.   Do you think you shall have
any share of confidence?

1714, August 5.   Christ Church.—The ingratitude and the
meanness of the bonfire makers is remarkable, but I expected no
other from them.

The Regents drive fast; it is to be hoped he who is represented
by them will like a gentler race when he is in the saddle.   He
has it in his power to establish not only himself, but his family,
if he would take the way which I believe your father would
suggest to him.   If they who are his justices should be his
counsellors, his reign will be uneasy, and should he stave off the
evil in his days, it would come upon his posterity.

I am afraid some will be for provoking him; it is certainly the interest of the late cabal to make an open breach betwixt him and the church party. I have some reason to think it is their design too. They may hope to escape in public troubles, or at least, if they are prosecuted, to say it is for the sake of their party and not their crimes. But I hope our friends will be on the defensive, and wait to see how they are used. I hope they will do nothing which may be a pretence for disgracing them. I mean not by this, that I would have them immediately give the Civil list for life. No; surely it will be sufficient to give it at first for one year, and there is a fair pretence that [it] is beneath you to give it for a longer term till the King himself is here to ask it.

I have yet no directions about binding your books. I have heard what passed betwixt your father and that fellow, though you would not tell me.

1714, August 7.—I thank you for your hint. I have not sold. I always thought the possession would be quiet. The struggle if any will be some time hence, when we see what we are to expect upon the revival and animosities of parties. I foresaw there would be a rise of stock. When it is known abroad how quiet we are here, I am apt to think money will be poured in from Holland. If so, it may rise above 92, but pray enquire of your uncle, who dealt with those who are vested in this trade, what he thinks will be the highest mark. I am resolved to sell when I think it is at that pitch. I will not run the hazard of quarrels here, which must certainly happen, unless that method be taken, which the warm men of both sides will oppose. But I would willingly sell as well as I can, since it is the only hit I shall ever have. 200*l.* odds is somewhat to one who knows now the utmost he is to expect in this world. I depend upon you for intelligence in this point.

I have had notice of the bonfires from several other hands, they were so remarkable that every one made reflections on them. I hear the word now from Lord B[olingbroke], and Ruffian is forgetting of old quarrels and reunion of friends; they begin pretty early to call for help.

Postscript. My duty to good Lady Dupplin and her lord. My Lord perhaps may have occasion to borrow a little philosophy of my Lady. I fancy some of his countrymen have been mumbling a thistle lately. I need not explain myself.

I forgot to tell your Lordship that little He[a]rne proclaims aloud in all places your munificence to him.

1714, August 10.—I have some obscure remembrance of your Lordship's speaking to me about a Witney blanket to make you a riding coat. Let me know in your next if you would have one, and of what colour you would have it.

Without doubt the late cabal are taking their measures, either how to make their court or stand upon their defence. The rebuke to Sir W. was seasonable. I believe they think their own game desperate, and will endeavour to draw the church party into an open breach with the present powers in hopes of heading them and being protected by them.

The small pox is very rife and very malignant here; a very pretty woman indeed, Captain Bertie's daughter, died this morning of them. I am glad I did not let Lord Dupplin come hither.

We have had a sore disappointment in our loss of Lord Weymouth.

Is Sir Humphry [Mackworth] returned? I long to hear how he and the Captain explain upon their meeting, I believe Sir Humphry will now venture to give him some strokes.

Dares the Dean of St. P[atrick's] appear?

I suppose you hear what Lord Marlborough gives out of your father, that Bothmar showed the now late Queen a letter from your father to the Prince to persuade him to come over, of the same date with that printed one which was written to dissuade him.

1714, August 12. Christ Church.—It was very mean in the V[iscount] but no other than I expected from his temper, but I thought he had had better sense than to think such a thing possible. Does he think after what has passed, they who are clear themselves will come in to save him; that is the meaning. The Ruffian's language is just the same amongst our gown; old quarrels must be forgotten, we must unite again, no doubt of it; and it is to be hoped the church party will unite, but exclusively · of them. No one will ever have to do with such villains any more. Ruffian caressed the Bishop of Bristol [Smalridge] very much when he met him in the House of Lords upon his last coming.

Postscript. I have not seen "Guiscard's Ghost," pray send it to me. I hear there is a ballad in which your father and the V[iscount] are both· abused; if you have it pray let me have that too.

1714,. August 13.—I am told that Ruffian has worked himself into the Duke of Ormond and Lord Poulett. I should be surprised at either's having any confidence in him. But most at the last, on account of the friendship he has professed, and I suppose still professes, to your father, and the very good correspondence too he has with the Bishop of Bath and Wells. But it is said that both those great persons visit Ruffian often. It is fit you should know this, and I wish you would enquire what truth there is in it; if there should be any ground for this report it would be great charity to prevent their being drawn in by one who has no aim but to use them, though in that which may ruin them, to promote his own purposes.

1714, August 14. Christ Church.—I hope to send you a Witney blanket before you go to Wimpole. How long do you design to stay at Wimpole when you are there? Though I fancy you will defer your journey and will hardly go now till the King comes, since he is expected so soon. It is as wise men thought it would be, both sides striving who shall bid highest for him.

Since I wrote on Friday, I am told that Lord Steward [Poulett] had quarrelled with your father before the staff was taken away. Is there any ground for this? I am certain that the Chancellor and his party reckon upon him as sure to them.

1714, August 17.—Your Witney rug went this morning by Badcock's waggon, that lies at the Oxford Arms in Warwick Lane, if it is not brought to you, pray send to enquire for it. There is enough to make two coats, that you may have one always dry.

Poor Altham died on Sunday night betwixt ten and eleven.

I hear poor Weymouth was very desirous to have been Privy Seal in the new scheme that was to have been opened. Did you ever hear of this before, it was certainly so. Do you think Sir Humphry was ignorant of this?

I have just received your Lordship's; pray no excuse for not writing to me, I expect it not but when you have nothing else to employ you. I am glad I am misinformed as to Lord Steward, but that which I wrote on Friday was on account of my hearing from a very good hand that Lord Steward often visited in Dean's Yard, and I heard since that Lord Chancellor says that Lord Steward had quarrelled with your father, and pretended at the same time that he had entered into intimacies with himself. I am sure this came from Lord Chancellor, but I never give credit, till I have enquired, to any thing he says.

I thank you for my venison, it will come very seasonably to make much of J. Drummond, whom I expect for three or four days.

1714, August 19. Christ Church.—The Bishop of Bristol has given us an account of an extraordinary conversation he had with Lord Chancellor. The Lord Chancellor took no ordinary pains to convince the Bishop how sincere a friend he had been to your father to the very last, and how he had laboured with the Queen not to displace him. He then gave the Bishop great assurances of the respect he had for him, and said he should be very uneasy if the Bishop entertained any unkind thoughts of him. Both parts of the discourse were alike true. *Quelle impudence!*

The boat which brings your books is expected here to-morrow. You may perceive how scarce water is with us.

1714, August 21. Christ Church.—I thank your Lordship for my own presents. I shall always value the picture of that lady, for the true honour and esteem I had for her. I think the prints of my Lord of O[xford] very good, but graver than his looks commonly are.

Lord Marlborough has been in our neighbourhood, but is gone to-day to dine with Lord Wharton at Winchington, in his way to town. At his coming to Woodstock, the flag on the church tower was displayed, and continued so whilst he stayed there. I have sent you the account I have received from the Bishop of Bristol of his conference with Lord Chancellor. You will perceive that you must not own to him that you have seen it or know of it, and pray show it to no one but your father and under the same caution. The rest of the letter was College business, you will see by it the Lord Chancellor in his perfection. It is plain what they aim at by this attempt on the good Bishop of Bristol, but at the time he delivered that scandalous paper against me to your father I was not estranged from him, but, had his own professions been to be relied on, in high favour with him. His impudence if possible is greater than his treachery. Nevil, though he has got his own money, has still in his hands a large bundle of notes for money from half-a-crown to seven pounds, borrowed of others in the neighbourhood upon Nevil's credit, and which Nevil could never yet prevail with him to pay. I have some thoughts of buying in these notes, and bringing a bill in his own Court against his Lordship for them.

Looking over the account of your father's library to-day in Nicolson's preface, I remembered the letter which I sent with the papers to your father which you told me was bound in the first volume with the letters. There are in that letter several private things, besides the account which I was able to give of those letters. Somewhat I remember particularly relating to Dr. Potter. I would not willingly have that part of the letter seen by those who may look into those papers. I spoke to your Lordship formerly upon it, I beg you would take it out the next time you go to York Buildings, and I will write another to be inserted there, to give the best account I can of those papers.

I thank you for the "Ghost," they are very good and very proper, but how comes his associate the Bishop of Rochester to escape? Methinks he would have been proper to have blessed the bed in which his Lordship was to solace himself with the sisters. If the poet is of your acquaintance and under your command, pray desire him not to forget to do due honour to the Bishop in the next edition.

1714, August 24.—I troubled you with a long letter last post, I hear since that the V[iscount] gives himself great airs and says there were designs formed for the Pretender, and that he is able and ready to make full proof of it. I suppose this is the effect of his resentment, because the offers he lately made for a reconciliation were not accepted, but I believe he will hardly get any one to believe that your father if he could have entered into such a design would ever have put himself into the Viscount's power.

T. Rowney's daughter is married this day to Sir Cloberry Noel.

Here is a report that is believed that the Master of Pembroke [Brickenden] is dead suddenly at his house in Berkshire. I believe the College will not suffer much by his death.

1714, August 26. Christ Church.—Has your Lordship received the box of prints, lately sent directed to Mr. Thomas, for which I sent you the bill of lading? Let me know in your next. Leers has sent me the account, and desires to know if my friend would upon some allowance let him draw for the money now, that he may put it in the lottery. But I have ordered him to draw a bill upon me dated the 1st of October to be paid in three months, that will make the money payable at Christmas, and he may negotiate the bill if he will put the money in the lottery.

The Attorney has reason to make friends if he could. I am going to tell you that which perhaps you know better than I. Leers tells me that the King comes over with a full persuasion that the late cabal had a design for the Pretender.

1714, August 29.—To-morrow I shall make a visit at Bucklebury. I have not been there since my return from Windsor at Christmas. I take this opportunity that I may pay my respects before the Lord comes down; I suppose he will be at liberty next week, if pleases to see his Lady.

One [Matt.] Panting, a Fellow of Pembroke, is likely it is said to be chosen Master. The Vice Chancellor is very zealous to pay his duty to the King, he has got an address ready and will be up with it this week. The verses, which are not yet ready, will be a good pretence for another journey.

1714, September 4. Christ Church.—Are you barbarians, do you make a jest of a poor man who has compassion for an unfortunate creature, that has seen many bad days, but perhaps not the worst yet? My duty to your father, and pray tell him I shall not be wanting to do my poor endeavours to comfort other than such widows when he thinks fit to put me in a condition of making pretences to them. But your father should not laugh at me, since he has found that by my advice at least I can help others, besides widows. I understand, though you have never owned, that there is no doubt now of Lady Harriet's being with child. I pretend, next to your Lordship, to the greatest merit on that point, it was certainly done at Christ Church. How will your father reward me for prevailing with my Lady to take that journey? Brother Hammond throws up his cap, and says it is a blessing on your endeavours, for your goodness to Peckwater. He bids me tell you he will be as good as his word, and keep count for you. It was lucky that I made my visit as I did, I saw an instance of tenderness so extraordinary, that I could not but be pleased at another's trouble. I was there when the account came of what had passed in town, the circumstances of it made the poor creature [Lady Bolingbroke] apprehensive of somewhat of a more dangerous nature that might follow. She burst into as great a concern for one who has deserved so little of her, as Lady Harriet could have done for you upon a like occasion, and should anything of that kind ever happen, I am certain she would part with all she has in the world to save him. But the gentleman, let him put on what airs he pleases in town, yet I am certain by what I saw, *spem vultu simulat*. But this to no one, except your father.

Your Lordship has never mentioned to me the famous coach that is shown in Drury Lane for one shilling to any one, bound with purple velvet and trimmed with gold, that was designed for the new ecclesiastical Privy Seal. Pray go see it and encourage as many as you can, it is a pity but it should be public.

I believe I must now lay aside all thoughts of seeing Wimpole till the next spring. Your Lordship will not stir out of town I suppose till the entry is over. The ill weather will be come before you can be settled at Wimpole, and the roads, some of the worst in England, that are betwixt this place and Wimpole, impassable to so bad a traveller. I hear preparations are making for the Coronation, pray let me hear, if it is known, how soon it will be. I hope you will walk as a peer there.

1714, September 7. Christ Church.—I am sorry for the end of your letter if that be so, we shall be in the state we have been for these last twenty years, but no one can foresee what the issue of new struggles may be, or where they will end. It will be the spoiling too of as fair a game as ever was played into a wise man's hands, and the only way by which it could be spoiled. I remember I heard your father tell a story of your great grandfather, that he with some others went to represent to King James the First the discontents of their country upon several heads. Your *Proavus* told him, "Sir, if the mischief from these things comes not in your own days it will in your son's." I leave your Lordship to make the application, I am afraid you have too good ground for what you tell me, but there can be no hurt in preparing ourselves for it. I am certain your Lordship will act like a man of honour and conscience, and I doubt not you would have done so, though God had not put you out of the reach of any temptation from want of fortune to do otherwise.

I shall be heartily glad to hear your Lordship and my Lady are in the country, it will be proper to allow you a week's time to settle yourselves there, nor could I conveniently come before Monday se'nnight the 20th of this month. But the roads betwixt this place and Wimpole are fit only for the strongest horse and the lightest man in England. And I am afraid before that time they will be impassable for one of my weight and little skill in horsemanship. At least I am afraid if I should be able to get thither, I should never be able to get home again.

1714, September 9. Christ Church.—I hear your neighbour acts the meanest part that ever man surely in his post did, and makes complaints to every one that he can get to hear them, of his miserable condition. That he is deserted by all his friends, though he has given no one occasion to use him so. Amongst other instances, he had the impudence to say that Dr. Stratford, whom he had done all that ever he could to oblige, had deserted him without any cause. Was there ever so rank a knave? I perceive he begins to stink for fear, I begin to think myself more considerable than I took myself to be yesterday. The man certainly has some apprehensions of me, and expects I should have a reckoning with me [*sic*, him ?]. I am sure of the truth of what I write to you. Dr. S[tratford] did not play so stinking a part as this is, when he was forced to fence against that man's subornation. But the fear that arises from reflections on his own villiany will be a greater plague to him than Dr. S[tratford] would ever return to him.

Postscript. Duty to my good Lady Dupplin and her Lord. I suppose she is in town to see the show. I heard of an old lady that went up last week, who said she had not long to live, but God willing she would see as many sights as she could before she died.

We are now in our horse races. Lord Pelham's horse won the Town Plate yesterday, and Lord Wharton's the Gentlemen's Plate the day before. You see the W[hig?]s carry it.

1714, September 15. Christ Church.—I have just received your Lordship's of the 11th. I am ashamed you should send your coach so far to meet me, but I desire you would not think of coming yourself. God willing I will be at the "Swan" at Newport Pagnel on Monday night, I must come thither in a coach, for though I hope I have got clear of the pain in my arm, yet it is still so weak that I cannot lift it to my head, much less hold a bridle.

1714, October 19. London.—I take the first opportunity to thank your Lordship for the kindness I met with at Wimpole. The state of affairs here grows every day to be more so as it was reported to us. The Duke of Northumberland is turned out of the Castle of Windsor and the Constableship of the Forest; and they are given to the Duke of Kent. The mob have lost their curiosity; it is said their attendance to-morrow will not be so numerous as has been usual on the like occasions. It is supposed that in a few days a party will be declared at Court against the Duke of Marlborough.

Time is short, and I have yet been able to pick up little; I hope against the next post to be furnished with more materials.

1714, October 21. London.—I am got safe from the Coronation. Nothing remarkable but that above twenty persons were killed by the fall of a scaffold. The Duke of Ormond stayed not dinner, but went off in a chair at the end of the procession and was followed by several hundreds huzzaing him. Most of the scaffolds filled with rabble at sixpence a piece for want of other spectators. A fellow with large horns on his head ran about the streets followed by much company.

Duchesses of Bolton and Mountagu declared Ladies of the Bedchamber. Scarborough turned out, I hear not his successor.

By all I can hear, I am confirmed in the necessity of all I presumed to suggest to your Lordship with respect to yourself and family. By all the love and respect I bear you, I beg you to think of it seriously and without delay.

1714, October 26. London.—Your father said this evening that my Lady should be made easy in all things. I will write at large about the public when I am at home. I can only tell you warrants are come to the Attorney for Mostyn and Smith in the room of Dupplin and Mansel. Your family must expect all the spite that can be shown, that still makes what we have talked of more necessary.

1714, November 1.—I left the town full of reports of differences betwixt the Duke of M[arlborough] and the King, and the same Duke and the P[retender] too. It is said too that the Whigs all agree in being angry with the Duke of M[arlborough] for engrossing too much to himself, but at the same time quarrel about their measures amongst themselves. H[alifa]x is for moderate measures, the others for going through with that they have begun. What ground there is for these reports, I cannot say, I believe some for all of them, but I fancy all are magnified beyond the truth. I believe it is certain that Lord Townshend has expostulated with the Duke of M[arlborough] for not keeping articles with him, he having promised to desire no more than to be declared General again.

Lord and Lady Dupplin are wisely resolving to suit their expenses to their circumstances, they are going to part with their house in town, and to retire wholly to the country, where his Lordship to show the command he has on himself will not have so much as one hunter.

Your father talks of being at Wimpole again within a fortnight, in his way to Herefordshire. I believe he will be with you again as soon as all things are removed from the old house, but he is not used to execute anything within the time he at first projects it.

Some distant overtures seem to be made by those who lately broke with your father towards a reconciliation. I know not how far they will be hearkened to, but your father will make no advances, but the lady [Masham] declares that she has no more to expect, and that she will have no more to do with your father.

I hear S[hrewsbury?] will be in town again within a month, it is said P[rior?] will continue where he is, and return no more to England.

1714, November 5.—You have heard of poor Radcliffe's death; it was a great mercy that God gave him the opportunity and heart to make so noble a will as he has done. 120,000*l*. in charity is what can scarce be paralleled in any age from a private man, and all gotten by himself by the fairest practice that ever any of the profession used, and himself living nobly too, all his life. Above 60,000*l*. is immediately to be laid out in charity, the rest is at present in annuities to relations, and to be laid out in charity by his executors, as the annuities expire. It is no small honour to Mr. Slaughter to be named as one of the executors of such noble benefactions. I suppose you know the executors are Mr. Bromley, Sir George Beaumont, Mr. Slaughter, and Beck the scrivener. 40,000*l*. for our public library. Amongst other uses John Hudson's place is to be augmented out of it to 200*l*. *per annum*, and a certain sum every year for ever for buying in what books are wanting. Two travelling physicians, to be as I think of University College, with 300*l*. *per annum* to each of them for ten years, to be five years abroad and five at home. They are to be chosen by the Archbishop of Canterbury, Bishops of London and

Winchester, the Lord Chancellor, two Secretaries of State, and
two Chief Justices, and the Master of the Rolls. 5,000*l.* as I hear
for the augmentation of the headship of University and rebuilding
the Master's lodgings. 600*l. per annum* to St. Bartholomew's
Hospital.

You hear of the reform in the Navy Office. Sergison
and Lyddal are rich, I am afraid poor Tollet is not in so good a
condition. But now those officers are turned out, who had been
kept in hitherto for their sufficiency by all parties, I suppose no
one will be spared. It is said Sir R[oger?] M[ostyn?], though
he had kissed the King's hand, will not have his place, but
Stamford.

Mr. Rowney and his lady are come home and beg their hearty
respects to you and my Lady. Tom, to show what an honest man
can do and to set a good example to his son-in-law, has got his
wife with child again. She is now breeding, and it is supposed may
lie in about the same time with her daughter, which affords us
good diversion.

1714, November 8.—There came news hither last night
that a paper was cried about the streets in London of your
father's having been shot on Hampstead Heath by four men
in visor masks. It came from Sir James Lumley's sister to
him, but it met with the credit it deserved.

1714, November 19. Christ Church.—I hear from a sure
hand that the old lady is resolved to stay in the country, I
heartily give you joy of it, you will now be provided to your
heart's desire, and it will save you so much money that I
shall hope, by the project of buying in of Lady Pickering, to see
you clear, and able to subsist with what you have at present only,
in spite of all your enemies, both in plenty and in honour. I
suppose my Lady will desire your father when he is in town
to be with her. When he is alone with you he will be a comfort
to you both. I hope you will part with your other house as soon
as you can.

There will be no mercy to any one. It is supposed N[ottingha]m
himself will not keep his ground long. St. Asaph [Fleetwood]
goes to Ely, and Willis to Gloucester, and you will be surprised
I believe to hear that J. Wynne is Bishop of St. Asaph, but
so it is, and obtained at Sir Roger Mostyn's desire by Lord
N[ottingha]m and by no other interest as I am told.

[1714, November.]—This is for your own perusal only. As
we were on the road I told your father with all the freedom
possible that Lady H[arley] would never bear any other
mistress than herself in the house where she lived. That he
must not think of putting you in that house unless that point
were gained. All the answer I had was that that would work easy
in time. I went with him to view the house. If you could have
it entire or with the reservation only of one apartment above
stairs to your father the house both for state and convenience

would be better than any other you could have; but according
to the present disposition there is one entire apartment above
stairs to your father. Three little rooms reserved to himself for
his closets below, two little rooms allotted to Mr. Thomas, two
good rooms to the library, and only a drawing-room and parlour
for common use. There is no room possible for your own use
but only one dressing-room, nor for my Lady's but a dressing-
room and closet. If your father live alone with you the apartment above would furnish him with a dressing-room and three
closets for his own use, and then if all below were left to you
there should be convenience enough for you, but according to the
present disposition there will neither be any room for you and
much less for your family. Besides other inconveniences of two
families it will not be possible to lodge both in that house. One
thing you may [be] certain of. The old Lady will go into the
country for this winter that you may have the whole house to
yourselves for your use at your first coming, and till my Lady is
out of the straw. That is a convenience which you should
certainly make use of. When you see your father again
at Wimpole, you will know what more you may depend on. You
need not put off your other house till then. I should advise my
Lady, when your father offers the house to her again, to tell him
plainly that she is afraid there will not be room for two families.
That will oblige him to speak out, and if he offers to leave
the whole house and to seek for a house for himself elsewhere
then it will be proper for my Lady to desire that he and the
servants that attend him should do her the honour to be with her.
This will put matters to a short issue, and if the point
is gained be a mighty convenience to all of you. I need
not desire you not to let any one know that I concern myself in
this, nor tell you how far I trust you in dealing so freely with
you.

As to other matters depend upon [it] that I have seen
every hour more reason to confirm me that all that I have said
to you in relation to your own private affairs is not only proper
but strictly necessary. You must without one moment's delay
put a stop to all sort of expense whatever that is not for the
support of your family, and you must turn your thoughts every
hour to consider where you can spare either in the number of
servants or any manner of expense either in your house or your self.
You must not think any frugality, be it never so little, useless.
You will find you will not be able to spare enough to bring your
own expense within the compass of your income, much less to be
able to answer the demands that may be made on you from your
family. I have made some enquiry into your father's condition.
His private debts are above double to anything he has to answer
them, without computing the known incumbrances on the estate,
for which interest must be paid. But you must be prepared for
all the mischief that can be done to him by those now in power.
Both Marlborough and Arg[yll] agree in (vowing?) his ruin.
All the Tories shall be received into grace. They desire only one
sacrifice and that is H[arle]y. Sacrifice is the word. You

may depend on what I say. And I believe I have satisfied your father that he cannot depend upon anything from those three Lords in whom he thought he had interest because he had deserved it from them. But they have promised their party to concur with them in anything against him that does not directly strike at his life. These things should be concealed as much as possible from my Lady, but they are very proper for you to reflect on. I do not think his enemies will be able to do him any hurt, but they will attempt it if their own divisions do not prevent it ; and this being the case I must leave it with your Lordship to consider how far it is necessary to put your own affairs on a foot on which they may last. You may, without care, be in a worse state than you were before your marriage. Upon your present resolutions the honour, the peace, and the plenty of your future life depend.

1714, November 24. Christ Church.—Dr. Radcliffe's body will be brought hither on Saturday, and lie in state in the Divinity School till Thursday, when it will be buried. The corpse will be attended with as great ceremony as Bodley's was. I expect Mr. Bromley here, but I know not yet whether he will come to meet the corpse, or only be here soon enough to be at the funeral. I perceive by a letter I had the honour to have from my Lord of Oxford to-night, that he will not be at Wimpole so soon as you expected him. I was afraid you might have been at Woodstock on Thursday, the day of the funeral, but now I believe you cannot be there so soon. Mr. Bromley will be much engaged in returning and receiving visits whilst he is here, but if you pass by whilst he stays I know not but he may desire to meet you too at Woodstock, if he can get from his company here. If he should not be able to come along with me, I shall beg leave to leave him for a night, and not fail to meet you.

Baker was recommended by our Dean, they may call him sub-preceptor, but he has no other business than to teach the children to read English. The Princess had taken notice at the chapel of Baker for reading well. I never heard that Philips had that post. They who made the new Bishop of St. Asaph [Wynne] will be often disappointed in him, and he himself too will not seldom be at a loss how to act. This promotion was the greatest chance in the world, and owing solely to Mostyn. I little thought Sir Roger would have made bishops, but he has secured a good interest to himself in Flintshire by this. The Bishop never had any fancy for his new patron, Nott[ingham], but he will be grateful, especially whilst his patron continues in the interest he likes. The Bishop is sensible he owes nothing on this occasion to the Whigs, either ecclesiastical or lay, but he was one of those who were in great apprehensions of designs against the succession. He owns now they were groundless, but he still thinks the Whigs are the most in earnest for maintaining it, and on that account will be disposed to join with them in things that are not very flagrant ; but he dares not be damned for them. They may, upon pretence of what they call necessary for maintaining the succession, often impose on him, but where anything is directly against his judgment he will never join with them. He thinks they drive furiously, and as he pretends to love truth and to endeavour to form his judgment right, he has the misfortune often to be of the opinion of the last book he reads or the last man he converses with. There is no fear of his old friends trusting him too far; but they will be a great check on him, and make him often whether [sic, very?] doubtful which way to vote.

Postscript. I hear from a good hand that the Whigs now talk favourably of Lord Bolingbroke and Harcourt, and point all against your father and Lord Strafford.

Domestic affairs go to your wishes; your father tells me the house shall be left entirely to my Lady. He seems to hope for somewhat from the disagreement that is certainly amongst those in power, but I am afraid they will agree in opposing. It is certain there will be no mercy to any, much less to any of your family; the measures show that somewhat desperate is designed, nothing less can support the present measures. If they can get a majority returned, they will not only support themselves but soon increase their number. But every thing of this kind is a fresh argument for your Lordship's going through with the retrenching of your own expenses. Every one should prepare himself as well as he can against the worst that can happen. You cannot imagine how much you will save by living in a place where you will be exempt from all parish duties. And if your father lives privately as a guest with you, that will be at least 2,000*l. per annum* saved to the family. I suppose you hear nothing from the Duchess.

Lintot printed the "Considerations" in the "White Staff," and we have reason to believe young Sym was the person who conveyed it to him. His father [Harcourt] has laid many trains to get visits and compliments from this place, but to no purpose, nobody went near him.

1714, November 29. Christ Church.—Dr. Radcliffe's corpse will be here on Wednesday, and the funeral will be on Friday. I have notice from Mr. Bromley that he will be here. I expect him to-morrow or Wednesday, he will be returned I am afraid before you pass by us.

1714, December 10.—A proclamation is come out for a thanksgiving, but none yet for dissolving Parliament. It is probable none will come till the thanksgiving is over.

I think they have now made all the changes they can even to the lowest offices, it is now time for them to try what effect these changes will have in the election of a new Parliament.

I suppose my Lord of O[xford] will not think of stirring till you come to town.

I suppose you go straight to the house in St. James's. Have you parted yet with the other house?

1714, December 15.—I suppose this may find your Lordship still at Wimpole. If it does I must desire you would employ somebody at Cambridge to enquire for Joshua Barnes's History of Edward III. None were sold in his lifetime but by himself. I suppose since his death what remained of the impression is disposed of, and it is most likely to be heard of at Cambridge. I would desire a copy in sheets if it is to be had so; if not, bound.

1714-15, January 25. Christ Church.—Mr. He[a]rne has already returned to me the book which you sent to him by me. He will allow me to be the arbitrator of all differences betwixt him and Mr. Wanley.

I believe Mr. Urry will soon trouble your Lordship with some proposals about his Chaucer, and beg your favour to get subscriptions for him. The subscriptions are to be all for his own use, he having not money but books from the printer, for his own pains in the editing.

Was there any thing remarkable on Thursday last, either in those who attended the solemnity, or in those who were spectators of it? Were the scaffolds for those who were to buy places full at Paul's?

Our elections in university and town were over yesterday. Does the reform go on amongst the military officers?

Postscript. Mr. Bromley, in great compassion to his old friend Archer, would not let his son be put up in Warwickshire. He has undertaken for Mr. Archer to the gentlemen, that he shall no more be a whimsical. Mr. [William] Peyto, a kinsman of Lord Willoughby's, will be the other for whom his Lordship undertakes.

1714-15, January 27.—We shall have a great struggle about the Margaret Professorship. All who used to mutiny against their own Governors and all the "Goodfellows" join for Delaune. The Sub-dean dissents from all his brethren and will alone of this House vote for him. We are afraid our Sub-dean has some secret correspondence still with Ruffian.

[1715,] February 12.—I bless God for His signal mercy to you, it is very remarkable that the child should come upon the day the mother was at age. It is a circumstance that will endear it to you, and her too; you may now wait with safety for settlements. I will christen it with a good will though it be a girl, but I see no use of my coming till the time of the christening. Should the little one be in any danger Mr. Garwood is always at hand. If it continues well, you will defer the christening I suppose till your father returns. It would be most convenient for me to come up with him, but my honoured Lady may command me. Only I would be in town as little as I can, and I cannot stir till after Friday next; on that day is the election for the Margaret professor. I believe we shall lose it, but I must not be absent. I kept Jack only till he had drank some hot wine, but the ways are very bad, deep and wet. I am afraid he will hardly be able to reach Brampton so soon as you hoped he might.

I am very much pleased with all the steps you have taken both to the old aunts and the Duchess herself, it will have its effect I hope at last. I knew not before that she was come to town. You are in the right to try the Bishop of L———, but how came you to know from himself of his interest in the Duchess. Are you acquainted with him? How did he gain it? Did he give institution upon the Duchess's presentation or upon yours?

My duty to my honoured Lady, my daily prayers wait on her. Pray take care that she have entire quiet and no flesh. Radcliffe was used to say that most that he knew that ever miscarried in childbed was by eating flesh too soon.

We kept the birthday, Bishop of Chester, brother Hammond, J. Urry and I. Old John kept the Bishop and Canon almost till twelve; if they offered to stir, John began "It is my Lady's birthday, therefore we keep holy day." This amongst ourselves. We drank you with "*Quos Deus conjunxit nemo separet.*"

[1715], February 18.—If my Lady's uneasiness proceeds only from her milk, I hope the physicians are in the right who apprehend no danger, but I shall be uneasy myself till I hear that she is easy as well as safe. Beg of her not to make too bold with herself too soon, nor to presume too much upon the strength she may fancy she has.

Delaune carried his point to-day by eighteen voices. Many accidents concurred for him, nor was it so much a combination for him as against the Vice-Chancellor and the Heads. Delaune had only two Heads for him, Brasenose and a Whig, the Warden of Wadham, and about six Doctors, the rest of his votes were all Bachelors of Divinity, near half of them jail-birds like himself, who had left the University for debt and had not appeared here before in ten years or more. He had rummaged the nation for them.

1714-15, February 24.—I bless God that all is safe. I hope one may trust it is so now. I hear too, by a hint from Morley, that other matters are dispatched too. I know you will allow me to observe to you the providence of Almighty God to yourself, that at such a juncture, and when your father had made so little provision to support the honour he is to leave you, that all should be so amply secured to you, without your being under any obligation to any one for it but to one who is herself a blessing to you infinitely beyond any thing else that she can bestow on you. Your own goodness will suggest to you the reflections that are proper upon so signal an instance of God's mercy to you. Your fortune is now in your own power, and if you persevere but three years in the method on which you have entered, you will pass the rest of your days in peace, plenty and honour, and no more fear the malice than you will have occasion for the help of the enemies of your family. This child at this juncture is a greater blessing than perhaps at the first reflection you may be aware of. It is no little security to your father himself. The prospect of the settlement of so great a fortune in his family will dispose many to treat him with more respect than they would have done otherwise.

1715, March 8.   Christ Church.—I hear nothing yet of your father, by which I presume I shall not see him until the next week.   And by your giving me notice that I may depend upon being brought up by him, I suppose you defer the christening till he comes.

John Urry has sent to his correspondent to order some papers to be immediately left with you.

Simon's rheumatism is returned, and they are afraid it will be as bad as it was before; if it should, he will hardly escape. But on Sunday night as his father was coming out of his chamber his Lordship made a false step and tumbled from the top to the bottom of the stairs.   They say he lay dead for a quarter an hour, but upon bleeding he is pretty well again.

[1715,] November 8.—Your friend Hearne is mad.   Upon being chosen 'Bedle,' he could not attend his duty in the Library so much as he did before; and what is worse, he would not do it. And when he was there he would neither assist Dr. Hudson himself nor help others as he ought to do, to the books they wanted. His salary from the Library was only 10l. per annum.   Dr. Hudson, who had been the great instrument to make him 'Bedle,' desired him to quit the Library, since he could not attend it; he refused. Dr. Hudson complained last year to the Visitors and desired them to declare the place void as inconsistent with the 'Bedle.'   The Visitors, in hopes that he would himself quit it, would not proceed to that.   But upon fresh application the Visitors yesterday declared the place void.   Upon this Hearne [has thrown up his?] Bedle's and Arch-typographus's places.   The Vice-Chancellor and others have done all they could with him to-day to persuade him to keep them, but to no purpose.

The Bishop of Oxford on Sunday last offered a paper styled "A Declaration of the Bishops in and about town," to the Bishops of Bristol, Chester, and St. Asaph to be signed by them.   The Bishop of Chester declined reading it, and said it was his fixed principle not to sign any public engagements but what the law required.   The Bishop of Bristol would not sign it, but gave reasons, I believe, in writing why he would not.   St. Asaph signed it.   I suppose you will soon hear of it in print.

[1715,] November 16.—I shall pay your compliments as you order.   I was misinformed in one particular I wrote lately.

The Bishop of Bristol did not give reasons for so doing it, but only a copy of what he had said upon public occasions, and offered to sign another of his own drawing up, which should be altogether as strong, as to the exhortation part, as that was which he declined to sign.   But it would not be accepted.   He is or certainly will be out.

1715, November 28.—Last week upon some words in Hamilton's coffee house, one of the officers here drew his sword and struck a scholar of Exeter. In the evening, at Line's coffee house, a student of our House, Mr. Bertie, James Bertie's son, and one Floyd a commoner, whose father was lately turned out in Ireland, and says he is related to you, were talking of what had happened at Hamilton's and said it was base to draw a sword on a man who had none. The Major of the regiment came in and heard them ; some words passed, the Major, one Duncomb, fell into a violent passion, struck Bertie with his cane, and pulled them both to the guard. This was about nine. With much ado, the Bishop of Bristol got them released from the guard betwixt eleven and twelve. There was nothing said reflecting on the Government or any ways relating to it, but I believe the young scholars, who talked to the officers with the same freedom they talk to each other, might use expressions which men in town do not use to each other. But nothing was said that could justify striking, much more imprisoning them. It is now under consideration what to do in this affair, and whether to make a public complaint.

[1715-16,] January 6.—I doubt not Neddy will prove an honour to us, and a blessing to his family. I suppose we may have his good mother's leave to make him as hearty a Tory as we think fit.

We have nothing to entertain you with from this place but the news of a marriage which makes some noise here. Mr. Alsop, who was engaged by twelve years' courtship to a woman here, has left his old mistress to wear willow, and married his predecessor's widow. I am afraid there is enough under his hand to occasion a prosecution in Doctors Commons. He was so unhappy too as to assure his old mistress under his hand, since last All Hallows day, that he would make good all his promises to her and marry her. When he was asked why he renewed his promise so lately when he had other designs, he said he was not then sure of the widow, and he had a mind to have two strings to his bow. It occasions much talk here, and it is said a little volume of love letters will be published. I am the more concerned on the account of the good Bishop of Rochester, this rogue having been his chief minister. C. Aldrich, Nicols of Westminster, and Bagshaw that was chaplain here, were the persons summoned to attend this honourable marriage.

[1716 ?] April 19.—I know not where you could have made a provision for yourself so well as in the place where you were. T. Rowney has given me some account of proceedings in their House ; they are allowed by all to be more extraordinary in so short a compass of time than the oldest members can remember during the whole time they have attended. I am out of pain, I confess, for my friends upon all accounts but one, but I lately met with a passage in a book I was reading which, upon reflection, I could not own but to be true, by many instances which I recollected:—"*Qu'il n'y a point d' innocence à l'épreuve du choix des juges.*" There is one thing makes for us, every judge in our case is making precedents which may be used against himself.

I met with a passage lately which perhaps has not occurred to you, it is in the late edition of Misson's Travels in volume one, part one, page 249. If you can meet with the book and consult that place, you will find that the band-box, which some pretended so much to ridicule, was a method of murder that was formerly practised with success. And I believe too you will be of my opinion, that they who tried it lately had either read this book or seen that which is mentioned in it.

1716, April 30.—The Bishop of Chester designs to dine with your Lordship on Thursday se'nnight in his way to Huntingdon, and I design to be at Wimpole before that, if I find by your answer to my last that it will be convenient to me to come at this time. If it be proper for me now to wait on you, I must desire you to send your chariot to meet me at the same inn it did the last time, at Newport Pagnel on Monday next, and then God willing I shall dine with you on Tuesday.

[1716,] June 13.—The friendship I met with, great as it was, is not that which gave me the highest satisfaction I found at Wimpole. I had that in what I saw in your Lordship, since I had an opportunity of observing that you discharged cordially as well as fully the two greatest duties of life, that of a husband and of a son. I hope God in recompensing will give you such a spirit of wisdom that your duty to your father will be so managed as to be without any inconvenience to yourself.

Postscript. I find everything in great confusion here. We have been every day expecting some mischief would happen. There have been quarrels betwixt townsmen and soldiers, and scholars and soldiers, every day for the last week. Three or four scholars have been wounded and several soldiers were beat soundly on Monday night by our countrymen of Jesus.

In coming from the race at Woodstock the Colonel drew his sword in Portmead on a gentleman of Lincoln, one Mr. Ettrick, the occasion said to be that the gentleman had reported that the Colonel and his officers had drunk confusion to the Church. Mr. Ettrick told the Colonel he hoped he would deal fairly, and only one of them fall on him, that he was ready to fight anyone of them. But the Colonel bid his officers who were with him draw their swords, and the Colonel slashed the gentleman whilst the officers stood about him with their drawn swords.

There has been an uproar at Gloucester upon a quarrel betwixt the mayor and the commanding officer of the soldiers. The officer drew up his soldiers, and the mayor the townsmen. The officer bid his men fire, but a captain of the regiment bid them not; the soldiers obeyed the captain. The major, who was the commanding officer, put the captain in arrest upon it. So things were when our intelligence came away. Much blood had like to have been shed.

[1716,] August 31.—On Friday as a sergeant here was beating up for dragoons at the end of Balliol wall, he turned to several scholars who were leaning on the wall, and asked them if they had a Pope in their bellies. Upon this some stones were thrown at him, one of the soldiers with him drew his sword, shook it at the scholars, and swore he would have their blood before he left the town. This soldier was one of the town, newly listed, by name Bull. One asked Bull in the evening why he would draw his sword, he swore again he would have the blood of those scholars. On Saturday evening the Captain was standing at the "Star" inn gate where he quarters, and saw four scholars coming through North Gate he whispered a boy, who ran across to Jesus Lane to an ale house, out of which immediately came six new listed soldiers with Bull at the head of them; the Captain made a sign with his head to the soldiers, upon which they went up to the scholars, looked them in the face, and cried "God bless King George;" one of the scholars answered, "We are all for King George, why do you trouble us, why don't you go to your quarters?" Bull cried, "God damn you, say God bless King George, George and Marlborough." Upon which one of the scholars cried, "Why then God bless King George and the Duke of Ormond." The soldiers, who had all clubs in their hands, immediately knocked them down, and fell upon them, and beat them when they were down. The people ran in, took off the soldiers and took up the scholars all bloody and bruised and carried them into the post house. The town rose, the "Star" inn gates were shut and barricaded, the Vice-Chancellor and Mayor came and with much ado hindered the people from pulling down the inn, and knocking the soldiers on the head. On Sunday night the people came together again, and began to batter the "Star" inn, the Vice-Chancellor came in time enough to prevent any other mischief but the breaking of the windows. On Monday the soldiers went off, the Captain having first given security for their appearing at the session. The scholars were Sir Harry O'Keit of Worcester College, and three gentlemen commoners as I think, one Creswick, Chester, and Castleman. None of them, that I own, were of those who were leaning on Balliol wall.

Postscript. I found when I was at Bucklebury that you had given Sir William Wyndham an account of our adventure as we came from the Tower; I hope it will be your turn next to be undermost, then I shall be even with you.

1716, September 20.—I suppose you are now happy, for I take it that Mr. Wanley must be with you since the books are put up. I have that catalogue I mentioned to you. When you meet with it, I believe you will alter your method. That will be good employment and amusement for another summer. Is my good Lady's room done and made fit for her to come into it again? You have taken care of yourself in the first place. Little Captain of Stoke was with me on Sunday night, he is much pleased to hear of your alterations.

Your tutor, my neighbour, is gone to Canterbury in order to
fetch a wife home. He and the lady are agreed, but it sticks
with old Isaac; he will not yet part with as much for a settlement
as the lady insists on. Whether the Sub-dean can prevail with
Isaac to come up to the lady's demands, or with her to abate
of them, a little time will show. But he is [in] a desperate
condition upon this difficulty. This age can show no example of
any one so far gone in love as he is. He comes up to the height
of all the noble heroes of romance in all points but the fighting
part. I know not how he would acquit himself, if there should
be occasion for any prowess, but for soliloquies he surpasses
Orondates. And in the midst of family discourse with his
servants, he will fall, without perceiving it, into raptures and
addresses to his dear Betty. I do not exaggerate matters I
assure you.

We have got the 500*l*. which Dr. South left us to our building,
and shall pull down the last side of Peckwater next spring. In
our new building, we shall observe Dr. Aldrich's model as to the
case, but we design to turn the inside into a library, and to make
it the finest library that belongs to any society in Europe. A
friend of mine may now be furnished with a proper p . . . (*torn off*)
if he should have any occasion for that he once hinted to me.
I have somewhat more to say, but I am afraid you who write
such short letters will think what I have already written too
much.

[1716,] October 31.—Last night we had a great disturbance
here, the major of the regiment ordered the soldiers to go round
the town and break all the windows that were not illuminated.
There had [not] been the least difference before since they were
here, nor was there any provocation of any kind now. Nor does the
major pretend any reason for his orders, but his own displeasure
against those who had no candles out. I believe he would
disown it now if he could, but it is fixed by oath upon him, by
one whose windows were broken and who heard him give the
orders for the breaking of his windows, and told him, "Sir, I
shall remember you"; upon which the major drew his sword,
and ran at him, and had killed him if the man had not got
within his door. The Mayor who came to quiet them was fired
at, the mace bearer's hat was shot through in four places, and
the Mayor's door is a good witness against them, by the bore of
the bullet. Poor Tom Rowney's windows were broke, and he
himself upon his coming out was insulted by several soldiers
who flourished their naked swords over him, but did not cut him.
No Colleges were meddled with, nor had any scholar any concern
any ways in this riot. The Lieutenant Colonel who commands
here lies ill of the gout at the "Angel," he pretends great concern
for what has happened. This is the best account I can yet send
you, but I suppose we shall have a more particular one when all
the affidavits are taken. I believe Tom and his townsmen will
be spirited up to make a public complaint.

1716, November 1.—It would be as improper for me to desire to know as for you to write the state of your affairs. I am concerned no farther than for the general event. Let us hear what happen, and whether any disposition be made to any one else to your prejudice. I take it to be a remarkable providence to you at [this] juncture, and I doubt not your own good reflections and, what is more, your experience of what has been in these last years, will prompt you to make the proper use of it, and not to neglect this fresh opportunity of always being able to make yourself and all who are related to you easy. I take a young lady's going off lately, and your own lucky coming up to town, to have been two considerable incidents towards this grand catastrophe.

Upon further enquiry I find the windows of that part of Balliol College which are towards Magdalen Church were broken. The Vice-Chancellor himself was cut, several pieces were fired about him, a blow aimed at him, but it lighted upon the lanthorn on his man's head, and beat one side into the other. The Vice-Chancellor read the Proclamation, upon which the soldiers where he was dispersed. If Tom Rowney's servants had not forced him into his house, he had certainly been murdered. Tom had been at the tavern that afternoon with his corporation, which made him a little more brave [than] usual. No scholar concerned but one Baker of Wadham, a candidate in physic and a constitutioner. He went with the soldiers from house to house and encouraged them to break windows. I believe the university will make an example of him.

Did your Lordship ever see Jasper Wayne's translation of Lucian with a dedication of it to William, Duke of Newcastle?

1716, December 11.—You must give me leave to enquire how my Lady's cold does. I have little else to trouble you with at present. I would humbly recommend lying in bed to her Ladyship as the most certain as well as easiest remedy.

The major is gone up with affidavits sworn by some constitutioners and soldiers in his justification. They are certainly as to the main false oaths. Our Vice-Chancellor and Mayor were not only so unwary as to take and sign these affidavits, by the Recorder's advice as it is said, but they took the affidavits as they were brought ready drawn up without ever examining the persons who swore to them, and two of the soldiers who were brought to swear refused to do it. Nay more, they let the major take the originals away with him, without so much as reserving a copy of them for themselves. The major may foist in what he pleases. I suppose these will be printed too.

1716, December 16.—Surely there will be no great occasion for the future for the parsons to preach up the vicissitude of human affairs, at least not to this generation, they see enough of it. The Whigs at present seem to be under the same agonies the Tories were about this time two years ago. I had a letter from one on Friday night. Recollect, if you can, the language that was used by the Tories when the late Duke of Ormond was disgraced, and apply it to poor Lord Townshend's case, and you will have what was written to me. But I beseech you to have so much pity upon us rusticated mortals, as to let us a little into these mysteries. You live near the fountain. Is the late dismission a particular punishment for the misbehaviour of the person dismissed, or only in order to the introducing of another ministry? If particular to him, what was the fault that could deserve such vengeance? If for a new ministry, who has thrown out the old one, or is to model the new one? It will not be easy for the Government to meet with others in whom the good people of the land can so thoroughly confide. The Government may expect to feel upon this occasion the resentments of Hare and Canon.

————*nec te tua plurima, Townshend, lubentem pietas, nec canonis infula texit.* But is your cousin Sunderland gone too, entirely gone? Is he not allowed to keep that little morsel of the Vice-Treasurership of Ireland? We apprehend here too some circumstances which may embitter the fall of our patriots. The rascally Tories here seem all certain that all the Tories who have been turned [out], those especially who received their doom by Lord T[ownshend], will wait upon him to condole with him. Pray let a little light into us. I know you are lazy, but methinks you may be content to take a little pains, were it only to grieve such a Whig as I am.

The honest officers here had twice this week taken care to assert their own authority, by affronting and abusing the Proctor and others as they walked after ten o'clock, but I am told to-day that the honest fellows seem a little crestfallen upon this news.

Postscript. Some prints say Lord T. is to have the Vice-Treasurership of Ireland for life; should this be so, he would gain by his dismission. Some travellers who came last night from London say your father was at the bottom of this wicked piece of work. I perceive his credit for politics is good still.

[1717,] March 16.—I will make you the first master of a discovery I have made. All Bentley's project for his new edition of a new Testament is stolen out of Toinard's *Prologomena* to His Harmony cap. 2. *De castigando Græco texta.* There Toinard tells you that he altered his Greek text, by comparing the variations of two ancient Vatican manuscripts with the vulgar version, and that to his great satisfaction he found the vulgar version and those manuscripts to agree in many places with the various readings in Fell's Testament. There is not one tittle besides this that Bentley pretends to do, only the comparing of more manuscripts with the vulgar version. Toinard is honest enough to own that he had his hint from R. Stephens. I think you owe me somewhat for imparting this discovery first to you.

A soldier was tied to the whipping post to-day, but not whipped, with an accusation affixed over him, for being perjured in marrying. It seems the colonel of this regiment gives an oath to the soldiers after they are listed that they shall never marry—the first oath surely of that kind that was ever administered.

[1717,] March 20.—I thank you for your very good news. You observe truly that a bill of indemnity is the most material point; they who have interest enough to carry that will be able to prevent any of the extravagant things they are talked of, and it will be their interest to prevent them.

I never was in much pain for the bill about the universities, it would have been so flagrant a breach of property, and so many private interests, besides that of those who are resident here, would have been concerned in it, that I can never think it would pass. Not but that I am fully satisfied many at the helm would, if it were possible, pass bills even to extirpate us, but I believe there has been much the same management in relation to us that was used to your father. They thought to have us frightened into somewhat mean and dishonourable, but they have been disappointed, though our Pates were thoroughly frightened and, if they had not been restrained by one or two of us, were ready to have gone into any form of submission. But I bless God the enemy knows not our weakness, and now we begin to take heart and to be stout again. The Bishop of Bristol has carried up with him a letter from the Pates to the Archbishop, to lay before him the motives he has to oppose any such bill. I have not seen the letter, but I am told there is nothing improper or unbecoming them in it.

The day of your father's release, by the method by which he is likely to come out, and by which I always thought he must come out, will be more glorious to him than that on which he had the staff.

Now I am out of pain for him, I should be glad to hear your own affairs were settled, both as to your bill and your agreement with Lady Francis. I should be concerned if your business should hinder my good Lady from enjoying the spring at Wimpole. I wish too you could get Vane in, you will not be able to use the timber you have purchased so dearly till that is done.

Here have been strange violences by the soldiers at Woodstock and at Kirtleton; one Captain Gilman here, on Monday morning betwixt four and five o'clock, broke open a house with the help of other officers, carried off a girl by force from her mother, who lay dying, brought her to the "Cross" inn and, as the girl swears, ravished her there, but no magistrate has yet courage enough to grant a warrant against him.

[1717,] May 10.—°Madam. It is with great satisfaction that I now write to you. For security, we clapped two more blisters on Neddy's wrists last night, he went to sleep, and without any

---

°This and the three succeeding letters, as also a later one dated June 9. are addressed to Mrs. Abigail Harley, at Mr. Auditor Harley's house in Lincoln's Inn Fields. The "Neddy" referred to ultimately succeeded his cousin in the title as third Earl of Oxford.

opiate slept till towards seven in the morning as heartily as any farmer could do. He waked wonderfully refreshed, his blisters succeeded very well and ran plentifully. His pulse continues to grow better, his fever indeed continues still, but is abated. His water sometimes is foul and breaks, and sometimes grows clear again, which gives us some apprehensions that this fever may end in an intermitting one. We are then sure of him. He was very cheerful to-day and laughed with me. I asked him if he wanted to see his mother or you, he said he would not by any means have you give yourselves the trouble of coming. Blisters are not very agreeable to him, but I presume to take a little authority upon me, and I will do him the justice to say he is as tractable in sickness as in health. You cannot hear again till Sunday's post, but I hope I send you now such news that you will be able to bear with one day's intermission. Mr. Auditor will be heartily welcome to us if he comes, though I do not design to let him take my trade out of my hands, for I take myself to be a better physician and nurse too than he is.

1717, May 19.—In spite of all the precaution the doctor and I could use, Neddy found a way yesterday of getting some victuals. It agreed so very well with him, that it was plain he wanted it. He had a purge to-day, which worked as well as could be desired ; he was allowed some wine and water and half a boiled chicken to dinner, and is mighty cheerful after it. We have nothing, I bless God, to fear, but lest he should desire to be well too soon, but I shall take care of that, though I can hardly in conscience preach mortification to one who has already undergone so much discipline. He gives his .duty and love, as due, to all the family.

1717, May 21.—Your nephew grows too strong for me, I shall have no authority over him in a few days but what will depend upon his own courtesy. He now sits up most part of the day, and walks across his room without any help from a stick. He is to be purged again to-morrow. He has three boils risen in the nape of his neck where his blister was ; none of them are yet broken, they are a little troublesome, but the doctor is glad of it, and says it is a sure discharge for any remains of his distemper. After to-morrow I believe I shall leave you to his own correspondence to give an account of himself. He longs for a letter from some of you directed to himself, almost as much as he does for victuals.

Postscript. This day came orders for the march of our soldiers, they go on Thursday and Friday. This is the best news we have had of many a day.

1717, May 22.—Neddy's physic has worked very well to-day, one of his boils is broken. The doctor allows him to go down stairs to-morrow, and to eat what he pleases, provided he does it with moderation. I shall now leave you to a more agreeable correspondence, his own. He designs to write to you to-morrow.

The wine is come, but no tamarinds along with it, which the nurse says were promised by his father. But I wonder Mr. Auditor has sent port wine: surely that, be it never so good, cannot be digested easily by a weak stomach, but must rather load it than strengthen it. I shall not let him venture on that wine for some days yet.

I pray God give a good success to what I suppose is now under debate in the House of Lords.

1717, May 29.—This place now affords matter for a letter. There has been a club lately set up here that call themselves the Constitution Club. It consists only of Whigs ; by that you may guess how numerous it is. I never heard of it till yesterday, but it seems they had for some weeks given out that they would have an extraordinary bonfire as yesterday and burn the Pope and Sacheverell. They had taken the room towards the street in the "King's Head," and the Marquis of Hartington was to be admitted at that time of the club and declared president, and his tutor Bradshaw of New College, who was Proctor four years ago, was. wise enough to assist at the initiation of his pupil. The bonfire, had it been made as it was designed, would have been large enough to have endangered the whole town. As they were piling up the bonfire some persons in the room over them threw out money to the mob, the mob in scrambling for it as it were casually overturned the fagots. Orders were given to rear them up again, but then the mobility could refrain no longer. They said they loved the King and would have a bonfire, but such rogues as the Constitution Club should not have the honour of making it. Every one that could get at the pile seized his fagot, and carried them all off to their own homes. · When the fagots were gone, the club prepared to light their candles, of which they had prepared a great quantity. But upon the first appearance of light, the mob saluted them with a volley of large stones, and forced them to quit their room and to retire to the back part of the house. No harm happened hitherto, the mob for two hours ran about the streets crying, " Ormond, Sacheverell." Their number was prodigious, so many thousands as never had been seen by the oldest man in this place. It was market day, and they had taken that occasion to come in from all the villages round us in expectation of this sport. They cried as they went along, " The rogues want to be at a civil war, we are ready for them, and we will give them their belly full of it." About ten o'clock they seemed pretty well dispersed, and it was thought all would have been quiet, but they had separated in order to rally. They gathered again about Paradise and fell upon the meeting house and demolished it in a trice. Some say they seized the preacher, and put him in the stocks, but they carried the pulpit in triumph, and were openly this morning gathering up the fragments of the meeting house, in order to wait on the pulpit at a bonfire this evening at Carfax. They were so numerous and furious, that nothing but disciplined forces could pretend to restrain them. We hope they will disperse of themselves to-morrow. They gave Oriel a token of their respect by breaking their windows, because several of this club are of that College. It is reported that the meeting house at Abingdon has undergone the same fate.

Sacheverell is in Derbyshire, and has taken possession there of 400*l. per annum* left him by his namesake, to whom he dedicated one of his famous sermons.

1717, May 30.—I had forgot to tell you that the mob waited on the Constitution Club as they came out of the tavern to their respective colleges, huzzaing, but not touching any of them. One of the club, one Hamilton, son of Sir David, of Oriel, went from the tavern to New College and when he was within the gate he fired a pistol loaded with bullets amongst the people. The bullets hit against the back door of New Inn Hall and did no damage. The mob would not disperse yesterday but employed themselves in picking up the fragments of the meeting house, to attend the pulpit in the evening. The Mayor came often, they would go off, but return again as soon as the Mayor was gone. In the evening the Vice-Chancellor and Proctors walked and cleared all the public houses; the mob were quiet, but would not separate. After ten, when the magistracy was supposed to be in bed, the mobility fell upon the Quakers' meeting house and gutted it in a trice. They went to his house who is speaker amongst the Quakers, and threw his goods into the street. As part of them were passing by Oriel, a gun was fired out of an upper chamber in that College, and wounded one of Brasenose, it is hoped not dangerously. The person who fired it was one Ingram, there are two of that name in that College, both of the club. Other shots were made out of the windows of that College. The mob turned, and broke all their windows and were with much ado restrained from breaking open the gates. Much work was made in the town for glaziers. The Recorder escaped not without marks of their respect. We are not quite free from apprehensions of further disturbance, the mob are so enraged at the shots from Oriel that they threaten vengeance to any of the club who dare to show their faces. But our governors are taking all the precautions they can to prevent it, they all will patrol this night, and orders are given in every College for all who belong to it to be within at nine, and the gates are to be shut. If you hear not from me by to-morrow's post you may conclude we are quiet again.

It is now said that Bradshaw was not with his pupil at the club.

1717, June 9.—I hear Mrs. Harley is concerned at what she has heard from my godfather, that Neddy has a little pain on his breast. I sent for the doctor, he assures me it is only a little weakness. I believe he judges very truly, for Neddy is quite rid of his pain as soon as he has eat his dinner. I believe this weakness was occasioned by the purge he had on Monday last, it was a good one, and he found himself weaker after it. I doubt not as his strength returns he will be free from his pain, it is much decreased already.

I hope in a few days to congratulate you all upon Lord O[xford]'s liberty.

Postscript. How came Mr. Auditor to be so tender of his old friend Cadogan? Was it from a motive of conscience, or had he any tockay?

1717, July 14.—I wish this may be the last I write to you in town. I long to hear you are going into the country. I suppose your father, who has stood an impeachment, will not fly an exception in the Act of Grace, but for the respect that is proper for the honour done to him in it. I should be glad to hear what he says, at least the substance of it, upon that occasion.

If you consult Meteren, but Strada chiefly, upon the indemnity published at Antwerp in 1570 or 1571, you meet with somewhat to gratify so curious a person as you are. Bentivoglio and Grotius have their remarks on it too, but short ones. I would recommend those passages to my godfather's perusal. Strada's authority, who was a Jesuit, cannot be doubted of in this point. When you are in the country, the story of Philip the Second and his son, Don Carlos, may afford you amusement and reflections too. You will meet with it in short in the historians of those times, but there was a little account gathered out of all the historians, and translated from the French in 1670.

1717, July 18.—The exception of the Att[orney] was a surprise to everybody, but most to him, though he had two or three days' notice to expect it, I suppose from Lord C[armarthe]n. By what I hear he is very uneasy at it, but they need not fear much from his resentment, and I fancy others will not put it in his power to make his peace at their expense. I am glad to hear you have thoughts at last of the country, it might be a useful amusement to you to read the history of the troubles in the Netherlands. The effects which you would see there of the oppression of a free people by a Spanish ministry, may suggest reflections not improper to you. The best account of those troubles, of those who wrote against the Spaniards, is Meteren.

I suppose you have heard that Alsop's mistress has recovered two thousand pounds damages. A pretty mulct, if you take too into the computation the load of infamy in this world and guilt in the next. Do you think your friend the Bishop of Rochester will help him to pay his fines? Bob Freind ought to have some pity on him, it was almost his own case.

You tell me you have received the picture, but you tell me not how you like it.

Postscript. My duty to my honoured Lady and your father, I congratulate my godfather upon the honour of his exception. I suppose this is instead of a present for his two embassies. At present it is only an exception; it is to be hoped, it may in the next Act of Grace, be a proscription.

[1717,] August 26.—Your friend the Attorney is returned to his old trade again, and is as very an attorney as ever he was.

He was here lately upon no other account but to endeavour if he could by threats or wheedles to bring the lady who has got a late verdict against a certain person to a composition, but he was forced to return *re infecta*. This I think was the proper work of an attorney, and somewhat beneath one who had been in the high station he once filled.

Mr. Bridges, your brother book-buyer, did me the honour of a visit lately and drank your health with me; he designs to wait on you at Wimpole before the summer is over.

As your Lordship's fame is justly in all places of literature, the widow of Mr. Budyer sent me a day or two ago to know how she might direct her deceased husband's catalogue to you. I told her your address, but said I was afraid the catalogue would make a packet too big for the post, and offered to convey it to you, but I have not heard since of her. Mr. Bridges has seen the books, they are choice but in no good condition, and I believe you have most of them. The widow wants to sell [them] in a lump.

Prior is in the country with the Duke of Shrewsbury. I know not whether we shall see him here before we leave it. The Bishop of Durham has been at Lincoln this fortnight; he is now in his life time vesting the College on the great benefaction he designs for them, to the value I believe of 40,000*l.* He drops too his benefactions of lesser note in other places, amongst others, 100*l.* to our library.

[1717,] August 30.—The man who copied Dr. Radcliffe's picture was gone as soon as I returned. But there is now one in town, one Miller, who has been much employed by G. Clarke, who will copy Mr. King's much better than the other could have done, I believe. I believe the man's hands are full at present, but he shall do it before he goes.

We had some ill effects of the storm here; we lost two trees in our long walk. I hope you have lost none in the beautiful avenue to your house. But the storm has done prodigious damage in Holland, it raised the water at Rotterdam so high, and it happened to be the fair time, that it overflowed all the rooms equal with the ground in all the houses in the town. It broke one of the dykes at Dort, it bore off the roofs of all the country houses in the campagne about Amsterdam, and shattered all the wooden summer houses to pieces, and if it had not changed of a sudden from the north to the south, in probability it would have broken down all their dykes, and laid all Holland under water. I had this account from Mr. Muyssart, a very honest Dutchman, who was here this week for two days with John Drummond. He is nephew and heir to Burgomaster de Haas, who was for the peace. He wants much to see your father, and will be much disappointed in returning to Holland without seeing of him.

Lady Mansel lay here last night in her way to Bath. She did me the honour to send [for] me, and I sat the evening with her. You may be sure I wanted not the stories current amongst the ladies of her opinion, but I need not trouble you with them. Your father will furnish you with them and no doubt tell you of the famous scolding bout betwixt the Princess and her Majesty of Munster, in the drawing room, upon the Princess saying, as her Majesty approached, "here comes her mock Majesty."

Methinks Lewis fetched a compass in order to go to Warwickshire. I suppose your father will give you the particulars of a brisk quarrel betwixt Don Lewis and poor Prior. Surely it is *impar congressus*, but I believe Don Lewis takes himself to be the richer of the two, and that supplies all other defects. Either I made some great blunder, or you mistook me. The Bishop of Durham, good man, never withdrew his benefaction. I, as Deputy Treasurer at present, am now in possession of the 100*l*. His benefaction to Lincoln is an augmentation of each fellowship 10*l. per annum*, an erection of eight or twelve scholarships, for gentlemen's younger sons of the Bishopric of Durham at 20*l. per annum* each; an augmentation of a living belonging to the rectory 20*l. per annum*; of four livings held with fellowships 10*l. per annum*; and purchasing all the houses betwixt Lincoln and All Hallows, and building there for his new scholars and others.

How came Heywood, who is a perfect stranger to you, to call upon you, with such a trail along with him? Had he no pretence for it but calling upon me, it would have been impudent enough if I had been there. Though I knew him twenty-five years ago, . I am a perfect stranger to his spouse and his fireside. Pray let me know whether he had any other pretence for calling on you.

The Bishop of Durham left us this morning, we mustered up all the horse we could in town to attend him out of town, and he relishes the respects that have been paid him full well. Barker, though he owes all he has to Lincoln College, was in town, but never went to wait on the old gentleman.

Lord Harcourt is in London, what will you say if you should hear that he is gone up to solicit for a pardon.

I need not write you news from Eywood. I heard from Neddy this week; he is well, but I find not that he thinks yet of coming hither again. But he promises to enter into indentures with me not to give breakfasts for the sake of showing his equipage. I shall not deliver them to him, but upon those terms.

Postscript. Merton College had like to have been burnt lately; one in the uppermost room over the gate house fell asleep without putting out his candle. The furniture was burnt, the ceiling, the floor, the man escaped; but the flame was seen by one passing by at one in the morning in the street. The walls in the gate house were very thick, which preserved the College.

1717, September 9.—I have had more strangers within these last few weeks than in the whole year before, though some I expected have not yet been here, and Mr. Thomas says your father's business will not let him stir yet. Lord and Lady Foley did me the honour to dine with me on Wednesday last in their way to Woodstock; you may be sure we remembered Wimpole.

The Bishop of Chester took care to observe to him how very
fresh venison might be brought from Brampton hither, but I did
not perceive that his Lordship made the application the Bishop
desired he should.   I was so fortunate to give my Lady such
content, that she has promised me her custom whenever she
passes this way.

My correspondents in town are suspicious of the journey of a
late (sic) man thither.   They think he has been endeavouring to
make his peace.   Lord Nottingham and Lord Car[marthe]n
were with him constantly whilst he was there.   Prior designs to
be with you about a fortnight hence.

I think it will be best for me to send up Charles King's picture
to you when you are in town again, as you must be when the
Parliament meets, you may then have it copied by what hand
you like best.

You have heard how the bishoprics are disposed of ; Holland
of Merton has the prebend of Worcester, vacant by Chandler's
promotion.   Our friend the Bishop of Hereford went to the
Archbishop of Canterbury to desire his Grace's interest for that
prebend in behalf of his brother Dr. Bisse.   I am amazed he
could be so mean as to apply there, when his brother too is
already so well provided for, and when his Lordship might
make further provision for his brother, if there were need of it,
by his own preferments.   How could he possibly hope he should
succeed ?   It is [very] plain now why he courted this
Archbishop so much and used to plead for him.   For this and
some other practices like it, I cannot help despising my old
friend.

1717, October 27.—My honest lad Neddy returned to us on
Wednesday last, he is very hearty, and I believe he has brought
his virtue entire to us, though he has been more than once upon
the Welsh hills with my godfather.   The good lad had more wit
than his father ; he would have had him to have stayed in the
country till he himself had come up to town, but the lad was
wiser.   We expect Mr. Auditor here about the middle of the
next month.

Pray explain yourself, who the old friend is who will not
make a good D.D.   I know no old friend of ours, amongst
the late creation.

I am glad if anything we could do was, as it was designed, an
evidence to Mr. Prior of the respect we sincerely have for
him.   You are very happy in having him so long with you.   Mr.
Fellows, the Master in Chancery, was lately here, to see a good
young man, his son, who had put out his ankle, and he gave
us, without any application to him, from the sole motion of
his own generosity, an 100l. to our library.   If Providence
raises up benefactors where we so little expect them, we shall
compass our building.

Old Mapletoft has been ill of a fever at eighty seven, but is got
over it, and likely now to live ten years more, to the Bishop of
Chester's comfort.   He lately published a little book of good

moral sayings of the old Greek philosophers, and I am to have a book for your father and one for you, which he presents you as a legacy to each of you.

I perceive you have had a true account of the reception the Pandar [Brinsden] has met with. Methinks the news of it should not make the master in haste to return, if he could. It is now hotly discoursed that all impediments are removed.

I give you joy of your new aunt. I suppose your uncle has made this match, to prove his capacity to be Prime Minister.

We have been much alarmed for some posts with news of a Royal visit to us, but we are not yet babes of grace enough for such a favour; the talk is over.

[1717,] October 29.—I take this opportunity of the Bishop of Chester's servant, of letting you know what I have heard of the Pandar, that we may compare the accounts we have had and see if they agree. I was at Bucklebury when a letter came from Brinsden to give notice of his being in England, he pretended then to abscond, and that he durst not own his being in England. I since hear he came over with Lord Stair's passport, and went directly to Lord Sunderland and was introduced by young Craggs to the King to present, as is supposed, a petition from his poor master, and it seems agreed that the reversal of the attainder will be proposed next session. Brinsden brought over letters to all Bolingbroke's old friends, he went to Longleat, but Lansdowne would not see him, and sent to him to be gone immediately out of his house. He went to Sir W. Wyndham's, Sir William saw him, but excused it to his friends that he could not do otherwise, being a trustee for his lady. Jemmy Murray, who I think was with Sir William Wyndham, bid the Pandar tell his master that he was a treacherous villain, and that he would cane him whenever he met him. This is my account, and methinks when the poor Lord hears it he should not be so eager for coming home. Neither the reception he is like to have from his old friends, nor the condition of his own private affairs, should make him wish to return. I am afraid he has not philosophy to struggle with contempt and want.

You say nothing of your going to town. I am afraid there will be a very poor appearance of our friends. By what I hear, there is a sort of agreement amongst them not to come up to Parliament. I will give you a paragraph I had in a letter last week from Baginton [W. Bromley's]:—"I do not hear from any one what our friends design to do, more than that it is thought many that are in the country will not come up if they can help it. I wait to know what others in whom I have a confidence will do, or would have me do."

I take those in whom he has a confidence to mean your father. If you would have him up at the beginning of the session, you must send for him. I understand it not. The Court will get what they want before the holidays, if the House is empty. Will it be necessary, on the account of your private bill, that your friends should be in the House?

Sir W. Wyndham made last week mighty entertainments for his neighbours; an amphitheatre was built in his park, gentry and commonalty for several miles round were invited to see sports or to bear a part in them, such as cudgel playing and other noble diversions. Rewards were allotted *tam rictis quam victoribus*, and entertainment *gratis* in booths for the several days of the diversion. I know not whether he proposed any thing but diversion, but the Government seems to think him considerable. A regiment of dragoons went down last week to his neighbourhood, I suppose to serve instead of constables.

1717, November 6.—The adventure I am going to tell you is so extraordinary that I would not deny you the diversion of hearing it. Your old acquaintance John Keill is married to a pretty woman, but to one whose quality and fortune are alike. She was a servant, niece to Harry Clements, her father was a book binder, the widow her mother has many other children, and earns by washing what she has not from the parish to support them. But John talks like a philosopher; he has been married five months, and says he likes his wife better now than he did before he married her. That she is that which is agreeable to him, that she is one who will live just as he would have her, and that he has more ease in his mind now than he had in his former life, and in this last point he is certainly right.

Sir John Doyly is put up by the Whigs for the county and Sir Robert Banks Jenkinson by our friends. I fancy Sir John Doyly will make nothing of it; it is hoped he will see it so plainly himself that he will desist. All the younger brothers of the Jenkinsons are christened Robert with another name too, that upon the death of any, there may still be a Sir Robert surviving.

1717, November 8.—I have received the favour of your Lordship's by Mr. Thomas, I am surprised to find you complain in it that Neddy is not come to us. I am afraid by this that mine to you in which I gave you a long account of Neddy is miscarried.

Lest my letter should have miscarried, I must repeat what I said of my honest lad. He is perfectly well, and as good as his best friends wish him. I do not find that his rambling on the Welsh mountains has in the least tainted his virtue. His father would have kept him still in the country, but to what purpose I cannot imagine. It was with much importunity that the good lad got leave to return to us.

I heard last night again from our friend, and have written to him this morning, and pressed him to be in town. He is ready himself to come upon any summons; should a line come to him from your quarters, it will certainly determine him.

1717, November 15.—Sir John Doyly seems resolved to stand it out, and the Duchess of Marlborough has sent orders to their agents to make interest for him, but we doubt not but he will lose it by a prodigious majority.

The little captain came hither on Wednesday with his lady,
she went yesterday towards Herefordshire, and he across the
country towards you, and designs to be at Wimpole on Monday.

Lord Harcourt appears in this election with a zeal he never
was known to do, and rather against Doyly than for Jenkinson.
He told Doyly hê would oppose him with all his might, as he
would any one else, even his own son, if he were set up by Lord
Parker or the Duke of Marlborough.

[1717,] November 18.—I believe you may safely presume that
I do not only excuse, but thank you too, for communicating that
which is so welcome to me in relation to your private affairs. I
pray God to confirm you in your resolutions, they are the most
proper you could take for your honour as well as for your ease;
and when the Act is passed, if my poor thoughts may have any
weight, not a stick of timber that was an inch thick should
stand in Welbeck—I had almost put in Brampton too—whilst
any incumbrance to the value of sixpence was left on you or
any that belong to you. But I understand not one paragraph.
I can assure you *in verbo sacerdotis*, I never heard any mortals,
but two, charge you with the least of crimes, and they too charged
you to your face, and with no other than what you confess, a
little heedlessness. If you would know the persons, they were
Morley and myself. I must bring in Morley to help to bring
myself off again. As to all other mortals, as far as I know, you
have the most reason to be satisfied of any gentleman in England
I ever heard of, in the general esteem of all that know you. I
would not say this, for fear of raising your vanity, if it did not
seem a little necessary at present to relieve under a contrary
sentiment. Here is an old swash buckler here, I mean old
Gifford, who never saw you but once, but was then so charmed
with you, that at the meeting of any company he constantly bars
any one else from beginning your health and claims it as his own
privilege. If you would explain that dark paragraph a little to me,
I would thank you, and tell you my thoughts of it.

I entirely agree with your Lordship in all your reflections, I
find my fears are too true as to a brother of ours lately disgraced.
I believe they will find disappointed Whigs not better Christians
at least than disgraced Tories. That same sermon I believe sticks
in his stomach, but he comes of a race that can digest retractations.
The person you enquire about is quite at the end of his politics,
this last blow has finished the despair he began to have upon the
dismission of the sober Earl of W[harton]. He pretends not to
any conjectures, but waits only in a maze for the issue of things.

I have no manner of apprehension from the other person, nor
need any that ever was engaged with him. His foible is too
well known. There is a sure way of dealing with him; any one
that dare crack a louse may keep him in awe, if there should
be any occasion for that method.

You own you would not come to town, if it were not for your
Act, and is not that a stronger reason against my coming, who
have not so much as a pretence of business, than any you can

give me for coming. I have done with politics and have subdued my own curiosity in that point. Though I own there is somewhat in the present face of affairs that would tempt one that was less a philosopher than I am now in that point. The good Bishop of Chester is as eager to be at the opening of the session as ever he was to be married, and that was enough in all reason. —*Nobis non licet esse tam protervis*, who profess myself a poor disciple to Robin Morgan. I heartily thank those who have given us a late quietus, I thank them for it, on my own account and their own too.

My most humble duty to my Lord and Lady Oxford, my thanks to my Lord for the favour of his, I shall do myself the honour to answer it by Mr. Thomas, when he returns. I shall take care of the enclosed.

My most sincere duty to my ever honoured Lady, I am glad to hear my Christian improves so much. I shall not disgrace her any more by that vile epithet of Little. I have too much concern for her to say any thing to her disadvantage. I hope she is big enough to be able to tend her brother, if she could have one. I wish your old tutor may not have infused some of his own qualities into you which he might well have spared. I hear a great deal of tittle-tattle in the next lodgings to me, but no crying out yet. I wish I could hear that you had been on the back of the Arab, but I suppose that is like other rarities, for sight once a quarter not for use.

1717, November 22.—Perhaps you will hear before this reaches you, that old " shoo strings " [Sir W. Whitlock] died on Wednesday morning. There are two who would if they could succeed him, your friend Simon, and Dod of All Souls. There is no possibility of preventing a dispute, but by putting up George Clarke ; that I hope will do it effectually, though it will not be without difficulty that G. Clarke will be prevailed on to serve. Dod is on the spot, and offered himself last night in several places. His hopes lay chiefly in the young masters who are warmest, but I fancy he sees the inclinations so general to another that he will not expose himself by persisting. Delaune, and all who had been obliged by Sim's father when he was in power—which were too many, to your father's shame be it spoken, who would not, as he was pressed to do, take the merit to himself, and not let others run away with his due—would I believe have tried what could have been done for Sim if there had been room, but as I take it they will be silent, since the gap is stopped. Had there been room for a trial, they would not have carried it, but they might have given us some trouble.

I have seen young Bentley's *Patronum non erubescendum*, every one takes it at first sight as a recantation of the old one. It is of a piece with every thing else he does.

[1717,] December 2.—Dod desisted on Thursday last ; we shall now have our election for county and university, without opposition in either, on Wednesday. We have done for the university the best that our present circumstances would admit

of here. No other but G. Clarke could have prevented a great
struggle amongst us, as they who were for Simon lay on the
watch on one side, and as this Dod actually set up on the other.
This Dod is a fellow of All Souls, a physician, a paltry insignificant fellow, but has some estate. He has been used to give
drink to young masters. In principles he is somewhat beyond
a Tory, he was put upon this attempt by the Bishop of Rochester
and Shippen, though both disown it, since nothing could be
made of it. But besides other good spirits, Dod himself affirmed
to the Bishop of Chester, if he stood it out I believe he could not
have polled fifty, but if the election were to have been by
scrutiny, as other elections are, I am afraid he would have had
more on account of his supposed principles.

I am much at loss to guess at the meaning of that paragraph
still. I thought your father had had enemies enough for the
whole family. I never heard of so much as one particular to
you on your own account, nor can I guess upon what ground
possibly any one can be so, but I shall wait with patience till you
think fit to explain, or till Providence brings us together again.

We expect the Auditor here on Wednesday and he will stay
with us till Friday. John Drummond with two polite Scotch
ladies will be with me on Friday evening and stay with me till
Monday. For the part of gallanting the ladies, I have already
appointed Mr. Thomas my substitute. I have sent the letter up
by T. Row[ney?]. Mr. Bromley came to town on Saturday was
se'nnight, and was in hopes of finding your father there. I hope
your father will not be much longer with you. Business seems
to call; I suppose we all agree pretty well in our reflections on
what has happened in the close of the last week.

[1717-18;] January 30.—The place where you are affords at any
time, and much more now, better materials for a correspondence
than that of my abode does. I know not what to tell you hence,
but about Neddy, and his life is so much of a piece, so very
regular and good, that it affords not any variety for a correspondence, and therefore whenever I say nothing of him you may
safely presume that all is as you would wish it.

Your own bill, I perceive, is in so great forwardness, and the
session is likely to last so long, that I suppose I may safely congratulate you upon the passing of it and upon the merit of your
own activity in it.

1717-18, February 1.—You write as gaily as if your bill had
received the royal assent that morning. I bless God we make
a shift to keep soul and body together, but not in the manner
you would seem to imagine. It becomes you indeed well, who
riot in plenty, to insult us upon our poverty. We know very
well that you carles of the laity think a poor parson luxurious,
if he barely supports nature and has not the fear of famine.
But as riotous as we are, if I had not had more comfort than my
dignity is able to supply me, the weather would have been too
hard for me. We have one blessing indeed, which serves instead
of plenty, and all other blessings, a thing called independency.

You will guess how we have lived by Mr. Thomas's meagre looks when you see him this week. He has been forced to keep Lent here in the carnival season. I hope you will have pity on him, and make him keep carnival in Lent. I never doubted of my friend the Attorney, but it is somewhat hard that there should be occasion for new instances of villainy to refresh men's memories. That which I told you of when I was last with you begins to show itself. He said he desired not to see a certain person in business again, that he was the last man in the world he would wish to see so. He seems to be afraid least that person's credit should rise again, and to be weak enough too to think that he can stop it.

I thank you for your hint of Sir John, but I had heard of that subtle device. It is hard a poor man should be found out and laughed at for the first sin he was ever guilty of of that kind.

You will hear of old Tom, he will lay himself at your feet to thank you for the honour you have done. As for the poor innocent young one, you must excuse him if the ambition of saying somewhat to you made. him impertinent, and charge himself with compliments to you.

The poor Duke [of Shrewsbury] has a wonderful escape if he recover. I should have thought the prescriptions he has had surer than any draughts his lady ever mingled in her own country.

[1718,] February 14.—°The Vice-Chancellor sent for He[a]rne yesterday about his preface, he has forbid him printing any more at our press. He has told his printer Rance that he will expel him the university if he prints any more for him. He has told He[a]rne that he will put him into the court and send for two Justices of the Peace and tender the oaths to him, for that he believes him a papist. How He[a]rne will get off, I know not. I am apt to think it will end at least in changing his quarters. Pray communicate this to Lord Harley.

The exportation of bullion on account of interest due to foreigners from our funds was what I was not aware of; that in a little time must drain us, and amounts to the same thing as a balance of trade against us, viz.: Debts due from England to other countries, nor can this have any remedy but by paying off the funds, for which I suppose we are in no condition.

I thank you for your care of my little commissions. When you next pass by Tonson's, pray tell him I will take up Lord Lempster's book and pay the other payment for it as soon as the book comes out, and see that added to the memorandum.

That rogue is certainly not married, but has the impudence to live here publicly with a whore under the name of a wife. The different accounts given by him and her of the place of marriage, and what Taylor says, are clear proofs. There needs no further search, this will end in his ruin.

Lord H[arle]y writes me word that Paleotti was taken out of the Bishop of Ely's house. How came he to have shelter there ?

---

* This letter is addressed to " Mr. Thomas at the Bird in Hand and Star, near the new Exchange in the Strand, Westminster."

Postscript. I had this morning a young valentine come to my bedside to claim me, Dr. Hudson's young daughter. Pray desire Agatha to lay out, as far as a guinea, no farther, in somewhat for a young girl of seven years old, knots or beads or any thing she thinks proper, for I am utterly ignorant what is so on these occasions.

[1718,] February 16.—I desired Mr. Thomas to let you know that your friend He[a]rne is in tribulation, and how he will get out I know not. He has condescended to apply to me to help him, but how to do it I know not well. I am afraid it will not be very proper for me to interpose for one who has so grossly and foolishly abused our founder, if there were no other exceptions. But if I should interpose, though I perceive he wishes himself out of this scrape, yet he is so proud and so stubborn that he will recant nothing. I believe it will end in his being obliged to leave this place, at the apprehension of which he seems not a little disturbed.

You seem to me to be somewhat disturbed that Neddy does so well here, and afraid lest he should come up to the credit you had here. My reason is, the pains you are taking to make him otherwise. Surely you are not wanting to throw temptation in his way. Ten dozen of wine at one lump is enough surely to try the virtue of one of his age. I pray God he may have enough to stand the trial.

Postscript. Pray send me a little good snuff. I have the honour of your Lordship's. Your reflections on the effect the prosecution of He[a]rne will have on him are very just, but there are some such things in his preface, I know not well how the Vice-Chancellor could avoid taking some notice of them ; and though He[a]rne will be more stubborn and more proud for it, yet he is very apprehensive of being obliged to change his quarters.

[1718,] February 18.—I perceive your Lordship has still a tenderness upon you for He[a]rne. For your sake, not out of any kindness of my own to you, I have done to-day what I can for him, but I believe to little purpose. The Heads of Houses have now an opportunity of being even with him, no one will resent any thing that is done to him, the tide is turned against him. Every one applies his general reflections to themselves in particular, and suppose that he thinks that no one here is good for any thing but himself. But "Premier" [Edward ?] Gwyn, who is his great confident, and a hearty solicitor for him, owns to me that though he is stubborn still, yet he begins to be concerned. That which gives me the greatest aversion to him is his remarkable ingratitude to the best friends he has ever had. I wish your Lordship may fare better than others have done. My neighbour the Sub-dean is his hearty enemy on this occasion, though once they were great cronies, but that is for his speaking against the marriage of grave Doctors, and from a slight mention which he

made in his preface of the Sub-dean himself, which Mr. Thomas can explain to you. Though I speak truth of him to you, I plead for him as much as his cause will admit of it, when my neighbour attacks him.

[1718,] February 27.—Mr. He[a]rne has been with me full of your Lordship's unexampled generosity to him. It is noble indeed, and fit for the Lord of Welbeck. But for all this, I can be pretty positive that you cannot get the missale nor so much, I am afraid, as a dedication. You may perhaps have a simple *honorifica mentio*, but you must own your political principles a little more plainly to him, before you can be deemed worthy of the honour Mr. Rawlinson has.

Tom Rowney has let me know by this post of the great honour you have designed to him and his family, but Tom at his age is shame faced, and says he has not assurance enough to accept it. Tom is like many fair ladies who through their modesty lose what they have a mind to, and I suppose, like them, will not be ill pleased to have his modesty overpowered.

Dod has been canvassing here again upon presumption of Mr. Bromley's death, and I am told that our friend He[a]rne, upon the report that Mr. Bromley was dying, broke out into great joy, and said now he should see Dod in. If upon enquiry I should find this true, I will stick closer to his hump than all the delegates together do.

Postscript. My duty to my most honoured Lady. Neddy, who is sitting by me, desires his respects to you both. Neddy tells me of a present of two books he has from you. This is right and a little more proper for him than ten dozen of claret.

[1718,] March 2.—I thank you for your news of my Lady Abingdon's being with child again, but I should have been better pleased if you could have sent me the same news of your own lady, *pudet hæc opprobra, &c.*

There was on Thursday, much to Mr. He[a]rne's honour, an assembly of the divan of the Heads of Houses upon him. An extract of passages in his preface, that were thought liable to exception, were laid before them. The result was, that the Vice-Chancellor was desired to consult with the Assessor how he could be prosecuted, and the Vice-Chancellor was farther desired to consult with the Delegates of the Press how far it might be proper to allow him to print here still. But there is no doubt but they will permit [him] to go on with " Neubrigensis"; and I am apt to think, but I will not undertake for it, that the other part will end in a private reprimand.

I thank you for the favour of your countenance this day to my friend Tom and his family. They are not a little proud of it, as I perceive by his epistle this day. There is not much politeness, but a great deal of heartiness. I have looked over the books you have sent Neddy, you are resolved he shall have *Gustus Eruditus.* It is very kind in your Lordship to form his taste so early by such dainties, but I hope you take care that our good friend the Auditor knows nothing of this. He would be more concerned at this little box than at the four hampers, he would dream of his boy's having as great a bibliomania as your Lordship has, and be afraid lest some of the acres at Eywood should in time be pawned for Aldus and Colinæus.

Now I am upon this subject, I must not forget Mr. He[a]rne desired me to enquire of your Lordship what part of Tully it was for which you lately gave 30*l.* He thinks it was for one of the first edition of *Natura Deorum*. Pray where and when was it printed?

1717-18, March 8.—I have had Mr. He[a]rne under examination, he stoutly denies that he ever expressed any joy upon the report of Mr. Bromley's being likely to die. He owns upon that report, for which he says he expressed great concern, he might have some discourse of Dod's being likely to appear again. I desired him to recollect what he had said upon that occasion. / pretended he could not, but the result seemed to be this, ` he expressed any joy for Mr. Dod's being likely to succeed, ˄ly upon a supposition of a vacancy, and not that he ˄ a vacancy, that he might succeed. Though I could not ˄g him to own so much directly, I shall now examine into ˄ne authority of those who charged him. His affair is still in the briars, and I know not when it will be out.

Neddy is very presumptuous upon the stock of the wine you have sent him. He invited me to solemnize this day, being that on which your father was stabbed, with him. I told him I thought it was more proper to celebrate the day in which he was acquitted than that on which he was stabbed. I could not convince him, but to compromise the matters he has invited me to keep that too. I have promised for that night, but I could not go to-night, because it is Saturday.

[1718,] April 10.—At two days' warning you may have a very good coach here, that will hold four easily, but it will cost you 5*l.*

I hear your retinue will be very numerous. When I resolved to wait on you, I had no apprehension that you and my Lady would be so well provided with friends to attend you. I wish you had been so kind to let me know it. Since you are like to have no want of friends, I believe I should not, if I had known it, have increased the number of them. But I suppose lodgings for the season will be taken for me, before I could send to stop it. Your two or three last letters have been very full, very particular and very instructive.

[1718,] May 1. [Bath.]—I am very glad I can tell you that nobody here wants you. My good Lady takes ample care of all her poor servants, and she herself is easy and cheerful, and much pleased that she has come hither. The waters agree wonderfully with her, and she perceives and owns that she is already much better than she was when she came. I attend in person at places where it is allowed to me to appear. When her Ladyship goes to

the play, I substitute my chum old Francis in my place, though he acquitted himself but indifferently last night, for after he had put her Ladyship in the chair, he did not go and sup with her. Now you perceive there is no occasion for you, I hope you will not think of seeing us till June is begun.

Miss Peggy is in perfect health and wantonness, and promises as fair as any lady of her years to be an admirable coquette.

My Lady Harley's play last night was crowded more than any that has been acted this year, but discord and faction will break out in places dedicated to ease and diversion. Lady Katherine Edwin would not go to the play, nor let Lord Manchester's or her own daughter go, and was so wellbred as to own her reason to be because it was bespoke by Lady Harley. But the ladies stand by us bravely, and have vowed revenge upon Dame Edwin, if she dares to bespeak a play this season.

The Duke and Duchess of Richmond are here. The Arabian and his spouse came in with a mighty train last night. The Duchess of Kent is come and the [Duke] expected, and [so] are the Duke and Duchess of St. Albans. I hope then we shall have a due complement of titles and garters. This place affords no more at present.

My most humble respects to the most excellent ladies of Eywood, all three of them, and to the lords of Eywood and Stoke.

[1718,] May 31. [Bath.]—I am glad you had the manners to write to my Lady from Stevenage, you will receive an answer by the "Higler," which is much kinder than you deserve. I thank God I can give a very good account of my charge. You could be so hard-hearted as to leave when she was out of order, and soon after you was gone, about four o'clock, her fit of illness returned, and she was very sick. But the worst of it is, that this is not an illness that is owing to any kindness from you, it is not of that sort which she should have, and which, if you were good for any thing, she would have. But I can now with great joy tell you that under my care she is so very well recovered, that we sat chatting last night till near twelve. She never was better in her life, I thank God, than in your absence. For my own part I find no want of you, but I cannot prevail on her to allow me to say as much to you from her. I find I can live here very easily without you, and I will dispense with your stay as long as you please, if you but send Morley to me.

The evening post informs us of great news from St. Albans. I hope we shall have from you to-morrow somewhat that we may depend on about that great man. Much depends on it.

Miss Margery is perfectly well, and Monsieur Guiney admires her almost as much as he does his own performance.

My duty to your father and my god-father. My respects to good Lady Dupplin, aunt Tabby and the convert, and to others as they ask for me.

Postscript. The rebels at Cambridge broke loose on the 24th of May, they grumbled about the streets all day, at night they attacked the meeting house, gutted it, and carried the pulpit a mile out of town in triumph, and burnt it with great solemnity. I hope some of the quieters of the nation will be sent to chastise them for this and to prevent any more of it.

Upon further information, we hear the outside of the meeting house was chiefly battered, but that the inside is not much damaged and the pulpit is safe. A virago, or man in woman's habit, crowned with laurel, led up the party to the assault. Many scholars are said to be concerned.

1718, June 15.—I found myself much more able than I thought I had been to bear travelling, and got home a day sooner than I proposed, on Friday night.

I beg leave to return my thanks for all the favours I had from you at Bath, and for your bearing with all the trouble I gave you there. I am obliged to you chiefly, for the satisfaction I had by your bringing me thither, of seeing my opinion as well as wishes answered in the great benefit my Lady has found by the waters. George Clarke came home a day before me, and as far as I can judge by a little conversation I had with him this morning, he is perfectly well in all respects.

The Bishop of Chester continues on the mending hand, but still looks wan, and is very weak. By the accounts I have had of him since I returned, he was in much greater danger than we apprehended. The Bishop of Bristol has nothing about him that shows that he was lately ill.

I found Neddy with a cold on him, but I think I helped to cure it the first night I came home. I have had him at confession, and he does own a sort of a hankering after those celebrated damosels, the Muses. I am afraid he will never have his father's approbation of such an amour.

The worthy Major has told you how we met; pray tell him I have obeyed his commands to John Drummond, and let John know how sensible the worthy Major is of John's steady and successful friendship to him.

The great Mr. Wanley has used the Bishop of Chester very unkindly, not to say rudely, in refusing flatly, with sturdiness enough, to consult some papers for him in your father's library. But he will leave the "Genoa Arms" for no one but you, if he would do it for you.

All here send service and duty to my Lady and yourself, and heartily pray for the same fruit to you from the waters [at Bath] which they suppose you chiefly wish for from them.

My respects to the worthy Major and Mr. Prior; pray tell Mr. Prior my memory served me right, that the word is λιβιρτῖνος that it denotes not men of any sect or opinion, nor ever was used to express any such thing; that the synagogue was that particular synagogue where Jews who were strangers, who lived at Jerusalem but had not been born there or in Palestine, worshipped; that as the Alexandrians, Cyrenians, &c., denoted those who came from those countries, the Libertines signified those who came from Rome, who were the sons of Jews who had been brought slaves to Rome, and freed afterwards by their masters. Which Jews, when made *liberti*, had a particular quarter in Rome, *trans Tiberim*, as the Jews have now in Amsterdam, where they lived by themselves.

1718, July 25.—I thought my godfather had been too old to go abroad again for pleasure, and I daresay he does not go upon politics, though perhaps some may suspect so.

The Warden of All Souls' and poor Charlett—to his no little mortification—are turned out of the Commission of the Peace. Some gentlemen too are displaced in the county. Those who are put in to supply their places are chiefly, as I hear, shopkeepers. It is said there are alterations in the commissions all over England, and chiefly amongst the clergymen who were justices.

The Bishop of Chester, I bless God, continues very well, and has lately met with very considerable evidence to confirm his own opinion as to the Archbishop's authority of conferring degrees. It is certain the Bishop of Chester has the right on his side, and I am apt to think it will appear so plain that the Archbishop will be obliged to give it up. Should it be so, it would be no little mortification to the Archbishop and credit to our friend. But no thanks to the great Mr. Wanley for his assistance upon this occasion.

1718, July 31.—My friend Neddy is well, and entered upon his sports, for he has sent me the first fruits of them, a pot of grouse.

Your Lordship was saying at Bath, that one volume of the "Magdeburgenses" was very scarce. I beg to know which it is and what is the title of it. I have a set of them which was my father's, and I would be glad to know whether it be complete.

Your friend Steady, being so eminently ingenious, has got the company of two wits for his entertainment, Pope and Gay. Lord Harcourt lends them Stanton Harcourt to live in this summer.

One Smithies some time ago got with some young men of Magdalen, and pretended to have been at Preston. They informed against him to the Vice-Chancellor for drinking the Pretender's health, &c. When he was to have been tried at the assizes, orders came down in the middle of the night to stop his trial here, and to remove it to the King's Bench. He is too to be re-examined, but the examination was taken by the judges out of the Vice-Chancellor's hands, who had committed him, and put to two sitting justices It is supposed the prosecution will be dropped, and confirms men in what they suspected, that he was a spy sent hither. It is supposed he would endeavour to turn the accusation upon the young men, if after having been accused by them, he can be capable of being an evidence against them.

[1718,] August 3.—You give me the highest satisfaction, when you are pleased to give yourself the trouble of imparting to me any thing that tends to the security or ease of your own affairs. I am glad you have ended with the Duke [of Montagu], but your

bill cannot come in till you have renewed articles with Vane, but your saying that you are in no fear of a chancery suit implies, I hope, that you either have agreed with him or are likely to do it.

I am a little surprised at what you tell me of J. H[udson]'s visit to you, and of your bounty to him. Surely he had no title to it, and if I may have leave to say so, would you search strictly into your own motive to it, I am afraid you would find that your largess was rather from ostentation than generosity, and that you had more regard in it to your own glory than to that "honest" man's merit. Do you remember what you observed to me at Newbury when I told you that Lord Carnarvon had sent John Hudson 200l.? You said he always placed his bounty wrong. It would not be amiss to apply such just observations to our own practice.

I condole with you for your loss, but I think our cases are somewhat different, you have timber and stone of your own, and money too for workmen, to enable you to repair. I wish I could say the same of myself upon those articles.

Indeed they were the "Magdeburgenses" of which you told me at Bath that one volume of them was very scarce and hard to be met with. That was it which made me desirous to know whether I had the scarce volume. I have twelve volumes.

[1718,] August 10.—You will be visited in a little time at Wimpole by a gentleman who leaves this place to-morrow, Dr. Savage. He has certainly lost no assurance by his travelling; he is full of himself as well as of his travels. Abroad he was looked on as a spy for the Government, he has somewhat I must own, both in his look and address, that always gave me a caution. His parsonage is within seven miles of you. I find he designs soon to be with you, and as to the account of his travels he will be entertaining enough.

Your Lordship and I will have no difference about "Magdeburgenses."

We have had very much mischief done in all the counties round us both as to men, beasts and houses by the late thunder and lightning. I pray God preserve you and yours from such accidents.

The Bishop of Sarum has had a great quarrel with his Dean and Chapter, for their letting the anthem "By the waters of Babylon" &c., be sung upon the first of August. He showed violent tokens of uneasiness all the time the choir was singing it. When he came out he said it was designed as an affront to him and the guest, and he would not bear it, but would complain of it. The thing was perfectly casual, a new boy who was to be tried having desired it might be in that anthem, as that he was best acquainted with. But if it really is any ground of offence, why does not his Lordship get an Act of Parliament to have it left out of the ordinary course of the Psalms, on the 28th day of every month?

1718, September 7.—I have just now received the honour
of a letter from your Lordship dated from Wimpole, but without any specification of month or day, unless your Lordship
says in it that you had been there above a fortnight. If your
Lordship means by that expression somewhat short of three weeks,
this letter must have been written some time ago, and ought to
have been with me sooner. I believe your Lordship will think
that I have expected to hear from your Lordship for these many
posts, as you are pleased to say you did from me, especially since
in the last I had the honour to write to you I had begged the
favour, though of one line only, to let me know by the first post
after you came down how you all got thither. I must confess I
have been often at a loss, not to say uneasy, in my own thoughts
for the reason of your silence. My only comfort was from my
innocence, not being conscious, upon the strictest search of myself,
of any possible occasion that I could have given for it. I was
thinking once or twice to have enquired the reason of it, but the
respect I thought due from me to you restrained me from it.
Since I could not but judge your forbearing to write to imply in
it a forbidding of me to do so. I think I may as safely venture
to stand the charge of forgetfulness of friends as the last Duke
of Buckingham thought he could that of covetousness. I have
commonly had the opposite imputation, and perhaps not without
some reason, laid to me, of being too troublesome to my friends.
So·much for myself. And as to your Lordship, if there were any
heterogeneous humours stirring in you, though I cannot possibly
tell how there should, I hope air and exercise have worked them
off, and so let us begin a new score.

Your letter came in the very nick, for to-morrow morning I
move towards Baginton. I had been there a fortnight ago, if
I had not waited for intelligence of the motions of a friend
of yours, which you well know are not very certain. At last I
was told they were further off now than they were a month ago
from being determined, and I was desired to wait no longer. I
hope to be at home on Tuesday, or at farthest on Thursday
se'nnight. At my return, I shall be able to give you an account
of our friend's health, which is not, I am afraid, yet so well as you
and I wish it. I expect to meet the Bishop of Chester there, in
his return. I believe he will call there on Thursday, but we
shall not return to Oxford together. The Bishop strikes off to
Northamptonshire, to Fawsly, and proposes not to be here till
Saturday se'nnight. I bless God he continues extremely well. I
shall bring with me from Baginton, C. King's age and the day
of his death. I shall meet with it there, or can send for it when
I am there from Aston. The Bishop of Bristol has had an ugly
mischance since he was at Bristol, his foot caught in a mat, and
he was thrown headlong down a pair of stone stairs. I bless
God he escaped with a bruise only of his left arm, he has not yet
recovered the use of that arm, and I believe he will call at Bath
as he returns, and pump it.

Your uncle called on me as he went home, and told me, much to my satisfaction, that all your affairs will be ready for the opening of the session.

My most sincere respects to the worthy Provost of King's when you see him. Does your Lordship hear anything of 1,500*l.* *per annum* fallen to Bentley by his Archdeaconry?

Have you seen a poem called the Oxford Toasts—if you have not, send for it, it is said to be written by a young poet Whig of St. John's, one Dive or Drive [Dry?]. Tom Rowney young and old and old madam herself are in, upon account of poor Mrs. Perry that lives with them. It is a piece of the most impudent scurrility that was ever published.

[1718,] September 19.—I returned home on Wednesday. I have been out of order since the day I set out, and am so still, but my complaint is such as I hope will soon wear off without any prejudice to me. I found our friend better than I expected, he looks as well as ever he did in his life. He eats well and sleeps well, but his pain in his side continues, it lately returned with such violence that he was forced to bleed, and it continued great too, after bleeding, though not at the height it was before; it began to abate again before I left him. If it be only what his physicians say, a weakness in the muscle, it will give him trouble upon every little cold, but no further damage. He desires [his most] hearty respects to you.

Sir Charles Holt knows not the precise age of Charles King, and that was the reason that no mention was made of it in the epitaph. But Sir Charles thinks our friend was in his 59th year when he died, on March 11, 1712[-3].

[1718,] September 24.—Charles King's monument is set up in Aston church. It is a village within a mile of Birmingham, where Sir Charles Holt's seat is.

The Bishop of Chester returned to us on Saturday, as plump and jolly as ever I knew him.

I take Mr. Bromley to be out of all danger as to life, but I wish his pain in his side may not disable him from attending public business. If it cannot be removed, and be liable to be increased upon every cold, I am afraid he will not be able to live in town, or if he could bear the town, would not be able to attend the Parliament.

I hear nothing of Neddy, it is not I assure you with my approbation that he stays so long in the country, but my opinion has not been asked, and I must not take upon me to offer it unasked, that might look like taking upon me to direct. I am told he stays till your father comes into the country, if so, we shall not see him yet in some weeks.

I hear old madam is moved at last. I congratulate you all upon it, she stood her ground and disputed it notably. You will now I suppose soon see somebody at Wimpole.

Mr. Coke of Norfolk, and his young lady, your cousin, were here whilst I was at Baginton. We are told they went to see Blenheim, and that the Duchess of Marlborough, who was there at that time, sent them word they should not see it.

1718, October 8.—It is as welcome [news] here as it can be at Cambridge, and I must own for my own part that I take a particular and I hope very innocent pleasure in hearing that an insolent knave [Dr. Bentley?] has been humbled. I beg your Lordship in your next would do me the favour to let me know who the six Heads were that were assessors to the Vice-Chancellor in an action of so much spirit as well as justice.

I believe there is no ground for what your Lordship has heard, of an order from Court to stop Hearne's prosecution. The Court can have no pretence or authority to interpose in such an affair, nor should we submit to it. But I am to think that Hearne's prosecution is dropped, but that will not do his business. The inhibition to print here continues still, perhaps too that may be removed under the new Vice-Chancellor.

Yesterday Dr. Shippen entered upon the Vice-Chancellor's office, he had some things in his speech that were more remarkable for their bravery than their discretion, and they might as well have been left out.

Lady Bolingbroke about two months ago thought she found some return of her stomach; she just tasted a little for two or three days of some odd salt meats, but her stomach flagged again, and now it will not bear asses' milk. She keeps her bed altogether, and I do not think that she can last three weeks longer.

[1718,] October 15.—I most heartily thank you for your account of Bentley, it is of more use to me than the private satisfaction I have from it. I gives me not a little credit in this place, where every one is eager to know the event of this affair, but no one has any account of it. It can pardon the Duke of S[omerset] a great many things for his interposing on this account. It is truly very handsomely done, and worthy of the office he holds. It is an obligation that ought to be gratefully owned by the university, it effectually screens them from higher powers, and I take poor Bentley's cause to be desperate. I know not whether a submission to one of his temper may not be a sorer evil than the loss of his professorship.

This place enables me not at present to make any returns to you, but I am going this day to dine with a pretty near friend of yours at Woodstock. I am amazed at his journey, at this season, and when his stay must be so short. The lady to whom he is going may truly be called the magnetic lady, who can attract in such weather and at such a distance. But yet, you and I should, I believe, think her such a one.

Your true steady friend Sir. W. Giffard has been for some time under a miserable fit of the gout, such a one as the old swash buckler never had before.

I know not whether I told you that John Keill had 200*l.* from Lord Carnarvon for his dedication, and he has laid out good part of it on his lately betrothed. He has bought her a gold watch, a white satin gown and petticoat, and a crimson nisdale, laced on the cape and down the sides with a broad galloon. Had she been an honest woman when he married her, I am afraid he would not have done so much for her.

Alsop is at last certainly gone to Rotterdam, which I take to be the completion of his ruin.

[1718,] October 22.—I most heartily thank you for your full and exact account of the proceedings against Bentley. I reckon the breach to be now as irreparable as betwixt his Holiness and the Gallican church. I am apt to think the Court will not [interpose?] at this juncture, though no doubt he will represent his persecution to proceed not only from the Tories, but the Walpolians too, which would be more likely to engage some of the ministry for him, but I suppose it must be brought into Westminster Hall, either by Bentley or the new professor. Who is likely to be chosen in his room?

Your blanket went up by the waggon yesterday directed to Mr. Thomas. I hope it is such as you will like.

I might not perhaps express myself clearly, but I meant only that if the Vice-Chancellor should adjourn the Court to Trinity College, he would do what I thought beneath him; I did not suppose he would do so. I own they have acted like men of mettle, and will retrieve the credit they had lost by their trimming conduct, to say no more of it, for some years past.

It was not our fault that Chaucer was not printed in the black letter, the Bishop of Bristol insisted long and heartily with Lintot upon it, but he also lately refused to go on with it on that condition.

Have you amongst your extraordinary collection a poem written by Scipio Capricius *de Principiis rerum*, in imitation of Lucretius' style? It is not ill done. It is at the end of Contarenus *de Elementis*. I ask because I never saw but one of them, which I have got by chance.

1718, October 27.—I know not whether I shall be the first that gives you notice of poor Lady Bolingbroke's death. She died on Friday morning about eight o'clock. Her father-in-law and his family, Mr. Packer and his wife, were with her. When her will was opened, it appeared that she had given all that she had left to herself, and had not before given to her husband at his leaving England, to Packer's second son, her godson, except legacies to servants.

Lord Harcourt has been in town these five days; he returns to-morrow to Cockrop. He has been very gracious in his visits; this morning he paid visits to the Bishops of Bristol and Chester. I take this for a certain sign that he is upon ill terms with Ruff, though no doubt he has some further aims too in this.

[1718,] October 29.—I thank you for the copy of the "Bedle's
Deposition." By the Vice-Chancellor's dismission it seems plain
that the Court will concern themselves in this [Bentley's] affair.
The ferment will certainly be high upon it, and it is not easy to
guess the consequences; they may be of an extraordinary nature.
By all means get Mr. B[romle]y to Wimpole, it cannot be much,
if at all, out of his road home. I am very glad to hear he can
bear such a journey. He[a]rne's affair is at last ended. Lord
Arran wrote a letter to desire that upon his submission he
might be forgiven and have leave to go with his book. The
perverse fellow's stomach is come down ; he has made a submission. He says it is nothing more, or very little more, than
he offered to the late Vice-Chancellor at first, but by what I hear
it must be more than I could have compounded the business for.
I shall insult him sufficiently upon this submission; he is now
rectus in curia, and has leave to go on with "Neubrigensis."

The Attorney had a copy sent to him of Lady Bolingbroke's
will ; he expressed mighty concern for the Lord, and blamed the
Lady in pretty coarse terms for not leaving every farthing she
could to him. All that ever she had to leave in the world I
am certain must fall short of 3,000*l.*, and it is all that she has
given to her family out of all the fortune she brought. I am no
ways bribed to speak for the poor lady, for she paid not what her
husband owed me, and now I may give it for gone. By the
Attorney's great civilities to our bishops, I take him and Ruffian
to be broken.

Your public reasons for not coming into Parliament are, I
think, over. You may indeed have private ones, which would
not appear for the county where you are. You may be afraid it
would expose your retirement to too much company. I could
wish you were in Parliament if it were on terms you liked. Since
you decline it, I hope Mr. Bacon will be pitched on ; my hearty
respects to him and to Mr. Prior.

1718, October 31.—I long to hear whether your neighbours
go on to choose a new professor. If they stick at that it will look
as though they were afraid lest they had made some false step.

If the Court come in it will be upon a supposition that this
has been carried on by Townshend's and Walpole's party, and the
ministry may be likely to prosecute it more fiercely upon that
suspicion than if Tories alone were supposed to be concerned in
it. We hear from town that the Chancellor begins to relent a
little. How true this is I know not.

Our bumpkins in this country are very waggish and very
insolent. Some honest justices met to keep the Coronation
day at Wattleton, and towards the evening when their worships
were mellow they would have a bonfire. Some bumpkins upon
this got a huge turnip and stuck three candles, and went and
placed it at the top of a hill just over Chetwynd's house, who
has bought that which was lately Stonor's, near Wattleton.
When they had done they came and told their worships that

to honour King George's Coronation day a blazing star appeared over Mr. Chetwynd's house. Their worships were wise enough to take horse to go and see this wonder, and found, to their no little disappointment, their star to end in a turnip.

Pray enquire if you can, and let me hear, how the Bishop of Chester's brother-in-law, Mr. Mapletoft of Clare Hall, voted on this late occasion, whether for or against Bentley.

[1718,] November 7.—I am glad your neighbours have such a stock of mettle, it is thought they will have occasion for it. I have heard from Mr. Bromley since his return to Baginton. He is very sensible of your kind invitation, and much concerned he could not wait upon you. But he says the trust he has will give him many opportunities of making you amends. He seems to wish you could have been prevailed on to appear for the county. You forget to tell me who is pitched upon by the gentlemen. I hear nothing of Neddy, nor consequently of your father, which surprises me not a little. Nor do I hear of any coach ordered down from London, but I shall expect to hear somewhat of them to-morrow night. I must do so if your father and uncle are at the opening of the session, as I cannot but think they will till I see the contrary. I am afraid Mr. Bromley will not be able to go up.

1718, December 2.—I am glad you are all together again. I hope now you are met you will have some regard to your own private business, though none of you have had much to the public, whilst those of you who are in Parliament would not attend it, nor those of you who are out of it stand to come into it. I am hard put to it here to excuse my Lord Harley for letting a Whig [F. Whitchcote] come into the county of Cambridge. Why would not Bacon stand?

One Morris of Jesus, a young master, who has a college curacy in Gloucestershire, preached on Sunday in the afternoon a sermon which gave very just offence. It was all in commendation of Bangorian doctrine, and it was brought very oddly from his text, which was "Let no man despise thee." But he said the exorbitant claims of the clergy were the only reasons of the contempt they met with. Neddy, who was at church, came and brought me in great wrath the first account of it. The Vice-Chancellor demanded his sermon notes. He readily delivered them, and said he could justify what he had said in it. He will certainly suffer what the statutes enjoin, which happens to be very light in this case, only a suspension from preaching, which many will think a reward rather than a punishment. If they who have been rakes with him are to be believed, the fellow is a notorious drunkard. It is certain at his curacy he cohabits with a woman as a man should with his wife, without owning her as such. And yet amongst other things he said no ministration from an ill clergyman could be of any validity. He delivered his sermon with great impudence, and is himself of known impudence on all other occasions.

1718, December 18.—It may be for aught I know to the contrary one of the many peculiar privileges which belong to you great men to expect letters when you answer none. But then you should let us know as much. It would be presumption otherwise in your poor vassals to write to you, till by your answer they are authorised to trouble you again.

It is Christmas time, rosemary and other greens abound, and we are now I think, as my brother South told Ruffian upon a certain address, when he bid him look up to the greens in the church, in a flourishing condition. But is it one of your Christian virtues, now you are so near being out of your own troubles, to divert yourself with the thought that your friends are entering into them? I hope we are prepared not only for this bill and visitations, but for worse too, if it comes. Otherwise we have been Robin Morgan's disciples to little purpose, but I know no one more concerned in interest to stop these things than you are. If I am turned upon the common again, I shall make straight to Wimpole. And I grow old and unwieldly, and if I am once lodged there you will find it very difficult to make me remove and quit my quarters.

You take no notice of what I said about Ruffian, what the town thinks of the late gracious reception he has had at Court.

The small-pox has been very much in town, we have many gentlemen and others of the College who have not had them, but only two have fallen ill, and both, I bless God, are like to do well.

Postscript. Morris appeared yesterday. He refused to sign a retraction which was tendered to him; upon that the Vice-Chancellor suspended him from preaching within the district of the University. The Bishop of Oxford as Professor assisted at the censure. Does this look as though we were afraid of visitations?

[1718,] December 22.—I cry "peccavi,"; you were in the right certainly to complain of my being sparing of my letters, though the balance was on your side.

It is a little hard though (if I may say so) that I must send you from Oxford the reason of some bishops voting at London. I think by the accounts I have had, that L[incol]n's part has been, as he managed it, the most scandalous. I had yesterday, from undoubted authority, the following story. He has an uncle, one Gibson, who is a man mid-wife, rich, without children, and a dissenter. His uncle came to him last year, when it was thought the bill would have been brought in, and told him that if he did not vote, as he has now voted, he must expect nothing from him. I do not say this was the only reason of his voting as he has done, but it was a good motive to come in aid of the prospect of a better bishoprick. I believe he has outdone what his uncle expected at least, if not what he required. I cannot get one word from you of what is said or thought of Ruff's late reception at Court. But you must let me tell you a merry story that is stirring here. It is said that upon the news of it

John Barber came to him, and asked him seriously whether he left the Chevalier. John desired him to be plain with him, "for," said he, "if your Lordship has left the Chevalier it may be time for me to leave the Kingdom."

Honest Ned is very well, and so good that if, as the good women say, your Lordship had not had my first love, Neddy might have set you hard. I think he is out of danger of being spoiled by any thing, except by his own father or mother.

My duty to my honoured Lady, and most humble thanks for the favour of her letter. Forget me not to my young mistress. A Merry Christmas, and many a one to you all.

[1719,] February 25.—You are beaten, but you have the support of brave men, the conscience of having done your duty, and that you have lost no honour, though you have lost the day. I must own those of my own cloth are grown insupportable and I shall not be surprised, if I should live, to see their truest friends to leave them, and to give them up to the cruel mercies of their enemies.

Here has been a very odd sort of a marriage at Merton, which gives some diversion here. The Warden has two nieces, they are nicknamed by the Fellows, Chloe and Daphne. They were invited on Valentine's day to drink tea at a Fellow's chamber. There were in the chamber, Cowper (Spencer's son), and one Russell another Fellow, in priest's orders, a famous constitutioner. In a frolic, as they now say, the Rev. Mr. Russell would marry the nymph Chloe, and Cowper was to be the priest. Cowper, after he had gone a little way in the office, boggled, and said it was too serious to be trifled with, but the parson and the nymph too called to him to go on. Upon that he took heart and read out every word of the office, the parties each of them answered distinctly and leisurely to their parts. At noon he went to the Fellows in the hall to tell how he had been married. Upon enquiry into the matter, all the grave men gave him joy of his wife. It is now a great question here, whether the marriage be good, much the majority of us are for the affirmative. It is thought parson Cowper too will be called to some account for his share in the farce.

1718-19, February 28.—You are obliged to your own father for the story of the bow. When he did me the honour to give me notice of your bill's passing, he told me how gracefully you made it. I think you come off very cheap with his Majesty.

I heartily thank you for your just rebuke, I shall endeavour to make the proper use of it. Being out of politics, and having strained my eyes with reading, I see not how I can employ myself better than in changing my condition, and in trying what I can make of it, both to amuse myself and to mortify my neighbour. Poor man, his philosophy fails him as well as somewhat else, he flies still like gunpowder at any thing that looks like a remote reflection upon his puissance. I wish for his lady's sake, that so great a tenderness be not a shrewd sign of guilt.

Mr. He[a]rne goes on without interruption in publishing those useful pieces of monkish antiquity, by which he is to immortalize his own name and reform us all. He is still as proper an object as he ever was of your Lordship's great bounty, for he has as high a conceit of himself, and as great a contempt of all others, as little a share of common sense, and as much insolence, as he ever had.

Cardinal Wolsey's statue is come down, and a very fine one it is, but we think it is made to look the wrong way. It looks full upon Dr. Lane's lodgings. If the connoisseurs prove to be of that opinion, we can remedy it, by making it change place with Bishop Fell's.

Postscript. Last Tuesday was a great confusion in St. Mary's. They in the galleries, upon some scholars being driven up and making a noise, thought the gallery falling. They crowded down and bore down those who were coming up. The Doctors and Masters took the fright and all crowded towards the porch. All the benches were overturned, many shins and noses broken. Some poor men were borne down in the passage and trampled on by those who were crowding out; they were much bruised but will do well.

1719, April 9.—I have indeed accounts of what passes at Westminster, but that does not make what come from your Lordship either less kind in you or less welcome to me. The campaign is opened and Ruff has made a very insolent incursion into poor Rob's quarters, but in my poor opinion there is somewhat as mean in what he does as it is insolent. It will be strange if such childish extravagant proceedings do not injure his character. But this is but the prelude, the storm will not be at the height till the election comes, then it will roar, and you will see Ruff, as you truly observe, display himself to the full. I envy your Lordship the diversion—I suppose you intend to be there.

· I wish our invasion may not be somewhat akin to the 40,000 Spanish pilgrims in the time of the Popish plot. The account in the last Gazette seems a very blind one, no name either of ship or master from whom the intelligence comes. This story of a return seems only to be to save our own credit, that we may not be thought to have alarmed the nation without any ground. A fleet that was victualled only for twenty days could not be designed for us.

Lord Brooks has won in these two days that are past seven battles out of ten. I think there is some news of moment for you.

1719, May 12.—I am very sensible of the honour of your Lordship's kind invitation to Wimpole. It is the highest instance of mortification that I can practise if I do not accept of it. There are none for whom I have that concern, or to whom I pay the duty due from me, with that pleasure to myself, as to the Lord and Lady of that place. Nor was I ever in a place which, on account of itself, was more agreeable to me than that spot. There is but one objection, which is itself too a temptation, that the way of living there is not so suitable to such a poor hermit as I am, and it costs much physic and fasting, when I am at home again, to get clear of what I bring with me from Wimpole. These are strong motives to one to accept of your Lordship's generous invitation, but after all I cannot help perceiving that I grow old, and less fit every day either to travel myself or to trouble others. And though it would be impertinent in one, in the insipid life I lead, to pretend to much business, yet some I have too, such as it is, which will not allow me as yet to be positive whether it will be in my power or no to pay my duty to you.

I suppose we shall see the Auditor here in a day or two; a forerunner, a hamper of Cyprus, came hither last night. I want much to see him on Neddy's account. He sent Neddy word that he had lodgings ready for him at Lincoln's Inn against next winter. My lad is afraid lest this is an intimation that he designs at that time to remove him hence. You cannot easily imagine how much this has disturbed him. Should that really be the Auditor's design, it would be the most unaccountable one that ever was in a father, not to permit his son to stay where his behaviour is beyond even what the fondest friend he has could have wished for, and to interrupt that in his child which most other parents strive and pray for to no purpose in theirs. But I will not presume the worst, and if I should find it so will say what I can to divert him from it. But should what I say be ineffectual, I must call in your Lordship's and your father's aid to prevent what will be truly so much to my boy's prejudice, as well as against his inclination.

Mr. Wanley's countenance shall have due honour paid to it when it comes, Neddy desires you would send one for him at the same time. I should be obliged to your Lordship too for a print of Shakespear. I heartily congratulate you upon the rarity you have discovered.

One Triplack, who says he was Lord Morpeth's tutor, came hither for a degree to qualify himself to hold a second living which he is to have from Lechmere. I am no stranger to his true character from other information than what may be discovered from his conversation. But at Decker's desire John Drummond recommended him, and we did him so much service, chiefly by the Bishop of Chester, that in a full house all the Heads and Doctors were for him, but in above 180 he lost it by 12. The masters said they would not enable foreigners to hold two livings, when they cannot get one; even the Constitution club was against him. He says he will try again. I know not but we might carry it, if it were worth while. He saw your Lordship's picture in my parlour, and to show his acquaintance with you said he would write to Lord Morpeth to get your Lordship's letter to recommend him more effectually to me, but I would not let him be so impertinent.

1719, May 14.—Mr. Auditor disappointed us last night, but we hope to see him this evening or to-morrow.

Mr. Garnier has been with me and informed me of your Lordship's generosity to him and kind reception of him. He told me one passage with a smile, and it made me smile too, as an instance of his own dexterity. He said when he was called on for a toast, he named the Bishop of Rochester, I suppose, taking your Lordship for a topping Tory, he thought that would be most acceptable to you.

1719, May 19.—Mr. Auditor came to me about nine on Friday night; he eat a bit, but say what I could, he would go to the inn at eleven at night. He was disturbed in the night, and had but indifferent rest. I cannot say I was sorry for it. He dined on Saturday with the Bishop of Chester; he went on that afternoon to Chipping Norton, and took Neddy with him. Robin was left with me, and has taken up his quarters in your bed. I have had much conversation, both to my diversion and instruction, with my young schoolfellow. I can assure you he does not degenerate; he has very good seeds in him of probity and sense too, and I doubt not but he will be a credit and comfort to you all. Robin rode out yesterday with Mr. Thomas to meet his brother on his return. He rode as far as Heythrop, and came home, you may believe, heartily tired. Neddy came back much easier than he went, his father had told him what had passed betwixt him and me. On Saturday morning I had much talk with the Auditor about Neddy. I found there had been a design, though not fully resolved on, of removing Neddy next winter, but upon what I said to him, he made me a solemn promise that he would never remove him but with my full and free consent. And he told this to Neddy at Chipping Norton, and repeated the promise to him. I suggested one thing to the Auditor, which I thought would be a good compromise, that if he thought it would be any advantage to his son with regard to his study of the law to converse with those learned in it, as soon as possible, he might give him his chambers in Lincoln's Inn, and let him spend two or three months there in the winter, and the rest of the year here. The Auditor seemed very fond of this, and I suppose the business will end in it. He told Neddy he should have his chambers when he would, and spend as much time there, and as much here, as he himself had a mind to. So the affair I hope is settled to all our contents.

1719, May 28.—The person who behaved so basely in the election at Wadham has paid dear for it. He had been induced to it by great promises, some think of the living of Marsh, vacant by the late Warden's death. He went the next day to the new Warden, to claim what had been promised. He was told he should be remembered when there was a proper occasion, but that he was young yet and might stay. News came too that Marsh was disposed of. This affected him so, to find he had lost his credit and was cheated into the bargain, that he locked himself [in] and never has been out since. He began to cry that he had injured an honest man who had been his friend to whom he never could make any amends, that he himself too was cheated. These thoughts became every hour more tormenting to him, and he is now with two keepers, raging and tied down in his bed. The new Warden and his party keep any one from coming to him, lest secrets should be discovered in his frenzy.

The College has lost probably as much by this election as it is already possessed of. The Primate of Ireland [Lindsay] gave them notice of a very considerable sum, which he would immediately settle on them if Gudlet [Gyllett?] was chosen, which he now designs to dispose of otherwise. Your father's schoolfellow, Mr. Doyly, sent them word that he had no relations, and was worth 3,000*l.*, which he designed to leave wholly to them upon the same condition, and it is taken for granted he will now think of some other way of bestowing it.

[1719,] June 7.—The person who preached on the 29th May is one Wharton (*sic*), a master of arts of Magdalen, and one who was chosen poetry professor about a year ago. It would be well if his sermon might be looked on as a poetic performance too. I did not hear it, but by the account I had of it it was a very indiscreet and improper one. My boy Neddy shaked his head when he gave me an account of it and said he was a very foolish fellow, but I am told it was guarded so that it is thought no hold can be taken of it by the law, but I believe no one that heard it did not think it looked rather forward than backward. But however it is like to make some further noise here.

One Medlicot (Meadowcourt), a constitutioner of Merton, has been with the Vice Chancellor to complain of it, and said if he could not have justice here, he would apply elsewhere. The Vice-Chancellor has ordered him to bring what he complains of in writing.

Duke Hamilton is here, under a pretence of paying his debts and taking his leave, but I am told he designs to leave part of his debts to be paid at another season. But he has behaved himself very rudely to the Dean since he has been here ; he has never been near him, nor cannot be persuaded by anyone to it. The reason he gives is still worse; he says when he came to the "Angel," where he has lived since he has been here, he sent to give the Dean notice that he was in town, and expected the Dean should have visited him first. This reason, bad as it is, is entirely false as to the fact, for he never sent any message to the Dean. Another reason he gives is that the Dean did not invite him to dinner as often as he did other noblemen. This, though not very proper to be urged, was true, but because he never was to be found in the College. The true reason I believe is, because his commons were stopped last Christmas for one day only, upon a general order to stop all who were in arrears for half a year. But after six weeks' notice had been given of the order a message was sent particularly to his governor five days before to give him notice that if one quarter's commons were not paid, his name with others must be stopped on the Friday following, for that it would be impossible for the Treasurer to make an exception of him only. And before the day came, the Treasurer himself spoke twice to the governor, who promised each time that it should be paid, but did not pay it, till after the commons were sent up on Friday. No notice was taken of this at first, as there was surely no reason there should, but a fortnight after no less men than the Vice-Chancellor, Delaune and the Warden of New College supped with his Grace, and stayed somewhat later than men of their stations use to do with young gentlemen. When they were warm Delaune jested on his Grace for being put out of commons. This has fired him so that he resolved to part with the Dean in this manner, and to complete the business the Vice-Chancellor to-day gave him a doctor's degree, when he was sure the Dean, who should have been the principal person attending on such occasion, could not upon the Duke's behaviour to him be there, and I suppose the degree was designed more as an indignity to the Dean than as a compliment to the Duke. But there was still a greater reason for this Duke's resentment against our governor. The poor Dean is not disaffected enough for him, and politics were at the bottom of all this worthy behaviour, and made use by those who thought it worth their while to put him upon playing so foolish a part. Our young fellows have given him an unlucky nickname, on account of his living at an inn, and not at a College, when he was dubbed Doctor. They have called him Dr. Angelicus, a name given to one famous in his generation, Thomas Aquinas.

1719, June 9.—Neddy writes to you this post, and sends you the charge given in against Mr. Wharton's sermon. The sermon as I am told was in such general words, and so guarded, that though no doubt all contained in the charge was intended, yet I believe the accusers will not be able to bring direct proofs of it. But though the preacher should escape, yet possibly the university may suffer for the sermon, and the judges may be thought not to censure, more for want of inclination to it in themselves than for want of matter for it in the sermon.

1719, June 11.—Had a caution been a security for payment, we might be justly blamed for calling on any one when we had their caution, but our case was as follows. Gentlemen would run beyond their caution, not only one but several quarters, and our arrears amounted to some hundred pounds, which was all out of the College stock, and which if we did not get in, the King our Visitor might oblige us to make it good out of [our] own pockets. We never called for payment till the arrear was so great that the caution would no longer answer it. After half a year due for commons and chambers and buttery, enough of a caution would not be left to answer another quarter on any gentleman commoner's caution. Therefore we were obliged to order that whoever at the end of one quarter did not clear for the preceding quarter should have his name stopped. This allowed every one half a year to pay in, and withal allowed them to be always one quarter in arrear.

This we thought was indulgence enough, we could not allow more with safety to ourselves, and the friends of gentlemen think this commonly too much. When we come to ask them for debts, they always say we should have made them pay the money when it was due, and not let them squander it on other things. This order was made in the middle of November and put up in the hall. At Christmas we took the names on a Monday of those who had not paid Michaelmas quarter. The Duke's name was there. To prevent any thing that might look reflecting on him, the Treasurer's man was sent to let him know that on Friday next we should be obliged to stop the names of all who had not paid Michaelmas quarter; that it would be impossible for us to make an exception for the Duke out of the general order; that if we should do so, no other nobleman or gentleman would think themselves obliged by it. The governor owned this to be reasonable and said he would pay it. The Treasurer himself spoke twice to the governor betwixt Monday and Friday. He still promised to pay it, but did not until after the commons was gone up on Friday. Whether this was done with a design to have a pretence for a quarrel I know not, but I believe your Lordship will agree that had you been here and been called upon for that from which we at the same time excused any other, you would not have thought yourself bound to obey the House. But this was no new thing, men of as great quality as the Duke of Hamilton have had [their] names stopped and thought it no reflection. But this is to show that what we did was reasonable though we should have had the Duke's caution in our hand. Though in truth he never laid down any caution, and we were so over civil as not to press for it. But though this might have made what was done more reasonable, yet we had no regard to that in our order. But he is gone, and there is an end I believe to this foolish affair. And I have troubled your Lordship with this long account only that you may be apprized of the strict truth if you should chance to hear any talk of it. It will not be for his interest to talk. Should he oblige us to justify ourselves, we must say many things he would wish should be unknown.

1719, June 12.—The bells rang for prayers as I was writing to your Lordship yesterday. I forgot I believe to observe to you that the compliment we paid to the Duke in sending or speaking thrice to his governor, betwixt Monday and Friday, was more than we paid to any other gentleman, who had no other notice than what was put up as usual in the hall. But as I told your Lordship formerly, part of his anger against the Bishop of Bristol was because his Grace thought the Bishop not to be altogether in politics as his Grace would have him. At the time that he behaved so to the Bishop of Bristol, he took care to distinguish the Bishop of Chester by his respects, and was fully of his compliments to him. To make, I suppose, his neglect of the Bishop of Bristol a greater affront to him, another reason of his displeasure to the Bishop of Bristol was the good advice which the Bishop, according to the duty of his place, had from time to time given him, and which the Duke's behaviour called for very often and made but too necessary to him. It seems he lays it down for a settled rule of his conduct that he will never be controlled or contradicted by any one. He is like to be a wise and happy man, and he had another maxim it seems when he first came hither, and which I assure you he strictly observed, that he would in every thing do contrary to what the Duke of Queensberry had done. You may guess by that what his life was here.

Your Lordship observes truly that persons of the highest quality, especially those who have *rictum et cubile* in his college, always use to visit the Dean first, though he were not a bishop. But had the Duke paid a visit to the Dean, I believe it would have been by no means proper for the Dean to have returned it to him at the "Angel" inn, whilst his Grace had his name in the buttery book. But enough of this gentleman; all this is written only for your Lordship's information. I hope we shall hear no more of him, nor have any occasion to let him hear of us.

Pray what is the impression of the seal with which your last was sealed. It seems to be some very valuable "antick." To me it seems to be Cupid showing his finger to Venus after it had been stung with a bee. Won't you give Neddy and me Mr. Prior's print [as] well as the others?

My duty to my ever honoured lady. I hope Mrs. Margaret continues well. It is observed that amongst the streets of new buildings one should have been called Tower Street.

1719, June 16.—I thank you for the good news of Lord Danby. I must have a concern for him, for the sake of his excellent mother, for whose memory I shall always have the utmost respect.

Nothing is yet done about the sermon, nor will be done here. The complainant said he would apply elsewhere, but I do not hear that he has yet done it, nor would he perhaps be much regarded if he should.

We are going on again with our library, as far as 500*l*. will carry it; but that is the utmost we can yet reckon on, both in cash and promise too.

[1719,] June 28.—I suppose this may find your Lordship still in town, having heard nothing of your quitting it. The poor Rector of Lincoln went last week to see the Bishop of Durham [Crewe], and has been seized there with the gout in his head. We expect hourly to hear he is dead. He will be a great loss to that society, and I am afraid we must stay till a new head is chosen before we can get the *Typicon*.

Meadowcourt has laid his complaint against Wharton's sermon before Craggs, the same which he laid here before the Vice-Chancellor. On Friday an express brought a letter to the Vice-Chancellor from De la Fay, by order of the Regents, to require him to proceed against Wharton according to the statutes of the university, to save them the trouble of taking other measures. Yesterday the Vice-Chancellor summoned six Doctors who were present at the sermon to assist him, and sent to Meadowcourt to appear and make good his accusation. He sent them word he had no more to offer than he had already given in his paper, and bid them pursue the orders they had from the Regents. The Vice-Chancellor summoned Wharton and required his sermon. He said he had it not, nor knew not where it was, and offered voluntarily words made of it. They then drew the general charge of Meadowcourt into seven propositions and gave him till nine o'clock to-morrow morning to answer them. I suppose he will give in as general a denial of them. I believe the Vice-Chancellor has done all that he can, and perhaps more than he was strictly obliged to, but I know not whether it will satisfy above.

One Jans, a clergyman, who had a good living in Oxfordshire, but lived for many years with the late Warden of Wadham in his lodgings, was bound for the late Warden for 300*l.*, and on Monday last arrested for it. He pretended to step only into his bed-chamber to fetch somewhat, and immediately shot himself. He is said too to have been one of the instruments in persuading the fellow that went distracted lately to play the villainous part he did in the late election.

Since I have written, we have had the sad news of the Rector of Lincoln's death.

[1719,] June 30.—Wharton yesterday gave in his answer signed with his own hand. In the preface to it he solemnly disclaims any design of reflecting on the Government, and then gives a round to every particular extracted out of the general charge. How far this will satisfy I know not. I believe they can proceed no further against him. If any thing more is designed, we, not he, I suppose, shall suffer.

The Rector of Lincoln is buried to-night in All Hallows Church, which was raised so much by him. We hope Dr. Lupton will be recommended by the Bishop of Durham to succeed him. When I see who is the new Rector I will apply again for the *Typicon*.

Your old servant Juggins died on Sunday, after being ill three days of a fever. I wish I may be able to send you as good brawn as I used to do, now he is gone.

A brother bookworm of yours, Mr. Bridges, is now in town, and drank your health with me last night.

Postscript. I pray send me two or three of the plans of your new [Cavendish] Square. George Clarke and others beg them of you.

1719, July 2.—We hope Dr. Lupton will be Rector of Lincoln. On Tuesday came on an election for three Fellows at Exeter. The Whigs presumed they should have had a majority, because one of the Tories, who had never had the small pox, was absent; but he lay two miles out of town, and appeared at the election. The votes were equal. Their statutes direct in such a case to call in the Vice-Chancellor. He was sent to and came immediately, and turned the election on the Tory side.

The same day, one Amherst of St. John's, who wrote the "Oxford Toasts," and some more such scandalous pieces, stood to be admitted actual Fellow, but he was rejected by a great majority. They have power of rejecting probationers, without assigning any reason. It is said the fellow glories in it and hopes to find his account in being rejected.

But they were even with them the same day at Wadham, where the new Warden and his party, out of two probationers, rejected one against whom there was not the least exception for either learning or manners. When the poor fellow desired to know of the Warden for what reason he was rejected, the Warden only told him he was too warm. They are now in their visitation at All Souls, but I suppose we shall not know what passes till the Archbishop determines upon the report made to him by the Dean of the Arches. There are mutual accusations of each other by the Warden and Fellows, and interrogatories put to both of them by the Visitor, but we are yet in the dark as to any particulars.

[1719,] July 8.—I am sorry I must tell you that there will be no thoughts of Dr. Lupton at Lincoln. Most of the junior Fellows were pupils to one Mr. Morley, who has been preferred some years in Lincolnshire. They have resolved upon him and the rest are come into them, and they yesterday sent two Fellows with a letter to the Bishop of Durham, to let him know they had pitched upon Mr. Morley, and that they hoped he would be agreeable to his Lordship, not if he should be agreeable. They had done better if they had spared their compliment. It is thought the old Bishop will take it very ill. There are considerable sums designed by him for the College, but not yet settled, which perhaps may now be otherwise disposed of. The old Bishop is much troubled at the late Rector's death, speaks not of him without crying, and sees no company. It is feared these accidents may hasten his death, for his stomach, which has hitherto been good, fails him and is almost quite gone. It is thought the young part of the electors dread Lupton too, as a disciplinarian.

The Dean of the Arches left All Souls on Monday in the afternoon. In the morning he admonished Littleton, Newsom, and Fiddes to go into orders within six months under pain of contempt. He intimated that the Archbishop would for the future rather restrain than increase the number of physicians. This was all he did, nor is it yet known whether the Archbishop will do any more upon his report.

1719, July 11.—I can now tell you the reception the Fellows of Lincoln had from the Bishop of Durham. He asked them, if they were determined to choose Dr. Morley, why they came to him. He said Dr. Morley was a stranger to him, that he was too old to make new friendships, that the late Rector was his friend, that Dr. Lupton was so too, that if his advice was asked he must recommend Dr. Lupton to them, that he did not recommend Dr. Lupton to them for his own sake, that Dr.

Lupton would rather lose by it, but for their own sakes that they might be gainers by choosing him. This last was home indeed, but I cannot yet tell what effect it is like to have; I know what it ought to have.

1719, July 19.—What I feared has happened. The Fellows of Lincoln yesterday chose Dr. Morley. We shall hear I suppose in a few days how the Bishop resents it. Dr. Lupton is with him.

I am a perfect stranger to this new Rector and care not to make any acquaintance with him. I hope Mr. Wanley has some acquaintance here by whom he can borrow the *Typicon* of him. If he has not, I will endeavour to borrow it by some other hand than my own.

Your friend Mr. Bromley was so well as to ride last week by Oxford, not through it, in his way to Lord Stawell's. He rode in one day from his own house to Woodstock. He desired his journey might be a secret to all here, but he was so kind as to give me an opportunity of meeting him at Woodstock; and I shall, God willing, meet him to-morrow night at Abingdon as he returns.

[1719,] July 28.—By a second order I met Mr. Bromley at Woodstock, not at Abingdon. I passed the evening with him on Monday. I cannot say he is quite well, but I bless God much better. For some days he feels nothing of the old pain in his side; when it returns it is much less than it used to be. I hope it will be quite gone before the summer is spent. We remembered your Lordship, he expressed a great sense of the kindness of your invitation of him to Wimpole when he was in Cambridgeshire. He was very sorry he could not then accept it, but believes he shall have an opportunity of waiting on you. He pressed me to go to Warwickshire, but I told him that having excused myself from waiting on your Lordship, upon your very kind invitation, that was a sufficient answer to all other invitations, even to his.

I hear the Bishop of Durham is disobliged to the highest degree with the election at Lincoln. I am not surprised at it.

Your news of the Bishop of London's marriage was surprising. Pray who is the lady like to be happy in his embraces?

I am afraid your Lordship has forgotten an humble request I made to you, of sending me two or three of the plans of your new square. G. Clarke presses me for one of them, and he must have that which I had from Neddy, if I can get no other.

I was in hopes that your last would have fixed the time in which you are to change your quarters. Neddy is very well, but a little impatient to receive his summons. He is pressed and eager enough to go to Eywood, and therefore looks upon every day you stay in town as a double delay to him of seeing Wimpole and Eywood too.

1719, July 30.—I send this by the gentleman who next to your Lordship is the person that is dearest to me. It is with unspeakable satisfaction that I can tell your Lordship that he merits by his virtue the same share in your esteem which he has by his blood in your affection, and that as he is the nearest male relation you have, he is the fittest too, that I know, to be made your friend.

The Bishop of Durham has let Lincoln College know that they must expect no more from him, and that they are much mistaken if they think what he has already settled is irrevocable, and that he had designed them a benefaction of 30,000l., but must now think of placing it elsewhere.

1719, August 2.—The Bishop of London's marriage with Mrs. Cornwallis is confirmed as certain from undoubted hands. Cannot the old man live without a nurse, surely he can want nothing else at his age? But I never heard of his having addressed himself to Mrs. Dolben, nor can I guess how he could have any acquaintance with her or opportunity of offering himself to her. If you have any other grounds for that than a flying report pray let me know them. I have seen Ruff's answer in Chancery and immediately fixed, as every one else does, upon that diabolical part in it to which your Lordship alludes. Whatever it be that he insinuates by that, it must be somewhat that he had in the utmost confidence from Bob, whilst they lived in strict friendship. The villain would now make use of it to ruin Bob. But I believe he will find himself disappointed. Bob writes us word that he has no apprehension of any thing from that clause, but the villain has showed his good will, and I am much obliged to him, for he takes effectual pains to make good all that ever I have said of him, for which I have sometimes been hardly thought of.

The new Rector of Lincoln has been to wait on the Bishop of Durham, but was received so very roughly by him as to give too much reason to fear that that great benefaction will be lost to the College.

1719, August 28.—Your Ruffs and Reeves are delicious food indeed, too good for such poor mortals as we are. But it is very good in your Lordship to give one a taste of what you enjoy, and shows me too what I have lost by not being at Wimpole. I am sorry to hear your new library was so calculated so much short of your stock of books as not to be able to hold half of them. It is a sign you did not know your own riches; one may apply to your *Bibliothèque* what was said of Lucullus's wardrobe, " *Exil domus est, ubi non et multa supersunt et dominum fallunt et prosunt furibus.*"

You will be forced to have recourse at last to what I once suggested of turning your greenhouse into a library.

I am very heartily concerned for poor Dr. Heathcot's death and more for the sad manner of it. I am concerned on my Lady's account as well as on the doctor's. I wish her Ladyship may meet with one she can trust as much and as safely.

I hope to see your father here in a little time, as he passes by. I have this day written to Mr. Bromley, to give him a meeting at the Proto's. God willing, Monday shall be celebrated here in the best manner I can. Tockay shall be poured out to my Lady's and your Lordship's health, out of half a dozen pints, the only stock I was ever master of.

1719, September 21.—I most heartily thank your Lordship for your kind visit, chiefly for your stay after my Lord O[xford] was gone.
Your bounty to Mr. Hearne was, as usual, very large, if we may judge of it by its effects. He went on Friday about one to Antiquity Hall and stayed there, with Rance his printer only, till one next morning. He lost no time whilst he was there, but plied the black pot fairly, and would let no health be drunk during the whole time, but Lord and Lady Harley, junction not division, he drinking it to Rance, and Rance returning it to him. I suppose your Lordship may be now in a fair way for a dedication.

[1719,] September 23.—The Bishop of Chester it seems was got to Eywood on Thursday last. I suppose he is now at Brampton. I thank God I can tell you that Mr. Thomas is quite well again. I hear the keeper of the ducks [Lord Dartmouth] met your Lordship about Thame ; he has brought two sons to Magdalen. I wonder who directed him thither; he could not have pitched upon a more unlucky place for breeding up his sons in his own political sentiments. If the youngsters suck in the air of that seminary they will never be hopeful.
Postscript. The knave He[a]rne has another insinuation, as he thinks, against us, *p.* 794 in his "Spicilegium," for letting a piece of ground that had been grazed about two hundred years be ploughed up. I wonder what put him upon picking quarrels with us, who have been friends to him, but not of the highest rank indeed. We have not done enough for him to merit our being abused by him.

1719, September 30.—I came home last night to attend my poor friend [Smalridge]'s funeral. He found the pain he had so long complained of in his breast to increase about ten at night on Saturday. The doctor was called, and blooded him plentifully. He rested tolerably that night, he awaked at six, and heard the clock strike, and asked the maid who watched by him what o'clock it was. She answered six. On which he said, then I thank God I have had a good night's rest. He turned about and without fetching a groan he died immediately. By the manner of his death, his distemper must have been a polypus in the heart.
My brethren who were on the spot immediately sent to the Bishop of Oxford to desire he would use his interest to be Dean, but he positively declined it. I believe he is not fond of it, but I believe too he thinks he could not have it if he desired it. Then they desired Dr. Egerton, who readily complied with them, and

went this day to town to push his interest. He is surely not *par negotio*, but I believe he would be better for us than any other that would be likely to be sent.

I am afraid the poor man that is gone has left his family but in indifferent circumstances.

[1719,] October 2.—I have already had a very kind, sensible letter from Neddy to condole with me upon our loss. I have nothing to say about it more than what your Lordship had in my last. We hear nothing yet of a successor, nor do I believe we shall in some weeks. I am not altogether in so much pain for the poor deceased family as I was when last [I wrote?]. I believe when goods are sold and every thing scraped together there may be a subsistence, though still scanty enough.

1719, October 5.—I am very much obliged to you for your great concern for us upon our present circumstances. I am not a little pleased to find that your thoughts exactly agree with my own. I had the same fears your Lordship has, and in answer to Neddy I wrote largely about them. I made it plain to him that he could suffer no further by this loss than in the advantage he had from the Bishop's own conversation. That he would still have the same tutors and the same friends to converse with, that no Dean that came could any ways affect him or his studies. That as he was now a bachelor, he would be under no obligations to have any correspondence with one whom he might not perhaps like. That any thoughts of leaving us would carry with them an unkind reflection on his other friends, as though there were none left who were either able or willing to serve him.

I have told your Lordship in my former letters all I know as yet about a successor. We may perhaps have one who may want somewhat of that little good which was in Ruff, but we can never have any who has so much ill in him. To your father's honour be it spoken, no ministry that hates, nor any that loved us—if such a thing could now be—can send us either so bad or so good a Dean as he did.

We hear the children of Edom rejoice, and cry " Down with it, down with it, even to the ground." But perhaps they may be disappointed in some measure. We begin to recover of her (*sic*) fright. I believe none of our gentlemen will have any thoughts of leaving us. Whoever comes will not make many converts amongst the present set, and it may require more time than may come to his share to raise up a new generation. I fear more for the Chapter than the students. Some of our brethren are old and drooping. I am likely to be here in a comfortable post.

[1719,] October 9.—I hope this will meet you returned from your ramble. The Bishop of Chester came home on Wednesday; they have crammed him in Herefordshire. He is more plump and jolly than ever I knew him in my life.

The circumstances of the house of mourning in my neighbourhood are, as I suspected, indifferent enough. They will be obliged to make money of all they can. The poor man had not many books of value; those which are most likely to bring a little money are in the enclosed note, which they will part with if they can privately, some to one, some to another, as friends may happen to want them, at easy reasonable rates to be set on them by some one who knows books. I believe your Lordship has all of them. There is an edition of the Councils, which if you have not already will be worthy of your library. It is the Louvre edition, perfectly fair, and nobly bound. The edition too of Cyprian by Fell, which is now extremely scarce, is in large paper, and entirely fair and clean.

We yet know not our fate, but as far as our information yet goes, we have most reason to expect Bolter will be our governor.

[*List of about sixty works on various subjects enclosed.*]

1719, October 13.—I have secured the Councils and Cyprian for you, if you like the prices when they are set, which I suppose will be reasonable. I did not think you could have occasion for any of the other books. I believe the widow has no mind to part with Devigne's prints, though if she would take my advice she should; but they being a present from a Royal hand she seems fond of keeping them. The good man indeed could not have laid up large fortunes for his children, but things might have been better than they are, if the wife had had a little more management.

Postscript. The Bishop of Durham has settled what he had further designed for Lincoln College upon the University, with a reserve to himself to appoint by deed or will the uses of it.

1719, October 28.—We now know our fate, Bolter has both the deanery and bishopric, and we expect him here in the beginning of the next week. How he will behave we cannot yet guess, but I believe by some accounts I have that he will be more a party man than is commonly thought.

The Prince has given the widow and family of our late governor a pension of 200*l.* per annum. Dick Hill was the chief instrument in procuring it.

The late Dean had many volumes of pamphlets, in which pamphlets of very different kinds often happened to be bound up together, which he had bought by chance together many years ago. Perhaps there may be amongst them some old pamphlets hard to be met with which your Lordship may desire to have. A catalogue is taken, but it is too big to send by the post; I will send it to you by Mr. Thomas when he goes up.

1719, November 2.—The "Louvre Councils"* are valued at 45*l.*, the Cyprian at 2*l.* 10*s.*, I think neither unreasonable. If you like the prices the books may be left with me and sent to you at leisure, as you shall order. You may pay in the money to Dr. Freind when you go to town.

The late Dean had two pictures which were thought good ones, one was brought from Italy by Mr. Nelson and left in his will to the Dean, the other was done by some "Flanderkin." You may have the pre-emption, if you please, and they shall be left at Dr. Freind's for you to see.

---

* Described in the List above referred to as "Conciliorum omn. General. et Provincial. Collectio Regia. 37 Vol. Paris, 1644. Bound in red Turkey leather. Gilt on the back and sides and leaves, and lettered on the back."

Mr. Clarke desired me to enquire whether you had received the letter he sent to you, with those verses of Mr. Prior not printed in his book. You will be pleased to take notice, if you have received it, either to him or me. I have tried Mr. Clarke about the letter, but I find he cares not to give any copy of it. I cannot much blame him. I believe you would do so if you were in his case, but he says he will take care when he dies that the original shall be preserved.

Yesterday [Queen's] College was consecrated by the Metropolitan of York, their Visitor.

Postscript. I suppose you hear a new war is commenced betwixt Ruff. and the Chapel vestry about the nomination to that Chapel.

1719, November 6.—The election at All Souls was ended last night at nine o'clock, the very last moment of time they had left to choose in. Three are chosen, and a devolution made to the Archbishop for the fourth vacancy. Brotherton of Balliol was chosen upon the first scrutiny on Tuesday morning, then the Fellows insisted to have Stephens—son of the honest gentleman in Parliament—Anderson and Jenkinson of our House, brother to Sir Robert Jenkinson. The Warden offered to agree to the two first, but said he could not in conscience—and he had too much reason for it—agree to Jenkinson, because he had appeared so very ill upon the examination. The Warden [would?] agree to one Thomas—who was of our House—that had appeared the best of all the candidates, instead of Jenkinson, but the majority of the Fellows insisted for Jenkinson. The Warden then offered to choose Stephens and Anderson, without coming to a scrutiny for the last vacancy, but the party would have all three or none. At nine last night, which was the last moment they had left for choice, two of the Fellows came over to the Warden, Tindall and Newsom, and made a majority for the choice of Stephens and Anderson. The fourth vacancy is devolved to the Archbishop, but the Fellows design to insist upon the choice of Jenkinson as valid, in order to deprive the Warden of his negative, but I believe they can make nothing of that point.

Our new governor came to us yesterday, and was installed this morning. He desired to have a private installation, and gives us an 100*l.* to our buildings, instead of the treat which the Deans are used to give in the hall upon such occasions. Nothing extraordinary or remarkable has happened yet. All, hitherto is fair and easy and, for any thing that appears yet, may continue so. At least it will be so for some time, for he leaves us on Monday and designs not to be with us again till the end of the spring.

Your old tutor is the veriest poltroon that surely ever was in such a place. It is impossible to express the mean, servile court which he makes to the new comer, who has not only sense enough to see it, but, if we are not all mistaken, to laugh at him too heartily for it.

1719, November 11.—Our new governor was recommended by the present ecclesiastical junto, whose recommendations only are regarded as to preferment, viz. Norwich, Sarum, Gloucester, Lincoln. We are told he received orders to wait on those four bishops and thank them, and that he was expressly forbidden to take any notice of the Archbishop of Canterbury. Accordingly he never waited on the Archbishop till the day before he came hither, when he could not avoid it, in order to know the time of his consecration. It is said too the Archbishop by way of rebuke told him that he was surprised to see him, for that the public news had given him reason to think that he had gone to Oxford. His Grace is said to be more affected with this slight, in relation to the preferment of his own college and the manner of putting it on him—such was the grossest that could be—than any other affront he has had. But his resentments I believe are valued much as they deserve to be.

I must not detain you from Calphurnia's conversation ; that will be full employment for you whilst she stays.

[1719 ?] November 11.—I believe all people agree in making the same reflections upon the late disgrace of some chaplains. I believe one of them expected another sort of return to this deal. As to myself I can only say *solamen miseriis socios &c.* though I think we were used with more tenderness and had not our disgrace notified with so much solemnity to the world. We expected upon this and have found accordingly another royal prorogation of the Convocation to the 14th of February. The Archbishop has given our Governor notice of it, declaring himself to have no hand in it.

[1719,] November 13.—Lord and Lady Foley called here on Wednesday night in their way to London. His Lordship designs his premier for us next Whitsuntide, and has desired me to have him entered immediately. I have recommended Mr. Thomas for a tutor to him. If he talks of it to you, when you see him in town, take care to second me.

Postscript. You will rejoice with me for Ruff's defeat yesterday in Chancery upon moving for a dissolution of the injunction.

1719, November 16.—I most heartily thank you for the enclosed in your last. Mr. Prior has at last met with a subject worthy of him, and the best pen has paid due homage to the greatest example not only of her quality, but of her sex too.

The books [the Louvre Councils, &c.] are here for you. Would you have them sent to your house in town? You may pay in the money to Dr. Freind at your convenience.

The picture brought from Italy by Mr. Nelson is a Madonna, the other is a half length of some Walloon general or admiral. No price is yet set on the pictures, nor do they know how to value them. If you like them I suppose you will have them at a reasonable rate. They will be left at Dr. Freind's for you to see them.

1719, November 28.—The little captain of Stoke took a bed with me on Saturday night, and went away again by six on Sunday morning in order to be at the opening of the session. I believe you think we remembered. He could not tell me when our friends in those parts design to change their quarters.

We have heard of the address you mention ; it is mean indeed. I should be glad to hear how it is relished by their own corporation. I should think that the promoters of it must lose many of their own friends by it. How was it carried ? Was it a surprise ? Was it proposed without giving notice of it before ? I would gladly know too whether ·it proceeded from themselves, or whether they were put upon it by their Chancellor. The last, though no sufficient excuse, would be the best that could be made for them.

1719, November 30.—Poor John Hudson died on Friday morning about six. Mr. Hall of Queen's had declared he would accept the place if chosen, but declared at the same time that he would never ask for it. But upon Dr. Hudson's death he was prevailed on to canvass publicly for it, but he was too late. The generality were set for Bowles the under librarian, an industrious young fellow, but too young for that place, for he had but this term two terms given him to enable him to take his master's degree. I was and all my brethren but the Sub-dean, and most of the House, on the losing side, as usual, being by virtue of our oath for merit. The Sub-dean left us at Delaune's instance, and would not call the House together to desire them to agree on their votes, which they were ready to have done if he would have proposed it to them. There could be no pretence of comparison betwixt the competitors, but the only objection pretended to Hall was that he had kept close in his chambers for some years, and would not attend the duty of the place.

I hear Ruff. has lately written a letter to the Bishop of St. David's in which he has been pleased to be very free with your father.

1719, December 24.—Our friend [Lord Oxford] is not at all to be blamed for his present stay. He could have done nothing in the House of Lords had he been there. His stay was concerted too with all his friends, even with Mr. Bromley, who had not intended to have been up till after Christmas, if the unexpected stop that was given to the Peerage Bill in the House of Commons had not given his friends an opportunity to press him to come.

The person in custody is not much to be blamed neither upon that account ; he thought and his brother too, as well they might, that no stop could have been given to the Bill. They did not think others would have been so mad as to have pushed it so, if they had not been sure of carrying it. When he [Lord Oxford] heard of the check given to it he would have come up if he had had time; but I own to you that it will be impossible to convince the generality that there was not some other end in it. And Mr. Bromley sent me word that no excuse would be admitted for him, but the taking of him into custody was the jest of the

House. I did not like that. But you may depend upon it that our friend has not yet done with politics, I take him to be deeper in than ever, from inclination as well as engagement. He might indeed have made use of this juncture had he been on the spot, and others would have been ruled by him. But I take the true reason of his stay to be because those who should will not be directed by him, or put themselves under him again. His spirit is too great to be concerned on any other terms. He lived last winter by himself, and his brother could not bring them to act under any regular conduct. Mr. Bromley, who was the only man who could have had influence on them in that case (though I question whether he could have had enough), was not able then to be in town. This I take to be the chief reason of our friend's rustication, he stays till necessity brings people to that which reason cannot. But though he could not have stopped a late bill had he been in town, yet he might have made advantage of the defeat. He might at least have kept the Tories from hearkening to the offers that are made them. As it is, I believe very few will bite. But Harcourt is very busy and I believe has assurance of being employed if he could prevail with any number of Tories to come in with him; but I believe he will meet with few that either like what he proposes or him. He was very early at Mr. Bromley's lodgings and called there several times, but the other would never be seen. This betwixt ourselves.

The Savage you mention had a title from Ruff. to be his chaplain, and promises of kindness from him, but has been so much disappointed by him that he has little dependence on him or respect for him.

I know little of Dr. Hudson's will, only I hear he has left to University College library those of his books which they wanted, and then to Bodley what is wanting there, and the remainder to be sold; but I will enquire further about them and his papers.

Certainly some bill was designed about empowering the King to visit us if the Peerage Bill had passed. And bills too of more moment than that against us would in all likelihood have been brought in; but I believe they would have found it difficult to have formed any bill against us so as to have answered their end and not to have made all the property in England precarious. But we are safe for this session, Lord Harcourt assures us we are so.

I thank your Lordship for your news about Trinity, and heartily wish a visitation may go on there. But we hear Bentley has at last prevailed with those scoundrels that depend on him to agree that the charges of the last visitation on both sides shall be borne by the College, which will bring a burden on the College of 1,300*l.* There should be a visitation for that only had they no other grievances.

You put a hard question to me when you ask me who can influence the Bishop of L[incoln]. For the present I can only say, his interest, and consequently any one in power. But I will talk with the Bishop of Chester and some others here who know him well, and endeavour to send you a more particular answer by the next post.

The Bishop of Chester is most heartily at your Lordship's service. If there be no dissolution—of which there is much talk —he will be up against the next meeting of the Houses.

Postscript. I am glad to hear you have used so much exercise this winter. John tells me you have been out with the dogs—once. Our Tories would do no more than vote against the bill. They would not speak against it nor come into any address against those who advised it. Their pretence was, lest they should do a kindness to T[ownshen]d and Walpole. If that be real it is wrong judged, should this ministry go out I do not believe the King would take on the others, he would think that putting himself into Hopeful's hands. I believe the true reason of the Tories was because they think the present [Ministers?] either are, or must be at last, inclined to another interest. Were that the case, it would still have been most advisable to have pushed them. That would not have lessened, but rather increased, their necessity of looking out else-where. It would have embarrassed affairs much. It would in all likelihood have forced the King to have broke with the Parliament, which was the thing they should have aimed at; for I do not believe he would have parted with his ministers, because he knows not where else to go.

I leave Neddy to speak for himself. I can give you [no?] farther account of what Ruffe wrote to the Bishop of St. David's but that it was somewhat intimating that he supposed your father had his reasons for not coming up. Your father only said Ruffe had been free with him, but he owed no account of his staying to such fellows as he.

1719, December 28.—I have consulted the Bishop of Chester and some others here, who knew L[incoln] well. All agree that no other answer is to be given to your question but what I have given already. If you can meet with any one power to speak to him, it will do; your uncle Sunderland could do it effectually. If the favour desired is for any honest Tory, it is to no purpose to ask it, unless some Whig will apply for it. His uncle, Dr. Gibson the physician as he calls himself, though I think only a surgeon, could do any thing. He lives in Hatton Garden, and is to make the other his heir to a considerable estate. He married Dick Cromwell's daughter.

[1719,] December 30. ··· I will not be positive as to the reasons of our friend's present conduct, but I believe that which I suggested is at least one motive to it. Perhaps present impracticability may induce him to suspend other thoughts, but I fancy they are only suspended, not laid aside ; but of this more when we meet.

As to the last thing I mentioned, that some gentlemen would only be on the defensive, and not engage in the offensive part, I am very positive. Could I show you the authority, which I have now by me for what I write, you would immediately agree with me.

Have you seen, but why should I doubt it, Steele's public recantation of all he has written against your father ? It is a very remarkable one, and a very handsome one, and I think he deserves the pardon he begs. I take it after all to be a sort of upbraiding of the present powers, for not having done more for him, who for their sakes had treated so ill your father, who had dealt so generously by him when he was a professed enemy. But be his motive what it will, the thing is right, and certainly galls others more than any thing would have done that had been written directly against themselves.

I expect Robert Freind here to-night. I shall then know how things stand at Westminster. My duty to my honoured Lady, and many happy new years to you both.

[1720,] January 20.—You may be sure you shall be served before any one else, except your own father; I have no tie upon me from him. From what I know myself of the boy [Bateman], I doubt not but he will do as well as any brought in by my brethren. I will therefore, without more ado, put him upon the roll to-morrow, but advise his mother to keep him at school as long as Dr. Freind thinks it proper.

Bishop of Bangor is made a justice of peace in the new commission for the city of Oxford.

What think you of the Attorney's going to France? Either he or his son is going, and speedily too, but I think it is the Attorney himself. For what end is the question.

1719-20, January 24.—I shall deliver the book to He[a]rne with the charge you give. Possibly this book may bring him to me, though I have invited him many times since the book came out in which he abused us he has always made an excuse and declined coming. I suppose his guilt made him afraid of some just rebukes.

You will place any respect on Sir W. Giffard very well. His sincere respect and, if I may use an improper word, fondness for you, give him a very good title to your favour. I suppose if you have him you will have the Triumvirate, G. Clarke and little T. R[owney]. All are very sincerely your servants. Sir William returns this week.

Postscript. How come Lord Lewisham and his brother to be sent to Magdalen? I thought their father had been a sharper fellow. He knows little of that place I perceive.

1720, January 31.—The present controversy about the play house is entertaining indeed, and fit for so great a hero as Sir Richard [Steele] against so mighty a Prince as His Grace of N[ewcastle]. This place is dull and barren, and cannot afford such momentous quarrels to entertain you with.

1720, February 2.—When I give your Lordship notice of any misfortune that befalls us, I am sure I write to one who heartily condoles with us for it. We had one here this morning. It is usual for our choristers to put out Christmas, by burning the greens in the hall, the day before Christmas [*sic*, Candlemas]. They did so yesterday at noon, for it was fast night and no fire in the hall. Some of the sparks of the greens had lodged themselves in the lanthorn of the hall, which was as dry as touchwood, and I believe too as rotten. Nothing appeared till this morning about five o'clock, when the lanthorn was all on fire, and no other part of the hall either inside or outside. We were in great confusion, and our governor Townsend, who should have directed all for us, happened to be out of town. It was a strong north-west wind, but I bless God we quenched it, with the loss of that part of the roof on which the lanthorn stood, and of the breadth of a window on each side of the lanthorn. No other part of the hall is damaged in the least, and all the rest of the roof entire. I cannot yet estimate our loss. I hope it may be within 400*l.*, but I speak by mere guess. I had not much of sleep last night before the alarm came, and rising on that, and the hurry since, have made me scarce able to hold my pen, but I was resolved to write somewhat.

1720, February 3.—Be pleased to send the enclosed by to-morrow's post to your father, either under your own cover, or otherwise as you think it will go safest. It contains nothing but an account of our misfortune, which I thought myself bound to send him.

Our damage is greater than I at first thought. Upon the best survey that can yet be made it will be about 600*l.* Townsend tells us it is one of the most curious roofs in England, for the work of it. The curious parts are all preserved, or where damaged, not so much but that they may be repaired.

Enclosure.

[To the Earl of Oxford.]

1719-20, February 3.—The concern your Lordship has always been pleased to have for us, makes me presume to trouble you with an account of a misfortune we have had. You will be pleased too to hear that it is not altogether so bad with us as you may fear perhaps from the first report of it.

It has been usual for our choristers to burn the day before Candlemas the greens which are put up in the hall at Christmas. They did so on Monday at noon. There was no fire in the hall at supper time, being fast night. We suppose some of the sparks of the greens had flown up and lodged themselves in the lanthorn of the hall, which by age alone must be very dry. Nothing appeared till Tuesday morning about 5 o'clock, when the lanthorn appeared all in a flame, but no other part either on the outside or on the inside, but the fire had gotten between the rafters and the lead. I bless God we quenched it, but not without the loss of that part of the roof on which the lanthorn stood, and of the breadth of a window on each side of the lanthorn. The rest of the roof and hall received no damage. We are told our damage is to 600*l.*, we must expect too some jests, besides our loss, and to be told that Christ Church does not now carry the lanthorn.

A friend of your Lordship, contrary to his design, was obliged by extraordinary business to go to town. When the affair was over, he immediately returned, and will continue at home. A

certain Attorney, well known to your Lordship, attempted early
and often to have seen him, but your friend was somewhat out of
humour and would not be visible to him.

1720, February 7.—Our charge will be much what I told your
Lordship in my last, but we shall upon this occasion not only
repair what is damaged, but improve and beautify too the hall,
and execute part of what would have been done if Lord Weymouth
had lived. We shall make two chimnies instead of the rotten
lanthorn, and arch the hall, and pave it with the best pavement,
from the common fireroom to beyond the present fireplace.

Townsend, who has had occasion now to take a strict survey
of the hall, says there never was in England a better building,
for fineness and curiosity as well as for strength and the goodness
of the materials.

1719-20, February 10.—Poor Neddy's compliments I am
afraid will hobble this year in prose, but what would you have
him do? His strain keeps pace with his cellar. Since you
have not thought fit to replenish that, you must be content with
what college "tiff" can produce, which will hardly rise above prose.
I own a silver writing equipage has somewhat more durable in
it than brittle flasks, but though that may give him more credit,
it is not so proper to produce poetry as champagne and burgundy.
In the present poverty of his cellar, he will be so gracious as to
keep the birthday with me, which he was too proud to do before.
Two old swash bucklers, much humble servants to my Lady and
your Lordship, are to meet him there, Dr. Hammond and
Sir W. Giffard. The old gamesters threaten hard that I shall
find that, upon so joyful an occasion, they can be young still.
I know not how I shall stand them. This I foresee, that my
Lady's health will be drunk by the letters of her name, and
that is no short one. If it be my fate to fall on this occasion,
there is none in which I am so much obliged to it, or can do it
so honourably.

1719-20, February 18.—Neddy did squeeze out a little metre
at last, but I think he has given you fair warning that it is the
last you are to expect from him. The father begins to stir in
him, and he is for somewhat a little more substantial than
poetry.

I am afraid there are few projects in which the Attorney is
engaged that have not somewhat of scandal in them.

Here is a tenant here, that is come to renew with us, that lives
at Mansfield, seven miles from Welbeck. He is well known to Mr.
Wenman, and drank your health heartily to-day at dinner. His
name is Litchfield. I perceive your character is gone before you
and they are in mighty expectations of your coming amongst
them. He tells me your woods at Welbeck are worse every day
for standing ; he puts a noble value on them. I heartily give
you joy of it.

1719-20, February 26.—I am very glad to hear of my godfather's
return in so good plight ; though the news is very welcome upon
his own account, it is not the less so for the good news he brings
of our friend John [Drummond].

This evening Dr. Bertie of All Souls was chosen professor in
Natural Philosophy in the room of Dr. Farrar, who died on Tuesday last. The place is worth 120*l.* per annum. The electors are
the Vice-Chancellor, President of Magdalen, and Warden of All
Souls. I suppose they have had good proofs of Dr. Bertie's
sufficiency for it. *Pudet haec opprobria nobis, etc.*

1720, March 6.—I hear from others as well as your Lordship
that the Attorney thinks himself sure of his point, but I agree
with your Lordship that he may be deceived, and that the knave
does more service as he is than he could in another post.

The visitation of All Souls is ended. The Warden has gained
all the points he insisted on, and some he never dreamt of. The
Fellows are humbled sufficiently. I cannot but say that, as far as
I know the controversy, the decision is very prudent and very
honourable. *Si sic omnia,* he would fill the chair he is in with
great dignity. The Fellows are laughed at heartily, which is no
little aggravation of their mortification.

What will you say if we poor Fellows of Christ Church are coming
in play again ? What will you give me for my hopes of a good
deanery? It is to be hoped particular benefactions may be the
consequence of a general one. Our governor gives us hopes that
we shall have some share of the royal munificence. It will be
the more extraordinary, since none of us ever more dreamt of it
than we have asked for it. It will show the man they have put
over us, as one they have confidence in, or is this a prelude to
some greater change? I fancy such benefactions must give
jealousies to some of their dependents.

1719-20, March 10.—I heartily thank you for the verses. Pray
be so kind as to send me another copy of the same author's, which
I hear is printed, called I think, the Conversation.

Our great men seem to be under no small difficulties, they can
have no peace abroad, it seems, without giving up Gibraltar, and
I see not how they can hope for peace at home, if they part with
it. Are we, who had nothing to do with this war, and who have
borne the chief part of the charge, and to whom the success of it
is entirely owing, to be the only losers by it, and to purchase for
every one else what he wants at our expense ? If the Utrecht
peace deserved impeachments, what will this do ?

1719-20, March 23.—I was much at a loss to know what was
become of you ; you seem to have dived for some time. I am
glad to hear you appear again at Wimpole. You and your fellow
travellers are great philosophers that are able to leave the town
when so much business is stirring. But your fellow traveller
has too much poetry to have his head turned to money, and I
think the walks at Wimpole a more proper place for one of your
quality than Exchange Alley, though so many peers condescend
to be brokers. I heartily congratulate you upon your new
employment; it will be no blot on your escutcheon. You know
I have often wished that you were bound prentice to Morley

rather than to Wanley, with all due respect to Mr. Wanley's profession. I shall be glad to find you so good a proficient as to [be] able to debate a point of improvement with the merchant. I am not sorry neither, as much as I am to preach up matrimonial concord, to find that you and my Lady have been married long enough to be able to be asunder for a week. This is Lent, and a little retirement is proper to the season, and may be of use to you on some temporal accounts of no little moment, as well as spiritual ones.

I am glad you have got the parsonage, but had well hoped it had been with a design to restore it to the church, and not to enclose it. I am afraid you are layman enough to say this is church language.

We have a royal grant for 1,000*l.* and are to have half as much from the Prince. Is not this somewhat of a reproach to your father? He squandered indeed upon us out of his own pocket, but he kept his mistress's purse close. *Quid non speremus*, when the Exchequer is open to us under your uncle S[underland]'s ministry.

Postscript. The suit is begun against the Bishop of Chester; the citation was fixed on the church doors of Manchester the 6th of this month, to summon him to show cause at the assizes why he hinders the King from filling that church.

1720, April 3.—Neddy was sent for on a sudden and went up, as much against his own as my inclination. His father is not aware of the prejudice he does him. Pray let his father know how uneasy I am at his being called away, and join with me in having him sent back as soon as possible. I suppose you see Neddy every day, pray thank him for his letter and tell him I will answer it next post.

I have enquired of Hudson's letters and papers, but there are none left. He had put all that he thought of any use or moment into Hall of Queen's hands, some weeks before he died.

John Bateman came down last night and I hope will do very well; no care shall be wanting of him.

The giving up of Carolina will mend the matter much, but I suppose they will ask the consent of the proprietors, or must the nation buy it of the proprietors for the French?

1720, April 15.—Can you tell me the secret of Ned's being set? Was it that he might not lose this noble opportunity of learning all the mysteries of stock jobbing? Will his father transfer his gains to Neddy? If he does I hope the boy will have grace enough to give them to pious uses, since he cannot know the true owners to whom they ought to be restored; I wish they may not prove a canker in Eywood.

Our History professor is dying, and numerous are the candidates. I wish I could say we had one fit one. We have one of our own House too, Mr. White. I am afraid he will be distanced, should he come within view all would unite in one to defeat him. The others are Mr. Warden of All Souls, Dr. Harrison of All Souls, Dr. Girdler of Wadham, Mr. Dennison of

University, Mr. Beckham of Oriel, Mr. Hall of Queen's. The last is the fittest, and for that reason I suppose he will be first distanced, and forced to give out. It would be blessed days with us if we had as many fit for it as pretending to it.

1720, April 21.—I am heartily glad my good Lady is prevailed on to go to Bath. I am glad too you do not go along with her, but I am afraid you do not forbear going from the proper motive. You seem to grow a fashionable husband, who can with so much indifference let my Lady go by herself. I hope I shall see you both as you go or return. I am not much out of your way as you go, but I am directly in your way if you return straight to Wimpole. I am not yet ill enough to be able to justify to myself the expense of a Bath journey. Possibly by the next year, I may have contracted scurvy enough to make it necessary.

We are busy here, but I am afraid not to much purpose. The aspect of the planets seems not favourable to Christ Church at present.

1720, April 24.—I assure you I have no aversion at all to Bath, but a great inclination. I always find great benefit from it. Nothing but the regard which one in my circumstances ought to pay to his pocket makes me forbear it, till necessity calls for it. But how come you to be concerned about my going to Bath, who design not to be there yourself? If I might be hearkened to, you should go too, and if you would observe proper discipline, it might be as useful to you as to my good Lady.

I told you in my last I did not like our present canvass here, I am every day more sick of it, and if we persist as I suppose we shall, we shall be laughed at most heartily.

You say there is no news with you, and yet Neddy and the Bishop of Chester give me notice of greater than has happened in some years. The Royal breach it seems is happily made up, I should be glad to hear on what terms. Are T[ownshen]d and Walpole taken into the treaty, or are they given up?

I am glad I shall get my boy again. I pray God he may have escaped the infection, and return without any tang of a stock jobber.

1720, April 28.—The honest Attorney seems to have met with some as treacherous as he himself is. I am afraid the world will not pity him much when he complains of it; his cake is dough. I suppose he sees an end of his present pensions as well as any farther hopes.

I believe all the world have the same opinion of the sincerity of this recon[ciliation], but however it may be strong enough to encourage them to attempt those things which nothing but their divisions restrained them from before. And if it is owing to any common danger, it may last till the fear of that is blown over.

The Tories have leisure to reflect on the prudence of their own conduct; they were not for taking any advantage against those that were in, lest [those] that were out should come in again. Your Lordship once gave in to that measure. They may in vain perhaps wish again for such an opportunity as they have had and not used. But as far as one can guess any thing at such a blind business, of which we have such obscure reports, Honest Dick [Steele] and they who are of his cabal will be the persons most lurched, and consequently most laughed at upon this occasion.

1720, May 3.—Our competitors are reduced to three, Harrison, White, and Dennison, who are now polling for it, but I have no great hopes for ourselves.

The business has gone as I thought it would, we are beaten near two to one. Harrison had 177, Dennison 104, White 92. Many in the scrutiny who had promised Dennison and White, when they saw Harrison would have it, went over to him. We could have given it as we pleased to any other but to ourselves, and we might once have had a chance for having it ourselves, but we had not sense enough to do either.

1720, May 5.—I was in hopes the account of the issue of our foolish affair would have been with you by Wednesday night. I gave my letter to Mr. Benson, who designed to have gone early by the stage coach, but your cousin Winnington came to town that night, who persuaded Mr. Benson to go with him in his coach, and they left not Oxford as I hear till twelve o'clock.

Our northern allies of Queen's from whom, upon the account of many obligations which were owned, we had an assurance of a body of auxiliaries of twenty-five, left us to a man. I am sure at least that not above three of them were with us, but this is not the first time those worthy men have done so, nor were they the only men who did so on this occasion.

It was remarkable that all the Whigs voted for Harrison, who is the most open professed Turk of this place. One of them, Scurlock of Jesus, a famous constitutioner, was taken into custody by two messengers on the day of election, and a messenger came along with him to the Convocation House when he came to vote. We know not yet certainly what he is taken up for, but he preached a sermon lately and dedicated it to Sir Richard Steele. I suppose it may be for some expressions in that.

I thank you for the picture, the original must be a great curiosity, but perhaps more proper to be preserved in the original only in your own cabinet, than to be engraven and dispersed in the print. I suppose you do not design these prints to adorn ladies' cabinets.

1720, May 8.—I beg your Lordship's pardon for disobeying your commands, but I assure you I shall neither burn nor return the print. I think it as great a curiosity as you can, and no ways improper for my own poor collection, though I cannot pretend to the honour of being a virtuoso.

This last election has made good only what, from all my observation, I was thoroughly persuaded of before, that we can never carry anything for ourselves, and may always, with common discretion, give it to anyone we please but to one of our own body. We might have done so now, if we had not been very silly fellows.

Dr. Mangey was with me this week, and I hear from him what mighty things St. John's expects from your Lordship's and my Lady's bounty. We have had, I own with great gratitude, more than we could ever have hoped for, and we are not so impudent as to pretend to engross your Lordship. But neither shall we [be] so far modest to a fault as to let St. John's run away with you. We shall still keep our claim to you, as I told Dr. Mangey. We think we have a better claim than St. John's, and a "Prior" claim too.

1720, May 17.—There are likely to be some new troubles in All Souls. Since Harrison has secured his point in the election, he is fomenting disturbances again there. The Warden has sent up a fresh complaint of him to the Visitor, but few pity the Warden. But I am afraid the University, as well as All Souls College, will find the ill effects of fixing that man here.

Dr. Hammond and Sir William Giffard both beg me to make their compliments and return their most hearty thanks for the honour you did them. When you see your old tutor, pray fail not to expostulate with him a little for debasing his own character so far as to assist at a private election, huddled up in Jerusalem Chamber.

1720, May 19.—We have heard of what has passed at Westminster. Our news here was exactly true, that orders had been given to take no notice of the poor late Dean, and the orders, it seems, were punctually executed. It is hard to say whether the inveteracy of this malice or the meanness of it were greater. It is amazing that a man should not see that he does more hurt by such a thing to his own character than to the poor man's that is gone. All the world cries out of it, as the most brutal thing that even Ruffe himself ever did. I suppose our wise governor may at last be able to open his eyes, and to see that this was designed as an affront to him as well as to his predecessor, and that no mention was made of the last Dean, for this reason amongst others, to avoid saying any thing of the present.

The news from France is extraordinary, and may well frighten all here that deal in such estates. Won't Mr. Auditor sell out upon it?

1720, May 22.—The Bishop of Chester is come safe to us, but he had a little disorder in his journey, which I hope will be over in a day or two. He has given me an account of what passed at the election, and of the general resentment of it. Surely this will finish Ruffe's character and satisfy the whole world of it. I am afraid there are some so unhappy still as to trust him. I wish they do not pay dear for it at last.

I thank your Lordship for the honour you did Agatha, I have not heard from her yet, but I make allowance for her business at her first arrival. I wish poor John were here too. The affairs of France seem likely to break out into some great confusion. In such a case, not only [John] Law may be sacrificed, but his countrymen too for his sake.

I have at last got lodgings for your cousin Foley, to Neddy's comfort, just by him ; those over the porter's lodge next to the back gate. I know not whether your Lordship remembers them, if you do, pray take care to inform my Lady Foley how stately and convenient they are.

1720, May 31.—Our Vice-Chancellor has been baffled, he had expelled a servitor, who had an exhibition in the House of 40*l.* per annum. The true reason was supposed to be that he might make way for a creature of his own. The reason he pretended was discourse of the young man against the Church, &c. The young man denied it with the utmost asseverations; offered to submit, if any such thing could be proved. The Vice-Chancellor said he had informations against him, but never would produce them, nor let him know who they were that accused him. Lee, tutor to the young man, and Brooks, the two seniors of the House and undoubted Tories, appealed to the Visitor, upon the point of the Vice-Chancellor's doing it without the consent of the seniors, as by statute he ought. The Bishop of Lincoln, the Visitor, restores the man without enquiring into the grounds of his expulsion, but because it was irregular. The Vice-Chancellor in wrath resolves to take another course and to expel him of the University by the Convocation. This was very improper at this time, and might have engaged the University in much trouble. He summons a meeting of the Heads, through whom it must pass before it can be brought into Convocation. But though he had taken care to have all his own creatures there, he could not get it passed, and I suppose there is an end of it.

1720, June 19.—I hope this will find you safe at Welbeck and full of the satisfaction of viewing some of the noblest manors in the world which you now call your own. A more solid as well as more honest estate, than any got in the extravagant acquisitions of the South Sea.

I have had the honour of a very kind letter from my Lady at Bath, she tells me she is better and that she is advised to continue as long as she can there. She seems too disposed to do so, and I shall endeavour by this post to confirm her in that good disposition. She tells me, if it suits with your convenience, she shall be willing to return home through Oxford.

The Bishop of Chester moves towards Chester on Tuesday, and I shall be going the same day to take a little fresh air for about a fortnight, at my poor hut, on the Berkshire Downs. Our new governor comes to us on Wednesday. I fear no great hurt from him, but the worst of it is that I expect as little good too.

I suppose you have seen in the prints that the Bishop of St. Asaph is married. He sent his resignation the next day, and a new Principal was chosen on Thursday, one [William] Jones, an honest man as to principles, and the best I think in other respects that that place [Jesus College] affords.

1720, July 5.—I was at my little cot in Berkshire when the favour of yours from Welbeck came hither, or I had sooner acknowledged it. I rode home this morning, a greater journey than I have taken for many years, and which I much doubted if I should have been able to go through when I attempted it. Am not I who value myself so much upon riding seventeen miles a fit person to undertake a journey to Brampton? Neddy was so good as to make me a visit at my cot, and to spend four days with me upon scraps of meat and classic authors. But I own I was somewhat unconscionable in getting him a stomach, when I had no victuals to give him; I used to make him ride with me sixteen miles upon the downs before dinner.

Dr. Edwards, who is here to take his degree, has given me hopes from your father of seeing him here shortly in his way to town. If you can learn when he designs to move, I beg you would give me notice. This weather and my poor villa tempt me to make short excursions, but I should burn my cot if it should be the occasion of my being absent when your father calls here.

Christ Church affords no news, we are still without a governor, but we have notice to expect him to-morrow. He sends word he has got the 1,000l. of the Royal bounty. I wish that may not be the best thing he ever brings with him hither.

A sad accident happened here on Sunday morning about two o'clock. Sir William Wheeler and one Statham, a gentleman commoner, both of Magdalen, and some others, with a stranger that lives in town, had been drinking all Saturday at a private chamber in Trinity. As they were coming home at that early hour, they picked a quarrel with two men they met in the street. Statham got the stranger's sword, and run one of the men through. It is thought the man cannot live. Perhaps Neddy may give you a more particular account of it. Lord Lewsom [Lewisham?] was one of the company, but by great fortune went away at nine o'clock. It is a pity but his father knew what an escape his son has had.

I know not whether you have heard how the Westminster cause has gone. The Chancellor was of opinion that Dr. Freind had a right to the master's garden, which could not be taken away without his consent. He said he thought the prebend[arie]s too had each of them such a right to the private garden as annexed to their houses, but he was not so sure of that, but he would not take upon him to decide anyone's property, and therefore referred them for a trial of those points to the King's Bench next term. Ruffe, when his counsel had done, begged leave to supply some defects he had observed in them, and made a long speech in great disorder and passion, chiefly to revile Bob Freind. When he saw how the cause was like to go, he flung out of Court in a great rage.

Postscript. Tom Rowney just now sends me word that certain news is come of Sim Harcourt's death at Paris. Tom adds what is scarce credible, that Sim had for his own share in South Sea 100,000l.

1720, July 6.—I have nothing to add, but that the news of Sim's death came to his father by a letter from Lord Bolingbroke on Monday morning. He died of a bloody-flux. He was opened, and his liver, &c., were found to be perished. I hear the news struck the father very much, and he was so ill upon it that Dr. Mead was sent for. I was under a mistake in one part of my news, it is the father and not Sim that has in South Sea and African to the value as it is said of 200,000*l.* Our governor came to us about an hour ago.

I wish my Lord Oxford joy of his gout, I am afraid he does not owe it to any great increase of stock in the South Sea.

Postscript. The Duke of Queensberry and Lord Carleton were presented this afternoon to their Doctor's degree, *honoris causâ.*

[To the EARL OF OXFORD.]

1720, July 12.—I give your Lordship joy of your gout, I am afraid it is not owing to the advance of your stock in the South Sea, though surely you have the best title to the gains of that company. But though your gout brings no increase of wealth to your Lordship, I hope it will of health.

I wish Lord Harley had not left Eywood before the account came which I sent him of Mr. Harcourt's death. I hear Lord Harcourt is in the utmost dejection upon it, but whatever reason he may have to be concerned at the loss of an only son, I am afraid he has much more reason to be troubled at the manner of it, if he has had a true account of it. I hear Lord Bolingbroke, at whose house Mr. Harcourt died, is much concerned lest Lord Harcourt should think that he encouraged that which occasioned his death. But I truly believe Lord Bolingbroke was innocent of that. J. Dr[ummon]d in a letter to me, a few days before the news of Mr. Harcourt's death, told me that Lord Bolingbroke though his landlord, would not drink with him.

[To LORD HARLEY.]

1720, July 14.—The opportunity I have of sending by an old college servant who goes to Bath for his health, allows me to write freer than I should by the post.

We yet know not what to make of our governor. All as yet is very quiet, he has hitherto concerned himself little, not entered into any acquaintance with any here, nor seems much to design it. The most he has is with the Sub-dean. We cannot yet judge whether his calmness be from a desire of being quiet, or from a want of capacity to form new models. I do not take him to be a very long-headed man. He seems to be pretty much in a wood, and not to know well to which way to turn himself. If he has any designs, he will not find it easy to get accomplices, the greatest part are prejudiced against him, and on their guard. They suspect him to be a friend of Bangor; nothing yet appears.

Never was son more lamented by a father than Sim, nor less lamented by every one else that knew him. Every one talks with great freedom of him, and no one ever knew him but had occasion to talk so. Had his capacity been equal to his inclinations he would have outdone his father. I cannot say more.

1720, August 2.—I made bold to send for some venison from Wimpole to entertain Lady and Lord Foley. My advice would not be taken in any thing; however I am in high favour, and have had a whole buck with a fine epistle from Witley. The buck came seasonably to entertain Lord and Lady Harold, whom Dr. Cheyne, much to my surprise, was pleased to recommend to me. I had the honour to gallant that Lady about the town for two days. The near relation she had to my Lady Harley commanded the utmost respect in my poor power.

Postscript. I have a strange story to tell you when I see you of the Duke of Wharton's giving 800*l.* to All Souls' building, and being turned "errant" Tory.

1720, August 4.—You need not doubt I believe of finding Neddy. Your uncle has had horses in town this fortnight, but he is so deep engaged in the South Sea that he is not likely to stir yet, though he says he is detained by Cavendish Square.

Be pleased to deliver the enclosed to my honoured Lady, and to let me know by the post after you receive this on what time on Tuesday next I may expect you.

Postscript. Duke Wharton has actually signed articles by which he obliges himself to build a particular piece of the buildings at All Souls, which will amount to 1,183*l.* He is to advance next week 250*l.* and to pay the rest proportionably as the work goes on.

1720, August 22.—I have some ill news for which my godfather will be concerned. Young Bridgwater, whom he recommended to us, was found dead yesterday in the evening in his chamber. He had always been a sober lad, and was particularly so on Saturday night, he complained about nine that night of a pain in his stomach. He was missing yesterday, in the evening his door was broken open, he was found lying with his head on the ground and his feet on the bed; it looked as though he had been striving to get up when he was struck. There was blood which had come out of his mouth and nostrils by which it was plain it was an apoplexy.

We hoped Neddy would have heard from your uncle last night, but not a word, I have put off my journey till Thursday, but if I see not your uncle here by Wednesday night I can stay no longer for him. I wish, too, I could be at any more certainty as to your father's journey. I defer my own waiting on you at Wimpole only in expectation of seeing him here.

We hope to hear of a fracas in Exchange Alley.

1720, October 24.—Give me leave to assure you that, amongst all your great qualities, the sincere kindness and condescension with which you can receive an old servant is one of which you have not the least reason to be proud. I have much cause to rejoice in your prosperity, on account of the share you so generously allow me in it. But I hope I can truly say that I take a much greater pleasure in it on your own account, and that it is with the utmost satisfaction that I think I may be confident that your mind will always be superior to your fortune, and that no blessings can be poured on you which you will not employ to great and noble purposes.

I find all here under dismal apprehensions of confusion and poverty. None rails more outrageously than a great Lady lately in our neighbourhood; she says she once thought there could not have been a worse minister than Oxford. But she owns these V———ns (?) are ten times a greater plague.

John Keill has had wonderful luck, he bought his subscription for which he gave 3,150*l.* of Waller, Aislabie's son-in-law. He is supposed to have been agent to his father-in-law, he now refunds the money to all who have bought subscriptions of him, and is said already to have refunded to the tune of 80,000*l.* I do not well understand the policy of this, and I am afraid it is not only from a principle of probity. I know not whether it may be a proper method to prevent a prosecution, but I am sure it is a plain confession of guilt.

We find here almost a total stop of payment of rents, even from those who were never used to fail a day. I wish we may be able to keep house, you have reason to wish so too. If we break, I am afraid the parish will send me with a certificate to Wimpole again.

Sir William [Giffard], Clarke, and I did ourselves the honour to remember your Lordship and my school fellow last night at Tom's. George is wonderfully pleased with your present, and charges me return his compliments and thanks for it. Tom comforts himself that, though he may have some share in the approaching calamity, yet he has none in the guilt of bringing it on us. His old friend the Attorney cannot plead that. I believe too he has fear as well as guilt. An express came on purpose to summon him to be in town without fail on the night Lord Sunderland was expected. Lord Sunderland wanted to speak with him first; this is a proof of no little intimacy. He set out the moment he received the summons.

We have so many vacancies here, that I shall be able to bring in Bateman student at Christmas.

My hearty respects to my schoolfellow, he must allow me to tell him as I am a theologue, that disappointments, though most sore, yet are of most use to us when we have least deserved or expected them.

1720, October 26.—I forgot to tell your Lordship in my last that the report about Decker was entirely without ground. The failure of Beck, and Decker's intimacy with a great Duke [Portland] were the sole occasions of the suspicions. Agatha assures me that there are not six men in the city of London so well in their circumstances as Decker, and Dick Hill, who is Decker's neighbour at Richmond, writes the same to G. Clarke.

Abel and his young honour will be here this week, I know not whether Lady Termagant comes along with them, but Abel shall not fail of meeting in me with one of Job's comforters as to his S[outh] S[ea] loss.

The Duke of Beaufort is come to University College with Mr. Dennison of that College, who was a sort of a governor to him at Westminster, and is now his tutor there.

Postscript. How goes on the canvass at Cambridge, I have given Mr. Bromley a full account of the state in which I left it.

[1720,] October 31.—Abel and his lady came hither on Thursday and left us this morning. He has dropped his young honour here. Abel and Lady Termagant are both sufficiently mortified, but Abel like Sir John Daw has recourse to philosophy in his afflictions. He supports himself as well as he can with the cordials he brought with him from John of Leyden. He showed me one thing you must take no notice of, a letter under Lord Carlisle's own hand, dated October 13th, entreating with great earnestness, as a favour that would be very seasonable and much acknowledged, that the last Michaelmas rent for the house might be paid immediately. I think this is a full proof of no little distress.

Abel is very angry with the reduction of the subscriptions to four hundred. He says he could have paid his, and now he is cheated by this reduction of his share of thirty-six millions. Much discourse we had, but I could suggest no other comfort to him but what might be had from a serious repentance for the share he has had in the infamous commerce. That with which he comforts himself most is that he bought in most of what he has at so low a rate that he hopes to be a saver at least. But I have some reason to suspect that he fibs, I dare not use a coarser word.

This day was our election for Fell's exhibitions. One Nash, one for whom I think your Lordship was concerned at Auditor Foley's desire, appeared so well that he was one of the two that were chosen.

Frank Annesley has been employing friends to the Bishop of Chester to desire them to make the two Mapletofts for him; but Frank happens not to be in the Diocesan's good graces, and in that case all his oratory is lost, he does *surdo canere*.

Postscript. Ruffe has been baffled in a motion he made in the Exchequer about the Chapel.

1720, Nov. 2.—I told you I would give our friend in Warwickshire a full account of what had passed at Cambridge, to the time I left you. I had last night his answer, which I shall transcribe *verbatim*, but I desire you would communicate it only to my schoolfellow [Prior]:—

" Mr. Prior has been very ill used by the Vice-Chancellor, and having no prospect of success is in the right to lay down. After the unjust and barbarous treatment he met with, and his behaviour under it, I should have been pleased to have had this respect paid to him. According to your account I conclude Mr. Finch will be the member, for I fear Mr. Willoughby will not desist, and I am mistaken if my friend does."

His Honour is left with us, and desires his service to your Lordship. I begin to hope the youth may do very well, now we have got him from his parents.

What think you of Walpole's being Earl of Walsingham and having the staff; he will deserve it if he can find an expedient, as they say he undertakes, to make all parties of the late gamesters easy. To show too his capacity, he is at the same time to get the Peerage bill passed, and the Septennial bill not continued but quite repealed, that the prerogative of the Crown may be as much at liberty as it was in former reigns to dissolve or continue Parliaments. These are great things to be undertaken in so stormy a season.

1720, November 4.—What Lord Anglesey wrote to Dr. Audly was surely *satis pro imperio*, but it is very agreeable to his present disposition. He is now at Blechingdon, and I hear from those who converse very intimately with him that he is under utmost concern for the success of his worthy kinsman. I forgot to tell your Lordship in my former that I had the good luck, before I got out of your grounds, to meet the Arab, and was not a little pleased that I had a sight not only of so true a horse, but so great a curiosity too.

We have had a confirmation of Ruffe's battle in the Exchequer. A motion was made against Herbert, in relation to New Chapel. Ruffe in his great prudence and nicety had worded the motion so that it was rejected with open contempt the whole court.

If they have any spirit left in Cambridge, they will never endure to be bullied by one who himself was so much obliged to them.

I beg my duty to my honoured Lady and my young mistress, and forget me not to my schoolfellow and Mr. Thomas.

I hear your cousin Packer is soused in the African. We are now told here positively that Lord S[underlan]d himself has been deeply engaged in South Sea, some say he has sold out, others that he is still in.

1720, November 9.—This was an unexpected turn at Cambridge, but how came the Pates not to be quick-sighted enough when they proposed the Provost to see the consequence of his being chosed. A majority of them is as much against B[entle]y as the young masters can be. I look upon this division to have been purely Whig and Tory, and to show what the Tory interest truly is, if it had not been broken. Pray be so kind in your next as to let me know for which of the candidates Cross is. The putting by of the Provost is a great blow to Annesly pretensions, if the present Vice-Chancellor is engaged for another. I think Cross is looked upon as a thorougher, though he succeeded Sh[erloc]k [as Master of Catherine Hall].

I have had a long letter from our friend Decker about the report that was of him. He has not for four months past had any thing to do in Exchange Alley upon his own account. He had sold out betimes, and had left nothing in any of the stocks but what was pure gains. At the time the report went of him he had written to the great banker in Amsterdam, Pels, who, as Decker thought might be pressed, to give him leave if he had occasion to draw at sight 100,000*l.* on him.

1720, November 14. — Methinks the Vice-Chancellor has done B[entle]y too much honour, and seems to make him too considerable. B[entle]y may rely perhaps in some measure on their dissensions, but more I am afraid on their weakness. Had not they given him advantages against themselves by their own mismanagement, they might have ended this dispute to their satisfaction long ago.

John Drummond is come to us again, and seems to be glad that he is. In the main, I believe he is able to say that he has lost nothing but his time. He is much as he was when he went to France. If there be any difference I believe it is rather to his advantage than loss. But he tells me that his countrymen here are universally undone. It is his opinion, who has seen what has passed abroad, that the only way to preserve us from utter ruin is to leave all things as they are, and that, if there should be any attempt to raise the stocks again, it would undo us, by the advantage it would give to foreigners.

[1720,] November 21.—It must be said of your neighbours that they act consistently with themselves, there is no danger of their degenerating into a more honourable character. Surely this not so proper a time for compliments; you will hear from Mr. Thomas what success such an attempt had here.

If the accounts, which are repeated to us every post, hold good, the great man you hint at will not be long in a condition to pay for such trumpery, as your Lordship justly calls it, and B——— will as certainly leave him in the lurch as he did Lord Halifax.

The Attorney, in expectation of South Seas rising again, bought in to the value of 4 or 6,000*l.* a fortnight ago at 215*l.* South Sea wrecks begins to be talked of now in the country, as well as in town.

I beg my duty to my honoured Lady and to my young mistress too. Little as she is, she has my heart more than ever any mistress had. If I took notice of her in proportion to my concern for her, every one of my letters would be a—" *Scriptus et in tergo, necdum finitus Orestes.*"

1720, November 23.—The little Auditor took a bed with me last night in his way to town. He enquired after your chimneys, he is positive they may be cured, be the cause of their fault what it will. But if it is occasioned only by the height of the old house, he says he knows a certain cure, and if it is a sure one, I am sure it is a very easy and simple one. It is only by making a hole on the tops of the chimney, on the side of them opposite to the old house. He will explain it to you better when you meet him in town.

If what he tells me be true, I must congratulate you, though the occasion of it be melancholy. He told me, he had heard that your uncle Nat had left all he had to your Lordship.

1720, November 28.—There were some circumstances in the affair of the font which I was forced to omit for brevity. I thought it would divert you. When you see Bob or the Bishop of Chester you will have an account of a long dialogue betwixt Ruffe and old Martin, the brewer, which will divert you more than the font. Ruffe only tampered with the old fellow for three days together to make him give false evidence upon oath; one of Ruffe's peccadilloes.

1720, November 30.—Since it was advisable for my school-fellow [Prior] to desist, I think the affairs at Cambridge have taken the best turn we could wish for the public, as well as for the disappointment of those who were so meanly industrious to disappoint my schoolfellow.

I forgot not to speak to the Bishop of Chester about Swift's verses said to be found in Mrs. Long's cabinet who died at Lynn. The Bishop searched all his papers but could not find them, nor could he recollect what he did with them. But he fancies you may easily hear of them at Cambridge; he had them from his brother, who told him they were common there.

Postscript. I suppose your Lordship hears of the new scheme for redressing our evils, but no one that I hear from seems to have any opinion of it. To me it seems utterly impossible that upon the new scheme any more interest can be paid than is received from the governor, much less fifteen *per cent.* as is proposed. I fancy it must make matters rather worse than better in a little time.

[To the EARL OF OXFORD.]

1720, December 1.—I received the enclosed on Thursday last. Mr. Bromley is still in the country; he had earlier notice than we had here that a prorogation was designed, and deferred his journey upon it.

I bless God that your Lordship is past the danger of your late distemper, but I must beg leave to say that none of your servants can be easy till you are in town, where your physician will know better what to advise than it is possible 'for him at such a distance.

1720, December 9.—Your good tutor begins to own that he is in the South Sea, but we cannot bring him yet to own for how much or at what price, though we know both. He is one of those who expect the Parliament is to work miracles to raise it again.

You will hear before this reaches you that Law is turned out of all; they offer to let him escape privately, but he is brave and resolved to stay and run the hazard of every thing they can do to him.

1720, December 19.—I am much surprised to find that little Robin has been kept in the country ever since your uncle went down, and we have notice to expect him here this week. It seems as odd to send him up at this time to town to be idle there during the holidays, as it was to keep him so long at Eywood. Mr. Edward I perceive has no thoughts of seeing us again till he comes up with his own father or yours. But by sending Robin at this time, I should guess that none of them have any thoughts of coming up soon after Christmas.

1720, December 23.—Robin came hither on Wednesday noon and was so kind as to be my guest till this morning, when he went up in the coach to London. He brought me a letter from Brampton, in which there was one enclosed to Palmer. Mr. Palmer goes down on Monday by Robin's horses. I believe

Palmer had not been sent for so soon if it had not been to get rid of the Archdeacon. I hear he had no mind to quit his quarters, but designed to keep all the livings as long as possibly he could. My letter, as usual, is not the plainest in the world, but as far as I can decipher it we are in haste to move, and perhaps shall not do it at all, at least till all the racket above is over.

1720, December 26.—I have read Dr. Middleton, and think all his observations just. I own Bentley's proposal to be a bubble, but however I am afraid I shall give in to it. But I hope I may be excused, since it will be the only bubble I have any concern in.

1720, December 28.—There are too many *participes criminis* to let the Directors be called to any accounts. I see nothing designed by the present scheme but to secure to themselves what they have gotten, and themselves from being called to any account for it. Nobody gains by it but the old proprietors, and they gain extravagantly. It leaves every one else greater losers and more discontented than it found them. Nor do I believe that the only evil that they hope to remedy by it can be stopped so much as for the present. But if it should, it will certainly in a few months recoil again upon them with greater violence. Indeed I am apt to think that if a dictatorial power were given to the ablest and honestest men in the nation, they could not help us. But the present scheme may probably hasten the evil day sooner than it would have come otherwise.

I hear that the Cambridge men pretend to take it ill that my schoolfellow did not give a vote at their late election. But surely it was unreasonable to expect it of him.

Postscript. I hear by this day's post that the Directors are in no great fear for themselves, but that the Ministers are in great fear of the Directors.

[1720 ?] December 29.—As to public news we are as in my last. The city continue in a high ferment about the quarantine bill, and the new bridge that is to be built betwixt Lambeth and Foxhall. There will be mighty opposition by the city to that bridge.

1720-1, January 2.—The new scheme does not seem to go down very glibly. There seems to be pretty strong physic used to make it pass that seems not much for the credit of it. They who wish it may pass expect not much from it, only they are for this rather than none, and willing to be at a certainty. Archibald Hutchinson is resolved to oppose it, and has one of his own to offer in lieu of it, which he thinks more equitable, and I doubt not but it is so. The more the merrier.

I have the good fortune to be much in Doctor Edmonson's good graces. He has favoured me with another letter, with some reflections on their late election. I find he is not a little satisfied with his own conduct, and pleased that Mr. Finch had such an opinion of him that he never offered to ask his vote, either by himself or his friends.

[1721 ?] January 6.—I hope this will congratulate you upon [your] own and my Lady's and my young mistress's safe arrival in Dover Street.

You have wisely enjoyed the country whilst nothing of moment passed in town, and have contrived to come just when business begins to open and thicken too. If you have as much leisure to write letters as you are like to have materials for them, I shall have an excellent correspondent of you. If the ferment that seems to begin improves, I shall wish our distant friend in town.

My most humble duty to my good Lady Dupplin. If I might presume that the honour I once had of her Lord's favour is not quite forgotten, I would congratulate him too upon his gains in the South Sea. When his younger children are largely provided for, I hope the overplus will go to support episcopal seminaries in his own fatherland.

[1721,] January 9.—You have sent me the news I most desire, and in which I can acquiesce with satisfaction, without any other, in telling me that my Lady, your dear one, and yourself are come safe to town.

As to fine things to be done by our senators, you know my opinion. Our evil admits of no remedy, were our senators as uncorrupt and as able as they should be, and we with them. The most they can do would be only like a man's delaying the evil hour of bankruptcy, by shifting his debts from one hand to another. That only makes it fall heavier at least. But what the issue of these things will be, no one can pretend to say. Nothing I am afraid that any good man can rejoice in. By a letter I had this morning from Neddy, I suppose your uncle is in town, he did wisely not to wait for a summons by the Sergeant. But pray tell him that I take it unkindly that he did not pass through Oxford. He has spoiled a speech, too, which I had prepared to congratulate him upon his coming up attended with the public officers, as I expected he would.

1720-1, January 12.—I am heartily sorry for the death of young Mr. Foley's wife; she is certainly a great loss to him, and in that, to all the family.

I am glad to find we are likely to live in peace. It is plain no attempt on the Lords House can do any hurt, and the scheme is carried in the Commons. Nor do I fear lest the secret committee, with carrying of which some warm men seem much pleased, should do any great matters. I am most concerned for the scheme itself, lest it should not effect the great ends for which it is contrived, of restoring credit and stilling clamour. Some, who are for putting the worst colour on every thing, gave out that it is calculated more to support those who propose it than to ease those who cry out for relief. But I hope the rise of stocks by the next post will silence that calumny.

Pray remember the epitaph; though it be a mournful ditty, I want it to make me merry.

1720-1, January 12.—The Bangorians were jockeyed yesterday at Merton, at the election which they had for five fellows. They, like the saints who are privileged, had agreed to cheat their own brother Whigs and the Warden too, and to bring in, without communicating with the others, all five of their own principles. The Warden smells this, and secretly treats with the poor remnant of Tories there, and at the election joins his Whigs to the Tories, and excludes all the Bangorians, and brings in every man he had agreed on with the Tories. I cannot yet tell you all their names, but a grandson of Bishop Stillingfleet and a nephew of the Warden of All Souls were two of them.

1720-1, January 14.—I never heard of the Latin epitaph upon the Abbot of Rochester. Is it upon some old Abbot who was famous for the same qualities the present Abbot is, or is it one upon the present Abbot? If the latter, pray by what hand is it? If you have a copy pray be so kind as to communicate it.

I hear the Attorney is published in the "London Journal" for being of counsel for the Directors, under the insinuation of a great person near Red Lion Square.

1720-1, January 17.—I have read, since I had the honour to write to your Lordship, the most entertaining epistolary performance that this age has produced. Mr. Prior could not come up [to it?], nor the famous Lord Rochester, were he alive. I mean the short and concise, but very significant, epistle of Timothy Watch. It ought to be printed by itself, on elephant paper and in the grand pica. I should be proud to be known to the worthy author.

I have just now a letter from Mr. Palmer, dated from Brampton, January 13th; I find my Lord of O[xford] had not then been downstairs and was so weak still that Mr. Palmer had not then seen him. I am sorry to find he recovers so very slowly.

All now seem to agree that the Directors must be hanged. As they please. I have nothing to do, either to tie them up or cut them down. But are they the only men that deserve this fate? Should not some of their judges, if they would be impartial, put their own names into the same bill, especially they who had possession or promise of stock before they voted for it.

1720-1, January 24.—I perceive by my correspondents this day, that the weather begins to grow hot in the House of Commons. Tom tells me that Aislaby was dismissed on Sunday night. Are not some others to follow him? Will the chief minister himself stand firm, when underlings are torn off? Who will be so charitable as to take the management of us in our present condition?

I told you formerly that John Keill had the prodigious good luck to buy his subscription of Waller, Aislaby's son-in-law, and had his money returned in South Sea bonds. John turned part of these bonds into money, how much I know not, but I believe the best part. The money he lodged into Middleton's hands, who lately stopped payment. Out of the frying pan into the fire. The Sub-dean tells me that he believes John had some other money besides that of the bonds he sold in Middleton's hands too.

1720-1, January 26.—Whoever transacts with your Lordship cannot but have everything to his satisfaction, unless he traffics upon a South Sea expectation of enriching himself by the ruin of the person he deals with.

I agree with your Lordship entirely. No doubt Knight's going was by concert, and it is likely with others besides D[irector]s. I fancy too, as you do, that after all the noise those gentlemen will not suffer what others expect, much less what they deserve. Nor do I see well how they can, without somewhat of the nature of a Bill of Attainder.

His Honour is come again to us ; we shall do what we can with him, but we shall never be able to answer Abel's expectation. He thinks poor parsons, in any way, can never give him enough for his money.

Madame Rowney is gone up to her spouse this day, and carries with her a piece of her own work, which she has been hard at this winter, which she designs to beg leave to present to my Lady. She hopes she may be admitted to make a morning visit, for she despairs of finding my Lady in an evening.

[1721,] January 29.—I had a full account of Ruffe's extraordinary motion, but he seems to be happy in some respects. Nothing he can do can make some people think worse of him, or others any thing ill of him. This, if any thing, should open men's eyes. How comes he to be so tender about perjury ? He himself has not boggled at [it?], more than once, upon much less temptation.

I had a letter last post from Neddy, he bids me now not expect him till Thursday next. He says he stays to see Palmer instituted, and the Archdeacon dislodged from Brampton. I find Neddy's Welsh blood is up, he gives the Archdeacon hard names, unless they are deserved. In that case, I was always a friend to justice, and should be no more for sparing an archdeacon than a director. Tom Rowney tells me the report of J. Keill's loss by Middleton is not true. He says Keill luckily got 200l. out of Middleton's hands, two days before he stopped payment.

They say it is talked that the Attorney is coming in again into his old post. I thought he would have liked better a private pension, and would have avoided such open play. But he can help them as little as any one else.

1720-1, January 81.—If our reports hold true we shall have some sport. Our patriots are said to be upon an Herculean labour of cleansing their own house. The Augean stable surely was not filthier. Should truth come out, the Attorney certainly would appear to have no little share. But though he was in early, and had stock at a very low rate, yet I fancy he was cautious enough to pay for what he had. That may exempt him from the censure others may have, though not from the guilt.

The detection and punishment of the authors of our misery, with the help of the new scheme, will no doubt restore our halcyon days. The present state of East India and Bank, upon the bare apprehension of the scheme before the bill is so much as brought in, give us a comfortable prospect of the redress we may expect from it. It is said there are lists handed about of the patriots in both Houses who entered into council with the South Sea for promoting their cause. If there are any such things, I should be glad to see one of them.

1720-1, February 5.—I most heartily thank your Lordship for the favour of your last. It has some important hints. I shall be very sorry if one person mentioned should be capable of such a thing. My concern would be more for the station than the man, but if it should be so, let shame fall where it is due. It will be better the iniquity should come to light, than be smothered.

I can easily believe any thing of my old friend Ruffe. It will appear by the list lately printed of those who have a vote in the South Sea stock, what interest his son-in-law has there. And it would be no hard matter to learn at what time he first had stock. I wish I had one of those lists.

The Tories, by the list you were so kind to send, seem but merchants of small wares, and to be poor pedlars in iniquity. It is a sign they are not used to it, but it is amazing to find men of such large fortunes playing at so small a game.

Postscript. I think it impossible that the Attorney should have the Seals, or any other place openly, whilst he stands excepted out of the Act of Indemnity. Nor do I fancy that to be his game at present, he deals rather in pensions, and no doubt he makes his bargain well there. But if W[alpole] and his interest should come uppermost, the Attorney may fall short in his pension. How stands S[underland]? Surely his own interest must grow weak as his own creatures go off and his opposites get strength.

1720-1, February 7.—I am amazed that none of my correspondents take notice of the gradual but constant fall of all stocks, since the new scheme that is to redress all our evils ·was voted. It alarms me, nor can I conjecture any thing from it, but a total failure in a little time of all public credit, and that we are gently going into the same condition our neighbours are.

Not a word from Neddy of your father's moving, I daresay it will be, as we conjectured, spring at least before he thinks of it.

Postscript. Stanhope's death may be some loss, at a time when others seem not very fond of the service. Perhaps it may be of some use on the point of Gibraltar and Port Mahon. No doubt the guilt of that, as far as it can, will be laid on him.

1720-1, February 10.—I am bound by many ties to put up my most cordial prayers for you and your Lady, on the day on which this I hope will wait on you. But I cannot, I think, put up a more comprehensive and more ardent one than that the doubt, which I daresay all who know you both have at present, may always continue.

28493

I shall not interrupt you further on this joyful day than to desire that my duty to you both, and prayers for you, may be received amongst those of your other servants who are now making their compliments to you. I suppose you will be so well employed on the good day, that I shall not expect to hear from you on Sunday.

1720-1, February 14.—The remission of the seven millions is too hard for my philosophy and puts me out of all patience. What ado is made about half a dozen! What shall we get by their being hanged, if we must pay seven millions for the ropes? It is surely such a thing as never was mentioned before in a free nation, to give seven millions out of the pockets of innocent people to increase the gains of those rogues, who have cheated you of twice as many more before. Were I on the stocks, for my own interest I should not desire it. It will be a just reason for those who are injured by it, to sink the stocks themselves if ever they have a juncture for it.

1720-1, February 16.—I have Neddy again at last, he brought me a letter from Brampton. I find by it that your father's nails, every one, both of hands and feet, are coming off, and new ones coming on. This may be painful to him, but I hope it is a great discharge of the venomous humour that has flown about him, and a good proof of strength of nature. As to Neddy, what I feared has happened. His mother has been cramming him, he is as fat as I am, I had almost said as your Lordship.

The Arch-deacon has been playing a very strange part. Your father is wonderful good in covering it as he does.

I hear of a very extraordinary appeal of Ruffe's. As far as I can judge of those things, I believe one of that nature was never brought into the House. Methinks those who are most his creatures should be ashamed of appearing for him in it. I know not upon what prospect he brings it on. I hope your Lordship will solicit heartily for Bob [Freind].

Do not you all conclude that the chief impeachers are returning again into full power, and that great changes are at hand?

1721, February 18.—Neddy tells me that your father's stomach is very bad still. Whether it is much weakened by long illness, or all the bad humour has not yet discharged itself, nothing would do him so much for that, or to clear his body of this humour which runs about, as Bath. He ridicules it, but I hope his doctors will oblige him to have recourse to it.

I am not disappointed in the report, nor shall I be, if we hear no more of the Directors. It is very plain matters must be hushed up. I fancy Knight will come, but he will be well instructed not to hurt himself or others. This will end probably in many alterations in great places. What turn the disobliged may take time must show.

Tockay is a medicinal wine, it must be a great quantity indeed of that to do so much hurt.

1720-1, February 23.—I have had a very kind and florid epistle from my good friend Dr. Tudway. He tells me Middleton is replying upon Bentley, but the main reason of his letter was to tell me that he designs, when your consecration is over, to set upon a large treatise of music and to dedicate it to your Lordship. He complains he was straitened in compass in the short essay he has written before the book which you have. But he will spend the remainder of his life in writing a full and just treatise, if that short essay meets with that approbation he hopes for from your Lordship. What he means by that last, I know not. If he means verbal approbation, I suppose he may have it as large as he may have what he will of it (sic). There are not I am afraid materials enough left out of which a satisfactory account can be drawn, but I believe his is as good as any can be given.

I hear Lord Gore and Sir William Wyndham are at Woodstock, with dogs of all sorts and denominations. Why did they not go to Staffordshire, if they can dispense with their attendance in Parliament? That is a better country for fox-hunting than Woodstock.

1720-1, February 26.—Shame belongs to nothing that I know of but sin, but surely not to our good deeds, and least of all to the best of them. Your letter, of which you say you are ashamed, was proper for your quality, proper for your integrity, proper for your spirit, proper for the character you always had, and I trust in God ever will have in the world. I have reason to be proud of the favour of all your letters, but that was without exception the most glorious one I ever had from you, and as such I esteem it, and shall preserve.

I entirely agree with you as to your judgment in the other part of your letter, and I have been of the same opinion ever since I was with you at Wimpole. But I should be glad to know my godfather's opinion, which I should rely on before any one's in this case. And your uncle's too, who on this point is a good judge too. Pray talk it with them at least. It concerns even such a poor fellow as I am to have one's [eyes?] open upon such apprehension, but much more one of your station and circumstances, that you prepare for the emergency as well as you can. I hear Colonel Churchill returns a *non est inventus.* Men I believe will generally make the same reflections on it, but I should be glad to hear how they resent it.

Postscript. My duty to my honoured Lady. I suppose she is comforting the Duchess of Buckingham. That lady will certainly be a decent, but do you think she can be a sorrowful, widow. Old Rub will be a loss. Not finding the news of Knight's escape confirmed by any of my letters this post, I fancy my correspondent T. Rowney was misinformed.

[1721,] March 2.—Neddy is in great glee upon A[islabie]'s commitment. I am forced to preach up Christian philosophy to him. I can allow him to take pleasure in seeing a wicked wretch humbled, but I am afraid he considers him as a family enemy, as well as a common oppressor, and finds it hard to confine his joy to the proper ground only.

Here is a letter to the Master of Trinity come to us. Who is supposed to be the author of it? I fancy it is a second part of Middleton.

I shall hope to hear from your Lordship, though one line only, every post till the little one is quite well again.

· I beg my duty to my honoured Lady, I pray God keep her from any fears about that which is dearer to her than herself.

Postscript. The epitaph and epigram are no secret. A gentleman who came down here brought them with him and I believe has made them pretty public. My schoolfellow [Prior] is talked of too for the author, upon no other ground that I can hear but that they are thought good enough for him, and they know no one else that could write them. I have religiously observed your orders to me.

1720-1, March 8.—A thousand thanks to you for the kindness of yours by this day's post. You must give me leave to rejoice for the news of it, on my own account as well as my Lady's and yours. Next to my little one's parents and her grand papa, no one could have been more dearly affected than I should have been with any thing fatal to her. I hope her physicians will be of my opinion, if the weather would change, to send her into fresh air.

I have the Pates' censure of Bentley; there is more work cut out for him, and perhaps for them too. I hope B. will think himself bound in honour to reply to them. I do not altogether admire the style of this censure. However the style as well as the subject here is somewhat better than it was in another performance of theirs of no very ancient date.

1720-1, March 5.—I have had an abstract of the report sent me by a friend, and upon reading it I am satisfied that we are no more to expect that any thing should be done at home than that Knight should return home. The parties concerned are too great, as well as too numerous, to allow of any such thing.

The honour your Lordship allows me of being your servant procures me compliments I had no reason to expect from Cambridge. I cannot but take satisfaction in them, as such favours to me are a proof of the respect that is paid to your Lordship. I had yesterday a kind letter from Covel, with a copy of the censure of B[entle]y enclosed. I did not think I could have lived so long in ignorance of your Christian name. I knew it not till last night when Dr. Davis's edition of Tully *De Divinatione* was brought to me. That book first informed me that it is Thomas. So learned a man, and that had opportuntity of informing himself by being in your neighbourhood, cannot surely be mistaken.

Postscript. I have the favour of your Lordship's, and rejoice with you for Mrs. Peggy's perfect recovery. A little want of strength is no illness. God bless your endeavours against Ruffe. Go on and prosper.

1720-1, March 7.—I have had some further account of the report, and particularly as to the state of the charge against Sta[nho]pe, by which I am fully convinced of the equity of acquitting him.

We see [m ?] to have a method of curing wounds, not by draining off the humour that feeds them, but stopping only the orifice. Legal doctors are used to call this the practice of empirics, and to suppose that the humour would burst out again with more violence in some other place. But this [is] out of my profession, I leave it to those to whom it belongs.

I beg my duty to my honoured Lady, and my dear young mistress.

Postscript. I hope you never forget me to my schoolfellow.

I have heard that the Chancellor eats his decree. This is a full proof to me of Ruffe's secret correspondence with S[under-lan]d. That can be the only means by which the Chancellor has been brought to retract. And this is a juncture in which S[underland] will be willing to oblige any one, especially one that is supposed, though I believe without much ground, to be capable of influencing a great many of a whole party.

1720-1, March 13.—I hope you will be in town again before Bob's cause come on. The great man that Ruffe corresponds with in secret is influencing all he can in his favour, and drawing off Bob's friends. I know nothing that can counter-balance this so well as if the Tories who are Ruffe's friends could be made to see what the interest is by which Ruffe works, and on which he chiefly depends.

We are here in some ferment. Our Recorder is dead. His second son stands for the place, and Sir Robert Jenkinson is put up by Lord Abingdon. The inclination of the electors is certainly for young Wright, and if the University did not interpose with a zeal very uncommon, not to say too violent, Lord Abingdon would be laid on his back, but by our help he will carry it.

I have seen old Rub's epitaph on himself. I am heartily sorry for it. It is a sad thing for a man to seem to glory in that which is not only his shame but too likely, too, the cause of misery to him. I see not of what use it can be to tell all posterity that he was an infidel. The epitaph imports little less. Were I Dean of Westminster I fancy I should never let it be put up. I suppose by *Improbus* he means *Impius*, unless he reckons cheating at Marybone and such peccadillos no breaches of probity.

Your neighbour Mr. Bacon is quarrelling with G. Clarke about a bill that is brought in to enable the colleges to part with lands and houses, to make room for Dr. Radcliffe's benefaction. As to the bill itself, I doubt whether I should have advised it, upon reasons relating to the colleges themselves. But Mr. Bacon can have no reason to think it, as he pretends, an affront to him. His opposition to it is from mere peevishness.

[1721,] April 5.—I bless God for your safe return to your own family again. Tudway indeed did give me a noble idea of the vast alterations that are projected at Wimpole. I could not but

admire them, though at the same time I begged leave to bestow one tear upon the loss of my beloved grove, and the old trees of the old avenue.

I most heartily thank your Lordship for your great service to church and state, in the share you have had in mortifying of Ruffe. I wish Bob may gain his point. But the point I most wanted is gained. The fellow is known, and his character exposed, by a testimony that cannot be eluded, his own insolence. I expect that his rage will every day produce some new extravagancies. I hear he does your father the honour of ascribing to him the opposition he has met with. I wish for the good of my good master's soul it were true. It would be the best atonement he could have made for preferring him. I wish I knew what the reasons are why your Lordship is not surprised at T[revo]r's being so thoroughly for him.

Your friend Sir W. Giffard has lost his wife, and is much afflicted at it.

The less Neddy stays in town the better.

Postscript. My hearty respects to my schoolfellow. I doubt not but he has had his share in the public service of humbling Ruffe. Is not S[underlan]d supposed to be decently retiring from public business?

1721, April 6.—I cannot but reflect that Ruffe by his insolence should draw upon himself so just a mortification, in a cause in which much might be said on both sides, but in which he had more to say for himself than in any that he was ever engaged in. But the most wicked men have their time limited. Probably he has now met with his stop and may decline, but never regain credit again.

I am glad you are so well pleased with Neddy's outside, but I hope you will find reason to like his inside still better.

How goes the chapel on? Do you think it can be finished this summer? I suppose not. Pray answer me seriously to that. You know I have a little reason to enquire. I suppose you will not think of consecrating it till every thing belonging to it, that is to be fixed in it at least, is completely finished.

Mr. Bromley tells me that Ruffe was once one of old Rub's executors, but struck out upon that illness which sent him to the Bath. He must have got into old Rub by very mean flattery.

I am told the Attorney droops, upon the apprehension of his friend S[underlan]d's going out. The Attorney carries it so far as to talk of retiring within a month into the country, and never more concerning himself in public business; not I suppose till more pensions or subscriptions are to be had. There seems to be a full hue and cry against S[underlan]d. All these addresses seem pointed at him.

[1721,] April 9.—I am mightily pleased to hear that my sweet grove and the old avenue have got a reprieve. I hope it will be for my life.

I am so happy as to agree with your Lordship entirely in all your reflections about Lord S[underland]. Some gentlemen we know have been and are still miserable dupes. Those too I am afraid who are the very chief of the party. And Ruffe has been the instrument used in deluding them, and he has kept up his credit with them by that very thing, which has given him an opportunity to merit elsewhere by betraying them. That alone should induce all who have any compassion for those gentlemen to endeavour to take them out of his hands, by showing him in his proper colours. He has got such a hold on them, by the treacherous part he has played, that nothing but what is very glaring can open their eyes. I hear how it has gone at the Chapter, and expected no other. I was always in my own thoughts against the expedient, and wished the House had been left to pursue its own warmth. It will now be returned with much disadvantage to the Lords. Could friends be rallied and the point carried, his mortification would be much greater now he thinks he comes with so much advantage. And if the opposition still should be warm, it would I doubt not once more [give him?] occasion to display those amiable passions he has. Should he carry the day his insolence will be insupportable. I have too good reason for what I suggest of the part Ruffe has played, and of the opinion that he has instilled of Lord S[underland] into those who take him for their oracle.

Neddy tells me his father is gone to take a ramble during the recess. Is Neddy gone with him? He says nothing of himself. The doubt of it hinders me from writing to him.

My hearty respects to my good school-fellow. He never did any thing more meritorious than to help to humble Ruffe.

Postscript. Is it known who was the mother of this young Herbert who is *hæres secundus* to old Rub? I am told by one who has most concern to know that he is suspected to have been by a daughter of his own.

1721, April 16.—Your Lordship forgot one thing, which I am concerned to enquire and which you can tell me, whether your noble chapel at Wimpole is likely to be finished this summer. I had another sweet letter on Friday last from Dr. Tudway. But the old man is so gay and so full of his compliments, that I am not able to keep pace with him.

I hear of a saying fathered on Lord Oxford, that the removing S[underland] to take in W[alpole] would be like a man's putting off one dirty shirt to put on another dirty shirt. It came to me from Warwickshire. It was added that it was reported to have been told the King as Lord Oxford's saying, and that his Majesty was much diverted with it.

[1721,] April 23.—I have seen a very remarkable passage on the answer to a late address. Does your Lordship remember Macbeth's speech to Banquo's ghost, "Thou canst not say I did it." Surely no thanks are due to the minister that drew up that answer. Does your Lordship know that Morley's rake that was

our student is married. Here was a little sorry girl that was a servant to a poor bedmaker here, when that fellow was with us. The girl afterwards went to a service in London, where this fellow met with her last summer and married her. I have been applied to to recommend to Morley's favour his new daughter-in-law, but I believe you will think I have declined that office.

I thank you for your account of Lord P———t's disposition. I hope all friends will be mustered to prevent the putting off the cause again.

[1721,] April 28.—We heard this morning that Mr. Herbert, knight of our shire, was drowned, yesterday as I take it, by a slip of a foot bridge betwixt his own house and Thame. I hear no other particulars. I know not whether you will hear this first from me. Sir John Doyly is said to be in town already making interest, but it is not said for whom.

1721, April 30.—Sir John Doyly canvassed here for my Lord Chancellor's son, but it is thought he would have set up for himself at last, if he could have met with any encouragement. But he had so little where' it was supposed he would have found most, that it is thought he has done with it, and that we shall be left to choose any one we have a mind to. It is thought Captain Bertie's eldest son, that was lately heir to James Norris of Weston, will be put up.

Our late knight is supposed to have been taken with an apoplexy, as he was going over the bridge. He was walking out alone into his grounds, as he used to do, about ten in the morning. There had indeed about five days before been a very hard bout, which might have helped it, at a meeting Duke Wharton had with the Tory gentlemen.

I have read Dr. Middleton's book with a great deal of pleasure, he is a very ingenious man. I shall epistolize my good friend Dr. Tudway very shortly with my thanks. I fancy Bentley will be as little in humour at the election as I hope Ruffe will be. I shall be full of expectation of news from you by Thursday's post.

1721, May 2.—Mr. Edward was this afternoon presented to his master's degree. He was graced with a numerous attendance of Heads and Doctors. I cannot say it passed *nemine contradicente*, there were three and I think no more of our perverse club against it. Mr. Sub-dean made a florid speech at presenting him, in which he vouchsafed to sprinkle a few good words on your father and yourself. I guess by that, and his talking more than ever he did against Ruffe, that he suspects the times are turning. But I will not forestall him. I suppose he will give you a copy of what he said. He sets out to-morrow towards the election.

Mr. Perrot, that married Duke Chandos' niece Bourchier, is set up for our county. I think there can be no doubt of his carrying it. Sir John now makes interest for himself, but he meets every where with so much discouragement that I cannot think he will persist.

1721, May 4.—I am heartily sorry for the news you have sent me of Lord Carmarthen. I pray God make him in some measure sensible before he leaves the world how he has lived in it.

I suppose the rejection of the bill in the Lords will be construed to be equal to a toleration of Arians and used by them accordingly. If they who encourage this can bring the nation to a division of orthodox and Arian, they will find it somewhat more fatal to the peace of it than Whig or Tory ever was. Though I doubt not they who encourage this, design through that to strike at Christianity itself.

The day was as shameful surely in the Commons with respect to our temporal goods. But I take it they have cut their own throats there. What they design to raise credit will I fear in a little time sink that and stocks too with it. There may be a little flourish for the present, but when once it appears that it is impracticable to pay our debts, as I think it is now, every man in his wits will desire to be out of stocks. And I doubt not but they who are in the secret have given up the seven millions, chiefly that they may sell to advantage.

Your Parmesan is most excellent.

1721, May 7.—I am afraid Bob has had a good deal of trouble in his contest. But one may safely say he would have had much more had he submitted to the insolence of his adversary.

It is now said we shall have no opposition in our county election. The Duke of Chandos, upon his new alliance, has brought over the Marlborough interest to his nephew Perrot. I know not how the Whigs will take it, they can do nothing without it, nor could they have done much with it.

I heartily rejoice with you for the news of poor Lord Carmarthen's recovery. I pray God he may make the proper use of the longer time that is allowed him here. But he has used that poor body of his so unmercifully, that I am afraid he cannot hope for any long time.

Postscript. I believe Dr. Middleton is generally right in supposing Bentley has no manuscripts but what have been collated before, but Bentley has had one collated which never was, I believe, made use of before, and the most ancient now extant ; and if Walker says true, will be of great use. An account is given of it at the end of Lamy's " Harmony," in the Appendix. I am amazed that Mills had it not collated. That " Harmony " was published many years before Mills' Testament.

1721, May 9.—I am going to my poor villa to-morrow for a little air. If the weather does not force me home again I believe I shall stay a fortnight or perhaps three weeks.

I am heartily sorry for poor Tom Vernon, I had a kindness for him ever since I came acquainted with him, upon drawing up the answer to your father's articles. If what he did were excusable in any one, it was in him. I am sure it might better have been excused than what Ruffe said for Aislaby in the

House of Lords. I am sorry this should happen on the Tory side.
The Whigs would have managed such a point more dexterously,
and not have punished it if discovered so severely. I believe
that has no place in their catalogue of sins.

Postscript. We are here at present full of noble " cockers."

1721, May 16.—I can hold no longer. I must enquire how you
and my Lady and Mrs. Margery do. I am here in a perfect
solitude, and find I can be easy enough in my ignorance
of the state of the rest of the world, public and private.
But my thoughts will be going to Dover Street, and
cannot be easy when they return without any account
of them. It is some step towards happiness for a man
to know what it is that has hold on him, and what he sits loose
to. And more still to know that those to which he is most
attached are those which he has most reason to value. But I
think a man can be assured of this by nothing but his own
experience of the want of them. You see my state ; it is in your
power by two lines to make it as happy as I desire it to be. And
if you will direct them for me at Mr. Thomas Smith's at Lamborn
they will come safe to me.

I find by the Bishop of Chester that you ventured to the school,
when you heard Ruffe would not be there. What is the state of
that poor place ? As miserable, and as little likely to be put
upon a better foot, as the nation itself.

I find by what I hear of reports from the public prints, that
the remission of the seven millions has had the issue I always
thought it would, of sinking stock instead of raising it. What is
to be done next ? Do they pretend to have any other resource?

1721, May 24. Little Shefford.—I must wait for the particulars
of Ruffe's gaining his cause, till I see the Bishop. But I hear in
general that it was through the Attorney's jockeying, and the
desertion of some Scotch peers. And no one that has the least
knowledge of either of them can be surprised at any treachery
from any of them. Upon the whole I believe Ruffe will find he has
lost more than he has gained. The point I was more concerned
for is gained ; his treacherous correspondence is now as clear as
sunshine.

I know not any thing that has happened to me of late that has
so truly grieved me as my missing of my godfather. I had left
it in charge with Neddy to send a messenger over to me the
moment that he should hear any thing of his coming. And I
had resolved to return the moment I had notice of it, though it
had been at midnight. But my godfather's consummate prudence
frustrated all my precautions. Could he have prevailed with
himself to have dispensed with a little of that, and to have let us
know a week before when he designed to call at Oxford, I had
avoided the misfortune I have had.

I hope you have a better opinion of me as a parish priest than
to think I would leave my parish before Whitsunday, though the
Bishop of Chester is at Oxford.

1721, June 4.—I have been with the Warden [of All Souls], and have had what account he can give me. They agreed, he says, in the gross with Thornhill, for both pieces of painting, and entered into no particulars with him. For the painting over the altar, Thornhill had 250*l*., but then Thornhill was at the charge of putting up the frame of boards, lath and plaster, on which the painting is. The painting of the roof is done upon canvas, stretched upon frames. For those roses, and for new painting the figures on the walls, and the two vases, Thornhill had 260*l*. 10*s*. But the old gilding of the buttresses of the beams that support the roof was fresh and wanted not to be renewed. Had that been to have been done, it would have come to much more. This is all the account I can get. I asked particularly if they had computed their charge by so much a foot or a yard, in either piece of painting. The Warden said no, but that they had agreed in the gross with him. If you want the dimensions, or anything else, let me know in your next.

Neddy saw his father safe as far as Morton in Marsh.

1721, June 18.—I agree with you in your reflection, only I would improve it a little. They should be scratched with scorpions and not with briars. I have been amazed on that account at the management of some men. But they can as little use, as create, opportunities. They have acted like men in pay. Perhaps they are so. But if I mistake not much, the thing itself admits of no cure. After all our tinkers can do, they will leave the kettle in as bad a condition as they found it.

I have had a hint, as though Lord Carleton was to be chief minister. Do you think there is any ground for it? I shall be amazed if one in his circumstances would meddle with such as are in ours.

Neddy dined with me to-day; Brother Hammond is drinking the waters at Bristol, and I am alone on Sundays. After dinner I went to see your noble present of the arabs to him. I liked them so very well, that he had much ado to hinder me from carrying them off. I thought they might appear to more advantage in my hall than in his room.

1721, June 23.—I have one secret that I can let you into. When South Sea stock was fallen, the Company itself took off the greatest part of the Attorney's stock at 600*l*., some was left in to keep up a show as though he had not sold. You see now the reason of his concern for them, and he had from the Government all the money that he put in there. It is a pity but these things were more known.

I suppose the Lord Chancellor's visit last week to Ruffe is no secret in town. He did it with great reluctance, but higher powers obliged him to it.

Postscript. Walpole has been to visit Ruffe, and S[underlan]d and Lord T[revo]r have been there together. Carleton, who is to come in play, is often in close conference with him. If all this does not open the eyes of the Tories, they must have a *gusta serena* in them. It is plain he is in the secret of the new scheme, whatever it is. I suppose he has engaged to bring in a party of the Tories to it. I have heard that some of the most warm were doubted of. I mean no less a man than W[yndha]m.

1721, June 25.—I must beg pardon for a mistake I made on Friday. It was Carteret, and not Carleton, who is in close and daily conference with Ruffe. Bob is under such resentment to Carteret, for the treachery with which he dealt with him, that he seems resolved to refrain from common civilities to him.

I pray God send you good news from Brampton, we could spare one lady there, but not your aunt. I have had a sweet epistle - from old Tudway, in which he desires me to recommend his duty to your Lordship. He seems to take me to have an interest in your Lordship to which I have no title, nor the impudence, I hope, to pretend to. I have just now the favour of your Lordship's. I cannot but be amazed at Lord Car[marthe]n's accepting.

Postscript. What is the Attorney disappointed in? He was talked of for Privy Seal. The Tories will find themselves most rarely bubbled. What junctures have they lost, and would do so again, had they as many more, under their present conduct. They will be the most contemptible set of men in the kingdom.

I hear Sir William W[yndham] is not to appear again for Somersetshire should there be a new Parliament. It would be to no purpose. Nor your cousin Palmer for Bridgwater. But Palmer talks of putting up for the county, but it is supposed can make nothing of it.

1721, June 29.—I heartily grieve with you for the news you have had from Brampton. I shall not pretend to say anything of her to one who knew her so much better than I can pretend to. May we all live so as to meet her again where I doubt not she is. Your uncle's loss will be easier as to the care of his family by his having so excellent a sister to supply his wife's place in that point.

I hear there will be more alterations, but I am of your Lordship's opinion, that all talked of are not possible. Nor can I see of what use those which are to be made will be, but only for those who come in to scrape a little. And there cannot be much gleaning after the late general plunder. I am afraid no change of hands can make those who are undone insensible of it.

I have had a letter to-day from Mr. Covel. He is finding out an office for me for which I am in no way qualified. I perceive your Lordship and he are not yet quite agreed upon the price of his knick-knacks. He invites me to see them, and says he would submit to my mediation and determination in that affair. I shall thank him for his kind offer, which I should readily accept of were I within reach, but shall let him know that my taste is not exquisite enough for me to pretend to judge of the value of such things.

One Franks of Merton, a clergyman whom possibly you may remember, who had Wood Eaton, and the fine cure of Gam Gay (Gamlingay) near you from that College, is thrown into the castle here for debts by his adventures in the South Sea ; and Painter, the late Rector of Exeter's daughter, has lost 1,200*l.* which her father left her, and is gone to service into Duke Chandos' family. I am afraid we shall every day hear of more of these instances.

1721, July 2.—My Lord Oxford will certainly be much concerned at your aunt's death. If I understand him right such a domestic affliction will sit heavier upon him than an impeachment. But the concern he will be in for your uncle, and his endeavour to comfort him, will make him suppress his own grief as much as he can, and help to divert it too. How different are our fates in this world! That which is so real an affliction to your uncle would be as real a comfort to my good master.

My neighbour Mrs. Rowney is under no little concern that she had not an opportunity of paying her duty to my Lady this winter. She had been preparing a piece of her own work, of which she had designed to beg my Lady's acceptance. I have comforted her as well as I can with hopes of better luck next winter.

To-morrow the Bishop of Durham completes his fifty-first year since his consecration. They say no English bishop ever was so long a bishop except Bourchier, Archbishop of Canterbury, who was fifty-two years bishop. Many of our Heads go over to-morrow to solemnize the day with him, and they are to appear in their Doctors' formalities and he is to receive them in purple velvet.

Hall of Queen's has married John Hudson's widow and she has given him money to take his doctor's degree. Behold the power of a woman! It has drawn a hermit [out] of his cell, that was proof against every thing else.

1721, July 9.—I have sent your Lordship as I promised a catalogue of the few Travels which I have. I believe there are scarce any amongst them but what are in your collection. I have met lately indeed with an account of two collections of Travels which are not as I remember in your collection, nor did I ever meet with or hear of them anywhere but in a collection of several · pieces of Mr. Locke printed at London, 1720, 8vo. In that piece called " Some thoughts concerning reading and ·study for a gentleman," p. 241, there is mention of a

Relation des Voyages en Tartarïe, &c., le tout recueilli par Pierre Bergeron. Paris, 1634. 8vo.

Le Grand Voyage des Hurons, situées en l'Amerique, par F. Gab. Sayard Theodat. Paris, 1632. 8vo.

Mr. Bridges and Bateman the bookseller are in town. They were with me last night and Tom Heron [*sic,* Hearne ?] was so very gracious as to come along with them, where your Lordship's health was drunk in the first rank of the *Literati.*

· 1721, July 17.—I find all your Lordship hinted about Ai[slab]y proves true. No doubt it will have the effect you suppose. I admire our great men, they act with a just contempt of the resentments of all concerned. This is a rare job for the Attorney, according to his own heart's desire. I may suppose that he is not as squeamish as Rosse was. No doubt he finds his account from the person concerned, as well as from those to whom he does journey work.

I hear B[olingbro]ke is not to be included in the act of grace, though he was once promised that he should. They still promise that he shall [have] the King's pardon. That, as the Attorney says, will reach only to life, but not restore either honour or estate. He must be very low if he can submit to come home upon those terms.

We in the country do not like the making of the malt tax a fund for a lottery. We are afraid it tends to the mortgaging of it at another time, for more than one year.

The present proceedings do not seem to me to tend either to a new ministry or a new parliament.

1721, August 5.—The horse-race which is in the beginning of the week at Oxford has obliged me to defer my return thither for a few days. But I shall be there again, God willing, on Thursday next, but I am afraid my·stay will not be long; for I have a strong impulse upon me, which I know not yet whether I can resist, to take a journey into Herefordshire.

I find the French papers have transcribed out of the English the news of a match for my dear young mistress. I have had many questions asked me about it, but I could very truly answer that I knew no ground for it.

The Attorney is now *rectus in curia*. We shall soon see whether he will have what he has earned so dearly. He seems to have left his friend B[olingbroke] in the lurch. Great promises were made, which surely might have been performed if the Attorney would have employed his interest for any one but for himself.

1721, August 10.—I believe your Lordship thinks I would deal seriously with you and not presume to recommend any servant to you, much less a chaplain, that I did not think every way proper for you. But if you look over England I do not think you will find one more fit for your purpose than Tom Thomas. He has those parts of learning, I mean the mathematics, which will be of great use to your Lordship in many of your affairs; nor should such a family as yours be without one well skilled in them. He will be a very good assistant or deputy to the great Mr. Wanley. But his learning though good is by no means the chief qualification for the post for which you design him. His temper is chiefly to be considered, and I know not one in the world more particularly fitted by that to live in so great and so good a family as your Lordship's. He is not yet in orders, but, if you are in haste, soon can be, and will go on purpose to Chester to get orders, I dare say, if you should desire he should come to you before Michaelmas, when the next regular ordination is.

I hope my friend Mr. Gurwood has left your Lordship upon a valuable consideration.

1721, September 5. Eywood.—*Post varios casus, post mille pericula, tandem venimus ad Patriæ sedem*, but could I have imagined the roads had been near so bad as I found them, a coach and eight horses would not have tempted me to have ventured. On Friday night your uncle's chariot met me at the Hundred House; and on Saturday night, tumbled and bruised by the wretched roads from the crown of my head to the sole of my foot, I reached this place. I received orders at the Hundred House from your father to go to Eywood, and not to come to Brampton. I was told he would meet me here, but I hear nothing of him yet. Your uncle goes over to-day to Brampton, but positively refuses me to go with him. He says he will bring your father here to-morrow. There is some mystery in this which I am not to be let into. All that is told to me is that your father has a mind to come and spend some time here, but- that the old Lady has hitherto refused to come. So my being here is to be made use of as a pretence for his coming, and for desiring her to come along with him. If this be true, and the only reason why I am not allowed to go to Brampton, the poor man is put to hard shifts for gaining his own innocent purposes.

1721, September 13. [Eywood.]—I thank your Lordship for the honour of yours which I received here. Your father came not to us till Thursday last. Next day came Baron Price and stayed till yesterday. I have had no discourse yet alone with your father, and I believe I shall have little. Though he says he has as much to say to me, and I suppose when my boots are on to be gone I shall be told that he wants much to speak with me. He gets strength every day. Were he where he could have proper advice, and be tolerably easy, I doubt not but he would soon be as well as he ever was in his life. By what he has dropped to me, and by what I learn from your aunt, he designs for the town, though I perceive your uncle is against his moving now. As well as he was last year, I hear your uncle takes the credit to himself of hindering him from coming up last year, but this betwixt ourselves. If I have opportunity I shall very freely speak my mind. I have left the friend I called on in my way hither in the utmost disposition your father himself could wish to concur with him in every thing. I have just had a hint from your father of some private transactions of your brother-in-law, and I perceive he is nearly concerned at them, and well he may. I must own that would have been the last thing I would have suspected.

Postscript. The book you mentioned against the Bishop of Chester can never be [by] Kennett. It is the product of Grub-street or some madman's.

1721, September 24. Little Shefford.—I bless God I am safe at my own hut again, but surely there are no such roads in any part of the world as in Herefordshire. If ever I could pretend to any merit from my good master it is upon this occasion. I defy any in the world, but himself or your Lordship, ever to induce me to go those roads again. I am amazed that I have returned with all my limbs sound. At the very top of the highest hill in Hereford-shire, in the place where there are precipices on each side, as the little captain was shewing me the way to Ross, my horse's heels flew up upon the rock and he came flat upon the ground with me, but I bless God I had no hurt. At Stoke I met your aunt Charleton and her wise husband. As I entered Ross I had an honour I very little expected. The people took me for their new bishop.

I thank God I left your father getting strength daily, I wish he may be prevailed with not to defer his journey till the weather and roads will make it more hazardous for him than it is at present.

I met here the account of the Bishop of Durham's death. No doubt that See will be supplied as well as Hereford has been. My godfather was positive that Duke Chandos by proper methods would prevail for his brother. I was humbly of opinion that the usual methods would not be allowed to take place in that case. I proved to be in the right, but none of us imagined the person who has it would have been pitched on. No doubt Ruffe will put in for Durham, as he did for Winchester, but I cannot think he will prevail.

1721, September 30.—I wrote to your Lordship again last Sunday, by the first opportunity after I arrived here, and before I had heard of poor Mr. Prior's death. I heartily [feel?] with your Lordship for the loss of so dear a servant to you, and bewail my own loss of a very ingenious friend. Neither this nor any other nation as far as I know, has any one of equal talents to him. Poetry is gone with him. The rest of the pretenders to it are but scribblers. He had signs indeed of weak lungs, but I did not think he had actually been in a consumption, but I have not yet heard of what particular illness he died. He had the last satisfaction he could be capable of, in dying with one who had been so noble and true a friend to him as your Lordship had been.

I go for Oxford again next Thursday. There has been a sad mortality this summer. I am afraid the succession of B[ishops?] is not likely to be better in its kind than that of Poets.

1721, October 20.—Last night I received a packet from Eywood, the enclosed were in it, and another from your aunt. But in case you were gone, I was ordered to burn your aunt's letter. If I may judge by Ned's letter, the purport of all was to press you, since you were so far on your way, to come on to Eywood. I have answered for you that they could not well expect that such a thought should come into you, whilst you expected every post to hear that Lord O[xford] had fixed the day for his journey to town. I perceive your father is still at Eywood, and that your uncle has no thoughts of stirring yet. Whilst he stays he will not let your father move. I am sorry for it. If the journey is not quite laid aside, it will be too late I am afraid either for his health or any business.

1721, October 23.—I wrote on Sunday last a pretty home letter to Ned; I desired him to show it to your aunt and his father. I know not how it will be taken, but I have guarded as well as I can against resentment. I pretend not to tell my own thoughts but other men's, that all suppose your father is kept against his inclinations by your uncle's importunity. And I ask, if anything fatal should happen, as it is likely it may in another winter, how your uncle would bear to have his brother's loss imputed to him, though he should know there were no grounds for it. I hope your Lordship will write, as you said you would, immediately to your uncle, to desire him earnestly to press your father not to lose the opportunity of this mild weather for his journey.

I am afraid you will not find poor Prior's estate as free from incumbrances as you thought it was. I hear from Agatha that my namesake, Frank Stratford, has a claim upon Prior for 1,495l. If this should prove a legal debt it will take place of all money legacies, and the special legacies, such as are left to you, will be safe, yet Mr. Drift and Madam Cox must submit to deductions if there is not enough besides to answer it.

[1721,] October 29.—I have heard from Ned; they were much concerned that their letters did not come to you before you left me. He says your father was very uneasy at the disappointment of not seeing you. I guess by that there are no thoughts of coming up soon, if at all. I perceive my letter galled somebody—as they please, *Liberavi animam meam*. If your father stays a few weeks longer, I shall never expect to see him more.

You will hear by the prints, before this can come to you, that the great lady [Marlborough] carried the election at Woodstock—it was carried by twelve. There were sixteen, twenty, guineas a vote. After all she had lost it if there had not been as usual great mismanagement on the other side.

The Viscount [Harcourt] has got 600l. of the King and 300l., some say 400l., of the Prince towards building Worcester College. I think this is an instance of power as well as favour. He has been made easy, you may guess which way. He went up to town on Thursday in good humour. He pretends to be positive that the Parliament will be dissolved in February.

1721, November 1.—I am glad you have fresh assurances of your father's health. It will I doubt not be for his health, though not of much use I believe as to any other purpose. All the business of the session will probably be over before he can be there. An opportunity was lost last winter that probably will not be to meet with again, and will be a just punishment on the Tories, if by screening S[underland] they have put themselves out of all hopes of ever recovering the game.

It is now said, there will be a new Parliament, and with such confidence, that I know not what to say to it. But I am afraid it will be such as the present is. There was some bickering lately betwixt Shippen and Walpole. When it was over Walpole came and sat by Shippen and said, "Will, you

are a happy man than can speak your mind." Shippen
answered, "Robin, why do not you do so, you can afford to do
it better than I. But shall we have a new Parliament as you
pretend?" Walpole replied "You must have one, this is worn out,
I am quite tired of it, but I hope soon to leave you." The last
words were supposed to relate to his going into the House of
Lords, he being said to have in his pocket a patent to be
Earl of Walsingham.

Your old tutor is as you supposed much elated with his new
honour, but knows so little how to manage it that there is
danger of his being mad with it. I keep at a due distance out
of harm's way, but he has had bickerings with the Bishop of
Chester in the Chapter and out of it. To-day was a gaudy,
when the undergraduates bring verses to us at our table to
desire a gaudy. The Bishop by chance observed to him that in
the title they had omitted Doctor of Divinity and Sub-Dean and
said "this is only to plain Tom Terry." He took this as a
designed reflection, and set into a violent passion openly at table,
and said he would not be insulted, especially now in the Dean's
absence—meaning I suppose since he was proxy—that he could
say things upon the Bishop, but he must not; the Bishop had
privilege; he should be punished, if he said what he could—
meaning I suppose the danger of *scandalum magnatum*—and at
this rate he went on, though he saw the whole table in
confusion.

G. Clarke desires me to tell you, and so does the Warden of
All Souls too, that there is only one copy of Jerome in the
Savilian archives. There is another in the Bodley Library.
Mr. Wanley said there were three, and, as I understood him, two
of them in the Savilian archives. If there is another, I suppose
it is in the Bodley archives. Pray enquire this of Mr. Wanley.

[1721,] November 6.—Neddy says your father leaves Eywood
this week—' say and hold '—and that he [Lord Oxford] will go
to town as soon as he has notice that a house is taken for him.

I find by my letters that poor Prior's will makes a noise in
town much to his disadvantage. Some malicious fellows have
had the curiosity to go and enquire of the ale house woman
what sort of conversation Prior had with her. The ungrateful
strumpet is very free of telling it, and gives such accounts as
afford much diversion. You know I suspected such things.

You say nothing to me of my namesake's letter to your Lordship
about his claim of a debt from Prior. As far as I understand the
case, my namesake has a very equitable claim, at least to that part
of the money which he paid down for Hales's share. It was at
that time a mighty service to Prior, and if it had not been paid
then, the whole intrigue of that stock jobbing would have broken
out, and have blown up Prior. I gave you notice I remember
in your little room at York Buildings of this very co-partnership,
but you would not then believe it.

The election at All Souls was carried on Friday for Mr. F.
Gwyn's son by a great majority of six voices. It is a great blow
to Harrison and his party.

1721, November 10.—The entertainment of one *Principe* of the *Literati* is surely a sufficient excuse, if you could need any for not writing to such a poor *homuncio* as I am. But what could bring our friend Mr. Bridges to Cambridge? Can that place afford any materials towards the history of Northamptonshire?

A sad accident happened here this week, one Ward, a senior fellow of Oriel, was found on Wednesday morning, in a chamber there not his own, but of one he had the use, shot through his head. He had been out of order sometime in mind and body, he was supposed to have done it in the night time. He was a very honest fellow, and designed for Provost, if the present [one] had gone off. Bowles the librarian is playing the same part in that society your tutor does in ours. He has offered himself to the Whigs there, but they won't receive him. Upon changing sides too, he has changed manners and taken up those of the Whigs, and keeps a wench here pretty publicly. That is somewhat new in this place, nor do I remember any instance of it before but in J. Keill, and he was forced to cover her with the name of a wife.

It is said the new Parliament depends upon the reports that will be made from the west, of what may be hoped for there. Ros. and Vincent are gone down to try what they can secure.

1721, November 13.—All the salaries of the judges of Wales as well as England were augmented at the beginning of this reign except Mr. Jeffries'. His salary is now ordered to be augmented as well as the others, and the arrears to be paid him from the time the others were augmented. This is said to be procured without his privity, by his friend the Viscount; he seems very uneasy at it, but it is thought he will take it. More of this when we meet.

1721, November 20.—I am afraid we shall have a disturbance in this place. Harrison and his party now canvass openly for a sorry fellow, Dr. King. Tim Thomas can give you an account of him. The design is only so far as yet appears to throw out G. Clarke.

We are like to lose one of the honestest men we have here, the poor Master of Balliol [Baron]. He is very ill of a rupture of an uncommon largeness, and has a dropsy, the jaundice, and a mortification too with it. Old Charlett seems to 'pick up his crums,' and I hope will get over this winter.

I have a most kind epistle from my worthy friend Dr. Tudway.

1721, November 24.—You to be sure have earlier notice than I have had, that Sir T. Powis's house is taken for our friend. I like the house and situation very much; but now that excuse is removed, I wish he may not take some months to settle things in the country before he can leave it. By mine of Wednesday last we were still at Eywood.

Postscript. My respects to Mr. Cæsar and the most excellent Calphurnia. Ruffe is doing everything possible to regain credit with old friends. He enters warmly into all opposition that is given. He knows he shall be despised by the others if they see he is not trusted by old friends. I do not find that he can yet gain ground.

1721, December 2. [London.]—I hope you and my Lady are safe again at Wimpole, as I am in town. But I hope your own air agrees with you better than a strange air does with me; I am afraid I have got the usual blessing of the town, a cold. I lodge in Westminster in Stable Yard at Mrs. Broughton's, the brick house that faces the gate that joins to the College chamber.

I had a letter last night from our friend in Herefordshire, he says he is in good earnest going home to dispatch every thing for his journey as soon as possible. He has been pleased to let me know the too sad reason he has had for deferring his journey so long. But no doubt your Lordship has had a fuller account of that than I have, or I should have sent you what I have.

Walpole has been ill. It is said he is now past danger; his illness has deferred the project of the engraftment, which he is resolved to push through the Parliament though the several companies should refuse to agree to it. His project is to aggrandize the Bank by it, and by that to govern the other companies, and consequently the whole kingdom. All wise men are of opinion that it will immediately sink the South Sea Company and ruin the others too at last. There will be a violent opposition to it. There is no doubt in these parts of a new Parliament, and it is said the opposition between the two ministers is greater than ever, and that the great struggle will be betwixt these two parties, and that each of them would choose rather to see a Tory in any place, than a Whig of the other party.

The Viscount's pension is no less than 5,000l. per annum, and he earns it dearly. He has now pulled off the mask, and votes openly in every vote with his masters. Lord W[harto]n says that Lord Cowper is at the head of the Tories and Lord H[arcour]t at the a—— of the Whigs.

1721, December 6.—The reason of detaining your father was to break a very scandalous match for your cousin Ned, in which your worthy uncle had engaged himself, upon the hopes of a mighty fortune. Your father, in his letter to Mr. Thomas, says it would have been the ruin of the family. In his letters to the Bishop of Chester and to me, he says it was unmeet in all respects, but his dear brother happened to be entangled in it by the prospect of a great fortune. He says he has put an end to it, but with great difficulty, and that it required a good deal of management. It was some great creature that was I believe as disagreeable in person and humour as in blood. For I find Ned had the utmost aversion to it, though he writes as becomes a son, and says his father's affection to him began it, and his tenderness to him at last put an end. Both your father and Ned refer me to our meeting for particulars, but both enjoin me with the utmost strictness not to take the least notice to his father that I know any thing of it. I can only perceive in general that it was very scandalous, much pressed by your uncle for the sake of money, and that the whole family have been in the utmost fright about it and abhorrence of it, and have with great difficulty brought your uncle off of it. But this has not been the only mischief that has happened by it. Your father by his delay in the country has lost a juncture, which I know not whether he will recover. Mr. Bromley had come up by your father's desire to meet him. Sir William Wyndham and those who were supposed to have headed a party in opposition to your father, now make their court entirely to Mr. Bromley, and as he has declared he will act with no man but your father, had your father been on the spot, I believe all old breaches had been made up by this time, and Mr. Bromley had brought the whole Tory party once again under your father. But your father having failed Mr. Bromley, he is going into the country again next week, and I cannot say whether there will ever be so fair a juncture again for it. As to affairs here, I find it still doubted whether there will be a new Parliament, though all the ministers swear still that there will.

Walpole's heart is set upon the engraftment, and Sunderland too comes into it, which is a proof to one that the pretence to a quarrel betwixt them two is a juggle. But I am told by those who should know, that the South Sea will never be brought to consent to it. In that case it is supposed Walpole will ram it down them. That may be done, but it will be a hard case.

No one seems to doubt but that the new Parliament, if there be one, will be to the Court's mind. The counties are most of them compounded already.

We are going to bully Portugal with a squadron, in a case in which they certainly have the right.

The Lords too go on to put questions about the debts of the navy and treaties, and are always baffled by 60 to 21, but they still protest and many good speeches are made.

Lord Wharton has left the Tories and returned to those from whom he came, and kissed the King's hand yesterday. The Viscount now votes in every question with the Court.

1721, December 12.—Your sister Kinnoull, with all those 'bearns' that are with her, is ordered by her Lord to follow him to Kinnoull, and is now I suppose on the road thither. She, poor Lady, writes to your cousin Popham that she hopes to see her still within six weeks. But Mrs. Bateman, from whom I have this, is of opinion that it is with a design to leave her and her children there, and to send those who are there to her. I must own I agree with Mrs. Bateman, who told me further that she was sure it was his design when he left this town. I wish you may ever see your sister again.

Here is a mighty struggle in the city at the ballot for and against the engraftment. The Court exert their utmost strength, and omit no means possible to carry it for an engraftment. But the ballot ran last night against it, and it was thought would do more so to-day. The ferment is great. Many suspect the present directors as much as they did the last, and are as angry with them. It is certain that most of them go entirely into the Court measures. Mr. Walpole's fate is supposed to depend upon the issue of this ballot, nor is that the only consequence that is expected from it.

Mr. Bromley left this place yesterday, he would have stayed
longer if I would have undertaken that he should have seen his
friend here before Christmas. But I have burnt my fingers far
in that already, and more than I will ever do again. I durst not
venture to give any further hopes of that nature.

1721, December 14.—Your Lordship's of the 11th was delivered
to me yesterday morning. I fancy by it that you are not ignorant of the name of the person designed for our young friend. I
was referred for that to our meeting, but if your Lordship
knows it, I hope I shall not be kept so long in suspense.

I wish your Lordship had been pleased to let me know when
I may hope to see you in town. But you take not the least
notice of what I said to that point, by which I am afraid I have
as little hopes of seeing you here as your father.

I have been confined to my lodgings for three days by a cold,
and am disabled by it to furnish you with much news, though I
think there is but little stirring.

The ballot was carried against the Court by 178. No means,
no arts were omitted to have turned it on the other side. Many
expect there will be some strokes upon it and that Sunderland
will take this advantage to give a lift to Walpole. This I can
assure you, that though. all the rest of the Court were zealous
against the question yet some of the most intimate creatures
that Sunderland has, Harcourt, Bateman, and Daniel Poultney
(Pulteney) were for it. The Lords go to oppose and protest,
Cowper at the head of them, who has gained great credit by his
management.

Lord Wharton's return to the Court is no news to you. There
is much talk of terms which he made, but I am assured he sent
the ministry *carte blanche*. When he first appeared after his
reconciliation in the House of Lords, he told every one that he
designed to make the Bishop of Rochester his confessor, and he
did not doubt of satisfying the bishop that what he had done
was reasonable; and he went that very morning to the Bishop of
Rochester.

Ruffe himself finds that all the world distrusts him, and is
using all methods possible that either impudence or artifice can
practice or suggest to him to save appearances in some measure
to the world, and to seem to have some credit with his friends.

1721, December 19.—The fortune you mention was not so
great that it ought to have tempted our friend, where other
things were improper. He might without doubt have such a
fortune every day in the year for his son, but as your Lordship
justly observes the vicinity was the bait. *O si angulus ille
proximus accedat, qui nunc denormat agellum.* I see your
obligations to the tawdry Duke, and it is very just that you
should have such retribution from one whom some of your family
have served so much, when he so little deserved it. But if I am
not much misinformed, you will still have much worse usage
from him, and not only submit to it, but serve him too in points,
to the damage as well as discredit of your family.

All I converse with are still fully persuaded that there will be a new Parliament, and I cannot see why there should not. I think there is no doubt but they will have one to their purpose, and that will answer all objections and may do anything.

I hear your uncle joins with Sir Archer Croft [at Leominster], and that they are sure of throwing out Carswell [Sir Geo. Caswall].

I am now told that S[underland] had nothing to do in the answer to the South Sea, that it was left entirely to W[alpole] and written all in his hand, as well as the contract with the Bank was. It is certain he has the odium of it, which grows very strong in the city. It is said he too is very bold still, and says he will force the engraftment on them. But he looks wretchedly, and many think him as uneasy in mind as in body. He is gone into the country to-day. Many still fancy this affair will end in his dismission.

Some things have happened at a new opera which have given great offence. It is called *Horidante*. There happens to be a right heir in it, that is imprisoned. At last the right heir is delivered and the chains put upon the oppressor. At this last circumstance, there happened to be very great and unseasonable clapping, in the presence of great ones. You will hear more when you come to town.

1721, December 21.—Sir Humphrey says that Walpole will be "gigged," and I find most people are of that opinion. It is supposed he will retire honourably to the peerage. The public cry designs Carleton for the Treasury, and Poultney for Chancellor of the Exchequer.

1721, December 23.—The cry continues as it did in relation to Walpole. Some say his health will never allow him to engage again in public business, and that his physicians have told him so. Others are still of opinion that though he could be able to go on with business, yet advantage will be taken from what has happened to give him an honourable dismission. It is said cabals are going on by the ministers, and some of the same nature that were talked of last winter, but I can warrant nothing of this to you.

Postscript. I have been so happy as to meet Calphurnia at the Bishop of Chester's, and shall make bold to wait on her without staying to be introduced by your Lordship.

Lord Rochester has a pension upon the Post Office for 2,000*l.* during pleasure.

1721, December 28.—The talk runs still upon Walpole's going out. The South Sea stock is risen to an 100 upon the hopes of it, and it is said it will be an 110 when he is out. But I find some, who have opportunities too of knowing how things run at Court, doubt whether he will go out.

Kennett's (Bishop) daughter is big with child, impregnated by his coachman, who owns her as his wife. Whether the marriage preceded or followed the impregnation, I cannot as yet say.

No news of our friend's having left Eywood. I fancy the thoughts of moving this way are suspended, till it be seen whether there will be a new Parliament or no.

1721-2, January 1.—You will have from Mr. Thomas an account of the new occasion of our friend's stay in the country. He says it would be determined of the last week, and then he would move, but I have done believing. I shall still doubt till I see. I confess he would put your election in Herefordshire upon the most proper and most honourable foot, if it will go there. But as the world is, it is straining the thing pretty far.

Things here, as far as I can hear of them, are in the same uncertainty they were. Some talk Carteret will be at the head of the Treasury, Pulteney, Chancellor of the Exchequer, and Compton and Treby the two Secretaries. Others with more likelihood, I think, suppose Walpole will keep his ground, and no alteration till the elections are óver, if then. Others still doubt whether there will be a new Parliament.

Letters were writ to some of both courts the last week to bid them to be on their guard, for that there were designs such a day against them. They are supposed to be a mere banter, but they put them into a foolish fright. Here are whispers as though a new plot would break out. Should any thing of that kind be broached, I suppose it is in order to continue the Parliament. Some talk it will be continued for the present for a year only.

This is the best trash I am able to pick up for your entertainment. I will relieve the scene a little with what the German doctor said, if you have not heard it already, who was to have been hanged for a rape, but had a pardon. When he was asked how he against whom the proof was so plain could get a pardon, he said the gallows be not for the German, but for the Englishman.

There will be a mighty opposition from the city to the building the new bridge a little above Peterborough House. It is thought it will be offered to the city to drop the Quarantine and the Bridge Bill, on condition that they will choose such members as the Court shall recommend. But such offers are likely to have little effect on them in their present disposition.

1721-2, January 2.—Harry Watkins is Secretary instead of King. The Chancellor told King he could keep him no longer, but to make his dismission less disgraceful gave him leave to resign. King still persists in canvassing against G. Clarke, but unless some very extraordinary charge should happen in the University, from what it was when I came away, it will be impossible for him to make anything of it.

It will be an utter shame to you in Cambridgeshire, where the Tory interest is so strong, if none are set up against the present members.

I shall be very glad of your duplicate Thevenot. I hope too you will bring up Covel's book with you. You promised me too the book of the gentleman who was with the King of Sweden at Bender. There was some other book too, of travels I think, but I have forgot the name. I want these books to help me to pass the evenings, when I am commonly alone in my lodgings.

1721-2, January 4.—It is confidently said, and I believe with good ground, that Walpole is relapsed, and dangerously ill in the country. It is thought too that Carleton will be prevailed on at last to come into the Treasury. S[underlan]d was never known to be so easy and so gay. Some are ill-natured enough to impute this to the ill condition of Walpole. I forgot to tell your Lordship that R. Morgan wrote a little while ago to know whether your Lordship would appear for Herefordshire. He pressed for an answer that he might be able to tell all others who applied to him, that he reserved a single vote for your Lordship.

1721-2, January 6.—Walpole is somewhat better, he is expected in town again to-morrow night. It is now said confidently that he will be dismissed honourably to the peerage. Compton is the man talked of to succeed him in the Treasury, but some still doubt of all this.

Postscript. Haldane has been named by the Court to a vacancy of the Lords of the Session in Scotland. The other Lords pretend that no one can be named without their approbation, and by a great majority have refused to approve Haldane. Argyll, Ilay and Stair are for the courts complying with them. Montrose and Roxburgh say if any one has been Advocate five years, he may be made a Lord of the Session without the approbation of the other Lords, and advise to insist upon the King's prerogative. And I am told it will be insisted on and Haldane crammed down their throats. I am told further that nothing is more likely to be resented nationally. Haldane was in the commission of the forfeited estates, and very unmerciful in the execution of it.

1721-2, February 23.—I pray God send you well to Wimpole, and continue you in the noble resolution you have taken. It is the only way to make you easy in yourself and as considerable as by your quality, your fortune, and your virtue you ought to be in the world. And is a slow, but sure, and the only way to retrieve the effects of some late management, and will effectually do it at last.

If your relation truckles he may, as you hinted in a former letter, hold longer than some think he will, but I doubt not but he will have a kick of the a—— at last. I pray for Robin on the same account you did.

I hear there are rods in p—— for us, that our wise Governor is got under the influence of Ruffe, and takes his advice how to manage us. But I believe he will make as little of the management of his College as he does of his private family. I have not heard this post from the Bishop of Chester, but your Lordship's hint is sufficient to let me know what is to be expected.

1721-2, February 28.—I hope this will find your Lordship easy, safe, and quiet at Wimpole. But though you are now in the midst of that you with so much reason chiefly delight in, your own admirable library, yet I hope you will converse more with figures than letters, and employ Morley more than Tim Thomas.

I am verily persuaded this will prove a providential event in your life, and the odd circumstances which for the present exclude you from any share in public affairs, by turning your thoughts entirely to your private ones, will be a sure foundation for your future ease and greatness.

We are told here that the Duchess has thrown up the cudgels at Woodstock, and that Wheat and Trotman will come in without opposition.

1721-2, March 2.—I told you that I had hinted my mind pretty freely in a letter I wrote to Neddy. I have heard from him since, but no answer at all to what I wrote, nor the least notice taken of it. I perceive they are deaf on that ear.

They say there is a great deal of money spent in the elections by a new sort of people that never appeared before. They spend out of their own pockets, and not upon the Court expense. They are generally, it is said, the new gentry, that have been raised by the late bubbles. No doubt such a set of men will be as mercenary as any other, but they will not serve without pay, and the ministers may be obliged to discard some of their old dependents, to make way for these new comers.

1721-2, March 5.—Neddy in his to me last week took notice that Lord O[xford] was still at Eywood, but gave no hint of any design to quit those quarters. But I fancy he will be moving upwards when he ought to have been going down, if he had been in town, about the time the elections come on.

The cudgels are thrown up at Woodstock. Clayton is put up by the Duchess at St. Albans.

I believe the little satisfaction you had too much reason to have in town has helped to give a relish to the country. I cannot blame you for being glad to be at present out of the way of questions and answers. But you must not expect to find every thing smooth when you show your face again in the world. I hear there are great grumblings at your not appearing for any place.

Postscript. I hear there is prodigious spending by way of ready money at Bishops Castle. They will only allow the great Duke one. The South Sea man puts up, I know not his name, who is resolved to outbid him for the other member, let him offer what he will.

1721-2, March 7.—Here is some whispering here at present, as though the Whigs of this place would go over entirely to King. I know not what to make of it. There is some ground I believe for it, but I can scarce think it will prove so; but if they do, they will not I am confident be able to carry it for him.

The impudence of these fellows here is prodigious. Harrison two days ago told an acquaintance of mine that his friend Doctor Stratford was staggered, that Lord Harley had set upon him earnestly for Doctor King, and the Doctor was at a loss what to do. My acquaintance was surprised, and said he would go and enquire immediately if it were true. I told him Lord Harley and G. Clarke were the two last men I had conversed with in town, at Lord Harley's house, and bid him judge by that of the truth of what Harrison said. I shall trouble you with a little news which is not of the growth of this place, because I am not sure that you will have it from other hands.

The news we had when I left you of the prevalence of your relation [Sunderland] is in the main confirmed to me, and I am assured it was at that time true and continues so, though the opponent has carried some things since.

The Viscount has been the great stickler in the matter of expunging protests and is said to have been the chief adviser of it. It is said he will be of the Cabinet, though I hear not yet in what post.

The most material is what I have from good hands. The Congress of Cambray, if it be opened, is not likely to be ended soon, at least not amicably, without we give up Gibraltar. The French and Spaniards are resolved to insist on that. Some fear they will insist too on Port Mahon.

1721-2, March 11.—We shall have all the foul play that is possible, but we must in spite of all they can do carry it by a great majority. But we desire our majority should be as great as we can make it.

You have your private reasons, no doubt, why you have resisted the importunities you have had to stand in the county where you are. But I cannot help wishing that it had been convenient for you to have appeared there. It would have gone far to have taken off all resentments for some transactions elsewhere, in that part of the world which had no immediate concern in them. It would have effectually have done it with every body, and in every place, as to yourself.

But all I can hear yet, the change is not like to be great as to the principles, though it may in the persons of the next Parliament. But it will be owing to the want of unanimity and concert among the Tories; I hear of many places where men might be chosen, if they could be prevailed on to appear.

1721-2, March 12.—I take the secret of some late transactions to be now out. Neddy tells me in a letter I had on Saturday that his father, on account of his health, had quitted his pretentions to Lempster. I suppose this is no news to your Lordship. I could not help telling him in my answer that it would have been kind to have let his friends know sooner, that they designed to withdraw from all public (*sic*). Perhaps some others would have done so too who were now engaged upon expectations and, as they might think, assurances of their joining with them. He tells me further that if our dear friend Lord Harley had come down he would certainly have been chosen. I could not help being a little warmer in my answer on that point. I told him that I was not let into the bottom of that affair, but that I believed your Lordship would have come if they from their quarters had given you any encouragement; that I not only thought it was your inclination, but believed too that you imagined your honour engaged in it;

that to all solicitations your answer was that you would stand
only for Her[efordshi]re; that you had run out of town to avoid
the confusion you were in, when questions were asked about that
matter. He says the Radnorians had pressed my godfather to
appear to be their knight, but that he seemed not inclined to
meddle with them. And no wonder, when he sees that no one
else of the family is to be in Parliament. I perceive poor Neddy
is not in the secret; he seems to intimate as though they were all
coming up soon, and it is high time to do so. If what I hear be
true, the country is grown too warm for them.

We must beg your Lordship to dispatch Tim to us on Monday
next. Our election is likely to be on Wednesday in Passion week.
Our mutineers give out that they will still persist; if they do
we must expect all the foul play possible, and we must use the
same precaution as though it were likely to be an even lay. I
believe it will be Tim's best road at this season to come by
Woburn.

1721-2, March 16.—I forgot to tell you that little Dartmouth
is gone up to London at the desire of your relation. Some of
the old pretences are still carried on, and hopes are given him
that he shall be taken in, but I think it not much matter how
this affair goes. If they banter him, his resentment can do
them no hurt; if they employ him, he can do them no service.

Twenty-six Scotch peers have met at Edinburgh, and engaged
upon honour to each other to choose no one who shall not first
upon honour declare that he will never vote for the Peerage Bill
as far as it relates to Scotland.

I believe the news I trouble you with hence is very stale
before it comes to you, but you should tell me if it is so, that I
may spare myself as well as you. A little scrub pamphlet to
allay people's resentments about the Quarantine Bill is Gibson
[Bishop of Lincoln]'s and is sent in packets all over England, to
be distributed gratis. This is very mean work that he submits to
for his hopes of London.

I hope on Saturday to hear that I may expect Tim Thomas
here on Tuesday.

There has been wise management at Westminster. Sir
Thomas Cross and Hutchinson are together by the ears, and are
advertising against one another. Does your Lordship design to
be at home again by the time that election comes on? If you
do, I hope you will vote for both of them. Reading has dealt
the most honourably of any borough I have yet heard of. They
shut their doors against Cadogan's brother·and another who
came with him, and declared that, though they starved, they
would not be bribed this election. They sent to two neighbouring gentlemen to come, and much ado they had to prevail with
them to appear, though they were to be chosen *gratis*.

The Bishop of Exeter [Blackburn] now at Exon, as he was lifting
up a sash window which flew up quicker than he expected, tumbled
out of the window, which was twenty feet high from a paved
court. But the proverb was on his side; he only bruised a
little one side of his head and shoulder.

1721-2, March 19.—When I told your Lordship what Harrison gave it out, about your Lordship's canvassing me for King, I hope you did not think that I had the least doubt of your respect to G. Clarke, or of your concern for us, but on the contrary that I mentioned it as an egregious instance of that fellow's impudence.

We shall have bustle enough I believe. They design to offer many votes, who have no names in any college books and have left the university many years ago. Perhaps our heads may be cloudy, but I daresay they are not more so than other persons' expressions are. I defy anyone to guess what they would be at by all they have said, and no doubt it was designed that men should not be able to guess at their meaning.

The little Captain's son is opposed at Hereford and likely to be hard set.

1722, March 21.—We heartily thank you for sending Tim to us, I leave it to him to acquaint you with what has passed at our election. There was a foolish opposition started against our City members, young Rowney and Sir John Walter, at ten o'clock on Monday night, by Counsellor Hawkins and young Wright. They polled seventy-nine out of twelve hundred voters and then threw it up. There is an opposition started up in Berkshire for the county by Grey Nevil; the election is to-day, but I cannot yet learn how it is likely to go.

I am heartily glad Sir J. Cotton puts up [for Cambridgeshire], and I should still be much more pleased if your county would have spirit to choose you, though you do not appear for it.

I hear there is great seeming intimacy between Townshend and Carteret. They affect to appear much together, and they have sent for the foreign ministers and told them that they shall certainly have the next Parliament at their command, and that they may write to their several courts that every thing will go smoothly.

The virtue of the town of Reading was occasioned by a sermon against bribery, preached by Reeves, a worthy man, put into that place by the late Queen's order. But the Court, it is said, will not permit such a bad example to be set, and money is scattered in such large quantities that it is likely to be too hard for the effects of the poor sermon.

The Bishop had his fall upon throwing up the sash to hearken whether the cathedral bells rung upon Rolle's and Drew's coming into town. Those gentlemen had been sent for by the citizens to oppose those who were set up by the Court. All the bells in town rung upon their coming into town except the cathedral bells.

1721-2, March 23.—I have to add to what Tim brought you that King applied to the Lord Chancellor, by Doctor Monro a physician in Greenwich, for his Lordship's interest in this place, and had a promise of it. King went over on Saturday last to the Lord Chancellor, who is now in the country, to thank him for the promise. The Lord Chancellor sent over hither on Monday and Tuesday Sir John Doyly and others who brought over for King four Whigs of Merton and about six of Wadham, whose names are now actually on the poll for King. His Lordship left his own chaplain, who is a commoner Master of our House, to vote as he pleased, because he said he heard his House was unanimous.

It was pretty remarkable that Meadowcourt of Merton, who informed against Wharton, and Wharton himself, both voted singly for King. The poll will be printed with proper observations, I will take care that your Lordship shall have a copy of it.

The election was carried in Berkshire for the two old members [Stonehouse and Packer] by above four hundred ; they had some hundreds more to have polled if there had been occasion.

There are three chosen at Abingdon, Hucks, Doyly, and Jennings. I know not which of them will be returned.

There was an opposition yesterday at Woodstock by Crispe and Clayton, but it was carried by fifty for Trotman and Wheat.

I have heard from Neddy that his father could not refuse the kind invitation he had from Lempster, though he had fully determined not to stand. I suppose there was solicitation by somebody else, as well as invitation from Lempster, that helped to change his mind. Ned is full of the opposition that is given to young [Foley of] Stoke at Hereford, where, as he says, the Tories put up one under pretence of opposing Africanus, but who is truly a creature of Coningsby's. Ned says it now appears how wise the measures were that were taken for the county. That you might have been chosen indeed, but the labouring oar would have been thrown on you in the county, as it is on young Stoke in the city. That now it is seen how prudent it was to insist, as was done, on a meeting before hand, &c. I have not taken the least notice of all these wise reflections in my answer. I perceive poor Ned is not let into secrets, but writes what papa dictates.

It is thought the election will go well at Coventry. There will be a right majority at Lichfield, but the returning officer, who was always thought a Tory and an honest man, has been bought, and will certainly return the others.

1722, March 26.—The prints and our friend William Thomas inform us that your Lordship at last appears for Cambridgeshire. I am heartily glad of it. I doubt not but they who have been so importunate with you to stand have taken care to make your election sure, as well as honourable. I cannot expect to hear from your Lordship in so busy a season, but pray desire Tim to let me know as soon as he can what the success is. May I hope to hear, when you are at leisure, whether anything from another part of the world helped to determine you to alter your resolution. I hope to hear that my godfather has complied with the invitation he has had from his old county.

We are in these parts in perfect quiet again, our own mutineers appear every day more and more to have been great scoundrels. We have proof that they offered money for votes, and pretended to engage the next parsonages that should fall in the university gift to those who would vote for them. There is a strange spirit stirring at Westminster, if it should be contagious, the Lord have mercy on some people.

1722, March 30th.—I heard last night from our friend in Warwickshire; he is wonderfully pleased that your Lordship appears where you do, and your uncle at Lempster. He enquires if I have seen a letter of Coningsby to the Corporation of Lempster. I have not heard of it but from him. I wonder Ned did not send it to me. At the same time I had a letter from the little Captain, he was just returned from Stafford. He says he had heard nothing of or from our friends at the other end of the county, since he left London. But he gives all for lost as to his son at Hereford. He complains loudly of the treachery of Hopton and Geers, who have put one Mayo there, a creature of Coningsby's, though they had given him solemn assurances that they would assist his son. He supposes your father might foresee better than others what these men would do, and seems to think that their present behaviour may be an excuse for your father's insisting on the terms he did with them. I find indeed by my last from Ned that this very use is made of what has happened at Hereford. Whether it was foreseen or no I cannot say, but it will be said now to be sure that it was foreseen. They seem to be laughing in their sleeve at Eywood, at the distress the little Captain is in at Hereford. Hopton and Geers by what I hear pretend only to put up Mayo in opposition to Africanus, but the issue of it is like to be the throwing out of little Stoke.

I am sorry I must tell you that poor brother Hammond begins to decline apace. I am afraid next winter, if he lasts to it, will set him hard. But this to yourself. I suppose now you will soon think of returning to town.

It was carried by the Mayor's vote against Cadogan's nephew at Banbury.

You will see by the "Evening Post" how poorly Erasmus [Lewis?] and John Dy—— are come off at Marlborough. I wonder who put them upon so foolish an attempt.

Postscript. I am told the Viscount, though he should have no place, will certainly be of the Regency. I shall not be sorry to see him in it.

1722, April 2.—I thank you for the account of your very honourable election, which Tom sent me by your order. I heartily give you joy of it. I wish we could have had accounts as much to our credit from other parts. But there must have been some strange management or we could not have been defeated with circumstances so much to our discredit. How could they possibly be so mistaken in their calculations? Treachery alone will never account for the odds betwixt 91 and 105. I am afraid the interest there is gone, as the other Auditor's too seems to be at Hereford, and in all likelihood both had been preserved entire not only in the county, but boroughs too, if the early offer had been embraced of putting up your Lordship with the little Captain. But then we were under [no] engagements to Africanus, and had thoughts of joining you with his son. There may be one fruit of the disappointment that has happened to both families. It may dispose them to be better inclined to each other, and to join against those who wish well to neither. At least it may check resentments that were rising on both sides, and hinder them from growing to an open breach. Who is to come into the town of Cambridge when Sir John makes his choice for the county?

Our election here for the county was to-day of the old members without opposition.

Ned tells me they have thoughts of a petition for Lempster, but the complexion of the new Parliament seems to give little encouragement to that.

I know not whether I told your Lordship that I am informed from a good hand that the Viscount will be of the Regency. I shall not be sorry for it.

1722, April 15.—Bowles was the person who took the poll for G. Clarke, and in whose hands the original bill was left, to be digested into that order and with those marks with which it is now printed. I suppose too he put it to the press, and corrected the copy. We do not apprehend here any mischief from the printing of it. They of Balliol are the persons who chiefly resent the printing, but their part, especially their Head's, was so foul, that it is fit they should be exposed for it. No one thinks the advertisement other than a sham. There is no fear of any account they can publish. King himself I believe will scarce show his head here again. I am credibly informed of a great load of debts and contracts on him. I am still of the same mind as to the success of a petition. What has the justice of any cause signified of late against a majority? Nor is the gentleman likely to meet with friends even from the same party he might most likely expect it. Besides some old grudges, there are fresh ones against him for being supposed to keep another person away. If he meets with any assistance from T[orie]s it will not be out of respect to him or his cause, but purely on your account. He has one thing indeed that may be of some use to him, the hatred to his antagonist.

As I am writing I receive the favour of your Lordship's. I am heartily glad the common miscarriage has had that effect I expected and hoped it would.

I thank you for putting me at ease about our friend Cæsar. I am satisfied to hear that your Lordship thinks him not to blame. I can wait for particulars till we meet.

It is no surprise to me that you hear nothing of our friend's coming up, he hates moving, and for aught I know may defer his journey till towards the end of this summer, supposing it possible for him to stay there. But if what the Baron said here was true, he cannot be at his own house. The negligence I mentioned to you when I had the honour to see you here, has made things much worse than when I was in those parts. The cry is very great. The other person, if he has the friendship he prétends, should show it in stopping this clamour, though it were without his friend's privity. I am heartily concerned, but I cannot be more concerned than I am amazed.

I am glad to find your Lordship seems to have any hopes of any good from this Parliament. It would be somewhat if we can be able to stand on our defence. *Quanquam O &c.* It grieves one to the soul to think that this mighty opportunity has been lost for want of concert and understanding amongst [us]. All considering men who have observed the disposition of the country are of that opinion. Management would have done it in a great measure, without money, or with very little. And that which would have been necessary would not have been felt if it had been levied amongst friends understanding one another in proportion to every one's fortune. More money has certainly been spent by particular men, though the game is lost, than would have carried it if [it] had been collected from all and laid out properly. But common sense was never the talent of our friends.

1722, April 18.—I have received the present of a book called "Jus Academicum." I suppose it is Dr. Colbatch's. I have not yet looked into it, but I doubt not but it is accurately done, coming from that hand.

The Viscount has lately refused our friend, Tom Rowney, a very slight ordinary kindness, which he asked of him. It goes to Tom's heart to meet with such a return to many faithful and expensive services which he has done for him for thirty years past, and in times when the Viscount very much wanted them. Tom's resentments at present are strong, I believe, and you will imagine I do not lie when I say I hope that this will occasion an entire breach betwixt them. The rest of the family are louder too than Tom. These men seem to think that no turn can ever come that can make them have occasion for their old friends again.

I am told from pretty good hands that our Governor is as weary of us as we can be of him, and that he will leave us as soon as ever he can, for a bare equivalent, without any advantage. But we are not likely to change for much the better. Who do you think is designed for us if the present scheme holds? That scandalous man Baker of Wadham, who is to go over with the King this summer. But keep this to yourself.

1722, April 21.—Your news [of Sunderland's death] was surprising, and is truly what Sir Humphry [would] call a stroke. It is obvious indeed to think all power may be thrown into his rival's hand, though you may have very good reasons for being of another opinion. My chief objection to what you think is, that they will be at loss for any other whom they can employ. This death may be worse for us in one respect and better in another. Church affairs can never be on so bad a foot as they were during his power. A few days will show us what consequences we are to expect. I should be glad to know any particulars of his death, and whether he showed any sense of religion ; I suppose not. I am afraid his death will throw a temptation in your way. I suppose his collection of books will soon be scattered. Here will be gleaning for my friend Mr. Wanley.

28493

I have heard from one who saw the Viscount since S[underland's] death that the poor man was inconsolable and in no little consternation. It is not impossible but I may have a visit from him this summer.

I have had a letter from Neddy full of joy upon the second defeat of Africanus, but still justifying the wisdom of their own conduct. He says what has happened will turn much to the interest of your family. I have told him with some freedom that all others I meet with, though friends to them, think quite the contrary.

1722, April 26.—I see by the "Freeholder," as well as by your Lordship's letter, that [Sunderland] had some form of religion at his death. But I cannot see for what reason men of his opinion, in which he was so open when he lived, as well as of his manners, should affect to act such a farce at that moment. The best that can be said is that possibly then they may have fears which they never felt before, and are willing to catch at any twig. But I see not how their confessors can think any few expressions of fear at that time a sufficient ground for giving them comfort, much less the sacrament.

I heartily wish Lord Morpeth well. By what I have heard of him he has many good qualities, which may possibly exert themselves more now his father-in-law is gone. He was not indeed always biassed by his father-in-law, but in some cases he might.

I hear Benson has played the fool in his visitation as Archdeacon in Berkshire. His speech was full of commendations, not only of the Government, but Governor too. He talked against popery, but he might have succeeded as well if he had preached up transubstantiation, as ————(sic). Such speeches can have but one end, to recommend the speaker to men in power, but they do as little service to a cause as they do credit to the authors. It is proper enough for a nobleman to understand architecture, but it seems beneath him to profess it as a trade. But perhaps the noble person that laid the first stone is a freemason. That has been an honour much courted of late by quality.

Postscript. I see to-day in a letter that though your Lordship and Dr. Freind were not at the laying of the foundation stone yet you both made a visit to Lord B[ingley?] that morning. For what reason, I pray? Did you think good manners obliged you to excuse yourselves to him for not attending him at the ceremony? If there might be some pretence on that account for Rob's going, I see not how there could be any for your Lordship's.

1722, April 29.—I am going on Tuesday for a little fresh air and retirement to my country hut; I shall be out I believe about a month.

We are told that Carleton is likely to have a great share in affairs. It will be a wiser step than I expected. The Viscount then will be kept still in pay.

Want of consent in the Scotch peers can never be pleaded again against the Peerage [Bill]. They have fairly given their consent by choosing those again who were for it.

1722, May 2. Little Shefford.—Your Lordship: and I do not differ. I can easily allow that at the last moment, the greatest libertines are most likely to have their fears. But I still wonder that they, and much more their confessors, can think a few acts of religious worship can at that time be of any service to them.

I have had a letter from Ned in which he talks of coming up soon, if others do not. By which I perceive that no one else has any thoughts of moving yet.

1722, May 12. Little Shefford.—I hope this will welcome you to town again. We have strange rumours here of the apprehensions and confusion that you are in there. If you lived where you could have as little certainty how things go, as I have here, you would not think a newspaper so dull a matter. But dull as it is, it may be of some moment now, and not be the only dull thing in the world that is so. We are told here, that one Muscovite begins to be afraid of another Muscovite. That is somewhat new in nature. *Feræ non nisi in dispar genus.* We hear too that the stocks have got a great alacrity in sinking. I cannot but congratulate all the friends I have that have any share in them.

The town of Reading, we are told here, is full of soldiers, and a camp marked out within two miles of it. They have the glory of being confessors.

Have you seen a book called the Miseries and Hardships of the inferior Clergy chiefly about London ? It is a notable book, but the author, we are told, is very profligate. But one of the same tribe was so spirited up by it, that lately in the cathedral of Winchester he preached very virulently against all other clergymen that had better preferment than he had. The Dean and prebendaries present sent the verger to him to tell him to come down ; but his assurance failed him not, and he went on. And he could not be silenced till the organs opened against him.

Be pleased to send any of those papers so dull to you, but comfortable to me, as I before desired.

Is the present hurly burly likely to hasten or retard your motion to Wimpole? I am afraid nothing can put another friend into motion.

Postscript. The "London Journal" informs me that your Lordship is about a purchase of books, that will amount to 10,000. I suppose this can only be Lord S[underlan]d's library.

1722, May 14.—I most heartily thank you for the favour of yours, and agree with you entirely in the reflection you make at the close of it. But we have been [more] "alarumed" in the country than you have been in town. My neighbours at Newbury believed heartily for two days together that 15,000 Muscovites were landed in Scotland. All I could say to comfort was, that they had a great way to go, and I hoped we should get our harvest in before they could reach us.

The story about Lord Sunderland's papers, is, as we country folk say, a very dark one. I am amazed that Lord Carleton should have that share he had in it.

I hear the Auditor writes that he will be in town next week, and bring Lord O[xford] with him. Does your Lordship hear anything of this? If it should be so, I shall leave this place sooner than I designed, but I fancy Ned will give me notice. If the Auditor had such a purpose, I believe he will alter it ; when he hears of the hurry in town, he will desire to keep out of harm's way.

1722, May 19.—I hope this will find you well at Eywood. I pray God it may find your father so too. What I always feared, a relapse by his stay where he could have no help, has in some measure happened. They must answer for it who for ends of their own have kept [him] in the country for two years, and gloried in doing it. By some particulars I have heard of his late relapse I perceive he had still great remains of strength in him, and had he been two years ago, or last year, where he could have had help, he would probably have been as strong a man as ever he was in his life. If it please God that he goes off, he is perfectly lost by staying where he is. Your good aunt foresaw this, when she told me in the garden that Lord O[xford] must go to town, and that no one would or should stop him. But she was mistaken it seems in the last part of her conjecture. How your father may be able to bear a journey now, I cannot say, but I think he should be brought up, though it were in a horse litter.

Postscript. Walpole lately made a visit openly to Ruffe. The Viscount a little before Lord Sunderland's death visited Walpole, by Sunderland's advice. The Viscount was to be Privy Seal and a Regent if Walpole would give way to it. The Viscount told Walpole that some persons apprehended it might be for his Majesty's service for him to be taken into it, and to appear openly in it. Walpole answered very frankly, that he did not apprehend it could be for his Majesty's service either now or at any other time.

1722, May 26.—I bless God that you have found things no worse, and I am glad that you are resolved not to trust to any promises of following you, but to bring our friend up with you. It is an amazing thing that he should be kept in such a condition as he has been for two years in the country. I find the physicians are of opinion that his case is paralytic. I am sure no time is to be lost in that. I hope any more fits may be yet prevented, since the late ones have gone off without help. Had he come up to town last Michaelmas, he would probably have escaped the touch he has had.

I shall be at Oxford next Wednesday.

1722, May 31. [Oxford.]—I returned to my headquarters yesterday. I am obliged to your Lordship and Ned for your concern for me, but I should rather attribute Ned's intermitting fever to the late fall of stocks than to his own concern for me.

As the stocks recover, I hope he will. I thank God I am at liberty, both in body and mind. Some of a different coat from from my own passed lately in sight of me, but I lay not directly in their road, though pretty near it. But one of my sphere and condition has as little reason to be concerned at their rumour of plots, as at the rise and fall of stocks. I have to do alike in both of them.

I am might glad that Lord O[xford] has found relief upon his purging, if that had been done under skilful direction immediately after that violent discharge he had, he would probably at this time have been a hale, hearty man. Nature then pointed out what was to be done. Never was there such an eruption which did not leave great dregs of itself behind it. And it is amazing that he was not forced up to town after that, in order to have his body cleared under proper direction; and that he should be permitted to stay where he is, and to let that humour get head again. I hope you will not be prevailed with upon any promises to leave him behind you.

As I write I receive a letter for Lord Oxford from our friend in the country. He tells me it is to compliment my Lord on his illness, and desires me to send it as I have opportunity. But I shall not send it by this conveyance, till I am expressly assured by himself that I may.

The story of the Viscount I had from honest Wainwright, and at the end of it he writes—I think I have very good authority for this. •

In a written news letter on Saturday last to our friend in the country was this paragraph. " Lord O[xford] is coming to town in a horse litter. His Lordship of late kept constant correspondence by letters with the last Earl of Sunderland." I send you this, as it was sent to our friend, that you may see what reports are flying. ,

A messenger has been to search several houses at Birmingham and, amongst others, two rich Quakers, but found no arms.

1722, June 2.—The war is commenced again at Westminster betwixt Ruffe and his Chapter about Battely's place, their late Receiver. Ruffe would have it for his son-in-law Morris. A great majority of the Chapter are for Battely's nephew. Ruffe upon this pretends to dispose of it by his own authority. No one so violent in this against Ruffe as his late friend Broderick. They mutually upbraid each other with ingratitude, but I have a story that will surprise you much more. Ruffe is making pretences to the good Duchess of Buckingham. I do not banter you. This is the report, and the belief too, of many in town. It comes to us from one of my own cloth, a dignitary and no fool, and who offered to lay ten guineas that it would be a match. I do not doubt but he is capable of such a thing, and I believe he has caressed Pope so much of late with a view of making use of him on this occasion, but I know not what to say as to the success. If I consider the lady and her character, I should think it impossible ; yet she dined with him last Monday at Bromley. The young Duke, the last Duke's natural daughter, Pope and Chamberlain came along with her. This in one of her quality and who knows so well how to keep her state, was an odd condescension to one who had not then been a widower a full month, if she designs no further favour.

Postscript. I had almost forgot to tell your Lordship that He[a]rne has published his Fordun and brought back his MSS. to me.

1722, June 5.—We hear Ruffe has been very uneasy upon the examination of Johnson, who was lately seized. He has another name of Kelly, but which was his true name, and which that he usually went by, I cannot tell. Ruffe had much dealing, as it is said, with this man, but the man behaved with great presence of mind, and has owned nothing that can be to Ruffe's prejudice. But there were some papers seized at Mrs. Barnes's, the woman where Johnson lodged, in which there was mention of a dog sent from France to some body in England. The woman upon examination was asked much if she knew any thing of a dog sent from France. She said she heard there was a dog sent to the Bishop of Rochester. By this it seems they have learned the cant name by which Ruffe goes in the letters. Carteret asked Johnson if, as he came from France, he did not stop at some place on the Kentish road. Johnson answered that he came up by water, but I suppose Carteret will be remembered for this question.

The quarrel goes on heartily about the Receiver. Ruffe has dropped his son-in-law and proposes another, for whom he thought he should [find] more inclination, but the Chapter stick resolutely to their first man. There are nine against him.

We hear nothing more yet of the plot. It is said they had the first notice of it from Sutton.. Some say they have the original memorial given in by Lord Lansdowne to the Regent. It is odd that one of his quality on the spot should give in a memorial. It is said that Churchill was sent to France, to desire that Lansdowne's papers might be seized, but was refused. Upon which it is said a Privy Seal will be sent over to require Lansdowne to come home. I believe they will not be much the richer for any thing of his that they can seize here.

1722, June 7.—I am told there is nothing in the enclosed [*missing*] but what I may venture by the post.

I hear further that in the papers lately seized, the person to whom the dog was sent pressed for a rising at the time of the elections, but a certain lord, whose name is not known opposed it.

It is said there is full evidence that 100,000*l.* has been collected and sent abroad.

Ruffe has now the dog that was sent.

1722, June 10.—I can now tell you the name of the dog which Ruffe has—it is called Harlequin.

It is said that by the accident of the dog, other cant names as as well as Ruffe's were discovered, but I cannot learn what they are.

I am entirely of your opinion as to her Grace, but the mufti of late has affected to talk much to all people of his vigour, and to let them know that he finds no alteration in himself from what he was twenty years ago. He carried down Chamberlain to his wife a little before her death. I doubt not but he took occasion to let Chamberlain know the state of his body, in hopes of conveying it by him to somebody else. But I wot well, the lady is too sharp to be put upon by such tricks in so serious a matter. But what I sent to you did not come to us alone, it is town talk. It was written to G. Clarke as well as to us.

The disposal of the Receiver's place for the share of the coal tax which goes to the repair of the Abbey is in the Dean of Westminster, the Chancellor of the Exchequer, and I think the Chief Justice. The salary is 50l. or 60l. per annum. Ruffe desired Walpole's consent to give it to his son Morris—a mean request. But it was to be a pretence for asking the Receiver's place to the College. Walpole positively refused it. Then Ruffe proposed one Wynne, a pupil and relation of St. Asaph, in hopes of bringing over St. Asaph by it from young Battely. Walpole agreed to that, but Asaph is not brought over by it. Walpole made a jest over the town of the conversation he had with Ruffe. It was chiefly to tell him how incapable he was made for business by his late affliction in the loss of his wife.

1722, June 14.—No doubt Lord O[xford] will be better for physic, it was what he wanted. The violent discharge he had was a plain indication that there was a load upon him which was to be removed. Though nature might throw off a good part of it by herself, she could not throw it all off without some help. It was much that she was able to throw off so much of it as she did.

I fancy you will hear soon that Lord Marlborough is gone off. Dr. John Freind was called to him at four o'clock in the morning on Tuesday last.

Sir John Walters died last Monday night at twelve o'clock. It is supposed his brother Bob, now Sir Robert, will be put up for this city.

Young Lord Sunderland is going to Paris for this summer, and returns about the time he is of age, towards the winter. He has refused being a Lord of the Bedchamber, which shows he is under his grandmother's influence.

The Bishop of Chester went for Chester on Tuesday.

I wish I could have been with you at my godfather's. I suppose it was in his romantic castle of Stapleton. That has somewhat in its situation more agreeable to me than any place I think I ever saw in my life.

Postscript. There was a talk once that the King designed to visit us, but we hear nothing of it of late. I fancy we shall hardly have such an honour unless we earn it first by some sort of modest application. I do not believe there is any disposition to do that.

The Bank and South Sea are not near agreeing as is commonly reported. Walpole sticks so hard for the Bank, and is so set upon lessening the South Sea, that the present treaty is not likely to be soon finished. I think I have this from very good hands. I think I told you in a former letter that Walpole said that if Johnson had not burnt his papers, they should have made a bishop a martyr. And so they would in one sense. He will certainly, if he is ever pressed, be a witness.

1722, June 16.—The little dog came from Rome. The Abbot claimed him by his name, and by the name of the person to whom the dog was sent, which was the feigned name for his lady, and concluded to be his own. It is said, this has explained several things in the deciphered letters, which are now applied to him. It is said too, there is a great deal against him, but not legal evidence to convict him, but he is not at a loss how to make his peace.

I hear the first intelligence of the wicked machinations came from young Sutton, and that he got from a lady under whose petticoats he was once seen to have his hands whilst she was at play. It is said she told him all she had heard a certain Lord talk, and that she put too some papers into his hands, which were sent over. It is rumoured too that Lord has been so far concerned, that a pension of 1,000l. per annum granted to his lady for his use—besides that to herself—on condition that he should live in France and be quiet, is stopped.

It is said too the Seal is offered to Sir Peter King, but he will not accept but upon his own terms. One of which is that Lord Trevor be restored, but they are [not?] disposed to give that place so, nor Trevor to accept.

You see I write all that comes to me, but I vouch the truth of nothing. But you will not be much concerned at that, if you are in the same disposition in the country as I am. Any thing there is welcome. But I wish I were with you for a few minutes, or had another way of corresponding with you. I have heard somewhat in which some particular persons are concerned, which I care not to send by this conveyance. I hope you have seen Thursday's " Flying Post," and read the martial equipage in which the Bishop of Durham appeared at the review—*An haec est tunica filii tui*, but it may be proper for a Palatine or Lord Lieutenant. I think he should be made General of the ecclesiastics, as Peterborough [Kennett] is of the marines.

1722, June 19.—I have nothing to add to what I wrote by the last post, but that Carteret is looked on as Premier at present. S[underlan]d had given impressions of him to the old one and the ladies, so much to his advantage, that he is thought to have the best personal interest at present.

Sir John Walters has left the Viscount a legacy of 1,000l., he has left his lady his whole estate during her widowhood. He has left the reversion of it to his brother, the present Sir Robert, to do what he likes with, but not one groat in present. We know not yet who will be put up, he, Sir Robert Walters, at present declines it. Old Tom Rowney is much pressed to let himself be named again, and joined with his son. He may certainly have it upon holding up his finger. At present he says nay, but I am apt to think he will be prevailed on at last.

Young Sunderland had a Garter offered him as well as Bedchamber place, but his grandmother told him, if he would despise their baubles, she would give him somewhat better than they would or could.

1722, June 21.—I trouble you once more before I leave this place with a few particulars I had last night. Upon the news of M[arlborough]'s death, Cadogan called Oughton, Macartney, Wills, and Honywood together; they are said to be his Cabinet. It was resolved there that he should ask to be Captain General, and, if refused that, for the Ordnance and the first regiment of Guards for himself, and for the second for Macartney. He accordingly asked to be Captain General, but was told it was designed there should be no Captain General. The Ordnance and regiment were granted. When he asked for the second regiment for Macartney, he was told it was already given to Lord Scarbrough. Argyll upon the news of M[arlborough]'s death was closeted with Walpole for two hours, but we see no fruits of it.

I know not whether you have heard that Lord Craven and Oughton had a rencounter upon some words about the Coventry election. They were parted, but Lord Craven had wounded Oughton and was himself untouched.

The war rages fiercely at Westminster. The Abbot, by a writing attested by Evans and Lowe, demanded of young Battely all papers relating to the College. Broderick got a paper signed by most of the prebendaries, requiring Battely not to deliver up his uncle's papers but to such persons and in such manner as the Dean and Chapter should appoint. Watton, who is Treasurer, has made Broderick his deputy, and he says he will cashier all the workmen and stop the wages of all the servants who have been put in by the Abbot's sole authority. Here is a noble field of contention opened.

1722, June 28. Little Shefford.—I have the favour of yours of the 19th, I am glad to hear you are moving at all. If you are once in motion, I hope you will set out for a longer journey at last. Pray give me as early and as exact an account as you can of your designed stages, that I may have time to get home two or three days before you come to our quarters. I expect my Lord of O[xford] and you will take up your quarters with me. I have sufficient room for you both, and if our Eywood friends come with you, the Bishop of Chester's house, which is now empty, will hold a more numerous company than they are.

The pleasure I take in this place is somewhat delayed by some neighbours that are not very agreeable to me. Lord Hartford has prevailed to have the camp that was designed to have been at Marlborough, pitched upon Hungerford Down. Only two regiments are yet encamped, but more are expected. Though I am at above five miles distance, I am afraid I am not out of the reach of "Moroders" (*sic*, marauders).

1722, June 30.—I am concerned that you are not able to give me a better account of Lord Oxford's strength and stomach. I cannot say whether relief will be had when he comes to another place. But I am pretty sure he has no chance for mending them whilst he is at distance from those who are best able to advise him. I shall depend upon advice from your Lordship of your motions, for I shall not stir hence till I hear when I may hope to see you in Oxford. Our friend on the other side of Oxford [Bromley ?] will be glad to hear that his designed journey is disappointed by yours. Had Lord Oxford stayed in the country till the ways cross the country had been passable, he has such a mind to see him that he would have made him a visit. If the account he has had of those ways had not discouraged him, I believe he had been with you before this.

The mufti puts on the best countenance he can, but is very uneasy, I hear, at the story of the little dog. It appears, I hear, that thanks had been returned to the lady for the dog, and that several letters had passed betwixt the mufti and Lord L[ansdow]ne. I am told that what concerns the mufti will make the greatest part of the narrative that is to be laid before the Parliament.

The great talk is now about what Lord Marlborough has left. They who speak most moderately say above a million of money is left besides land, and what separate estate the Duchess has. Not one farthing is left to any charity, or to any old friend or servant. I hear the will was made in March last, and that there is a clause at last to desire the Legislature to confirm the disposition he has made. But I hear withal that several of the family are already contriving to defeat this disposition.

Upon the late agreement betwixt South Sea and Bank, stock jobbing is said to be revived with as great eagerness as it was two years ago, and as much court made to the present directors for subscriptions as ever were to the former.

The war goes on fiercely betwixt the Abbot and his brethren. Eight of them have already signed a paper, forbidding the late Receiver's nephew to deliver any books or papers to them. Two more I suppose have signed it by this time, so that a strong confederacy is formed against him.

Your worthy tutor made this week a fine entertainment for our Governor, the Warden of Merton, the Provost of Oriel, and the Warden of Wadham [Baker]. I wonder most at the last, because he passes for a scoundrel with his own party, but he is supposed to be designed for our next Governor, and your tutor like a wise man makes his court betimes. This I think is plain dealing and pulling off the mask.

1722, July 21. Little Shefford.—I have the favour of your Lordship's of the 15th I shall be at Christ Church again God willing on Thursday next, and wait there with no little impatience for the honour of seeing your Lordship and the good company that comes along with you. If it please God that you reach me safe, I hope you will recruit yourselves there by proper rest for the remainder of your journey.

I shall be very sorry to have any thing dishonourable appear against the person you hint at, but such things have been in the world. My chief hope that the information may be false is because it comes, if I understand you right, from those he has . lately quarrelled with upon egregious treachery, as he says, on their side. Your Lordship judges like a wise and good man, in wishing to avoid any retrospect. But I can easily believe that all with you are not of the same mind. Should any foul play appear, or be believed, a breach is unavoidable, and that will be uneasy to both families.

I hear Argyll and his brother Ilay quarrelled when they were last in Scotland, and that Argyll bid him begone out of his house, and told him he had been misled long enough by him.

Now Walpole has gained his point of patching up an agreement betwixt the South Sea and Bank, he begins to open the further design he has against the South Sea. The discourse is hot again of reducing their stock to twenty millions, and converting ten millions into annuities at five per cent. redeemable by . Parliament.

Carteret sent to invite your old tutor to dinner, when he was at the election; caressed him much, and since that sent him a present of some of the champagne which he had from the Regent. I believe you will agree that such uncommon favours, from one who is nòt much used to take notice of those who have just claims of gratitude from him, to one so little known to him, are not without good ground. I suppose our Governor has given assurance that he is true and trusty, and for their purpose.

The prints perhaps will tell you before this that the President of Magdalen [Harwar] is dead. Grandorge, Lydal, and Butler are put up for it. I suppose one of the two last will have it, because they are least proper for it.

A very extraordinary thing has been done in the Isle of Man. The good and primitive Bishop of that place required a man who had been guilty of fornication to do penance before he would receive him to communion. The man readily submitted. The Deputy Governor to the Earl of Derby threw the man, for submitting to the ecclesiastical censure, into the dungeon, and for this and some other acts of censure, purely spiritual, took upon. him to fine the Bishop and his two vicars general. Upon their refusing to pay the fines, he sent them all three to prison, by a file of musketeers. That Bishop both acts and suffers like an apostolical man. The whole island have that veneration for him that they would at this time tear their Sub-Governor piecemeal, if the Bishop himself did not restrain them. What the consequence will be, I cannot yet guess. He is by Act of Parliament under the metropolitan of York. Had he done anything irregular, the complaint against him should have been carried thither. I hope that metropolitan will make a noise at least, should he be able to do nothing else.

Postscript. The camp in my neighbourhood moves in a few days to be joined to that at Salisbury, where his Majesty is expected to review them.

1722, August [22]. Saturday.—I am glad to hear you are at last upon the road, I hope I shall see you early on Monday. At least I depend upon it that you will not bait or eat anywhere till you come to me, and I hope you will let Mr. Cuttle or some one else come before, to let me know about what time I may expect you. I send by Mr. Cuttle the two letters I have received from my Lady for you. Yesterday about three o'clock the Bishop of Rochester, who was sitting at the deanery, encompassed as usual with books and papers relating to his domestic quarrels, was seized by six messengers. They immediately searched his pockets for papers. When they took away his pocket book, he said they should not take that without sealing it, for there were bank bills in it. He desired they would let his servant shave him before they carried him off, but that was not allowed. He was carried straight to a Committee of Council at the Cockpit. Some of the messengers stayed afterwards, and searched the house for papers, and carried off every scrap they could meet with even from the close stool. After he had been about an hour at the Cockpit, he was sent to the Tower. He desired he might first go back to his own house, but could not prevail for that. All the favour he could obtain was to be sent to the Tower in his own coach, rather than in the barge that had been provided for him. This is all I yet hear, if any thing more appeared to-day I am promised to have it by this night's post.

1722, August 23.—Griffith waits on you with this, to beg you would let me know by him how my good Lord Oxford does after his fatigue yesterday. I hope a day's rest will enable him to come out in good time on Monday. Pray let me know too, whether I may hope that you will stay Tuesday with me, or whether you purpose to go forward.

Postscript. I will take care to have Neddy's bed ready for Robin. I shall not have room for him, but I shall be able to lodge my Lord and Lady, and yourself, and my Lord's servant to lie next to him, and your servant and my Lady's woman too, with great convenience. Have my Lord and Lady separate beds? We can provide for that too, if you think it proper. I wish you would let me know what you think my Lord's stomach would be most likely to relish.

[To the EARL OF OXFORD.]

1722, August 30.—I beg leave to return my thanks to your Lordship and my Lady Oxford for the honour you have been pleased to do me. I could have wished for the sake of your Lordship's health that I had received it some months sooner, but I hope still, if Providence has any mercy in store for us, that the assistance which your Lordship may now have will once more make you a hale man again.

[To Lord Harley.]

1722, August 30.—I hope this will find you well after your journey, and in the midst of your joy, on the celebrating of the day in which the happiest couple in the three Kingdoms were joined together. I could not omit the first opportunity of returning you my thanks for the honour of your visit, and paying my duty too to your Lordship and my Lady on this day, and of wishing you for many years the continuance of the mutual happiness which this day gave you.

A gentleman who came down hither on Monday pretends he went to see Ruffe in the Tower, that he could not indeed see him, but had an account from the warder that he was perfectly easy and unconcerned. I do not see the use of so false a report, unless it be to hinder some others from being too much "alarumed" at his imprisonment. If anything particular occurs about him, I hope you will communicate.

1722, September 1.—I wrote you one line yesterday, I had time for no more. You will perceive by that the account I had of what the Attorney says agrees with what you have heard. It is not hard to guess what they aim at by confining. Ruffe, and I believe his old friend the Attorney will be the man employed to manage it with him. But if he thinks himself safe, wind and limb, he will never squeak. If convincing be all they hope for, they had better have let him alone. They have done him a kindness, his confinement will give him merit and credit too. There was no occasion to satisfy the world of that which they knew already. Ruffe will be so far from being concerned that he will be pleased to have it made more public if it is without danger to himself.

I thank you for my new paper. Scrub as it is, you would find it comfortable if you were as I am, in a perfect solitude.

Postscript. I do not hear that one gentleman in these parts had the curiosity to go to the rendezvous at Sarum. That is somewhat odd. They seem to have been as insensible as your Silurians to their superintendent.

1722, September 5.—Bob [Freind?] has been so kind as to spend three days with me, he will be in town on Sunday night and soon after wait on your Lordship. I will not anticipate what he will say to you. I shall only tell you that what discourse he has had with the Viscount was agreeable to what we had heard. That perhaps there may not be enough to reach life, but any thing else short of life. And the Viscount assured Bob that Ruffe would never be able to do any one mischief any more. He seemed to intimate that he would be tried by a common jury, that itself is a strong presumption that they think they have good evidence against him. But I believe, by all I can yet hear, that the evidence is particular as to him, and not likely to affect any one else. Nor can I hear that he himself has it much in his power to impeach others if he should be disposed to it. When the scene opens, I believe it will appear that his folly has been as remarkable as any other quality in him.

I am glad to hear by little Robin that Lord Oxford holds well.

1722, September 8. Little Shefford.—I find upon my coming hither that Africanus has parted again with that estate which he had bought of Lord Bolingbroke and has given up the bargain, too, which he had made for Doleman's estate adjoining to it. Here are odd reports in the country, as though strange fellows with his livery on them were in his house for other purposes than to attend on him.

It was thought the Lord of Bucklebury might have fair hopes of returning home by the interest of his friend who now comes in play. But I hear fresh application has been made for that purpose, and he has been flatly refused, and it is thought his old friend will not spoil his own court by pressing too earnestly for him.

1722, September 9. Little Shefford.—You have sent me the best news you could in telling me that you hope my Lord O[xford] is somewhat better. I do not wonder that Dr. Mead has altered his prescriptions. I should have wondered if he had been so lucky in them at a distance as to have found no reason to change them. Radcliffe was surely in the right, that a man might as well draw a face as prescribe for one he did not see.

Our guards are returned again to our neighbourhood and some regiments are encamped in too near neighbourhood. There seems to be great precaution against these parts, though as far as I know them they are as little likely as any in the kingdom to give any disturbance.

I believe the Bishop of Chester will be at Oxford again by the end of this week, and designs to be in town the first day of the opening of the Parliament. You will easily believe that he is a little eager to see how the scene opens upon Ruffe.

There were some odd things in the last paper you sent me, but the stocks are to me the signs of the times, and sufficient ones for any business I have met with the world. I judge by their rise or fall what general apprehensions are.

1722, September 15.—When I had the honour to see you, you told me that your superintendent had ordained one who had suffered but a year before for forging orders. But I remember not well what the punishment was, whether he had done penance or stood in the pillory for it. The latter is the most proper punishment for such a crime. Can you tell me, too, whether that notorious young villain that was of our house lately, and that has been ordained by him, had been able to get testimonials from any one?

Postscript. The Attorney is gone up again. He pretends to be positive that Ruffe will be tried at the King's Bench bar. He says there is one witness besides circumstances.

1722, September 22. Little Shefford.—I have read above half of old Covel's book [on the Greek Church] since I have been here. It is very tedious and full of repetitions. But there is reading in it and some valuable things; if any one would be at the trouble of making an abridgment of it, it would be a useful book. He more than once refers to accounts which he designs to publish in another book; I take it to be an account of his travels. Is any such like to be published whilst he is alive?

1722, October 5.—The Bishop of Chester left me this morning. The members for town and county go up to-morrow. G. Clarke sets out on Sunday. Mr. Bromley will be in town on Saturday night at his old lodgings in Clarges Street. He tells me that he hears that most of the members will be up. I am told too, that this Parliament as well as the last will be opened with impeachments. But your Lordship who is on the place must know these things better than we poor fellows here, *ad quos vix tenuis famæ perlabitur aura.* I am much concerned for my old friend my Lord Orrery, but I hope there is no other ground for taking him up but the general jealousy of the times. I should not have suspected him for these affairs. I daresay he has had nothing to do with Ruffe, though he was his tutor. There has been nothing but a mere civil correspondence betwixt them for some years. I hear Lord Carleton was much concerned at the apprehending of Lord Or[rery].

Our Vice-Chancellor is sworn into his office again to-day. He is now entered on his fifth year, which no one ever did before since John Owen's time. I am afraid our Chancellor has done a very unpopular thing in naming him again; I wish that may not be the worst of it.

1722, October 9.—Parliamenteering would not do well to one with such a family as Affleck has at any time, and much less after losses in the Bubbles that I am afraid are not inconsiderable. But he has a foolish project in his head which he will never compass; nor, if he could, would his being in Parliament in the least conduce, though I fancy he thinks it will.

You will be more numerous than ycu were in the last Parliament, but not strong enough surely to carry any one point, though all the malcontent Whigs should join with you. No, nor to oppose the repeal of the *Habeas Corpus,* and yet that is the point on which one would think, if on any, an opposition might be made to purpose.

My old friend Dr. Cheyney has been pleased to recommend some more of his friends to me from Bath. I was fetched from the Audit House yesterday to three gentleman who had brought me a letter from Dr. Cheyney. I was once thinking not to have gone home, but when I did, the gentleman proved to be the famous Mr. Law and his son, and Lord Sommervile, a young Scotch lord. Though I was no stranger to Law's character, yet I did not grudge a bottle of wine, for the sake of a little conversation with one who has made so much noise in the world. He spent the evening with me. I put him upon talking of his own affairs, and he entered into them very readily. He seemed to take it as a great reflection on him, as he well might, that anyone should think our South Sea scheme to have been formed on the plan of his Mississippi. I perceive he takes our projectors to be great bunglers.

The little Auditor spent Saturday and Sunday with me. To-morrow I expect Abel and his lady and the babes.

1722, October 11.—You have indeed a very full number, but they seem to me to have little ground for hopes, who with such a number durst not struggle for the Chair. It is said your first point of debate will be the *Habeas Corpus*. If that goes through both Houses, no one can doubt what is to be depended on.

I spent the evening yesterday with Abel, he is gone forward this morning. He seems to have his fears and to think that he is in some danger for having protested so boldly as he did last winter. I did not endeavour to allay his fears, but told him I thought he was more obnoxious on account of his known intimacy with Ruffe. I fancy he will not protest again in haste, unless he has very numerous company to bear him out. He owned to me that he had been a very considerable loser in the South Sea, but he named not the sum.

Postscript. I have read the letter to the Clergyman about Ruff's commitment. I do not take it to be [the Bishop of] Lincoln's. I am told it is one Croxall's, a poet.

1722, October 13.—I fancy you may already see that it would not have been inexpedient if some of our friends had been sooner in town. I hope all here are convinced that the Government have lost nothing by Lord S[underland]'s death, and that apprehensions that his influence would be wanted are groundless. They always I confess seemed so to me. I own I am pleased to hear who the person [Harcourt] was that moved to add the words *are or*. I perceive he has his old friend at his heart. That was a home thrust under the fifth rib. *Hoc juvat et melli est non mentiar.*

We have now a full confirmation of the utmost that was suspected of King. I know not what he can make of it, nor is it yet certain that others will think him creditable enough to make use of his offers. I hear two of our Heads bless God that they have not drank a bottle with him for six months last past. You know the Act limits information for words to that time.

1722, October 16.—You are in the midst of your battle, I suppose, whilst I am writing to you. I am wishing that you may die like men of honour, for I cannot have the least hopes of any thing else. *Quanquam O!* If our friends had had common sense, and had entered into any measures about the late elections, they might have had the game in their own hands. This is a reflection that abates much of the satisfaction one can have in hearing that they fall honourably.

I am mighty glad to hear that Lord O[xford] was at the debate, there was great enquiry here after that; and to hear that he was there added not a little to the great indignation against an old fellow soldier of his, who has changed sides. We already see the utmost that is likely to be done by the Convocation, and if I should come up I find I am not likely to have any other call but my desire to pay my duty to your Lordship and my Lady.

As things are, I believe it is best that we do not sit. It is much to be doubted whether there could have been a majority that would have agreed in what was proper. But if there should, it is certain they would not have been allowed to do it.

1722, October 18.—I heartily thank you for the account of what passed with you, which you were pleased to send me by Mr. Thomas. I think you may now go play, your numbers are not likely to increase after a defeat. It is not hard to foretell the event of the seven years that are to come. And they who ride the fore horse must be as great bunglers as they who oppose them are, if possible, if they leave themselves open to any attack when they are to renew their power. I cannot but make one reflection on your weakness, that in your first debate and in so full a house you durst not oppose the main point, though so obnoxious, but only endeavoured to compound for a little shorter time.

1722, October 21.—I am extremely obliged to you for giving yourself so much trouble in the midst of the business you must have, to let me know so much of what has passed with you, though your own modesty would not let you tell me that part which would have been most acceptable. But other friends supplied that part, and set it in its proper light, as well knowing how welcome it would come to me. May God enable you to go on, and as your heart is as good, may your abilities appear as eminent as ever your father's were. Not that I think that any speaking is in these days of much moment, but we must do what we can, though we foresee little fruit of it. And it will be great satisfaction to your own mind, as well as joy to all who honour you, to be able to say *si Pergama lingua defendi possent.*

There can be no ground surely for what was mentioned as to have been offered on the demise of the Queen. If Ruffe could have had such a thing at all in his head, he could not at that time have gone those lengths. But if there should be any truth in it, I beg leave to observe that the discovery of it now must have come from the Attorney, who at that time, you know, was in the strictest intimacy with Ruffe.

You do not think but that in the midst of jealous and unsettled times I have some pleasure to see the Attorney act the part he does.

1722, October 25.—I wish you may be in a state to be on the defensive. I am afraid you are not in any point that others would in earnest contend with you. But I do not apprehend that they have any other points this session, but a few more troops and the remission of the two millions. And I believe you do not think you can stop either of them. Our member for the town in Walters' place was chosen yesterday without opposition, a young gentleman, unmarried, of 1,700*l. per annum,* and money in his pocket. His name Knowles, a relation of Tom Rowney's, and brought in by his interest.

I am told the apology for the suspension of the *Habeas Corpus* in the last "London Journal," was written by Hereford. It is great condescension in one of his station to scribble for common news writers. What he has now written is as little reconcileable to some things written by Bangor, as some things written by Bangor were to others written by Hoadly.

Postscript. I would observe one thing to you, which I know not whether it occurred in your debates. That in King James's arbitrary reign when a Tory Parliament was sitting, and plots both in England and Scotland which broke out in both Kingdoms to actual rebellion, there was no thought in any of those betrayers of their country, the Tories, to suspend the *Habeas* &c.

1722, October 26.—I am afraid the Master of University has not many hours to live. He was struck on Wednesday not (*sic*) at St. John's where the Ordinance then was, and has not had any sense since. It is thought one Cockman will succeed him, he is the best of those named for it.

Some new stock jobbing is going forward. The Viscount sent to Blechingdon to procure the consent of his College [Worcester] for putting their whole fortune, 14,000*l.*, into the South Sea. Accordingly consent under the College seal is gone up for laying of it out in stock. I suppose a rise is expected, and designed, upon the submission of the two millions, and conclusion of the congress at Cambray. What is thought will be the event of the last?

1722, October 28.—Your public news is very categorical. I think the victors may now go play, as old Colonel Astley told the Parliament generals, when they had defeated, near Stow, the last body of troops under the Colonel which the King had left. Business of much moment has been despatched in a few days. How many shillings in the pound this year, three or four?

Who is this Mrs. Spelman talked of for her fidelity to the Duke of N[ewcastle]?

Postscript. Poor Charlett is alive still and that is all. We may not only have a worse than he, but have little hope I am afraid of having one so good.

You seem not surprised at the great sum I told you was by the Attorney's management to be laid out in South Sea stock. I wish he may not do this with a design to sell his own stock to them. That would be a bite of which he is very capable.

1722, October 30.—Your countryman Saloway's sermon is like to have much credit here. The Bishop of Oxford is extremely pleased with it, and with the prefaces as much as with the sermon.

King's modesty is as remarkable as any of his other good qualities. He is come down to us again, I thought we should have seen him no more.

Charlett is come in some measure to his senses, but sinks apace; he cannot hold long.

1722, November 5.—It is not hard to guess what the issue of any contest about elections will be when the Court concerns itself. I only wish my old friend H[utcheson] may in his present defence be of a piece with himself and not flag in his spirit. King goes on to deny his having made any offers to Walpole, but he has one plea for himself I was not aware of. He says if he had gone to Walpole, why might not he go to him as well as G. Clarke go every day to the Viscount. Is not the last as great a ———— (*sic*) as the first? It may be somewhat difficult to answer this.

All Souls may perhaps have some new trouble, they ended their election last night. The parties were equal, so they agreed to take one of each side. They agreed to take no notice of a founder's kinsman, one Wood, a gentleman commoner of our House. But he immediately entered an appeal, and will I fancy be relieved by the Visitor.

Postscript. This Layer seems a very stubborn fellow.

1722, November 8.—The event of your debate is no other than I expected, but I should be glad to know how my friend Hutcheson behaved himself on this occasion. I had heard the poor man was somewhat dispirited. I hope he recovered himself, and kept his credit though he lost the day. Does your Lordship know the names of the three clergymen who came as witnesses on Lownd's side? The Roman Catholics are all alarmed at the report of the tax designed against them, and hastening up to town from all parts of the country hereabouts.

1722, November 13.—I am told that Dr. John Freind spoke very well in the debate of the Westminster election, and had a reflection in his speech on the Viscount. I should be glad to know what the last was.

The poor Master of University lies in a wretched condition, without any sense. It is impossible I think that he should last long so. The College is equally divided, five and five for Cockman and Dennison. If the senior Fellow's voice be allowed in this case to be casting, as I think it ought, Cockman will have it. There will be an appeal to the Doctors of Divinity as Visitors. The words are *absente magistro* the senior Fellow's vote carries it. The appellants pretend that *absente* extends only to the living.

Not one man in this place now opens their (*sic*) month here for the Viscount but his old friend Delaune. He does it heartily and observes on all occasions how happy the University is who has such a friend as he is to us in power; and tells his comrades that the Viscount's moving to add the words *are or* to the Suspension Act was out of tenderness to R[uffe] to prevent his being brought to a speedy trial, and to keep him in prison till men's animosities against him were cooled. I think the Viscount could not have had a more proper advocate.

1722, November 15.—We have neither intrigues at Court, nor contests about elections, nor plots nor trials, to supply new matter to us. We have neither insolence of enemies or folly of friends to afford us variety. But all is as downright hum-drum with us as your old tutor's conversation is with others out of his own doors or with his own wife within them. Your Lordship threatens to mortify me. Robin Morgan, who is a philosopher in deed and not in word, would tell you that what the world through wrong judgment commonly calls mortification is upon a due estimation of things the most refined and exquisite of pleasures. And in that sense I can allow that the more you honour me with hearing from you, the more you will mortify me. How is your election like to go at Westminster ? Is there any spirit, any resentment stirring ? It seems to me one of those things by which, though you may not gain much if you are victors, yet you may lose very much if you are worsted.

1722, November 17.—No doubt our good friends the Tories will be much exalted that they have been allowed to carry the Stafford election. We shall be apt enough to think the day may be our own again. A little thing contents us. This election indeed is, as we say, better than nothing, but it is but cold comfort for the suspension and augmentation.

A citation was fixed to-day at All Souls, to summon the Warden, Officers and Fellows to appear at Lambeth on the 10th of January next, in the case of an appeal of a founder's kinsman. The College, as much as it is divided on other occasions, will be very unanimous in making all the opposition they can in this case to the Archbishop's power, but I believe to no purpose.

You forgot to tell me the numbers by which the little Captain's election was carried ; but I had them from the Bishop of Chester.

1722, November 18.—The poor Master [of University College] died last night. The Fellows continue equally divided. There will be an appeal I believe to the Doctors of Divinity, who are the Visitors, but as far as I can yet guess it will go for Cockman, who will have the senior Fellow's vote. How is your election at Westminster likely to go ?

1722, November 21.—I am sorry you were only passive upon a late occasion, but I hear my old friend the Viscount took care to distinguish him in another place by his zeal, on that as well as all other occasions.

Poor Charlett has died in very bad circumstances I am afraid as to his temporals.

1722, November 22.—Is there such a thing as a step that some men can boggle at? It should seem so by making the election only void. I am glad to find even such slender remains of shame. I am afraid I must not call it grace. My most humble respects to Mr. B[romle]y, how does he think the next election at Coventry will go? The tide it seems is turned in your own quarters. I take it to be of some moment, but what will not a camp and suspension do? It is happy for G. Clarke that he is laid up with the gout, it may be a good excuse for not accepting a challenge. King is gone up with a resolution, as he told his cronies here, to call Walpole, Bromley and Clarke to account. But I suppose the next news we shall hear of him will be that he is in the Fleet.

Some of your House who are come here say you shall adjourn for five weeks at Christmas and at your meeting again go upon the Lords in the Tower. I suppose then it must be by impeachments. Do you hear any such thing? We are amazed that we hear nothing to-day of Leare [Layer?]'s trial.

Postscript. When will these Travels come out that give an account of the King of Sweden?

1722, November 27.—I have read King's advertisement, and see not but that the main of what has been charged on him may be true, though this advertisement should stand good. He denies that he either *went* to Walpole, or *wrote* to him upon any occasion, but he does not deny that he ever *sent* any one else to him upon any occasion. He denies indeed that he ever gave a *commission to any one* to make overtures in his name, about informing, &c. And perhaps that might not be directly offered at first, but was to be the consequence of his being returned into Walpole's service; or the person employed by him to Walpole, who is said to be his brother-in-law, one Withers, a hearty Whig, might assure Walpole of this, as that which he knew King could and would do, and do this too with King's knowledge, without having King's express commission for doing of it. As to any answer to it, I see not to whom that belongs but to Walpole himself. The report came from him, and he is the person who alone is obliged to make it good. But I suppose he will hardly condescend to enter into an advertisement combat with King.

It is not yet known what part Layer is like to play upon his conviction.

1722, November 29.—Your concern is very just for the death of that poor Lady, who gave an excellent proof of the goodness of her own temper, in being so kind a mother-in-law as she was.

Surely the bill now depending with you is a more real persecution than ever the dissenters complained of in former reigns. Can they press this bill who thought the restraint of occasional conformity a hardship?

Can you learn what Walpole says to King's advertisement? He ought to answer it, he gave occasion for the reports. I fancy Shippen will take notice to him of it. You might learn from him what Walpole says to it. Surely this bustle will bring to light the proofs of this matter, and produce those who were either employed by King to Walpole, or desired by King to introduce him to him.

Postscript. I am afraid your joy is but short-lived. The bill depending seems to have an ugly aspect towards property. Hence, I suppose, as well as from particular application, the great opposition to it. But I much doubt whether in other cases, though of a trying nature too, you would have so much company.

1722, December 2.—We are somewhat impatient to know what will be the issue of King's advertisement and insult upon Dod. No one thinks it will be proper for Mr. Walpole to enter into a paper combat with King. But it is supposed that he is bound in honour, by what way he thinks most decent for himself, to let it be known that what has been reported of King came from him, and that he can make it good.

1722, December 4th.—I thought there had been no petition against our friend Cæsar; since there is one, though upon never so frivolous a pretence, I am afraid he cannot hope to keep his place [for Hertford].

The election at University is over, but will be contested, though I think there is little ground for it. The statute says the Master shall be chosen *per canonicum electionem.* By the canons regularly, there should be to make an election, not barely a majority of votes for one candidate, but a majority of the whole number of voters, but the same canons allow no man to vote for himself, and by the custom of the College the senior's vote is casting. To avoid these two last points, Dennison did not vote for himself, but threw away his vote on one Ward. Four others voted for Dennison and five for Cockman. Dennison has appealed against the election as invalid, because a majority of the ten votes were not for Cockman upon a strict interpretation of the words *canonica,* and if you could suppose all the voters had given their votes *bona fide,* with an intent to make an election, perhaps there might be weight enough in the objection to oblige them to go to another election. But since the Visitors are to go *secundum conscientias,* and it is plain one vote was given, not with an intent to promote but to hinder an election, I do not think there is much weight in what is objection to the election, but that it will be judged very good.

1722, December 6.—The gentleman to whom the words about K[ing] were spoken has written about them to the person that spoke them, but I hear not yet of any effect his letter has had. Perhaps the person that spoke it might have feigned most of what he said to make his own court. If it should be so he is a greater villain than the person he represented as such.

We are to meet this day about the election of University, I know not whether we shall enter into the merits of it to-day, though I think there is no ground for this bustle. Your Lordship shall know the event when it is over.

1722, December 11.—This morning Cockman took quiet possession. When we noble Visitors met, Dr. Hammond put in a protestation against all their future proceedings as null, the three days in which we had cognizance being lapsed. It was signed by Hammond, Burton, Stratford, Carter, Provost of Oriel, Terry, Clavering, Moulden of Pembroke. Then Cockman appeared and read a protestation in the name of himself, and of those Fellows who chose him, against any further proceedings in this cause. The protestation was not received because he called himself Master in it. Our noble court was somewhat disconcerted. The advocate on Dennison's side desired further time to consider. He would have had till Thursday, they have given him till to-morrow in the afternoon. What our noble Visitors will then do, I know not. I thank God we have rid our hands of it, but the King's Bench must determine this at last.

Postscript. The Provost of Queen's signed our protestation to-day in court with this exception, that he took the three days not to be expired till Monday, which we had fixed to Saturday.

1722, December 16.—What was in the Pretender's ships? Were they full of dragoons or ammunition? Or were they employed upon small traffic to help him to get a livelihood? Were they pleasure boats? Surely they will not forbid him to keep a little small craft upon either of the two last occasions.

1722, December 18.—Dennison and his party proceeded yesterday to a new election of Dennison, but I am told there is some confusion amongst them. It is said that all who took upon them to void Cockman's election will not venture to confirm Dennison, but are afraid of burning their fingers any further. But I am not certain how that affair stands.

1722, December 29. From Mrs. Broughton's in Stable Yard near Dean's Yard, Westminster.—I fancy you were as little a stranger to the place of my abode here, as to the time of my coming hither. It is plain you knew the last so well, that you took care to get out of town before I could get into it. And I suppose you will have no thoughts of returning to it, till you hear I am gone from it. I have had the honour to wait thrice on my honoured Lady, and she is so good as to allow me to dine with her to-morrow above stairs. I paid my duty to my old master, on Christmas day in the evening, and to my great comfort I had him alone for three hours. I dined with him on Thursday, but there were many others there. All my observations of him tend I am afraid only to confirm me in those thoughts I had when I saw him at Oxford, but I care not to dwell on so melancholy a subject.

I have not yet been at Lord Kinnoull's. I shall call in a day or two, though were it not for the good lady, I wish I could say mistress of that family, I should keep my due distance. Your uncle sent Robin to me on Monday night to invite me to dine with him on Wednesday, but I was pre-engaged, and obliged to make my excuse as I did to my honoured Lady and your father for the same day. As I came from waiting on my Lady on Wednesday, I passed by your uncle coming thither; he looks very well, but I have heard nothing further of that family. But the person that has loaded me most with un-deserved honours has been Abel. He prevented my respects to him, and came to me himself the moment he heard I was in town with his own and his lady's compliments. Upon my returning the visit, I had great caresses from both, and pressing invitations to make their house my own whilst I-stay here. Your father would make me vain; he tells me the good lady designs me for her second. So much for private correspondence.

I fancy there has been no great change in the face of public matters since you left this place. Though differences continue still, the talk of changes is said to be over. No ground yet to expect that Or[rery] or any others in durance will be bailed. The Regent has interposed vigorously against the Catholic bill, but the person who promotes it says that, for that very reason, it shall be driven through. They will show those abroad, as well as those at home, that they are in no fear of them. I am told the same person is not so forward as he was to augment the troops—the reason when we meet. If men can be reasonable and quiet, and let things remain as they are, perhaps there will be no more prosecutions about the plot. But if they are impertinent, and press to be let into the bottom of what is discovered, they must thank themselves if they who are provoked, when they are not furnished for prosecutions in inferior courts, have recourse to Parliamentary methods.

Postscript. Since I wrote the Auditor has been with me and we have chatted an hour or two. I wish I could give you as good an account of your father as of your uncle. I think I never saw him better in my life.

1722-3, January 3.—Pray thank Mr. Harley for the favour of his. Since my last to your Lordship I have waited on Lady Kinnoull, who will look better when her red spots are gone than ever she did in her life. Yesterday I paid my duty in Dover Street, and found all well there. I dined with your uncle and spent the evening with your father. He is very deaf still, and must be so till he can prevail on himself to keep better hours. But in other respects I thought him somewhat better than when I first saw him. All other affairs continue as when I last wrote to you.

, There are nothing but conjecturals as to what will be done when you meet again. The Speaker [Compton] has been very ill, but is on the mending hand. However some think he will not be in a condition to attend the service of the House at the time to which you are adjourned, and that you may be adjourned for a week longer upon his account. You will have heard that Lord Carlisle on Friday last received a letter from Lord Townshend to let him know that the King had no further occasion for his service. I can hear of no other reason for his dismission but his reproof of Williamson for his behaviour to the prisoners. You have heard no doubt, too, of the battle between the Bishop of Rochester and Williamson. Reports are very various. Williamson has made an affidavit that the Bishop collared him, struck him, and threw him down. A pretty odd affidavit for a great officer to make—that he was beaten by a gouty bishop. The story by the Bishop is very different. Williamson and White, the Major of the Tower, came to visit him ; the Bishop ordered both his servants to stay in the room. Williamson said upon that he would have two warders up. The Bishop said, and surely with reason, that there could be no occasion for warders when superior officers were there, and when he was not conversing with suspected persons. Williamson ordered one of the Bishop's servants to call up warders. The Bishop bid his servant not to stir. Williamson then desired the Bishop to dismiss one of his servants that they might be two and two. The Bishop gratified him in that. Williamson after that insisted still to have one warder, and bid the servant call him. The Bishop said he should have no warder, and bid the servant not to stir. Williamson then said he would call one himself. The Bishop was nearest

the door, and got thither first, and set his back to it. Williamson, in coming round the bed, entangled his foot in a little chair
at the bottom of the bed, and was thrown down flat on his back.
The Bishop protests he did not, I cannot see anything else he
did which could be on any account improper.

1722-3, January 5.—The talk is very general and warm that
the plot is to be laid before the Parliament. Opinions are
different about the consequence of it. Some talk of impeachments, others only of proper addresses from both Houses. It is
as hotly talked that Carteret is to be Groom of the Stole, and
Pulteney Secretary. The Prelate since his late quarrel with the
gaoler is confined to his room and not allowed to come down
stairs to speak through the grate to his son and daughter, and
upon complaint, no redresses, but the order confirmed by friend
Carteret. I am told by one who has good intelligence that
Walpole went out of town much out of humour upon being pressed
to come into a new German treaty, which he did not like.

1722-3, January 8.—We hear nothing more of King's advertisement, nor shall we. I hear Walpole says to private men that
what he had said of King was true, but there will be nothing
made public against him. The talk grows daily that there will
be a narrative of the plot laid before the Houses. It is said
Walpole has taken Bland and a chaplain with him into the
country, and trunks full of papers in order to draw it up. But I
meet with no one that thinks any thing can be made of it. You
say not when you design to be in town. There will certainly be
a further adjournment. The Speaker will not be strong enough
by the time you are to meet to be able to attend the House. I
have seen Kinnoull and was received with great demonstrations of
joy and friendship, to a degree that seemed to me to proceed from
a consciousness of guilt, which he would willingly hide. I have
just come from my Lord of Oxford ; his hearing continues as bad
as it was, and in all other points he is much as he was. I believe I
may now tell you with some assurance that some sort of narrative
is preparing in order to be laid before the Parliament. I hear
nothing yet but conjecturals as to the further use that is to be
made of it.

1722-3, January 19.—Lord Harcourt sets up for a benefactor
to [torn, Oriel?] and would have us give up an alms house for
ground to build a chapel for them. Your old tutor is in great
haste to give up the site of our College to oblige his Lordship. I
learn his Lordship [is] afraid of opposition from his old friend
Stratford. This betwixt ourselves. I have no interest now in
[torn], however I believe difficulties may . . . . ted which
his Lordship will not be able to surmount with all his skill and
all the interest one of his power may have amongst a parcel of
mercenary fellows. Some think this only a feint in his Lordship,
and that he foresees or desires difficulties may be started to bring
him off.

1722-3, February 23.—I forgot to tell you yesterday, that
Browne, one of the proscribed, preached the Latin sermon
yesterday, before the determining bachelors.   He prayed openly .
for Cockman as Master of University College.. All the bachelors
immediately turned their heads and looked on the Vice-Chancellor.   He was in some confusion, but he may perceive by this
in what disposition the Fellows are to submit to him.

1722-3, February 24.—I have brought the young gentlemen
safe to Christ Church.   I bless God we are all well, only a little
weather-beaten.   I beg leave to pay my most humble thanks to
your Lordship and my Lady for all your goodness to me in
town.   Be pleased to tell my Lady that the new bride of Balliol
occasions much discourse here.   The majority of his brethren,
the Heads, condemn the match.   The young men of the College
laugh heartily at their governor, but hope to find their account
in their governante.   You may imagine the debates are not
less amongst the ladies, but their assemblies are divided on the
point.   The graver part seem resolved at present not to visit
her.   I have not yet been out to learn any other news, if there
should be any.

1722-3, February 26.—On Saturday in the evening the Vice-
Chancellor sent to the Doctors to meet him yesterday at University College at one o'clock in the afternoon.   He gave no
summons to any who had protested, nor any summons to any
of the College to attend.   There met this day, the Vice-Chancellor,
Delaune, Hole of Exeter, President of Corpus, Newton of Hart
Hall, Brabourn of New Inn Hall, Fenton of Edmond Hall, Hunt
of Balliol.   I cannot learn that there were any more.   They
locked themselves up, and admitted nobody but Dennison, whom
they called in once.   The Vice-Chancellor pressed unanimity
much, and encouraged those who were backward and timorous.
They resolved that Boraston the senior Fellow should be ordered
to deliver up the keys of the Treasury to Dennison, that Nevil
and Taylor, two Fellows in possession of the Master's lodgings for
Cockman, should give up the lodgings to Dennison, and Browne
the Bursar pay to him what was due to the Master, before
Thursday se'nnight, upon pain of suspension, and if they incurred
suspension and submitted not within seven days, upon pain of
expulsion by the 14th of March.   It is hard to say whether the
proceeding be more irregular or extravagant.   I am told
many were drawn in upon assurance that the Fellows would
be intimidated and submit.   I believe they will find themselves
mistaken in that, and if they dare then venture to execute their
own resolutions a fair way will be opened to Westminster Hall.
Postscript. I hear since I wrote that Fenton, the Principal of
Edmund Hall, withdrew from the rest and would not act with them.
Dr. Haywood of St. John's was dragged in much against his will
by the President; it seems he has some favour depending in the
College.   Martyn, the junior Pro-Proctor of New College, was
one too who had no more to do there, supposing they had a legal
power, than your footman. They not only did not summon any

of us who had protested, but no other Doctors in town who had
not protested, of whom they did not think themselves sure.
Their decree was fixed up to-day, in which they adjourn themselves to Thursday se'nnight. If I can prevail on others to
appear with me, they shall have more company then than they
expect, and such as will soon make the room too hot for
them. If all who are against them would but act, we are two
to one now in town against them. When they had locked
themselves up, they opened their court with a bottle of wine.
Pray communicate this to Mr. Bromley.

1722-3, February 27.—I have enclosed to you a copy of our
famous decree made on Monday last by our Visitors. I would
only observe that, if they had power, what they require of the
Fellows, if submitted to, might not excuse them from punishment.
For though they should submit, yet if afterwards their friend,
Mr. Denison (sic), should refuse to certify under his hand their
submission, they would still be suspended and at last expelled.
The other blunders are too obvious to be observed, the grammar
and sense in it is just as good as the law and reason of it. This
made by these few men locked up without ever summoning even
those who did not protest against them, if they [had ever?]
before differed from [them], without ever summoning the
parties they pretend to punish, or giving notice to them of
any complaint against them, or hearing any proof of such complaint, and upon proof admonishing them to do their duty by
such a time, or then they would consider what further to do—
the usual constant method in all courts of this nature that have
full legal powers.

1722-3, March 2.—We had a remarkable struggle here on
Friday for the Curator's place vacant by the death of Sir
Christopher Wren. The event of it will have its consequences
here, but I could not know it soon enough to send it to you by
that day's post. That place has been usually bestowed by way
of compliment to the Vice-Chancellor for the time. The present
Vice-Chancellor has made more attempts than one to get a
surrender from Sir Christopher. He has for the last two years
doubted of his own interest in the Convocation, but to remedy
that he took other precautions, sure ones as he thought. The
Curator must be chosen out of the delegates of Accounts. They
are named by the Vice-Chancellor and the two proctors. The
present delegates are the Heads of Brasenose, Magdalen,
Exeter, Oriel, Corpus Christi, St. John's, Trinity, Pembroke, All
Souls. The present Vice-Chancellor, whenever he made any one
the compliment of naming him a delegate of Accounts, asked him
at the same time for his vote for himself in case of Sir Christopher
Wren's death. He did so particularly to the President of
Magdalen last November, who promised him his vote. All Souls
is already a Curator, and having secured, as he thought, Magdalen,
he apprehended no opposition. When he had notice on Wednesday of Wren's death, he immediately went to Magdalen. The
President repeated his promise, and said he would recommend

him to his House, but there appeared a strange aversion in the whole university to the Vice-Chancellor. The men of Corpus [wished] to put up their Head, but he said he had promised the Vice-Chancellor and was under obligations to him not to let himself be named in opposition to him. Many went from several colleges and desired the Magdalen men to put up their Head, and offered them their assistance; they applied to their Head, but he still declined it. At last they begged of them to put him up without his consent. It was Friday morning the day of election before they could be prevailed on to do it, but at last they did. All the Pates, Whig as well as Tory, out of deference to the Vice-Chancellor's authority, stuck by him. Our Sub-dean was the only Canon who was at the election; he solicited our House man by man for the Vice-Chancellor, but could only get two of the whole House to go along with him. Only eight of our House were at the election, of which five were against the Vice-Chancellor; the rest stayed at home. The issue was that it was carried for the President of Magdalen against the Vice-Chancellor by 96 to 65. All who stayed away, had they come, would have been against the Vice-Chancellor, and in that case he would have lost it by above an hundred.

Never was there a public mark of detestation so remarkable in all its circumstances ever fixed before in this place on one in his post. The Masters cried aloud in the Convocation House that they hoped this would be fairly represented to the Chancellor [Arran], and that he would see by it how his Vice-Chancellor was esteemed and beloved, and that they should have no more of him; and indeed it is high time for our Chancellor to look about him, if he thinks it worth his while to preserve any interest here. If he continues to countenance this man and his cronies he will find a great majority here revolt against it. When the affair was over, as the poor proscribed Fellows came along the street, every one ran up to them to give them joy of the Vice-Chancellor's disgrace.

Be pleased to communicate this account to Mr. Bromley. Dr. Haywood, the most considerable both for learning and morals of those who signed the decree, has written a letter to the Vice-Chancellor to take shame to himself, to beg pardon of the poor men whom he has wronged, to desire his name may be withdrawn from the decree, and that at the next meeting his own protest may be entered against himself. This is the substance of a very handsome letter, in the beginning of which he does me too much honour by attributing the change of his opinion to his discourse with me.

I have seen Tim, but if he did not bring more money than he has news with him, I am afraid he has fared very hard upon the road.

1722-3, March 5.—I hear you are in the report, or rather appendix to it, though not in the Plot. I give you joy of your escape. It is well so you had so wise a father. But I have a quarrel to you, that the true reason of your journey last year into

Herefordshire should be kept such a secret to me. But could you think that any of your finesses could escape Ruffe's sagacity? It is hard though that he who has so great talents should not employ first to guard himself, and that one of great penetration into other men's motions should have so little circumspection as to his own.

It is generally thought, I find, that somewhat extraordinary is designed. I want only to hear the issue of Thursday's debate. If such a thing be voted, I shall easily guess what the success will be. If these things go on you will not go to Wimpole so soon as you imagined?

Postscript. Was there any thing in Ruffe's letters about the patriarchal power, or insisting upon great secular offices as well as the Archbishopric?

1722-3, March 9.—Our noble Visitors met again yesterday. Mr. Dennison was called and asked if the Fellows had submitted ; he said no, but he made it his humble request to them that they would be pleased to allow them longer time. Upon this they were so gracious as to allow them till the second of May. The grimace of this was good to seem to do at Dennison's intercession (*sic*). What the aim of it is I know not. It can be of no use, unless they begin to be sick of the business, or have a mind to drop it leisurely. But I scarce think that, and to me the affair seems not capable of accommodation by reference.

I have the favour of your Lordship's. They do me great honour who suppose me to have such influence in the University. But the gentlemen ought not to be defrauded of any part of their own merit. I can affirm that I never had occasion to speak of this election but to two persons, one of our own House and one of another House. Had I been so busy as they think me, I should I suppose have used my interest against him in our House, where I have still a little, and where many stayed at home whom I could have sent against him, and some voted for him that I could at least I believe have kept at home. The Warden of All Souls [Gardiner] voted for the Vice-Chancellor. I believe some who did not appear for the Vice-Chancellor were at least as good friends as he to G. C[larke?]. I fancy Christ Church were as steady and as numerous as Brasenose. No one doubts, I believe, of Blechingdon's friendship to G. C[larke], yet he differs from the Vice-Chancellor heartily in University cause, and has been used brutally upon their account by his old friend the President of St. John's.

1722-3, March 10.—I am informed this morning that an appeal was lodged on. Friday with the King against the Vice-Chancellor and his adherents, and was received with all the favour possible. Keep this as yet to yourself, though it cannot be long a secret. . When I first suspected it, I sent for Mr. Cockman to stop it at least for some time, that our mad men here might have leisure if they pleased to come to their senses. I must do Mr. Cockman the justice to say that no one could be [more] ready to do it than he was. Before I spoke to him he

had written to London to stop it, but he had left an appeal ready
drawn at London, to use if there should be occasion. And the
Fellow who is left agent for them there put in Mr. Cockman's
and the Fellows' too, even after he had received Mr. Cockman's
letter to stop it. Our great men may see what is to make men
desperate. Though I did what I could to stop this, yet I cannot
in my judgment blame them for having recourse, after the
usage they have had, to any one from whom they could hope for
relief. I have discovered, too, that there has been for some time
all possible encouragement given underhand to these Fellows to
apply where they do for relief. But they had never taken this
step if the last decree had not driven them to it. Now *jacta est
alea*; our Visitors must stand to the consequence of what they
have done. Pray communicate this to Mr. Bromley. The
malignity of the planets seem to shed their (*sic*) influence at the
same time on Ruffe and his creatures.

I have read the report, but cannot say that I am much wiser
than I was when I was in town. But by the result of your
debate on Friday, I find it has all the effect they who drew it
could wish for in your House. Who is Hacket, with whom
Ruffe was to be reconciled and to act when he came out of the
country? Not a friend of ours surely. Musgrave must be much
out if he could have such a mad thought.

Postscript. I fancy our grandees rely upon the Viscount to
help them out of the scrape. No doubt he will help them as he
does R[uffe].

1722-3, March 11.—By a letter I saw last night from Dr.
Henchman, I perceive Mr. Cockman's letter which came on
Friday night was too late to stop the application to the King.
The agent left in town for the Master and Fellows had been with
Lord Carteret on Friday morning, and acquainted [him] with
their business, and was appointed by him to bring the petitions
on Saturday morning. Upon this, he says, he thought himself
not at liberty to stop upon Cockman's letter when he came to
Carteret on Friday morning. Carteret told him the matter had
been laid before the King, who received it very graciously, and
bid him assure them that all dispatch possible should' be given
to their business. Now they are in for it, no one can foretell
the issue. But no doubt they who have it now will make
the most of it they can, for their own purposes. Pray acquaint
Mr. Bromley with this.

Your Lordship says it is plain what the chief aim is in pursuing
Ruffe, others will be sufferers. What is the aim besides
humbling him? I guess not what you mean.

1722-3, March 12.—I have another humble petition to you, and
of a little more moment, though not in my own behalf, but of one
who deserves it much better. It is for the sake of honest Wainwright. It is very usual for those of your Lordship's quality to
give instruments to your lawyers, by which you constitute them and
retain them counsel for you, with a certain fee of two or three
marks a year, as you please. Could Wainwright be honoured

with such an instrument by your Lordship, he would not expect, nor is there any reason he should, to be employed in your business any more than he is now, unless in opening a cause, or any under job which your usual counsel, or Oliver Martin, would not care to be concerned in. At least he would not hope for any share in your business but what you would be disposed to throw on him without such an instrument, till your other servants fail, and his own age and experience be greater. But such an instrument would be of great use to a beginner in the world, by the credit it would give him, and without entitling him to your business would certainly be a means to bring other grist to his mill. But if what I have presumed to beg be on any account improper or inconvenient, I hope you will be so good as to excuse me, and to suppose it never mentioned to you.

Tim comes to you with the addition of another character, but no more money I believe in his pocket than when he left you. I suppose he carries off with him all due to him here, but as corn goes I fancy it may all be left upon the road before he reaches you.

By what I still hear, our grandees, as I hinted in my last, rely upon an Egyptian reed, that will run into their hands that lean upon it. I begin to feel in me compassion for Ruffe. The manner in which they treat him plainly shows they are determined to come at him and to lay him low. I could not have imagined such a number could be brought into such extravagant proceedings. May God grant him to make the right use of it, and to own before Him in secret that what he meets with is due to him for other sins, though not for those crimes for which, or from those hands by which, it is laid on him.

1722-3, March 14.—There seems surely to be somewhat more than party in the eagerness of the present prosecution. It seems to come from a spirit of resentment in one you may remember who upon a certain breach was supposed to influence those he could to stick to one man, in order to keep out another. In others without doubt there is a pleasure in exposing the profession through R[uffe]. Somewhat of this kind in many I suppose, else there might be punishment without acrimony.

You need not fear there will be time found for the affair of University [College], assurance was given that all possible dispatch should be used. I do not see how any one can be affected in this case but the men immediately concerned in it, but it may be expected that this may create further divisions in this place, and increase their interest in it.

I just now hear what has happened to Dr. John Freind. You may be sure my friendship to the family gives me no little concern.

1722-3, March 21.—I was surprised last night with the news of my cousin Dolben's being brought to town in custody of two messengers. I am told she has been examined and is confined more closely upon it. Yet no [one] hears as to what she was examined, but only in relation to some conversation she had with

Mrs. Hughs. It must be long ago surely, if she had any conversation with her. Mrs. Dolben I believe has not been in town since the other is said to have returned. You may be sure I am in some concern for so near a relation. If you can learn from Mr. Affleck, or any other, any particulars which are supposed to be laid to her charge, pray be so kind as to communicate. Your Lordship may not have leisure to write them, but Tim may.

Our noble Visitors are now in for cakes and ale. To make the appeal odious, it is given out I hear that it will be a Royal visitation on the University. But that is idle. Nothing can possibly be brought in question upon this appeal but .this particular affair of University, nor can any one have any concern in it but the thirteen who took upon them to void Cockman's election, and the seven who proceeded to suspend and expel those who would not submit. They indeed may all of them be liable to a *Quo Warranto* in the King's Bench. But I do not apprehend it will be carried farther than to declare what they have done to be without due authority, and therefore null. Dr. Newton, one of the Visitors, is publishing a case on Dennison's side.

1722-3, March 24.—Dr. Newton's performance is published. I would have sent it to you, but that I suppose you will have it from the booksellers in town before this can reach you. The poor man has been very ill informed by those who furnished his materials to him. I am willing to suppose the best, and not to think there has been any want of ingenuity in himself; but his quotations and facts are as false from the beginning to the end as his reasonings, nor is there one true position or one right inference in the whole.

We had like to have been in a flame here last week. The President of Trinity as Pro Vice-Chancellor had, in the Vice-Chancellor's absence, given leave to a servitor of University to have a letter from the Chancellor for one term for his bachelor's. The Vice-Chancellor when he returned was in wrath, and said he would stop the letter because Mr. Dennison's consent was not first had, though Dennison was out of town at the same time the Vice-Chancellor was. The Masters got it, and vowed they would [stop] all other letters and business till that letter was passed. Upon the Proctors representing this to the Vice-Chancellor the gentleman was pleased to pull in his horns and to let the letter pass.

Postscript. How comes Pulteney, who is so severe a prosecutor of the Bishop of Rochester, to put up Charles Aldrich for your preacher who was the Bishop's chaplain, and creature and tool too, to as infamous a degree as so poor a wretch could be. Charles too is mentioned in Lawson's evidence, printed in the report, for one who frequented Bromley, whilst the plot was in agitation.

1723, March 26.—I thank you for the comfort of your last. If it holds good, those I am concerned for may have some more trouble, but are out of danger. As for the first, though I wish it to no one, much less to my friends, yet by the just dispensation of Providence every one commonly has their share, of some sort or other. And some of that in this world is often of main use to make us wish for the happiness of the next. But I beg your pardon, you will think I am transcribing a paragraph out of a sermon.

You must give me leave to expostulate with you. I am told my patron, my Lord Harley, and all his relations voted for the rider to the Bishop of Durham's bill. You may say, I suppose, that it was only with a design to quash the bill itself. But you must allow me to say that you took a very dangerous method. Should both parties in the Lords agree, as they did with you, and take you at your word, your poor friends may smart severely for your joke. Besides your rider itself is nonsense. Many of the estates which would bear the best fines would by your wise rider be wholly excused from any fine at all. How many estates have we and others, upon lives, which have paid no fine at all for above twenty years last past? If it could be just or equitable to have such a clause at all, it ought to ascertain the fine to such a fixed value, a year's or what you please, and at the same time oblige the tenant, under sufficient penalties, to give in the full value of the estate. And then you laymen would get little by such a clause. But I do not like these jokes in the laity, they seldom get such things in their heads and move them; but though they fail at first, they revive them again and pursue them till they carry them. Our best security is that you are too much in danger yourselves to be at leisure to new model us.

1723, March 28.—I thank you for your good news that my relation is likely to be at liberty again. I hear poor Ruffe could not forbear intemperate behaviour to Williamson before the serjeant of the House of Commons. If you hear what it was, pray let me know. Nature must be very strong that could not be restrained by his present circumstances.

I hear poor Newton is so pleased with his own performance, that he designs a supplement to it in a few days. The parties in that cause are summoned to attend the Attorney General on the 5th of April.

I have once in my life had the good fortune to please Mr. He[a]rne, and to be highly in his favour. He has thanked me wonderfully for the share I have had in that cause. He is the most zealous solicitor in the university for Cockman and his friends.

Harry Watkins is with me again in his return to town. Master Edward [Harley], and he and I, shall presume to drink your health to-day at dinner.

1723, March 31.—The gentleman who gave me my intelligence is a most sincere friend and servant to your Lordship and your family. He was misled I suppose by common report, as one who was with me here last night, and who is much your servant, had been also. He read to me your Lordship's name out of a catalogue of Tories who had voted for the clause, when I was enabled by your letter, which lay on the table before me, to contradict him.

What violence on the motion on Friday! Where will these things end? But it is pretty plain what will become of Ruffe, notwithstanding the opinion which I find some have, that he may still have a chance to escape.

1728, April 2.—I hear Mr. Edward leaves us at the end of this week. I suppose the lady is ready, and that as soon as Passion Week is over, he will be entered upon the great business of mankind. I could heartily wish he had spent two or three years abroad, before he had been tied down to work for the continuation of the family. I shall send by him that sermon of Burnet's, which I promised to you. I have another present for your library; it is as I take it one of the commandments of the Grand Signior, which as those you had from old Covel, but this is somewhat finer. The beginning is in golden flourishes, and the paper is pasted upon green silk. Harry Watkins found it among his father's old papers. I have given it to Hunt and Gaynier to decipher for me. As soon as I know what it is, I will send it to you.

The Vice-Chancellor has lately dismissed poor Gaynier from being deputy to Wallis the Arabic professor, and has put in a young Fellow of Magdalen College. The Fellow knows not the letters, and began to read the very hardest book in the language, Pocock's "Carmen Tograi," but read only the Latin translation. Hunt and another of Hart Hall attended his lecture, and when it was over asked him, as the Statutes empower them, questions. He gave them ill language. They complained to the Vice-Chancellor. The Vice-Chancellor begged them to hush it up, said he was sorry he had put one in unfit, but could not now help. The Fellow in his next lecture reflected on them. They complained again and demanded he should produce his lecture. The Proctors came along with him to bully for him. The complainants, who had the Statutes to defend them, stuck to their points. The Vice-Chancellor again begged them to drop it, and said the man should make them public satisfaction in his next lecture. They would be content with no other satisfaction but his being turned out. The Vice-Chancellor again entreated them to put it up for his time, and then they might do what they would. But I believe they will pursue their point.

1728, April 4.—Mr. Edward brings with him Burnet's Sermon on Fletcher's father, which I promised you; it is but small, but has all the value which such a thing can have by being scarce. I do not believe there is another of them in England; Burnet bought up all he could. It was designed to make his court to Fletcher's widow. It is a proof of that which was charged on him by Lesly in the remarks on the Sermon on Tillotson, and which Burnet denied so heartily in his answer to those remarks, viz., that he once set up for mystical divinity, or if he was not, he was somewhat worse, a great hypocrite, and pretended to be so, in hopes of engaging the widow by it. And perhaps that was the truth of the case. Lord Bolingbroke lost the title-page when I lent it to him.

1723, April 6.—Gaynier's Life of Mahomet is finished. He will be in town in a few days to make his presents to his benefactors, amongst whom your Lordship is chief. There is a proper mention of your Lordship's library and just respect paid to your worthy librarian, to whom my service if you please. If Gaynier meets with encouragement he will go on to publish an Arabian Geographer, that has been much wanted and very proper for the understanding the story of Mahomet or any other Arabian history.

1723, April 9.—Is banishment thought a greater instance of lenity than imprisonment at home? I should not think so were I of Ruffe's age, and had that want of foreign languages which he has, not to mention other inconveniencies. But perhaps it is designed as the greater punishment. Notwithstanding the vile usage I have had from that man, I cannot help now feeling some compunction for him. May God grant him to make the proper use of what happens to him, upon reflecting that what he had practised so long to others is in so short a time returned sevenfold into his own bosom. Were his son here capable of any kindness, I should be ready to show it, but he is such a creature - as would alone be a severe affliction to any other father.

I hear I am represented as the great incendiary in the cause of University. Your Lordship was so good as to give me a hint of it some time ago. It will not be long now before the world will be able to judge who were the incendiaries in that cause and who the peacemakers. But the thing that is surest is the bustle in the Curator's place. It is a great honour to me, to suppose so many men, a dozen of whose faces I know not, should pay that deference to my opinion as to [be] influenced by it, only upon supposing it. They will scarce allow this honour to me in any case but in one, where they want some excuse for so remarkable an instance of hatred, and would throw it upon any other cause rather than a detestation of their own actions.

1723, April 12.—I hear Ruffe is now indeed affected with his circumstances, it is thought he will not be able to support his spirits when his defence comes on.

I have it from a sure hand that the Attorney exults and is in great joy; it is so great, that with all his skill he cannot conceal it. The time is come that he has been watching for during these last four years, and he has made use of. What have I lived to see betwixt these two men; righteous art Thou, O God, and just in all Thy judgments!

1723, April 15.—My accounts still continue to tell the concern Ruffe begins to be in for his present circumstances, and well he may. For I hear from a sure hand that one tittle of alteration is not to be hoped for in the bill in any respect. Nay, it is said that all which some unreasonable men think hard is, in a due estimation, downright mercy. Perhaps so. The Psalms as I remember mention a sort of mercies that seems to have some resemblance to this. But I am astonished at the policy of those who quitted the House when the clause was brought. I am told it was at Ruffe's own desire. Not unlikely. It is so very peculiar and so impenetrable to poor common mortals. That clause well managed might have taken up a fortnight, if not much more, in debating it. Not a comma in it, but should have been opposed singly.

Your cousin tells me he is to be put up, upon the vacancy which is expected in your county. Better late than never. But it is hard to give a reason why that which is so proper now would not have been much more so at this time last year. His coming in now may be of some use to himself but not of much use to any other purpose. He may help indeed to carry a sprig of rosemary to the funeral of poor brother Hammond. Your most sincere servant declines apace, he cannot have many weeks of life left, perhaps not many days.

Postscript. As soon as my turn here is over next Sunday, I believe I shall be going to Berkshire, where an evening " Post " will be no little consolation in my solitude.

1728, April 25.—There was an election at Oriel on Friday last. Five honest men were chosen, one by ten votes, four by nine votes, against the Provost and three in the first case and four in the other. The Provost refused to admit them, and designs to insist upon a negative ; a claim that was never heard of before in that ancient foundation. I suppose the Bishop of Lincoln, their Visitor, will allow it, and himself claim the nomination, as upon a devolution, though there is not the least colour for it in the statutes. But our Doctor Visitors have set the example, who roundly affirmed all power where not expressly taken away was lodged in Visitors by the nature of their office. They too once had designed to proceed by way of devolution. They were sufficiently told of the danger as well as absurdity of their doctrine. It recoils upon them sooner than I expected.

Postscript. Since I wrote I have received the favour of your Lordship's. I wonder you should not think R[uffe] likely to be disconsolate. If I were in his state I believe I should feel it. He certainly did so when I wrote to your Lordship, though I hear he is now pretty easy again. As to the Attorney it is pretty plain why he should exult, if you remember what I told you three years ago, that he said to a friend of ours that ———— was a villain, and he watched his time to be revenged of him. He has met with it, and has begun to be as good as his word, as you will hear when you come to town.

1728, April 27. [Little Shefford.]—I thank God I am got into the country at last, and have a hearty relish of it, though I have but very indifferent company to converse with, no one but myself. It is for you great ones to be perfectly happy and to be able to have company as well as place that is agreeable. Though I believe you too sometimes have some alloy to your satisfaction, and though you can command what you like you are forced to bear too with those whose room you would rather have than their company.

My neighbours here trouble their heads about the Plot as little
as I do. Our chief concern here is for want of rain. We suffer
as much by it as you can do in Cambridgeshire ; and if this dry
weather should hold a fortnight longer I shall have no great
reason to brag of my being a farmer.

1723, April 30.—There was one odd thing at the sessions last
Saturday at Newbury. A clergyman had high treason sworn
against him, the highest of high treason, a downright attempt
to list men for the Pretender. One man swore directly that he
offered to settle an estate of 14*l. per annum* on him, to engage
him for himself and any others for that purpose. Some say he had
been endeavouring to deal with the "Blacks" for that purpose.
His name is Power, he was formerly a commoner of Christ Church.
His father is at present minister of East Hamstead near Reading,
where Sir William Trumbull's estate is. The man's character is ill
enough on all other accounts. My neighbours who bring me
the story say his design was to inveigle others, and to discover
the enemies of the Government. It is certain the man behaved
as though he apprehended no danger to himself. He offered at
no defence of himself, nor showed any concern at his accusation.
I have but an imperfect account, but expect a letter. But there
must have been treachery or treason, and he deserves to be
hanged for either of them.

1723, May 3.—I beg your pardon for mistaking your meaning
as to R[uffe]'s behaviour. You had very good reason to wonder
that he should not be better prepared for that he had so much
reason to expect.

I have had some hint of a conversation with a certain person,
but I am bid to expect no more till I can have it *tête à tête*. I
can easily suspend my curiosity for a few weeks. Nothing from
that quarter will surprise me.

I told you of a clergyman committed for high treason, I can
now give you a more particular account of it. This Power was
curate to his father at East Hamstead. His father, though a
vicar in Berkshire, lives at Bristol and has 300*l*. per annum.
This son his curate was so scandalous that Lady Trumbull sent
to the father to remove him, or she would complain to the bishop.
This son went not long since with three of Evans's dragoons,
without any warrant, to search a house, as he pretended for some
of the "Blacks." He found only a country fellow or two taking a
pot of ale, but committed such disorders there that the people
of the house got a warrant, and carried him before Mr. Barker,
son of Surgeon (?) Barker, a justice near Reading. Barker committed him for a riot, but kept him for a week in the constable's
hands, to see if any one would bail him. He was so scandalous,
no one would. Barker asked him if he thought his own father,
if he were there, would bail him. He frankly owned he believed
he would not. To gaol he went, but he told Mr. Barker he
would send him a paper, if he would promise to return it, that
would justify him in what he had done, or to that effect. A

paper was sent, signed at the top, and countersigned at the
bottom, being as pretended an authority to converse with the
Blacks in order to discover them, and leave also to talk treason,
and to make any reflections he pleased on any of the Royal
family. In a little time the man was bailed by Mr. Fellow, a
justice in those parts. Both his bail together were not supposed
to be worth five pounds. These things made a noise, and at the
sessions Mr. Jones of Ramsbury, seconded by Mr. Shirly a
clergyman my neighbour, moved to have the matter laid before
the grand jury. Mr. Barker was called on for an account of the
paper; he owned he had seen such a paper, but could not remember the contents of it. Being much pressed, he owned he had
taken an extract of it, but as I think, he said he had it not about.
Mr. Jones and Mr. Shirly still pressed to have the matter laid before
the grand jury. The other justices opposed it, no proof appearing as they said against him. Whilst this was in debate, three
men from Ockingham came and swore high treason against him,
for speaking treason, and for endeavouring to list them for the
Pretender. This was not to be withstood. The fellow muttered
somewhat of a paper, which he intimated would indemnify him.
He said Colonel Negus had procured him the paper, and how
should the King's enemies be discovered but by such men as he
was ? That the three men swore against him to save their own
lives, he having already informed against them to my Lord
Chancellor. But to gaol he is gone for high treason. If you
know Mr. Kent, the member for Reading, he perhaps can give
you a fuller account of it.

If Robin is not called off from his business, I believe he will do
extremely well. I have taken upon me to alter one direction his
brother left, that he should read nothing but classics for half a
year. His tutor beginning a mathematical lecture, I ordered
him to take Robin into it immediately. I am obliged to his
brother for a letter and should be for the continuance of his
favour, but cannot pretend to make him a return in kind from
this place.

The warm weather may cheer Lord O[xford] a little. I wish,
but I cannot say I hope, it will do more. As for good Madam,
fear not but she will bury you as well as your father.

I have been confined since I was here with a distemper proper
enough for one of my bulk. I am now on horseback again. I
have a horse that I make a tolerable shift with, but I cannot
say I ride with that security, nor consequently that pleasure, I
did on old Black.

1723, May 9.—I doubt not but the great affair that is going
on in your parts will be finished, but to me it seems to go somewhat more heavily than it did. I fancy many who are engaged,
and will go, wish it had not been begun. But my old friend the
At[torney] does not bear his share with that alacrity I thought
he would. I hear indeed he was very hearty upon an incidental
point, but they say he is tongue-tied upon the main point. I
wish, for the sake of his soul, that his shyness were owing to his

dislike of the business. But I am afraid it may be ascribed to a meaner motive, he would not give enemies opportunity to observe the consistency of his present and former notion. He knows how open he is to personal replies upon this occasion.

I hear my old friend Charles Aldrich has taken care to convince his new friends, by his late sermon, that he has contracted no political malignity by his former intimacies with the Bishop of R[ochester]. But there was no occasion for poor Charles to lay in so fresh a stock of merit. His former qualifications gave him a good title to some dignity, if perjury, matricide, incest and the last degree of stupidity may be thought to deserve any thing. I wonder who cooked up Charles's sermon. He could not, I believe, so much as transcribe it himself. I wonder how he read it. He must have had recourse to his old crony Alsop. But Charles, I hear, has lately had another piece of merit. Upon the vacancy of a trustee's place in the school at Henley, he admitted Lord Parker ; and the new Dr. Herbert, who is to be next Canon of Christ Church, was sent down to him in a coach and six to negotiate that important affair.

I long to hear who has Ely. The Cantabs have claimed a sort of right by custom to have it given to one of their University. I know none of the present set, that is a Cantab, that can put in for it but Benjamin [Hoadly]. No doubt he will. Should he have it, I suppose Hereford will be happy in Dick Smalbroke.

1723, May 11. Little Shefford.—I heartily condole with you for the confinement of worthy Dr. Colbatch. I must beg, when you see him again, that you would let him know that no one has a greater concern than I have for his trouble. Surely the interest of the Cambridge men is very low with their great patrons, that they cannot prevent things being carried to such extremities as these are.

Postscript. I am very glad to hear that R[uffe] supports himself so well under such long and constant fatigues. Anger and resentment, which I hear yet subsist in him, are certainly very useful to him on this occasion, and furnish him with that extraordinary supply of spirits which his affair requires.

I make no reflection on the news you send me, because I like better being in my poor village, lonely and obscure as it is, than in the *Grand Monde* with my friend Dr. Colbatch.

Postscript. Mr. Harley told me in his last that a clause was offered and received by the committee to extend the tax on R[oman] C[atholics] to the Nonjurors. Is it to bring in the Nonjurors to ease the R[oman] C[atholics] and to bear a share in the 100,000*l.* laid on them, or is it to lay the same tax in proportion on the Nonjurors, over and above the 100,000*l.* to be paid by the R. C. ?

1723, May 18.—I was much surprised at Annesly's and Commyn's leaving you in the vote you mention. They could not but see that you who were for it designed by it to excuse all. But if it were to pass upon [some ?] what reason could possibly be alleged why it should not in equity be laid too on others ? They might perhaps say that since they could not exempt all, they would exempt some. Bnt that still makes the hardship greater on those who are loaded. I am afraid that which would not pass in a clause will much less pass in a bill, where nothing else depends on it.

Mr. Edward has been wonderful kind in giving himself a great deal of trouble to inform me largely of what has passed. It is now over, and I shall say no more, but that I wish what has happened to Lord T[ownshend] and Lord Denbigh may be the worst consequences of this affair. I believe I may safely say that R[uffe] himself has met with more concern for him than he would have had upon any other occasion whatever, and that too in a great measure from those from whom he had least reason to expect it. But what could be the meaning of the Attorney's withdrawing upon the last vote, after the part he had acted in all former votes? This was pure grimace. Sense of decency, out of regard to past friendship, should surely have tied his tongue at least upon former occasions, as well as have obliged him to [be] absent upon this. But I think Lord L[echme]re has, in a contrary way, outdone even the Attorney.

I heartily wish I may hear our friend Dr. Colbatch is released.

Postscript. Poor Brother Hammond declines so fast that I shall return to Oxford sooner than I designed, and be there on Friday next.

1728, May 27.—Dr. Hammond died about eleven o'clock on Saturday night. I suppose this may find you at Wimpole. I was willing you should know our loss, and your own too, of a very sincere servant to you, as soon as you could. We shall soon have his successor.

The Bishop of Chester is safe with us again. Our deceased friend has left directions for a very private funeral. Mr. Biggs is his executor. The chief of what he has left to him is an estate of 60*l. per annum*, and perhaps about 2 or 300*l.* besides his household goods. The good man had the heart to give, while he lived, the most of what he had saved, having given in his life time at several times about 1,000*l.* to the College, and I believe near 1,500*l.* to his relations.

1728, June 6.—I hope you had that which I directed to Wimpole to give you notice of Dr. Hammond's death. The successor shows how kind their intentions are to us, but I hear there is some difficulty in it. It seems he is only a Lambeth Doctor; that will never be allowed here. And should he not desire a degree in the usual form from us, he will be treated only as a master of arts upon all occasions, which I suppose he will not much care for. On the other hand, if he asks a degree, it will be a public acknowledgment of the inferior value of his Lambeth degree. That will never be done I believe with the Archbishop's allowance, but I leave those concerned in it to solve this difficulty.

The Vice-Chancellor yesterday proposed a scheme for settling the late Bishop of Durham's benefaction. He began wisely by proposing the articles that were most reasonable. When he found opposition, he solemnly averred that what he proposed was agreeable to the Bishop's own intention. But all would not do, so great is the aversion to any thing that comes from him, that every thing he proposed was denied. Few of our House were there, they who were readily came in to what was reasonable, though they would have opposed other things had they been brought on; but nothing will go down during this man's mayoralty.

I give you joy of your old tutor's coming in for his share of Dr. Hammond's preferment. He has now the reward of the part he has acted here of late years, and I hope they who foretold this may be allowed now to have spoken from foresight and not from resentment.

Postscript. To whose interest is B[olingbroke]'s return owing? To the Attorney's alone? Is he so powerful? Is it thought B[olingbroke] will return before his attainder is reversed?

1723, June 11.—On Thursday I return again to my hermitage, where an evening " Post," whilst you are in town, will be as before a great favour ; and my butcher, Mr. Joseph Brunsden, at Lamborn, must be the medium of our correspondence.

No doubt the Attorney will claim the chief merit in B[olingbroke's] return, and promise to himself much support from it, though some who pretend to good intelligence think the Attorney had little share in it. I find it occasions many speculations in town, but I fancy some of them either are not designed or will not be found practicable.

1728, June 15.—I cannot have too much of this place during the summer season, I find the exercise and air of it as agreeable to my health as the quiet and solitude is to my inclination. What should I do at Oxford, there are but three in the whole town, when the Bishop of Chester is absent, that I have any correspondence with. I must go about a fortnight or three weeks hence to receive John Drummond and the Laird of Blair at Oxford. And I suppose I may return hither again in a week, and stay, without being called home, till the end of October.

Our new Brother at Christ Church is likely to be in great difficulties about his degree. We are now very certain that he was sent by London, on purpose to involve the university in difficulties. That man is possessed with an implacable spirit of revenge on both universities, because Oxford refused him a degree and Cambridge would not allow him *ad eundem.* But if we are but steady, as I hope we shall be, I think we are in this case upon very sure grounds, and can never be compelled by any thing, but an Act of Parliament, to allow Bradshaw, on account of his degree from Lambeth, the privileges of a Doctor with us.

I have not seen the " True Briton." If it be proper and not too big to be conveyed by the post, I should be glad to see it.

Postscript. What say you to a great lady's presents to R[uffe] ? A 1,000*l.* in a bill ; and fine, proper suits of apparel, one of them of purple velvet embroidered with gold. What is all this a sign of?

Would not she have had him, if he had stayed? Or would not she still have him, if he should return, whilst he can be presumed to have life left in him? I cannot much doubt of it.

1723, June 18.—We have sure information that our new Brother is sent to us upon the charitable view that he will be the most disagreeable to us,- and put the university to difficulties about his degree. Perhaps the pious authors of this counsel may be disappointed in both their views. I take the university to be upon a sure foot, and our new Brother will be mortified, unless he submit to that which those who send him at present seem not disposed to allow him to submit to.

The trials of our " Blacks " are over and, to our comfort though to our disappointment too, nothing of treason or even of sedition appeared upon any of the trial. The extraordinary commission had no other business than to give due correction to the old sin of deer stealing. .

1728, June 23.—You have acted the part of a Christian hero in paying so much respects to one in distress, who had made such base returns to you and your father too for the extraordinary kindness he had received of your father, without ever having had any title to it by any service, respect, or affection to him. I hear he has had a comfortable *viaticum* to support his spirits ;ʼthat, and the incense offered to him, have helped to keep him up pretty well here. I wish he may not find that they flag when he is abroad, where all old correspondence will be entirely cut off, and the want of language will make it difficult to enter into new, if that were a thing to be done with any comfort by one of his age in a strange country.

His suspicions of the Attorney I believe are very true, and his resentments very just, and I, who am no stranger to the honour, gratitude, and friendship of both of them, cannot but admire the justice of Providence in permitting one of the brethren in iniquity to be the instrument to punish the other. And I should still have more reason to acknowledge this, should I live, which is not impossible, to see the person now humbled to retaliate in full measure what he now receives to his old friend. I shall long to hear what the message is that he has left for him.

I suppose you are no stranger to the villainous letter wrote by one of Dennison's party, if not by himself, to the Attorney-General. But it has recoiled, as it ought, upon the author. Such a practice could come from none but some of Ruffe's disciples, the Vice-Chancellor or Delaune.

Since I wrote I have the favour of your Lordship's of the 20th. I have not had the "True Briton" for the two last posts, so I suppose it is stopped. I can easily believe that the reports about the contribution of the great lady and others were much beyond truth. I always thought so. I entirely agree with your Lordship that if they came from friends they were highly foolish and did much prejudice. I believe they came chiefly from enemies *ad invidium faciendum.*

Notwithstanding L[ondon's] charitable design to us, our new Brother must submit to ask formally his degree, if he will live as a Doctor with us. We have a rule that if any who is a gremial with us take a degree, even at Cambridge itself, he shall never be allowed *ad eundem* with us, but must take it again regularly, if he will be such with us. And a reasonable rule it is.

1723, June 27.—I thank you for your last favour to Shefford. I shall soon desire a renewal of it, for God willing I shall be there again on Tuesday next. I find at my return an empty stall. We hear nothing yet of our new Brother. They are convinced I believe that they should be baffled upon a contest, and will condescend to let him petition for his degree.

I hope to drink your health with John Drummond this evening.

1723, June 30.—I am now pretty full of company, but I would not omit to thank your Lordship for enabling me to entertain them. The venison is perfectly good, and you will believe the founder is not forgotten. Here are to be with me to-day, the Lady who is the head of the Kinnoull family, and the Countess of Errol, who has the constableship of Scotland in her, but I am afraid there is more of title than substance left to the family.

I hear my old friend is returned, which I confess I do not well understand. But the place in which the Attorney was first to have met him occasions speculations not much to his advantage. I wish him well, but he will have a difficult game to play.

1723, July 31. Christ Church.—I suppose you will have seen my godfather before this can be with you. You will have learned from him our misfortune, and how dearly we had like to have paid for our good nature in changing coaches. I bless God we had no hurt, and pray tell my godfather what happened was not ominous as he said it was. The braces of the stage coach held out, and brought me safe home. We had one pleasant adventure. As we were getting into our new coach, and bid the fellow drive to the deanery, he took Bob for Ruffe, "Oh" says he, "I know who you are, you are the late Bishop, I will take care of you I warrant you." And as we came out of the coach, he cried "God bless you, my Lord."

1723, August 1.—I thank you for the favour of yours by yesterday's post. It was the more valuable because written after such a journey. It was with no little uneasiness to myself that I left the town the day my lady was expected there.

I am sorry to find upon perusing this new Act that my lady must either swear or register. But I am afraid it is too certainly so, and no doubt the very utmost advantage will be taken of any omission.

Postscript. Yesterday's terrible rain has obliged me to defer going to Berkshire till to-morrow, that I may give time to the downs to be dried a little.

1723, August 3. Little Shefford.—I bless God, I am at my
hut again, and I begin to have a better opinion of myself than I
had, because I find I have still some taste of my own homely
doings here, after what was enough to have destroyed all relish
of them, I mean your Lordship's elegant and nice as well as
kind entertainments.

Ned and Robin spent the evening with me before I left Oxford.
I know not whether I debauched them, or they me, but we three
alone chatted till past eleven.

I find great confusion amongst my neighbours about your last
Act for taking the oath or registering. Many women as well as
men, who have forty shillings or three pounds *per annum,* who
never heard of a state oath in their lives, and scarce knew who
was King in Israel, are told they must leave their harvest work
and trot a foot fifteen or sixteen miles, to take oaths or register.
The poor creatures are frightened out of their wits, and think
their copyholds are to be taken from them, and any one might
have answered for their good behaviour, though they had never
been obliged to this new engagement.

I heartily pity you who are obliged by your business to stay in
town this weather, but that is one of the blessings that attends
your high station.

1723, August 8. [Little Shefford.]—Archdeacon [Gery] died
lately, possessed as Mr. Bromley hears of a great collection of
books and some MSS. Mr. Bromley knows not but some, and
especially the latter, may not be improper for your library. They
are in the hands of a farmer in Mr. Bromley's neighbourhood,
who was executor to Gery; they cannot in those hands be much
valued. Mr. Bromley is promised an account of them, and as
soon as he has it, he will give your Lordship or me further notice
of it. Mr. B. takes our friend Mr. Wanley to be nearly
related to the farmer's wife. Your Lordship once wrote to me
that the Abbot had left a message to be delivered to the Attorney.
I forgot when I waited on you to enquire about it. If ever you
heard it, pray communicate it.

I go to Oxford to-morrow to wait upon Lord Orrery, who is
coming there with his son, though he does not settle him there
till Michaelmas. But I shall be here again on Monday.

1723, August 14. Little Shefford.—I think I told you the
Archdeacon's name was Gery. He was one of the Archdeacons
of Lincoln diocese, but of which part I know not. Nor know I
the name of the farmer who was his executor.

The news about the " Raw minister " is agreeable to what was
rumoured when I was in town. If he is out of credit, it will not
I suppose be long before he is out of place too. The sooner the
better.

1723, August 24.—I could have wished myself with you at
Richmond. I doubt not of your being very easy there. I am
sure the master of the place took it sincerely for a very great
honour to him to see you there, and the company, the place, and

entertainment would all contribute to make you pass your time there pleasantly. I could wish you would attempt the raising of the Ananas at Wimpole, it would be a noble curiosity, and the expense is a trifle to what I apprehended it till I had talked with Sir Matthew [Decker].

I hear Dr. Blechingdon has had an apoplectic fit, it is doubted whether he can recover, but if he should he must be in a condition in which life can be little desirable. The chief canal of the Viscount's intelligence in our parts is stopped, I suppose.

I thank you for the news of Lord O[xford]'s being better. I wish it may not be owing only to the warmth of the weather ; that which is a trouble to most is certainly a benefit to him.

Postscript. My diocesan [of Salisbury] Willis was to have held his primary visitation this week. The days were fixed for every deanery, and public notice given to all the clergy to bring in their children to be confirmed. Upon the death of Winchester his Lordship appears not but sends his chancellor. Many poor clergy, who can have no notice, may bring their children with them and find no Bishop to confirm them. No doubt his Lordship is employed on that which will be of more use to the church of God, the getting of a better bishopric for himself.

1723, September 14. Little Shefford.—I hope by due discipline that I have in some measure subdued my cold. The most mortifying part of it has been that I have lost the advantage of this fine week for riding. I heartily wish you the benefit of a little country air, though it be but for a few weeks, for I cannot think it proper for you, much less for the ladies, to be at Wimpole after the middle or at farthest the end of October, though you should not be called to Parliament. And I am apt to think you will not have that call so soon as you seem to expect. I was assured when I was in town, by those who have always had good intelligence on that point, that there could be nothing of that till February at the soonest.

I heartily pray God that Lord O[xford] may go on to grow better, and that the change may prove to be from some more durable cause than the extraordinary warm summer which we have had.

I hear from Oxford there was a venison dinner on Thursday in the Audit House. The Bishop of Chester taking physic was not there. There was no restraint on them. The governor was invited. The healths proposed were Gibson, Hoadly, Blackburn, &c. Some there were not a little astonished. indeed it was the first time that those names were the current healths of that place.

Postscript. If B   be gone on the account you mention I doubt not but he has carried with him that which will make him very easy, wherever he is to be.

If this be so, it looks still as though W[alpole] prevailed ; but one would not think so by some late promotions.

1723, September 21.—I was in hopes, when I saw what you wrote of the General that which I received last post, of the dismission of Carteret. A friend of ours wrote to me with great assurance that a house was already taken for Carteret at Paris, and that he was immediately to go thither. He told me at the same time this report about the General. However I take the continuance of this report about the General to be a good confirmation of the former, since it is so likely to be a consequence of it. This is doing of business. T. Rowney writes me word that one Wilson, who keeps a tavern at Gloucester, has been barbarously used, as I understand him, by the gentlemen in red,

The season is now perfectly right for riding. I was upon a full pace to-day on the downs for near four hours. I have got a little ugly cropped horse exactly to my mind.

Postscript. There are a thousand comical stories stirring here about the poor people that go in to take the oaths.

1723, October 5.—We yet know not who will succeed Egerton at Christ Church, we are told a friend of Lord Townshend's is recommended, who is a Cambridge man. We cannot learn his name, but it is said his being a Cambridge man is an objection. I have heard of those who swallow camels and strain for gnats. Formerly any one's not having been of the College was thought a just exception to his pretensions. That has been overruled, and I suppose this new exception may be so too.

1723, October 9.—Next Tuesday, God willing, I shall return to Oxford, and lay up my hulk there for the winter.

The poor man that is sent abroad [Atterbury] must have somebody to quarrel with where ever he is. There has been a disturbance betwixt some servants of his and his son-in-law's family. He enjoined the servants of each family not to converse with each other, though they were in the same house, till further order. Two were discovered holding a secret correspondence and were dismissed upon it, and are come to England. These things already have made him the jest of that place. It is thought his son-in-law cannot live with him, but must soon leave him.

1723, October 16. Christ Church.—Since I wrote last to your Lordship I received the enclosed list of Dr. Gery's MSS. from Mr. Bromley. He has not seen any of them but those written in his own hand, and he gives no character of them. He says the man who is now possessed of them is grown purse-proud and pretends to breed his son a scholar; he sets on that account a high value of the MSS., and says he won't part with them. But Mr. Bromley takes Mr. Wanley to be his next relation and believes Mr. Wanley might persuade the man to part with them, if you should have a fancy to them.

The Duke of Somerset went yesterday with a great equipage through this place to wait on her Grace of Marlborough at Blenheim.

Enclosure: "A Catalogue of MSS." A Latin Bible, fol.; *Plauti Comed.*, fol.; *Tullii Offic.* fol.; *A. Gellii Noctes Atticae*, fol.; *Statii Papirii Surculi Thebaidos, Lib. 12,* fol.; *L. Juni Moderati Columellae Rei Rusticae, Lib. 13,* fol.;

A Latin Comment. on St. Paul's Ep. fol. ; A Latin Comment. on the Canticles and *Synonyma Beati* Isodori, 4to. ; Berentrand Exp. of Apocalyp., 4to. ; *Oculus Moralis*, 4to. ; A Piece of old English Poetry, 4to. ; An old Psalter, Latin, 4to. ; Anonymous Treatise of Divinity in English, 8vo.

King James's Speech to Parliament, 1620; and the Genealogies of the Nobility in his reign.
An Account of the Pedigrees of several Families.
A copy of the Heralds' Visitation of Leicestershire 1619, by S. Lennard, Blewmantle, and Aug. Vincent, Rouge-rose, Officers of Arms.
Many medals and coins.
[*The last items are in W. Bromley's handwriting.*]

1723, October 25.—I hear the affairs that have been mentioned in the prints are not so bad as they have been represented; that the gentleman and his son-in-law parted very good friends. One of R[uffe]'s men would have been doing a little with the daughter's maid, and when he was forbid conversing with her, pursued her by letters, which were conveyed by one of Morris's men to her. The maid complained, Morris insisted to have the man turned off, and offered to turn his own off at the same time. R[uffe] yielded with some reluctance, but it is said the masters parted friends.

Here has been a sentence given by the Bishop of Lincoln as pretending to be Visitor of Oriel, by which he would void the late election of five Fellows at Oriel, and take the nomination to himself, the most arbitrary and groundless that ever was given I believe in any case. He pretends to give the Provost a negative, contrary to the plain words of statute and the practice of four hundred years. And upon voiding the election he claims the nomination to himself, without the least colour for any such pretence. If the Fellows can be well supported, this cause may make near as much noise as ever the case of Magdalen College did.

It is not yet certain that Dr. Egerton will quit his canonry, he will keep it if he can. One George Lavington, one that was of New College about seven years ago, puts in for it. He is recommended and supported in his pretensions by Ben Hoadly. He is chaplain to Lord Coningsby, married his daughter's maid, and was made prebendary of Worcester by him. We know nothing of him but what we have from the Whigs, who own him without any reserve to be of a very infamous character as to his morals. God's will be done. But I defy him to be worse than my neighbour.

1723, November 15.—I have been for this last fortnight confined with a cold. I have gone through all sorts of discipline, and bled too at last. But that which never failed before to ease has not yet relieved me. Gibby Burnet's history came seasonably to entertain me during my confinement. I have a much worse opinion of his understanding, as well as of his morals, since I read it than I had before. It is a strange rhapsody of chit-chat and lies, ill tacked together. There is a strong tang of enthusiasm in all the accounts he gives of himself. It is plain that in most things he was very ignorant, and very silent in those of which he could have given the best, I mean the Popish plot. There are great omissions from the original draft, and they are made so clumsily that they are obvious to any one upon a cursory reading. They are I believe such as chiefly related to himself. Certainly there was most reason for those omissions, and they were made chiefly by the persuasion of Johnstoun. But there is enough left to show that he played a double game during the Popish plot, and betrayed both parties to each other. There is a peculiar venom runs through all his book against King Charles and Archbishop Sharp. His comparison of King Charles to Tiberius is monstrous. Both these men knew him, and dealt with him always accordingly. Sharp had once convened him, and would have deprived him of his orders and have excommunicated him, if it had not been for the intercession of Bishop Scougal. It is amazing that he could give such an account as he has done of Sharp and the Privy Council in relation to Mitchel, when he owns at the same time that a contrary account was extant, written by one Hicks. That pamphlet of Hicks is called Ravillac Redivivus, fol. 1682. You ought when you read Burnet's to confront Hicks's account with it. He has omitted the whole account of his treachery to old Grimston, with relation to the Bill of Exclusion, which I have so often heard from your father. All passages printed in Lesly's *Associations* and Cassandra's are omitted, except one in relation to Sharp's murder, and part of that too is omitted. But I hope the omissions will be supplied out of true copies of the original which are still extant. I never knew any book more open to be lashed. But it would be too tedious to mention more of the lies and absurdities that offered themselves to me upon a very hasty perusal.

1723, November 25.—I assure you I was far from disapproving your passive conduct. I cannot recollect the words of my letter, but either they were contrary to my thoughts, or I supposed you would understand in a proper sense, what I might write with a view of answering any one's curiosity who might peep into the letter.

The Westminster election has answered my expectation. I never doubted but those poor misled people would upon proper application come to their wits again. Is Layer likely to be obstinate after the conviction? If the gallows frighten him, it is to be hoped there may be enough discovered to stop their mouths who pretend yet to doubt of the plot, at least of the greatness of it. We heartily thank you for laying the load on the Papists, rather than the Protestants. They who are eased by your proceedings will not much trouble themselves to consider either the equity, the necessity, or the policy of them.

There has been above 3,000*l*. spent on both sides at Warwick. Sir William Keyte, who is returned, is a Tory indeed, bating that,

I hear a mighty good character of him in all respects. He was
bred up by Mr. Cockman, who is now put up to be Master of
University, and has I am told so great a kindness for his tutor
that he will stick at no charge, if there should be occasion, to
support his cause. That affair is likely to make more noise and
bustle here than I think there can be ground for.

1723, December 3.—The poor injured men of Oriel have
moved for a prohibition in the Common Pleas. It is ordered,
unless cause be shown why it should not issue, the first day of
next term. It may be a long suit, and if the poor men are
supported it must make a great noise in the world, and make
the character of their pretended Visitor more scandalous, if
possible, than it is at present. If you enquire in your neighbourhood at Cambridge, you will find that about June last he ordered
his son, who has always designed for the civil law, to take his
bachelor of arts degree, to the surprise of everybody. Afterwards a certificate was got for his learning and morals, that he
was qualified to be a member of any society in either university.
This was some months before ever the cause came before him.
By which it appears that he and the Provost of Oriel had long
before the cause was heard settled betwixt themselves what
should be done in it. Every one must be bachelor of arts here
before he can be capable of being Fellow of Oriel. But I may
venture I believe to foretell that his son will never be allowed to
go out *ad eundem* here.

Abel and his lady called here last week on their way to town.

1723, December 7.—We met yesterday about the appeal
against the election at University. Much squabbling we had;
there were twenty-six Visitors, but two of them had no right to
be there. Many of us were clear that our power by the statutes
expired if we did not determine within three days. Others
thought they had time as long as they pleased. We divided, ten
for hearing it to-day within the time prescribed by the statutes,
sixteen for putting it off till Monday. There seems to be a party
set to turn the poor man, by any method though never so
extravagant, out of his headship, to which he has as undoubted a
right as to any shilling he has in his pocket. If he should have
spirit, this may be an affair that may prove of very fatal consequence to the whole university. The Vice-Chancellor and
Delaune, instead of being judges, are canvassers and managers
for Dennison.

Postscript. Mr. Bromley is much concerned for Cockman,
having by his interest first brought him into the world.

1723, December 13.—The Attorney-General has not yet made
his report about University, but he gave very plain indications at
the last hearing that he should make his report in favour of the
King's title to be Visitor.

What your Lordship is pleased to write of Bentley is of a piece
with all his other acts, both as to the assuming of authority and
as to the exorbitancy of the punishment. Surely he could have

done no more with the concurrence of the senior Fellows, if the young fellow had actually made a breach in little Moss's body. But for a bare declaration of goodwill, a reprimand, and an interdiction of his lodgings to him, would have been abundantly sufficient.

1728, December 18.—Our noble Visitors met yesterday, they voided Cockman's election, and the Vice-Chancellor called in Dennison, who is not the senior Fellow, and ordered him to proceed to a new election, and to act as senior Fellow. The Vice-Chancellor, I suppose, presumed Boraston to be absent because he did not appear in court. The man was really gone out of town, but that was more than the Vice-Chancellor knew. Dennison, when the Visitors were gone, got to the buttery book and struck out Mr. Cockman's name. They go to a new election on Monday. Here is sport for Westminster Hall.

Postscript. These withdrew from yesterday's work, besides the eight protesters, the President of Trinity [Dobson], the Warden of Merton [Holland], Dr. Holdsworth, and Dr. Evans of St. John's. Both the Proctors withdrew themselves too. Only thirteen gave sentence out of twenty-nine who were in town, and of twenty-eight who attended. Vice-Chancellor, Delaune, Bridge, Wile, Moss of St. John's, Master of Balliol [Hunt], Dr. Wilks of Trinity, Dr. Davis of Magdalen, the Heads of Jesus [Jones], Exeter [Hole], Corpus [Mather], Brabourn, Principal of New Inn Hall, Newton of Hart Hall.

1728, December 19.—I hear not what the session is likely to be opened with, nor of anything extraordinary that is likely to come on, but Bolingbroke's bill. That was not long since despaired, but now his friends begin to have some hopes again. I am told it will in a good measure depend upon some changes that are expected before the sessions. What those are my friend could not learn, but they must be to Walpole's advantage, if Bolingbroke's interest depends on it. And yet Carteret [certain]ly not only kept, but gained g[round]. And if, as the Gazette tells us, [we shall] have peace abroad, I fancy Carteret will maintain his ground too at home. I take Walpole's interest to depend not upon any great liking to him, but the necessity of their affairs ; but a little time will show us what we are to expect in these matters.

It is said the bill for ascertaining our fines is drawn up and has been perused by the ablest lawyers. If that come in I think our friends should consider well how to behave in it. It will be a high strain of virtue in them to come in to support those bishops who have done, and still do, all in their power to ruin them and their friends. Few honest men are now left in any preferments that are likely to be affected by this bill, and not one honest man likely, upon present views, to come into any future vacancy. There are none but the Universities likely to be affected by this bill, for whom any honest gentleman can have any concern. I think our friends should at least frighten

[*torn*] . . . . tes, and if they do at last oppose
the . . . . to manage so as to let the
bishops know that they themselves are saved, for the sake of the
Universities which they are endeavouring to ruin.

We have had warm work this Audit. We caught our brethren
at most scandalous faults in their accounts, particularly in
allowing a bill to Egerton, for work done seven years ago, and
which upon a solemn examination in Chapter six years ago had
been resolved not to be allowed to him. We made them cry
peccavi, and say they would do so no more, but we insisted to
have it retracted. That they refused. The Bishop of Chester
and I said we must then enter our dissent to it, with our reasons
for it. They agreed to it, but when we had entered it in the
Chapter book, they said it was a reflection on them, and ordered
it to be struck out. Upon that we withdrew and said we would
come no more to Chapter—as we shall not—looking upon the
liberty of our vote as infringed. We have entered another protest to-day which I suppose will be struck out too as a reflection.
But I am very glad of [such an] honourable occasion of having
. . . . them. Your old tutor, though he
was not here when the act for paying Egerton's bill was made,
and though he was forced to own openly that it was wrong in
every circumstance, yet said he would main[tain?] it, since
it was done. He proposed an act, that the other act should
never be drawn into precedent. He was heartily laughed at for
his wise expedient, and told that it would be a plain confession of
the iniquity of what was done, as well as a fruitless precaution
against the like. But he stood to his tackle to support what he
owned was unjustifiable, and to strike out our dissent.

1723, December 30.—I am very glad your brawn pleases, I
believe you will have time to eat it in the country, if your return
is designed, as I guess it is, to be at the sitting of the Parliament.
Though the King be landed, yet he comes so late that I believe
they must have a week longer to adjust their business.

I have not yet condoled with you for the loss of Lord Mansel.
One part of his character was very commendable, his honourable
behaviour to your father. I hear he died of a broken heart,
partly for the loss of his son, but much more for the marriage of
his daughter.

1723-4, January 8.—I must refer your Lordship to the Bishop
of Chester for an account of our melancholy condition here.
Perhaps he will not tell you all. Your old tutor used his Lordship in Chapter very brutally, worse than ever he did me, and
without any provocation, and could have no motive to it but to
merit with his new patrons, by being very impudently, though
very stupidly too, rude to the Bishop. You shall have it when we
meet.

1723-4, January 12.—Honest Wainwright was so kind as to send
me the Speech. I wish your news may hold true, that we shall
have only one shilling in the pound. But the Speech seems to
intimate that we must expect the same we had last year, though
it hopes there may be no occasion for more.

There is no mention of the state of affairs abroad, but the observing that the augmentation of our forces has given weight and credit to our foreign negotiations insinuates that the continuance of the same augmentation will be necessary to preserve our credit abroad. And that seems to intimate that all is not settled yet there, though no doubt we should have had the same paragraph if the Congress of Cambray had been ended.

You may be sure all our hearts are full of joy and gladness, upon so authentic an assurance of the present happy situation of our affairs. And surely we may be allowed after the trouble we have been in, from our apprehensions of pestilence and rebellion, to refresh ourselves a little with the innocent diversion of masquerades.

The Speech seems to intimate as though there was a project on foot for paying our debts. Very good news indeed, if it be no ways akin to the last. It is said Walpole has a scheme for it. Some say one shilling per pound on land is to be mortgaged for a large term of years. I am afraid we poor country folks should think that somewhat worse upon us than the South Sea. I hope there is nothing in it, it would be a great damper of our present exultation.

1723-4, January 26.—You cannot surprise me with any thing that you tell me from your own House. You know my thoughts pretty well on that head. I have given over all home politics, ever since I saw the management about the new Parliament. Perhaps they may think, with reason, that they have more occasion to continue their additional forces than they had to raise them.

The town I believe was very calm and insipid. I began to be concerned for my friend the Bishop of Chester, lest he should be out of humour with it. But this strange accident will raise, I suppose, a little ferment; at least it will furnish some new conjecturals to support conversation a little.

I hope Lord Oxford has had no return of his fainting fits.

Postscript. Here is a report that the late Duke of Ormond was much in favour with the Prince of Asturias. It is to be hoped the young man will have more wit now he is King.

1723-4, January 30.—I suppose Mr. Bromley is now with you in town. His son, who will be soon in town too, called on me on Tuesday. He was to have paid his duty to your Lordship when he returned from his travels and stayed but four days in town. You were then gone to Wimpole. He will [call] on you again very soon. I never knew any one more improved than he is. Those things one would have wished otherwise in him are quite worn off. He is returned a good-natured, well-behaved, sensible, sober, honest gentleman. I wish your cousin Ned had gone along with him. If you ask some close questions you will find he had some curiosity whilst he was abroad.

Have you seen Gibson's sermons before the Society for reformation? The last paragraph about masquerades I think ought to be publicly complained of by those concerned in the late Queen's affairs, for the sake of their own credit as well as her honour. I should be glad to hear it was brought into the House of Lords, be the issue what it will. The French minister too ought to complain to the King of it. It is as impudent as it is groundless.

If Baron Scroop comes into the Treasury my godfather will have a friend there, but can any one that has been honoured with his acquaintance be proper for a post of so much confidence?

1723-4, February 4.—The verses are very good, and, as your Lordship truly observes, have a true taste of human life. May one enquire who is the author? He need not be ashamed of them. Who is Tr——? I know of no Trevor that now belongs to the Court, and yet that is the only name I can think of at present that rhymes to endeavour.

I have heard talk of the bill your Lordship mentions of putting it into the King's power to recall whom he pleases. But as a friend to the other person [Bolingbroke], I should not wish to see an attempt to make him easy by that method. Many who would be for him upon a direct bill will be against that way of serving him, if it is understood right, for that :—

1. It gives up the power of Parliament in having any share in repealing that which they had enacted.

2. It puts a very great and I believe a new power in the King which was never heard of before.

3. It puts it on the ministry to show grace to those who can give them money, and to exclude from it all who cannot.

I much question whether such a bill, when it has been talked of, and considered a little, will pass in the present House.

The town is employed very properly, for such a set of mortals as are there at present. What more suitable business can be found for them, than quarrels about operas and the ladies that belong to them?

1723-4, February 10.—All joy and happiness to you, upon the good day on which I hope you will receive this, and a continuance for many, many years of the blessings it has brought you. I am very sorry I cannot have the honour to assist at the celebration of it, but I shall keep [it] as well as I can here. I have bespoke your cousin Robin, old Sir William, and a friend or two more to assist me, and I believe the healths of the day will go round as often here as they will in Dover Street, unless old Sir William's courage fails him, which it never did yet.

I did not think Arbuthnot had had a genius for such performances. Your Lordship is much in the right, that he has no reason to be ashamed of it. Pope has the credit of it here, and has no reason to be displeased that another's child is laid to him. It does him as much credit as any of his own.

I shall return your Lordship my subscription money to Pope by the first opportunity I meet with. Had I known of it a week ago, I could have sent it up with other money to Mr. Thomas. I am a subscriber in obedience to your Lordship; it is a little prodigal in a country parson whose benefice is worth but 60*l.* per annum to pay five guineas for that in English which he can read in Greek.

The transaction at Westminster is a very comical one and much for the credit of the moderation Prelates, it shows too their sense as well as their temper.

I shall be very glad to see Motray['s Travels].

1724, February 18.—I meet with no one but what is very glad to hear how the great man you mentioned has been mortified. I believe no one that ever got and spent so much money as he has done, ever got, by spending it, so little goodwill. The more I think of the bill you mention, the more I believe it will meet with opposition if men are aware of the consequences of it. However fair the title may seem, and the consent of all may be thought to be had to it, yet it is indeed reversing an Act by other powers than that which enacted it, and giving power to the Crown which it never had before. I fancy no precedent of this kind can be pretended.

I live in expectation of Motray, as full as it may be of silly stuff. A man that converses with men or books must hope for little diversion from either, if he has not the skill of picking a little from those which are silly.

I wish this late weather may not have pinched Lord O[xford]. I am sure it pinched me, though I am not so old or crazy as his Lordship, though I am crazy enough.

1723-4, February 23.—It is likely enough I may sometimes be whimsical, and take more precautions than are necessary for my health. That is a usual effect of a solitary life. But that was not my present malady. I had a violent return of my cough. I bless God it is pretty well over, and I hope to be out again in a day or two.

I hear Fiddes' Life of our Founder [Wolsey] is despised, as no doubt it deserves, in town; I always thought it a vain ridiculous design. But I am afraid the success of it will not cure him of being conceited of himself, or troublesome to others.

The Duke of Beaufort here has been in great danger with a violent cholic. They almost despaired of him, but youth preserved him. It came through extravagant drinking after hard exercise, and young as he is, he will drink and swear with any cocker in England. This to yourself. It is owing entirely to the company he is brought into by his tutor, who ought to be hanged for it. *Hic fiunt homines.* No doubt his relations, who endeavoured lately to have taken him out of his guardian's hands, will make proper advantage of this for our credit.

1723-4, February 27.—I have some news that will be very agreeable to your Lordship's curiosity. At Sandford, three little miles from us, where one Powel, a papist, is impropriator, there was occasion a few weeks ago to pave the church. In order to it, it was necessary to take up the steps that lead into the church. Upon the taking up of the first step, they found upon the side of it that was turned to the ground, a fine image of the Virgin with an imperial crown on, designed for the Assumption, and eight angels about her. A great deal of the blue and gold left upon the image. This, no doubt, was placed there to conceal it from the Commissioners that were appointed to destroy such images, and was forgotten, and lain undisturbed ever since. It is to be brought into the Museum.

Sir Nathaniel Floyd is giving them a building at All Souls which will cost him 1,200*l*., and will finish their new quadrangle, all of it, except the turning of the hall.

[1724, March 1.] St. Taffy's.—I thank you heartily for your last. The spirit rather increases than flags, and a diabolical one it is. It may be very just that Providence should permit him on many other accounts to be distressed by these men, but that no ways alleviates the implacability of their malice. He certainly deserves nothing on that account for which they pursue him. But I doubt not but they are under apprehensions, and without any reason, of designs in the Attorney, if he could bring in his associate to help him to undermine them. And these apprehensions will not be lessened, if there be any ground for that which is told us with great confidence by those who come from town, that Sir William Wyndham is to have a considerable post and the Duke of Somerset to be again Master of the Horse. Sir William's son [is] to marry Lady Dye Spencer and to be made Earl of Northumberland. We hear, too, Lord W[alpole] is to be made a Duke, and the father, to show the excess of his vanity, is to take Garter without a title.

I suppose your next may tell me that young Mr. Quin has already opened in your House. I take him not to want necessary assurance.

1723-4, March 5.—I had not Motray till Tuesday last. He is impertinent and silly beyond the reach of any expression, he is the veriest Frenchman I ever yet read. What does he pretend to for religion—I fancy a papist, though I suppose he has much the same religion as he has sense. But after all I am glad I have him, for the account he gives of the poor King of Sweden. Though his account is a very imperfect one, yet I think it is the best we have of what passed whilst that King was in Turkey. There is I own in that poor King's character something very extravagant and near approaching to madness, but yet there are many things very great, and I cannot read his fate without a great concern. La Roque (Larroque) I have, and it is certainly the best account we have of that spot he treats of. Quesnel I have read, but he is nothing but a merry fellow that gives you an account of himself and his companions, rather than of the countries he went to. The others I shall send for.

I doubt but W[alpole?] may if he pleases have the thing passed by very great numbers, but if only a few of his own party would be disobliged by it he may not be willing to hazard that for the other. Nor indeed can I see that he will let it be done, unless he could some way find his own interest in it, and how he will do that I see not.

1723-4, March 8.—That your Lordship mentions was as stupid as it was barbarous. However I take it for certain that those ninety seven who joined in that question did by that in effect declare that they would join in opposing another, if it should be brought on. And if any Tories should join them in that case, and others be absent, the opposition might be greater than is commonly expected. I do fancy that business will be dropped for the present. It is plain to me that these men have jealousies of their leaders. If there were any conduct in our friends, care would be taken to improve these jealousies. Do these men think that neither they themselves nor any of their generation shall ever have occasion for mercy and compassion ?

Postscript. Since I wrote I have received a letter from my dear young mistress, which I esteem more than I should letters patent for Winton or Durham. I shall preserve it accordingly. My most humble duty and hearty thanks to her.

1723-4, March 12.—Your Lordship's judgment is very becoming your own goodness. The case is hard indeed. It may be very just in God to permit the poor man on other accounts to be used so by such cruel men, but that does not lessen the barbarity of that unrelenting, hardened race. Since it is dropped now, I am apt to think it will never be revived. Oh, the honour of the Attorney! Has he no resentment for having been made a tool to lead his dearest friend into a snare? Or was he in the secrets? Many will be apt to think so if he shows no resentment on this occasion, as I will answer he won't. I am afraid the poor man himself may begin to wish that he had not given himself some of the airs he did last summer.

Your Lordship observes very justly that it is pretty odd for one at that age to plead *heat* in excuse of himself, who was never famous for much of it in his youngest days.

1723-4, March 14.—There are very quick turns in my old friend's affair. There must have been some extraordinary service to earn so sudden a change of counsels. They must be speedy if they design anything. They have but little time to turn themselves in, if you are to rise in Passion Week. Whatever the event be, by that which has passed lately in your House I perceive the opposition will be more violent, and perhaps too more numerous than was once expected, and though it should be baffled, may leave ill blood behind it. What is become of the project for paying our debts, which [we] were made to expect from day to day. Is it gone in fume? Or is it deferred to be opened at the time the treaty of Cambray is finished.

I am glad Mr. Gwyn may have an opportunity of showing his parts before he is turned out.

Your Lordship's appetite seems keen for the country. I wish it may hold, but I own my fears lest I should not hear of your leaving the town till much about the time that others are returning to it.

Postscript. I am sorry for that you write about Mr. Bridges. I hear it too from other hands. He will be a loss to the *Res Literari* and to his private friends.

1723-4, March 19.—I am heartily sorry for our loss of Mr. Bridges. Do you hear how his books are disposed of? If they should be sold, perhaps there might be some picking for your Lordship.

Dr. Freind's fate could not be doubted. Several Whigs must have joined you, or the number of those for him would not have been so great as it was. I am glad he is gone off with so much spirit, I think there is no reason to be concerned on his own account, that he is not continued in the House. I always thought it an attendance not very suitable to his profession. I suppose neither of the great men you mention will ever make use of him as a physician.

If any thing be done for my old friend this session, it cannot I believe in so short a time be by any other way than by an act of grace. And they will find it not a little difficult to extend grace to him without naming him—for which I suppose there is no instance—and not comprehend others at the same time, as I believe they design not. I am apt to think it will be put off to another session.

We hear that by the help of Lunn the Jews have carried it against Jesus Christ.

1723-4, March 23.—I thank your Lordship for the account of 'what passed with you. It is plain the great man may carry the point if he pleases, but he never intended it, or does not care to break even with a few desperadoes on the other's account, or may be influenced by both reasons. Though I am told too of a stronger reason, that his antagonist at Court opposes it, and that the umpire will not allow any thing to be brought on in which both do not agree. Be the reason what it will, I take it for certain that my old friend will be dropped this session at least. It was odd that no one seconded Miller. Several of those men are certainly hearty against it. I take the motion to have been as much against the Attorney as against his friend. Had it come to a question, though lost by a great majority, I believe the Attorney would have been uneasy upon it.

1724, April 8.—Here is a report here to-day that the Bishop of Winton is struck with a palsy, and is to be succeeded by Exon. If there be any thing in this, it must come cross the country, for he was at Farnham.

The project for preachers at Whitehall is managed in such a manner as is not likely, I am afraid, to work the wonders expected from it. No indifferent men, none that would go many though not all lengths perhaps, are to be taken notice of [in] it. It is declared none must hope for a share in this bounty but they who are staunch Whigs, and openly profess themselves to be so. I am afraid this will not increase the number of honest thorough Whigs ; rather unite and confirm, than break the perverse Tories. You will allow me some concern to see so great a project, through ill management, not likely to be improved to the ends it was designed for.

. 1724, April 10.—There was no ground for the report of Winchester's death. There has been another election at Oriel to-day, where six Fellows chose two very worthy men against the Provost and two who were with him, but he insists on his negative and refuses to admit them.

There is talk of an address to be proposed to our Convocation, to thank for the late bounty of the Whitehall preachers. But that affair is managed so ridiculously as well as scandalously here, that should any such address pass the the Heads, and be brought before Convocation, I am confident it would be thrown out by great numbers. That would be rare work.

I am pretty well informed the great ones above are dissatisfied with the management of our wise Governor, and want to remove him, and to put in Bradshaw, not Tanner, as I once thought. That man would bustle a little more, but to as little purpose as the present gentleman. I hope your next will tell me when you return to town.

1724, May 13. [Little Shefford.]—I am returned again to my hermitage; since there will be no occasion for my attendance on your Lordship this summer, I believe I shall not stir hence till I return to my winter quarters. I most humbly thank you for your kind invitation to Wimpole, but not only old age, which makes me lazier if not weaker than I was, but other business will oblige me to deny myself the greatest satisfaction I am capable of in this world.

1724, May 21.—I thank you for the favour of your note on Mr. Thomas's letter, bad as the news was. · I must beg the continuance of it though it should be more melancholy. I presume not to beg it from your own hand, you may be in too great a concern to write. But be pleased to order Tim Thomas to let me know how things go, I own I expect the worst. Bleeding may give a little present relief, but I am afraid nature is too far spent for any one to hope reasonably that our friend can continue much longer.

I hear a letter came on Sunday last to the Vice-Chancellor, signed at the top " Ge. R." countersigned " Townshend," to be communicated forthwith to the Convocation. It was three sheets of paper, full of favour and affection, and to give notice of a new establishment, for a Professor for modern history, in each university. Surely somewhat more than appears is aimed at by this great profusion of favours on a sudden. I wish they may be distributed with such prudence as not to defeat what is aimed at by them. Some are so unreasonable as to doubt whether this be a full equivalent to the university for the suit to support the Archbishop's degrees, or to the church for the new Archbishop. I hear a letter was proposed and passed the Convocation in answer to his Majesty's letter. But in my poor opinion this was using his Majesty with too much familiarity, though the letter be sent up by a Bedell in one enclosed to Lord Townshend, to be delivered by him to the King. No doubt a solemn address, attended by the most considerable of the body, was expected.

· 1724, May 23.—I received this morning from Oxford, not having yet my letters from Lamborn, the news of the death of my Lord Oxford, my honoured and only master. The long reason your Lordship has had to expect it has I hope in some measure prepared you for it. The integrity with which he served his country in the midst of temptations, as well as perils, his universal capacity for it, and the unblemished honour with which he is gone out of the world, as they are the proper grounds of comfort for your Lordship upon this juncture, they will also, I doubt not, be a means to assure to your Lordship the continuance of the protection of God to you, for his sake as well as for your own. My concern upon this occasion is chiefly, I own, upon another account. His decay and death, and some other late events, forebode to me what we are to expect. The removal of those who alone [are] likely to prevent what we dread, or in any measure to redress, is a token to me that Providence is likely to permit it to come on us. But these thoughts are not seasonable now, nor at any time, but for our private use. I hope I need not assure your Lordship that if my own duty to you, or concern for you, could be greater than it always has been, that which I paid, inviolably as I hope, to your great father, would, as it ought by right of inheritance, be devolved to you.

Postscript. I beg your Lordship would be pleased to deliver the enclosed with my duty. I need not say that it is not to the Dowager.

1724, June 8.—There is one topic which I did not think proper to mention in my last, which is as proper to afford you comfort as any that can be suggested to you. I mean the satisfaction you must have from reflecting in how tender a manner you paid your own duty, upon the most trying occasions, to such a father. If your Lordship may justly glory in having had such a father, I am sure he was blessed, in the judgment of all others as well as of himself, in the best of sons. To my knowledge he thought it a blessing, that did not only support him in all his troubles, but far outweigh them. And you have reason to bless God for those troubles which ended so much to your father's honour, and gave your Lordship too an opportunity of showing to the world so great an example of filial piety.

1724, June 21.—I thank your Lordship for the favour of your last. I should scarce have troubled you again so soon from so barren a place, but that a very odd story has been brought to me from Oxford, which perhaps your Lordship may have heard more of in town. It is said the Viscount four days before his lady's death had a consult of physicians, and pressed them to tell him sincerely their opinion, for that it was of great importance to his affairs to know it. They told him they believed she could not live three days, upon that he called his coachman and ordered him to have the coach ready next morning, and drove him directly to Lady Walters at Sarsden, and was there at the time of his lady's death. The gentleman who came to me from Oxford and told me this is a worthy honest man. I am sure it is believed at Oxford, but I will not answer for the truth of so extraordinary a story. If it be true it needs no comment.

1724, July 1.—I am by further accounts now persuaded of the truth of that I wrote to your Lordship about the Viscount. It was so monstrous that I could not at first give entire credit to it, though it was brought to me by a very honest man. Should he succeed, I am afraid it will be as little for the lady's credit to admit of his address under such circumstances as for him to make it. The woman that is gone, though in many respects disagreeable, had a right by the relation she had to him to have the common forms of decency observed to her. Though she was not very proper to excite affection, she had highly deserved respect and gratitude, if one who has saved another from a jail may be said to have deserved any thing of him.

I have heard somewhat of the affair in which our old friend is embarrassed, but not enough to be able to make a clear judgment of it. I suppose your Lordship means the money deposited in his hands. I know not who advised him to act the part he does, but I fancy he will not let go his hold till he has such authority for it as shall indemnify him at least, and prevent any after reckoning. I take him to be on the sure side of the hedge. He has the money in his hands. In my opinion they have the worst of it who want to have the money out of his hands. He may perhaps lose some credit, but men of his climate value not that much if by losing credit they do not lose gelt too. But they who want to have the money again must, I am afraid, submit to some things of very hard digestion before they can come at it.

I hope, as your Lordship observes, that the French raise their demands so high, that they may compound with us the better for that which they most desire. I trust it is so, because I see the demands have not yet affected Change Alley. Should they make these demands that they may have a pretence to break with us, methinks we should not be so indolent upon it. But our best security, if I am rightly informed, is the inability France and Spain are in, from their own poverty, to disturb their neighbours.

1724, July 22.—Our late brother Egerton, your Lordship's present diocesan in Herefordshire, is got into a fine scrape. He met lately near Whitchurch a loaded cart, the driver of which refused to give way to him; upon this the bishop was dormant in him, and the nobleman alert and predominant. He swore at the carter like a dragoon, and beat and bruised the poor fellow with the butt-end of his whip. The rude rustic has been so uncivil as to employ a noted attorney for such matters to take the law of his Lordship. His Lordship has offered two guineas by way of composition, the attorney insists upon an hundred and says he doubts not to have lusty damages against one of his character for swearing and striking. Thus the case stood when heard last of it. It comes on, if not compounded, at these assizes, and I question whether my late brother does not love money well enough to run the hazard of being exposed at a public trial, if he can hope to save any thing by it.

Postscript. Since I wrote I have received my ring, for which I most humbly thank your Lordship. It is, as it ought to be, dear to me both for the person by whom and him for whose sake it is bestowed on me, and though I have, I hope, at the same time in my mind more substantial things of another nature to preserve dear my old master's memory to me.

1724, July 25.—Your Lordship will have heard before this can come to you of the change that will be at Christ Church. The new Governor may perhaps make a little more bustle, but will serve no purpose, good or bad, any more than the old one. But I am amazed at the taste of the great men, that can think Hugo fit to be Primate. Here will be a proper occasion for our old acquaintance Jonathan to revive his talents.

1724, August 4.—I am but an indifferent horseman, but when I have my Lady's leave I would surely go much farther than the distance is betwixt Shefford and Newbury to pay my duty to her Ladyship. Spinam (Speenham) Land at the entrance to Newbury is the proper place for her Ladyship to bait; and the "Bear" is the best inn. Newbury is just the midway betwixt Reading and Marlborough. If her Ladyship should have a mind to go the best part of the journey in the morning, she might bait at Hungerford, which is twenty-two miles from Reading and eight from Marlborough, and the "Bear" inn there too is a very good inn. I shall depend upon notice from your Lordship of the day and place.

I live in a place where new books are never heard of, our intelligence reaches no farther than to the price of corn at the next market. But when I send to Oxford I shall enquire for my friend Cheyney's book; I should be glad to meet with anything that may contribute to health whilst we live. As to long or short life it is not much worth while to be very solicitous. I expect some nostrums.

They must know our new Governor [Bradshaw] very little, or be very weak in their own judgment, who have great expectations [of] him. There is an old maxim, which I believe will hold as true for the future as it has done hitherto, *nemo dat quod non habet.* He certainly will do them no more service than Hugo has done, he may possibly make them some more enemies than Hugo did. He will be more *busy* than Hugo was, but not to any more purpose. I expect more from him out of the College than in it. He will attend the meetings of his brother Pates, be pressing or opposing things which he may think will recommend him above, and possibly raise some intestine broils amongst the Heads, and inform against them to the ministers. He may perhaps at home give port sometimes. He loves his bottle, and if he will give drink he will meet with those who will help him to drink it. But farther than this I apprehend nothing, either without or within doors.

1724, August 15.—I must beg leave to divert your Lordship a little with a soliloquy of your old tutor. He thinks it seems the Government have done him great injury in not naming him to succeed his friend Hugo, and could not forbear lately to make his complaints of it, as usually, to himself. "I have been nine years Sub-dean, and could govern the College I say as well as Dr. Bradshaw, and am as loyal as he for the heart of him. I say I shall not care to serve long under him."

Honest Dr. Fowke I hear is to be the new Canon, he has earned it by a part that has outdone even your tutor. It is too long for a letter, but when your Lordship sees Bob, if you ask him, he can give you some account of him.

1724, August 23.—The master and his brother surprised me last Saturday night about eight o'clock. They stayed with me Monday evening. The master is now beyond dispute plumper than your Lordship. I am afraid his father has stayed so long in looking out for a fortune great enough, that whenever the master marries, he must scarce hope to see the proper effect of it. I congratulated him very heartily upon the approaching marriage of his sister. There is not a gentleman in England upon every account more desirable than Mr. Verney. The young lady will indeed have occasion to show her great goodness and discretion in her behaviour to her mother-in-law. She is of the first rate of the Termagants, and upon a fair trial of skill would I daresay outdo our old dowager.

What I wrote to your Lordship about your old tutor is now no secret. He cannot forbear expressing his resentments to others as well as to himself. It is now said Hugo insists for him, and that he stands fair for it. I know not whether this be given out to banter him or upon any ground. But there seems to be some stop put to the disposing of that preferment, and we are told Tanner is talked of for it as well as Bradshaw and your tutor. If they would give it to any of our own growth, I fancy the new Primate would be able to get it for his own convert, honest Peter Fowke.

The Viscount and his lady that is to be are preparing their wedding clothes. She is to be married before Michaelmas, for then she quits Sarsden to Sir Robert. She is said to have great settlements and to expect an addition of honour to her spouse.

1724, August 29.—My duty to my godfather. I hope it is for some very good purpose that he stays in town, when a marriage, to which I am sure he wishes so well, is coming on in the country. We are now sure who will be our Governor. Bradshaw that was first named is the man, and Clavering, who has Llandaff, is to keep his professorship with it. As little regard is had to suit men's different preferments to the proper business of each of them as to their own capacities. How the bishopric of Llandaff and deanery of Hereford will be consistent with a Regius professorship in Oxford, I cannot see. There will too be no little inconvenience to the College, for want of one to hold the offices. Poor Tanner I believe must be summoned to do duty, and in that case will have reason to wish that he had kept Ely.

Your old tutor has exposed himself to be laughed at heartily by taking people's banter of him for earnest, but he has made such loud professions that he would be Sub-dean no longer, that I see not how he can come off of them.

Postscript. I expect to see some sport when I return to Christ Church. I have letters thence just now, which tell me that our Sub was in high expectation last week of being Dean ; that the old *ab origine* Whigs roared at it, and cried what would become of their pretensions if converts had such encouragement. But upon Bradshaw's being declared, the poor Sub cannot forbear showing the greatest dissatisfaction and to Bradshaw himself. Their bows to each other are very short, and their looks very shy. This it is likely will in a little time afford some diversion.

1724, September 2.—Possibly my next letters from Oxford may furnish me with somewhat to entertain your Lordship with. Their new Governor is expected every day, and I fancy his Sub will not be able to command himself enough at the installing of him as not to show some visible marks of resentment at the injustice done to his own merits.

1724, September 5.—I do not remember who was the author of that satire in block letter which your Lordship mentions. If the book was in verse, it was probably Skelton's the poet laureate, some of whose verses Fiddes quotes out of a satire written by him against the Cardinal.

I know not but I may have John Drummond here to drink your Lordship's health over your venison. The news letters come regularly. I propose at present to go from hence on the 1st of October to Oxford, but my stay there will not be long.

1724, September 25. [Oxford.]—An ague has obliged me to return hither a week sooner than I designed. I may thank myself for it, by presuming too much upon my strength and by walking by the river's side an hour after sunset. But I hope the worst is past. I am so weakened and tired with the discipline I went through last night, than I can write no more now.

1724, September 28.—I believe I have such a share in your Lordship's good wishes that you will not be ill pleased to hear that I missed my fit last night. But I am still but so so, and have not yet done with the nasty draughts of the bark. I can now from my own experience advise you to guard against so troublesome a companion as an ague is, and I take Wimpole soil at this time of the year to be likely enough to give you one.

1724, September 30.—Your old tutor seems to have digested his resentments. A bottle of port has worked wonders and brought on a good understanding between them. He goes in with our Governor, as he did with Hugo, after nine o'clock prayers, and was lately met unluckily coming out of his Governor's lodgings past one in the morning. This is known to every under-graduate, and they easily see from it what government they are to expect.

Is not this Trefusis that Sir John Cotton has married a daughter of Craggs?

1724, October 1.—I had the honour yesterday to receive safe from Shefford your Lordship's of the 22nd, directed to Lamborn. Your Lordship may perhaps think I had received it sooner by my mention of Sir [John] Cotton's marriage in my last. This is as quick dispatch as the Viscount's. But Sir John is the person purchased and not the purchaser. Such a fortune will be a noble support to him. Is the lady tolerable as to her person? His end is obvious enough, but what was the lady's? Cavaliers who drink so very hard as our friend Sir John, are not thought to be the most likely men to answer what the ladies chiefly propose to themselves. I have heard it whispered as though there was no ill understanding betwixt the lady and Sir John in Trefusis's life time. Yesterday the Viscount was to conclude his famous marriage. It [was] deferred till yesterday to save Michaelmas rents. Never was known such an extravagant change from a penurious wretch, who has all his life before sponged upon others, to a profuse prodigal, and for the sake of a woman nearer 50 than 40, whom he can feel indeed, but has not been able to see for these ten years past. 1,200*l. per annum* rent charge, added to the 800*l. per annum* from her former husband. Great presents of jewels and plate, country house and Cavendish Square house. The last to be richly furnished with damasks and velvets brought on purpose from Genoa. And it is said the lady says she will show him what it is to live. I look upon this as a plain crack in his head, and the beginning of the fall of his understanding, if of nothing else.

I should have told your Lordship in my last that I am afraid our old friend Sir William Giffard has not many more days in this world.

Postscript. I am told this afternoon, and I believe it comes from the Viscount's family, that there are to be ten days of open house at Sarsden, and ten after at Cockrop, and then the lady is to be carried to court, and the husband to be made a duke. I have heard for some time that there was to be an increase of honour upon this marriage, but I scarce think it will go to the highest step.

The Duchess of Marlborough made Lady Walters a visit upon the prospect of this marriage, and presented her with a set of Japan dressing equipage, which had belonged to the late Queen, and been valued by her. The Viscount and Lady Walters together returned the visit to the Duchess.

1724, October 12.—My neighbour on the other side has been at a loss for a curate for his parsonage. He had his living he says from the Chancellor and must therefore have one that is not obnoxious. There was none upon enquiry in his own College of whose affection to the Government he could be sufficiently secure. One of New College was recommended—"How is he affected to the Government?"—"Ask your present curate, he knows him well."—"I cannot rely on what he says, he was put in by Dr. Hammond."—"The gentleman has taken the oaths."—"Ay, that may be, that is no proof."—"He is an honest man."—

"Honest is an ambiguous word, I must have one that is discreet and yet stirring, and that will keep the people together upon the right side upon any election."—At last he has taken one Parkinson of Wadham, who is one of the Lord Chancellor's pensioners there.

1724, October 14.—Yesterday I had the honour to hear from my Lady Oxford, with an account of her having been confined for a week to her chamber, and that she was going to Lady Paulet. Her Ladyship mentions not to me what her illness was, but if it was the cholic, I am certain there is no other safe certain remedy for it but the Bath waters. Radcliffe, who would allow the Bath good for nothing else, owned it was a specific for the cholic. And if her Ladyship finds any thing of that distemper I hope she will be prevailed on to spend some considerable time longer at the Bath.

I design at present to be at London early, and to pass the best part of the winter there, but I will not resolve upon any certain time for my journey till I hear when your Lordship designs for Bath, and whether you come through Oxford. If you take this road, I will not be absent when you come here.

I most humbly thank your Lordship for communicating to me so many particulars. I had heard some of them before, enough to satisfy me that all the others are true. That particularly about Ruffe, though there are different accounts of him. Some say he has prevailed to have all he has quarrelled with discarded. Others, that he has been told his advice was not wanted. In general, it is certain that he has quarrelled with everbody he was most intimate with, and has roused amongst those poor desperate wretches as great a bustle as ever he did elsewhere.

I am far from having any disadvantageous opinion of Wimpole, I think it for the summer as delicious a spot as is in England. I cannot indeed think a ground that at bottom is clay, and consequently that holds water as much as that does, to be wholesome in the winter.

The Viscount says the Parliament will certainly sit on the 12th of the next. I suppose your Lordship will be at the opening of it.

Sir William Giffard, contrary to the expectation of his physicians, is still alive, but he cannot, I think, last long.

1724, October 17.—Poor Giffard is still alive, but drooping. G. Clarke has been forced to leave him upon a summons from Dick Hill, who is ill too, and who, I fancy, designs to leave G. Clarke some concern in his will.

I hear Mar has written a letter to the King, owning the letter taken about Erskine's to be his, and begging pardon for it. This looks like a prelude to his coming over, but if he comes, it must be upon the same foot Bolingbroke had his pardon, without honour or estate. And if that be done again, it may possibly occasion some notice to be taken of both pardons in Parliament. Ruff has played the devil abroad, but there are different accounts of it. Some say he made complaint of those who had the management and had interest enough to have the powers of two of the chief superseded. Should this be so, it is probable that was one of them, and this may be the occasion of his present measures. Others say Ruff advised not to have any Scotch or Irish trusted, and wrote that he could not serve unless they were all removed. The answer said to be given to him was that his advice was not wanted. Should this be the account that is true, I know on what side Ruff is by this time. All agree that he has set them together by the ears abroad, and that the Government here never did a wiser thing for themselves than in sending him thither.

I hear exactly the same account of Bolingbroke's affair that your Lordship does. He is upon the History you mention, at least pretends to be so. As far as I understand, it is only an account of what passed whilst he was in the Pretender's service.

I hear your countryman Lord North has not been able to prevail with his mother-in-law in Holland to let him take out thence part of his wife's fortune for the payment of his debts. He is retired upon it to Paris, not being able to return hither.

Our worthy friend the Viscount, I hear, begins already to be weary of the change of his house keeping, and is come again to the usual diet of loins and legs of pork. But fondness continues as yet, and the old fellow kisses so heartily that the smack is heard three rooms off. Blechingdon preached there last Sunday, the rogues here say his text was out of Genesis, 18th chapter, 11th verse. The Viscount carries his young lady to Court on Monday. It is supposed he puts in for her to be of the Bedchamber to the Princess in Lady Grantham's room.

The new Metropolitan that is to be is returned from the west, where he has been distressing all the clergy that agreed not with him in politics to the very utmost of his power, and has parted with them in the most provoking manner possible. One of them that was to preach before him took· his text out of the 12th of the Revelations and the 12th verse : "The devil is come down unto you, having great wrath, because he knoweth that his time is but short."

Postscript. Great intercourse and compliments and frequent visits pass betwixt the Viscount and the Duchess of Marlborough. I think I told your Lordship that she had made the Viscount's spouse a present of a Japan dressing equipage that was the late Queen's and of which she was very fond. The Viscount has power for sending for what venison he pleases, and uses it very freely to save beef and mutton at home. He has had three does already this year.

I heartily pity poor Mrs. Hay, they will convict her, but they cannot be so barbarous as to take her life. I heard of all Kinnoull's usage of her from T. Dod when he was with me. But as I observed before to you, is it to be wondered at from one who uses such a wife, and his own family, in so vile a manner. But if I am informed right, he is likely to pay for it in this world, and will not be able to get so much as bread in a little time. Should that be his case, whatever was done for his wife and children, I think he ought to be left to die in a ditch.

1724, October 26.—On Friday night our new History Professor came down, with the royal donation of the professorship to the University for the King's life, and of the patent to himself only for one year. They have made it a very precarious tenure to the professor himself. He is to take out a new patent for it every year under the sign manual. They are resolved to keep him to his good behaviour. Notwithstanding their resentment of our non-addressing before, Lord Townshend has sent with the donation a most gracious letter to the University. By many circumstances it is plain they desire to have a public address, and I think it is not difficult to imagine why they desire it, both with regard to themselves and to us, and no doubt they will have one. The matter is to be before the Pates to-day. Our new Governor came down here the same day that the Professor brought the donation, and he had been with Lord Townshend the morning before to receive his instructions; he returns too to town next Friday. That it is plain he came down with no other view but to promote this address, and I suppose he will take to himself the merit of it. And the ministry perhaps too may ascribe it to him, and think they have done a fine thing by giving us a new Governor. But he will have no other share in it than any other Pate, and he might have spared himself the journey if he had not proposed to himself new merit. The address would have passed without a single vote to oppose it if he had been absent. Nay, I doubt not but every one there will be as forward in it as he can be.

Postscript. I am now told the business of the address will not go so easily amongst the Heads as it was thought it would have done. Your Lordship shall hear more next post. I should be glad to know whether Cambridge do anything more upon the instruments being brought to them.

[The Rev. Dr. Stratford to the Rev. T. Thomas.[*]]

1724, October 28.—Pray tell my Lord my first thoughts about our address proved the truest. It passed the Heads without any difficulty, out of nineteen only four thought the letter which they had formerly sent sufficient; they were Vice-Chancellor himself, the Warden of All Souls, Brasenose and Lincoln ; all the rest with both the Proctors came in roundly for an address, and the person who proposed and managed the debate for an address with great noise and warmth was Delaune.

Our Governor was very modest in the address, he only said that if the University thought fit to address he could assure them it would be kindly taken and they would be well received. It appears by many circumstances that the ministry had set their heart upon bringing us into an address; we cannot yet

---

[*] This letter, and the one which follows dated Nov. 4 and referred to in that of November 6 *post*, are printed from copies in Thomas's handwriting, with the dates and a few words inserted or corrected by Lord Oxford.

guess at all their ends in it. The Vice-Chancellor is to draw up the address and no doubt he will be very cautious, but I know not what others may offer to insert, or how the Masters may relish anything extraordinary in it.

Our Heads had more to say for themselves than I knew in sending only a letter upon the notice they had that such a benefaction was designed. When King James I. in 1605 annexed a canonry of Christ Church and the parsonage of Ewelme *in perpetuum* to the Divinity professorship, a much more considerable benefaction than this, the Convocation did no more than decree *Litterae Gratulationae* to be sent.

1724, October 30.—Our grandees go up with their address on Friday this se'nnight. The compliment I suppose will be over before I am in town, and I shall be so unhappy as not to have a share in that solemnity.

Things look but untowardly for Madam Villeck ; her cause was put off on Wednesday till this day on pretence that the Attorney General was indisposed, though he was very well at eight o'clock at night at the Rolls on Tuesday. There are suspicions upon this that she may not meet with all the dispatch she expects. That which is done to-day will probably give us more light.

[The Rev. Dr. Stratford to the Rev. T. Thomas.]

1724, November 4.—Our address passed yesterday in a full Convocation very unanimously, but our Governor has had occasion upon it to discover himself. In the beginning of the address it is said, *In full confidence that their address will be received with the same favour that their late letter was*, they, &c. Our Governor proposed to leave out that clause at the meeting of the Heads when the address was first read, because, as he said, it was well known their letter was not received kindly. The Vice-Chancellor asserted that it was, and had my Lord Townshend's letter to produce for a proof of it. Our Governor was seconded by the Wardens of Wadham and Merton, but the other Heads stuck to their clause and over-ruled them. Then our Governor proposed a clause by which they were to promise to instil good principles into the youth ; part of that he proposed was admitted and part rejected. He took this so ill that he resolved once more to attempt to have the alterations made to his mind in Convocation. He desired the Masters to be at the common room yesterday after dinner with a design to propose to them his alterations, and to tell them that if they would stand by him he would propose them in Convocation. This was a very extravagant as well as unusual method and very improper for his station ; but whether his emissaries had brought him word that it would not pass in his own House (as it would not have done with the majority) and much less in Convocation, or whether some friend had suggested better advice, he sent the Masters word after dinner that he should not come and only desired that they would be at Convocation. The thing had taken air and the eyes of the whole Convocation were upon him; had he moved anything he had been cut down immediately. That dashed him, it was thought, not a little, for he was silent and offered nothing. The Dean could have no view but to recommend himself by an excess of zeal; the address of itself is brimful of loyalty.

1724, November 6.—In my last to Tim, your Lordship has the conclusion of the affair of our address; as far as is proper for a letter. The rest must be reserved till we meet, which I hope we shall do soon, for I am apt to fancy your Lordship will now come to town, and take your place in the Lords' House and go thence to Bath. I am very glad my Lady stays so long at Bath. The two greatest scoundrels in this business of the address were Delaune and Hunt of Balliol, and yet if any two in this place were ever more open, as well as more warm, in their disaffection than others they were the men. The last now makes great court to our new Governor, but I am told he is run into great necessities by his extravagance upon his alliance with the noble blood of Sheffield. Our Governor I hear is gone up in great wrath upon his disappointment, but I believe he has done his business by it in the University, and not a little prejudiced himself too in his own House. His friends above may see that they may safely depend upon his zeal, but not much upon his interest. One part of the clause he would have had in was, "the *only* support of the church of England, of all the Protestant interest abroad, and of all the Protestant Universities." The last was surely somewhat very ridiculous. I fancy our Governor, nor any of the ministry, if catechised, could tell the names of the tenth part of the Protestant Universities, so little have we to do with them.

Our Chancellor I suppose will not go with the address, for the same reason the Duke of Somerset declined going, because he had not been taken any notice of in Lord Townshend's letters.

I am afraid Bentley will have the advantage in the present dispute. The trustees are nominated by Craven's will, the senate had no power to make any alteration.

The French lady has her money, she stays now to solicit her friend's other affair.

I shall lodge at Mr. Battely's in Dean's Yard, Westminster.

1724, November 12 [London].—You will have seen our address and the gracious answer in the Gazette. Lord Townshend made a splendid entertainment for all that came from Oxford. The Bishops that attended the address dined with them. His Lordship gave in an elegant speech fresh assurances to them of the kindness with which his Majesty received this address and was resolved to treat them. But our poor Vice-Chancellor, who had never been at Court or with great men before, to the no little surprise of the company, made no answer to the compliments. I am assured the Royal speech to-day will be full only of grace and favour. No notice of parties, or complaints of disaffection, but only gracious assurances of favour to all subjects without distinction.

Postscript. I have dined with some who heard the speech; it is, as I told you it would be, nothing but tranquillity. We are happy if we continue in the condition we are, and to do as we have done. All the same, the same forces are necessary to preserve the continuance of that respect which at present is paid to us abroad.

1724, November 17.—The poor Vice-Chancellor was in a maze, he had never seen a King or Secretary of State before. The address was of his own inditing, that you may easily guess; it is not over polite. But the matter and thought, though not the words, in that clause about privileges, were suggested to him by the Bishop of Chester.

I never knew so dead a calm as we are in here at present. Young begins to solicit for his bill of divorce, he says he has agreed with his wife about the alimony; I think it is 400*l.* per annum.

I am glad you have such a prospect of succeeding in your election. If you carry it only, as you justly observe, by a small majority, it will be reversed here. The expectation of the town is against you. Your Lordship will be in such a hurry that I cannot expect to hear from you, but pray tell Tim that I expect that he should give me an account how the election goes.

1724, November 23.—I condole with you for your defeat, but I suppose it was no surprise to you, when you [knew] with what weapons the enemy managed the war against you.

I suppose your friends in the House of Commons were beaten too yesterday, in the only stand they expected to make this session, upon the army. But I have not yet seen any one by whom I could hear how matters passed.

Ruffe has managed things so abroad that he has thrown them into the utmost confusion. The Government never did a wiser thing than in sending him thither. Lately the cry went for Ruffe against Mar, but now it is said that every soul there, even Lansdowne, is turned over to Mar against Ruffe with great bitterness, who with no less fury acts alone against all.

I hope you will come and comfort yourself among your friends in town for your disappointment. Methinks, too, you should desire to hear the debates about Young's divorce.

Postscript. I just now hear that poor Giffard is dead. He has left T. Rowney and G. Clarke executors. His estate, which may be better than 4,000*l.*, after some legacies to servants, to be equally divided amongst his brother's children.

1724, November 28.—The reading of Norton's letters to Mrs. Young gave great diversion yesterday to the House of Lords. The sick, lame, and blind attended it, and crawled out of doors to share in the entertainment.

Postscript. The case against the Bishop of Chester is revived with great violence, and many very unfair circumstances. I always apprehended this would be the return to our address.

1724, December 6.—The return which I expected and foretold is made to our address, though I was not believed but rather smiled at when I suggested my fears, that if the ministers got the address they seemed so much to desire, they would afterwards prosecute the Manchester cause with more violence than they had done hitherto. But I remembered an unlucky story, that when the Lower House of Convocation had upon many promises been betrayed by Atterbury into an address that the church was safe and flourishing, within six weeks, by way of making good the promises of favour to them, a letter was sent from the Queen countersigned by Sunderland, requiring them to submit to the bishops and threatening to punish them if they did not.

On Tuesday last was se'nnight the Bishop's solicitor having heard by chance that the Manchester cause was upon the list to be heard, he went to the solicitor of the Crown and expostulated with him for not giving him notice of it. That solicitor seemed to make light of that. The Bishop's solicitor told him that the bill of exceptions had not been made part of the record, as had been agreed. Paxton, the Crown solicitor, said surely they would not insist upon such trifles. Watson, the Bishop's solicitor, desired Paxton to go with him to Baron Gilbert. The Baron told Paxton he dealt unfairly, for that he had in his presence agreed to make the exceptions part of the record. The Baron immediately called for the bill of exceptions and signed it. Paxton said they did not think the exceptions of any moment. The Baron very justly replied that then he had less reason to apprehend their being argued. The two solicitors went from the Baron to the Attorney General. Upon Watson's complaint of the unfair dealing, the Attorney General only said he did not think they would insist on things of so little weight.

The Attorney General moved next day to bring on the cause but agreed to defer it till next term, because it had been brought late upon the list. Raymond was not in court. Prat and Flat (sic) said indeed it was time to end this cause, and that the poor man had been kept long out of the favour the King designed him. Fazakerley, the Bishop's counsel, said the delay had not proceeded from them, they had always been ready, but that the Attorney had not represented the whole of the cause to the court, that there was a bill of exceptions that was by agreement to have been part of the record, and he prayed an order of court to make it so. The court said they must adjust that among themselves. Paxton offered to Watson to make the exceptions part of the record, if he would give bond not to appeal to the House of Lords. Watson asked him what he meant by such an offer, that he (Watson) had no power to give any such consent. On Friday night Watson gave notice to Paxton, that he would move the court again next day for an order to make the bill of exceptions part of the record. Paxton's own hand was produced in court, where he promised it. The Attorney and Solicitor both came out of other courts to oppose the motion with great warmth, but it being matter of right, not favour, the court could not longer refuse it, and made the order as desired. This long account I suppose will sufficiently explain what I hinted at in my last, and show your Lordship the true meaning of the gracious answer to our late address.

Nothing is expected till after Christmas, nor much then. Some say the Irish halfpences will be brought into Parliament, because they begin now to be vented in England. Probably the affair of the masters in Chancery will come there, it cannot well be settled in any other place. But the ministry, it is thought, will beforehand prepare the scheme they would have pass. It is supposed this affair will end in the dismission of the present Ch[ancello]r. But his successor is not yet settled. King and Trevor are talked of; Trevor dined lately with Townshend and Walpole.

Bolingbroke's bill will certainly come in after the holidays, but it is not yet generally agreed in what manner it will be brought in. I am sure that at present promises are made to the lady that there shall be a repeal of that part of the attainder which disables him to inherit his father's estate. But this is the most favourable bill that can be hoped for. Others say that to that partial repeal a clause of banishment will be added. But if it is not part of the bill when brought in, I believe it will be moved to add it to the bill, and many think the bill will not pass without it. Bathurst is now the chief if not sole manager for Lord Bolingbroke. I know not that this place affords any thing more than I have mentioned. I never knew so dead a ca m.

1724, December 12.—Nothing from my neighbour can be a surprise to me, but there seems to be in this that relates to Tim more of stupidity than malice. But what occasion can he have to enquire whether Tim be in priest's orders? It is to know whether there will be occasion at Christmas to admonish him to take them.

The House of Commons has afforded somewhat this week that has pleased all parties, but the North Britons that are to suffer by it; because they could never yet be brought to pay the malt tax they are exempted from that, but by way of equivalent sixpence per barrel additional excise is laid on them, and the drawback which was allowed to them, upon the exportation of corn, is taken away. The debate was betwixt the Scotch and the ministry. The Scotch pleaded, and I believe truly, that it was a breach of the Union. I do not hear that any other answer was given but that it was not the first breach, and this was necessary. They threatened to leave the House. You will easily think they were not much believed as to that. Cockburn said their drawback was taken away only to favour the exportation from Norfolk. It was carried by 138 against 41. Only Wade, Lawson, Plummer, Bernard, and two more whose names I have forgot, were with the Scotch. I find they who are not much satisfied with the regularity of this, yet think the Scotch have no complaint, who went so violently into the taxing of the papists, and all other exorbitant bills.

A grand jury was called in Dublin to find the bill against the man who printed the pamphlet for which the proclamation came out. The jury twice brought in the bill *ignoramus.* That jury was dismissed, and another called of the most substantial merchants in Dublin. They instead of finding the bill brought in a presentment, a thorough one indeed, against Woods and all his "accomplices," who by fraud or any other means should attempt to vent those halfpence in that kingdom, &c.

Here is a poem in town, I cannot yet get the sight of it, but I hear it is an excellent one, called the Fable of Prometheus stealing Jupiter's golden chain, by the connivance of Venus, and leaving a brass one instead of it. You will not be at a loss for the author of it. I am told Jonathan's picture is put up by the magistrates in the town hall at Dublin.

Postscript. At the time I am writing there is a great meeting of the bishops at the Archbishop of Canterbury's house here in Dean's Yard, to consult what to do to put a stop to masquerades. No doubt they will come to some worthy resolutions. I suppose all will end in some application to the King.

1724, December 17.—On Wednesday night the report was made by the Committee of Council about the masters in Chancery. There are 60,000*l.* deficiencies, five of them have given in, in their accounts, 6,000*l.* in an honourable person's hands, meaning the sum which they gave to the Lord Chancellor for their places. It seems one said, if this enquiry went on, his place would be worth nothing, and therefore he would be so true to his family as to give in what he had given for his place, as part of the account. The others stared at him at first, but when they found he persisted in it they thought him a wise fellow, and did the same. It was proposed, upon the report of the Chancellor, to order the money now in the masters' hands to be paid into the Bank. He promised to make an order for it as yesterday. What will be further done, when this comes into Parliament, cannot yet be guessed. Some think the Chancellor will be out before, most think he cannot stand it, but a few are of opinion that he may still keep in. A great deal of the securities paid into the Bank will consist of securities upon rotten houses, in and about the town, which paid perhaps ten or twenty per cent for the loan of the money.

I am told his Grace of Canterbury proposed taking some methods to stop the masquerades to his brother of York first, but he did not approve it. I suppose he was afraid the lay masqueraders might retaliate on him. Upon that his Grace of Canterbury summoned only the bishops of his own province. It was proposed to consider of some reasons to be laid before his Majesty against masquerades. At a second meeting, it is said, it was referred to the three bishops of this church here to draw up the reasons. If it be so, they will make rare work of it, but nothing further is yet done, and I am apt to think that York, by London, will take care to banter it and quash it. It is said private masquerades grow numerous, and are more diabolical than the public, bad as they are.

The bill against the city of London will perhaps make some noise ; there was a division upon the motion for it of 130 odd to 49. Mr. Walpole told them, if any one had objections, it would be time enough to offer them when the bill was brought in. The purport is, as I am told, to give the mayor and aldermen a negative upon the common council, and to abolish some other privileges which are not used as the ministry would have them. It is surely the highest attempt of this nature that ever was made, and much beyond the taking away of charters in King Charles's and King James's days. There at least was a form of law, and a sentence in Westminster Hall.

I have seen all the Irish pamphlets. All here are of opinion that Jonathan wrote the whole fable, I must own I think so too.

1724, December 22.—The Lord Chancellor now seems to be given up by all the world. On Friday the Council required him to order the masters to give in such security as the Judges should require that they would not alienate the securities which they had in their hands, and to commit any masters to the Fleet who should refuse to give such securities. He thought this hard and boggled at it, but it being insisted on, he consented. It is said Newcastle whispered him that he would have reason to be glad if he came off without an impeachment, and upon that he submitted. My godfather thinks the ministers will endeavour to screen him, and to let him fall as gently as possible. It is thought they care not for the precedent of a minister's being exposed for a corruption. There may be somewhat in that, but others think the matter is gone too [far] to be stifled, if any were disposed to do it, and that he must be obliged to refund, either by bill or impeachment. As I was going to see your worthy aunt to-day, as I passed by the Lord Chancellor's house I saw your cousin Townshend coming out into his chariot. It was a court day too. I leave you to make your reflections. There is much talk that Cadogan will be stripped of all or in part. It is said .corruptions have been discovered in the management of the robes, and that the poor Turks have been cheated of their appointments ; a mortal sin no doubt. Some say Poultney designs to lay down. Bolingbroke's bill will be brought in without any clause of banishment. They are not sure that no such clause will be offered by others.

I hear there is a scandalous paper goes about of a copy of verses by way of dialogue betwixt the Devil upon Ben, and a certain statue upon a steeple in Bloomsbury. I hope no one will presume to send it to your Lordship.

[1724,] December 25.—I told your Lordship in my last that I saw Lord Townshend on Tuesday last coming out of the Chancellor's. That was looked upon by some as ominous, but I am informed, very well I believe, that it was to a quite contrary purpose. The Chancellor had desired to know whether he was to go out or no during the holidays, that he might regulate his own motions accordingly. Townshend was sent to him, with the

Duke of Devonshire, to assure him that he should not go out, at least during the session. I believe this to be true. They have no mind of a precedent of a minister's being exposed for corruption. It is not known where such a precedent would stop. Some think he will not go out till the King returns again from abroad, but I believe it is certain he will be kept on till his affair about the musters in quite over, that if he should go out afterwards it may be with as little slur as possible. At another time this matter would have been pushed too far to have been stopped. It cannot still be kept out of the House, and I suppose some means must be found to pay in the deficiencies before it comes. Should there not, I suppose the matter cannot yet be stifled, but if the money that is wanting can be found, I am apt to think there will be strength enough to prevent any farther enquiries. Some noise there may be, but that will be little regarded.

As I am writing I receive the favour of your Lordship's, and find you judged right in thinking they would not let impeachments be brought against any of themselves. I beg leave to repeat my thanks to your Lordship, and to assure you again that I little expected the amends you are so good as to make me for a mischance that could not be prevented. The bill for Bolingbroke will be brought in, in as favourable a manner as possible in all points, but that of restoring him in blood. And I have reason to think, that he himself will come over as soon as his bill is passed. The bill against the city will be carried with a high hand. Time alone must show us whether any of these things will afford you any diversion upon your return to town.

1725, April 1 [Oxford].—I heartily bless God that you are out of doubt of Lady Margaret's having had the small-pox. It is the greatest blessing God could have bestowed on you, except one other which I hope too you have sure reason to expect. Two such blessings in one year are great compensations of Providence for your father's troubles.

Your neighbour's illness is very unseasonable for his friend Bolingbroke's affair. Should your neighbour recover, he will scarce do it soon enough to be able to attend that business. Do you hear any thing how the election goes at Launceston? Was there any opposition to the Doctor [John Freind]? Bob dined with me yesterday in his way to Tedsworth, where we did ourselves the honour to remember your Lordship, and all that belong to you. I long to hear that my Lady is past all doubt as to that we apprehended in her, as well as Lady Margaret is as to the small-pox.

1725, April 4.—I thank your Lordship for giving me so good an account of two persons for whose welfare I am so nearly concerned as my Lady Oxford and Lady Margaret. I am now determined to go to Bath to endeavour to wash off some scurvy that has been floating about for some time, and which I ought indeed to have prevented by repairing thither before this time. Sir Humphry has offered to call on me here next week, and to carry me with him. I suppose I shall have the pleasure too of Mrs. Alice's conversation, as well as of his.

A gentleman lately happened unluckily at dinner before your old tutor to say that the late Chancellor had sold all his livings. Your tutor was in no little fear and concern, and fell a stroking his belly, and repeated with great earnestness six times together, "Indeed sir, I came honourably into mine; indeed sir, I came honourably into mine, &c." The gentleman, who had no suspicions of him before, began to entertain some, upon this uncommon earnestness to prevent suspicions. But though he has lost one patron, he is resolved if possible to earn some other. He now begins to closet young men, and to tell them if they expect to be trusted with pupils they must give proofs of their affection to the Governor. "Sir, I have taken the oaths." "The oaths, what is that? Every one takes oaths, are you zealous for it? Will you do as you are directed? Will you choose such *Parliament men* as you shall be directed?" "No, sir, I can never promise that upon account." I think this is going the utmost lengths, nor could I have believed it, as frail as I know him to be, had I not had very sure authority for it.

1725, April 7.—I bless God for the good news of all kinds which you confirm to me. You may be certain that which we suspect and hope shall be an inviolable secret with me till it betrays itself. I hope Arbuthnot, as well as you, is convinced that Lady Margaret's illness was the small-pox. I am glad you are going into the country, though I hope you will not stir till you see the City bill over, though you have no prospect of throwing it out.

1725, April 8.—Have you seen a book called "An Enquiry into the Ideas of Beauty and Virtue"? It is Dean Berkeley's, it is worth your reading. I have but one objection, that in some cases he seems to think better of mankind than I am afraid they deserve, and than facts as attested by our best histories will allow.

1725, April 17. [Bath.]—I bless God I got safe through the rain hither, I am afraid my friend Sir Humphry will find the roads very bad next week. My godfather seems to have no occasion for the waters yet, but if he holds on he may perhaps in a little time, as hardy as he is. I cannot hear that Mr. Jeffrys has as yet found the relief he hoped for here, but he seems not to me to live up to the dignity of his fortune and quality. He and my godfather have each of them one little room in the same house, and eat at the common table with other boarders in the house. Harry Watkins begs his most humble duty to your Lordship; he would be well if he could totally forbear the relapses which his good nature sometimes occasions. But I hope to finish his cure, I shall exercise my authority and put him under proper discipline. I have already began it by forbidding absolutely my godfather in an evening, and I shall allow their congress but rarely too at noon.

I thank God I begin already to find that these waters have their usual effect on me.

1725, May 5. [Bath.]—I thank you for the honour of yours from Welbeck. I was much surprised to hear of your journey thither, which I did first from the master, but I was much pleased too. And I am glad to hear you are gone farther. May you take such journeys once a year.

I did myself the honour of writing to my Lady from this place, and she was so good as to answer me immediately. She tells me her health is bad still, she took no notice of something I presumed to hint at a distance, but I take her silence for a confirmation. And I hear from other good hands that all goes as we could wish, and I heartily bless God for it.

I have had a return of the ague I had in September last. My godfather, who gave his other friends fevers, gave me I am afraid my ague, by walking me by the river side in a cold east wind. But I have not heard of it since Sunday se'nnight, and I was able to go last week to Wells, and to spend six days there, where your Lordship was constantly remembered by the good old Bishop [Hooper] with all respect possible. I thank God I left him without the least decay in any part of his understanding, nor with any in his body worth notice. A little trembling when he writes in his hand, and such a weakness at eighty-five in his eyes that he is afraid he must at last use spectacles. I think he is likely to last many years.

I hear my old friend's bill goes on very heavily. The great ones pretend they cannot govern their dependents, and have already given way twice to them. Possibly it may be so clogged as to prevent the chief ends that were aimed at by it.

Postscript. My hearty respects to my brother Timothy and to the merchant. I hope the merchant will teach you his trade, and make your Lordship as " errant " a landjobber as he is.

1725, May 17. Bath.—Sir Humphry is here, and spends his time chiefly in playing at whist with his landlady and his two maids. He begs his respects to your Lordship.

The letter to put off the Act at Oxford was devised by a party that had been formed secretly against, but I expect to hear by the next post that upon a second letter it is put off, though not without a struggle. There are many who desire to have the opportunity of an Act to recommend themselves. Others think this is not a season for compliments, when the cause that has been so long depending has contrary to promises been called for, and the judgment that was against us affirmed. There has been an appeal lodged to the House of Lords, but I suppose that will only gain a little time.

1725, May 29. Little Shefford.—By the account I have of your being at Dupplin, I suppose this may reach Morpeth before you pass by it again. The visit you have been so good as to make to that excellent lady was as worthy of yourself as it must be comfortable to her. Indeed it must be the greatest comfort to her that she was capable of receiving in this world, in her present circumstances. But now you have seen the good land of Scotland, I dare say nothing but the same good strong motive can ever

engage you to go into it again. I shall long to have an account
of your peregrinations, and of the accommodations you met with on
the road in that land of promise. If merchant Morley's own
cargo failed him, I am afraid the places where you baited would
scarce afford him bohea and loaf sugar.

I thank God that I am got to my hut again, and the noise I
have been in at town and Bath has only served to endear the
quiet and privacy of this place to me. But I hope you have met
with better weather towards the northern pole, than we have had
here in our southern climate. The cold and rain as yet confine
me within doors, which is the only grievance I have to complain
of here. I thought to have brought Harry Watkins with me
hither, but he had a relapse the morning we were to have come
out, but I hope it was a short one, and that it is over before this
time, and that I shall soon see him. I paid my duty to my good
Lady Oxford, the post before I left Bath. I hope you will find
the grand affair so well advanced at your return that it will be no
purpose to continue on me the injunction of secrecy. Indeed I find
it has taken air, for several have enquired of me if I knew anything of it.

1725, June 7.—I bless God I continue well here, in very bad
comfortless weather, which has confined me to my house ever
since I came hither.

It was very suitable to your Lordship's goodness to
bear with a journey even through part of Scotland, to give the
good lady [Kinnoull] you visited the greatest comfort she can
have in this world, except from her reflections on her own truly
Christian behaviour under her present circumstances. I am very
sensible of the honour she did me in remembering me. My prayers
for her are as sincere and as earnest as my esteem is great. I can
say no more. I beg my most humble respects to her when you
write.

The widow was in good health, and in perfect good humour,
and entertained me very agreeably and very graciously below
stairs, when I was not above with her father. My scoundrel circumstances will not allow me to aspire to any thing more from
her, and if she continues as she is a little longer I suppose she
may be past it, as well as I.

I hope your Lordship will meet at your return to town with
the satisfaction of seeing that you have so much reason to pray
for past the ordinary seasons of disappointment, and that you will
make your poor servant here happy with a confirmation of it.

1725, June 19. Little Shefford.—I heartily bless God for
your Lordship's safe return so far in your way home from so long a
journey, and through such craggy, scrubbed ways. The ill
weather, which has been here without intermission, has brought
my ague again. But I am once more rid of it, and hope I shall
hear no more, if the good weather, which we have had for a day,
holds.

The fraternity of his Majesty's chaplains is honoured with your old tutor. He and Charles Aldrich are proper ornaments to it.

1725, July 8.—I hope this will come to welcome you home. I heartily bless God for preserving you in your health and from all other casualties in so long and perilous a journey. In all other respects I am sure you must have reason to be pleased with your adventure.

I had heard of that which was feared at home, and bless God that it is over for the present. It is very happy that you are returned, to prevent as far as may be any new occasion for such fears. One word from you will, as it ought, in this case be of more weight than all that physicians or any other friends or servants can say. God forbid that when we have such a fair prospect of having that we have so long prayed for, we should be disappointed for want of a little care, or by presuming too much upon our strength.

If you have any acquaintance among the Red Ribbons, I suppose your Lordship will have business enough upon your hands for a week or two, in making your compliments to them. What a piece of pageantry! Lord Stanhope, it is said, has paid pretty dear for his jests on them.

1725, July 7.—I am glad the impertinent part of my letter happened not to displease your Lordship, but since I wrote I am more convinced of the necessity of those precautions. I hear from more hands than one, and good ones too, that great notice has been taken of the non-appearance of a friend of mine.

People will soon be disabused as to common expectations. Had not the South Sea convinced me that there is nothing so extravagant which the generality will not run into, I should have been surprised at the present opinions. No one in their wits could think there could be ground for them.

Postscript. Your Lordship and others may have one advantage from the present forwardness of others, to be rid fairly for the future of their impertinence. Should they upon disappointments set up for malcontents again, surely they cannot expect that others will be so weak as to give in to their resentments. If they renew old language, others may with honour turn their deaf ear to them, and refuse to have any thing to do with them. It will be some comfort that they who are content to be quiet may now without reproach be so.

I am told Sir S[pencer] C[ompton] is to be in the House of Commons again, and probably Speaker, that he will be content to share the power with W[alpole], and that the new Parliament will be called as soon as ever this is up. If any of these things be true I think it is pretty plain what the measures will be.

1725, July 14.—I thank you for your good news that all is safe. I pray God continue it so till its maturity, and then to bring it well into the world.

Robin writes to me that young Murray writes to him from London to secure his chambers when he leaves them, for Lord Dupplin. I suppose this is perfectly without your Lordship's knowledge, or you would have mentioned it to me. The chambers indeed are the best in the College, but as I take it Lord Dupplin must be upon a frugal foot. It will cost a good sum to furnish those chambers in any tolerable manner. The rent is at present 12*l. per annum*. Mr. Watkins has been offered more and may have it every day in the year, though I would not let the rent be raised whilst the master and Robin were in it. I suppose by the hand by which this comes to Robin that it proceeds from Lord Kinnoull himself, who cares not directly to write to me. But is his Lordship to be Mr. Watkins' paymaster? Would Harry or any one else trust his Lordship for one Scotch bodle? I should be glad to have your Lordship's thoughts on this point. Out of duty to your Lordship, and the great veneration I have for the excellent mother, and my affection to the young Lord himself, I should be glad to do any thing to serve him, but the points I have hinted require a little consideration.

It was lucky for you that you had not the curiosity to see Glasgow, when you were in the land of promise. You might have been suspected for having fomented the rebellion of the True Blews. It is remarkable that the first disturbance should be amongst them who are the heartiest Covenanters in Scotland, and the only men too who have got by the Union. What becomes of the Carles, have they submitted yet?

Postscript. I hear poor Wainwright is out of his Bankrupt commission. I wish his friends could give him a little encouragement in his profession. Does King set up for a more staunch Whig than Jekyll, that he turns out whom the last put in?

1725, July 24.—I have heard, since I wrote last to you, that Kinnoull's affairs are in a very bad condition, and not mended by any late favours to him. I am heartily sorry for it, on the account of his excellent wife and poor "bearns." But I have not the least concern on me, on his own account; but I am sure this intelligence is a very good reason why I should not advise any friend I have to have any thing to do with [him]. If your Lordship sees Robin, pray instruct him to give the answer you mention. I have heard from the Bishop of Chester, who is on his visitation. He is very well and hearty, he has had bad roads, but business, of which his hands are full, always does him good and gives him life and spirit. That is a very happy constitution.

Postscript. By my letters from Lancashire, they seem to have some other account of affairs amongst the North Britons than we have in our prints. It is represented more favourable in our prints than their neighbours think it.

1725, July 27.—I hear your noble present is come safe to Oxford. A thousand thanks to you for it, I hope I shall value it as I ought, both on account of the person whom it repre-sents and of him from whom I receive it. I long to see it, I believe I shall go over for two or three days n⸱⸱

1725, September 10.—I have got Forman's letter, and entirely agree with him as to the main of it; we have been, and are like to be, the bubbles of Europe. But there are some few facts, as well as some judgments, in which I think he is mistaken, particularly that of Stanhope, though he seems to write of him out of gratitude for favours received, the best excuse I confess, if there could be any entirely good, for partiality. But who is this Forman? English or Scotch? He seems to have been concerned in the Preston business.

Postscript. Our last accounts from abroad seem methinks to intimate that we are likely soon to come to an open breach with the Emperor. But that I think cannot affect the English, though it may be the German, dominions.

Bell Tyrrel, one well known to the master and Tim, and to them I design this news, a girl worth 4,500*l.*, has been pleased to steal a husband not worth a groat, a young rake whose only employment was to be master of the horse to Lord Abingdon. Though she has not, I think, done worse than she had like to have done four or five years ago; she had then like to have stole a fiddler.

Forman's letter, and that which probably will come on next session in relation to this affair, will give a fair handle, if there was any one to manage it, to justify your father's conduct, and to return proper compliments to his impeachers.

1725, September 29.—I hear we put on airs at the Imperial Court very different from our old ones. We have been bullied, and we now bully in our turn. A little time will show us the consequence of it. I am told the King is not expected till after Christmas.

I have some choice papers relating to Ruffe to show your Lordship and my godfather when I see you again.

If this find you in the country, I beg my respects to all at Eywood.

1725, October 11.—The Attorney and his gay though old lady come to Tom Rowney's to-day, and spend two or three days in town.

Yesterday the sermon was in the afternoon here. The Bishop of Gloucester is at the Deanery, and he, the governor of this place, and their brother of Llandaff sat in the Deanery, within hearing of the preacher, and not one of them left the table to come to church. I have been enquiring whether old Fell's ghost did not walk last night. Nay, poor Dr. Aldrich always laid down his pipe on such an occasion, though he would go to it again when sermon was done.

1725, October 17.—I was mistaken in one circumstance, but not a material one, in the account I gave you of our three prelates. It was not at the Deanery but at Clavering's that they dined, near enough in all conscience to the Church.

1725, October 19.—God Almighty be blessed for His great goodness to you. You have now the utmost that I daresay you yourself do wish for, or your friends could wish for, for you.

And had your good father lived to see this day, he would I daresay have thought it a full and ample recompense from God in this world for all his own troubles. I beg my compliments to my honoured lady upon this very joyful occasion, and to Lady Margaret too, who I daresay will be as fond as any one of her little brother.

1725, October 21.—I most heartily thank you for your great goodness in giving me an account, by Tuesday's post, that all continued well with the mother and the precious babe. The little gentleman has already had influence as far as to this place. Every friend I have here has done me the justice to think me so much concerned upon this occasion as to make me a visit on purpose to congratulate me.

This joyful occasion had almost so filled my thoughts as to leave no room to congratulate your Lordship upon another extraordinary piece of good fortune, which I hear has happened to you. I suppose one of so just a taste as your Lordship thinks it the greatest that could happen to you, next to the birth of Lord Harley. At least you will, if you have my good friend John Drummond's sentiments. It will be well, in that case, if you do not prefer it. I hear your Lordship is become a burgess of the " auncient and gude city of Edingborough "; an honour no doubt preferable to red or blue ribbons, and that alone was wanting to complete your happiness as well as your dignity. I wish you may bear your good fortune with due moderation. It seems to come thick upon you.

I beg my most humble duty to the good Lady in the straw, and to dear Lady Margaret.

Postscript. I hope the little one will have no gripes that are dangerous. I would only hint that our friend Radcliffe was for giving young babes as little as possible. He frankly owned he knew not what to do with them, and was for leaving Nature, if it were possible, to do its own work.

1725, October 24.—No words I can use can make such a loss as you have had easier to you and my Lady than it would be otherwise. God and time alone can do that. And as to the part I take in it, I believe you as little doubt that I grieve with you now as that I rejoiced with you before. The most proper reflection for all our comforts is, that since it has pleased God that my Lady at such a distance of time has bred again, as you are both young enough, by God's blessing and proper care this loss may be soon repaired. I shall think it my own duty, upon this occasion, rather to hasten than to defer my journey.

1725, October 26.—I most humbly thank you for your account of the continuance of my Lady's health under her late affliction. I hope in God, it is an earnest to you both of your future blessings. I have a strong persuasion on me that upon proper measures she need not doubt, through God's blessing, of children of stronger vitals.

1725, October 28.—I shall have somewhat to entertain your Lordship and Tim with upon my coming up. My honest brother Fowkes has done a thing, the most extraordinary that ever was done in this place, and especially by one who has his view on the deanery. But it is too long for a letter. The College is in a flame upon it.

1725, November 26.—I heartily give you joy of the good news you had [from] Scotland before you left the town. It is no little comfort to have an affair so very desperate to be retrieved as far as it is possible to [be] done. And honest John by pressing his brother William in this point has shown his regard to your family as much as he ever did in many former affairs.

Perhaps you will have heard before this reaches you that Mr. Walpole sent on Thursday to the insurers to advise them to beware of insuring the Ostend ships. This has filled the city with rumours of war, and an expectation that orders will be given to sink the Ostend ships. The apprehension of war is revived strongly and increases every day, and I am afraid upon too good ground.

Letters from Ireland tell us that the great man there [Carteret] has lost his temper as well as his question, and is in a rage as well as confusion. His private secretary has been sent over at an hour's warning, it is supposed to have instructions in some point of moment. It is said a committee of that Parliament, which sits to enquire into abuses of the revenue, makes fresh discoveries every day. Notwithstanding reports given out that North Britain submits now readily to the malt tax, I have undeniable evidence that it is with the utmost reluctance that it is crammed down in every part of that country.

1725, November 27.—Twelve men of war are ordered to be got ready immediately. They are to be ready if possible by Christmas. Politicians are not agreed on the place for which they are designed. It is generally thought they are to winter at Copenhagen.

It is said that to induce the Dutch to come into the new treaty, we offer to agree to demolish the harbour of Ostend, and to submit to have no trade with Flanders but through Holland.

The trial of Huntridge, on Wednesday last, makes a great noise. He lived on the wall of New Park, and had some words with a great man. He was prosecuted for concealing deer stealers. He had many witnesses to depose that they heard those who swore against him own that they were to have money for swearing. A horse stealer had been pardoned, and came in as a witness against him. After a long trial he was acquitted, upon which there was a great shout quite through Westminster Hall. The mobility will have it that a great man was concerned in the prosecution.

1725, November 30.—The Irish grow every day more mutinous. It was desired of them to provide for the 50,000*l*. which they owned to be a deficiency, allowed but unprovided for by

Parliament. It was said the supplies already given would not only provide for the current service, but be sufficient too to pay interest at 7 *per cent.* for that money, till the principal could be paid off. A debate upon it, carried on very warmly by the mutineers. Papers were brought in, saying there had been a mistake in the former account given in to the House, and two sums, one of 6,000*l.*, the other of 5,000*l.*, paid by the King's order, had been omitted. The King's letters for payment of those sums produced and read, but ordered to lie on the table without any regard had to them. The Court doubting of their success proposed to adjourn, that they might have time by proper methods to bring them to a better temper. It was carried against adjournment. Then the main question put, and carried against the Court by nine. The mutineers increase. This is the best account we have yet, but a more perfect one is expected, more, it is feared, to the advantage of the malcontents. Poor Stilletto ! Thou art gone !

The Poles have dismissed all the Protestant officers out of their troops. Upon their application to the King, he has given them a month's pay and ordered Fleming to put them upon vacancies into the Saxon troops. The Emperor is very stiff and stubborn ; he will yield nothing to us. He has secured the Pope, and is negotiating with all other powers that can be of any use to him.

The two great prelates differ about the bishopric of Chester. York is said to have sent an express to Hanover for Gilbert, and London to have written earnestly to the King himself for Anget.

What would you say to a new Parliament ? This will surprise you. What if this should be Sir Robert's last refuge, if he should find himself pressed in this Parliament ? I have a very odd, but very true, story to tell you about this when we meet.

We say here that your Lordship slunk out of town, to avoid being invited by your new countrymen to St. Andrew's feast.

1725, December 2.—I have seen some private letters of moment from those too who are in the interest of this Government. They abundantly confirm all I wrote of the sturdiness of the Emperor. His minister, Count Coningsek, at the Hague tells the States he is ready to treat about all other points, and doubts not but they may be accommodated if they desist from Ostend. But as to the trade of that place he had orders to tell them that his master will not so much as let it be mentioned ; that his glory was concerned to make good his promises to protect it. This is the language too of all the Emperor's other ministers in other places. They declare they will not enter into any treaty at all about it. Coningsek desired the States to stay and hear what the new Spanish minister, Sir Philippo, had to offer to them. He said he doubted not but he would offer such terms to them as would convince them that it will be more for their advantage to enter into the treaty of Vienna than into that of Heren Hausen.

It seems unavoidable that you must have war or give up your trade. I do not find that they have any other hope left to avoid it but that the Emperor may be frightened, and give up the Ostend trade, if the Dutch come in with us. But this to me seems a very slender hope. The Emperor and Spain will hinder the Dutch if they can from coming in with us, but will not I believe desist from their own projects if the Dutch should join against them. It is plain that Spain is as deep in this project, be it what it will, as the Emperor. They are both closely united in it, and both as far as yet appears seem to point their whole design against England. As to the Dutch, it is said that Haerlem is prevailed on to consent to come into the treaty of Heren Hausen, but that Dort and Delf keep out still, but it is hoped they may be brought in before the King returns.

It is said the Emperor has sent the Duke of Holstein word that he always was for him, and opposed, as far as he could, the stripping of him of his dominions, and would assist him to the utmost of his power to recover them. The Prince of Cellamare is gone to Rome; he was the Spanish Embassador, who managed the intrigues in France against the late Regent. He is said to be gone thither to meet some malcontent Frenchmen, in order to raise disturbance there. The French letters give a sad account of the young Bear's behaviour to his Queen. He not only never speaks to her wherever he meets her, but lies too now in a separate apartment.

I gave you a hint in my last of some suspicion of a new Parliament; the ground of it was this. You know Mr. Dawney, my Lord Downe's second son; he has a living in Dorsetshire. Walpole sent to him lately by Lord Scarbrough to ask him if a prebend of Westminster would be agreeable to him. You may be sure the answer was that it would, if conditions were not required that could not be complied with. A week after Scarbrough came again to him, and told him that only one condition was insisted on, and he should certainly have the next prebend, viz. that upon the next choice of Parliament men for Dorsetshire, he should vote for Peter Walters, and another whose name I have not heard. Mr. Dawney honourably declared he would not upon any terms forsake the interest of the gentlemen his friends. This looks as though Walpole had a new Parliament in his view, in case he should find himself pressed in Parliament. It is not probable that he would insist upon a vote now for a vacancy four years hence. Strangeways indeed has used Lord Walpole very roughly; no doubt it is determined to be revenged of him and to throw him out. But it is not likely that he should provide for this four years hence.

Postscript. The two great prelates are at open defiance of each other about the succession to Chester. York insists to have Gilbert. London presses for Anget. All the bishops are said to join with London against York. It is said the difference betwixt York and London was so high that they speak not to one another.

Alterations are talked of in the law. The Master of the Rolls [Jekyll] to be a Lord, the Attorney [General] to be Master of the Rolls, Lutwych to be Attorney. Three Judges, Powis, Dormer, Tracy, to have their quietus and a pension.

1725, December 4.—The Dutch mail yesterday brought news, not very agreeable, that Mr. Finch had left Warsaw. Stocks fell upon it. But that which concerns us more is the resolution of the Ostend Company, who in a full meeting at Brussels gave power to their directors to do as they should think fit in the following points proposed to them:—the setting up a trade to the north and a fishery for whales and herrings, the settling a trade with the West Indies, the building a fort and settling a factory on the coasts of Coromandel and Bengal, the not making a dividend this year but applying their money to extend their trade. These are not the resolutions of men that are likely to quit this trade.

It is plain we must lose our trade or engage in a war. Many think we shall chose the former. It is said one of the secret articles betwixt us and France is that England shall not guarantee the succession of the Austrian family to the Empire; and that the Emperor knows this and said he should then think himself at liberty to recall his guarantee of the Protestant Succession. Townshend asked Staremberg upon what ground the treaty with the Czarina was made. Staremberg answered upon the same the treaty of Hanover was made, to secure the peace of Europe.

Postscript. I find Sir Robert's friends begin to apprehend that a storm is gathering against him.

The town of Glasgow have demanded of the King's Solicitor in Scotland to assist them, in the absence of the Advocate, to prosecute for murder the officer who ordered his soldiers to fire. Sir Robert asked Baron Scroope, as a lawyer, what the Solicitor must do. Scroope told him the Solicitor was obliged by his office to do it.

1725, December 7.—The Parliament sits the 20th of January. The proclamation for it is signed. There is said to be great tampering with the Tories. This, if true, may make it probable that Poultney, as reported, is at work in good earnest. Poultney's party is said to increase. It is reported too that the great man should say that the Tories came in so fast that he knows not what to do with them. That is likely enough for him to say. I think I told you in my last that Lutwych is said to have positively refused the Attorney's place. The present Attorney must, as they say, be dismissed, not preferred. I hear no more of Jekyll's barony. Nothing more that I hear stirring.

1725, December 9.—It was thought the King would have been here during these light nights, but now it is said he will not set out till the light nights in the next month. And I believe it true, for I am sure, notwithstanding the reports, none of the family is set out to meet him, nor have they any orders about it.

Three Dutch mails due to-morrow. Here is a strong report that the Pretender's wife has parted from him. She pretended a visit to the convent of St. Cecilia; when she was in she dismissed her equipage, and sent letters to the Pope and to the Cardinal Secretary, to give them notice that she was retired for the remainder of her days. It is said John Haye wrote a letter to her to let her know that if she retired upon any suspicion of the Pretender having commerce with his wife, that he could convince her, by very sufficient proofs, that there was no ground for any such suspicion; and that she answered him smartly, that neither he nor any of his were able to give her any uneasiness, that if she had had any reason for complaint he would be the last person to whom she should make them, and required him not to trouble her any more with his impertinent letters. This is the sum of the report. I know not what to think as to all circumstances, but I believe there is some ground for it, and that it may be of fatal consequence to the Pretender that [he] gave out that the reason of Haye's hatred to him was that, because upon some displeasure that Madam Sobieski had taken to John Haye, he had advised, upon being consulted, John Haye to retire till he could make his peace. John Haye expected that Mar should have offered to support him against the lady, but it is plain by this that the displeasure to John Haye has been of some standing. But there is another thing may have contributed to this retreat, the bringing in again of Jemmy Murray. This last gentleman had, not long before he left the Pretender's formerly, affronted the lady in gross terms. No doubt she must be uneasy to see him brought in again upon her. Both Haye and he are ministers of Ruffe's recommending, who has very happily, to the blessing of the Pretender's cause, been sent abroad.

1725, December 9.—I forgot in my letter to beg your Lordship would give leave to have your name used to Alderman Child in behalf of Dr. Girdler for the lecture of St. Dunstan's. You know his character, and what he has suffered for being an honest man. Were your father alive he would be heartily concerned for him. It will be of great service to him, if your Lordship will be pleased to order Mr. Thomas to tell Alderman Child that you would take kindly any service he does to Dr. Girdler.

1725, December 14.—The news I sent you of the retirement of the Chevalier's wife is true. I guessed exactly at the reasons. She said she could not bear any longer the insolence of John Hay and Jemmy Murray, the two new pretended Earls of Inverness and Dunbar. She had forbid Hay's wife her apartment some time before she retired. All other circumstances I wrote to you are true, but I can warrant no farther, though a great many stories go about here, as that he caned her, &c. But it is certain, I believe, that all that has ever happened before to that man has not been so much to his prejudice as his wife's parting from him. This is a ripe precious fruit of Ruffe's ministry.

I hear there is great wrath at Christ Church against Wigan for his speech at the Bishop of Chester's funeral. It is reported here that they threaten to expel him, but I cannot think they will be so extravagant. I hear he spoke in it very handsomely of your father, as well as of the Bishop. I am sent to him to beg a copy of his speech, if he is willing to give one out. Bolingbroke is come to town, but I have not yet seen him, but he has signalized his return by a very dishonourable action. He has made strange havoc at Bucklebury, he has cut down all the trees in the grove and about the house, that were a defence as well as ornament to it. He has cleared all the hedges round the estate, he has marked 1,100 trees to be cut that are so small as not to be valued at half a crown a-piece. In short he seems resolved to ruin that estate entirely to the utmost of his power. And this . has been done without notice to Packer, whose son has the reversion. Poor Packer is come to town with his son to get an injunction to stop cutting, but they are helpless creatures. Were they not so he durst not have used them as he has done. A man of sense and spirit would make him fly his country once more upon better reason than he did before.

An express came on Sunday from Hanover. The prints tell you several days in this month on which it is thought the King may set out, but I find they at Court who should know best expect him not till next month. Three mails came in yesterday, but no news by any of them. Townshend was expected at the Hague to try what he can do with the Dutch.

1725, December 15.—I thought your Lordship would not be ill pleased to see the enclosed [*missing*]. He [Wigan] carried one expression in my. letter farther than I designed it. I told him I thought your Lordship would not be ill pleased to see any thing that mentioned your father with respect. He understood it as though your Lordship had employed me to desire a copy of his speech. Our Governor and my brethren are much provoked. They dare not fall on him directly for the speech, but they are trumping up again the old business of his refusing young Fowkes' theme. On Saturday last the boy offered his theme again to Wigan in the hall. Wigan said, "*Non est mei ingeniijud icium ferre de tuis scriptis.*" The boy began to say "the Dean"—Wigan interrupted him, "*Quid vis tibi loquere Latine si Decanus jussisset temandata sua ad me deferre, jussisset te etiam ea Latino sermone exprimere.*" The boy began " Decanus, Decanus," but could get no further. Wigan said "*Abi et disce Latine loqui, non est meum in hoc loco audire aliquem nisi Latine loquentem.*" It is confidently said they are resolved to proceed against him for refusing the theme. It will be rare sport. What they will do I cannot imagine, nothing they do can be justifiable. To deprive him of his rhetoric reader's place for three or four days before Christmas will be ridiculous. To deprive him of his librarian's place, for that he has done as rhetoric reader, will be extravagant. But I will not take upon me to answer for what they may do, but do what they will they will do more prejudice to themselves than to him.

1725, December 18.—You will have the other speech which you desired, and Wigan's too entire as soon as the man returns who has it.

No news since my last. The King will be in Holland on the 23rd it is supposed. If the wind is fair he may embark on the 24th. Great struggling about the Dutch to keep them from coming into the Hanover treaty, and to bring them into it. A little time will show what is to be expected from them. They who understand them best still think they will not come into any offensive alliance.

I have two little pieces of news that are of some moment, and that I have from good hands. Fréjus, the King's preceptor, is so dissatisfied with the Duke of Bourbon's management that he offers to retire, and, it is thought, will do so. The French Court have supported the expenses at the marriage and since at Fontainbleau by monopolizing corn and provisions in this time of scarcity, and themselves selling it to the people. The people have perceived it at last, and are not, you may believe, the less discontented with them for it.

Postscript. I can now tell you, I think from sure hands, that Gilbert will be Bishop of Chester. It is not commonly known, nor will it be declared till the King returns. London, after all his burning, knocks under. Next to the Archbishop's own promotion, this is the most remarkable that has ever happened in this poor church.

1725, December 21.—A mail came in on Sunday, but brought nothing more than that Townshend was at the Hague, and the King to set out as on Friday last. They seem to have some more hopes that the Dutch may be brought into the Hanover [treaty], but if they are, it will be on their own terms, and on condition that we be the aggressors. The letters from France continue to tell us that the misery of that kingdom increases daily. The late method they have taken, by lowering their money to induce people to bring it out, has had a contrary effect. They lock it more than ever. Money grows scarcer, and provisions dearer every day. Fréjus and all others are endeavouring to withdraw themselves that they may have no share in the present management.

1725, December 23.—Bolingbroke when he left England reconveyed all his wife's estate to her; she immediately conveyed it to Lord Stawell and Sir William Wyndham for the payment of his debts, &c., giving the inheritance to Packer's eldest son. All this was done for his benefit with his consent. By this settlement, the Government could not come in upon that estate till the debts were answered. I know Chandos's and all other claims were allowed by the Commissioners, and more money has been raised than will answer all the ends, for which the estate was vested in Stawell and Wyndham. However, they now, as Packer tells me, make use of their power at Bolingbroke's request, to make this havoc and destruction to raise some ready money for him. And Bolingbroke has drilled him with hopes of accommodation till the time is past for moving for an injunction, and, though he had promised him that he would stop the cutting of the wood, now tells him he will go on with it. This is very dirty work for men of such quality to be concerned in. Packer's counsel tell him, and I believe truly, that the trustees have no power to do this. But they know it is more hard to get redress for a damage than to prevent it, and they certainly rely upon poor Packer's weakness and inactivity.

I have been to wait on B[olingbroke] but found him not at home, but he knows I have been there. But he is in such a disposition to me that I question whether I shall see him at all. I have two degrees of original sin in me, which are not to be washed out, the respect I paid to his late wife, and the being supposed to have a greater regard to your father than to him. I may tell your Lordship a secret, which I would have continue so with you. Upon hearing what he was pleased to say, upon the notice he had of my having been to wait on him, I have sent him word, by a friend, that I have nothing to reproach myself with in relation to him, that I am ready to pay all respects due from me, but if it be disagreeable to him to have me wait on him I shall not trouble him. I shall conduct myself according to the answer I receive, which I believe will be that he desires not to see me. This makes me too believe that though others may desire to see your acquaintance with him renewed, he himself has had no desire or thought of it, and I the rather think so, because I have sure and certain intelligence that he is resolved to have done with the Tories and to observe no measures with them, but to throw himself entirely into the opposite party.

Fréjus did come back again at the Duke of Bourbon's desire, but the letters from France still continue to say he will retire, and many others with him. A general crash in their government is apprehended. The Spaniards have presented another memorial to demand Gibraltar and Port Mahon. It is said our great man declared openly that we shall have no war, that he will lay down if we have, and it is not thought, that since bullying will not do, that we shall be quiet.

I thank God the judge grows better at Bath. I shall let him know the honour your Lordship does him to enquire after him.

I take it for certain that Gilbert will be Bishop of Chester; but London still, as it is strongly reported, continues to oppose him, and has prepared a memorial against it to be given to the King at his return. It is said Newcastle has promised to present the memorial to the King; that I much doubt of. It is said the Bishop of London, to induce Walpole to join with him in opposing Gilbert, has offered to consent to let Hare be Dean of Paul's, and Sherlock Bishop of Chester. But I take York to have a better interest in Sir Robert, than the Bishop of London. It is said too that Gilbert is to marry a relation of Sir William Strickland, and that Sir William has got a promise from Walpole for him. London has been soliciting on his brethren to join with him in the opposition to Gilbert, but some, who think York to have the best interest, have refused him. Be the event what it will, they say the breach is irreparable betwixt York and London, and may probably spread itself farther amongst the bench.

Postscript. I remember my Lady was telling me once of meat [cooked]down to a glue, and made up in hard cakes like chocolate cakes, one of which dissolved in warm water would immediately make a porringer of broth. She said many used to take them with them on the road when they travelled. Does her Ladyship know where such things are to be had, or has she the recipe for making them. They would be very convenient for my way of life.

The last mail brings notice that the Dutch are likely to come in, that the Imperial Minister has used high language and had as good returned to him. We are not a little uppish on this here.

They go on at Glasgow to prosecute Bushel the captain for murder, it is thought he will stand trial and that the Government will endeavour to support him and bring him off; if he should be condemned, he is sure of a pardon.

1725, December 29.—As to my own affair with my old patron I can yet tell you no more than I did in my last. I have had no answer, but I shall exactly keep to what I then told you I proposed, and not be so impertinent as to press for admittance unless I am told that it will be agreeable.

Public news we have none, but what you have in the papers. The Dutch have acceded to our treaty. We shall not I suppose be let into the private articles upon which they have done it. The Imperial minister bullied them very heartily upon it. They had a report at the Hague that Spain was dissatisfied with the Court of Vienna, but I believe there could be no ground for it, because Ripperda, upon his return to Spain, was much caressed by the King and Queen and immediately declared Secretary of State for foreign affairs.

You have I believe by this messenger a famous manifesto sent to you. Another letter is come over from John Hay, in which he says his master is entirely easy now, since he has discovered all that was passed to have been the management of Lord Mar, who employed Mrs. Sheldon, who had been dismissed upon Jemmy Murray's coming, to incense his wife. But I do not find that this last letter gives any one a better opinion of their prudence than any of the former had done. The bishops here have got it amongst them that Ruffe has been the occasion of the quarrel betwixt the Pretender and his wife, and laugh heartily. I believe they are in the right, and they may well laugh at it.

Peter Foulks is Sub-Dean of Christ Church. Your old tutor quitted his place of power. There was a general joy upon his dismission, and I am afraid he is the most contemptible man that ever was in the place. They durst not offer, after all their menaces, to pass any censure upon Wigan. When they came to tell noses, the Dean and honest Peter were left alone, the rest would not burn their fingers in such warm work.

Postscript. Bentley is come to town with his Terence and Phaedrus; the first to Prince Frederic, the other to Prince William. He calls Hare in his preface *Quidam Clericus.*

1725-6, January 1.—I can now give your Lordship a better account of the accession of the States to our treaty; they offer to

come in but with restrictions. 1. That they will have nothing to
do with the affair of Thorn. 2. That they will not be bound to
guarantee the treaty of Westphalia. 3. That England and
France shall guarantee to them the payment of the subsidies due
to them out of the revenue of Flanders, in case payment should
be stopped upon their coming into the treaty. These are some
of the restrictions. The rest are not yet known. That affair is
not yet over, but we hope now they are come so far, that they
may be brought further. Stock sank on Wednesday to 117, upon a
rumour of a war with France. A man came on Monday night
into Child's coffee house, and offered even wagers that France
would declare war against us or we against them in six weeks
time. On Wednesday the rumour was hot in the city. I can
find no other ground for it but Horace Walpole's coming over
with bag and baggage. Some say he came away abruptly, that
his wife was past her reckoning, and was designed to have lain in
in France; others that he has been soliciting three months to come
over, and came now only to have his wife lie in here. I am apt
to think this last true. There was a report too in the city that
the Jews had private letters that the Pretender was to come
shortly to Vienna, but surely things are not ripe yet for that. It
is now said that in the struggle for Chester, London would carry
the day, that Blackburn wrote to Lord Townshend for Gilbert, and
was answered in general terms that the Court would be ready to
oblige him in any request. That Gilbert wrote at the same time
to young Townshend, with whom he had an acquaintance, and in
answer was advised to apply to the Bishop of London, for the
Court would not make a bishop against his inclination. I am apt
to think this true.

I hear Thomas Terry takes occasions now he is out of his place
to swear [at] his governor. There will be civil war there. I
think I told you that they were forced to drop the business of
Wigan. He is come off with flying colours, but upon his being
left out from being rhetorick (*sic*), some of the mutineers there
have made a couplet :

Would you have all as dull as he that does preside,
Keep Sherman in, and Wigan lay aside.

1725-6, January 4.—I hear not that my postscript is confirmed,
but by authentic accounts from France, Bourbon and all his
creatures are in a tottering condition. Indeed it will be
absolutely necessary for them, I believe, to try if a change of hands
will in any measure revive credit amongst them. They are
sure it will grow worse, if possible, every day, whilst he continues in. Some are positive that Stanhope has given notice
of a secret negotiation betwixt France and Spain, a preliminar-
y of which is the dismission of Bourbon and all his adherents.
We are very uneasy here at the prospect of alterations in France.

For want of other news you must be content with some from
Christ Church. The Governor there neither invited the gentlemen on Christmas day, nor the Masters on New Year's day. He
seems to signify to all his subjects that he has no regard for
them. One Blith, brother to the Irish lord, a commoner bachelor,

lately brought an epistle to ask leave out of town, and by mere mistake inscribed it *Revd. &c., Johanni episcopo, &c.* John was the name of the famous president Bradshaw. When the Governor met with *Johanni*, "What is the meaning of this? all the world knows my name is William." He went on, and instead of *necnon hujusce Aedis Decano Dignissimo*, met with *nec, &c. Dignissimo*. "*Nec Dignissimo*, this is done to affront me, you shall not go out of town, and I will consider of punishing you, as you deserve." As he was going lately to the audit house, there were several standing under the hall stairs who pulled off their caps, but poor Jesson the chaplain had his back to him and saw him not, and kept his hat on. The Governor came up in wrath to him, and asked him how he came not to pay the same respect to him that others did, and would not admit of his true excuse of his not seeing him. One Whitfield, an undergraduate student, a bold lad, used as he came out of church to look the Governor in the face; the Governor sent for him, and wisely said, "What do you look me in the face for as you go out of church, do you think I will be brow-beaten by you?" The boy was as ridiculous as his Governor was absurd; he answered, "Upon *my honour* my Lord I had no design to affront you." "Upon your honour, how long pray have you been a lord?" These are rare methods to secure respect, and this is the man from whom they promised themselves such mighty things, and of whom we were to be afraid. The breach betwixt Thomas Terry and the Governor is now pretty notorious. Thomas jokes on him before all companies.

1725[-6], January 5.—I must beg leave to explain myself as to the consequence of M[orley]'s death. I am a stranger to Peter Walters, but by the character I have heard of him I feared that if he were left in the trust, without a majority to control him, he might give you much trouble. It was in view of that trust solely that I apprehended any consequence of his death, and your Lordship is the best judge how far you might be affected by it in that point. As to any other consequences, per-haps I agree pretty well with your Lordship.

York and London both seem sure of their point, London says he has all with him, except the women. If it is to be carried by them he has nothing to say. It will now be soon decided, but if I were to wager, it should be on York's side. London mentioned Peplo, soon after our friend's death, as a pastoral man, and I know not if he could not carry it for Auget, who was Sund [er-land]'s man, he would push for Peplo, and no doubt that would be to show his regard to our late friend's memory and to the universities.

I want much to see the pamphlet about the importance of Gibraltar. I have heard it much commended.

I hear Mr. Pope is with your Lordship. I beg my respects to him.

His Majesty has certainly had experience of the comfort of being in a storm. When he was seen on Monday off Rye his yacht was alone, and separated from all the others; but they say he who steered that course in the storm did like a seaman.

I leave the rest of my paper open for news, if I can meet with any. The Chester and two Irish mails that were to have come in on Monday are lost.

I told your Lordship there was a report that Sir Robert would throw up; it was so strong that the Bank sent some of their members to him to enquire if there was any ground for it, and that he upon retiring was to be Duke of Northumberland and Carteret to be Treasurer. He answered that he was heartily weary of the Treasury, and could he honourably go off, nothing the King had in his power should tempt him to continue; but he had no thoughts of leaving it yet. He did not think it would be proper for the King's service for him to leave it at this juncture, and he promised them that, whenever he did think of leaving it, he would give timely notice to them and all his other friends for them to take what measures they thought fit; that there was nothing in the report of his being a duke. That he had honour as much as he cared for in his son, that he knew not indeed the King's mind as to Lord Carteret, but he knew nothing of his being Treasurer.

The surveyors of the window tax have made a report to the Lords of the Treasury, that there were 4,800 houses empty this winter within the city and liberties of Westminster.

I have been out to-day on purpose to have picked up some news, if there had been any. Townshend's impatience was the occasion of their embarking contrary to the advice of all the seamen. It is thought the King will not stir from Rye till to-morrow morning, and not be in town at the soonest till Friday. A mail last night, but nothing new, all in the same uncertainty. The Dutch will not come, but with restrictions. They will gain as much and hazard as little as possible. We are in great fears lest France should not only leave us, but hop upon us.

1725-6, January 8.—On Thursday evening a man came into the Bank, and offered any wager that Port Mahon was then in the hands of the Spaniards. He was treated as one that was employed to sink stock by such reports. He said that to show he was confident of the truth of that he said, and was not afraid to stand by it, they might take his name and place of abode. Stock fell upon this to 115. Yesterday, some letters by the Dutch mail confirmed this news; they said the Spaniards had landed on a sudden 8,000 men and seized it. South Sea bonds immediately fell to par. I will not yet warrant this news to you, but I find some believe it.

The rumour is very strong that France is leaving us; it has been talked for some days, that the Emperor is to exchange with France that which he has in the Netherlands, for that which the French have in Alsace. This is the most probable scheme that could have been thought of for uniting those powers. Should [there] be any ground for it, good night to us.

It is said the King has got a flux from his tossing at sea, and that is supposed to be the reason of his short stages.

1725-6, January 13.—His Majesty has had a fair escape. Sir Robert says in confidence to friends, that they have managed so abroad that they shall have no war; that he wants only the malt tax and two shillings *per* pound. But it is hotly discoursed that care will be taken this session to have the two shillings levied *ad plenum valorem*, in the northern and all other counties, as well as here about London. They pretend to be sure that France will not desert them, but by some authentic accounts I have had, which cannot be conveyed in a letter, the Duke of Bourbon is there upon a ticklish foot.

It is now said that the Dean of York will be Bishop of Chester, Gilbert Dean of York, and Hare Dean of Paul's. It is likely enough that this may be designed, as the most likely method to accommodate the difference betwixt the two contending prelates. This too would account for the Dean of York's resignation of Winwick, which he had engaged to do, when it was given him, before he accepted any bishopric. But some of the Dean of York's friends are positive that he will not accept it, if offered to him. Nor can I think the bishopric alone would be worth his while. It is said there is a struggle still about our canonry, but I hear not the competitors.

There were such letters as I mentioned to the Jews about Port Mahon, but they are supposed to have been written in concert, to affect stocks. The talk is revived that Newcastle goes to Ireland, Horace to have the seals, Carteret to go to France.

Poor Neighbour did some dirty work to screen Llandaff, but they never came to vote about officers. It was agreed beforehand that Terry should go out and Llandaff stay in. Terry expected they should have entreated him to stay him, and they were resolved to take him at his word when he offered to quit. Llandaff, as I am told, desired another year to make up his accounts, in other words, to get in money to pay his balance. Authority is at a low ebb here, they are divided amongst themselves, and the students detesting and deriding both of them. It is said there is a struggle still about our canonry, but I hear not who are the competitors.

I thank your Lordship for the favour of yours of the 11th; surely it is too cold weather for my Lady or Lady Peggy to stay longer in the country. If you have anything done this session, it will be on the first day. I hope you do not design to stay beyond that in the country.

1725-6, January 15.—We are afraid the Dutch are retreating faster from the Hanover treaty than they advanced to it. The Emperor's minister makes them great offers:—to secure to them the barrier treaty, to secure to them the subsidies due by that treaty, to secure trade upon the foot of the Munster treaty, to stint the trade of the Ostend company to three ships a year. One of the chief of the States has proposed this to their East India Company, and desired them to draw up such a project to be shown to the Emperor as will content them.

The Dutch Ambassador at Madrid writes to Holland that the quarrel betwixt the Pretender and his wife is feigned, that he is expected at Madrid, that ships are getting ready in Spain, and that it is suspected an attempt is designed on Scotland. I believe the Dutch minister has written this, but I do not find that it gains any credit here.

Stocks sink still, upon an apprehension, as I am told, that our great men are selling out.

Master was with me this morning and is very jolly.

Surely we shall see you at the opening of the session, it is to be opened in the evening with a masquerade.

1725-6, January 18.—To the astonishment of all the world Peploe is Bishop of Chester. The contending bishops have had a hearing before the ministers, and *verba brigosa* passed betwixt them. London had procured letters from some of the rankest men in those parts to recommend Peplo as the person that would be most acceptable and popular in that diocese. He has carried it. York is under the highest resentments, and his opponent triumphs as much. But I do not believe he could have pitched on a man that would have been so disagreeable to all sorts of men in that diocese, or that would have made such a figure on the Bench, as this is like to do. Godolphin has resigned the deanery of Paul's, but not his residentiaryship. Hare will be Dean. That was the composition betwixt London and the ministry. Gilbert is to be our Canon, Stillingfleet Dean of Worcester, and one Mordaunt, a late convert from popery, prebendary of Worcester.

More stock comes to market than can meet with buyers. Foreigners are selling, chiefly Spanish Jews, who have most of any foreigners in our stock. They are said to be put upon this by the King of Spain.

Postscript. If your Lordship has no thoughts yet of returning to town, I must beg to know whether you will be pleased to give me authority to subscribe any sum for you to Dean Berkeley's design. I have promised him to apply to my friends, but I have deferred doing it because I would willingly have the honour of having your Lordship at the head of my list, if you think fit to be a subscriber. No money will be called for till there is sufficient subscribed to build a college, and maintain the Head, three fellows and five scholars at least. That may amount to 20,000*l*. There is already subscribed above 3,000*l*. Underneath is the account of some sums subscribed :

Lady Betty Hastings - - - - -	500*l*.
Lord Pembroke - - - - - -	300*l*.
Lord Arran - - - - - -	300*l*.
Duke of Chandos - - - - -	200*l*.
Lord Perceval - - - - - -	200*l*.
Mr. Hutcheson - - - - - -	200*l*.
Sir R. Walpole - - - - - -	200*l*.
Auditor Harley - - - - - -	100*l*.

1725-6, January 25.—I have my *quietus*. I was so much a servant to another person that I could not be a friend to him. Ill offices had been done him with his wife, when he was abroad.

If I did not do them yet I ought not to have been indifferent where he was concerned. He shall not put himself upon the foot of expostulating with me. He cannot think of living on a foot of friendship with those who had abandoned him in his distress. Would your Lordship have me say anything directly to Dr. Stratford? No. I am not upon a foot to make a breach with any one. I shall do the Doctor no harm. If I chance to meet him anywhere I shall be civil to him. I have no more to say.

I think this fairly implies, though it does not directly say, that he would not have me visit him. I shall certainly understand it so, and have no reason I think to be sorry, since I have sufficient witness that I have done all that could be incumbent on me. I must not be forgiven, a supposed regard to your father and poor Dice; and the last, in my conscience, as little as the first. Though I believe the money is at the bottom of all, but not a word of that. I forgot to talk with you about the havoc at Bucklebury, but that will keep till we meet again. Pray burn this as soon as you have read it.

Sir John told me this morning that Pulteney is said to have been alone two hours with the King in his closet. That the ministry have made up the quarrel betwixt the Chancellor and the Master of the Rolls, and that they are endeavouring to accommodate all private differences amongst themselves. these things are so, they are as sure a sign as I know of a way.

1725-6, January 25.—Lord Townshend told the Lords on Thursday that he had that day received an express that the Dutch had acceded to the Hanover treaty. A mail came in on Sunday night, and I can aver to you that the States adjourned till Wednesday next come se'nnight, without acceding. And I have very good grounds to believe that when the States meet again, that affair, if done at all, will not be done so soon as some are pleased to imagine, or at least to give out.

It is said Walpole has sent to the Jews to let them know that if they continue to sell out stock with a design of retiring they shall find that, notwithstanding the laws lately made in their favour, there are enough left to keep them in England.

1725-6, January 29.—I have some strange stories to tell you of my neighbour your old tutor, fresh ones come out every day. It is a question whether they are more profligate or more absurd, but they are too long for a letter, I must stay till we meet.

I am told the German councils run all for war, that the speech was designed to have been in effect a proclamation of war, if Walpole had not hindered it. That he was for trying once more what could be done by negotiations, but it is said that they wait impatiently for notice that the Dutch have acceded. If they come in, it is supposed we shall change our language and breathe nothing but open hostility.

That rogue Bentley abuses openly our poor friend that is gone, the Bishop of Chester. Calls him a worthless silly fellow, a mere rat, good for nothing, had no learning, he write a book, he never could write a book, extols the preferment of Peploe, he was the proper man for the Government to pitch on, the fellow before him was a Jacobite, the gentlemen of that diocese are all Jacobites. Peploe is proper to keep them in all. It is [   ] that this fellow should use such language; our friend had always lived well with him. The rogue can have no inducement to it but to make his court as he thinks to those who have preferred Peploe.

I now hear that the Emperor's minister has given in a memorial to tell the Dutch that if they accede to our treaty he will look on it as a declaration of war, and take his measures accordingly. The Dutch are frightened, and it is thought they will not come in to us, or if they should at last, it will be with many and great restrictions. But instead of coming in, they talk in Holland of sending Hop to Vienna, and old Buys hither, to endeavour to make up matters. We shall look very simply with our treaty, if the Dutch will not come in.

A debate yesterday in the House about the army. The number of Tories was so small, that they thought not fit to divide. The Whigs that were against the Court yet said at this time they were for the army. Shippen and Wyndham both spoke; the last is said never to have spoken better. Shippen did not directly oppose the army at this time, but said he wished they had some security from the throne that the army was not to be perpetual, and would not be desired when there was no occasion for it. He observed it was our misfortune that the Prince who now threatened us was one to whom our King was a vassal. Upon this there was a great cry by Walpole and others "hear him." They were in hopes that he would have said somewhat to give occasion for sending him to the Tower, but he kept within bounds, and the word he had spoken was too notoriously true to be taken notice of. Mr. Verney spoke, and observed amongst other things very justly that his Majesty saw only the opulent part of his dominions, and wished he knew the condition of the other parts, of which the gentlemen who lived there were witnesses.

1725-6, February 1.—I told you Sir William Wyndham was said to have spoken very well, I had it from a friend of his. But I hear his speech gave great content where I suppose it was not designed to do so. There were some compliments in it to the King, upon which the courtiers thanked him, and some of them visited him upon it.

It is said, upon what grounds I know not, that Sweden and Portugal are come into the treaty of Vienna.

The Court give out that they have notice from Spain, that the old Spaniards are against a war, and that the King threatens to retire again if the Queen persists to have a war.

The paragraph in the King's speech about the Pretender is said to be in relation to Duke Wharton's negotiations with Ripperda and Prince Eugene at Vienna in favour of the Pretender. We say we know all that passed, and that his proposals were debated in a council of the Emperor's, called on purpose, but that Prince Eugene, after the council, declared he would have nothing to do with it.

Poultney and the great man are sparring every day against each other. It is said the great man loses his temper every day and did so particularly on Saturday.

1725-6, February 3.—This place affords not much to entertain you. You see by the Gazette how we endeavour to support our sinking credit by the notice of the States of Holland, but they tell us not the restrictions with which they come in. The consent of six other Provinces is necessary, and then all to be laid before the States General. There will be no haste I believe in that affair.

I find by our friend Mr. Bacon that Sir William Wyndham's speech has raised jealousies of him. Bacon expected they would have divided upon the army. Wyndham concluded with saying that at this time it might be necessary to continue the 4,000 men, and gave up the question. Walpole in his speech on Saturday last had been very hard upon stock jobbers, who took advantage of poor peoples' fears to sink stocks. He was supposed to mean Poultney and his father Gumly. On Tuesday Walpole was saying how he thought us in a good condition; that he could have all the money of the next year at three per cent., that he verily believed we should have no war, &c., but says he "I will promise nothing, least a friend I have in a corner should call upon me to make good my promise." On that Shippen rose up, and assured the House that friend would always be ready to appear whenever he was called on. He recapitulated what Walpole had said on Saturday against stock jobbers, and then pointed it all directly upon him, and supposed that he had sold out on purpose to sink stocks that he might buy them, with a design to raise them and sell again. He went on with great violence and insolence, he said he would do anything to bring such a bear to the stake; that as much as he detested a bill of pains and penalties, he would readily come into it to make such a monster spew up his ill-gotten wealth, &c. Walpole rose in a great passion, and protested solemnly that he never since he had been in his place had by himself or agents sold 20l.; that if that member knew he had, he ought to accuse him. That he called upon him to do it, that he challenged him to produce anything against him, that if he knew of any such thing it was his duty to acquaint the House with it, that if he had no ground for what he said he ought to recant the injustice of his insinuations. That he himself equally detested those who could be guilty of such practices, and those who could insinuate such things against others, without any ground for their accusation. The warmth was great on both sides, Shippen made no reply, but it was once thought he would have been called to the bar. After all it is said that Walpole did sell out 30,000l. of Bank Stock, though in such a manner that legal proof cannot be made of [it].

I am told the last masquerade was so infamous that even some of the great patrons of that diversion were scandalized at it.

There is a report to-day that the other States and the States General are come in, but it is not yet believed; but the Dutch news has as yet had no great effect in the city. Stocks rose to ten per cent., but fell again in a little time to eight. It is certain that Spain as well as the Emperor gave in a memorial to tell the Dutch that they should look upon their accession as a declaration of war. We shall now see what those powers will do, but we are very gay upon the news we pretend to have had from Spain, that the old Spaniards are much dissatisfied with the Queen and Ripperda. And we say we are in hopes there may be a revolution there; but we say that if Spain does anything against us, we will not leave them a ship swimming on the sea. We talk of sending a squadron under Hosier to the West Indies to intercept their galleons, and that ten more ships will be put in commission.

There is said to be a misunderstanding betwixt Walpole and the Banks. It is said it appeared visibly on Tuesday in Walpole's speech when he looked up to the gallery, where there were crowds of citizens, and said he saw many who had been locking up their money for three months past, in hopes of making advantage of the public necessity, but he doubted not to manage so that they should be disappointed, and not get one farthing. There is to be a lottery for 1,200,000*l* , but the subscriptions for it are not to be at the Bank, but to be taken in at the Treasury, and the money to be paid in and paid out there. The great man says he will have all the money for this year's service at three per cent.

Lady Lechmere is very ill, some say upon the ill treatment she has had at home, for her late management at Bath. Her fits seem somewhat hysterical, she has perpetual swoonings. Her mother is gone to her, and lies by her night and day. But the worst of the story is to come. The report is hot that under pretence of physic she has taken poison.

Postscript. The States of Holland are come in with all the restrictions I formerly mentioned. We are to pay the States 129,000*l*. per annum if the Emperor should stop their subsidies on their accession. It is said too that at the instance of the Dutch we agree to demolish not only the trade but the harbour itself of Ostend.

1725-6, February 5.—It is now said every where that Lady Lechmere is dead, and I meet with no one that doubts that she poisoned herself. She was said to die yesterday in the evening, but he was in the House of Lords in the afternoon. Her debts are variously talked of, some say 5,000*l*., some 10,000*l*., but all agree that he will pay no more than he can be compelled to.

On Monday will be the most busy day, as it is said, of the session; the debt of the navy comes on. It is said there are many irregularities to be produced. The Master of the Rolls has promised to exert himself.

My deafness still continues on me, and my head is still stuffed. When you come to town, I am afraid I must cup.

The talk in town is that the Emperor will remove the East India Company from Ostend to Trieste in the Adriatic Gulf. We cannot pretend to stop them there, but it is likely the Algerines would make bold with them sometimes.

1725-6, January 8.—I gave you false intelligence on Saturday, but it was the whole discourse of the Mall that day. Lady Lechmere is alive and like to do well, but all agree that she had dosed herself. They say she was saved by taking too large a dose of laudanum, it made her sick and came up again.

The Duke of Somerset's marriage is at present the entertainment of the town, no one of the Duke's own family had the least suspicion of it till it was over. He had with her 5,000*l.*, but has made settlements proper for a Duchess of Somerset.

Lord Essex is married to the Duke of Bedford's sister. He was married on Thursday last, but it was kept private some days. It was first published by Lord Bolingbroke, who at table where the sisters and others were, that were come up in expectation of being at the marriage, drank to my Lord and Lady Essex. Lord Bolingbroke is the great governor of Lord Essex, and has undertaken to extricate him out of Peter Walters' hands. It is said the family stopped the match till Lord Essex promised to have done with Peter Walters.

It is said the last mail brought an account of a new letter to the States, in stronger and more threatening terms than the last, in case of their accession.

Dr. Freind speeched it yesterday in the House upon the petition about Wycombe election. There were some things which seemed to reflect upon Walpole's management of elections. He was not in the House, but his creatures Pelham and Lord Tyrconnel fired upon Dr. Freind. But Dr. Freind's side carried it, to hear the election at the bar of the House on this day fortnight.

The Wycombe election occasioned the postponing of the business of the day till to-morrow, when warm work is expected about the army. Poultney and the Master of the Rolls promise to exert themselves.

1725-6, February 9.—The account that Lord Nottingham gives of the match is that he had no reason to expect it, till six weeks ago he received a letter from the Duke of Somerset to desire him to give him leave to make his addresses to his daughter. That when he was received, the Duke desired the utmost secrecy; he had with her only the usual portion of the daughters of that family, 5,000*l.*, and he is said to have presented her with 2,000*l.* of it on the marriage day.

If reports are true, the Emperor is far from receding. It is said he has not only sent another letter to the Dutch, in a higher strain than the former has, but that he has sent a message hither, to put us in mind that we are an Elector of the Empire, and that if we enter into any engagements to his prejudice we must expect to be put under the ban of the Empire.

I can tell you from undoubted authority that Ruffe is at the bottom of the wise management in the Pretender's family. That he supports Hay and his wife, commends the letters and manifesto, and the publication of them, and says the Pretender's conduct on this occasion has done him more service than any thing that ever happened to him.

Walpole in a speech a few days ago in the House, speaking of his projects for raising the money this year at three per cent., said he would take [upon] him to say, without the spirit of prophecy, that the golden days were coming when the only contest amongst those to whom money was due from the Government would be who should be last paid. I am afraid, one that had taken upon him the spirit of prophecy, and been allowed to do so with reason on other occasions, would scarce be believed on this.

1725-6, February 12.—The resentment of the haughty letter from the King of Spain is said to be that which brought in the three towns of Holland which stuck out; four other Provinces were come in since. Gelderland and Over Issel were not come in when the last letters came away. The Spanish ambassador has told the States that he is sorry he is come too late, that his stay will be short, that he expects orders to leave the Hague, as soon as they have formally acceded to the Hanover [treaty].

The same sort of letter is expected here from Spain to the King, with that which has been sent to the States.

The Emperor's new Resident has not yet had audience. The Emperor used to give our Princes the title only of Serenità, but when the present Emperor came over hither to be sent to Spain, Leopold wrote a letter with his own hand to the Queen in which he gave her the title of Majesty. The public credentials from their chancery at the same time gave the old title only of Serenità. Since that time every minister from the Emperor has brought a private letter with the title of Majesty. That compliment is now dropped. The new Resident is come without such a letter, but he has been told that he must have no audience till he produces such a one.

His Majesty at the opera on Tuesday last, as the Duchess Dowager of Ancaster, who sat next to him, chanced to stretch out her hand towards him, told hold of it and kissed it publicly. She was surprised, but rose and made him a low courtesy. The ladies clapped their fans to their faces, and tittered. The whole house was astonished. This was thought to be pretty near to a declaration of love. It was thought the ministers would have been at her levée next morning.

The debate on Wednesday turned upon the question, which you see in the votes, for a commission to state the debt of the nation. It was moved for by Daniel Poultney, the division was 262 to 89. No Tories that I hear of spoke. Fifteen Whigs only with the majority.

1725-6, February 14.—If you design to be in the House of Lords at all this session, you ought to be there on Thursday. Your father's name will probably be much mentioned in both Houses on that day, at least there will be opportunity and occasion for it. This is the day appointed to consider the late treaties. The meeting of Dr. Busby's trustees, which was appointed for that day, is put off upon the expectation of a debate, though I see not how now there can be a very long one in

the Lords, where there are so few to manage it; but if there
be any spirit and sense in the Commons, it will appear on that
day.

1725-6, February 19.—I wish you had been here on Thursday
to have countenanced by your presence the debates which were
so much to the honour of your father. Compliments were made
by Lord Scarbrough in the Lords House to Lord Strafford upon
the treaty of Utrecht. Strafford said he was glad to receive
those compliments, but there had been a time when he and all
concerned with him in that treaty had wanted these compliments.
Strafford spoke very handsomely in the Lords upon the late
Queen and her ministers, so did Wyndham and others in the
Commons. Auditor Foley spoke to nothing else but to your
father and his ministry. Not one word upon that point was
said in answer by any of the opposite party. Your Lordship
will have heard that the sole point in both Houses was to
promise to engage in a war to support the German dominions if
any attack should be made on them. The numbers in the
Lords were 94 to 15, in the Commons 285 to 107.

Newcastle produced Stanhope's letter in the Lords, which
said Ripperda had sent for him and told him that one secret
article in the treaty of Vienna was that the Emperor was to
assist Spain with 30,000 men if Port Mahon and Gibraltar
were not delivered, and Spain was to furnish the Emperor
with money to pay 30,000l. if any disturbance was given to
the Ostend trade. Horace Walpole in the Commons, and
Townshend in the Lords, owned that Don Carlos was to marry
the Emperor's eldest daughter, by which in case the Emperor
has no son, the Empire with all its dependencies will come
to Don Carlos, and if his elder brother die, Spain too; and
if the King of France should go off, a claim to that kingdom.
Men of all sides seem to think these things must end at last
in a war. It was said in the House stocks would rise upon
their vote, but they have sunk.

Your Lordship was yesterday chosen unanimously by
Dr. Busby's trustees to succeed my Lord Carleton. Your humble
servant was put in nomination with the Archbishop of York to
succeed the Bishop of Chester. Nottingham, Dorset, and Finch
for York; Aylesford, Dr. Freind and Bridges for me. It was com-
promised at last by choosing York now upon a promise to bring
me upon the next vacancy. Dartmouth promised Aylesford to be
there, but came not. Aylesford brought Dartmouth the day before
to the House of Lords, but when it came to the vote he went over
to the Court, which was remarkable in one who had such a share
in the late Queen's ministry.

Postscript. Carpenter has received orders to go immediately
through France to throw himself into Port Mahon, of which he
is governor.

1725-6, February 22.—All politics are suspended till we hear
what effect our late votes have abroad. Opinions are divided.
Some think they will frighten, and prevent a war, others that

they will irritate and hasten it. It is said 18 men of war go to
the Baltic, and 12 to the Mediterranean, where they are to be
joined by 12 French men of war. I know not whether I told
you that [Thomas] Lewis of Hampshire left his friends on
Thursday last, and declares himself an humble servant of the
great man.

Sir William Wyndham's speech, though well as to the treaty of
Utrecht, did not in the close of it give content. He declared
himself for the Hanover treaty and for all the address except
the last clause, for supporting the foreign dominions. His friends
say he he had no authority from them to say this, for they
approved neither.

Robberies increase in the streets daily. Mr. Shirley was
robbed on Friday last in St. James's Street, and a hackney coach
was robbed on Monday night in Dover Street, and two chairs in
Hanover Square.

The town is now full of enquiry after Harry Nevil (or Grey). On
Friday he wrote an affectionate letter to his wife, another to
Walpole to desire him to take care of his wife, and another to a
friend to come to a place named, and to take care of his carcass.
He went out with a pair of pistols. His friend came to the place
to which he was directed, and found Nevil had been there, but
was gone. Nevil went to a fishmonger's who hires a salmonry
of him, and took up 400l. due to him. It was concluded from
this that he had changed his purpose of killing himself, and was
gone abroad. It was said yesterday that his wife had said she
knew where he was, and that he was well. Some said his servants
had found him in the city, with his pistols by him, and had
brought him home to his wife; others that he was at Billing
Bear, his seat in Berkshire, where he had shot but not killed
himself.

1725-6, February 28.—Without doubt Nottingham and Finch
called on you for no other reason but themselves to acquaint you
that you were chosen a trustee, and to pay their compliments to
you upon it, and by that to show you what share they had in
doing it. The world is much changed. The trust is to dispose
annually of 700l. per annum in charities to poor clergymen of
Lincolnshire, Buckinghamshire, Oxfordshire, or Middlesex, and
to poor housekeepers. Through inadvertence so many have been
brought in who are Whigs, that there was danger of their having
a majority, and then the charity would probably have been per-
verted and applied chiefly to make votes at election. If it please
God that I ever come in, I believe we shall be a sure majority,
and have it in our power to preserve this noble charity.
Dartmouth is a trustee, and promised Lord Aylesford to be there
for me. Had he come there would have been a majority for me,
and though that would not have done, for there must be six at
least, to choose in another trustee, yet it would have been a good
reason to have insisted that the others should comply with them.
But Dartmouth failed; I wish one reason was not my declining
to bring in his son student. Poor Aylesford was very much out
of humour upon his failing there, and his voting the day before.

My landlord Battely ought regularly to have acquainted your Lordship with your being chosen, but I took it upon me to do it.

I heartily wish you had been in the House on Thursday. If the adding of but one vote could be a reason for any one's absenting, it would be a reason for every one's doing so. I cannot tell you the names, but I believe you may pretty well guess them, and I fancy you may see most if not all in the protest, though the protesting Lords were jockeyed. The King appointed to be attended with the address at two o'clock. This was much sooner than usual. The Lords who designed to enter their protest found they had not time for it, and desired the leave of the House to have the time for entering it prolonged. This was denied them, upon which, on Saturday, they protested against that denial. No bishop to be sure with the minority, and only one Whig—the Earl of Bristol. Bathurst was against dividing, but when they did divide, he went out with his old friends. I think you are all much wanting to yourselves in not improving this opportunity further. The affairs of Europe justify your father's measures so fully that his enemies are and must be always under confusion of face, when the impeachments are thrown in their faces. It is a pity but that it was done more, and that the articles were reprinted one by one, in some public paper.

Harry is not, that I can learn, certainly heard of yet. It is generally thought that he is in Holland. He is a deplorable instance of what a man may come to by a total neglect of his affairs. I hear of no expensive vice that he had; he lived perfectly well with his wife; he had coming in 9,700*l.* per annum, in as good rents as in England. His northern estate was left charged with 40,000*l.*—the money given for Grey's pardon—which with moderate care might easily have been cleared. But he never could be brought ever to take an account of his condition. His friends pressed him much, as encumbrances grew greater, and offered to clear him if he would confine himself to an allowance they proposed. He never would hear of it, but went on in a thoughtless, expensive way. ' The interest upon the 40,000*l.* amounted to 12,000*l.* Upon this the mortgagee foreclosed him and entered on his estate. This is said to have driven him to that he now does, and now all other creditors crowd in.

I am told, and it comes from Court, that we had not a true account of Stanhope's letter. That he wrote that the Queen was in council when Port Mahon and Gibraltar were demanded; that the King of Spain was silent, but the Queen made the demand in an imperious tone. That when Stanhope answered that it was not in the King's power, that they could not be delivered without the consent of Parliament, she replied, why does he not call his Parliament and get their consent? Tell him if he does not the King of Spain will take measures to force them from him. But I hear to-day a piece of news of more moment, if it hold true, that Count Palmes, the new Resident from the Emperor, came on Friday to Lord Townshend, and told him the Emperor desired of all things to live in amity with England. ' That he

owned he owed as much as Prince could do to that nation, but
that the Elector of Hanover had behaved so in the Empire that
his conduct must be resented. That the Emperor had designed
to have fallen first upon the German dominions, but since
England by the vote the day before was made a party to the
quarrel he would begin with England. That they expected such
a vote from the Parliament, but that, however, they did not look
on it as the sense of the people of England, which they knew to
be otherwise, but only of a party in Parliament. It is rumoured
that Wager is to go immediately and sink hulks in the port of
Ostend to ruin it. The Dutch will come in if we will agree to
demolish that harbour; they would have had it done at the treaty
of Utrecht, but your father refused it. The consequence of it
would be that all our trade with Flanders must be through
Holland, by which we should lose, and the Dutch gain, 500,000*l.*
per annum.

The last masquerade was fruitful of quarrels. Young Webb
had quarrelled at the "Coco [Tree]" with Oglethorp, and struck him
with his cane; they say that quarrel was made up. Webb went
afterwards drunk to the masquerade and met a German who had
a mask with a great nose. He asked him what he did with such a
nose, pulled off his mask, and gave him a slap of the face. He
was carried out by six grenadiers. They say merrily that Webb
has begun the war. Sir John Hobart and Sir G. Oxenden
quarrelled after the masquerade was over at the King's Arms in
the Pallmall. Reports are more to the advantage of Hobart's
gallantry than of Oxenden's. Some say Hobart, when locked up
in his house, got out of a window to meet Oxenden, but Oxenden
had taken care to have himself put under arrest. Others say
Hobart is under arrest, and that Oxenden absconds. His
Majesty is said to have stayed at the masquerade till five in the
morning, and had a hot supper for him in one of the little rooms.

Postscript. Sir Robert Rich said yesterday in the House of
Commons that Harry Grey was certainly dead, though the family
would not yet own it.

1725-6, February 26.—An express came yesterday from Spain.
I cannot learn particulars, but in general it is said to bring fresh
assurances of war. Portmore is ordered immediately for Gibraltar
as well as Carpenter for Port Mahon. All officers belonging to
regiments in either of them are to be gone under pain of being
immediately cashiered. Six ships are ordered to be sheathed
immediately. It is supposed they are to go to the West
Indies. It is confidently said twelve more ships are to be
put in commission. Great is the difficulty of manning the fleet,
the volunteers are few. A battalion of the guards is to go on
board the fleet, and it is said six regiments are ordered from
Ireland for the Straits. Sir Robert, as some say, has changed
his note and begins to own that we are likely to have a war.
The new lottery goes on heavily, it is thought great part will be
drawn for the benefit of the Government.

His Majesty had a hot supper provided for him in one of the
private rooms of the opera. Fabrice and three ladies supped with

him. He said, as he went to supper, that he had only one
diversion, and it was hard that people's incivilities would not
allow him to enjoy. He stayed however till betwixt four and
five, though he still meets with new rebukes. One came in like
a drawer, and cried as he went along, " Coming, coming, sir, we
are very full to-night." "Is there no room empty," a shrill voice,
supposed to be a boy's, cried out amongst the crowd : " None but
the King's Head."

Here is a story among the Jacobites that Madam Sobieski received the sacrament on Christmas day, and was waited on
afterwards by twenty-two cardinals to whom she declared upon
the sacrament that she had received that she had not left her
husband upon the instigation of any person whatever, but upon
weighty reasons which she did not think fit to own. When this
news was brought to the Chevalier's Court, Madam Hay, as it
was said, ordered things to be prepared in the Chevalier's Protestant chapel, and sent for Berkely, the chaplain, and desired
him to give her the sacrament. It seems she had some declaration to make. Berkely refused it and said she who had occasioned the parting of man and wife was not in a fit disposition to
receive it. She in great wrath sent for Cooper, the other Protestant chaplain. He said he was of his brother Berkely's mind,
and that if he could prevail, she should not have the sacrament
till she had done penance through Rome in a white sheet, with a
taper in her hand.

1725-6, March 1.—The last mail brought orders from Holland
to sell much stock, but though there were many sellers, there
were no buyers. That helped to sink the stock. But another
thing contributed more, the report is very hot again that France
is leaving us. Sir Robert does what he can to bear down this
report, but it is now common amongst men of the best fashion at
this end of the town, and it was even said yesterday that Lord
Townshend was to go to France to try if he could prevent it.

1725-6, March 5.—The suspension of news continues, till we
hear how our late addresses are relished abroad. The talk of
France abates, but no one doubts but there are some intrigues
going on to draw France off, though we cannot yet guess what
the issues of them will be. Lord Townshend said on Monday last
that the Court of Vienna talks now in a more pacific strain.

The reason now appears of Lewis of Hampshire leaving his
friends in the late debate. He is to be a peer, and the honour
to be entailed on his daughter and her issue, and she is to be
married to Sir Robert's second son.

I am told that among papers given in at the end of the last
session there are some which can be proved false and which
would sit heavy upon Sir Robert. It is he himself would give
some thousand pounds to have them out. To prevent their being
used against him it was violently carried in a late debate not to
make use of any papers given in a former session, after the prorogation of that session. Pulteney is said to have had a meeting with some Tories, to know if they would assist him in

prosecuting those papers. They are said to have been very cool upon the matter, and in effect to have declined it. I shall not be surprised if this be true.

I am not used to invite your Lordship to buy pretty knick-knacks, but one has been showed me lately which I cannot help mentioning to you. It is a picture of Archbishop Sheldon drawn by Cooper in miniature. As far as I can judge it is a very extra-ordinary one. It was a family piece, and is to be sold by one who married a grand daughter of Sir Joseph Sheldon, one English, house-keeper at Hampton Court. He was sent to me with it by the Vice-Chamberlain to desire I would show it to your Lordship. I know not what he asks for it. He says he will let no one else see it till your Lordship has had the refusal, and I have promised him to show it to your Lordship, if you come to town before I leave it. I should be glad only to know whether you think you shall be in town by the 30th of this month. I stay till that day only, because I am promised that on that day I shall receive the money for the Angel Inn, which I have agreed to part with. I shall certainly, God willing, go for Oxford on the 1st or 3rd of April. If your Lordship has no thoughts of being in town before, I must write somewhat to you which I would speak if I could see you.

1725-6, March 8.—I am told that Lord Trevor is Privy Seal in the room of the Duke of Kingston.

There will be a smart debate to-morrow about the bill to enable the Treasury to compound with Hambden. It is a scandalous bill indeed.

Some say the French army is preparing to march across the Rhine into Germany if there should be occasion. The Spanish Ambassador here says we must wait to see who strikes the first blow. I find some who in common discourse pretend to expect no war are of another opinion with their friends in private, but all yet is uncertain as to that point.

1725-6, March 10.—I had not the picture on my hands when I received your Lordship's last night, but I immediately sent for it, and it was brought to me this morning. The lowest price will be twenty-five guineas, no unreasonable price as far as I can judge of these things, but that I confess is but very little. It is perfectly well preserved, both picture and case.

Public affairs are in the state still they were when I wrote last. The wise think we must have war at last, some sooner, some later. The talk still continues about negotiations between the Emperor and France. It is now said the Duke of Bourbon is to marry the young dowager of Spain. That indeed would reconcile him at once to both his sworn enemies, Spain and Orleans, and in that case no doubt he goes entirely into them. It is said the Emperor has ordered 20,000 horse and as many foot to be ready to march.

Lady Ferrars' cause is referred to King, Harcourt, Trevor. After so many years' law and expense it is like to be compounded upon the terms that were offered before the suit began. What a blessing law is!

Bolingbroke after much teasing has his final answer, that he must expect nothing, for this session at least, and I believe I have good authoriy to add for no other. He seems to be playing a desperate game. He is struck on, as I am told, with Poultney against Walpole. This comes from his own friends. He takes to drinking again, is very expensive, and has but one comfort in view, that his French lady is said to be in an ill state of health.

The lottery does not fill, the time has been prolonged, and the terms too they say must be bettered. Four per cent. for blanks is talked of.

There are letters which say the Imperial Court change their language, that Prince Eugene advises the granting the investiture of Bremen and Verdun ; that the Turks are going to fall on the Muscovite conquests in Persia, and are marching a great body towards Hungary. Were this much credited I suppose stocks would rise and the lottery fill.

1725-6, March 16.—I left off my bark by my doctor's order on Monday and entered upon Spaa water and steel, but this morning I found somewhat that looked like a slight return of my ague. I shall stay long enough in town to get rid of it, I hope, and Oxford will be altogether as good an air as London if I should have any return. I propose not to go into the country till the beginning of May, not then unless I find myself hale and free from all symptoms of my distemper, but go I must at the time I propose. I shall have stayed longer by a fortnight than I proposed. I shall have come to my utmost tether. Neither my pocket or business will allow me to be here longer. I must go, and by good husbandry prepare for next winter. But I am afraid I shall not see your Lordship whilst I stay here. I thought the letter Mr. Vaughan brought would have told me when to expect you. By your silence I suppose those thoughts are over. Be pleased only to let me know so much that I may write what I would say if I saw you.

I have sent the picture by Ned Vaughan, I wish you may think it worth your money. I am no judge either of the performance of the painter or the value of his work. I can only say that I believe that it is very like the little, smirking, wise man. It is very like all the best pictures which any of the family have of him. I shall be glad to hear your Lordship's thoughts of it.

An express came in on Saturday morning from Vienna ; the report was hot on Saturday and Sunday that the Emperor was dead, but surely without any just ground. Possibly the express might bring word that he was ill or worse than he had been. Here would be joy on such accident. But perhaps without much reason, as he would die without issue male, without marrying any of his daughters, or so much as giving the investiture to any of them of his hereditary dominions—which, however, if it had been given, would be questioned by the next Emperor—there would be a scramble for his dominions, and wars about a successor. All Germany would be immediately in a ferment, and another consequence, in all probability, would be a reunion of France and Spain. The last would attempt to seize all they had given up in Italy, and France would invade Flanders and we and Holland be left alone to oppose them. But I believe we shall have no ground to improve these speculations, and we shall not know what to guess as to any other affairs, till we hear how our late votes are relished at Vienna and Madrid.

Swift is coming to town. [Erasmus] Lewis has had a letter from him dated from Chester. He designed in his way up to ˅ stay two or three days at Oxford.

No other news of any kind. Hampden's petition and Wycombe election, both very scandalous, are the only subject of talk. I know not what is done on the first. I believe what Sir Robert hinted, but would not propose, will be followed, to take half the estate to the public, and to settle the remainder upon his wife and brother.

Postscript. Bolingbroke is certainly in the state Hinton thought him. He is going, if not gone, into the country for constant residence, and to come to town only as occasion requires in the summer. His credit runs as low with all others as it does with the ministry. I never met with that book Hinton saw in his closet. I hear [he] begins to doubt of the success of his lawsuit with Packer; he owns it has broke his measures. He depended he says on the money from that sale for the new buildings that he designs. I hear not how he is with Trevor, but I dare say nothing farther than civility betwixt them. Some think Simon expected the seal.

1725-6, March 19.—An express came in from Madrid on Wednesday morning which was sent to demand some categoricals. It went and returned in a month's time. The contents of the answer are not communicated. Some who belong to the great ones say Ripperda is unintelligible, and gives obscure answers, which they know not what to make of. The city suspect the worst, because it is concealed, and stocks have fallen upon it. The express was sent back on Thursday morning; the great ones say it will return with peace, but the city does not yet give credit to them. Hosier's squadron, that was to go to the West Indies, is said to be stopped till the return of this express. If it goes at last, they say it is to go directly to Portobello or Carthagena to attack the galleons there.

The votes tell you of the scandalous things going on in the House of Commons. Your cousin Hampden's bill goes on heavily, but Walpole says the House must do somewhat in it, and give directions in it. They will not, he says, take it on themselves. Hampden acts like a madman; he has been ranting in the Treasury, and says they shall not make him retrench his way of living.

1725-6, March 23.—I am sorry I shall not see you before I leave this place. When I am at Shefford you may be sure I shall not think of stirring till next winter at least, if then. If your Lordship's business will not allow you, who have a coach and six every minute at your command, to come from Down Hall to town, much less will my business allow me, who have only two poor horses, to neglect both my harvest and to come above three-score miles from Shefford to Wimpole. Had I seen you I had somewhat to have said that I shall not upon any consideration whatever trust to paper. That which I wanted to write, if I did not see you, is to beg your charity. I have not been troublesome to you or my Lady on that head; I have always forborne you, whilst the poor late Bishop of Chester and others were picking your pocket for good purposes. But I now want a few guineas, beyond what I can afford myself, to help some poor lads with necessaries, bare necessaries, to go on with their studies. I know not a better charity in the world, or one more extensive in the fruit of it. I am taxing your uncle, and I beg you would send your orders to Mr. Thomas, to give me what you find yourself disposed to in your own heart, for so good a purpose.

I have sent you the Bishop of Bath and Wells' letter, there is nothing in it about Arbuthnot's book more than compliment. But though I send this letter to you, I do not give it to you, and I desire you would return it to me before I leave the town. My journey is fixed, God willing, for Monday se'nnight.

It is said the express that is sent back to Spain is to demand once more a direct answer; and in case it is not given to declare that their not giving it shall be looked on as an act of hostility. One of Hosier's squadron is already sailed, with orders to the ships in the West Indies to meet him at an appointed station. He is to sail with four others within seven days, and one stays behind to carry the last orders to him upon the return of the express from Spain. We are here in no little ferment upon the expectation of a message from the King to both Houses. It is said the purport will be to desire a vote of credit to enable him to raise what money and men he pleases, particularly to pay 12,000 Hessians, and besides to lay before the Houses the usage his ministers have met with abroad. This is not likely to raise stocks. Sir Robert is said to be against it, and to be much out of humour. His own creatures in spite of all he can say sell out stock every day. The lottery is in such discredit that many think it will be dropped. But that which is likely to give the finishing blow to Sir Robert's project of raising all the money at three per cent., is the necessity the East India and South Sea Companies are likely to be under to raise the interest of their bonds. Their bonds are brought in so fast upon them that it is thought they can have no way to stop demands but by raising the interest to five per cent., and they have it now under consideration.

1726, March 26.—I am very glad I shall be so happy as to have an opportunity of paying my duty to my Lady before I leave this town. I shall keep the secret of her jaunt. I will call on Tuesday evening to know how she does after her journey, though she should be too much tired to allow me to see her. As for her stomach, you must not I am afraid hope for any alteration in that by any thing but by Bath water.

I must beg to have the Bishop's letter again. I cannot well [part] with such a proof of his friendship to me, and perhaps the last too of this nature that I may receive. Nor can I think that I can justify it in good manners to part with any such paper written in freedom to me without the knowledge of the person who wrote it, nor can the letter be any use at all to your Lordship.

I dined yesterday with Sir Humphry, where you may be sure you were remembered. His son and daughter Berkshire will be in town next week. Sir Humphry left the House in the midst of the debate yesterday. He said there had been some fine smart strokes upon his governor before he came away, and he supposed there would be. I can give you no particulars of the debate; I can only tell you the result was no more than was expected, carried for the question by 270 odd against 80 odd.

It is said the Spaniard has declared that he will look upon our sending of a squadron to the West Indies as a declaration of war, and that the moment he has notice that it is sailed, he will seize all our effects in the West Indies and Spain.

1726, March 30.—I take the liberty you are pleased to allow me of suggesting to you that you have erred, but you have erred as we say on the right side, not by defect, but excess. Your generosity is greater by much than I could have desired or hoped for. I should have thought my petition for a few guineas fully and nobly answered by ten, but I hope your Lordship will find the effect of the prayers of the poor souls that will be refreshed and comforted by your munificence. I should be prouder of being almoner to your Lordship than to any crowned head. But your Lordship can have no occasion for such an officer, but in the subservient part of distributing your bounty. You have a head to direct as well as a heart to bestow your bounty, and I perceive that if I ever have the honour of being called in to give my poor thoughts I shall have more occasion to restrain than to excite your bounty.

I have left with Mr. Thomas some of the things I would have said, if I had seen you. One I should never have mentioned if the person concerned had not returned to England, as I thought he never would when I heard it. You will perceive it is from indubitable authority, and though I do not think it proper by any means to stop correspondence or to check any common observation of civilities, yet it is a ground to you for caution and to be on your guard, and in that view only I thought myself indispensably obliged to impart it to you. There is somewhat more of greater importance that I should have said, but I own I do not give credit to it myself. However, I do not think it is utterly to be despised, but is ground enough for your Lordship and any one else to put their private affairs upon as sure a foot as they can and as soon too as they can. I have nothing to add of public news to my last, only I am told this morning, by one who has reason to know but did not believe it before, that there has been remitted by Spain to Vienna, to the value of 800,000*l.*, a million of pistols. The ministry give out otherwise, but this gentleman, though heartily in their interest, tells me they are not to be regarded on that point. This is the surest argument I know that there will be war, and it is an argument that I think cannot be answered.

Your Lordship's great condescension and goodness, for I will not call the expressions compliments, are too great for me to receive, and therefore I shall not pretend to answer them. But if your Lordship can prevail on yourself to take such a romantic journey as to surprise me at Little Shefford, I believe you are persuaded that the joy I should have would be equal to the honour done to me, and though you would meet with nothing fit to entertain you, yet possibly there might be somewhat in the newness and oddness of the scene that would divert you.

1726, April 6. [Oxford.]—I bless God I have had a safe and pleasant journey. Dr. Freind came with me hither, and went on this morning for Witney.

I had the honour to spend several hours with my Lady on Friday last. I can see no cause to alter my opinion, that she must not expect a stomach or strength till she has been again at Bath.

I find Lord Dartmouth has entered his son a commoner; he is to be brought in student by the Dean, I suppose, because the Dean has put him to one of his own creatures. I suppose this is by Townshend's recommendation.

This poor place is in a wretched condition as to all parts of its government. It is a peculiar providence of God that there are so many of all sorts who do still extremely well in it, under so total a want of discipline and encouragement, but I shall not trouble your Lordship with any of our ridiculous stories.

1726, April 28.—I saw your cousin ["Abel" Foley] once before I left the town. I must do him the justice to say that I neither observed or heard any thing but what is to his credit. I never saw any gentleman return from so long travels with so little affectation or foreign airs. He is returned as plain an Englishman as he went out. [His] father designs to have him to wait on his Majesty, and Lord Townshend is to introduce him. This was mentioned to me to see how I liked it. I only said I hope he did not design his son should frequent that place, and turn a courtier. I thought there were many reasons against that, and I believed too it would be less expensive to him to continue a country gentleman. Now their thoughts are upon settling him in marriage; that is certainly right. I was told I should be consulted upon it, with a compliment, because I was a particular friend. I said my mind was known, and I had but little time then at my command. However I appointed an hour, but the father was hindered from coming at the time he appointed, and I could not wait for him, so I can tell you no more of that.

All Souls and the University itself have truly had a great loss by the death of the late Warden [Gardiner]. It is said Bertie and Levet are likely to be returned to the Archbishop. We have had extraordinary diversion in the canvass for a *Custos Archivorum*. My good neighbour has in it, if possible, outdone himself, and exposed himself so far as to have doubted whether he is laughed at more abroad or at home. But I must refer your Lordship to Tim for particulars, which I know he will have from his correspondents here.

I beg my most sincere respects to Dr. Colbatch, he is a worthy, considerable man. I know not Dr. Middleton, but by that I have heard of him and seen of his writings he deserves the opinion very justly your Lordship has of him.

I think I wrote to your Lordship from town how brutally Bentley speaks of our friend the late Bishop of Chester, though he always lived well with him; and with no other view but to make his court to [the Bishop of] London.

1726, May 2.—Yesterday Wilkins, the Prussian, was with me to desire the use of my *Marmora Oxoniensia*, with Dr. Mills' corrections. He told me he had been promised by Mr. Wanley the use of Lord Oxford's. I told him if he was to have the use of Lord Oxford's he did not want mine; that Lord Oxford's had been transcribed from mine. He said he understood by Mr. He[a]rne that your Lordship's was one that belonged to Togree [Dr. Thomas] Smith. I said your Lordship might, for aught I knew, have that which had belonged to Togree Smith, but I was sure you had a book that had been corrected by mine. In short I positively refused him the use of mine. This man had been recommended by poor Dr. Grabe to me and others and subsisted I believe by the friends Grabe procured him some years. When his great benefactor, Grabe, was dead, he gave out that he died a Papist and of the pox. He was a spy here whilst he was living in a great measure on the kindness of the place, and gave constant accounts to Wilcox—as it was said—of every thing he could pick up, and no doubt added some inventions of his own. Charlett had been very kind to him, lent him the use of his study freely, and would leave him there often many times alone. He once, in Charlett's absence, rummaged amongst a great many of the boys' exercises which poor Charlett had thrown aside, and met with one in where there was honourable mention of the late Duke of Ormond. He pockets this, and sends it up to his correspondent. Poor Charlett, who I dare swear had never read it, had like to have been brought into a plot. This man afterwards was recommended by some German to the Archbishop, he was taken in first at Lambeth as librarian, afterwards made chaplain, and has gotten a 1,000l. per annum in spiritual preferments. He married lately a daughter of Lord Fairfax, a natural, that lived at Canterbury with one to feed her and nurse her, for the sake of 4,000l. which she had. He has heard of my book, and says he cannot learn what is become of Dr. Mills' own book, and would have my book that he may publish it and get a penny. I am sure there can be no edition worth a groat without my book or your Lordship's, if Dr. Mills' own book is not to be met with. I would freely lend mine to any worthy, good man to make his best of it, but I think such a one should have the advantage rather than this gentleman.

1726, May 4. Little Shefford.—I wrote to your Lordship the day I left Oxford, about a modest request of Wilkins to me. I believe I then forgot one circumstance relating to him that is pretty material. When the Archbishop took him into his family, he sent him to Oxford to get a master's degree. His character was so well known that great opposition was made to it. The Archbishop employed all hands to get it passed, amongst other our then governor, poor Dr. Smalridge, but all would not do, he was refused. Great was the resentment at Lambeth about it, and I am apt to think it was no little motive since to all the violent proceedings in Peplo's case.

1726, May 17.—Surely that needs no excuse which merits so much thanks, as your long letter does. Wilkins could but have one end in enquiring after your parsonages, viz. to see if any of them were good enough for his worship, and then to cast about how to get it of you. But the gentleman is now full of greater dainties. Such a man, a foreigner, has 1,000*l.* per annum in preferments, whilst so many worthy men of our own country are starving.

I am so fully possessed of Dr. Middleton's character in all respects that I extremely long to be known to him. I am not certain from your Lordship's letter whether he has been at Oxford or designs to be there. If he has not been there, if I knew the time when he designed to be, if very extraordinary business did not hinder, I would certainly go over thither. I have not yet seen Hare's book. I have had an account of it from Bob, and I expect it every day with great impatience from Oxford. It will be a controversy very fruitful of diversion to the *Literati*.

I very well know the melancholy subject that employed you and John, you may lament it, but I know not how you will remedy it. The difficulties will grow upon you every day. I know but one thing certain, that your Lordship must in a great measure keep the mother and all her " bearns " into the bargain. It is a strong argument with many others to oblige you to look sharply into your own affairs. Be as private as you will in your relief of them, the gentleman [Kinnoull] will trust that you will not see them starve, and impart his own money, when he has any, to them accordingly. Nay I know not whether if he were sure that you would let them starve, that he would not do so too.

I have seen Newton's book [" University Education?"]; I had one presented to me. I have the same opinion of it your Lordship has—*rir justus probus innocens timeris*. He is one full instance, of many, that a man of good intention and warm zeal, with but half wit, is less capable of being advised or dealt with than the rankest knave alive. The man in the main meant well. He warped indeed pretty much in the case of University College, in doing ill to bring about a good end as he thought; but it is come home to him. And this book has made his character as well known to the rest of the world as it was to this acquaintance.

I will not answer that young Abel may not be more disposed to Court than the old one could wish. If he is, and madam likes it, the fate of that family is seen. I was told indeed by two gentlemen, your Lordship's friends, that he was turned Whig when he was abroad. They pretended to be sure of their intelligence from more than one that had been with him there. I was much concerned at it, and enquired seriously of the old man that was with him if there were any ground for the report. He assured me there was not more than once with great solemnity. He said the only occasion that could possibly be for it was that young Abel had, by his advice, conversed with great caution, and avoided entering into foolish conversation when begun by others, perhaps to entrap him. That was certainly right, but as the young gentleman has great reserve for his age, he may have deceived the old man. Should it prove so, I believe the foundation was laid for it where it is little suspected.

1726, May 18.—I have read Hare with wonderful pleasure. He has not spared his old friend, and I think he has exposed him for his ignorance as well as for his plagiarism. If B[entley] were not the most impudent man alive he could not show his face, but we shall have more sport. B[entley] must at Hare again, or the world will suppose he owns himself laid on his back. By the advertisement at the end of the epistle, and by somewhat dropped in the epistle, it should seem as though some other person were writing against B[entley]. The more upon his bones the better. Hare's compliments to Dr. Middleton are very handsome and justly due to him. But I could not but observe that when he mentions those who wrote about Phalaris the malignity of his temper prevailed on him. He owns they had discovered two notorious instances of B[entley's] theft, but not a civil word to them, though he is free of his compliments to all others who have written against B[entley], But this is agreeable to the inveterate spite he had always to us, though without any cause ever given for it by us to him. When he was asked once abroad, by a friend of ours, if he knew the gentlemen of Christ Church, he answered insolently, "I neither do nor desire to know any of them."

Postscript. The gentlemen of Oriel have carried their cause against the Provost in every point. The jury found for them without going from the bar. This is much for the Bishop of Chester's credit, who alone supported and directed them. This too I take to be a sure precedent for University College. Though Oriel cause was clear yet much more may be said for University. And indeed the plea of my brother doctors is so ridiculous that Comyns, who you know is cautious enough, is now grown very sanguine and advises Cockman not to try the cause, but to demur to the plea, which counsel never advise but when they judge themselves sure, because there is no after game to be played if the demurrer should not be good.

1726, May 28.—I go on Tuesday to Oxford to be ready to receive Mr. Mattaire on Wednesday, who is coming to show his spouse Oxford. I suppose they will be with me till Saturday or Monday.

1726, June 6.—My guests are here and make a much longer visit than I expected, I must not say desired. I thought they would have left me this morning, but I believe they design not to quit their quarters this week, nor perhaps then if my affairs would allow me to stay here longer. I could do well enough with my old schoolfellow, but his wife and daughter-in-law, I must confess, are too polite for me; they should have a landlord that has a better taste of such conversation. By their being here I shall have the happiness of being here when Lord Kinnoull comes. Murray had letters yesterday that his Lordship will be here with Lord Dupplin to-morrow. I know not whether he will visit me, if he does I shall return it. But as for four years past he has not been pleased to take any notice of me, I think it would be ill manners of me, who am so much inferior in rank to him, to presume to offer other civilities to him than I have had the honour to receive from him.

1726, June 12.—Lord Kinnoull came hither on Tuesday. I met him on Wednesday morning at the deanery. Upon that, when he left the Dean, he called in on me. I waited on him at his inn on Thursday and stayed near two hours with him; I have not seen him since. I took care to turn the conversation upon his father[-in-law] Oxford, and the condition in which we were when he left the ministry and that we were in at present. I gave his son the best advice I could before him, and told Lord Dupplin that the greatest service we could do him would be to prepare him to resist the influence of the ill examples he would see in the world when he left us. The father agreed with me entirely both in morality and politics, and talked like a Tory. I perceived by old Grey, who came with him, that he expected an entertainment from me. He told Grey they should meet with no good wine at Oxford, but at my house. That was obliging, but I told Grey that as his Lordship had not been pleased for four years past to take any notice of me, I, who was so much his inferior, durst not presume to offer greater civilities to his Lordship than I received from him. Grey assured me he would tell it him home, and I daresay he will.

I am desired to recommend to your Lordship's goodness the case of one Mr. Latin, in an affair in which your Lordship is concerned with my Lord Thanet and my Lord Morpeth, as you have the care of the Duchess of Albemarle. It is for a debt due from the Duchess to one to whom Mr. Latin was lately executor. Dr. Henchman, at whose desire I mention this to your Lordship, does not say the debt is strictly legal, but highly equitable. But your Lordship will best judge of that when the case is laid before you. I shall only add that your Lordship may have Mr. Latin's character from G. Clarke. Mr. Latin's fortune was ruined chiefly by his honourable behaviour to his master the Duke of Albemarle, with whom he went to Jamaica. Upon his return to England he could not take the oaths. He has subsisted chiefly by the kindness of G. Clarke, the late Primate Lindsay [of Armagh], and others who were bred with him here, when he was of Wadham College. I do not believe there ever was a man of a fairer character and more universally beloved and esteemed by all that knew him, nor that has met with harder fortune in the world. He is now seventy, and in great want. If there is room for kindness in the case in which he applies to you, your Lordship cannot meet with a more [deserving?] object of it.

Poor Harry Watkins is here, but much out of order, and I know not when he will be able to proceed on his journey to London. He is skin and bone, under a visible decay, how far his doctor may retard his end I know not, I am pretty sure he can never restore him.

1726, June 13.—Mr. Mattaire brings up my *Marmora* with him to town. I think he is determined to undertake a new edition of it. He is peculiarly qualified for the only thing that is wanting to make a complete edition, the knowledge of the dialects. And by the help of my book and Togree Smith's, which I know he may have from your Lordship, he will not only make a very fine edition, but the poor man too, if he manages right, will put a good penny in his own pocket. I hear my friend Wilkins is in a great rage and threatened before he left this place, and does so too in town, what he will do to me.

You will have heard of the sad accident which happened to Alsop last Friday night or Saturday morning. By the accounts we yet have of the condition he was in that occasioned the accident makes it still more deplorable.

Postscript. I saw in a letter from Dr. Hale that Wanley is going to be married. Dr. Hale did what he could to dissuade him on account of his condition, Wanley answered that he was betrothed and would marry. Hale told him, I believe, as freely as he writes, that his condition is so very bad that he cannot last long. It is pity the man cannot be hindered from such egregious folly, that his poor relations may have what he has. No woman can think of marrying one in his condition but to strip him.

1726, June 20.—I long to see Dr. Middleton's book [   ] No doubt the world will divide into parties upon it. I take his to be a branch of the war against Bentley, and Mead has drawn it upon himself by his unreasonable espousing of Bentley; but some of the *Literati* said when Mead's speech first came out, that all about   in honour of physicians was a mistake.

I am afraid poor little Dupplin is too well acquainted with the state of domestic affairs and has too deep a sense of them. I sent for him before I returned hither, and as I was talking to him with the utmost kindness I could, he burst into tears. I asked him if anything troubled him; I told him I would not press him to know it, but if he thought fit to acquaint me with it he might be assured of the most faithful advice I could give him. He said nothing, but as I went on saying what I thought proper to him, he burst into tears twice over.

1726, June 23.—The Premier and his brother of All Souls called on me last week in their way to young Bromley's. They came from your cousin Popham's at Littlecote. They said Mr. Popham had showed them your uncle's book which he had given to Mr. Popham when he called on him in his late Bath journey. But Mr. Popham must have strangely mistaken your uncle, for he showed this book to the Gwyns, and I suppose he does so to every one else, as your father's composure. I set the young gentlemen right, as I shall do any others that I meet with under such misinformation. Mr. Popham talked too of somewhat of your father's relating to the peace in his ministry, that was shortly to be published. I did presume to say, that as far as I knew anything relating to the family, I never heard of such a writing, nor did I believe any such was to be published.

1726, June 27.—Poor Dupplin's case is worthy certainly of the utmost compassion, but nothing more can be done than what your Lordship mentions, by all kindness possible to him to encourage him to apply hard to his studies.

Things look as though we should be the aggressors. If the old renegade is gone, I suppose the war will break out this year. As they please, Little Shefford will be one of the last places it can come to, except by fury.

I hope Middleton's paper will come this week by Draper's wagon, that lies at the King's Arms on Holborn Bridge and comes out on Thursday.

I long to hear how the case stood about the *Marmora*. I have some obscure remembrance that I let Lord Kinnoull have my own book, which was corrected by Mills himself, and had a book which was my cousin Sheldon's on beautiful large paper, corrected by the book which Mills corrected, which I kept. In such case, Kinnoull's book will be of greatest authority, though I doubt not but my own was very exactly corrected. And I must beg your Lordship would not only desire the Dean of St. Patrick—to whom I pray my service—not only not to let any but Mattaire have his book, but that he would let Mattaire have it, that he may compare that which he has from me with it. But in this case, I am strangely mistaken if your Lordship had not a *Marmora* of your own corrected by mine.

Postscript. The miss of the family of the Abels will be no little misfortune to me. I shall only save some pounds by it. Do you hear anything more of young Abel? What ply he is like to take. Whether he frequents the Court, and is likely to strike in with them? Is any match talked of for him?

1726, July 2.—It is certainly so, and it shows what a fine fellow I am, and how fit to have books of such moment with the learned, that I could, for the sake of keeping the large paper, part with the book that had the original corrections. Not that I doubt in the least that the corrections in my own book are not very exactly copied, but still the book Swift has is of greatest authority. But if we keep our own counsel, it will probably never be known farther than it is at present where that book is; and if your Lordship and I keep the secret, and your Lordship is better at it than I am, it can never be known that mine is only the copy, and Swift's the original. For I have imparted that secret to no one but to your Lordship, but pray get Swift's book into your hands as soon as you can, and push on Mattaire, as I shall do, to publish his advertisement. When he has given public notice, I know he will go through with it. He may do it afterwards at his leisure.

1726, July 10.—Mead and his friends too are very uneasy. They own Middleton has hit a blot, but they think that should not have been taken notice of in one of Mead's character. But that on which I perceive most stress is laid, in order to lessen the thing by bringing an imputation on Middleton himself, is that Middleton is obliged to Mead; that Mead was a friend to Middleton when he was under prosecution and got 'him set free sooner than he would have been otherwise. I know not what ground there is for this; I apprehended the contrary. I thought Middleton and his friends apprehended that Mead screened Bentley, and that they should have had the better of him if Mead had not prevailed on Sunderland to protect him.

Postscript. I condole with you truly for the loss of poor Wanley. He was certainly in his way the completest servant you could have had in Europe. Since he would marry, I am glad his money is gone to a poor episcopal Scotch minister's daughter.

1726, July 14.—I suppose your Lordship has seen the two volumes of Toland's posthumous Tracts. In the second volume I meet with somewhat to which I was not wholly a stranger, though I did not think it had gone quite so far. I fancy your uncle could explain somewhat there to you. I think it I own dangerous as well as improper for anyone to deal with such cattle, upon any terms or any occasions. It is plain Des Maiseaux is the man who has written his Life, but though he has printed what Molyneux wrote to Locke in Toland's favour, he has not printed what Locke wrote in answer to Toland's; nor has he told of Toland's being cudgelled most severely by some of Marlborough's ruffians. I find the rogue in his letters is very free with the Dean of St. Patrick's and poor Prior, and has two or three impudent lies upon Christ Church.

1726, July 18.—I hear things go on at a wretched rate at poor Christ Church. The governor's jealousy of designs in his subjects to affront him in everything they do or say and their contempt of him increase every day. And this is the formidable man that was to convert and new model the whole society. He will I am afraid be the occasion of dividing it. They cannot be long without being divided into distinct parties of Whig and Tory, a thing hitherto unknown in that place. But I begin to pity our poor governor, the contempt of him rises to a degree higher than what he has done deserves, and the sense he has of it makes him do more foolish things every day to show his sense of it.

1726, July 23.—My lady errants have left me. What makes the stocks rise, is it the King of France's illness? Do we apprehend his death would be of any advantage to us? It would probably cause a new ferment in the world. We have had many of late

The world is in a pretty odd situation, that neither minister or Prince of any considerable power abroad can be changed but it produces all alteration of measures over all this part of the world.

1726, August 4.—I am sorry for the circumstance of poor Mr. Dennis burning his papers, he was a curious man and a scholar; I fancy there must have been somewhat valuable in them.

Have you any thoughts yet of a successor to Wanley? *Haud illum invenies parem!*

1726, August 8.—The news of Wharton's conversion is very surprising. Can anyone that reflects on the father and grandfather avoid observing the events of their family?

1726, August 17.—The young Queen may have had her *viaticum*, few of her quality die without a suspicion of somewhat of that kind. It is certain her death will be very convenient for the affairs of France at this juncture. It may too occasion a change of measures in other Courts, as well as in that of France, but the present prospect is so confused that I think nothing more can be gathered from it, but in general, that it cannot clear up without some notable alteration.

1726, August 31.—I forgot in my last to thank you for your banter about the stranger that was come to town. I did suspect after I had written to you that it was my godfather. I suppose he came now to buy a pair of stockings, the last time I remember he wanted new ruffles.

Do you know what made Swift return so soon to Ireland? I thought he had come to end his days here, at least to stay some years.

1726, September 15.—Lord Abingdon at Oxford Race was affronted by the mob, and used very freely, for having altered the race posts. In revenge he would not give the brace of bucks he had promised to be run for by freemen's horses. This has raised a mutiny, and they are ripe for a revolt against his Lordship. Her Grace of Marlborough strikes in, and begins to employ all Oxford tradesmen. It is given out, too, that she will give a plate of 50*l*. the next race, and two brace of bucks. There is like to be fine sport in Oxford. The great Berties are like to lose all their interest unless the University interpose with all their might in their behalf, and I know not, as things are, whether they will do.

1726, September 17.—I enclose according to your order the superscription that is marked again, it is not charged indeed, I paid nothing for it, but to what purpose this mark, when the observation is false too, the frank being as like to other franks as any man's hand at one time can be to itself at another time. I had another superscription so marked last week which I did not trouble you with. The frank was struck out, and it was charged nine pence, but nothing was charged for it in the postman's bill, so he asked nothing for it.°

*Annexed is cover of a letter addressed to Dr. Stratford at Lambourn, with "Frank, Oxford," in the corner, and the words "not like others," written above. Also some remarks at back in Lord Oxford's hand.

1726, October 2.—I am heartily sorry for poor Mr. Pope's misfortune. I hear Abel and Abelina with their younkers have been making a tour in Herefordshire, but the chief business was to call on Auditor Foley, and to be carried by him to wait on Lady Scudamore. It is not hard to guess the meaning of that. Should it do, it would make them great indeed in that part of the world. I have not yet stirred out, and have seen Dupplin only out of my window, but I perceive he was well.

1726, November 1.—Your cousin Robin was so kind as to spend an evening with me in his way to town. I understand by him that his father proposes to pass the winter in the country, and that Master and his lady set out for Herefordshire next Monday. I cannot think this a season proper for such a journey with a little one, and I should think a winter's rustication as little agreeable to a young lady as it is proper for Mr. Auditor himself. He will be overrun with the spleen, but I hope Master will be so kind as take Oxford in his way.

I never doubted of four shillings in the pound ; thecharge this year, beyond what was given for it, certainly comes to two shillings *per* pound, so that we have already spent the two shillings that is to be paid next year, and if there should be occasion, as no doubt there will, and for more, for the same expense again, we must anticipate again, and be always in debt for half of the year's tax.

I have not yet heard from J. Drummond, but I suppose you do not wonder to hear that he is grown very fat. No hog that is put up for fatting is ever crammed more than he has been for four months past in Fatherland. My neighbour does not cram more on a Gaudy day, when he purges beforehand to prepare himself for it. But the worst is that in this condition our friend John cannot be prevailed on to lose a little blood. I am terribly afraid of a blow some time or other.

1726, November 13.—Your Lordship surprised me much. I must be as great a brute as one not far from me if I can ever forget the noble offer you have made me, and the very handsome and generous manner in which you have done it. I am no stranger to the value of the living, and I know not any neighbourhood I should choose as soon as the friends I have there. Were I fifteen years younger, or had I a wife and children, I would most thankfully accept your offer and settle and spend my days there. I think any one who has that living ought to spend most of his time there. At my age, I ought not to think of beginning a new course of life, and unless I could resolve to live most part of my time there I should neither make the return I ought to your Lordship's great goodness, nor could I give to the world a reason for accepting it that would not be unbecoming one in my age and circumstances. I cannot think it would be a grateful return in your clerk to your Lordship, or proper for my own character, to put a curate into such a place, that I might have the overplus to put into my purse, or to spend at such a distance, when I do nothing for it. But I shall always have as warm a gratitude to your Lordship, for the goodness and generosity of your offer, as if I had accepted it.

1726, November 21.—You desire I would forgive you. I am glad you are so merry. Men commonly are so when they put the figure on their friends. This is a very notable one, to desire forgiveness for offering me a living worth 400*l. per annum*, as I now understand Presteigne is. I shall most heartily thank you to my grave for offering me the greatest means you ever had, or probably ever will have, in your power of showing your friendship to me. May I be allowed to say too that I value the offer, and in the manner too it was made as much, as it is an eminent proof of the honour and nobleness of your own temper, as for being so great an instance of your goodness to me. But though your Lordship has shown so signally that you wish well to me, yet I daresay, when you consider all circumstances, you do not in your private judgment condemn me on any account for not accepting the offer, unless it be for a foolish weakness, not much in fashion I confess, for not catching at anything that might bring in some money to me. Had your father thought fit to offer it to me, when it was in his power, I truly believe I should thankfully have accepted it, and have made my chief residence at least there. But now it is too late in the day for those things. Your Lordship has done very agreeably to your own character in disposing of it [to] your chaplain. And all who have the honour to belong to you will no doubt by that disposition be encouraged to serve you with zeal as well as fidelity, when they see their service so sure to be considered in a proper season.

1726, December 2.—I believe I know of some applications, that either have been or would have been made to you, if you had given opportunity for it. Abel, Abelina, and the Abelings were here last week. Abelina said, if she might have directed you, you should have disposed of it otherwise than you have, to a near relation, your aunt Charlton's son, a second son, who is not indeed yet fit for it, but is designed for orders, and it might have been kept for him. I immediately said if it would have been proper to dispose so of it, why should you not have given it in trust, for one of your sister's sons, who out of the many she has might well spare one for orders. *Ad quod nihil erat responsum.* I had forgot then that Abel has a living of his own worth 600*l. per annum*. I shall certainly ask him, when I see him again, whether it will not be as proper for him to reserve that as your Lordship to keep Presteigne for his sister Charlton's son. I find they are in good earnest to get if they can Miss Scudamore for Tommy, measures are taking for it. I cannot blame them, if they can compass it.

The application you mention was a very extraordinary piece of impudence indeed. It shows there are always those in the world who will not lose anything for want of asking; I remember I first suspected that man of double dealing in Prior's affair. You and Prior would not at first come into my opinion, though soon after it was evident.

1726, December 8.—There may not perhaps be much occasion for your regard to the Parliament, and yet there was one day last session when I heartily wished you had been there, and I believe when you heard.of it you wished so too. If I mistake not there may be more than one of those days next session. And I fancy your honour will prompt you, not only to attend then, but to speak too, and to put out all your sails. I dare engage you will have wind and tide both of your side. But why a special summons, as the news say, to all the peers to attend next session, if the session, as is reported, is to be opened with the attainder of three peers? Poor Lansdowne! I fancy you will feel in yourself some compassion for him.

I had almost forgot to give your Lordship joy of the promotion of Mr. Verney. But it looks as though there was some rub in the way. I hope he has not managed like some indiscreet ladies to have scandals without joy.

I think Master told me that at your Lordship's recommendation young Wigan was to have the case of Lord Poulett's son, and to have an 100l. *per annum* settled on him for life. Is it so?

Do you know that, by Sir Robert's interest, the King allows somewhat for the maintenance of Dup[plin] here?

1726, December 20.—I am not a little proud that I happened to jump with your Lordship in the same opinion of the influence a late match might probably have on poor L[ansdowne]'s affairs. Bob writes to me last post, that is said, that upon this match his affairs are made up and that he is to come home. But what will he do here? What figure will he make? How will he live? It is a strange match. See the fate of great families. Your relation's asking your opinion about accepting the offer made to him is just like men's asking their friend's opinion about matrimony. They are always determined before they come so far and only want a friend's authority to excuse themselves to the world for that which they know well enough they shall be blamed for. I have been so lucky, as well as your Lordship, to observe that this was working last winter, and I designed to have let your Lordship have known my observations had I seen you before I left the town. But I am much pleased for more reasons than one that he wrote to your Lordship, and had the answer you mention. You are certainly right in the person that has been employed in this affair. I wish our friend John were rid of such an acquaintance, he gets nothing but scandal in return for much claret which that spunging fellow soaks there.

Newton's statutes though printed are not sold, but given only to particular friends. He and I have not visited since the University affair, but I will try to get your Lordship a copy, and hope I shall do it.

I have read Gulliver, and I may own to you, with pleasure too. I durst not own so much to long Thomas when he was here. His lady was wonderfully delighted with them, but grave Thomas was in such wrath against them that I durst not come in to the lady's aid, and own that I had read them. But I

referred her to Mattaire, who I told her would help to support
her in that point against her lord.

Your Lordship has been extraordinary good in recommending
young Wigan, but I am amazed that he should not embrace the
offer. He has indeed some fortune of his own, but not such as
not to need what this offer would have brought him. But never
surely was there an age in which men made such estimates of
their own merit, and expected to jump, at their first appearance,
into such a fortune as their forefathers would have been glad to
arrive at after threescore.

The Rabbit affair is as great a monster in its kind as any,
even this age, has produced. I suppose you have seen the ballad
on it; it has given, I hear, an occasion to the ladies of our age to
show their modesty, in talking modestly upon it such things as
their mothers would have thought an affront to them to have had
any spoke in their presence.

If our friend B. has lost his lady, I am sure he will be heartily
out of humour; never wife will be lamented more. I think her
great fortune is to go to Greenwich Hospital.

Wharton, North and Grey, and L[ansdowne] were said to be
the three to be attainted. It is now said Mar will go to pot for
L[ansdow]ne; but Mar is attainted already.

1726-7, February 22.—My chine and fowls and black puddings
are come. When will you send in your pie with a hard name?
Let it be any day except to-morrow. What think you of Friday?
My fowls wont keep beyond Saturday. Settle it with Mr. Thomas,
and let me know by him.

1727, April 20.—On Tuesday night I was much surprised with
a visit from my old acquaintance the Dean of St. Patrick's; he
sat chattering with me till twelve o'clock. He dined with me
yesterday; Dup[plin] and young Arbuthnot were his company.
He went in the evening for Tidsworth. He is as little altered, I
think, of any man I ever saw, in so many years' time.

1727, April 23.—Should I have the honour to see your Lordship at my poor hut, I should accost everybody that came into it
after you, with Evander's compliment in the Eighth Ænead to
Æneas:

Limina quondam
Mortimer haec subiit; haec illum regia cepit.
Aude hospes contemnere opes, et te quoque dignum
Finge Deo, rebusque veni non asper egenis.

You know the fate you have to expect, but you will meet with
a welcome that if I mistake you not will supply to one of your
disposition all defects.

1727, April 26.—It is my misfortune to be always the first to
find out rogues, but not to be believed till it is too late to prevent
the mischief they do. I was the first who found out Atterbury,
but no one then would hearken to me. I was the first that foretold
what Carteret would be, but they who were sufficiently convinced

after by their own experience thought me at that time at the very best a rash fellow. I must be so vain as to put you in mind that I first told your Lordship and poor Prior, by somewhat I observed in Newcome's acting, that he was then betraying Prior. You neither of you then were of my mind, though I own you were a few weeks after. The fellow is a " thorougher," and is every way qualified to be at the top of the ladder, and he may be there in time.

1727, May Day.—I am glad you called on [Jekyll, Master of the] Rolls. He was brother-in-law and owed his fortune to your father's most implacable enemy, old Summers (Somers) ; and he himself was a Whig virulent enough in all conscience. Yet he acted the fairest part to your father of any of that set of men ; not out of the least personal regard, I believe, to your father— I believe he had as little of that as any of them—but out of regard only to the justice of the cause. But that motive was more for your father's honour as well as his own.

What I first said to you about Newcome was when Prior stood to be Parliament man at Cambridge. Upon somewhat Newcome dropped I found he was not sound. Prior did not think so then, but soon after it appeared that he was dealing underhand for Annesley at the time he pretended to serve Prior.

1727, May 6.—Your Lordship is not pleased to take notice whether you saw the Dean of St. Patrick's before you went to Wimpole. I suppose you did. Did he vent himself to you about Lord Carteret ? He opened with great freedom against him to me ; he had reason indeed. There was a very ingenious man, who had been introduced by the Dean to Carteret at Carteret's own desire. Carteret had seemingly entered into great friendships with him, and had invited himself often to his house, and lived very freely on him. He had frankly promised him any preferment in his gift. When the preferment fell which the man most desired, being very convenient for him, though of no great value, Carteret told him he could not give it to him, though he esteemed him much, because he was suspected to be somewhat of a Tory, and gave the preferment to a Frenchman recommended to him by the Duchess of Kendal.

1727, May 15.—Poor Christ Church, I hear, is a great combustion. Gregory, the history professor, has declared he will appear for a lecture on the 11th of next July in order to appear for Proctor next Lent. A great majority have declared vehemently against him, and put up the censor Manatou. It is supposed this fellow would not have ventured on this if he were not assured of being supported to the utmost of their power by the Dean and Chapter. I will not believe till I see it that they will act such a part or use threats and violence to bring over votes. If they should, I believe they could not carry it ; but if they go this way to work the College will be in a wretched state. We must have Tim up from Presteigne.

1727, June 17. Little Shefford.—I was misinformed as to
Swift's being with you. I perceive you had not when you wrote
received any notice of the King's death. I hear Strafford,
Scarsdale, and many others of that sort have been to make their
compliments; in that case I see not why your Lordship should
stick out.

1727, June 19.—Your next will tell me, I suppose, how you
have been received at Leicester House. I can but smile to think
how unconcernedly we poor rustics go on with our hay harvest,
whilst you are in such a hurry in town.

1727, June 26.—We are all in haste to make our compliments. I hear our governor carried up little Dupplin to help
out the show. I hope his appearing may be of some service. I
doubt not but my good neighbour *waddled* in the crowd. But
our governor has been baffled basely in his attempt to set up a
proctor. He has been forced to throw up the cudgels, and to
compliment the man he opposed. Pray be so good as to tell this
to my landlord, and that there will [be] no occasion for Tim to
leave his duty at Presteigne. Be pleased too to let my landlord
know that I received the box very safe on Saturday, and heartily
thank him.
I beg when you write to Dr. Middleton you would give my most
humble thanks to him. I have read his book with a great deal
of pleasure, but it is a pity any of his time should be lost upon
such a couple of scrubs. Though Tim thought he could hardly
spare time to come up to us, he must find some to spare, to ride
about the country, now Master appears. But Tim is a light
weight, and will dispatch a good deal of that business with ease.
I hope for the honour of the family, now Master appears, he will
not let himself be baffled. Make the old man bleed freely.
Perhaps that is designed to be thrown on you, but I hope you are
on your guard.

1727, July 1.—I agree with you that things must be in a great
measure, if not wholly, in the same track. Nor can it be otherwise
if they consider who is to be Premier. But the world seems to
me to be as mad as they were in South Sea days. Every one expects to make his fortune, but I doubt not they will be as much
disappointed in preferments as they were then in estates.
An old friend of yours and your father's too came up I believe
to town on Tuesday last. I suppose you will have seen him before this comes to you. By that he writes to me he is likely to
be in your Lordship's predicament.
Will your Lordship forgive me if I am very impertinent, and
presume to suggest anything to you on a point in which I am
perhaps the most improper of all men to suggest anything, and
your Lordship has the least occasion for any such suggestion ?
I myself want most to be advised to caution, and your Lordship
the least of any man I know. God be thanked you have a good
stock of it acquired as well as natural. But still out of my duty
to you, and concern for you, I will beg leave to say *abundans*

cautela non nocet. Unless we have been much misinformed, or there has been a very unaccountable change, next to a miracle, you have other tempers to deal with you than you had. Should any handle be given, though I am fully persuaded none will by any chance, advantage would be taken of it. A great man too, on your Lordship's foot, is always less obnoxious to others the easier he is in his own private affairs. With these two precautions the part you think fit to act may be safe I hope as well as honourable.

You are all I suppose fully employed on preparing for the Coronation. I hear Lady Foley says her robes will cost her more than 400*l.*, but I suppose she will not grudge. She will want indeed for her circumference some-more yards of velvet and ermine than other ladies. This between ourselves.

1727, July 15.—As to our friend, to whom there are objections, I suppose he knows the world well enough to be satisfied that one in his condition has always spies on him, who are not only to watch him, but to lead him too if they can into discourses that may be to his prejudice. Very often some of his own family are employed to observe his unguarded moments, and they commonly do that honest office who seem least likely. No wise man would be troublesome either to himself or others by unnecessary jealousies. But caution cannot be too great, nor observation, whilst it is kept in a man's own breast, of all who come near him, either within or from without, especially if any one seems to be more assiduous and prying than either his acquaintance or post can require. An old friend of mine, above thirty years ago, preserved his life and fortune by having had the precaution to mark, by single words, in his pocket book, the places and company he was in every day. He was enabled by it to defeat a malicious design that was laid to have ruined him, and but for this would have done it.

Stock jobbers swarm in this part of the world, and the vilest of them. If reports have any truth, incredible sums are offered for votes. The party seem to have orders to lavish money at any rate to secure their point, and there can be no doubt of their success. And the next assembly will probably have a greater number of that set of men than any yet has had. The vilest surely of men, and much more pernicious to their country, than any officers civil or military.

1727, July 29.—I hope this will welcome you to town. You find I suppose the Attorney gone. God have mercy on his soul! I am afraid he did not apprehend his end was so near. If you meet with any circumstances of his death or will, I should be glad to hear them.

Many have taken on them to reprove you of late; I suppose you may now in your turn laugh at them. I never was one of the sanguines, but I own the present turn is beyond my expectation. The run seems to be upon those who were creatures to the late Lord Sunderland. The quick dismission of Berkeley was a great surprise. I think he was cousin german or second cousin to Sir

Spencer. Now the Attorney is gone and [Lord] Berkeley dismissed, I take Bolingbroke, as he is the most obnoxious man in England to Court and ministry, to be also the most friendless man ; a happy state to one of his temper and in his circumstances. What was the particular pique against Young, that his great patron could not keep him in? Room might have been made for Clayton without dismissing him.

What a stupid part has North and Grey acted. Do he and Wharton think they serve the cause they espouse by their worthy conversions? Were I on that side, I should look on them as hired to do what they do. But it is of a piece with the rest of the politics of that party.

The talk of an opposition in the University by one Mosely is come to nothing already. Our knighthood of the shire went a begging. Tom Rowney was much pressed to take it, but would not bite at it. One Sir William Stapleton, a West Indian, formerly of Christ Church, a rake then as I hear he is still, is to be [the] man. He has but little estate in Oxfordshire, and that by his wife Mrs. Paul.

1727, August 5.—My friend Auditor Foley has been so kind as to send me a buck. He writes to me that Abelina has carried the day, and will not let Abelin stand for the county. Was there ever such a termagant, to insist to have her will in a thing that so little belongs to her, so proper for the young gentleman, and in which the honour and interest of the whole family is so nearly concerned? And may not I say too, was ever any one so henpecked as poor Abel. I find the Viscount, as I always thought he would, has made our friend Tom Rowney one of his trustees. He has given a great proof by it of his opinion of Tom's honesty, to lay such a trust on him, after his very ill usage of him. But it was no little degree of assurance to lay such a burden on one whom he had used so ill.

Postscript. My poor friend Tom is in great doubt whether he shall accept the trust. He would reject it with indignation, but an uncertain prospect of getting Newnham for son Ned, if it should fall whilst he is trustee, I fancy that will determine him to take it.

1727, September 2.—This comes to bring you very bad news. The horse races were last week at Oxford, and at the Mayor's feast on Saturday poor old Tom Rowney was seized with an apoplexy. He was thought to be past recovery on Wednesday, and I am afraid he is dead at the time. This is the effect of "phlethory and a continuando," and want of a due abstinence :— *Felix quem faciunt aliena pericula cautum.*

We have had the greatest struggle that ever was known in this county, but we have carried the day.

Packer	1620
Stonehouse	1558
Lord Vane	1319

Lord William Pawlet, who displayed himself at our election as eminently as he does on other occasions, thought fit to insist upon a scrutiny. But we are in no pain about that. Bad votes and foul management were not on our side.

1727, September 11.—This brings you some news that will not be very agreeable to you. The Bishop of Bath and Wells was taken ill about eight days ago. The physician that went to him from Bath, and returned thither on Wednesday, said he did not believe the Bishop could live till next morning.

Postscript. I am told Gloucester [Wilcocks] preaches the Coronation sermon. If so, it is likely ecclesiastical and civil will be of a piece.

1727, October 1.—I could not let Lord Dupplin go without my duty to you. His own looks tell you that all is well with him in all respects, and make any thing I could write of him needless. And as to anything that is passing here, he can tell you much better than I. Pray send him to us again as soon as you can, and if you have any anecdotes you may write them to him. He tells me that our old lady [Oxford] designs to walk at the Coronation. Is it possible? I should not have doubted her inclination, but I thought her age would have been an effectual hindrance. Nor could I think her quite so extravagant as to buy robes at her age, if her purse could afford it. Does poor Lady Kinnoull walk? I am afraid not. I suppose her husband undertakes to excuse her.

1727, October 7.—The design of the old Countess is so very absurd and extravagant that I could not have believed it, had I not had it from you. I perceive that vanity can as little be extinguished by age as another passion.

I had the "Craftsman," I thank your Lordship, last night. The great man's enemies have not lost their mettle, though they are disappointed of the places they lately hoped for. As far as I can guess, by the dim light I have, the conjuncture is like to be more favourable to them, and much worse to the nation in general, than it has been yet. I am afraid we are in a worse state than we were before the preliminaries, with which we were so much exalted.

Pray give my friend Dupplin an account how poor Mr. Windsor came to be jockeyed at Cambridge.

I must not detain you longer from trying your Coronation robes, that will be full employment till that piece of pageantry is over. I have two poor brethren here in a disconsolate state because they are not summoned to make part of the procession. They begin to suspect that they are likely to be dismissed from their chaplainships.

1727, October 12.—Your last has given me much ease. I was really vexed at the old Countess's absurd design of walking.

I perceive the "Craftsman" was to come out on Monday on account of the City election; I beg the favour of it. Should the Tories carry it against Whigs, Court, Ministry, and the three great Companies, it would be such a proof of their strength as never any party gave before.

My duty to my kind Lady and dear Lady Peggy. Could I be
so happy as to have an hour's conversation with her, I doubt not
but I should have a better account of the whole show from her
than from any one else that was there. Did not Lady Foley
walk? Mrs. Verney told me her ladyship pretended to be above
that vanity, but I offered to lay a wager on nature's side.

1727, October 26.—What is the meaning of "Princess Royal"?
Have we had any precedent for this in our own Courts, or is it
new, in imitation of the French?

1727, November 20.—The signification of your pleasure, in all
cases where I am at liberty, has the obligation with me of a
lawful command. It was always my opinion that the right of
voting in all public places is only a trust to be employed strictly
for the ends designed by the benefactor. I know no one so likely
to answer that end in the case of a Poetry professor as in being
directed by Mr. Pope's judgment. I beg my service to him. I
shall be proud of an opportunity to show my respects to him by
endeavouring to serve anyone he is concerned for, but what is
Mr. Spence, Whig or Tory? It is of some moment to know that,
if I am to serve him with others.

Your Lordship has certainly assigned the true reason of
S[herloc]k's accepting, but that is but a bad motive in any case.
Much worse to one in his circumstances, for a place of that
moment, where he can never be able to do any part of the duty.
Possibly Hare may have made the promise you mention, if there
was occasion for it and it was required of him, and he was just
as much in earnest as old Ruffe when he swore to Mr. Bromley
that he would lay his bones in Christ Church, and not take any
other preferment, no not the Archbishopric of Canterbury if it were
offered to him, because he was fitter he thought for our deanery
than the Archbishopric, and could do more good in it. I take it for
certain that Hare has his view on the Archbishopric, and sees, and
will use too, the means to merit it.

I am told that Mr. Cæsar has made his terms with the ministry, and for that reason the ministry threw all the interest they
could command into him against Cæsar (sic). It is said, too, his
Majesty was somewhat angry at this. Does your Lordship hear
anything of this?

1727, November 23.—I had last night a letter in behalf of
Mr. Spence from Dr. Arbuthnot at Mr. Pope's desire. I have
told the doctor that I had before received your Lordship's
command. I perceive Mr. Pope is very heartily concerned for
Mr. Spence, but there was no occasion to employ any one besides
your Lordship to me. If I could not do a thing at your
command, the whole world besides would be to no purpose.

I am afraid our peace is to come by the carrier called Tom
Long. It is not easy to see through the mist of the present
intrigues. I am afraid to speak out my own suspicions for fear
of being laughed at as a fanciful man.

Has Lord Berkeley made his peace ? I see by the prints that he is confirmed in all the places he had, except that of the Admiralty.

I have been expecting the rector of Presteign for these two days, he is to bring me my eyes, which I sent up to be repaired. I am almost blind for the want of them.

1727, November 28.—I give you joy of being initiated into the Society of the Virtuosos. You chose a very eminent god-father to answer for you. I am afraid his pretences to natural philosophy are much upon the same grounds as those he makes to divinity, in which he would be thought to be an adept. He had better stick to moral philosophy ; he has talents for that, and if he possessed other virtues in as high a degree as he does one, he would be a perfect man. I mean a virtue, of no ordinary rank, called patience. Thanks be to his stars, that have taken care for his daily improvement of it, by the constant exercise of it that he has at home.

The carrying of two in the City, under the present circum-stances, is a great victory. Had all that were influenced by Bank, South Sea and East India, by custom house, excise, post office, &c., and all that did not vote at all, been left to themselves, it must have been carried by at least 4 to 1. Great use might be made of such a disposition, were there any able head to manage it. But as that is wanting, it is likely it will not signify much. How is the Chamberlain's place like to go? Should that be carried against a Lord Mayor, the prevalency would be indis-putable.

Your Lordship does not tell me whether you think there is any ground for that I mentioned about Mr. Cæsar.

I humbly conceive that zeal will abate in proportion to the pensions. We live not in an age that loves to serve upon dry duty. Indeed it is a crying scandal that such a one as the D[uchess] of K[endal?] should have or take a pension.

1727, December 14.—There is no love lost betwixt Bentley and the two new bishops. There may be one good happen from their promotion, to expose Bentley, they may perhaps help to relieve the College.

My notion of our present condition is that let the Ministry design, if that were possible, to be very honest, yet they know not how to help us. They are not so much to be blamed now, for I see not how they can do otherwise than they do, but they are to be blamed, and ought to be hanged too, for what has been doing for twelve years last past, by which we are brought into our present state. As we are, if we could have the ablest and the honestest men that ever the nation had in all ages alive again for a wish, I see not how they could much help us, unless by such methods of strict religion, self denial, parsimony, unanimity and public spirit, as we may safely say in the present state of morality among us are impossible to be brought about.

Perhaps the session may be put off for some days longer, if they should not be able to tell us by the day appointed, whether we are to have peace or war, as I believe they will not. Were the French as hearty, as we say they are, sure that point might be soon put out of doubt.

1727, December 17.—I hope some particular compliment was made to Prince William, in the prologue or epilogue. Methinks they should get him entered of the school, though he never came there, and choose him a steward next year. Your neighbour may have interest enough for this, now his glory is high upon Townshend's recovery. It is sad though that Townshend will be so disabled by this severe illness that he will not of a long time, if ever, be fit again for business.

Who is likely to be Speaker? We have reports here that the old one will not be chosen again. Should it be so, will it be at his own desire, or is he to be laid aside? Methinks the last "Craftsman" seems pretty broadly to insinuate that the great man's interest was tottering at Court. I cannot believe it.

Do not men's suspicions increase? Can they think that France, if they were in earnest, could not put an end to this shuffling in Spain, and make them give, one way or other, a direct answer? Who is this mistress of the Duke of Grafton who has forged his name? What was her name? It is a great pity that his Grace was not obliged to pay the money, it would have been a just mulct for his whoring.

We have strange stories here of Colonel Howard's having sent to demand his wife, and having been offered money in lieu of her, which he refuses. But I suppose there is no ground for them.

1727, December 19.—I hear Mr. Spence and his competitor, one Jones of Balliol, are very busy already, though the election will not be till the next Act. I have not yet seen Mr. Spence, but I believe I shall secure him a pretty good interest in this College.

1727, December 28.—Nothing could hinder me from waiting on you at the Westminster feast but the affair I mentioned to you; but money, as Peter Birch said, is a serious thing. And I am mistaken if it does not grow more serious every day. I am amazed that the stocks hold up so high as they are, and much more that South Sea and East India should pretend to reduce their interest at Ladyday to 4*l. per cent.* Do these times promise so much peace and security that people will be likely to venture their money with such bodies for 4*l. per cent.*? And suppose men bring in their bonds, how will either of the Companies pay them off, even though the Bank should come in to help them. I entirely agree with Sir Thomas Hanmer; I am afraid there is ground for the utmost of his fears.

That which passed betwixt the gentlemen and a foreigner shows that *expellas furca licet usque recurret.* And it is likely to show itself more every day, as accidents happen to provoke it, and they are not likely to be wanting.

1727-8, January 2.—I have received orders from the Master to put off his coach. I expected them, and cannot blame him for staying with his beloved as long as he can.

I am glad your Lordship approves the reason of my deferring my own journey. I believe I shall every day be more convinced that is a very good reason. I am amazed that the world are not generally more apprehensive of our condition than they seem to be. The removing of one out of the way is but a poor shift, and can not be of much use. It is not men that the great man has reason to be afraid of; he knows how to deal with them if that were all. His difficulty is to struggle with affairs themselves; they seem inextricable. How he will get out of them I cannot see; but his enemies seem not only to grow upon him, but to crow over him, and write in such a strain as though they were sure his fall was near. Whether they have any ground for this, or it be done only to frighten him, and to hearten others against him, I cannot say, but he may now remember the swarm of pamphlets which came out with impunity against your father in the end of the Queen's reign and the beginning of the late reign. He has no reason to complain if he is served in the same way he served his predecessors.

1727-8, January 11.—Our condition is perhaps such as it never was since we were a nation. We are not likely to have any peace but upon terms dishonourable and detrimental, nor any peace, I am afraid, that will be durable upon any terms whatever. I defy any man to guess what the issue of the present intrigues will be. I dare not tell my own thoughts, not only because it may not be proper by my conveyance, but lest too I should be thought too fanciful.

1727-8, January 15.—I hope this will find you pleased with the entertainment you have this day. It is no little disappointment to me that I could not wait on you and partake of it. I hope to be there another year, unless the Parliament should be put off then too. It would be odd in me, who have no excuse for coming to town but to see my friends, to come thither before they are come.

By Horace's going round by Holland, it is plain some alteration is proposed in the measures that had been taken. My old friends the Dutch are not of the family of the " Hasty's." They will take sufficient time thoroughly to canvas any thing that is proposed, nor will they come at all into that we propose if my obscure guess at it should prove right.

1727-8, January 18.—I hope the entertainment in the hall was not increased in proportion to that in the school. I perceive there was a profusion of compliments. It would be hard if they should be lost and not turn to accounts. We have this to say:—there has been no want of will in us. Was old Peterborough there? I am told he is sending or has sent his grandson to Balliol, and that one Coningsby, who was of St. Mary Hall, has entered himself of Balliol to be his tutor. This Coningsby is the person whose sermon two years ago on the 30th of January, in which the bishops were reflected on, gave so much offence. It is odd that Balliol should pitch on such a man. I know not the man ; I have heard well of him. I am sure he has the worst end of the staff. I am glad the young gentleman is not sent hither.

1727-8, January 21.—A sad accident happened here on Thursday night or Friday morning. Two demys of Magdalen going home betwixt one and two, met a townsman, a glover and his wife, and some other company going home. One of the demys would kiss the man's wife. There was quarrelling. I know not particulars, but the demy was stabbed two inches deep into his belly, with a pair of scissors as they say. It is said now there is a possibility that he may recover.

If Horace has not brought the ultimatum I know not when we are to expect it, but I fancy his business was to concert new measures in Holland, and by the silence upon his coming I believe the Dutch take time to deliberate, as I thought they would.

1727-8, January 23.—I expressed myself unfortunately when I enquired if the entertainment in the hall bore proportion to that in the school, I meant eatables and drinkables. I thought that was so good last year, that it could not well be increased this year.

I heartily wish my Lady would put herself in your neighbour's hands. If she sees you uneasy at her being in other hands than those you think safest, I fancy her tender affection to you will induce her to comply with you, though not out of regard to herself, yet to make you easy.

Our brother Tanner goes up to-morrow to be chosen Prolocutor. He will have three offices in places pretty distant, Prolocutor, Chancellor of Norwich, and Treasurer of Christ Church.

Here is a report that the Dean of Westminster is dying, and that our friend Bob is to succeed both in bishopric and deanery. I know that deanery is in view, betwixt ourselves, but I can scarce think it will be compassed, much less with the bishopric. But I am apt to think somewhat of that kind is in agitation, because I have not heard thence in some posts, though I want an answer about some business of his own. If you hear any thing of this, pray communicate.

1727-8, January 25.—You are wonderful good in condescending to let me know so often what passes with you. I entirely agree with you in your judgment of the event of our present transactions. One may see I think the conclusion with half an eye. All that has been agreed is to be made good, but it is not yet to be owned either at home or abroad. The Parliament is to despatch money. I suppose there will be some general address, to leave the terms of peace to his Majesty and to acquiesce in what he shall think proper. Other affairs are to come on first abroad, and towards the close of all private articles will be produced and made good, and France I suppose is guarantee for this. I wish we may come off so well. What dull rogue is that in the Whitehall

Evening that talks of "Harley tricks" at this time of day?
Does he think he serves his party by reviving the mention of
your father's days?

I have seen "The Lord and no Lord." An old friend of mine
and his fine old lady are handled very coarsely in it. If the
knight keeps his ground, my old friend I am afraid will not have
quiet days. Yesterday by chance I met with some letters I had
from him and the late Viscount, which I had quite forgot. I was
amazed at the strain of kindness in them, but such is this world.

I hear our governor is gone up to put in for Westminster,
where a vacancy is expected, and that Bob is talked of for this
place. I heartily wish it might fall to his lot, it would be as
proper for him as for us. But I believe they would sooner give
him Westminster than Christ Church. They are very unreasonable who take exceptions to a few insignificant compliments.
But I expected it would be so, and if any consideration is had of
him, he will hear a great deal more [of] it. Were there any
ground for such reflections, they ought not to fall so much on
the elder as younger. He was always more warm in his words,
as well as deeper in his dealings.

1727-8, March 5.—The combatants entered the lists yesterday.
They began at two, and they alone held on the debate till seven.
Pulteney is allowed by his adversaries to have borne up better
than was expected. He said he would keep his temper, and did
so for a good while, but at last, as the enemy say, he first lost
his temper. The great man lost his too, but not so much, as the
enemy say, as Pulteney. After seven Barnard came into the
debate instead of Pulteney, and Sir William Strickland and the
worthy Mr. Verney in aid of Sir Robert. What Mr. Verney said
was to justify Sir Robert in assuming some expenses ought not
to be reckoned as public debts. Pulteney's party would not have
come to any question at that time, and Mr. Cholmly of Vale
Royal moved to leave the chair, but carried in the negative by
250 to 97. Then the question passed that six millions six
hundred odd thousand pounds of the public debt incurred before
1716 had been paid. This was owned from the beginning by
everybody. Then came on the debate what new debt had been
incurred since. Sir Robert owned at first that 8,500,000*l.* had
been incurred since. With much ado at last he admitted the
debt upon the civil list, which is one million more, to be a public
debt; that will reduce the debt paid to two millions only. But
the further consideration of this, which is the only material
point, is adjourned till Thursday, when Mr. Pulteney is to show,
if he can, that more debt is incurred. As it is, Sir Robert is not
thought to have gained or Pulteney to have lost much, and the
debate is allowed to have been of use. I suppose the Master will
give you a more perfect account.

Sir Nathaniel Curson, much to the surprise of Mr. Bacon, left
his friends on Thursday last in the debate about the King's
answer. They say there is a barony in abeyance to which he has
pretensions. But he returned to his friends yesterday.

Baker, a man who wants a hand, has the residentiaryship of
Paul's ; his character is as poor as any man's well can be.

Postscript. All unprejudiced persons allow Pulteney had the
better, but the Master will give you a full account.

We have, as is said, an express from France, which says France
has had an express from Spain, which informed them that the
Queen of Spain was in a rage at the first notice of the alterations
we proposed, and said the English would never be contented, and
she would have no more to do with them, but that, upon second
thoughts, she said the preliminaries should be signed as we
proposed. That the King of Spain continues ill still, which is
supposed to be the reason of her agreeing, if she has agreed.
But we own no preliminaries are yet signed, nor can we say
when they will be signed.

1727-8, March 7.—Upon occasion of the entry of the Dutch
Ambassadors, the combat that was to have been renewed to-day
is deferred till to-morrow. I leave the account of it to the
Master, for I shall have little opportunity of knowing particulars,
but as to the last day's fight all impartial men own Pulteney
had the better. A Whig owned to me freely that though they
had strength on their side, the others had justice. And that he
never saw the great man so much disordered and out of
countenance as he was at that debate. He designs to come off
on Friday, by a ridiculous distinction of an increased debt from
an incurred debt, as though I should mortgage an estate for
2,000*l.* and afterwards add another 1,000*l.* to the mortgage, that
increase of 1,000*l.* to the debt was not the incurring of a new
debt. This is all he has to say, but it will pass, and he will have
votes pass in his justification. I must tell you one thing which
you will scarce hear from the Master. The Master told me he
was sorry for his brother Verney, he was out in what [he] said.
But others of Verney's friends say he spoke very ridiculously,
and of that which it was plain he was utterly ignorant, and
Barnard lashed him and exposed him sufficiently for it.

Our affairs abroad are certainly growing worse every day, but I
must reserve them till I see you again.

Dr. Busby's trustees met on Wednesday, but for want of your
Lordship to make up a due number they could neither sign some
leases nor choose your humble servant trustee. They have
adjourned till Wednesday next at twelve o'clock, upon a
presumption that by that time your Lordship will be in town.

1727-8, March 9.—I leave the account of yesterday's debate to
the Master. It ended as was expected, Pulteney has gained credit
though he lost the question. Barnard, who spoke excellently well,
declared that when the report was made to the House he would
debate it again, article by article, and move to have it recommitted.
One may easily foresee the success. The great man artfully communicated to the House, towards the end of the debate, the news
that the King of Spain had declared he would sign the preliminaries in the manner we desired. This news was reserved for this

moment. I was told on Monday last that they had it, but some Dutch gentlemen tell me that on their side the water they do not think we are nearer to a peace for this.

1728, March 31.—Delaune is dying of a dropsy. You were used to tell me that the water I drank would bring a dropsy on me. He has a dropsy which has not been brought on him by drinking water.

1728, April 2.—The physicians tell Delaune he cannot last a month. The canvass for his Headship [of St. John's] is very open in the College; Holdsworth and Holme, both Doctors in Divinity, are the competitors, the first it is supposed will carry it. The competitors for his Margaret professorship are supposed to be many, but none as yet appear.

1728, April 8.—I doubt not but we must pay for any thing we have abroad as well as at home. All the world acts now upon the same principle, and we have managed so wisely that every one makes demands on us which we must comply with. But I will not believe yet that Spain upon any terms has agreed to leave us in quiet possession of Gibraltar; or will think themselves obliged to stand to any bargain that termagant lady may have made, if she has bubbled us of any money.

Young Murray showed me a melancholy letter on Sunday night from poor Dupplin, in which he owned that he and his brother could not yet come down, because the father could not furnish them with any [money]. He talked of a place his father soon hoped to have by the Duke of Devonshire's interest, and then he hoped they might get somewhat to bring them down. Be that as it will, I advised Murray to write to have the Colonel sent down by the stage coach on Thursday. He may be entered of the College and matriculated on Friday, and return again on Saturday. He may then stay at Westminster, if his friends please, till within a month of midsummer, but it will be much to his prejudice to lose this term here.

Divines say practice should follow conviction; I shall believe your Lordship approves fasting when I hear you have your set stated times for it, which you observe strictly, without dispensing with them upon any occasion. Forgive my concern that makes me impertinent on this topic, but I am fully persuaded that it would conduce more to make you easy, healthy, and lively than any physic you can take, nay as much as constant exercise itself, and would supply the place of exercise, when that cannot conveniently be had.

1728, April 11.—I thought the debates upon the debts would end, as I find they do, in a panegyric upon the great man; no doubt the debates were brought in for that purpose. But since all without doors are fully satisfied of the truth of that representation, I question whether in the long run it will turn much to his advantage. How did the Finches vote in this last debate? Were they against the great man, as well as they have been in the late elections?

1728, April 14.—I promise you I will never trouble myself more about Abel's concerns, let him be never so importunate with me for my opinion.• The true reason of this management is that I told your Lordship in town, the son will not marry unless the father will promise to settle 2,000*l. per annum*, and hopes to bring him to it by seeming averse to marriage ; the father will not make that settlement unless the mother will give him 15,000*l.* of her money, and hopes to bring her to it, for the sake of getting such a settlement for her son.   And he manages so wisely to get a point he will never gain, when he has it already in his power, if he knew how to use it, and may have all his wife's money, if he will but charge upon his estate, and leave the son to pay himself or his mother.   But I will never have any more to do with any of his domestic affairs, I foresee confusion enough in them.   The good Earl has too much reason to think himself trifled with, and so I suppose will any one else be that shall ever have to do with them.

1728, April 21.—I must heartily thank your Lordship for the trouble you have been pleased to take to give me an account of Abel's wise proceedings.   I am abundantly instructed how to deal with him for the future, though I take all this to be owing to the She.   It is plain their view is upon nothing but money.   There would be no need to look out for a wife for the young master, if they had the views they ought to have in marrying him.   He would be welcome anywhere, but it is evident that no regard will be had to family, education, sense, temper, virtue or person, nor to anything but to money.   And I wish I may not be a true prophet that it is likely they will meet the blessings they usually do who marry on such views.   But who do they think will have the daughter ?   If they regard only money in disposing their son, do they think any one will take the daughter for any other reason ?

1728, April 30.—I reckon you will not be absent at the time of the extraordinary masquerade, and hear at least what passes in it, though you should not bear a part in it.   All our newspapers are full of the great preparations making for it.   What is the occasion of these unusual doings ?   Why is this to exceed all other masquerades so much ?   In lewdness I suppose too, as well as finery.

Your Lordship I suppose has had an account of the doings at Cambridge.   Did any thing very remarkable pass there ?   They are to be the favourites.

To-morrow this poor College will be like a great hulk without any one to steer it.   Brother Tanner leaves, only poor Burton and I.   No proxy in the College, nor consequently any power to give degrees, or do any other business of any kind.   The less we have of human care, the more I hope we shall have of God's good providence.

Postscript.   Delaune holds out still to everybody's wonder.

1728, May 2.—We have a report here that it is still remem
bered who was and was not chosen Chancellor here in the
beginning of the late reign, and that it has been declared no visit
shall be made to this place. Can you confirm this news to me?
I am sure I should get nothing by a visit but a great racket in
my lodging.

In the fourth volume of Anderson's book your Lordship was
pleased to bestow on me, in the second part of the volume,
towards the end, there is an account day by day of what passed
betwixt the English Commissioners and the Scotch that came to
accuse their Queen. But the account of the seventh session is
wanting, and was not I suppose to be found, neither in the Paper
Office or Cotton's Library, from one of which places those papers
were taken. But I have met with it here, amongst some other
papers concerning Mary Queen of Scots, in a collection of papers
belonging to Archbishop Sancroft, which Dr. Tanner has purchased. He has given me leave to transcribe a copy for your
Lordship as well as for myself, and I shall make Sedgly transcribe them in a print hand, allowing as large margins as in the
printed book, and on the same sort of royal paper, so that they
may be bound up with our books, and this will make our books
a little more complete and valuable than other books of the same
edition.

1728, May 7.—Upon looking over my unbound books, I find I
want the two last volumes of Mr. Pope's Odyssey. I suppose I
might be in the country when public notice was given of their
being published, and so miss of them. If your Lordship will be
pleased to direct Mr. Thomas where he may have them for me I
have written to him to pay the remainder of the subscription.
Mine is the large paper quarto. Did your Lordship ever show
Bob the letters betwixt Mr. P. and his friend? Bob would be
wonderfully delighted with the sight of them; I dare engage for
his secrecy.

Tanner has all that were left of Sancroft's papers, but if I
understood him right, some books and papers had been parted
with before he came in to purchase. His purchase came to
near 200l. as he said. By some of the volumes I have seen,
Sancroft was a great but no very judicious collector. He binds
together too a strange medley of papers, that have no relation at
all to one another, and a great deal of riff-raff amongst a few
good ones.

1728, May 12.—My brother Gilbert, the Dean of Exeter, was
here for three days to fetch in his money. He never came once,
whilst he was here, within the inside of the church, but his
equipage drew the eyes of every one on him. His servant is a
black, who rides before him with a long gun, and he himself rides
with pistols, with holsters that would become a major-general.
Did the little Auditor tell you that when he and Lady Scudamore happened to send last year half a buck a piece on the same
day to the Bishop of Hereford, that his Lordship kept the
Auditor's half buck, which happened to be the fattest, for his own

use, and sent for his butcher, and haggled with him a long time for what he would allow him for Lady Scudamore's half buck, and took it out of him in money or meat? This was great diversion to Lady Scudamore.

1728, May 13.—A letter is come from the Chancellor to represent to the Heads and Convocation that he had entered *caveats* in behalf of the university after Dennison's trial; that he since had the opinion of Dennison's counsel, that the university was not bound by the verdict in Westminster Hall, and that he has sent them the state of the case upon that trial and the opinions of the counsel upon it, and hopes they will take such measures as will be proper to preserve their right. I wonder his Lordship should be so unadvised as to send such a letter, only at the instance of Dr. Shippen. The case is false stated, and it is somewhat odd to desire the university to determine themselves upon the opinion of the counsel on one side only. But it appears for what this was. Unluckily there was to be a hearing before the Attorney on Saturday night. It was insisted by Dennison's counsel to defer the hearing till they could know whether the university would espouse this cause, whose right they said was not determined by that which had passed in Westminster Hall. Cockman offered to put off the hearing if Dennison's counsel would engage the university would espouse it and appear in a fortnight. That they would not undertake. The cause was heard, and the Attorney declared his opinion that the university right was bound by the verdict in Westminster Hall. This letter was to have been a pretence for delaying the hearing before the Attorney. But it comes unluckily just after the Attorney has declared his opinion, and I find it goes down so heavily here that I need not stop my journey. I question whether it will pass the Heads, or if it go through them whether it will go down the Convocation. But if it passes both, the utmost they pretend to is to have a delegans appointed to consider of it, who may be ready perhaps with a report a year hence, when the Crown, in whose hands it now is, has settled all.

1728, May 14.—I wrote you a scrawl yesterday which I am afraid you could hardly read. The Chancellor's letter was proposed yesterday in the meeting of the Heads. For bringing it into the Convocation only three, the Vice-Chancellor, All Souls, Bourchier of Alban Hall; the others did not downright reject it, but more decently voted to defer reading it for a week, till they could hear what Mr. Cockman had to say and could know the report of the Attorney and Solicitor upon the late hearing. They were, Magdalen, Magdalen Hall, Queen's, Trinity, Jesus, Wadham, Edmond Hall, and the two proctors. And yet advantage was taken to bring this in when Cockman had fewest friends upon the place. I am apt to think it will be put off again next Monday, and so on till it is quite dropped. It was asserted by some at the meeting who had been present at the meeting, and who appealed to Bourchier to deny if he could what they said, that the representation was false in fact. The

Chancellor is very unhappy to be prevailed on to send such things with his authority and recommendation hither.

. 1728, May 19.—I go for Shefford on Tuesday.

There is a surmise stirring that the Princess Amelia may return from Bath through Oxford. If it should be so I suppose her parents may meet her here, or else they will hardly see us this summer.

I know your Lordship will be so good as to remember the London "Evening Post" to comfort a poor hermit.

1728, May 20.—What makes Swift's little pamphlets so scarce; surely he will send your Lordship a copy of them? It will be said now that he writes out of pique and revenge. It is given out that he was much disappointed when he was last here; that he was in hopes, by the interest he had in a certain lady, to have exchanged his preferment in Ireland for as good in England. Nay, that at last he would have quitted all he had in Ireland, for 400l. *per annum* here, but could not get it.

Postscript. The Chancellor's letter is thrown out by the Heads of Houses :—For bringing it into Convocation, Brasenose, Shippen; Trinity, Dobson; All Souls, Niblett; Alban Hall, Bourchier.

Against bringing it in, Magdalen, Butler; Magdalen Hall, Coates; Edmond Hall, Felton; Queen's, Gibson; Jesus, Pardo; Wadham, Thistlewaite; Balliol, Lee; Proctor Reynolds, Proctor Manatou. The Vice-Chancellor did not vote.

So I hope there is an end now of an affair as wicked as vexatious. I am afraid there will be some prejudice for the future to any recommendations from our Vice Chancellor.

1728, May 23.—You were pleased to say in your last that you had demolished Hare. On Monday at Oxford, just such another honest man, one Dr. Shippen, was demolished. I gave your Lordship a short account of the event. Of the Heads, who were absent, two of them had been warm men, whilst under Dr. Shippen's management, against Cockman, but could not be prevailed on now to appear. It is to be hoped they repent. All other absent men would to a man, if they had been there, have been for Cockman, but the ferment amongst the Masters surprised me. I own I thought if the letter had come amongst them it would not have been thrown out without difficulty; but I was soon satisfied it would have been rejected by above two to one. Nay, one who understands them perfectly well offered me any odds that it would [have] been lost by above two to one.

I am afraid Mr. Cockman owes this success to the general hatred of Dr. Shippen as much as to the goodness of his cause. I took care last winter that the Chancellor should know what the event of a letter would be, if he was drawn in to send one, but only one person had credit with him. His Lordship must be content with the consequence of it.

1728, May 25.—I supposed when Abel broke off so dishonourably with one much too good for him that his design was in the city. Yet how have I heard Abelina detest such a match! It is very likely they will meet with the reward due to them in such a match. Sure Abel's head is turned. He complains that his youngest does not behave with duty to him. Is it the way to increase his son's respect to go with him to a bawdy-house? Pray who was the duchess that was dressed so? Was there any particular allusion by such a habit and such chains?

Postscript. Do you know that Ruffe is turned out of his premiership?

Who is the author of the Dunciad? Is not Pope? I want a key to the names, I cannot decypher many of them.

I hear this morning from Oxford that the President of St. John's [Delaune] died last night. I am apt to think Jenner of Magdalen will be Professor and Dr. Holmes President.

1728, May 29.—I heard from Bob that my old friend [Atterbury] was dismissed. They who have dealt with him ought to look to themselves. He will without doubt go over to others if they think it worth their while to receive him. But I want to know for what he was dismissed, and indeed whether he was dismissed or quitted. If the last it might probably be with a·view of making his peace elsewhere.

If it be not too much impudence in me I would desire the continuance of the " Craftsman " as well as the London " Evening Post." The "Craftsman " is the chief support to our spirits in the country.

1728, June 5.—I would beg leave to put your Lordship in mind of Swift's manuscript. I had his leave to see it and your Lordship promised to get it of the gentleman who has it. If you will be pleased to send it sealed up in a cover by Colonel Haye when he comes to us, it may remain safe with him till my servant calls on him for it. I suppose the Colonel will now in a little time come to stay with us. When does poor Dupplin return? This loss of time will be an irrecoverable damage to him.

You tell me not whether Mr. Pope himself is not supposed to be the author of the Dunciad. If the advertisement in one of our newspapers be true there has been some insult lately made on him. This would be somewhat more than a paper war.

1728, June 13.—You have not said any thing to me about the election, though I hear you were there. I am told *Rex* and *Regina* were declined through all the cases in the Latin speech; that I expected. It is said too there were compliments in the speech to the blue ribbon. That I own is a surprise to me. Was there any ground for such a report? It is said too the election was but slenderly attended, but there could be no reason for such a report whilst your Lordship was pleased to honour them with your presence, though you should have been alone there.

I have read Mr. Pope's Dunciad often with a great deal of pleasure. I am sure it must be his, because no one else could write it. Nor had I ever any doubt but from the first paragraph in the preface; but that might be written by some friend. I should be glad to know whether he has been insulted lately, as a late advertisement seemed to insinuate. If it was so, it was very barbarous to attack so weak and little a man in a manner in which he was so unequal a match for them. I beg you would give my most hearty thanks to him for the kind present of the Dunciad, which I am sure must come from him.

Postscript. I see our friend He[a]rne is in the Dunciad. I cannot say that he has much wrong done him, but he is not used to pass by such things. No doubt Mr. Pope will, by head or tail, be brought into the next *prolegomena* or appendix.

1728, June 22.—I am glad Mr. Pope's corpuscle is safe, he cannot afford to spare any of his body, as I could. But visitations of wit sometimes end in hearty drubbings :—

Ludus enim generit trepidum certamen et iram
Ira truces inimicitias et lugubre bellum.

All great men in what kind soever must expect some alloy to the glory of their merit, from the envy that will pursue it.

1728, July 6.—Our great ones may at present very justly look upon themselves as absolute. There is nothing at home that can in our present circumstances give them any disturbance. Any thing that gives rise to any trouble here must come from abroad; but I do not think they ought to look upon themselves as settled till they see the success of the negotiations abroad. It is using, I think, a very modest word to say that appears as yet doubtful. There is one thing too at home that may deserve some reflections from them, the strange spirit that continues in the city of London. We find too it is a contagious spirit, and has infected the city greatest in extent and trade next to London, that of Norwich. I cannot imagine any reason for the uneasiness of such bodies, but some decay which they feel in their trade. That is the only article that uses to affect them. But it is plain here are great uneasiness ready to be increased and to break out, upon any juncture proper to inflame and favour them. And should not things abroad go to our wishes, I will not answer that there may not be a ferment run again through the nation, somewhat like that which was in Sacheverell's case.

1728, July 11.—Ruffe's friends give out with great industry that he was dismissed at his own desire and with great kindness. Both perhaps are true, but they tell not that he had been for some time endeavouring to make his peace here before he desired to be dismissed in the other place. And yet that is certain, and I suppose he desired his dismission in order to facilitate his negotiation here. But it was not known there I suppose that he was treating elsewhere. He applied here not by any persons on the spot but by some acquaintance he had abroad. But he could not succeed. He has now cast off one and cannot be received by any other. It is now given out that he is retired and writing a history of his own times that is to come out after

his death. I believe not a word of this, if there should be any
such thing, it will just be of as much credit as old Gibby [Bur-
net]'s.

1728, July 13.—There is a book written by one [William] Smith
about University College; he is a minister in Yorkshire upon a
College living. He is now, as he tells you in his book, seventy-
seven; he was an old peevish blundering fellow when he was at
Oxford and the common plague of the whole society. The whole
book is a confused rhapsody of lies and blunders; he has
slandered in it every one that he ever knew. He has abused poor
Charlett, to whom he had great obligations, and has several pages
upon Tom He[a]rne, who will not, I suppose, die in his debt.

1728, July 17.—If the news hold true of the King of Spain's
death, we continue still to have strange luck in deaths. It must
probably cause alterations in their measures; exclude the
termagant Queen; and unite them again with France, but
without doubt upon the condition of France's procuring Port
Mahon and Gibraltar for them. If France has a Dauphin, they
too will alter their language and talk to us in another strain
than they have done hitherto.

1728, July 22.—I am very impatient till the post comes. I
long to know what your neighbour [Dr. John Freind]'s illness is
and what the event of it is like to be. Should he be carried off, it
would be a very remarkable disappointment to one who was just
entering upon the utmost of his aims and wishes. I am afraid too
it would be no small check to his brother's hopes. He must in
that case be content with a prebend, and glad if he can get that.
There has been a famous quarrel at Christ Church, your old
tutor wanted a coach house to be built for him at the College
expense. A very unreasonable request of that which not one
of his predecessors ever had. He desired the Dean to propose it
to the Chapter. The Dean civilly told him he could not do it till
an estimate had been made of the charge and more Canons were
in town. Upon this he was very uneasy all the Chapter, and the
election of the new students; nay he could not at dinner eat his
venison in quiet. After dinner he broke out, and gave the Dean
very foul language. The Dean was wise enough to make his
return in the same dialect. The quarrel lasted long, to the great
diversion of all present. It was wholly personal, in calling one
another names, which though they should not have given to each
other it is likely both might in some measure deserve. Tanner,
who writes me this, says he had not time for particulars. When
I hear any of them you shall have them. This is rare sport for
the students.

1728, July 31.—The poor man is gone. May I ask you from
whom you had your daily accounts of his illness? They were
truer than his nearest friends sent that were about him. It is a
very remarkable event in all its circumstances, and would
suggest variety of reflections. One reflection every one ought to
make, how little life is to [be] depended on, and how prepared

we ought always to be to quit it. The extremes of both sides will be glad, we shall now see whether his great acquaintances are persons of honour and will remember his brother for his sake. But I am pretty sure a prebend will be the most now.

1728, August 10.—I have been told lately that the poor man's constitution was broken, but I was with him often, I never heard him complain of it, nor did I ever observe any thing from whence I could guess it. He has not left his equal in his own profession. He might I believe have managed his politics a little better, but he consulted with nobody. Bob always "hunted underPole" to him. Had he excused himself from being physician in waiting, on account of its being inconsistent with his other business, as Radcliffe did to King William but offered readily to attend when called upon any occasion, he might have had as much power, and not much less money, and no one could have made the least exception to it. I am afraid he hastened his end by too great fatigue, but I shall know more when I see Bob next week in his way to Bath.

1728, September 14.—I had a letter this week from good Dean Berkeley. In spite of all discouragements he is now on the high sea in prosecution of his design. He calls first at Rhode Island, to purchase there with his own money pasture for supplying his College with flesh meat, the want of which was by some, who opposed the design, made a great objection. God who moved him to lay the design, has given him a spirit proper to prosecute it.

1728, October 14. Christ Church.—Here is a difference betwixt the Bishops of Oxford and Bristol about the consecration of Blenheim chapel. I cannot say that I have all the particulars of it exactly, but as I have yet heard, her Grace of Marlborough desired the Bishop of Bristol to consecrate it. He acquaints the Bishop of Oxford, who took it not well that another should be desired to do that office in his diocese, and said he was ready to do his duty, but, however, if her Grace desired it should be done by the Bishop of Bristol, he consented, provided that his own register and secretary attended. The Bishop of Bristol would not agree to that. Upon this the Bishop of Oxford would not give leave that the Bishop of Bristol should perform the office. The Bishop of Bristol pretends that Woodstock was not in Oxford diocese, because it was not in Bladen parish, and that being too a Royal chapel, it was not under the Bishop of Oxford's jurisdiction. I believe neither of these pretences will hold, but Sarah has been attacked by so many people for offering to affront the Bishop of Oxford that she has deferred the consecration till spring, and it is thought will then drop the Bishop of Bristol, to his no little mortification.

I suppose you hear that Blandford's marriage with the Dutch lady [de Jonge], sister to the Countess of Denbigh, is now owned.

1728, October 28.—Some of the street robbers have come hither and made some attempts, but many strangers are seized, and we hope soon to suppress them here. A strange discovery has happened here, one Jennens, son to a very good family in Warwickshire, cut his throat in May last and threw himself out of his window at the Temple. He was of Trinity College, and a sober, ingenious, virtuous young man in all appearance whilst he was there. There were found in his *scrittoire* several letters from one Stevens of Trinity, who is son to Serjeant [Henry] Stevens, now a regent master, in deacon's orders and designing for priest's orders, curate of a village near Oxford, and probationer fellow of Trinity. The letters were full of blasphemy against Christianity; he declares himself a deist, and that he made it his business to propagate deism. He brags in them of the converts he makes, gives directions to Mr. Jennens how to proceed in that work, almost in every line extols Bangorianism, says he finds it difficult to bring men to deism, but through Bangorianism, that it is sufficient at first to bring them to Bangorianism; and a great deal more of such horrible stuff. The friends of the poor gentleman that destroyed himself imputed his end to such principles, and resolved to put the letters of Stevens into hands that might prosecute him. I had extracts of these letters two months ago from a friend of ours in Warwickshire, and was told it was designed to send these letters to the Bishop of Oxford. I confirmed them in the design, and the originals have been sent to the Bishop, and by him communicated to the Vice-Chancellor, and a prosecution is begun in the Vice-Chancellor's court. The man, I am told, when he heard where his letters were, swooned away and, when he came to himself, said he was undone; but owned he was still of that opinion, but was sorry he had endeavoured to bring others into it. He is since gone off. His father has been here, and declared a great detestation of his son, and himself struck his name out of the College book. But that signifies nothing, but to show the father's abhorrence of his son's principles, for his father had no authority to expel him. One Cater of that College, a bachelor of arts, mentioned in these letters, is since gone off too. Cater designed for orders too, the last ordination, but was stopped by the Bishop of Oxford upon his receiving these letters, though it is said Cater was yet only as far as Arianism, and dispersed books to propagate that amongst the young lads. Lord Aylesford, who by marriage is a relation to Jennens, has been very zealous in prosecuting this business, and offers himself to come down, if there be occasion, to be a witness at the trial. But I fancy Stevens will not appear in Court. I suppose we shall be called persecutors in town, but these are new things in this place, and it is time to put a stop. This accident occasions a little correspondence betwixt your uncle and me.

1728, October 25.—I bless God that I hear by Mr. Thomas that you continue still without any sign of your fever; he says you are very weak, that I am not surprised at, and that the diet your doctor allows you is not likely to give you strength soon. Your diet treats you very judiciously, the more slow your recovery is the surer it will be. I hope there is no danger now but of a relapse by presuming too soon upon your strength. Even when strength returns you must consider that your whole body for some

time after such a shock will be very tender, and liable to be
disordered upon the least thing that is irregular or even improper. But I hope since God has brought you within sight of
death, and by His great mercy rescued you from it, you will learn
by this illness to be more cautious how you manage your health
for the future; and perhaps my doctrine of fasting may be a
little more palatable to you than it has been.

1728, October 21.—They have been I hear in no little confusion
in town upon the apprehension of the King of Spain's death.

Stevens was last Friday expelled the University by sentence
in the Vice-Chancellor's court. He did not appear in court by
himself or proctor.

1728, November 26.—There was a meeting on Monday
se'nnight about publishing a programme in relation to Stephens.
Only four Heads were there. Our governor, who appeared then
to be against the thing, moved to have it adjourned because so
few were present, which was agreed to. They met again to-day,
only eight there. Whether the weather or the occasion hindered
others from coming I know not. Four for the programme, the
Vice-Chancellor, Corpus, Trinity and our Proctor. Four against
it, our governor, Jesus, your acquaintance Felton of Edmond
Hall who is gone into them, and the Proctor of New College.
Our governor gave reasons against it, very proper to come from
him, that it would make Stevens too considerable; that it would
make men abroad think we had more infidels than we had; that
it would be a reflection on the tutors to admonish them to take
care of their pupils, and what they had no authority to do.

Warm words I hear passed betwixt our governor and Corpus.
The true reasons of our governor's opposition are to make his
court above, and to oppose the Bishop of Oxford, who is supposed
to have advised this. London too is at the bottom, and he to be
sure out of opposition to Oxford, for I hear his cousin, Gibson of
Queen's, read a letter from him to some of his brethren, against
this programme; I cannot yet learn what the letter was. I hope
the Vice-Chancellor will bring this on again next Monday, and
take care to have the meeting better attended. In the mean
time, till we see the issue of this affair, communicate this I pray
only to the Master.

1728, November 28.—I told you in my last that London had
written a letter hither, about Stevens's affair, but I could not
certainly tell what was in it. I must do every body justice. It is
differently reported. Some say it was that the University ought
to make some public declaration upon this occasion. As soon as
I can learn the truth you shall hear it, but our governor has
engaged himself in a cause very worthy of his episcopal character.
Some say the Whigs design to make a party cause of it, and
I think there is some ground for this report. I heartily wish they
would put the credit of their party here on such a point.

1728, December 1.—I was sorry to see in last Thursday's
prints that the Turkey company was resolved to use their interest

to have Stanyan continued; but I hope [what] was inserted
there related only to the disposition they were in about a month
ago, and that they have been mollified since. I should be sorry
to have that project disappointed; so convenient a one will not
be soon met with again.

Abel and his family came to town last night, and are gone
on to-day towards London. The world is well changed and
thoroughly reformed when that family travels on a Sunday.

1728, December 2.—Our Heads met again to-day, sixteen present. Our governor opposed the programme as warmly as before,
and added one wise argument, that it would infringe the authority
of all the particular Visitors of Colleges. Principal of Jesus
seconded him, and Wadham spoke a little on his side. But when
it was put to the vote only our governor and Jesus voted against
it; the rest threw it up. Our governor looks somewhat simply
upon this very ridiculous attempt.

Postscript. Your acquaintance Felton would not vote at all.
He said he would have voted if he could have told which way
would have been for the good of the University. I think I told
you he is a new convert to Whiggism. At former meetings he
was directly against the programme, but numbers now staggered
him.

1728, December 5.—My news as to the main part is true.
The point of moment I mentioned was the recalling of Zinzendorf,
one part of that is now owned, that he is gone from Soissons
with bag and baggage. The other part, his disgrace, you will hear
of I believe as soon as he is come to Vienna; that he is disgraced at
least in appearance. That Welderen brought this news was a
circumstance only which I had from another hand and not from
him who sent me the principal points. Though I still believe
Welderen came not upon private business only, he might have
that or might pretend that, and yet have private instructions for
other affairs. The stocks begin to show what men's apprehensions are upon the recalling of Zinzendorf.

Do you not remember it was said lately in the prints that the
Wild Boy was come to town and had been at the play house. I
wish some unlucky rogue do not think he may have occasion
soon to make an allegory of it.

1728, December 8.—Our new Prince will afford without doubt
entertainment for conversation and materials for correspondence.
I shall expect to hear some of his *Bon Mots*, and who are his
favourites as well as his officers. Do you think the ladies are not
busy, and laying designs to engage him? Happy the lady who
has the good fortune to please most.

I have a book in 12mo. or small 8vo. called:—"The Adventures
of (Mr. T. S.) an English merchant taken prisoner by the Turks
of Angiers and carried into the inland countries of Africa, &c.,
written by the Author and fitted for the public view by A.
Roberts, &c., London, printed and are to be sold by the Messrs.
Pitt at the White Hart in Little Britain, 1670."

In this book towards the end, p. 240, is an account of a town and all the inhabitants of it, and everything else in it, petrified, on account of———. It says it is four or five days' journey distant from Tripoli. A note at the bottom of the page pretends that an account of it had been printed fourteen years before, under the name of Sir Kenelm Digby. But I look upon the whole book as well as this passage to be a mere fiction. I never met with any other account of any petrified town.

1728, December 9.—If the account I have heard of the gentleman you mention be true, I doubt not but he will repay the visit to the ladies who waited on him and be as willing to bestow his favours on them as they can be to receive them.

I cannot think there is any thing in the report of Prussia's investing Embden. He lies surely at too great a distance from it. Should he march from Cleves, the Dutch must have notice and be before him. Should he march from Brandenburg, he must go through Hanover. I have sent you the programme; it is but poorly drawn, and some expressions are not English. But those were not the exceptions our wise governor made, who displays his wisdom every day more upon every occasion whatever. We have had two such sermons lately from Llandaff, as I believe never came before from Christ Church or any other pulpit; most wretched stuff. But his episcopal zeal was strangely stirred in both sermons against the ladies' riding habit.

1728, December 15.—I can guess at no foundation for a strong report of peace, but a design to keep up the stocks a little, that they may sell out before the war breaks out. They who talk this most, believe least of it.

Should it be moved to annex Gibraltar and Port Mahon it can be with no other design, but that either the keeping of it, and a war upon that, or the giving it up, may come from the Parliament, and not from the ministry, as it must do if it be once annexed by act of Parliament.

This refusal of the whole tribe of the Finches has a bad aspect, and may seem to threaten the taking away that they have, instead of giving more. I shall send directed to your Lordship by Godfry's wagon on Tuesday a piece of brawn, of which I would humbly beg my Lady's acceptance. I wish it may prove good, for our poor cook that used to make it is dead, this was made by his brother.

How come you never to mention to me our friend Auditor Foley's daughter's marriage with the parson of his parish? I conclude you must have heard of it. Nor did Abel say any thing of it. I hope the father bears it like a wise man, but the many examples he has seen of such marriages should have made him look out for a husband for the girl. That is one of the things that will do itself. The parson though is inexcusable, the Auditor had been not only his patron, but kind friend too.

1728, December 19.—I must beg leave to differ a little from your Lordship. Should the news of the Chevalier's death be confirmed, I do not see how it could be of any help to the ministry, or any use they could make of it. I think quite the contrary. But we will " confer " notes on that point when we meet.

By the book which you say you have seen, I suppose you mean "The Adventures of the Merchant T. S." But I take it all to be a fiction from the beginning to the end. If there be no other authority for a petrified town, I cannot imagine how any one can ground anything in it fit for the Queen's perusal, and yet I never read or heard anywhere else of a petrified town.

How does our friend the Auditor bear his misfortune? Did he ever take any notice of it to you? If I mistake him not he is like to bear such a thing as well as most men.

1728, December 23.—I never thought my scrub book could have been of the value I find it is like to be. I was once going to have thrown it into the fire, but I have learnt from this instance as well as from some others to find that no book can be so contemptible for which one may not have occasion. I fancy Mr. Fowke will not be able to find this petrified city in any other travels.

If this story should prove to have any truth in it I doubt not but the virtuosi will confidently apply Lucan's verses to it; and it would be the best ground that ever has been found for the fable of Medusa. But I cannot imagine, if such a thing is true, how we never came to have any account of it either from Greeks cr Romans or in later ages. This is my grand objection. Certainly these countries were known, at least as far as this city is said to be seated, better in former days than they are now; and so remarkable a thing could not have escaped notice.

1728, December 28.—I most heartily thank you for your account of the "London Journal." If the person you mention is the author, it is plain he is in great distress, and has very little to say for himself. The "Craftsman" will have great advantage against him from this paper. There was a report that the printer of the " Craftsman " was seized and his papers all carried off. I suppose it was groundless, because there was no mention of it in the last prints. It is a sure sign things go ill when they are shifting the blame from one to the other. If Stanhope has mettle he will resent what is said of his kinsman and patron. I doubt not but in a little time we shall have them come to the impeachments and laying the blame of them upon each other. The Tories have a fair game before them if they had any that had spirit and conduct to manage it. I forgot, as I designed last post, to observe to you that the very last passage in the " London Journal" seems to be a terrible threat to an old acquaintance of mine.

We expect the Commission here very soon that is to put an end to the differences at University College. Oxford, Llandaff, Bristol, Tanner, are of it, and Drs. Paull and Sayer. It is said it is to be over before the Parliament sits down. Dr. Henchman, who comes as advocate for Cockman, takes up his quarters with me, though I believe there will be little occasion for an advocate. I am apt to think Dennison and his party will not appear.

1728-9, January 6.—The British lay an unreasonable stress upon the succession to Tuscany and Parma. If I mistake not much, though we may oppose it now when we cannot have our own points, we had actually agreed to settle them on Don Carlos by that quadruple alliance to which Spain acceded; and it is ridiculous to pretend that a succession to those territories would be formidable to all out of Italy as well as in it. Are not Milan, Naples and Sicily, dominions of thrice the extent? Are not they supported by the power of the German empire? And yet we thought them so little formidable in one Prince, though of such vast dominions elsewhere, that when he had not Sicily, we perfidiously broke a treaty to get it for him.

I hear they design to do somewhat against Bolingbroke for his scribbling. I believe they think him the author of more than he is. But I see not what they can do to him, unless in the cause that will come on this winter betwixt him and young Packer. If that goes against him he may probably go abroad again.

1728-9, January 12.—I know Carteret drew up that letter which the late King transcribed with his own hand. W[alpole] was once told that he had a fair opportunity by letting it be produced of being even with Carteret. He said "True, but that we must not do." If W. is pressed hard, and should think he may escape himself by sacrificing Carteret, no doubt he will do it. I fancy I shall live to see Carteret called to answer for it. But as your Lordship justly observes it is impossible that such a letter could have been written with the privity of T[ownshend] and W[alpole]. I am sure that single letter is a more proper subject for impeachment than all the articles together in all the four impeachments of famous memory.

1728-9, January 13.—I am amazed that inscription was not blotted or torn out. No doubt it will be printed. Tories and Whigs will agree to promote that, but I do not doubt it will be made use of to the prejudice of Bob himself. Do you know who bought the book? The price for the letters you mention shows what extravagancy men are capable off.

I am amazed my old friend should go on to provoke those who will have it in their power within few weeks to give a cause of great importance to him against him. He will be very uneasy, if that cause goes against him in every branch of it. And his enemies will have this handle, that equity is certainly against him, if the letter of the law should be for him. I am mightily pleased with the Considerations; I wonder who the penman is. They are in the right way of quoting against him, the pamphlets he himself wrote against the late Queen and your father. I take the report of sending Pulteney to the Tower, to be only *in terrorem*. Should they do so extravagant a thing, they would lose much more than they would get by it. They would alarm all the world.

1728-9, January 19.—Your Lordship surely judges very right of his Excellency [Carteret]'s present disposition and of the reason of his late civility to you. He dreads that letter being brought upon the stage as in the course of affairs it is likely it may. He has been screened hitherto for the sake of him that copied it, but should another person be pressed hard, no doubt he will give up his Excellency if he thinks he can excuse himself by it. That letter would be a just ground for an impeachment, which he would do well to think of, who went as heartily into the impeachment of others for measures for which they deserved the thanks of their country.

I thank you for the story of the madman; they may call him mad, but that demand was no sign of it. I wish some of our friends had known it and followed it. Should that which is aimed at be had at last, I believe it will be hardly purchased; but if nothing, as I am much afraid, should come of all our compliments how silly shall we look! Sir John certainly wants to get somewhat. All who deal with him should take that caution along with them. I wish him well, but things seem to go hard when one of his profession makes his court by a scrap of poetry.

1728-9, January 21.—I thank you heartily for the "British Journal," but surely the fellow writes booty (sic). I suppose Roger Manly is a feigned name. He has [not?] told all the truth, but he is pretty near it, and has said more than any honest man could ever have hoped he would. If this should be written by the bare allowance of the great men, it is plain they design to give up Byng and Car[teret], and the credit too of the late King into the bargain; and they hope to come off themselves by pretending they did not approve but could not stop that which they own they were privy to. Here might be fine sport made both within and without doors, were there any to manage these points to the most advantage.

Never surely was there an age in which we have such illustrious proofs that the most worthless men are the most impudent. With what face could our governor ask to have a prebend of Westminster added to that he has?

1728-9, March.—I am sure no bishop since the Restoration was warden of Manchester at the same time he was bishop of Chester till the present bishop, and I am pretty confident no one ever was so before the Restoration. No bishop of Chester since the Restoration was indeed ever warden at all till this man, except my father. Dr. Henchman convinced me thoroughly that the statutes of that College, which were made in Charles I.'s time, do not make the bishop of Chester local Visitor, but only give him the power of visiting there in his ordinary jurisdiction of bishop, which he could not have had in a royal foundation but by express grant from the crown. Indeed it is plain to me from the statutes, that the Crown has reserved to itself the general power of visiting. I am sorry we shall not have you to-morrow.

1728-9, March 22.—I thank you for the enclosed, the minority is less than I expected. Dr. Henchman saw your Lordship yesterday, he has promised me that he will endeavour to retrieve his original opinion and send it to your Lordship. But he seems apprehensive that, in the trial of the Manchester cause, the King's Bench declared the bishop of Chester Visitor. His opinion, he says truly, though it should be right cannot be set against the decision of that court. I asked him if that point of the bishop's being Visitor was argued in court. He said he could not say it was. I asked him if that point was not taken *pro confesso* without being examined or any judgment given in it—which I take truly to be the case. He said he could not say but it might be so; he had heard only a confused account of that trial, but he would enquire particulars of Fazarkely who was concerned in it.

1729, Good Friday.—This Manchester bill raises my indignation. It is an improvement of that bill, by which, in the late Queen's time, all the charters of the cathedrals of the new foundation, which were really invalid, were by Act of Parliament made valid, and all prior acts done illegally upon those charters were confirmed. This is a new extraordinary method, to enable by Act of Parliament one part of a corporation to oppress the other, and depriving the oppressed of the benefit of the law. Whereas supposing a charter or statutes defective, yet every one of the body has a right to enjoy them, as they are at the time they are admitted to it, and no alteration can with justice be made, but with the consent of the whole body. But that is not the case here. All the difficulty was owing to themselves, by their putting a man into a place that was truly inconsistent with that he had before. But there was an obvious remedy for that difficulty, which was made use of, by recourse to the King's Bench. And now comes an Act of Parliament to deprive the oppressed of that legal remedy, and to put them in a state under which they can have no relief under any oppression. And this to screen a man who has done very illegal acts, and to take him out of the power of the common law, whereas in equity, if any Act of Parliament extraordinary, it should be to punish him, if the common law would not reach him. I could almost wish myself in town, to talk this over with my friends, though it is not my business, who am archdeacon of Richmond, to quarrel unnecessarily with their man, and therefore name not me. Poor Harbin may wish well, but he has not a head to be master of this case. Fazarkerly, who I suppose will be counsel, is perfect master of it; and would Anglesey and Bingley be at a little pains to make themselves masters of it, there would be ample room to expose the person who has been put into that church, to expose those who put a man into a place so inconsistent with that he had before, and to expose the extraordinary methods that are taken to cover and justify the illegal acts which he has done, and to enable him to do more for the future, without any remedy against him, and to deprive others of the common benefit of the law.

1729, Easter Day.—If this Manchester bill pass, I am afraid both universities will think their foundations are made precarious by this instance. The authority which takes upon it to alter a statute relating to a Visitor, may do it in any other point, as well as that of Visitor. And it has been thought an illegal arbitrary act to alter any thing to which men have a right under the great seal, without the consent at least, if not the express desire, of all concerned in the corporation. The universities will have reason to think this an ill return from old T[revo]r for taking in two of his sons to partake of the charity of one of their noblest foundations. I wish somebody would suggest this to him.

I think I told your lordship, that on the 5th of November last, as I think, or on some such day, the sheriff of Lancashire, who lives at Manchester, went in procession to a bonfire, and the bishop followed him with a dissenting minister on each hand of him. The sheriff amongst other healths drank to the immortal memory of King William, the "founder" of the protestant religion. So far my correspondent, a very worthy man, is sure was true. He says farther, he is credibly informed that the bishop pledged the health in the terms it was proposed by the sheriff. Were this story known to Anglesey and Bingley, they might make some use of it, and it might show what the person is for whose sake, and to screen and support whom in arbitrary illegal proceedings, such extraordinary bills are brought in.

1729, April 3.—I am glad Lord Anglesey is so zealous against the Manchester bill. I hope your Lordship, Lord Foley, and all your friends will assist him. It is a scandalous bill, and I wonder old T[revo]r would be employed in such dirty work. You see by the case sent to your Lordship, that there is just ground to doubt whether the Crown be not Visitor already. If it is so, this bill gives the Crown nothing, but takes away a great deal from it. But suppose the bishop of Chester sole Visitor; at best the bill is unnecessary, for in the case when the bishop is also warden, either the bishop against the fellows against the bishop (*sic*) may upon any grievance have recourse to and relief from common law, as the fellows had lately against the bishop's illegal acts, as they may now safely be called, since the King's Bench has called them so. There can be no occasion to alter a constitution settled under the great seal by such an extraordinary proceeding, unless it be evident that without such alteration no relief can be had upon any just grievance, but this bill is plainly to bar the fellows from having recourse to common law—the privilege of all Englishmen—and to put them under another power, by which they who would oppress hope to have the advantage. Do the proceedings of a bishop that have been judged by the King's Bench illegal deserve such a reward, or one rather of another nature? But surely some stop might be put at least to this bill by having the statutes referred to the judges for them to give their opinion who is Visitor. Nor can it be proper to proceed, till you are sure the Crown has not already that power you pretend to give. When you are sure of that it may be proper to consider whether it may be more legal to leave the fellows to have recourse upon exigency that requires it to the law, or to create a new power, unknown to their statutes. And if this power of altering charters and statutes by Act of Parliament for sinister ends be allowed to ministers, no one knows when any foundation is secure, be it never so firmly established by law. If it should be said in the debate—as likely enough it may by London—that the late bishop had a design to have had the wardenship annexed to the see of Chester, I hope somebody will be ready to answer that it is true, but that he was never so absurd or so wicked as to design to be Visitor of himself, but in the bill for annexing it to have the visitorial power transferred either to York or to the Crown. There may be full room for Anglesey to expose the present bishop, if Anglesey will but take a little pains to inform himself of the cause,

A sad accident happened here two days before I came. The youngest son of Frank Annesly's, who is of Queen's, had some company with him drinking a bowl of rack punch. There was one Field of Trinity, who whiffed some tobacco in Annesly's face. Annesly told him if he did so again he would do him a mischief. The boy foolishly repeated it, and Annesly without more ado stabbed him betwixt the ribs with a pen-knife. At first it was hoped the pen-knife had stuck in the bone, but now it appears it went betwixt them, and the boy's life is despaired of, and Annesly is gone off.

1729, April 7.—Your Lordship judges very truly of the drift of the Manchester bill. The sole end of it is to debar the fellow, when oppressed, from having recourse to that which is the privilege of all Englishmen, the common law. By those who come to see me, I find we are "alarumed" at it here, and think it may [be] a precedent to break in upon any part of our legal establishments whenever those who wish not well to us are disposed to it. They lay on our T[revo]r plentifully, for seeming to have the chief concern in a bill of such pernicious consequence to us, at the same time that he has two sons whom he is pleased to allow to partake of one of the noblest of our charities.

I am, I bless God, tolerably easy to-day, but I live in dread of a return of my fit. My doctors insult me now for not having followed their advice. I perceive if my fit returns they design to let me undergo a great deal more pain before they will do anything to relieve me.

1729, April 8.—After I wrote to your Lordship yesterday I had a return of my fit. The pain was as severe as ever. The symptoms after the pain was gone were more favourable than usual. They have given me physic to-day which torments me without relieving me, and I know not whether the pain I have be owing to my physic or a return of my fit.

The prints say Lord Lansdowne is come to town. Do you hear anything of him or upon what terms he comes?

[1729, April 11.]—As yet I hear of no return of my fit. The doctors tell me I am better; I am sure I am low and weak.

If the termagant of Spain pretends to be disposed to peace, I am afraid she is upon some new juggle.

1729, April 13.—Accounts from Spain I find differ. A correspondent of mine that you may guess at says he has seen letters of good authority that say the Emperor rules there still and is not likely to dispose them to peace whilst he can get subsidies from them. Should they fail it is thought the case would soon alter.

Postscript. I hear there is a satire on the subscribers to Gay. Could you send it?

1729, April 14.—This is the first day I have been allowed to come out of my bedchamber into my study. I hope I am better, but low and weak still.

Pray let me hear if there be any confirmation of the termagant of Spain's eagerness for peace. If it be so it is somewhat extraordinary, and it is not easy to guess what can be the motive of it.

1729, April 15.—After all my bark my fit returned again last night. It was not quite so violent I think as some former ones but it lasted longer, from five in the evening till six in the morning. The doctors must say somewhat, but I am satisfied that tho' they are able men and very careful of me they know not what to make of my illness. I must wait to see what this will end in. *

1729, May 6.—I shall not trouble your Lordship but upon ordinary days, unless anything extraordinary happens. I hope I get a little strength, but it is very slowly.

I am desired to write to your Lordship in behalf of Mr. Manatou, who desires to succeed Mr. Langford in your chapel. He who was proctor of the University and censor of the College last year is in my opinion humble enough to desire a reader's place.

But I beg all my humble requests to your Lordship may be understood to be upon a supposal that you have no one else in your view.

I beg my duty to my Lady and Lady Margaret.

THOMAS WYATT to the EARL OF OXFORD.

1729, May 8. Oxford.—Last night about six o'clock my dear master died, went away very suddenly without sigh or groan. I am very sensible this is very unwelcome news to your Lordship, but I thought it my duty to acquaint your Lordship.

---

* Many brief letters of Dr. Stratford follow this, referring entirely to the progress of his illness.

INDEX.

H

Rhine, the, 429.
Rhode Island, North America, 467.
Rialton, [Francis Godolphin], Lord, son of the Earl of Godolphin, 17-19.
Rich, Sir Robert, 427.
Richmond:
    [Charles Lennox], Duke of, 237.
    Duchess of (1718), 237.
Richmond, Surrey, 280, 364.
    Archdeacon of. *See* Stratford, Dr. William.
Ripperda, Duke of, Secretary of State for foreign affairs in Spain, 412, 419, 421, 424, 431.
Rivers, [Richard Savage], Earl, sent to Hanover, 10, 15.
    illness of, 126.
Robbers, street, 47.
Roberts, A., book edited by, 470.
Robinson:
    Dr., [John], Bishop of Bristol, 44.
    ——, as Lord Privy Seal, 48, 51-53, 61, 73.
    ——, report that he is to be Bishop of London, 157.
    ——, as Bishop of London, 171, 191.
    ——, marriage of, 258, 259.
    Mrs. (married to Lord Wemys), 115.
Rochester:
    John [Wilmot], Earl of, alluded to, 287.
    —— Life of, 182.
    [Henry Hyde], Earl of, pension of, 311.
Rochester:
    Bishop of. *See* Spratt, Thomas; Atterbury, Francis; Bradford, Samuel.
    "Abbot of," 287.
Rogers:
    [John], Archdeacon of Leicester, guardian to Lord Huntingdon, 88.
    ——, beadle of Christ Church, 63.
Rolle [John], 317.
Rolls, the:
    Master of, 207; *and see* Trevor, Sir John; Jekyll, Sir Joseph.
    chaplaincy of, 52.
Roman Catholics, proposed tax upon, 339, 341, 359.
Rome, 406, 428.
    a dog sent from. *See* Atterbury, dog sent to.
    Jewish quarter at, *trans Tiberim*, 239.
    Convent of St. Cecilia at, 407.
Roper, Abel, 61.
Ros. [Rossiter], 307.
Ross, co. Hereford, 84, 163, 304.
    living of, 71, 78.
Rosse, General, [Charles], Member of the Committee of Inquiry concerning the South Sea Company, 302.
Rostock, book printed at, 23.
Rotterdam, 225, 244.
Rowney:
    Ned, son of Thomas, sen., 450.

28493

Rowney—*cont.*
    Thomas (old Tom, the Senator), M.P. for Oxford City, 14, 16, 19, 29, 33, 34, 47-49, 51, 55, 56, 58, 71, 72, 77, 79, 86, 88, 89, 115, 120, 124, 129, 144, 145, 153, 181, 182, 188, 193, 207, 214, 232, 233, 235, 268, 277, 280, 287, 288, 291, 321, 329, 348, 351, 366, 390, 402, 450.
    ——, his friendship for Dr. Stratford, 123.
    ——, promotion designed for, 164.
    ——, narrow escape of, 218.
    ——, windows of, broken by the soldiers, 217.
    ——, mentioned in a satirical poem, 242.
    ——, death of, 450.
    ——, house of, 178, 181.
    ——, son of. *See* Thomas, jun., *below.*
    ——, daughter of, 202, 207.
    ——, son-in-law of. *See* Noel, Sir Cloberry.
    —— ——, family of, 58, 193, 235, 321.
    ——, relative of, 337.
    Mrs., his wife, 122, 153, 171, 181, 207, 288, 301.
    Thomas, jun. (young Tom), 171, 233, 242.
    ——, as member for the City of Oxford, 317, 329.
    "old Madam," 242.
Roxburgh:
    [John Ker], Duke of, 313.
Royal:
    Family, 407.
    Society, History and Transactions of, 29, 169.
Royston, [co. Herts], 174.
Russell, [John], fellow of Merton College, 248.
Russia, [Catherine], Czarina of, Austrian treaty with, 407.
Rye, co. Sussex, 414, 415.

S

S., T., book by, 470, 472.
Sacheverell, Dr., [Henry], 5-8, 17, 23, 39, 53, 72, 73, 76.
    said to have preached another man's sermon, 79.
    burning of in effigy, prevented by the people of Oxford, 222.
    "his House." *See* Oxford, Magdalen College at.
    ferment concerning, 465.
St. Albans, [Charles Beauclerk], Duke of, 237.
    [Diana Beauclerk], Duchess of, 237.
St. Albans, co. Herts, 237, 314.
St. Andrew's feast, 405.
St. Asaph, Bishop of. *See* Fleetwood, William; Wynne, John.

2 K

Y

Z

ERRATA.

p. 24, *line* 28; *for* cause *read* course.

p. 41, *line* 37; *for* Ti *read* Te.

p. 55, *line* 10; *for* [Kent] *read* [Shrewsbury].

p. 71, *line* 28; *for* unreasonable *read* unseasonable.

p. 218, *line* 28; *for* Wayne *read* Mayne.

p. 219, *line* 36; *for* Prologomena *read* Prolegomena.

p. 219, *line* 37; *for* texta *read* textu.

p. 299, *bottom line*; *for* gusta *read* gutta.

p. 302, *line* 36; *for* Tom *read* Tim.

p. 311, *line* 17; *for* Horidante *read* Floridante.

p. 354, *line* 13; *for* which *read* such.

p. 354, *line* 19; *for* Gaynier *read* Gagnier.

p. 355, *lines* 1 *and* 5; *for* Gaynier *read* Gagnier.

p. 362, *bottom line*; *for* invidium faciendum *read* invidiam faciendam.

p. 376, *bottom line*; *for* Literari *read* Literariæ.

p. 439, *line* 32; *after* Dr. Middleton's book *insert* "De Medicorum &c."

p 442, *line* 8; *for* illum *read* ullum.

p. 447, *line* 8 *from bottom*; *for* Manatou *read* Manaton.

p. 463, *line* 25; *for* Manatou *read* Manaton.

HISTORICAL MANUSCRIPTS COMMISSION.

REPORTS OF THE ROYAL COMMISSIONERS APPOINTED TO INQUIRE WHAT PAPERS AND MANUSCRIPTS BELONGING TO PRIVATE FAMILIES AND INSTITUTIONS ARE EXTANT WHICH WOULD BE OF UTILITY IN THE ILLUSTRATION OF HISTORY, CONSTITUTIONAL LAW, SCIENCE, AND GENERAL LITERATURE.

Date.	—	Size.	Sessional Paper.	Price.
				s. d.
1870 (Reprinted 1874.)	FIRST REPORT, WITH APPENDIX . . Contents :- ENGLAND. House of Lords ; Cambridge Colleges ; Abingdon and other Corporations, &c. SCOTLAND. Advocates' Library, Glasgow Corporation, &c. IRELAND. Dublin, Cork, and other Corporations, &c.	f'cap	[C. 55]	1 6
1871	SECOND REPORT WITH APPENDIX AND INDEX TO THE FIRST AND SECOND REPORTS . . . . Contents :— ENGLAND. House of Lords ; Cambridge Colleges ; Oxford Colleges ; Monastery of Dominican Friars at Woodchester, Duke of Bedford, Earl Spencer, &c. SCOTLAND. Aberdeen and St. Andrew's Universities, &c. IRELAND. Marquis of Ormonde ; Dr. Lyons, &c.	,,	[C. 441]	3 10
1872 (Reprinted 1895.)	THIRD REPORT WITH APPENDIX AND INDEX . . . . Contents :— ENGLAND. House of Lords ; Cambridge Colleges ; Stonyhurst College ; Bridgwater and other Corporations ; Duke of Northumberland, Marquis of Lansdowne, Marquis of Bath, &c. SCOTLAND. University of Glasgow : Duke of Montrose, &c. IRELAND. Marquis of Ormonde ; Black Book of Limerick, &c.	,,	[C. 673]	6 0
1873	FOURTH REPORT, WITH APPENDIX. PART I. . . . . Contents :— ENGLAND. House of Lords. Westminster Abbey ; Cambridge and Oxford Colleges ; Cinque Ports, Hythe, and other Corporations, Marquis of Bath, Earl of Denbigh, &c. SCOTLAND. Duke of Argyll, &c. IRELAND. Trinity College, Dublin ; Marquis of Ormonde.	,,	[C. 857]	6 8

Date.	—	Size.	Sessional Paper.	Price.
				s. d.
1873	FOURTH REPORT. PART II. INDEX - -	f'cap	[C. 857 i.]	2 6
1876	FIFTH REPORT, WITH APPENDIX. PART I. - Contents :— ENGLAND. House of Lords ; Oxford and Cambridge Colleges; Dean and Chapter of Canterbury ; Rye, Lydd, and other Corporations. Duke of Sutherland, Marquis of Lansdowne, Reginald Cholmondeley, Esq., &c. SCOTLAND. Earl of Aberdeen, &c.	,,	[C.1432]	7 0
,,	DITTO. PART II. INDEX - - -	,,	[C.1432 i.]	3 6
1877	SIXTH REPORT, WITH APPENDIX. PART I. - Contents :— ENGLAND. House of Lords : Oxford and Cambridge Colleges ; Lambeth Palace ; Black Book of the Archdeacon of Canterbury ; Bridport, Wallingford, and other Corporations ; Lord Leconfield, Sir Reginald Graham, Sir Henry Ingilby, &c. SCOTLAND. Duke of Argyll, Earl of Moray, &c. IRELAND. Marquis of Ormonde.	,,	[C.1745]	8 6
(Reprinted 1893.)	DITTO. PART II. INDEX - - -	,,	[C.2102]	1 10
1879 (Reprinted 1895.)	SEVENTH REPORT, WITH APPENDIX. PART I. Contents :— House of Lords ; County of Somerset ; Earl of Egmont, Sir Frederick Graham, Sir Harry Verney, &c.	,,	[C.2340]	7 6
(Reprinted 1895.)	DITTO. PART II. APPENDIX AND INDEX - Contents :— Duke of Athole, Marquis of Ormonde, S. F. Livingstone, Esq., &c.	,,	[C. 2340 i.]	3 6
1881	EIGHTH REPORT, WITH APPENDIX AND INDEX. PART I. Contents :— List of collections examined, 1869-1880. ENGLAND. House of Lords ; Duke of Marlborough ; Magdalen College, Oxford ; Royal College of Physicians ; Queen Anne's Bounty Office ; Corporations of Chester, Leicester, &c. IRELAND. Marquis of Ormonde, Lord Emly, The O'Conor Don, Trinity College, Dublin, &c.	,,	[C.3040]	[*Out of print.*]
1881	DITTO. PART II. APPENDIX AND INDEX - Contents :— Duke of Manchester.	,,	[C. 3040 i.]	[*Out of print.*]
1881	DITTO. PART III. APPENDIX AND INDEX - Contents :— Earl of Ashburnham.	,,	[C. 3040 ii.]	[*Out of print.*]

Date.	—	Size.	Sessional Paper.	Price.
1888 (Reprinted 1895.)	NINTH REPORT, WITH APPENDIX AND INDEX. PART I. - - - - - Contents :— St. Paul's and Canterbury Cathedrals; Eton College; Carlisle, Yarmouth, Canterbury, and Barnstaple Corporations, &c.	f'cap	[C.3773]	*s. d.* 5 2
1884 (Reprinted 1895.)	DITTO. PART II. APPENDIX AND INDEX - Contents :— ENGLAND. House of Lords. Earl of Leicester; C. Pole Gell, Alfred Morrison, Esqs., &c. SCOTLAND. Lord Elphinstone, H. C. Maxwell Stuart, Esq., &c. IRELAND. Duke of Leinster, Marquis of Drogheda, &c.	,,	[C.3773 i.]	6 3
1884	DITTO. PART III. APPENDIX AND INDEX - - - - - Contents :— Mrs. Stopford Sackville.	,,	[C. 3773 ii.]	[*Out of Print.*]
1888 (Reprinted 1895.)	CALENDAR OF THE MANUSCRIPTS OF THE MARQUIS OF SALISBURY, K.G. (or CECIL MSS.). PART I. - - - -	8vo.	[C.3777]	3 5
1888	DITTO. PART II. - - -	,,	[C.5463]	3 5
1889	DITTO. PART III. - - -	,,	[C.5889 v.]	2 1
1892	DITTO. PART IV. - - -	,,	[C.6823]	2 11
1894	DITTO. PART V. - - -	,,	[C.7574]	2 6
1896	DITTO. PART VI. - - -	,,	[C.7884]	2 8
1899	DITTO. PART VII. - - -	,,	[C.9246]	2 8
1899	DITTO. PART VIII. - - -	,,	[C.9467]	2 8
1885	TENTH REPORT - - - - This is introductory to the following :—	,,	[C.4548]	[*Out of Print.*]
1885 (Reprinted 1895.)	(1.) APPENDIX AND INDEX - - - Earl of Eglinton, Sir J. S. Maxwell, Bart., and C. S. H. D. Moray, C. F. Weston Underwood, G. W. Digby. Esqs.	,,	[C.4575]	3 7
1885	(2.) APPENDIX AND INDEX - - - The Family of Gawdy.	,,	[C.4576 iii.]	1 4
1885	(3.) APPENDIX AND INDEX - - - Wells Cathedral.	,,	[C.4576 ii.]	[*Out of Print.*]
1885	(4.) APPENDIX AND INDEX - - - Earl of Westmorland; Capt. Stewart; Lord Stafford; Sir N. W. Throckmorton; Sir P. T. Mainwaring, Lord Muncaster, M.P., Capt. J. F. Bagot, Earl of Kilmorey, Earl of Powis, and others, the Corporations of Kendal, Wenlock, Bridgnorth, Eye, Plymouth, and the County of Essex; and Stonyhurst College.	,,	[C.4576]	[*Out of Print.*]
1885 (Reprinted 1895.)	(5.) APPENDIX AND INDEX - - - The Marquis of Ormonde, Earl of Fingall, Corporations of Galway, Waterford, the Sees of Dublin and Ossory, the Jesuits in Ireland.	,,	[4576 i.]	2 10

Date,	—	Size.	Sessional Paper.	Price.
				s. d.
1887	(6.) APPENDIX AND INDEX - - - Marquis of Abergavenny, Lord Braye, G. F. Luttrell, P. P. Bouverie, W. Bromley Davenport, R. T. Balfour, Esquires.	8vo.	[C.5242]	1 7
1887	ELEVENTH REPORT - - - - This is introductory to the following :—	,,	[C.5060 vi.]	0 3
1887	(1.) APPENDIX AND INDEX - - - H. D. Skrine, Esq., Salvetti Correspondence.	,,	[C.5060]	1 1
1887	(2.) APPENDIX AND INDEX - - - House of Lords. 1678-1688.	,,	[C.5060 i.]	2 0
1887	(3.) APPENDIX AND INDEX - - Corporations of Southampton and Lynn.	,,	[C.5060 ii.]	1 8
1887	(4.) APPENDIX AND INDEX - - - Marquess Townshend.	,,	[C.5060 iii.]	2 6
1887	(5.) APPENDIX AND INDEX - - - Earl of Dartmouth.	,,	[C.5060 iv.]	2 8
1887	(6.) APPENDIX AND INDEX - - - Duke of Hamilton.	,,	[C.5060 v.]	1 6
1888	(7.) APPENDIX AND INDEX - - - Duke of Leeds, Marchioness of Waterford, Lord Hothfield, &c.; Bridgwater Trust Office, Reading Corporation, Inner Temple Library.	,,	[C.5612]	2 0
1890	TWELFTH REPORT - - - - This is introductory to the following :—	,,	[C.5889]	0 3
1888	(1.) APPENDIX - - - - Earl Cowper, K.G. (Coke MSS., at Melbourne Hall, Derby). Vol. I.	,,	[C.5472]	2 7
1888	(2.) APPENDIX - - - Ditto. Vol. II	,,	[C.5613]	2 5
1889	(3.) APPENDIX AND INDEX - - - Ditto. Vol. III.	,,	[C.5889 i.]	1 4
1888	(4. APPENDIX - - - The Duke of Rutland, G.C.B. Vol. I.	,,	[C.5614]	3 2
1891	(5.) APPENDIX AND INDEX - - Ditto. Vol. II.	,,	[C.5889 ii.]	2 0'
1889	(6.) APPENDIX AND INDEX - - House of Lords, 1689-1690.	,,	[C.5889 iii.]	2 1
1890	(7.) APPENDIX AND INDEX - - S. H. le Fleming, Esq., of Rydal.	,,	[C.5889 iv.]	1 11
1891	(8.) APPENDIX AND INDEX - - - The Duke of Athole, K.T., and the Earl of Home.	,,	[C.6338]	1 0
1891	(9.) APPENDIX AND INDEX - - - The Duke of Beaufort, K.G., the Earl of Donoughmore, J. H. Gurney, W. W. B. Hulton, R. W. Ketton, G. A. Aitken, P. V. Smith, Esq.; Bishop of Ely ; Cathedrals of Ely, Gloucester, Lincoln, and Peterborough, Corporations of Gloucester, Higham Ferrers, and Newark ; Southwell Minster ; Lincoln District Registry.	,,	[C.6338 i.]	2 6

Date.	—	Size.	Sessional Paper.	Price.
				s. d.
1891	(10.) APPENDIX - - - - - The First Earl of Charlemont. Vol. I. 1745-1783.	8vo.	[C. 6338 ii.]	1 11
1892	THIRTEENTH REPORT - - - - This is introductory to the following:—	,,	[C.6827]	0 3
1891	(1.) APPENDIX - - - - - The Duke of Portland. Vol. I.	,,	[C.6474]	3 0
	(2.) APPENDIX AND INDEX. Ditto. Vol. II. - - - -	,,	[C. 6827 i.]	2 0
1892	(3.) APPENDIX. J. B. Fortescue, Esq., of Dropmore. Vol. I. - - - - -	,,	[C.6660]	2 7
1892	(4.) APPENDIX AND INDEX - - - Corporations of Rye, Hastings, and Hereford. Capt. F. C. Loder-Symonds, E. R. Wodehouse, M.P., J. Dovaston, Esqs., Sir T. B. Lennard, Bart., Rev. W. D. Macray, and Earl of Dartmouth (Supplementary Report).	,,	[C.6810]	2 4
1892	(5.) APPENDIX AND INDEX. House of Lords, 1690-1691 - - -	,,	[C.6822]	2 4
1893	(6.) APPENDIX AND INDEX. Sir W. Fitzherbert, Bart. The Delaval Family, of Seaton Delaval; The Earl of Ancaster; and General Lyttelton-Annesley.	,,	[C.7166]	1 4
1893	(7.) APPENDIX AND INDEX. The Earl of Lonsdale - - - -	,,	[C.7241]	1 3
1893	(8.) APPENDIX AND INDEX. The First Earl of Charlemont. Vol. II. 1784-1799.	,,	[C.7424]	1 11
1896	FOURTEENTH REPORT - - - - This is introductory to the following :—	,,	[C.7988]	0 3
1894	(1.) APPENDIX AND INDEX. The Duke of Rutland, G.C.B. Vol. III.	,,	[C.7476]	1 11
1894	(2.) APPENDIX. The Duke of Portland. Vol. III. -	,,	[C.7569]	2 8
1894	(3.) APPENDIX AND INDEX. The Duke of Roxburghe; Sir H. H. Campbell, Bart. ; The Earl of Strathmore; and the Countess Dowager of Seafield.	,,	[C.7570]	1 2
1894	(4.) APPENDIX AND INDEX. Lord Kenyon - - - - -	,,	[C.7571]	2 10
1896	(5.) APPENDIX. J. B. Fortescue, Esq., of Dropmore. Vol. II.	,,	[C.7572]	2 8
1895	(6.) APPENDIX AND INDEX. House of Lords, 1692-1693 - - -	,,	[C.7573]	1 11
	(Manuscripts of the House of Lords, 1693-1695, Vol. I. (New Series) See H.L. No. 5 of 1900. Price 2/9).			
1895	(7.) APPENDIX. The Marquis of Ormonde - - -	,,	[C.7678]	1 10

Date.	—	Size.	Sessional Paper.	Price.
				s. d.
1895	(8.) APPENDIX AND INDEX. Lincoln, Bury St. Edmunds, Hertford, and Great Grimsby Corporations; The Dean and Chapter of Worcester, and of Lichfield; The Bishop's Registry of Worcester.	8vo.	[C.7881]	1 5
1896	(9.) APPENDIX AND INDEX. Earl of Buckinghamshire; Earl of Lindsey; Earl of Onslow; Lord Emly; T. J. Hare, Esq.; and J. Round, Esq., M.P.	,.	[C.7882]	2 6
1895	(10.) APPENDIX AND INDEX. The Earl of Dartmouth. Vol. II. American Papers.	,,	[C.7883]	2 9
1899	FIFTEENTH REPORT. This is introductory to the following:—	,,	[C.9295]	0 4
1896	(1.) APPENDIX AND INDEX. The Earl of Dartmouth. Vol. III. -	,,	[C.8156]	1 5
1897	(2.) APPENDIX. J. Eliot Hodgkin, Esq., of Richmond, Surrey.	,,	[C.8327]	1 8
1897	(8.) APPENDIX AND INDEX. Charles Haliday, Esq., of Dublin; Acts of the Privy Council in Ireland, 1556-1571; Sir William Usaher's Table to the Council Book; Table to the Red Council Book.	,,	[C.8364]	1 4
1897	(4.) APPENDIX. The Duke of Portland. Vol. IV. -	,,	[C.8497]	2 11
1897	(5.) APPENDIX AND INDEX. The Right Hon. F. J. Savile Foljambe -	,,	[C.8550]	0 10
1897	(6.) APPENDIX AND INDEX. The Earl of Carlisle, Castle Howard -	,,	[C.8551]	8 6
1897	(7.) APPENDIX AND INDEX. The Duke of Somerset; The Marquis of Ailesbury; and Sir F.G. Puleston, Bart.	,,	[C.8552]	1 9
1897	(8.) APPENDIX AND INDEX. The Duke of Buccleuch and Queensberry, at Drumlanrig.	,,	[C.8553]	1 4
1897	(9.) APPENDIX AND INDEX. J. J. Hope Johnstone, Esq., of Annandale	,,	[C.8554]	1 0
1899	(10.) Shrewsbury and Coventry Corporations; Sir H. O. Corbet, Bart., Earl of Radnor, P.T. Tillard; J. R. Carr-Ellison; Andrew Kingsmill, Esqrs.	,,	[C.9472]	1 0

Date.	—	Size.	Sessional Paper.	Price.
				s. d.
1898	MANUSCRIPTS IN THE WELSH LANGUAGE. Vol. I.—Lord Mostyn, at Mostyn Hall, co. Flint.	8vo.	[C.8829]	1 4
1899	Vol. I. Part II.—W. R. M. Wynne, Esq., of Peniarth.	,,	[C.9468]	2 11
1899	Manuscripts of the Duke of Buccleuch and Queensberry, K.G , K T., preserved at Montagu House, Whitehall. Vol I.	,,	[C.9244]	2 7
1899	Ditto Marquis of Ormonde, K.P., preserved at the Castle, Kilkenny. Vol II.	,,	[C.9245]	2 0
1899	Ditto the Duke of Portland, K.G. Vol. V. -	,,	[C.9466]	2 9
1899	Ditto J. M. Heathcote, Esq. of Conington Castle.	.,	[C.9469]	1 3
1899	Ditto J. B. Fortescue, Esq., of Dropmore. Vol. III.	,,	[C.9470]	3 1
1899	Ditto F. W. Leyborne-Popham, Esq., of Littlecote.	,,	[C.9471]	1 6
1900	Ditto Mrs. Frankland-Russell-Astley, of Chequers Court, Bucks.	,,	[Cd.282]	2 0
1900	Ditto Lord Montagu of Beaulieu, Hants -	,,	[Cd.283]	1 1
1900	Ditto Beverley Corporation - - -	,,	[Cd.284]	1 0
1901	Ditto the Duke of Portland, K.G. Vol. VI., with Index to Vols. III.-VI.	,,	[Cd.676]	1 9
1901	Ditto Ditto. Vol. VII. - -	,,	[Cd.783]	2 3
	Ditto Chichester, Canterbury and Salisbury Cathedrals; of the Corporations of Berwick-on-Tweed, Burford and Lostwithiel ; and of the Counties of Wilts and Worcester.	,,	[Cd.784]	[In the Press.]
	Ditto Sir Geo. Wombwell, the Duke of Norfolk, Lord Edmund Talbot (the Shrewsbury papers), Lady Buxton and others.	,,		ditto.

Lightning Source UK Ltd.
Milton Keynes UK
UKHW02n0456160218
317658UK00016B/569/P